XNA™ GAME STUDIO EXPRESS: DEVELOPING GAMES FOR WINDOWS® AND THE XBOX 360™

JOSEPH HALL

THOMSON

™

COURSE TECHNOLOGY

Professional ■ Technical ■ Reference

ISBN-10: 1-59863-368-6
ISBN-13: 978-1-59863-368-9
Library of Congress Catalog Card Number: 2006909738
Printed in the United States of America
08 09 10 11 12 TW 10 9 8 7 6 5 4 3 2 1

Publisher and General Manager, Thomson Course Technology PTR:
Stacy L. Hiquet

Associate Director of Marketing:
Sarah O'Donnell

Manager of Editorial Services:
Heather Talbot

Marketing Manager:
Jordan Casey

Senior Acquisitions Editor:
Emi Smith

Marketing Assistant:
Adena Flitt

Project Editor:
Jenny Davidson

Technical Reviewers:
Wendy Jones and Andrew Rollings

PTR Editorial Services Coordinator:
Erin Johnson

Interior Layout Tech:
ICC Macmillan Inc.

Cover Designer:
Mike Tanamachi

Indexer:
Broccoli Information Services

Proofreader:
Kim Benbow

Thomson Course Technology PTR,
a division of Thomson Learning Inc.
25 Thomson Place
Boston, MA 02210
http://www.courseptr.com

FOREWORD

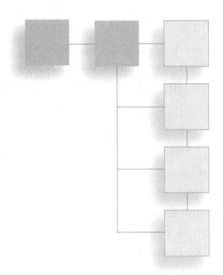

You're in for a treat.

The book you hold in your hands is destined to become a classic of XNA programming. Hidden within these pages, you will find clear and detailed guidelines for taking you from knowing nothing about XNA to becoming an expert. Unlike in other books, the examples here are useful and completely functioning, rather than snippets and "test programs" that you will find in other places. Not only that, but they are also clear enough to get the idea across in context. The use of context is invaluable, because there is nothing worse than having a code snippet with no idea of how to use it in anything other than a test-harness. I know that Joe has spent a lot of time on these examples, because I've heard of little else from him for the past eighteen months or so. I've never known anyone to put so much sincere effort into the example code for a book. And if that's just the effort put in for the examples, then you can imagine how much painstaking effort he has put into the text itself.

I've known Joe Hall, the author of this book, for a few years now. In fact, on my first meeting with him I noticed that he had a copy of one of my books on his bookshelf. That's a sign of obvious good taste and intelligence. All jokes aside though, Joe is one of the best programmers I have met. Now, I'm being completely immodest here when I say there are probably only about four or five people I can say that about. (Of course, this could just mean that I haven't met many programmers.) Let me put this in perspective, however. I am used to being the "go-to guy" for obscure technical problems. Even then, every now and then I'd run into problems that I couldn't answer—so I'd ask Joe. And he'd answer them. Instantly! Without even blinking! Yep. He's smart alright. Having worked on the original Xbox team, he's in a great position to have a head start on the XNA. And that's just what he's delivered in this book: a great head start on XNA development. You'd be crazy not to buy it.

A little more about XNA: I must admit, I was surprised when Microsoft released the XNA beta for the Xbox 360. Given the closed nature of console development, and the jealousy with which console manufacturers guard their API secrets, it is a bold and challenging move by the big M to lay it all bare for the average guy in the street to start coding games. Even though there are (necessary) limitations to what the amateur developer is permitted to do, it's refreshing to see. I'd like to see other console manufacturers follow suit. Let's see if they do. If they do, then I'd like to use the books that Joe will write in order to get up to speed.

If you've got the idea from this foreword that I think that Joe is a very smart person, and I think that you should buy this book, then you are 100% right. If you're leafing through this in the store, go to the checkout and buy it immediately. You know it makes sense, and you will appear instantly smarter and more attractive to the opposite sex*. If you're reading it at home, then you're obviously on the right track. Play some loud music to drown out the clamoring of your new groupies banging on your door for a date, and get coding the next Geometry Wars-killer.

—Andrew Rollings

Author of *Game Architecture and Design, Fundamentals of Game Design, Andrew Rollings and Ernest Adams on Game Design,* and *The ZX Spectrum Book—1982 to 199x.*

*results may vary

ACKNOWLEDGMENTS

Writing a book is not a solo effort (although it can sure seem that way as the deadlines go whizzing by). Without question, the people who made this book possible more than anyone else are my wife, Tina, and my three girls, Zoe, Abby, and Mary Frances. They've been very supportive during this process as I've had to miss bedtime stories, soccer goals, cheerleading events, and playtime sessions. I've been tucked away in my home office for nearly a year, and my wife hasn't had very many nights off during that time. I truly appreciate the sacrifices that they have made for this project. People frequently ask me if I'll ever write another book. My typical (joking) response is, "My wife says I won't."

Of course, you wouldn't be reading this now if it weren't for the folks at the publishing company. Emi, Jenny, and the people that they work with behind the scenes have shown great patience with this writing novice as he has struggled to understand the processes and terminology of an industry in which he has no experience. Thanks to them, I've been able to focus on the content of the book, ignoring the details of how my simple text magically becomes the book that you see now.

Wendy Jones was kind enough to take over the technical editing for the book when Andrew Rollings had to step out of that role due to job demands. Wendy's no slouch in the area of game programming. She's a published author, herself, with two titles on DirectX programming, the most recent of which (*Beginning DirectX 10 Game Programming*) should hit the shelves just before this book. She also has several commercial game titles, from two big-name game companies, to her credit. Thanks to her valuable feedback and input, many of the topics that are covered in this book are explained with greater clarity or in more detail than my original drafts offered.

Andrew Rollings is a recognizable name among students, hobbyists, and professional game designers alike. I owned his first book (*Game Architecture and Design*) long before I met him in person. His was one of 15 or so books that I kept at the office, and I was thrilled to hear that he would be working with our team to produce an important application. During that time, I gained a new respect for his programming and design skills. Luckily, it didn't take too much in the way of bribery, blackmail, and threats of bodily harm to persuade Andrew to write the foreword for this book. I think that one of the most valuable assets that a man has in his life is his reputation. I'm grateful to Andrew for lending his name to this project, and I appreciate his kind words. Don't let the foreword fool you, though, Andrew is a card-carrying genius, complete with his very own degree in Physics.

There are several chapters in which I used media that was given to me for inclusion in the book or was a part of the public domain. I thank the creators of that content within the chapters in which it is used, so I won't list them all here. There was one person who was kind enough to create a background music loop for me, but I never got the chance to use it in the examples. I'm including it on the CD, and it's sure to make an appearance in one of my future gaming projects. Thank you, Dr. James Conely, for your efforts. I'm sorry that I couldn't incorporate your work before my deadlines overtook me.

I just have one more "thank you" to report before we move on to the actual content. I would like to thank Todd Bryant, a software developer at Yellawood, for becoming (to the best of my knowledge) the first person to pre-order my book. Just minutes after I learned that the book had been listed on amazon.com, Todd forwarded me a copy of the e-mail confirmation for his order. At that point, I moved all the way up to 102,379th on Amazon's best seller list. Thanks, · Todd!

ABOUT THE AUTHOR

Joseph Hall has been a professional software developer for more than 16 years. He worked as a programmer for Microsoft and IBM, and he was the software architect for a Fortune 500 bank before starting his own consulting company in 2006. Joe makes his living writing desktop, web, and mobile device applications for businesses, but game programming is his passion, and it was gaming that got him into programming in the first place. He was a member of the original Xbox team and he joined the Visual Studio .NET team just after the Xbox was released in 2001. Joe applies his unique blend of development experiences to help you explore the exciting new arena of game development for the masses that is known as XNA Game Studio Express.

Me and my reasons for being.

Contents

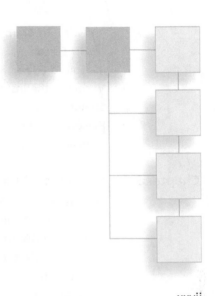

INTRODUCTION

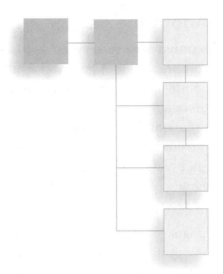

About the Book

This book is divided into four parts. Part I, "Building Blocks," (Chapters 1–12) introduces you to the XNA technologies and takes you through the process of setting up and configuring your development environment to create games for Windows and the Xbox 360, and it explores the major feature areas of the XNA Framework APIs by developing example games that demonstrate each. Part II, "Genre Studies," (Chapters 13–18) builds on what you learned in the earlier chapters to write six actual games. In Part III, "Components, Libraries, and Tools," (Chapters 19–24), you learn how to segment your code into generic component libraries so that you can reuse your work, rather than reinventing it with each new game. Part IV, "Tasty Bits," (Chapters 25–31) explores more advanced concepts like threading, performance tuning, and localization.

Each of the four parts of the book begin with an overview of what you can expect to learn in its chapters, and every chapter ends with review questions and exercises to help ensure that you understand the concepts that are covered. The games and example code in this book were designed with a focus on illustrating the concepts that are covered within the chapter in which they are developed. As a result, they are not polished, commercially viable titles. But, they are a great place for you to explore and experiment with the XNA Framework, and they provide a good starting point for you to bring your own gaming visions to life.

About the Reader

I would love to say that you should buy this book if you're able to read and comprehend written text. I would love to say that you can pick up a book and a compiler and start writing games after just a weekend of reading. I can't say that, though. I've made every attempt to make sure that someone who is new to game programming can easily follow the progression of ideas and concepts from introduction to implementation, while still keeping the interest of those programmers who have dabbled in game development or have written complete games, but this book will not teach you how to program.

If you have had any experience with writing programs (on any platform, in any language) you should be able to follow the examples in this book without any problems. If you don't know what loops, variables, methods, and arrays are, then it's time to pick up a good introduction to the C# language to which you can refer as you read this book. Games are frequently trivialized since they lie squarely within the realm of recreation and entertainment, but game programming is actually one of the most cerebral forms of programming that you'll ever do.

I hope that I haven't scared you off. If you have a passion for games, and you have a vision that you would like to see come to life, then I firmly believe that you can make it happen, and I believe that this book will help you. I just don't want you to think that you'll be developing the next *Quake* or *Gran Turismo* in a weekend, especially if you've never written a line of code in your life. Read the book. Answer the review questions. Work through the exercises. Modify the example code. By testing your assumptions, you'll be able to know when you've mastered the material. Then you can combine those core concepts in different ways to create great games.

Contact Me

If you have any questions, notice any errors, have general feedback, or have suggestions for topics that you would like me to cover in future editions of this book, a new book, or in an article on my website, please e-mail me at xnabook@codetopia.com. I'll try my best to reply to every e-mail that I receive. You can also reach me on MSN Messenger (joehall_xbox@hotmail.com) or on Xbox Live (groundh0gXNA).

My website is http://www.codetopia.com/. That's where my blog lives. I hope to coordinate the launch of my redesigned website with the release of the book. I plan to post articles, provide downloadable content (like XNA game libraries and games), and host a forum for questions about the book.

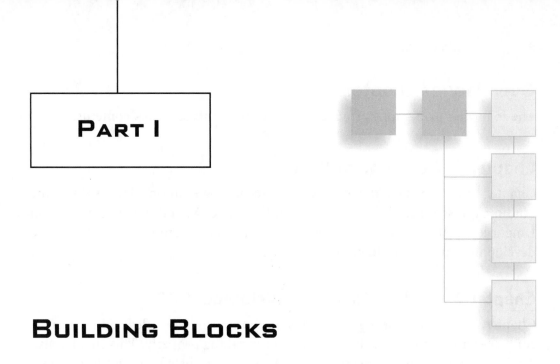

PART I

BUILDING BLOCKS

This section introduces the basic concepts behind writing cross-platform XNA games. As you work through this section, be sure to experiment with the example code. Don't just read the chapter text and follow the examples verbatim. You'll do your best learning when you test your assumptions and find them to be invalid. Working through issues will ingrain what you've learned much better than merely reading some printed text.

As you read each chapter in this section, don't focus too much on how something was done; try to understand why it was done a certain way. In programming, there are many paths that lead to the same result, each with its own pros and cons. You may think of a better way to accomplish a given task. Use the code from these chapters as a starting point for your own creations.

As you progress in your understanding of XNA and of writing managed code, take this concept a step further and try to understand why the Framework APIs were designed using the interfaces that you see. What do you think those APIs are doing with your data? How do you think they're processing your requests? How would you have written the API? What interfaces would you have used to expose that functionality to other developers? Why do you think the XNA Framework developers made the design decisions that they made?

Overview of Chapters

The following paragraphs provide an overview of this section's contents.

Chapter 1: Overview of XNA

Chapter 1 provides a good overview of the technologies upon which XNA Game Studio Express is based. XNA, Visual Studio, Direct X, and the .NET Common Language Runtime are introduced, and each component's role in the game development process is described.

Chapter 2: Setting Up Your Development PC

Chapter 2 takes you through the steps of configuring your development environment and making sure that everything is working properly. This chapter also discusses several content creation tools that you can install and use to generate audio, graphics, and 3D models for your games.

Chapter 3: Using Visual C# 2005 Express

Chapter 3 walks you through the basic features of Visual C# 2005 Express Edition. In this chapter, you will learn how Visual Studio solutions and projects are laid out, how to build your games, and how to identify and troubleshoot problems within your game code.

Chapter 4: Using XNA Graphics for Basic 2D

Chapter 4 introduces you to the basic features of 2D graphics within the XNA Framework. The example code for this chapter demonstrates loading images from the hard disk and using the graphics APIs of the XNA Framework to draw those images to the screen. Along the way, you'll learn how to manipulate your game images by scaling, rotating, tinting, animating, and tiling them, and how to vary their opacity (transparency).

Chapter 5: Using XNA Graphics for More Advanced 2D

Chapter 5 expands on the previous chapter by introducing some more advanced 2D graphics concepts. In this chapter, you will learn how to capture the game screen into an off-screen buffer and process it, pixel by pixel, to derive new images. The example code for this chapter captures the game screen, converts it to a black-and-white image, and then applies a warp effect, similar to the refraction of water.

Chapter 6: Using XNA Graphics for Basic 3D

Chapter 6 introduces the topic of 3D graphics programming in XNA. The example code for this chapter captures loads in several 3D meshes, animates them, and renders them using several different HLSL shaders. The player is able to navigate this virtual world using a free-moving camera, which he can manipulate using his Xbox 360 Controller or keyboard.

Chapter 7: Using XNA Input for Controllers

Chapter 8 shows you how to write code that allows the player to interact with your XNA games using the Xbox 360 Controller (for Windows or Xbox 360). Within this chapter, you'll develop an XNA game that allows the player to pilot a ship within an infinite grid. The state of all the controller buttons (except the media button, which is reserved for system use) is displayed on the game screen, and the player can engage the controller's vibration motors by pressing the A button.

Chapter 8: Using XNA Input for Keyboards

Chapter 8 shows you how to write code that allows the player to interact with your XNA games using the keyboard. Within this chapter, you'll develop an XNA game that allows the player to pilot a ship within an infinite grid, shooting photon torpedoes at will. (Tell me again, which one's Will?)

Chapter 9: Using XNA Input for Mice

Chapter 9 shows you how to write code that allows the player to interact with your (Windows-only) XNA games using the mouse. Within this chapter, you'll develop an XNA game that responds to mouse movement and mouse clicks, allowing the user to manipulate a grid of colored cells.

Chapter 10: Using XNA Audio

Chapter 10 explains how you can use the Cross-Platform Audio Creation Tool (XACT) and the audio APIs of the XNA Framework to add music and sound effects to your XNA games. The example code for this chapter demonstrates basic audio programming concepts by playing, and allowing the player to manipulate, three audio cues. The first is a background music clip that loops indefinitely. The second is an audio clip of my eldest girl telling a story that the listener can play, pause, stop, and restart. The third is a cheesy laser effect that plays whenever the player presses the A button on his controller. The laser effect was designed in XACT so that each time it's played, the pitch and volume of the effect vary slightly. The player can adjust the volume of the music loop and sound effects independently.

Chapter 11: Using XNA Storage

Chapter 11 demonstrates the storage APIs of the XNA Framework. The example code for this chapter lets the player design an image by stamping flowers all around the screen, then provides a way for them to save and load their artwork.

Chapter 12: Xbox 360 Considerations

Chapter 12 describes the issues surrounding writing games for the Xbox 360 game console. The text walks you through the steps of establishing a connection to your console from your development PC for deploying and debugging your XNA games on the Xbox 360.

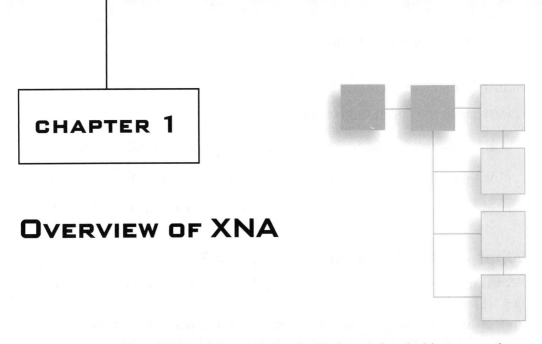

CHAPTER 1

OVERVIEW OF XNA

Microsoft recently introduced a line of products for hobbyist, student, and novice computer programmers, distributed under the "Express" moniker. These tools allow the average home user to explore and experiment with software development without investing a lot of (or in most cases, any) money. You can develop utilities, desktop applications, websites, relational databases, and more using tools that have traditionally retailed for hundreds of dollars.

Now, Microsoft hasn't gone completely mad. The Express versions of their developer tools don't have all the features of their commercial counterparts, and (as you might expect) support for the Express line is pretty much limited to peer support via the MSDN forums.

In general, there is no restriction on what you can do with the applications you develop using the Express tools. You can use them in a production environment or even sell them as commercial products. (There are some noteworthy restrictions when developing games for the Xbox 360 game console, which we will discuss later.)

In August of 2006, Microsoft released yet another Express tool, this time targeting aspiring hobbyist and student game developers. That new tool is XNA Game Studio Express.

In this chapter, you will learn:

- What XNA Game Studio Express is

- How managed code benefits game developers and designers

- What components make up the XNA Framework and how they work together

- About alternative means of distribution for your finished game

What Is XNA Game Studio Express?

XNA Game Studio Express is a set of tools based on Visual C# Express 2005 and the .NET Framework 2.0 Common Language Runtime (CLR) that makes it easier for students and hobbyists to write games for Windows and the Xbox 360 game console. XNA Game Studio Express includes a set of managed libraries known as the XNA Framework, which allows developers to use managed code to create DirectX-based games.

XNA Game Studio Express also includes a set of tools known as the XNA Framework Content Pipeline, which makes incorporating content into your games easier. And, of course, XNA Game Studio Express includes MSDN-style documentation, how-to's, and example code that help you understand how all these components work together and how best to use them to make your game development tasks easier so that you can focus on what really matters—writing great games. All of this is made available as free downloads, and there's a large community of XNA game developers that support each other and share tips, tricks, and ideas.

Note

While you can use the XNA Framework and XNA Game Studio Express to develop commercial Windows games, you cannot use these tools to develop commercial Xbox 360 games. You can share your creations with other XNA developers using Xbox Live, but you cannot package your titles for distribution to off-the-shelf Xbox 360 game consoles or share your titles with gamers who don't have access to XNA Game Studio Express or subscribe to the XNA Creators Club service.

Microsoft is scheduled to release a professional version of the XNA Game Studio suite in the spring of 2007. This new edition of the toolset will allow you to develop a commercial version of your title that can be processed through the normal certification process. Of course, your title will still need to get approval from Microsoft before entering the retail distribution chain.

Tip

If you're still a little confused about the terminology and the roles of each of these components, don't worry. That's why you're reading this book.

This new offering from Microsoft combines two technologies that haven't traditionally been very closely related—DirectX and managed code. If you're familiar with one of those technologies, you're likely not as savvy in the other. That's not to say that there haven't been efforts in the past to merge the ease of use of managed code with the performance benefits of DirectX. Microsoft has delivered two Managed DirectX (MDX) APIs in the past.

Note

Technically, there has only been one official MDX release. Version 2.0 of the MDX APIs never progressed beyond the beta stage. The XNA Framework will replace MDX moving forward, and Microsoft will provide migration guides to help you move any existing MDX code from MDX 1.1 and MDX 2.0 Beta to the XNA Framework. MDX 1.1 will continue to be supported via Microsoft's standard support policies, but MDX 2.0 assemblies will no longer ship with the DirectX SDK now that the XNA Framework has been officially released.

The majority of this book deals with using the XNA Framework and XNA Game Studio Express to develop games for Windows and the Xbox 360 game console, but I want to provide a quick summary of the underlying components on which these tools are based.

What Is Visual C# Express 2005?

The Microsoft Visual Studio family of integrated development environments (IDEs) is the industry standard toolset for writing applications for the various Windows platforms. Visual C# 2005 Express Edition provides a simple, streamlined interface to create, build, debug, and manage your Windows programming projects using managed code that's written in the C# programming language.

When coupled with XNA Game Studio Express and the XNA Framework, this world-class IDE can now also be leveraged to write games for the Windows and Xbox 360 game console platforms using DirectX and managed code.

A Brief History of DirectX

When Windows first entered the PC consumer market, it addressed several very real needs. Before Windows, programs monopolized a PC's resources. To run one application, you had to close another. And application developers had to write special-case code to support a wide variety of video cards, audio cards, and peripherals for all but the most basic of programs.

Windows provided a unified platform that application developers could target. This new platform provided (cooperative, at first) multi-tasking services and memory management services so that several applications could run simultaneously. This new platform also provided hardware abstractions that allowed application developers to target a single set of APIs for devices like printers, video cards, and audio cards.

For standard applications like spreadsheets and word processors, these abstractions were a godsend. They allowed the application developer to focus on the functionality of his application rather than the low-level inner-workings of the various hardware devices that were installed in his users' PCs.

For game developers, however, these abstractions resulted in unacceptably slow interactions with the hardware. Most games in the early days of Windows required users to completely exit Windows and start the game from the command line.

Microsoft's first attempt to address the performance needs of game developers was WinG, the predecessor of the DirectX APIs that we know and love today. DirectX provides a set of APIs, separate from the standard Windows APIs, to access hardware devices.

These APIs, and their underlying device drivers, are highly optimized for performance. While DirectX provides game developers with a method to write high-performance games that run within the Windows environment, it's not the easiest API in the world to master. A veteran game developer can do amazing things with DirectX, but it can be a little intimidating to folks who are new to game programming. XNA Game Studio Express and the XNA Framework attempt to mask that complexity, allowing game developers to focus on their game's content and game play.

What Is Managed Code?

On most development platforms, source code is compiled directly to native binaries that can be loaded and executed on the target processor (CPU) with no supporting runtimes or libraries. The executable file that's created for these platforms contains the actual instructions for the targeted processor.

For managed code, your source is compiled to an intermediate language (IL). This IL represents the instructions of a virtual, platform-agnostic CPU. This

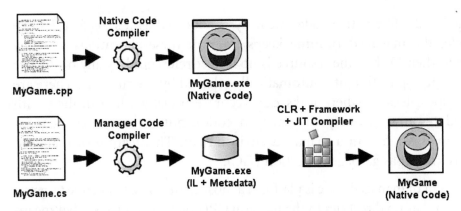

Figure 1.1
Comparison of a native executable with a managed executable.

virtual CPU doesn't actually exist anywhere but in software. To run managed code on an actual CPU, there needs to be some intermediary between the managed executable and the physical processor. This intermediary, known as the runtime, is a program that was compiled to the target processor's native instructions. The runtime then acts as a virtual CPU, emulating the non-existent, virtual CPU on the physical CPU. This concept is illustrated in Figure 1.1.

Emulating virtual CPU instructions sounds inefficient, doesn't it? Actually, for most applications, you would likely see only nominally lower performance over the same basic native code. But most managed code runtimes (Microsoft's included) support a feature known as just-in-time compilation (JIT). The JIT compiler takes the intermediate language that was generated by the managed compiler and generates native code that's optimized for the targeted physical CPU just before the code is actually executed on the physical CPU. While there is still some overhead imposed by having the runtime layer between your application and the physical CPU, JIT compilation closes the overall performance gap between your managed code and its native cousins.

That sounds interesting, but why include the additional complexity? What does targeting managed code offer an application developer that they wouldn't normally have when writing native code?

A major benefit comes in the area of memory management. In traditional languages that compile to native executables, memory leaks are a common problem. It's easy for developers to forget to release system resources that they allocate, especially when complex code paths or exception handling are involved.

In managed code, like native code, memory is allocated as it's needed. Unlike native code, the managed runtime keeps track of these allocations and any references to them. When the resource is no longer referenced by any of the live objects in your application, it's automatically released by the runtime. There are still a few special cases where leaks can occur (especially when dealing with unmanaged resources from your managed code), but memory management basically comes for free in a managed environment. This feature of managed runtimes is known as garbage collection (GC).

Another benefit of managed code is platform agnosticism. Since your code targets a virtual CPU, it has no direct ties to the physical CPU on which it runs. That means that your managed code should be able to run on any platform that provides a runtime for it. For instance, (in theory) an application written in managed code could run on PCs, handheld devices, mainframes, or even game consoles.

Your code will run on any platform on which there is a compatible version of the managed runtime and its supporting libraries. That's the key to XNA's ability to run your games on both Windows and the Xbox 360. Since both platforms support the Common Language Runtime (CLR) and the XNA Framework APIs, your games can seamlessly transition between the two platforms.

Having code that can execute on any platform is neat, but without access to components beyond the CPU, your code won't be able to do anything useful. In addition to the runtime, managed environments also include a set of APIs that allow you to access the native OS features via abstractions that won't tie you to a specific platform. These APIs include classes that allow you to access the file system to read and write files, utilize the user interface components of the operating system (like buttons, checkboxes, and menus), control peripherals (like printers), and access media components (like the sound system and screen).

What Is the Role of XNA?

Accessing the native host components through an abstraction layer is generally slower than accessing those same resources natively. In the case of the printer or file system, the performance difference isn't very noticeable. The device itself is slower than the abstractions—your code spends much of its time waiting for the device to complete issued commands.

But in the case of components like the graphics system, the cost of abstraction is much greater. Updating millions of pixels every second requires a lot of CPU power, even when using native code. Thanks to advances in graphics hardware, a lot of that graphics processing can be offloaded to the graphics card itself by way of specialized programs that run on a secondary CPU that's embedded on the graphics card, known as the graphics processing unit (GPU). By running these specialized routines on the GPU, your application is only responsible for coordinating the efforts of the GPU and for shuffling required data to and from graphic memory.

The XNA Framework includes a set of managed libraries that provides access to these advanced hardware features using a technology known as DirectX. DirectX is a set of drivers for these devices and a set of unmanaged (native code) APIs to access them. Of course, DirectX (and XNA) provides access to more than just the graphics hardware. Support for input devices and audio are provided by the XNA Framework via managed wrappers to the XINPUT and XACT components of DirectX.

In addition to providing a managed code interface to the hardware and DirectX APIs, the XNA Framework includes a component known as the content pipeline that makes it easier to use content that was created using third-party and custom tools—content like textures, 3D objects, music, sound, and other game data.

The .NET Framework is fast becoming the leading platform for developing general-purpose Windows applications. The XNA Framework relies on .NET Framework components like the Common Language Runtime and the core class libraries, but the XNA Framework has been specifically designed and optimized for developing games. As an added benefit, the XNA Framework APIs are highly portable between Windows and the Xbox 360 console so that games written for one platform can be recompiled to run on the other with little or no modification.

Note

The XNA Framework has been developed to provide cross-platform support for your games targeting Windows and the Xbox 360 game console, and with good design your games should run on both platforms with few or no source code changes. But you still need to provide a project for each platform, and any platform-specific code will need to be conditionally compiled out (using #if XBOX360) for the other platform. Binaries that you generate for one platform will not run on the other—you must build each project type separately.

Figure 1.2 illustrates how the various XNA components work together to help you develop games for Windows and the Xbox 360 game console.

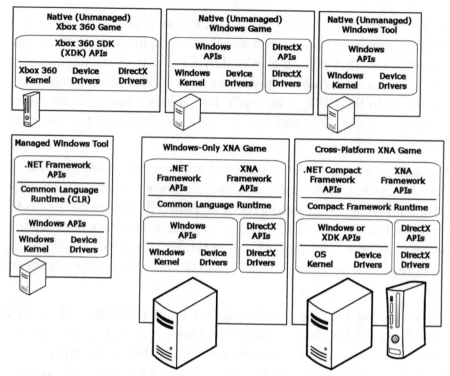

Figure 1.2
How your game runs on Windows and the Xbox 360 game console.

When you're accessing the file system, managing threads, or dealing with arrays, you're using the .NET Framework. When you're playing music, rendering 3D objects, or displaying a heads-up display in your game, you're using the XNA Framework. These two frameworks complement each other, greatly simplifying the Herculean effort of writing great games.

Note

> You may be wondering what the XNA acronym stands for. It doesn't stand for anything. The official XNA FAQ says that the letters X-N-A are a recursive acronym that expands to XNA's Not Acronymed.

What Is C#?

Until now, the description of managed code and its role in developing games on the XNA platform has been in generic terms. Now it's time to move from the general to the specific.

The managed runtime for the XNA Framework and XNA Game Studio Express is Microsoft's .NET Common Language Runtime (CLR), version 2.0. This runtime supports many programming languages, and each of the languages that are supported by the CLR have access to a common set of APIs known as the .NET Framework.

In addition to providing abstracted access to system components, the .NET Framework also includes a collection of data structures and algorithms that makes life easier for the developer. Tasks like string manipulation, network communications, thread management, and application security are greatly simplified by the .NET Framework.

Note

The runtime for your Xbox 360 titles is actually a trimmed-down version of the CLR known as the Microsoft .NET Compact Framework 2.0. The Compact Framework is designed for platforms with limited resources like cell phones and other handheld devices. This specialized version of the Compact Framework runtime trims a lot of unneeded fat from the full CLR and is highly optimized for the Xbox 360 console.

The CLR may support many languages, but the only officially supported language for creating games using the XNA Framework is C# (pronounced "see sharp"). C# is a close cousin to Java and C / C++ that has been adopted as the language of choice for developing Windows applications by millions of programmers worldwide. If you're familiar with those languages, you'll find that your transition to C# will be rather easy.

What Role Does Managed Code Play in Games Today?

As a standard for Windows application development, C# is often used as the language of choice for writing the tools that support game development. And C# has been used to write some really great Windows games. But for performance-critical applications, game developers typically use languages that target native code, like C and C++. Before the introduction of the XNA Framework, C# wasn't really the best option for developing high-performance games like first-person shooters or 3D racing games.

While C# is a relative newcomer to the area of game development, managed code has been used to script game objects and AI for a while now. Many times, developers will embed script parsers for game logic and use native code only for those areas of code where performance is critical.

Native game code is the domain of the expert programmer. Using scriptable objects makes it easier to have level designers implement basic object interactions and frees up the more experienced developers to handle the tricky, more technical areas of the code. As an added benefit, having your designers implement object interactions eliminates the communication barriers between the designers and the developers who often seem to speak different languages.

Of course, there's a time investment in getting the designers started and in supporting them in their efforts; but typically, developers find that the designers are able to use the scripting engines in ways that they never envisioned, leading to incredibly creative and innovative level designs. And since the designers don't need to rely on the developers to make changes to the code whenever they want to tweak their designs, the overall turnaround time is reduced, and the designers can try many more variations on their themes than would typically be possible in an often-too-tight product development cycle.

The XNA Framework makes it easier for individuals and small teams to reap the benefits of reduced development times and lower levels of complexity typically seen when using a scripting engine, while also gaining the performance benefits of native (JIT'ed) code that targets the DirectX APIs. Now you don't need to be a veteran game developer to write great, commercially viable games. Of course, those veterans will be able to make the XNA Framework do things that a novice can only dream of, but in the realm of traditional native code, most entry-level developers would have a heck of a time just trying to get their game project off the ground.

Summary

XNA Game Studio Express makes game development easier and more approachable for novice, hobbyist, and student developers by providing out-of-the-box support for many of the most common game programming tasks. By using XNA and managed code, your ideas will move from doodles on a napkin to playable games on your PC faster than ever before. Your code will be more robust and crash-resistant. And you'll be able to do all of this without emptying your wallet.

In this chapter, you learned what XNA Game Studio Express is and how it can help you to write games for Windows and the Xbox 360 game console. You also learned what managed code is and how it can make life easier for game developers. In the next chapter, we will get these tools installed and prepare your PC so that you can start bringing your game ideas to life.

Review Questions

Think about what you've read in this chapter to answer the following questions.

1. What are two benefits of writing applications in managed languages like C#?

2. Can I develop commercial Windows games using XNA Game Studio Express?

3. Can I develop commercial Xbox 360 games using XNA Game Studio Express?

4. What is DirectX? How does DirectX help me to write video games?

5. What is the role of the XNA Framework with respect to DirectX?

Exercises

EXERCISE 1. Write down a game idea that you have. Try to be specific in your description of the game play. Where does the action take place? What entities and objects exist in your game world? How do they interact with each other? Don't focus on the technical aspects; just document your idea from a game player's perspective. As you progress through the book, consider how what you learn can be used to implement your idea. Revisit your notes frequently, revising them as you go. When you feel comfortable with the tools and technologies that you're reading about, start fleshing out your design, and start writing a prototype—a playable "proof of concept" of your game idea.

EXERCISE 2. Pick a game that you enjoy playing. As you progress through the book, start thinking about how that game was designed and written. How would you write it? When you've reached the end of the book, try to write a simple clone of this game. Don't focus on the overall game. Try to break it down into smaller, more manageable components that you feel comfortable writing. Then put those components together to create the more complex whole. Don't worry about making a commercial-quality game. Just try to capture the essence of what makes the game enjoyable.

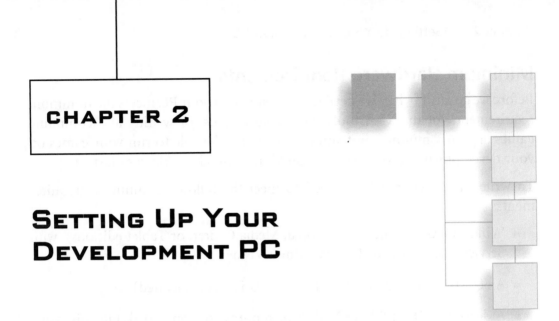

CHAPTER 2

SETTING UP YOUR DEVELOPMENT PC

Now that you have a basic understanding of what XNA Game Studio Express and the XNA Framework are, it's time to prepare your development environment so that you can start writing games. This chapter covers the steps required to download, install, and use the XNA tools.

All of the core software listed in this section is available as a free download from Microsoft's website. Before you start downloading and installing components, you need to make sure that your operating system will support them. At the time of this writing, XNA Game Studio Express supports Windows XP SP2 and Windows Vista. You can use the Professional, Home, Media Center, or Tablet editions of Windows XP, but you must have SP2 installed. All flavors of Vista are supported as of the release of Microsoft XNA Game Studio Express 1.0 Refresh.

In this chapter, you will:

- Prepare your PC for game development

- Identify, acquire, and install the software necessary to write games for the Windows and Xbox 360 platforms

- Verify your installation by building a simple "game"

Minimum Hardware Requirements

Before we go any further, we need to make sure that your PC meets the minimum requirements for the XNA tools. The requirements for writing and compiling games are fairly minimal, but you'll also want to be able to run your games on your development PC (so that the "build, test, tweak" cycle goes faster).

To write games, your PC will need to meet the following minimum requirements:

- Windows XP (Home, Professional, Media Center, or Tablet editions), with Service Pack 2 installed, or Windows Vista

- A 600MHz CPU (a 1GHz or faster CPU is recommended)

- At least 192MB of RAM (256MB or more is recommended, but this is an area in which you shouldn't cut costs—I don't have a development PC with less than 1GB of RAM)

- At least 500MB of free hard disk space (that assumes that you only install the compiler and the managed runtime, but you'll need at least 1.3GB free disk space for a full install; again, this isn't an area to cut costs—your game content will eat up more space than you think)

To play the games that you write, your PC will also need the following:

- A graphics card that supports DirectX 9.0c and Shader Model 1.1 (or later; 2.0 is recommended since some starter kits require it)

- A sound card that supports DirectX 9.0c (most, if not all, do)

- An Xbox 360 Controller for Windows (not strictly necessary, but very nice to have for testing if you plan on writing games for your Xbox 360 game console); the Xbox 360 Controller is the only joystick/game pad device that XNA supports.

Installing the Software

If you have ever installed any trials, betas, community technology previews (CTPs), or release candidates (RCs) of any of the following software, you need to uninstall them before you begin setting up your development environment.

- XNA Game Studio Express

- The .NET Common Language Runtime 2.0

- Visual C# 2005, Express Edition

Some components support side-by-side installations, where multiple (officially released) versions of the same component can be installed in parallel. In general, though, betas and other unreleased versions don't play well with their officially released counterparts. Also, support for betas and other non-standard installs is limited. If you have problems when using a non-standard configuration, you'll have a harder time getting help.

The specific versions of the software listed below were current as of the writing of this book. If there is a later version available by the time you're ready to prepare your development environment, then by all means, use the more recent version. If you have any issues, please be sure to read the release notes for the component that's giving you problems.

Microsoft provides extensive documentation and support for their products on their website. If you cannot find a solution to your specific problem on the Microsoft.com site, your favorite search engine, or in any of the related FAQs, visit the MSDN forums at the following URL:

http://forums.microsoft.com/MSDN

Most of the following tools and components support two modes of installation— online and offline. Using the default installer, you're actually only downloading a bootstrap application which, in turn, connects back to the Internet to grab the remaining bits. I personally prefer to have the install media, so I like to download the ISO images and create a CD from them (offline installation).

Visual C# 2005 Express Edition

You can download Visual C# 2005 Express Edition from the following URL.

http://msdn.microsoft.com/vstudio/express/visualcsharp/

Visual C# 2005 Express Edition allows you to create more than just XNA games. You can write most types of Windows applications using this tool. That's going to come in handy in later chapters when you learn how to write tools to support your game development efforts.

You can download Visual C# 2005 Express Edition as an ISO file. ISO files are virtual images of physical CDs. You can burn the ISO to a CD using any CD-ROM burning tool that supports ISO images. Alternatively, you can use a virtual CD-ROM driver to mount the virtual disc as a drive that's accessible in the same way that any physical drive on your system is accessed.

Note

If you have Visual Studio 2005 Professional (or another edition of the retail IDE), you don't need to uninstall it. Visual C# 2005 Express can be installed side by side with other Visual Studio editions.

When you install Visual C# 2005 Express Edition, version 2.0 of the .NET Common Language Runtime is installed automatically if you haven't already installed it. If you already have another version of the CLR, you don't need to uninstall it. The CLR supports side-by-side installations.

If you have a beta or preview release of the version 2.0 CLR installed, play it safe and uninstall it now, before proceeding with the Visual C# 2005 Express Edition install.

Once you start the installation program, you should see a screen similar to Figure 2.1.

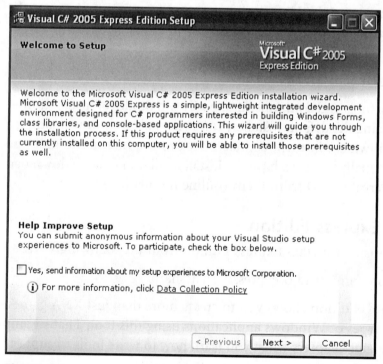

Figure 2.1
The Visual C# 2005 Express Edition installation dialog.

Go ahead and accept all the defaults when prompted. By default, the flowing items will be installed during this process. The required disk space for these components is around 1.5GB.

- Microsoft Windows Installer 3.1

- Microsoft .NET Framework 2.0

- Visual C# 2005 Express Edition

- Microsoft MSDN 2005 Express Edition

- SQL Server 2005 Express Edition x86

Note

If you're running a little short on disk space, the most obvious component to exclude is SQL Server 2005 Express. You can always install it later via a separate download, but it's worth installing now if you're able. We won't use SQL Server 2005 Express in any of the examples in this book, but chances are good that you'll want to experiment with it later, and it's actually a great product. Remember, the primary audience for Visual C# 2005 Express is application developers, and it can be used to write more than just games.

The installation can take some time to complete. Now would be a good time to take a break and grab a coffee. Don't stray too far from your computer, though. You may be prompted to occasionally reboot during the installation process.

Once you've successfully installed Visual C# 2005 Express Edition, register it by selecting Register Product from the Help menu within the IDE. You must register Visual C# 2005 Express Edition before you can successfully install XNA Game Studio Express. Registration gives you access to tons of freebies like royalty-free icons and images, eBooks, and components. Plus, you'll get access to the MSDN Flash—a newsletter for developers who use Microsoft technologies.

If you're installing XNA Game Studio Express 1.0 Refresh, you'll also need to install Service Pack 1 for Visual C# 2005 Express Edition. Read the release notes for the service pack before installing. There are certain conditions that may make the installation take a while to complete (up to an hour in some scenarios). There are several flavors of this service pack. You'll want to download VS80sp1-KB926749-X86-INTL.exe. See the readme file for the XNA Refresh for more information and the download link.

MSDN Library for Visual Studio 2005 Express Edition

MSDN stands for the Microsoft Developers Network. It's a huge repository of articles, technical documentation, and example source code to help you develop applications for Windows and the web. While you'll be primarily focused on the XNA Framework, there are several useful classes in the standard .NET Framework that you'll frequently find yourself referencing, and the MSDN Library also includes complete references to the C# language as well as the Visual C# 2005 Express IDE.

While the MSDN Library is available as a separate download, it was already installed when you ran the setup for Visual C# 2005 Express. The only tweak that you may want to make to the default installation is to enable the searching of online MSDN content so that you can get up-to-the-minute information.

To configure Visual Studio Help to use online content, follow these steps:

1. Open Visual C# 2005 Express.

2. Click the Tools menu.

3. Click Options.

4. Make sure that Show All Settings is checked.

5. In the tree view on the left, select the Online node from the Help branch.

6. Select the Try Online First, Then Local option.

7. Click OK.

These options are shown in Figure 2.2.

XNA Game Studio Express

At this point, we've prepared your PC for general Windows application development. This next step will install the bits needed to write games.

Note

It's very important that you run Visual C# 2005 Express at least once before you install XNA Game Studio Express. If you don't do this, some of the options for Xbox 360 game development may not show up on your menus. Just open Visual C# 2005 Express, and then close it. Once you've done that, you're ready to continue.

If you messed up and installed XNA Game Studio Express before opening and closing the Visual C# 2005 Express IDE, you're not totally out of luck. Just uninstall XNA Game Studio Express, run and exit Visual C# 2005 Express, and then reinstall XNA Game Studio Express. It may seem silly, but following these steps will fix the bad registry juju.

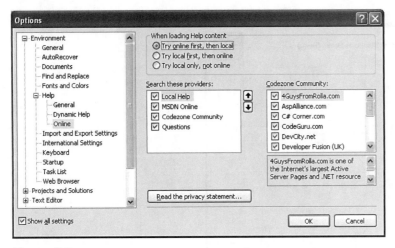

Figure 2.2
Configuring online help using the Options dialog.

You can obtain the setup program for XNA Game Studio Express by visiting the following URL:

http://msdn.microsoft.com/xna/

Again, just run the setup program and accept all defaults. The installation progress screen is shown in Figure 2.3.

The XNA Game Studio Express setup program will install the current version of the DirectX runtime files, if they haven't already been installed on your PC. The installer will also add a rule to the Windows firewall to allow your PC to communicate with your Xbox 360 game console on the local subnet.

Note

You may be thinking, "Hey! Why is XNA messing with my firewall settings?" XNA Game Studio Express communicates with your Xbox 360 console via a network connection to deploy and debug the games that you write. If your firewall restricts communication between your development PC and your Xbox 360, you can't perform these tasks.

If you're using a third-party (hardware or software) firewall that isn't updated during the installation process, don't worry. I provide the configuration details in Chapter 12, "Xbox 360 Considerations."

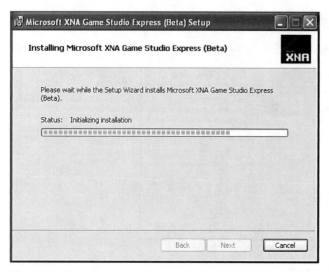

Figure 2.3
The XNA Game Studio Express Setup dialog.

For news, tutorials, peer support forums, and other XNA goodies, visit the following URLs:

http://creators.xna.com/

http://forums.xna.com/

http://www.xna.com/

Optional Software

The components listed in this section are either not strictly required or are already installed by one of the tools listed previously. They're worth mentioning here, but you can safely ignore them if you don't have the disk space or the patience.

Microsoft .NET Framework 2.0

As I mentioned earlier, the installer for Visual C# 2005 Express Edition will install version 2.0 of the common language runtime for you, if it's needed. If you want to install it yourself, you can download it from the following URL:

http://msdn.microsoft.com/netframework/

I won't detail the install steps for this component here. Just run the installer and accept all the defaults.

DirectX Software Development Kit

Installing the DirectX SDK is not required, but as you get more experienced in writing XNA games, you may find some of the tools in the SDK useful. If you have the space, go ahead and install it now.

http://msdn.microsoft.com/directx/sdk/

I won't detail the install steps for this component here. Just run the installer and accept all the defaults.

Paint Program

Unless you have an artist to generate your game content, you're going to want to install a paint program. There are several cheap and free image editors available, but there are a few features that you'll want to make sure that your chosen package supports.

- **Transparency**—The XNA Framework supports single-color and alpha-channel transparency, so it would be nice if your paint program did as well.

- **Layers**—This isn't strictly required, but it's really nice to have. You create images by layering partially transparent images over each other to form the final image.

- **Vectors**—This isn't a requirement, but it makes life a lot easier. Vectors are shapes that can be rotated and scaled without losing their original look. Pixel-based images become "blocky" or "pixilated" when rotated or scaled.

- **Adobe Plug-ins**—This isn't a requirement, but there are a lot of free and commercial effects plug-ins that can make the lamest of programmer art look more polished.

- **Many Supported File Formats**—I suggest that you get a program that supports the PNG image file format at a minimum. PNG is a versatile format that is easily compressed, easily viewed in a variety of programs, and it's fully supported by the DX tools and the XNA Content Pipeline.

The industry leader in image editing has been Adobe's Photoshop, but I've never been keen on shelling out their asking price. For the last several years, I've used a paint program known as Paint Shop Pro, from a company called JASC. Corel has since acquired JASC and repackaged Paint Shop Pro, and I honestly haven't kept up with their changes. For the especially cheap, there's a free paint program out there that claims to do everything that you (the hobbyist game developer) would need—the GIMP.

I can't tell you which program to use. Each has its own benefits and short-comings. And there's a strong sense of community that surrounds each product, so it's hard to get unbiased feedback. Download a trial (or in the GIMP's case, the full product) and try it out.

3D Editor

Like paint programs, there are many 3D modeling tools out there, each with its own positives and negatives. Search the web to see what other people think of their chosen program. Download a trial and play around, or find a free alternative (such as Blender).

Note

I personally love 3D Studio Max, but I'm too cheap to pay the multi-thousand-dollar price tag. So, I use a cheap, yet powerful 3D modeling program called Nendo. It looks like development on my little tool stopped quite some time ago, though. I don't know what it is about me and content creation tools. I seem to have a reverse Midas touch. Just pray that I never order anything from your favorite software company.

Sound Editor

Like paint programs and 3D modeling programs, there are many sound editors out there, each with its own positives and negatives. Search the web to see how other people rate their chosen program. Download a trial and see what you think.

Verifying the Install

Let's take a minute to make sure that everything has installed properly by compiling and running a simple Windows game project.

Launch Visual C# 2005 Express. If this is your first time using the IDE, you may see a dialog that tells you that the IDE is being prepared for its first use. Once the IDE has finished loading, you should see a screen similar to Figure 2.4.

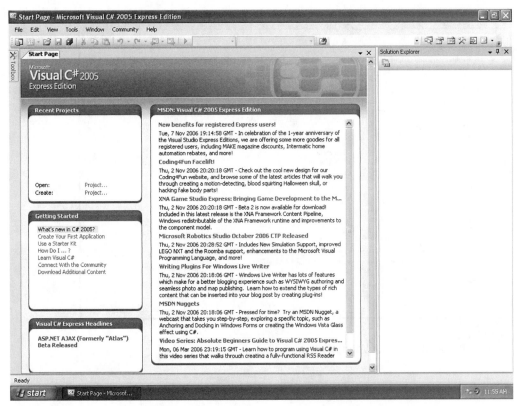

Figure 2.4
The Visual C# 2005 Express Edition IDE.

To create a new project, click File, New Project. The New Project dialog will appear. There are several options available to you. Select the Windows Game project type and click OK, as shown in Figure 2.5.

Now you have the default Windows game project. All of the game examples in the book will be derived from this project type. If you run this project without making any changes, you should see a window with a blue background, as shown in Figure 2.6.

If static blue screens aren't your thing and you want to verify your installation with a more interesting test, create a new Spacewar Windows Starter Kit project, as shown in Figure 2.7.

Starter kits are a way that example code can be distributed to the XNA community. Spacewar, shown in Figure 2.8, is a nice example of what a hobbyist can

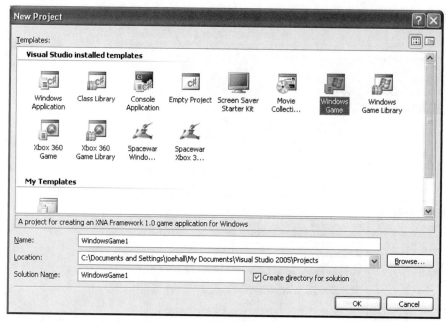

Figure 2.5
The New Project dialog with Windows Game selected.

Figure 2.6
The default XNA game, a (cornflower) blue screen.

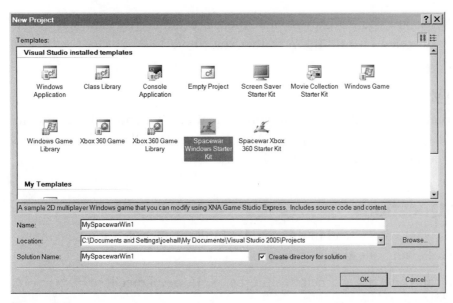

Figure 2.7
The New Project dialog with Spacewar Windows Starter Kit selected.

Figure 2.8
The opening screen of the Spacewar game.

do with XNA Game Studio Express, and there are some great new starter kits available for download from http://creators.xna.com/.

Summary

In this chapter, you installed and configured the tools that you will use to write your Windows and Xbox 360 games. You then verified that everything was working by compiling and running an XNA game project.

Review Questions

Think about what you've read in this chapter (and the included source code) to answer the following questions.

1. Where can you go to get help from other XNA developers?

2. Besides games, what other applications can be developed using Visual C# 2005 Express? How might that be helpful when developing your XNA games?

3. What is the MSDN Library? How can you view up-to-the-minute updates to the XNA Framework and Game Studio Express documentation?

4. List some of the features that image editing software should support to make developing XNA game content easier.

5. What is a Starter Kit project? What starter kit is included when you install XNA Game Studio Express? Where can you find more Starter Kit projects?

Exercises

EXERCISE 1. If you haven't already, create a new Spacewar Starter Kit project, and then compile and run it. Things will be easier if you have an Xbox 360 Controller plugged in. After having played the game, identify the game objects. Describe how they interact with each other.

EXERCISE 2. After having played the Spacewar game, take a peek at the project files. It may seem a little overwhelming if you are new to game programming, but I'm not asking you to dissect the source code, just notice how the programmer segregated the code into separate classes. Think about the rationale behind the design (screens, bullets, ships, helper classes, etc). Does the design make sense to you? Would you have logically grouped the game's functionality differently? Explain.

EXERCISE 3. Visit http://creators.xna.com/. Click the Education link, and then click the Starter Kits link. You should see a list of Starter Kit projects that have been distributed since XNA Game Studio Express was released. Follow the instructions to download and install these starter kits. Create new projects based on them. Revisit Exercise 1 and Exercise 2 for these new kits.

EXERCISE 4. Use your favorite search engine to find several cheap or free content creation tools. Test drive several applications. See what folks are saying about them on the web. As you progress through the book, use these tools to create content for your games.

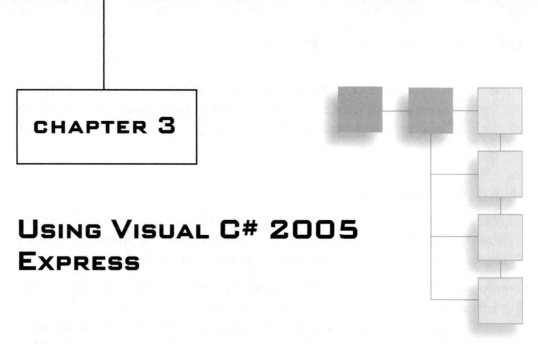

CHAPTER 3

Using Visual C# 2005 Express

Now that you have your development PC set up, it's time to learn about the tools that you'll be using to develop your games.

In this chapter, you will learn:

- The various Visual C# 2005 Express project types

- How projects are laid out

- How to build programs

- How to debug programs

The Visual C# 2005 Express IDE

The Visual C# 2005 Express IDE allows you to write more than just games. Hard-coding game data is tedious, and when your game gets big enough, managing all that hand-crafted data can be overwhelming. It's times like that when you'll want to write a tool (a Windows application) to provide a simple interface for generating and managing levels and other in-game data.

The Visual C# 2005 Express IDE groups related source code and media files into a collection known as a project. Related projects can be grouped into a higher-level collection known as a solution. Whenever you use the Visual C# 2005 Express IDE, you'll be dealing with a single solution that contains at least one project.

Different projects produce different types of programs. Each project type is configured to support its own unique output. Let's take a moment to cover each of the available project types and how they might be useful in your game development efforts.

Windows Application

This project type generates an executable (an EXE file) that runs in Windows. Whenever you double-click on a desktop icon or select a program from the Windows Start menu, you're running a Windows application.

You could write your game as a Windows application, bypassing XNA altogether, but interacting with DirectX would be more difficult, and you would have to spend a significant amount of time reinventing the XNA wheel for common game tasks like the game loop and capturing user input. Since we have the XNA Framework to help us write our games, we would be better off using this project type for what it was intended.

The most common use for this project type in your game development efforts is in developing programs to generate your game data. For example, you could write a level editor as a Windows application that provides a simple user interface to read, edit, and write files that your game can then use to initialize internal game data whenever the user progresses to a new level.

Windows applications spend most of their time waiting for the user to do something like click on a button. When the user clicks on that button, the Windows application is notified via a message from the operating system. That message is commonly referred to as an event. When the application receives this notification, it performs some task and then waits for the next message. This type of development is known as "event-driven" programming.

Console Application

Like its cousin the Windows Application project, the Console Application project type generates an executable (an EXE file) that runs in Windows. Unlike a Windows application, a console application runs in the Windows console (also known as "the command prompt"), and it does not follow the event-driven model.

Console applications are task oriented. They perform some tasks to completion, then exit. User input comes from command line arguments that are passed to the application when it starts up. The console application can prompt the user for text input while it's running, but there is no rich graphical user interface.

This type of application is handy for automating pre-build or post-build tasks and for tasks like converting data files from one format to another. We will develop a console application in Chapter 20, "Game Font Maker Utility," when we write a utility to convert Windows TrueType fonts into bitmap images.

A Quick Detour: Classes and Objects

Before we talk about the next project type, I need to define what a class is. All C# programs are made up of one or more classes. A class is the definition of an object. So, what's an object? The short answer is "everything"—everything in C# is an object.

Objects are in-memory representations of real-world things. Computers process streams of 1s and 0s. Humans think in terms of more abstract concepts. How would you describe a dog to a computer? Ultimately, your description has to be a stream of 1s and 0s, since that's the only language that the computer understands. It's the role of the C# compiler to convert a human-readable description into a machine-readable description.

Classes are the way that we describe objects to the C# compiler. A grossly oversimplified class for a dog might look something like this:

```
public class Dog
{
    public int NumberOfLegs = 4;
    public void Speak()
    {
        System.Console.WriteLine("woof");
    }
}
```

That class describes the attributes (properties) and behaviors (methods) of a dog that we're interested in. Now that we've defined what a dog is, the C# compiler can convert our textual description into a form that will ultimately become an in-memory instance of a dog object. Objects are instances of classes.

Every object in your game will be represented by some construct in code. The construct that best relates to real-world objects is the class.

Note

If you're scratching your head while you read this, it may be time to pick up a book on C# programming before you go too much farther. These concepts are fundamental to writing C# programs, but an in-depth study of object-oriented programming and the C# language is beyond the scope of this book.

I've been programming for a while and C# is a relative newcomer to the programming scene, so I've never read a book on C# that targets beginners. Based on a quick scan of the web, it looks like most folks recommend Eric Gunnerson's, *A Programmer's Introduction to C#*. I also have a lot of respect for Charles Petzold's early Windows programming titles (for C++), and I would imagine that his *Programming Microsoft Windows with C#* would be a good reference for Windows and GDI+ programming (useful when you start writing tools to support your games). Neither of these books will have any content on XNA; they're just a good start to get the fundamentals of OOP and C# programming in general.

Whatever book you choose, don't just follow the examples. You learn by doing, not by reading. Following printed instructions won't make you a great programmer. You need to deviate from the examples and experiment to see how things work. (The same is true of this book, too.)

Class Library

Class libraries are collections of classes that can be used by other applications. The output of this project type is a dynamic link library (or DLL) file. On their own, they don't do anything—you can't run a DLL. Windows applications and console applications can link to the DLLs generated by this project type, then instantiate and use the embedded classes as if they were contained as source code within their own project.

This is very handy if you have some common functionality that you want several applications to share. Just update the DLL, and the applications inherit your changes without recompiling. (Assuming that you don't "break the interface" by changing the signatures of existing methods or properties in your previously deployed classes, of course.)

Empty Project

All of the other project types generate projects that are pre-configured with the options that best suit their output types, and they include rudimentary "stub" code from which you can build your own custom code. This project type is exactly what its name suggests—a completely blank slate.

Windows Game

The Windows Game project type generates an executable (an EXE file) that can be run under Windows. References to the XNA Framework DLLs are automatically added for you, and the new project contains stub code that fully implements the simplest XNA game—a solid blue screen.

Unlike Windows applications, games are not event-driven. Games have a main loop that is continually active, constantly processing player input and updating the state of objects that exist within the game world. This loop (commonly referred to as "the game loop") executes dozens (or even hundreds) of times every second. In this way, objects in the game appear to be active, even when the player isn't.

For XNA games, the game loop is managed for you. Your game exposes methods that represent certain high-level game state changes or stages in the game loop processing. The most notable of these methods are:

- **Initialize**—This method is called when your game first starts up, just after the game object has been instantiated and the graphics device has been initialized. In this method, you will perform start up tasks like setting your game's screen resolution and creating any game objects that will exist as long as the game is running.

- **LoadGraphicsContent**—This method is called when your game is ready to load graphics resources. Typically, this method isn't called very frequently, but it is important to note that graphics resources can be unloaded and reloaded at any time during the lifetime of your game. For example, dragging a Windows game from one monitor to another may result in an unload and reload of graphics resources.

- **Update**—This method is called once per iteration of the game loop. This is where the real logic of the game is processed. Within this method, you will process player input and update the state of all of your game objects. For example, if you discover that the player is pressing the A button on the controller, you will create a bullet object. On subsequent calls to the Update method, you will move the bullet along its trajectory until it leaves the screen or collides with another game object.

- **Draw**—This method is generally called once per iteration of the game loop. In this method, you will render any game objects that are visible to the player. It is important to note that the Draw method will not be called if the game is struggling to keep up with the requested frame rate. In that case, the Update method will continue to be called with every iteration of the game loop so that the state of the game objects may continue to be updated.

■ UnloadGraphicsContent—This method is called when your game is ready to unload graphics resources, for example, when the game is exiting. Typically, this method isn't called very frequently, but it is important to note that graphics resources can be unloaded and reloaded at any time during the lifetime of your game.

Windows Game Library

Like the Class Library, the Windows Game Library project type compiles to a DLL and contains shared code that a Windows Game project can reference as if it were its own. Any updates that are made to the DLL are propagated to all the games that refer to the DLL, without having to recompile each game.

This project type is useful for creating components that can be shared across multiple games. For example, the keyboard-aware game pad that we create in Chapter 19 is implemented as a reusable Windows Game Library (and also as an Xbox 360 Game Library) that is shared by several of the examples in this book.

Xbox 360 Game

The Xbox 360 Game project type generates an executable (an EXE file) that can be run on the Xbox 360 game console. References to the XNA Framework DLLs (specifically built for the Xbox 360 game console) are automatically added for you, and the new project contains stub code that fully implements the simplest XNA game—a solid blue screen.

Please read the description of the Windows Game project for more details about the programming model of an Xbox 360 game. The beauty of the XNA Framework is that it provides seamless, cross-platform support for Windows and Xbox 360 games. The core concepts are the same on both platforms.

Since Xbox 360 games cannot be launched from Windows, you will need an Xbox 360 game console connected to your development PC via an Ethernet network to run and debug your Xbox 360 games.

Note

All of the games and examples that we develop in this book will focus on the Windows Game project type, but we will ensure that the code that we develop for Windows will also work on the Xbox 360 game console. The reason that I'm focusing the text of the book on Windows Game projects is that you can easily compile, run, and debug your creations on the same machine.

Every example in this book has two solutions—one for a Windows game, and one for an Xbox 360 game. These two projects share the same source code, but each produces executable code that will run on its respective platform.

Xbox 360 Game Library

Like the Class Library, the Xbox 360 Game Library project type compiles to a DLL and contains shared code that an Xbox 360 Game project can reference as if it were its own. Any updates that are made to the DLL are propagated to all the games that refer to the DLL, without having to recompile each game.

Starter Kits

Starter kits are a way that example code can be distributed to the XNA community. XNA Game Studio Express comes with a Starter Kit project called Spacewar. Spacewar is a great example of what a hobbyist can do with XNA Game Studio Express, and there are some incredible new starter kits that are already available on the xna.com website, with more on the way.

When you create a new Starter Kit project, Visual C# 2005 Express generates a new solution and a new project that contains a complete, working game. You can poke around the code to see how the authors accomplished what they did, and you can experiment with the code to see how your changes affect the game.

Nickel Tour of the Visual C# 2005 Express IDE

The Visual C# 2005 Express IDE contains a number of windows, menus, and toolbars that you will use to write your games (see Figure 3.1). The IDE is highly configurable—allowing you to move, dock, float, hide, and show individual panes.

Code Editor

This is where the magic happens. You type your C# game code into this pane. It has several features that make your coding life a lot easier.

- **Syntax Highlighting**—As you type, the code editor colorizes words and symbols that it recognizes as having special meaning. C# language keywords, class names, strings, numbers, comments, and other bits of interest stand out from the rest of the code, making it easier to catch typos.

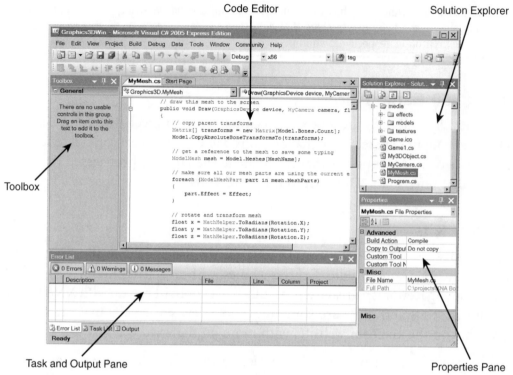

Figure 3.1
Anatomy of the XNA Game Studio Express IDE.

■ **Code Completion**—As you type, the code editor will try to predict what you're typing and provide a list of alternatives that you can use to automatically complete what you're typing, or simply ignore. This list of alternatives also includes descriptive text regarding each option. For example, if you're typing code to call a method on a class, the code editor will display an unobtrusive prompt listing each parameter of the method as you type, along with a brief description of its purpose.

■ **Refactoring**—The code editor provides another handy feature that lets you make sweeping, global changes to existing code. For example, let's say that you have a property named PlaeyrOne in a certain class that you're referencing in dozens of places, scattered throughout your code. You notice that there's a typo in the property name and you want to change it. The refactor function will rename the property for you, and then scan the project and update any references to the property that it finds.

Toolbox

For game projects, the Toolbox is not very useful. XNA games are created purely via code. There is no designer for an XNA game. On the other hand, Windows Application projects make extensive use of the Toolbox.

When editing a Windows application, you can drag components (like buttons and textboxes) from the Toolbox onto the designer (a layout tool that replaces the code editor when you are designing Windows forms). Then you can hook events from these controls to methods in your application.

Solution Explorer

The Solution Explorer provides you with a list of all the projects, project files, and project references that are contained within the currently loaded solution. You can edit files by double-clicking them in the Solution Explorer. You can edit solution or project properties by right-clicking them in the Solution Explorer and selecting Properties.

Properties Pane

Depending on what you have selected in the designer or in the Solution Explorer, the Properties pane may display properties for the currently selected item. For example, the Text on a button is a property and the Asset Name of a media file is a property.

Task and Output Pane

This pane contains several tabs that help you to manage feedback that the IDE may present to you.

- **Task List**—This tab lists the tasks that need to be addressed before you consider your solution complete. Such tasks may include unresolved syntax errors, compiler errors, and user-entered tasks.

- **Error List**—This tab lists all the errors that were generated by the compiler. You can filter this list to show or hide errors, warnings, and messages.

- **Output**—This tab displays all the messages that were generated by the build process. This output is similar to the text that you would see if you ran the compiler from the command prompt, outside of the IDE.

Building Games

Source code becomes an executable program via a process known as a build. Within the Visual C# 2005 IDE, you initiate a build from the Build menu when you click Build Solution (which tries to reuse unchanged files from previous builds to speed up the process) or Rebuild Solution (which performs a complete build, ignoring any intermediate build files).

There are two basic types of builds—Debug and Release. The Debug version of your game includes extra information that the IDE uses to aid you when you are debugging your game. The Release version of your game is optimized for speed and size. While you're developing your game, you'll want to make sure that you're using the Debug version of your game, and when you're ready to share your new creation with other players, you'll want to create a Release version of the game.

To change the build type, you simply select the desired option (Debug or Release) from the Solution Configurations dropdown list, located on the Standard toolbar, before you build your solution.

The following steps will take you through building and running the simplest XNA game.

1. Launch XNA Game Studio Express from the Windows Start menu. After just a few seconds, you should see the Visual C# 2005 Express Edition IDE.

2. From the main menu, select File, and then New Project. The New Project dialog appears.

3. Click on the icon labeled Windows Game, and then type **MyFirstXnaGame** in the field labeled Name. Note the value that's contained in the Location field; we'll need it later.

4. Click OK. A new XNA game project is created, and you can start adding your own code. This default project simply displays a blue screen.

5. To build your new game, select Build > Build Solution from the main menu.

6. To run your game, select Debug > Start Debugging from the main menu. The game displays a (cornflower) blue screen and waits for you to tell it to exit. You can shut your game down by pressing the Back button on your Xbox 360 Controller, pressing ALT+F4 on your keyboard, or by clicking the X in the top-right corner of the game window.

By default, your new solution should be located under your My Documents folder, in a subdirectory labeled Visual Studio 2005\Projects\[name of your solution]. Once you've performed a successful build, you should see a subdirectory within your project directory, labeled "bin." Within that directory will be subdirectories that relate to the platform and build type that you specified in the IDE—for example, "x86\Debug." These directories contain the actual executable files for your game.

Debugging Games

The Visual C# 2005 Express IDE includes powerful debugging facilities. You can step through your code, line by line, while it's running. While your program is paused, you can examine the values of any of the variables at that stage of execution, you can see what supporting DLLs (Framework APIs and Game Libraries) have been loaded, and you can examine the Call Stack to see what method calls lead the execution to that specific line of code.

The following steps will take you through debugging the XNA game that you created earlier.

1. Return to the MyFirstXnaGame project that you just created. Make sure that the Build mode is set to Debug by selecting Debug from the Solution Configurations dropdown list on the toolbar within the IDE.

2. Replace the existing Draw method with the following code.

```
protected override void Draw(GameTime gameTime)
{
    int x = 0;
    x = 1 / x;

    graphics.GraphicsDevice.Clear(Color.CornflowerBlue);

    // TODO: Add your drawing code here

    base.Draw(gameTime);
}
```

3. Build and run the project.

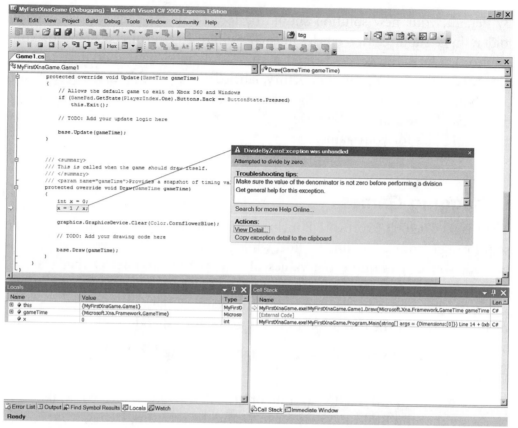

Figure 3.2
Debugging our intentional exception.

The code that we just inserted will generate a runtime error (known as an exception), which will cause the game to crash. If we were in Release mode, the crash would have resulted in the standard Windows dialog: "This application has encountered a problem and needs to close." Since we ran the game in Debug mode, the IDE traps the exception, pauses the game, and presents us with some tools to help identify the problem.

The first tool that the IDE presents to us is a dialog, shown in Figure 3.2, that describes the exception and lists some tips to help us fix it.

Notice the windows at the bottom of the IDE. The window to the left is labeled Locals, and it contains the values of any variables that are currently in scope. The window to the right is labeled Call Stack, and it shows the method calls that lead us to the line of code that caused the exception.

The Watch window is available in the same area as the Locals window. You can access it by clicking on the Watch tab. Like the Locals window, the Watch window shows you the current values of your variables. Unlike the Locals window, you can specify which variables you would like to watch. You can also hover your mouse over a variable in the source code editor to examine its current value.

The Immediate window is to the right, next to the Call Stack window. You can access it by clicking on the Immediate Window tab. This window allows you to print or change the values of variables and to make calls to your methods. Type **?** **x** and press Enter in this window to see the value of the variable named x. For detailed instructions on the usage of this window, see the "Immediate Window" topic, found in the Visual Studio 2005 Express Edition's documentation.

Not all programming errors result in an exception. Sometimes you'll want to break into the debugger at a specific location. For those times, you can set a breakpoint. Just before the game executes a statement that has been marked with a breakpoint, execution is paused and the IDE presents the same tools that you saw when we trapped an exception.

Once the debugger has been invoked and the game has been paused, you have several options for stepping through your code. You can:

- Resume execution of your game by selecting Debug > Continue from the main menu (or by pressing F5 on your keyboard). Execution continues until another breakpoint is reached or an exception occurs.

- Step over (execute) the current statement, breaking on the next statement, by selecting Debug > Step Over from the main menu (or by pressing F10 on your keyboard). The current statement is executed, and the debugger breaks on the statement that immediately follows it.

- Step into (execute) the current statement by selecting Debug > Step Into from the main menu (or by pressing F11 on your keyboard). This is the same as Step Over, but it allows you to step into methods, breaking on the first executable statement in the method.

- Step out of the current method by selecting Debug > Step Out from the main menu (or by pressing Shift+F11 on your keyboard). If you used Step Into to step through the statements that make up a method, Step Out will resume execution of your game's logic until the method returns. The debugger will break on the statement that follows the method call in the calling method.

Sharing Your Creations

For Windows games, you can simply distribute the executable that you create using XNA Game Studio Express, along with any media files that the game uses. The .NET Common Language Runtime supports a distribution method that's commonly referred to as XCOPY deployment (where you literally copy your game to another machine and execute it like any other application). There are also several third-party applications available that will package your application files into a setup package that can be delivered on CD, floppies (does anyone still use floppies?), or over the web.

The Visual C# 2005 Express IDE does have a Publish function under the Build menu that will allow you to distribute your Windows game via a UNC network share, removable media (like CD-ROM or DVD-ROM), or the web. It's not fancy, but it's free. For more information on the Publish feature of the IDE, please read the relevant documentation in the MSDN Library, which you installed in the previous chapter.

In the case of the Xbox 360 game console, your deployment options are rather limited. To share your XNA creations with an Xbox 360 user, you'll BOTH need to have the following:

- An Xbox 360 game console with a hard drive

- An active (Silver or Gold) subscription to the Xbox Live service

- An active subscription to the XNA Creators Club

- The XNA Framework runtime environment for the Xbox 360

- A Windows XP SP2 PC with a network adapter and XNA Game Studio Express installed

Once all those requirements are met, you can share your XNA game with the other user by sending him your entire project—all the project files, all the source code files, and all the media that are used by your game. The user then builds your project and runs it on his Xbox 360 game console just as you would.

You probably think that this sounds like a lot of trouble. You're right. But remember, the purpose of XNA Game Studio Express is to allow hobbyists and students to write non-commercial games and participate in a community of like-minded developers. It's not a way to bypass the approval process and licensing fees that are normally associated with commercial console game development.

Note

The XNA team at Microsoft has announced publicly that they would like to streamline the process by which developers can share their Xbox 360 games with other players (including those without the ability or the desire to install software development tools on their home PCs). They're trying to create a viable business model that will make the process easy for all involved—quickly pairing game developers with game players, while protecting end users from malicious applications of this new technology.

As of the XNA Game Studio Express Refresh release, there is a process for distributing your code to other XNA game developers without distributing your source code, project files, and game media.

Summary

In this chapter, you learned how the Visual C# 2005 Express IDE manages the source code and media files for your game, and how it generates the final game executable. You also learned how to step through your code, line by line, to identify problems and fix bugs. In this chapter, we discussed deployment options for Windows and the Xbox 360 game console, and we talked about using the Visual C# 2005 Express IDE for writing tools that help us to create, process, and manage game content.

Review Questions

Think about what you've read in this chapter to answer the following questions.

1. What are the two basic build modes for your games? What are the major differences between each?

2. List four ways to inspect the value of a variable in the debugger.

3. Where are your game's executable files located?

4. What is a starter kit? Where can you find them?

5. What is refactoring? How is refactoring performed within XNA Game Studio Express?

Exercises

EXERCISE 1. If you haven't done so already, be sure to follow the steps listed for building, running, and debugging your games. This information is fundamental to your game development efforts. Be sure that you know how to use the debugger to examine the values of your variables and step through your game's executable statements. Also be sure that you know where your solution, project, and executable files are located.

EXERCISE 2. Rebuild the MyFirstXnaGame in Release mode. Be sure that the error that we introduced is still in the source. Then run the game by selecting Debug > Start Without Debugging from the main menu. Describe what happens.

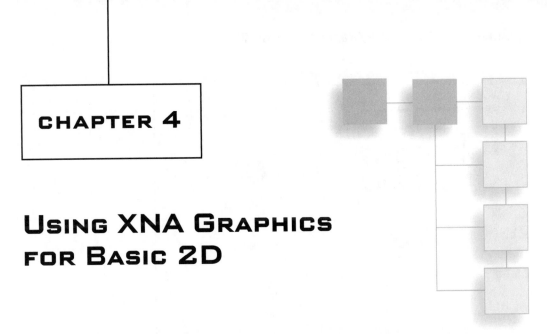

CHAPTER 4

USING XNA GRAPHICS FOR BASIC 2D

Sprites are the basic building blocks for 2D graphics programming in games. They are also used in 3D games as the basis for particle effects, heads-up displays, and text rendering systems. In this chapter, we will develop an example game that demonstrates the most common sprite drawing functions. Our example game (shown in Figure 4.1) will load several textures from the hard drive, and then scale, rotate, tint, fade, animate, and apply depth sorting to sprites that we create from those textures.

Every API that we discuss in this chapter is described in detail in the documentation that was installed when you set up your XNA Game Studio Express development system. This material is a good introduction to the basic concepts of 2D graphics programming, but you should also refer to the XNA documentation as you develop your own games.

In this chapter, you will learn how to:

- Load an image from your hard drive and display it in your game

- Use sprites for simple animations

- Rotate and scale a sprite

- Apply color tinting to a sprite

- Change the opacity of a sprite

- Draw sprites that are properly layered, regardless of the order in which they were actually drawn

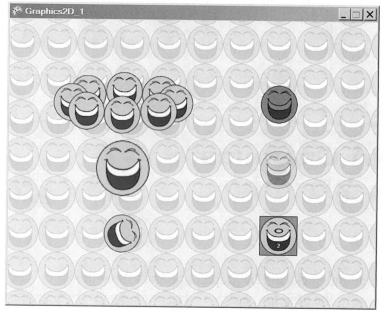

Figure 4.1
A screen shot of the example game that we will develop in this chapter.

Terminology

Before we get too much further, we need to define some basic terms that are common to 2D graphics programming under the XNA Framework.

What Is a Texture?

A texture is an in-memory digital image that is internally represented as a two-dimensional array of color values. These color values are called pixels, and they represent the most basic building block of any digital image. Individual pixels are identified within the texture using a pair of coordinates, typically labeled X and Y (or U and V). X represents the column position of the pixel in the two-dimensional array, and Y represents the row position. The top-most row has a Y value of zero, and Y increases as you move down the image. The left-most column has an X value of zero, and X increases as you move across the image to the right. The screen, itself, is conceptually a texture. It is represented as a two-dimensional array or pixels, and it uses the same coordinate system.

What Is a Sprite?

A sprite is a two-dimensional image that is integrated into a larger game scene. It is a subset of a texture that can logically be treated as a texture, itself. The width and height of the sprite are independent of the parent texture's resolution. Sprites provide a logical grouping of pixels which can be positioned and animated independent of each other. They make it easier to break large textures into multiple, smaller images in memory. Of course, a texture can contain just one sprite (as is the case in most of the sprites in this chapter's example game).

What Is a Sprite Batch?

The SpriteBatch class manages the drawing of your sprites to the screen. You begin a batch using the Begin method, draw as many sprites as you like using the Draw method, and then call the End method. Any settings that you assigned to the batch are applied to all of the sprites that are drawn within the batch. The SpriteBatch class is designed to take advantage of graphics hardware optimizations, and it can handle certain common tasks (like depth sorting) for you.

Files on the Disk to Textures in Your Game

Any digital image file can become an in-game texture, but the XNA Framework only supports one image format, internally. This format is proprietary and undocumented. Luckily, the XNA Content Pipeline provides support for a good number of graphics file formats. The pipeline converts your image files into XNA's native format as they're imported in Visual Studio. When you add a supported image file to your project, the pipeline works its magic and your image is available as a texture in your game.

I prefer to work with PNG source image files. PNG files are fully supported by the XNA Content Pipeline, they're supported by most image editing software packages, they can be previewed within Windows Explorer and all modern web browsers, they support transparency and alpha channels, and they compress well (using lossless compression). If you're not able to work with PNG files, the DirectX SDK provides a tool for creating transparent and masked images from BMP source images. For the examples in this book, I created all my game textures in a third-party image editor and saved my work as PNGs. The only time that I've had to use the DirectX Texture tool is when I was creating specialized textures for the 3D chapter.

When you create a new XNA game project in XNA Game Studio Express, the simplest code that represents a working game is generated for you. This game clears the screen to a shade of blue and waits for you to press the Back button on your Xbox 360 Controller. The source code for this game is contained within the Game1.cs file, and it is decorated with TODO comments that tell you where to insert your custom code. The example that we develop in this chapter starts from this base.

Just after the class declaration, we'll add a few variables to store our sprite textures, along with a reference to our one and only SpriteBatch instance.

```
public class Game1 : Microsoft.Xna.Framework.Game
{
    GraphicsDeviceManager graphics;
    ContentManager content;
    // the one and only sprite batch
    protected SpriteBatch m_batch = null;
    // our game textures
    protected Texture2D m_texSmiley = null;
    protected Texture2D m_texAnim = null;
    protected Texture2D m_texTile = null;
```

Now, we can load our textures from the disk. In the LoadGraphicsContent method, add code similar to the following.

```
/// Load your graphics content.
protected override void LoadGraphicsContent(bool loadAllContent)
{
    if (loadAllContent)
    {
        // initialize our sprite batch
        m_batch = new SpriteBatch(graphics.GraphicsDevice);
        // load our textures
        m_texSmiley = content.Load<Texture2D>(@"media\smiley");
        m_texAnim = content.Load<Texture2D>(@"media\smileyAnim");
        m_texTile = content.Load<Texture2D>(@"media\smileyTile");
    }
    // TODO: Load any ResourceManagementMode.Manual content
}
```

Those lines prepare the SpriteBatch for use, and load our textures into memory. Once loaded, we can draw the textures to the screen. The content variable is an instance of the XNA Framework's `ContentManager` class. This class is responsible for loading content that has been processed by the Content Pipeline. When we added the image files to our project, the standard graphics pipeline importer and processor converted the PNG image file into an XNA-friendly file format known as an XNB file. The XNB is a proprietary media file format that XNA uses for Windows and Xbox 360 games. You don't need to understand the inner workings of the Content Pipeline just yet. We'll cover the pipeline in more detail in a later chapter.

The Content Pipeline assigns a unique name to every media file that it processes. We'll use that name to load our textures. The smiley texture is a smiley face with a transparent background. The `smileyTile` texture is a fully opaque, grayscale image of the same smiley face, with a light gray background. And the `smileyAnim` texture contains five fully opaque variations of the smiley face that we will use as a simple animation.

The Heartbeat of an XNA Game

Unlike Windows applications, NT services, web services, and web applications, which spend most of their time waiting for events to process, an XNA game is constantly running, actively processing data. Games are real-time simulations that manage many objects simultaneously, gathering player input, updating objects, and drawing the current state of those objects to the screen in a fraction of a second, only to do it all again a few microseconds later.

This always-active process is driven by the game loop. The game loop is responsible for several tasks, but the most important of these is repeatedly making calls to your game's `Update` and `Draw` methods. That's the heartbeat of your game. XNA manages the game loop for you. You add code to your game's `Update` method to process your game objects, and you add code to your game's `Draw` method to render the current state of your game objects.

The `Update` method for the example game that we develop in this chapter is only responsible for maintaining two member variables. One records the time that has elapsed since the last call to the `Update` method (measured in seconds), and the other tracks the total time that the game has been running (also measured in seconds). Visual Studio was nice enough to add this method for us when we created the game project, but we have to add the member variables and updating logic ourselves.

```
// used for game state calculations
protected double m_TotalSeconds = 0.0;
protected double m_ElapsedSeconds = 0.0;
/// game logic such as updating the world
protected override void Update(GameTime gameTime)
{
    // Allows the default game to exit on Xbox 360 and Windows
    if (GamePad.GetState(PlayerIndex.One).Buttons.Back ==
        ButtonState.Pressed)
        this.Exit();
    // track elapsed time since last frame, and since the game started
    m_ElapsedSeconds = gameTime.ElapsedGameTime.TotalSeconds;
    m_TotalSeconds += m_ElapsedSeconds;
    base.Update(gameTime);
}
```

In addition to the code that we added to track the elapsed game time, there is an
if statement that polls the current state of the game controller, exiting the game
when the player presses the Back button. That line was automatically added to
the source code when we created our new game project. We will cover player
input in detail later in the book. Ignore that line for now.

The SpriteBatch Class

The SpriteBatch class allows you to use the same settings to draw multiple
sprites. To draw a sprite, you call the Begin method on the SpriteBatch object,
draw your sprite using the Draw method, and then call the End method. In our
example, we'll be using two different batch settings, so we'll call the Begin and End
methods twice, drawing two separate groups of sprites. Here's the Draw method
for our game, which uses the SpriteBatch object to draw several sprites on the
screen during each frame of the game.

```
/// render game objects
protected override void Draw(GameTime gameTime)
{
    graphics.GraphicsDevice.Clear(Color.CornflowerBlue);
    // draw typical sprites
    m_batch.Begin();
    DrawBackgroundTiles(m_batch);
    DrawTintedSmiley(m_batch);
    DrawFadedSmiley(m_batch);
```

```
    DrawAnimatedSmiley(m_batch);
    m_batch.End();
    // draw sprites that require special batch settings
    m_batch.Begin(
        SpriteBlendMode.AlphaBlend,
        SpriteSortMode.FrontToBack,
        SaveStateMode.None);
    DrawOrbitingSmileys(m_batch);
    DrawScalingSmiley(m_batch);
    DrawRotatingSmiley(m_batch);
    m_batch.End();
    base.Draw(gameTime);
}
```

The first batch of sprites uses the default settings of the `SpriteBatch` class. The sprites aren't scaled, rotated, or sorted before they're drawn. The second batch of sprites uses a different overload of the `Begin` method. This version of the `Begin` method allows us to handle the rotation, scaling, and sort order for our sprites.

The Background

The background for this game is drawn using the most basic form of the `SpriteBatch`'s `Draw` method. The background is made up of a grid of `smileyTile` textures, drawn side by side, one over another, until the screen is filled. To make the background a little more interesting, we will update the position of the first cell in our background tile grid over time as a simple, subtle animation. The other tiles are aligned to the first, so they too will be animated along with the first tile.

The background will scroll to the left at 50 pixels per second. The background will also oscillate up and down, varying its vertical position between 200 pixels up and 200 pixels down in a cycle that repeats roughly every 11 seconds (33 degrees per second). This vertical offset is calculated using the sine trigonometric function. The sine function takes an angle (expressed in radians) and returns a value between −1 and +1.

To animate our grid, we simply multiply the maximum vertical distance that we want our tiles to move in a given direction (200 pixels in this case) by the value of the sine function. The result is a number that lies between −200 (200 pixels up) and +200 (200 pixels down).

```
// offset from top, left of screen to start drawing our tiled sprites
protected Vector2 m_BkgrTileOffset = Vector2.Zero;

// number of degrees to increment with each passing second
protected const float BkgrDegreesPerSec = 33.0f;
// draw the background for our example
protected void DrawBackgroundTiles(SpriteBatch batch)
{
    // calculate angle and convert to radians
    double degrees = BkgrDegreesPerSec * m_TotalSeconds;
    double radians = MathHelper.ToRadians((float)degrees);
    // calculate the tile offsets
    m_BkgrTileOffset.X += -50.0f * (float)m_ElapsedSeconds;
    m_BkgrTileOffset.Y = (float)(200 * Math.Sin(radians));
```

Once we've adjusted the location of the first tile, we need to make sure that it's not too far off the visible screen. Otherwise, we'd be drawing sprite tiles that can never be seen (since they're not on the screen). That's a waste of processing time. As long as the first tile is at least partially visible on the screen, and it covers the screen pixel that's located at the coordinate (0, 0), it's ready to be rendered, along with the other tiles that make up the background.

```
// make sure that the first tile isn't too far left
while (m_BkgrTileOffset.X < -m_texTile.Width)
{
    m_BkgrTileOffset.X += m_texTile.Width;
}
// make sure that the first tile isn't too far right
while (m_BkgrTileOffset.X > 0)
{
    m_BkgrTileOffset.X -= m_texTile.Width;
}
// make sure that the first tile isn't too far up
while (m_BkgrTileOffset.Y < -m_texTile.Height)
{
    m_BkgrTileOffset.Y += m_texTile.Height;
}
// make sure that the first tile isn't too far down
while (m_BkgrTileOffset.Y > 0)
{
    m_BkgrTileOffset.Y -= m_texTile.Height;
}
```

We need to draw enough copies of the tile on the screen to fill the viewable area, and avoid drawing any tiles that are completely outside of the viewable area. The following code does just that.

```
// init current tile location with location of the top, left tile
Vector2 loc = m_BkgrTileOffset;
// draw our background tile in a grid that fills the screen
for (int y = 0; y <= SCREEN_HEIGHT / m_texTile.Height + 1; y++)
{
    loc.Y = m_BkgrTileOffset.Y + y * m_texTile.Height;
    for (int x = 0; x <= SCREEN_WIDTH / m_texTile.Width + 1; x++)
    {
        loc.X = m_BkgrTileOffset.X + x * m_texTile.Width;
        batch.Draw(m_texTile, loc, Color.White);
    }
}
}
```

Tinting Sprites

Take another look at the preceding source snippet. Notice the `Color.White` parameter that was passed to the `SpriteBatch`'s `Draw` method. That parameter is the tint of the sprite. In the case of our background tiles, we requested a white tint, which renders the sprite in its actual source image colors. You can tint a sprite using any color. The following snippet does this by making our smiley face pulse from red to normal tint.

```
// pulse smiley between red and no tint
protected void DrawTintedSmiley(SpriteBatch batch)
{
    // use simple sine function to pulse our tint between red and white
    double degrees = m_TotalSeconds * 120;
    double radians = MathHelper.ToRadians((float)degrees);
    float bias = (float)Math.Sin(radians);
```

Colors are expressed using three values—red, green, and blue. Using these three primary colors, we can represent just over 16 million unique colors. There are several ways to represent these three values in XNA. We'll be using the `Vector3` structure in this example. The constructor for `Color` that accepts a `Vector3` object expects the components of the vector (X, Y, and Z) to be in the range 0 to +1.

Since we're using the sine function to smoothly transition between shades of red, and the sine function returns values that are in the range −1 to +1, we need to clamp our values so that they lie between 0 and +1, ready to represent our chosen color. To clamp a value that's generated by the sine function (−1 to +1), we'll add one to it (0 to +2), and divide the new value by two (0 to +1).

```
// clamp the output of sine (-1 .. 1) to the (0 .. 1) range
bias = (bias + 1.0f) / 2.0f;
// get our new color
Vector3 v3Color = new Vector3(1.0f, bias, bias);
Color color = new Color(v3Color);
```

Next, we just pass our calculated color into the Draw method, and our sprite will be tinted for us.

```
    // draw our sprite at the specified location
    Vector2 loc = new Vector2(440, 108);
    batch.Draw(m_texSmiley, loc, color);
}
```

There are many uses for tinting within your games. As you progress through the various examples in this book, notice where tinting has been used to provide feedback to the player, without having to load and manage multiple tinted source textures. In the chapter on top-down scrollers, tinting is used to let the player know when his ship has been hit. In the chapter on bitmap fonts, tinting is used to draw text in different colors.

Transparent Sprites

When I said that colors have three components, I lied. Colors actually have four components. The red, green, and blue components define the color of every pixel that you see. The fourth component is the alpha value (or opacity) of the color. When the alpha value is 1.0f, the pixel is fully opaque. When the alpha value is 0.0f, the pixel is fully transparent. The following snippet is a variation on the previous theme that makes our smiley fade into and out of existence.

Notice that the red, green, and blue components are all set to 1, making the color white, which indicates that we don't want our sprite to be tinted while we're playing with its transparency.

```
// fade smiley in and out by varying the opacity of the sprite
protected void DrawFadedSmiley(SpriteBatch batch)
{
    // use simple sine function to pulse between transparent and opaque
    double degrees = m_TotalSeconds * 66;
```

```
        double radians = MathHelper.ToRadians((float)degrees);
        float opacity = (float)Math.Sin(radians);
        // clamp the output of sine (-1 .. 1) to the (0 .. 1) range
        opacity = (opacity + 1.0f)/2.0f;
        // get our new color
        Vector4 v4Color = new Vector4(1.0f, 1.0f, 1.0f, opacity);
        Color color = new Color(v4Color);
        // draw our sprite at the specified location
        Vector2 loc = new Vector2(440, 218);
        batch.Draw(m_texSmiley, loc, color);
}
```

Similar effects can be achieved using your image editing software. Drop shadows and glow effects that modify the alpha values of your source texture work without any extra code in your game. For an example, see the chapter on using player input from the game pad, found later in this book.

Animated Sprites

Sprites are static collections of pixels. You can change their location over time to create simple animations, but there will be times when you need more complex animations, like running or jumping characters. For those scenarios, you can create a series of sprites that contain the individual frames of your animation, and store them in a single texture. When you want to play your animation on the screen, you simply select the appropriate sprite from the series and draw it to the screen in its proper position.

In the following method, we will implement a simple frame-based animation by cycling through five animation frames at 10 frames per second. We need to track the current animation frame, and the time that the current frame has been on the screen. We'll store those values in member variables.

```
// current frame of animation
protected int m_AnimFrameNum = 0;
// delay between animation frames, and time since last frame change
protected double m_AnimFrameElapsed = 0;
protected const double m_AnimFrameDelay = 0.1;
```

Whenever our drawing method is called, we'll update the time that we've been on the current frame.

```
// draw animated sprite where individual animation
// frames are contained in a single texture, side
```

```
// by side, and drawn to the screen in rapid succession
protected void DrawAnimatedSmiley(SpriteBatch batch)
{
    // increment elapsed frame time
    m_AnimFrameElapsed += m_ElapsedSeconds;
```

If we've been on the current animation frame longer than a 10th of a second, we'll move on to the next frame and reset our elapsed time variable. When we reach the last frame, we'll start over with the first frame, looping the animation indefinitely. Rather than store the number of frames in a constant, we'll take advantage of the fact that each sprite in our animation is square (has the same width and height).

In our example, the number of frames can be expressed as the texture width divided by the texture height. Our source texture has five square sprites, placed side by side. Each sprite is 66 pixels tall and 66 pixels wide. The source texture is 330 pixels wide. So, the result of our formula is 330 pixels wide / 66 pixels tall = 5 animation frames.

```
// is it time to move on to the next frame?
if (m_AnimFrameElapsed >= m_AnimFrameDelay)
{
    // our frames are square, calculate the number of
    // frames in the texture
    int frameCount = m_texAnim.Width / m_texAnim.Height;
    // add one, take modulus of the frame count to keep
    // the index within the valid range
    m_AnimFrameNum = (m_AnimFrameNum + 1) % frameCount;
    // reset the elapsed counter, start counting again
    m_AnimFrameElapsed = 0;
}
```

Now that we know which sprite we want to draw, we can calculate the location of the frame within our texture, and then call out to the XNA Framework's graphics APIs to draw it for us.

```
// select the current animation frame, based on our index
Rectangle rect = new Rectangle(
    m_AnimFrameNum * m_texAnim.Height,
    0,
    m_texAnim.Height,
    m_texAnim.Height);
// location is constant for this example
```

```
        Vector2 loc = new Vector2(440, 328);
        // draw the selected sprite
        batch.Draw(m_texAnim, loc, rect, Color.White);
    }
```

We will use a similar technique to draw the backs of the playing cards in the chapter on card games found later in this book.

Scaling Sprites

The XNA Framework also provides routines for changing the scale of a sprite. In the following method, we will vary the size of our sprite from 50 percent of its original size to 150 percent of its original size, using the sine function.

The DrawScalingSmiley is the first of several methods that will take advantage of the more advanced settings of the sprite batch. To make things a little easier, we'll also define some constants that we can use when we don't want to specify a rotation, scale, or sort depth for our sprites.

```
// constants to ignore draw options that we're not interested in
protected const float NO_ROTATE = 0.0f;
protected const float NO_SCALE  = 1.0f;
protected const float NO_LAYER  = 0.5f;
// scale the smiley sprite from 50% to 150% of its original size
protected void DrawScalingSmiley(SpriteBatch batch)
{
    // use sine function to animate between extremes of scale
    double degrees = m_TotalSeconds * 66;
    double radians = MathHelper.ToRadians((float)degrees);
    float scale = (float)Math.Sin(radians);
```

Since the sine function returns values that are in the range −1 to +1, and we want values that are in the range 0.5 to 2.5, we'll need to clamp the raw value into a usable number. We can add 1 to the value to bring it to the range 0 to +2, then divide that by 2 to get the range 0 to +1, and add 0.5 to get a value that's in the range 0.5 to 1.5.

```
// sine generates a value between -1 and 1,
// clamp value between 0.5 and 1.5
scale = (scale + 1.0f)/2.0f + 0.5f;
```

Now that we know the scale, we can call out to the framework to draw our sprite for us.

```
// draw our sprite at the specified location
Vector2 loc = new Vector2(200, 250);
batch.Draw(
    m_texSmiley,          // the sprite texture
    loc,                  // location to draw the smiley
    m_rectSmiley,         // bounds of our sprite within texture
    Color.White,          // no tint
    NO_ROTATE,            // no rotation (zero radians)
    m_originSmiley,       // the center of the texture
    scale,                // our calculated scale factor
    SpriteEffects.None,   // draw sprite normally
    NO_LAYER);            // constant layer depth
}
```

Notice the m_originSmiley variable that was passed to the Draw method in the preceding code snippet. When using the standard functionality of the SpriteBatch, the anchor point of our sprites is (implicitly) the top-left corner of the sprite. When using the more advanced drawing methods, we need to specify an anchor point. In most cases, the center of the sprite is an ideal candidate. When rotating or scaling sprites, using the top-left pixel as the anchor would require us to constantly adjust the location of the sprite as it was rotated or scaled. Using the center of the sprite as the anchor means that the sprite will remain in the same on-screen position, regardless of its scale or angle of rotation.

This example applies a uniform scale to the sprite (the width and height are scaled by the same amount). The XNA Framework also provides a method of applying non-uniform scale to a sprite. By passing a Vector2 object (instead of a float value) to the Draw method of the SpriteBatch class, you can assign a different scaling factor

Rotating Sprites

The XNA Framework also provides routines for rotating sprites. In the following method, we will rotate a sprite at a fixed rate of rotation (66 degrees per second, clockwise). Note that the rotate variable in the following code snippet is redundant, but I left it in there to parallel the other methods that we developed (which take the sine of the angle in radians).

```
// rotate smiley at a constant rate
protected void DrawRotatingSmiley(SpriteBatch batch)
{
    // increment angle of rotation
```

```
double degrees = m_TotalSeconds * 66;
double radians = MathHelper.ToRadians((float)degrees);
float rotate = (float)radians;
// draw our sprite at the specified location
Vector2 loc = new Vector2(200, 360);
batch.Draw(
    m_texSmiley,            // the sprite texture
    loc,                    // location to draw the smiley
    m_rectSmiley,           // bounds of our sprite within texture
    Color.White,            // no tint
    rotate,                 // our calculated rotation angle
    m_originSmiley,         // the center of the texture
    NO_SCALE,               // no scale (1x times original)
    SpriteEffects.None,     // draw sprite normally
    NO_LAYER);              // constant layer depth
}
```

Sprite Depth

The XNA Framework also provides routines for sorting sprites by their distance from the player. We'll use this functionality to animate eight sprites, orbiting around a single point. As the sprites move along their orbital path, they will be drawn in front of and behind each other, based on their progress.

```
// how many smileys are orbiting?
protected const int ORBIT_COUNT = 8;
// draw several smileys orbiting around an invisible point
protected void DrawOrbitingSmileys(SpriteBatch batch)
{
```

The orbit path is a circle, but we'll be squashing the vertical movement of the sprite to create an illusion of perspective. We need to know the position of the first sprite, but we'll calculate the position of the other sprites by dividing the number of degrees in the circle (360) by the number of sprites that are in orbit. Since the XNA Framework likes to work with radians rather than degrees, we'll express the number of degrees in the circle in radians (2 × Pi radians = 360 degrees).

Note

If you're wondering why the XNA math APIs use radians instead of degrees, just keep reading. I'll give you my spin on it.

```
// calculate the angle for the first sprite
double degrees = m_TotalSeconds * 33;
double radians = MathHelper.ToRadians((float)degrees);
// calculate the angle between each sprite (the delta)
double delta = 2.0 * Math.PI / ORBIT_COUNT;
```

For each sprite that's in orbit, we need to calculate its on-screen position. We'll use the sine function to calculate the Y coordinate and the cosine function to calculate the X coordinate. The center of the orbit is located at (200, 140), so our calculations will generate values that are relative to that point on the screen.

To give the illusion of perspective, we'll squash our circular orbit into an elliptical orbit by making the change in X much greater that the change in Y for our sprites. Our sprites will move between –90 and +90 horizontal pixels, and between –20 and +20 vertical pixels.

```
// variable to hold the location of each sprite
Vector2 loc = Vector2.Zero;
// for each smiley that's in orbit
for (int i = 0; i < ORBIT_COUNT; i++)
{
    // determine trig values for sprite to calculate
    // each sprite's position on the screen
    float cos = (float)Math.Cos(radians + delta * i);
    float sin = (float)Math.Sin(radians + delta * i);
    // calculate the position of each sprite
    loc.X = 200.0f + 90.0f * cos; // [110 to 290]
    loc.Y = 140.0f + 20.0f * sin; // [120 to 160]
```

We'll use the depth sorting feature of the SpriteBatch class to ensure that sprites that are higher on the screen are drawn behind sprites that are lower. The sorting order is a configurable option that can be specified when you call the SpriteBatch's Begin method. The settings that we passed from our game's Draw method dictate that sprites with lower depth values will be drawn in front of sprites with higher depth values.

Our background tiles are also sprites, and they could, in theory, fight for position with our orbiting sprites, but they were drawn using a different rendering batch, so their depth is ignored when sorting our orbiting sprites. If enabled, depth sorting applies only to sprites within the same batch.

```
// calculate sprite depth as function of its
// Y location so that higher smileys are drawn
// behind lower smileys. sine generates a value
```

```
// between -1 and 1, clamp value between 0 and 1
float layer = (sin + 1.0f)/2.0f;
```

We're ready to draw our sprites. The order in which we draw our orbiting sprites doesn't matter. The drawing APIs will sort them before they're actually drawn (when we call the End method on our SpriteBatch class).

```
// draw our sprite at the calculated location
batch.Draw(
    m_texSmiley,           // the sprite texture
    loc,                   // location to draw the smiley
    m_rectSmiley,          // bounds of our sprite within texture
    Color.White,           // no tint
    NO_ROTATE,             // no rotation (zero radians)
    m_originSmiley,        // the center of the texture
    NO_SCALE,              // no scale (1x times original)
    SpriteEffects.None,    // draw sprite normally
    layer);                // our calculated layer
    }
}
```

A Tangent on Radians

You're probably wondering why XNA uses radians rather than degrees for its math functions. I wasn't involved in the design or implementation of the XNA Framework, so I don't have the source code to reference. What follows are my assumptions, based on my (arguably limited) knowledge of trigonometry, calculus, CPU architectures, and general programming concepts. If you don't have any interest in those topics, feel free to skip the next few paragraphs. I've just included this section for the curious.

Hardware-Accelerated Floating Points (FPUs)

In the early days of game programming, CPUs did not have specialized hardware to process floating point numerical data. Everything was integer-based, and floating point numbers were handled by the software. To speed things up, game developers would use fixed-point math for their calculations and replace the slower trig functions with custom routines that interpolated between values that were stored in a pre-calculated array.

Today's PC processors have instruction sets and registers built into the CPU that are dedicated to working with floating point numbers. In many cases, floating point operations can be performed just as fast as their integer-based counter-parts. Many of those instructions (like `fsin`, `fcos`, `fptan`) work with radians.

General Programming

As an API developer, you have two choices if you want to take advantage of hardware acceleration. You can store the results of your intermediate calculations in the native format of the hardware, or you can convert your data to the native format before passing it off, and then convert the results back to your internal format.

Our game can work with decimals, radians, or hoggies (a unit of measurement that I just made up where one hoggie = 3.85 degrees), but somewhere between our code and the FPU, our values will have to be converted to the native format of the hardware. Those conversions aren't free.

Why waste CPU cycles converting numbers when you can just store them in an FPU-friendly format? Handing raw data off to the hardware will always be faster than converting the data every time it enters or leaves the FPU.

The Math

The FPU expects radians. The math APIs use radians internally so that they can avoid wasting CPU cycles by converting data to and from degrees every time a method is called. That doesn't explain why radians were selected as the unit of measure in the first place.

What Is a Radian?

A radian is the ratio of an arc length to a radius. There are 2 Π radians in a full circle (360 degrees).

Given a circle of radius R, the length of the segment on its circumference that spans a given angle can be expressed with the following formula.

```
length(angle) = radius * angle
```

This formula expects the angle to be expressed in radians. If we want to work with degrees, we'll need to tweak it.

```
length(angle) = radius * (angle * Π / 180)
```

Notice that we've added a multiplication to our formula (the compiler is smart enough to combine "Π/180" into a single constant).

For the same circle, the area of the sector (pie slice) that spans a given angle can be expressed with the following formula.

```
area(angle) = ½ * radius² * angle
```

Again, this formula expects the angle to be expressed in radians. If we want to work with degrees, we'll need to tweak it.

```
area(angle) = ½ * radius² * (angle * Π/180)
```

And again, we've added a multiplication to our formula.

Think back to your high school trigonometry class. You'll see that our formulas for length and area give us the standard definitions for the circumference of a circle and the area of a circle when the radius is 2 Π radians (360 degrees).

```
circumference = 2 Π R
area = Π R²
```

Calculating Sine

The sine function can be defined as the sum of a series of numbers. As you expand the series further and further, you get closer and closer to the value of sine for the given angle. Or stated another way, the series converges on sin(x). The formula looks something like this.

```
sin(x) = x - x³/3! + x⁵/5! - x⁷/7! + ... + (-1)ⁿ * x^(2*n+1)/(2*n+1) + ...
```

You can't sum this series to infinity. You just need to take it as far as you need to so that you get a reasonable approximation of sin(x). The calculator in Windows tells me that the sine of 3 radians is roughly 0.141120. Let's see how well our power series approximates sine.

```
sin(3) = 3 = 3
sin(3) = 3 - 3³/3! = -1.5
sin(3) = 3 - 3³/3! + 3⁵/5! = 0.525
sin(3) = 3 - 3³/3! + 3⁵/5! - 3⁷/7! = 0.091071
sin(3) = 3 - 3³/3! + 3⁵/5! - 3⁷/7! + 3⁹/9! = 0.145312
sin(3) = 3 - 3³/3! + 3⁵/5! - 3⁷/7! + 3⁹/9! - 3¹¹/11! = 0.140874
```

We only had to calculate the first five or six items in the series to start getting values that are close to the actual value of the sine function. The further we go, the more accurate our approximation will be.

The formula calculates the sine of a given angle, expressed in radians. Would it work if we used degrees? Nope. The formula expects x to be expressed as radians.

We could change the formula to use degrees by tweaking each term in the series, or we could convert the parameter to radians before processing, but ultimately we need to use a radian angle.

Radians Are a Natural Choice

I could cite formula after formula that might be used in your games to calculate trajectories, angular momentum, torque, and a whole slew of other things. In each case, we'll either be peppering our code with "Π / 180" conversions or we'll just use radians directly.

Note

> The code for this chapter (and the other chapters) is not optimized. I've written the code to favor readability and illustration of concept over speed and elegance of design. You will often find me embedding conversions from degrees to radians within the game logic. This is yet another case of "do as I say, not as I do."

Summary

In this chapter, you learned how to load textures from the hard drive and break them into sprites for use in your games. You learned how to draw sprites to the screen and alter their position on the screen. You also learned how to apply simple drawing effects to your sprites to distort them, allowing you to draw a variety of on-screen sprites using a single source sprite. In the process, you learned how to write code to rotate, scale, animate, tint, fade, and depth sort sprites.

Review Questions

1. What is a pixel? How many pixels does an image have if its horizontal resolution is 640 and its vertical resolution is 480?

2. How many components does a `Color` have? What are they called? How do they affect the color of the pixels that you see on the screen?

3. What static method in the `MathHelper` class is used to convert degrees to radians?

4. What range of values does the sine function return? What range of values does the cosine function return?

5. Two overlapping sprites are drawn on the screen. The first has a depth value of 0.33f. The second has a depth value of 0.75f. Assuming depth sorting was enabled in the sprite batch, which sprite will be drawn in front of the other? If depth sorting is not enabled, which sprite will be drawn in front of the other?

Exercises

EXERCISE 1. Change the `ORBIT_COUNT` member variable from 8 to 100. Rebuild and run the game. Describe what you see.

EXERCISE 2. In the game's `Draw` method, change the sort mode of the second call to `Begin` from `SpriteSortMode.FrontToBack` to `SpriteSortMode.BackToFront`. Rebuild and run the game. Describe what you see.

EXERCISE 3. Pick one of the `DrawXxxSmiley` methods and modify the rate of change for the demonstrated effect. For example, change the assignment to the degrees variable in the `DrawScalingSmiley` method from `"m_TotalSeconds * 66"` to `"m_TotalSeconds * 360"`. Rebuild and run the game. Describe what you see.

EXERCISE 4. Modify the code in the `DrawScalingSmiley` method to apply a non-uniform scale to the sprite. What happens if you specify a negative number for the vertical scale factor?

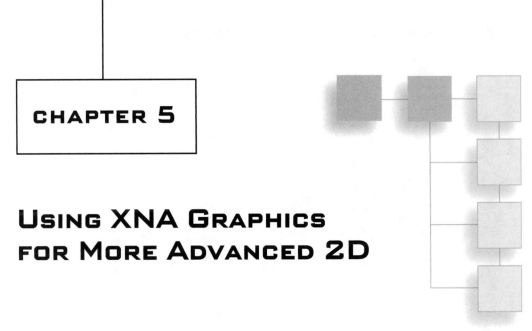

CHAPTER 5

USING XNA GRAPHICS FOR MORE ADVANCED 2D

This chapter will expand on the last chapter by presenting some more advanced 2D graphics concepts. We will develop an example game that draws several orbiting smileys using the same basic methods that we used for the example in the last chapter. When the user presses the A button on his Xbox 360 Controller (or the space bar on his keyboard), the game will pause the main animation, capture the current game screen, convert the screen image to black and white, and then manipulate the captured image using a simple warp effect that mimics the refraction you might see if our smileys were under water.

All of the work in drawing the new animation will be done using custom code that we write, drawing each frame of the warp effect pixel by pixel. We will also implement the same warping animation using the standard XNA Framework libraries. Having two implementations of the same effect means that we can compare them side by side, observing how each approach affects the performance and quality of the resulting animation.

In this chapter, you will learn how to:

- Combine multiple sprite effects to make your animations more interesting

- Capture pixel data from a game screen into an array of `Color` values

- Better understand how pixels map to on-screen images

- Implement a warp effect, roughly similar to the refraction of light through water

- Generate texture data using code and draw generated images to the screen

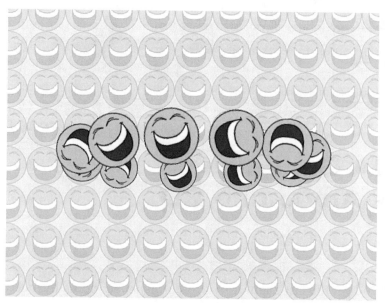

Figure 5.1
A screen shot of the example game that we will develop in this chapter.

The Main Animation

We'll start with the rotating smileys from the example in the last chapter. We'll use the same animated background, so I won't list that code here. But, we will be making some changes to the rotating smiley code, since they're now the focus of the example, rather than just a small part of a larger screen.

The smileys will orbit around a point at the center of the screen. Each smiley will get larger as it nears the player and smaller as he moves away. When the game starts up, each smiley will be assigned a random rate of rotation. The rotation rates will be between 1 and 50 degrees per second, and the direction of the rotation will alternate with each smiley. Rather than orbiting within a fixed plane, the smileys' orbits path will seem to tilt up and down as they move. See a screen shot of the game in Figure 5.1.

Let's take a look at the code. We need to declare some member variables to track the number of smileys, their progress along the orbit path, and their angle of rotation.

```
// used for game state calculations
protected double m_TotalSeconds   = 0.0;
protected double m_ElapsedSeconds = 0.0;
// how many smileys are orbiting?
```

```
protected const int ORBIT_COUNT = 11;
// what is the rotation rate of each smiley?
protected int[] m_rotateSmiley = new int[ORBIT_COUNT];
```

We'll calculate the location and scale of each smiley every time. We just need to know the angle of the first smiley's orbit position to calculate the rest. We'll calculate that angle by multiplying our rate of orbit (33 degrees per second) by the number of seconds that the animation has been playing. That's the orbit position of the first smiley. To calculate the positions of the other smileys, we can simply divide a complete orbit (360 degrees, or 2 × `Pi` radians) by the number of smileys that are in orbit to give us the number of degrees (or radians) between each smiley.

```
// draw several smileys orbiting around an invisible point
protected void DrawOrbitingSmileys(SpriteBatch batch)
{
    // calculate the angle for the first sprite
    double degrees = m_TotalSeconds * 33;
    double radians = MathHelper.ToRadians((float)degrees);
    // calculate the angle between each sprite (the delta)
    double delta = 2.0 * Math.PI / ORBIT_COUNT;
```

Knowing where the smiley is along the orbit path doesn't tell us where he is on the screen. We'll go ahead and create a local variable to store those calculations and fill it in later.

```
// variable to hold the location of each sprite
Vector2 loc = Vector2.Zero;
```

Next, we'll calculate the angle of tilt for our orbit plane. Like the rate of orbit, the angle of tilt is calculated by multiplying the rate of tilt by the number of seconds that the animation has been playing. We'll get the sine of this angle (a value between −1 and +1) and use that to offset our smileys on the screen.

```
// calculate a virtual tilt for the orbit plane
// to make the smileys look like they're on a
// tilt-a-whirl at the state fair
double degTilt = m_TotalSeconds * 33;
double radTilt = MathHelper.ToRadians((float)degTilt);
float   sinTilt = (float)Math.Sin(radTilt) * 2.0f;
```

We now have enough information to start placing our smileys on the screen. We'll be using simple trigonometric functions to calculate the location of the smileys. By combining the outputs of these simple functions, we can create more complex animations. We need to process each smiley, so we'll need to create a loop. Our first task within this loop will be to calculate the trig values that we'll be using for the smiley.

```
// for each smiley that's in orbit
for (int i = 0; i < ORBIT_COUNT; i++)
{
    // determine trig values for sprite to calculate
    // each sprite's position on the screen
    float cos = (float)Math.Cos(radians + delta * i);
    float sin = (float)Math.Sin(radians + delta * i);
```

Next we'll center the smiley on the screen, then calculate his actual position using the results of our trig functions. Remember, our trig functions return values that lie between –1 and +1, and those values are calculated based on the angle that we provide. For the same smiley orbit angle, we will always get the same value (between –1 and +1). Calculating our on-screen position is as simple as multiplying this value by the maximum distance (in pixels) that we want our smiley to travel in a given direction.

To make our orbit look like it's in a plane that's roughly parallel to the floor, we need to choose a maximum difference in smiley location that's wider than it is tall. In the orbit, each smiley moves along a perfect circle at a constant rate. On the screen, the distance that the smiley covers horizontally is much greater than the distance that he covers vertically. The orbit is squished on the screen. It's not a circle any more; it's an ellipse.

We'll pick a horizontal distance of 200 pixels, and a vertical distance of 20 pixels. That means that our smiley will travel horizontally between –200 and +200 pixels from the center of the screen, and travel vertically between –20 and +20 pixels from the center of the screen. If we weren't applying tilt to our orbit, we would now be done calculating our smiley's location on the screen.

To make the tilt a little easier, I'm going to cheat. Rather than throw any more math into the mix, we can just use the raw output of our trig function to manipulate the vertical location of the smiley, as is. Since the trig functions return values between –1 and +1, we can just multiply the vertical distance by this value to negate it (–1), cancel it (0), use it as is (+1), or anything in between. Without applying tilt, we get the same basic animation that we saw in the last chapter. For a given angle, the location of a smiley on the screen is always the same. By adding tilt, we get the same range of vertical motion, but over time the vertical offset is reversed, moving the smiley below the origin rather than above (or visa versa).

```
// position at the center of the screen
loc.X = SCREEN_WIDTH  / 2;
loc.Y = SCREEN_HEIGHT / 2;
// offset, based on orbit progress
loc.X += 200.0f * cos;           // [120 to 520]
loc.Y +=  20.0f * sin * sinTilt; // [200 to 280]
```

We also want to give our smiles a sense of perspective by scaling them as they orbit so that smileys that are further away from the player appear smaller than smileys that are closer. To make things simple, we can use the vertical offset (ignoring tilt) to know which smileys are further away. The higher the smiley is on the screen (again, ignoring tilt), the further he is from the player.

```
// calculate sprite depth as function of its
// Y location so that higher smileys are drawn
// behind lower smileys. sine generates a value
// between -1 and 1, clamp value between 0 and 1
float layer = (sin + 1.0f)/2.0f;
```

Since our background tiles are also sprites, we need to make sure that our smiley that's furthest from the player is never drawn behind the background tiles. Our background tiles are always at layer zero. As long as our smiley's depth is greater than zero, we're okay. So whenever a smiley's depth is zero, we'll set it to a value that's slightly greater than zero but guaranteed never to be greater than any other smiley.

```
// avoid conflict with background (at layer = 0)
// by choosing a value just above zero
if (layer == 0) { layer = NO_LAYER; }
```

The actual scale of the smiley is a function of his depth (or his distance from the player). The depth of a smiley is a value between 0 and +1, since that's the range of values that the XNA Framework expects when drawing depth-sorted sprites. When the smiley's depth is +1, the smiley is as close as he can be and should be drawn at the largest scale. When the depth is 0, he's at his furthest point from the player, and we should draw him at his smallest scale. I've decided to draw the closest smiley at 150 percent of his original size and draw the furthest smiley with no scale applied.

```
// scale the closest smiley to 150% and the
// furthest smiley by 100% to give the illusion
```

```
// of depth as each smiley completes his orbit
float scale = 1.0f + 0.50f * layer;
```

The last thing we need to know before we can draw our smiley is his current rotation angle. We can determine this angle by multiplying the rate of rotation for the smiley by the number of seconds that the animation has been playing.

```
// calculate the rotation angle for this smiley
float rotate = m_rotateSmiley[i] * (float)m_TotalSeconds;
rotate = MathHelper.ToRadians(rotate);
```

That's it. We're ready to draw the smiley using the standard XNA Framework graphics APIs.

```
        // draw our sprite at the calculated location
        batch.Draw(
            m_texSmiley,          // the sprite texture
            loc,                  // location to draw the smiley
            m_rectSmiley,         // bounds of our sprite within texture
            Color.White,          // no tint
            rotate,               // rotate each smiley at a random rate
            m_originSmiley,       // the center of the texture
            scale,                // scale between 1x and 2x normal size
            SpriteEffects.None,   // draw sprite normally
            layer);               // our calculated layer
    }
}
```

Capturing the Screen

Up to this point we haven't really introduced anything that wasn't covered in the last chapter. It's time to dig a little deeper into the inner workings of how images are stored, manipulated, and drawn within the XNA Framework's graphics APIs.

Our source images and the final image that we see on the screen are all made up of collections of pixels. A pixel is the smallest graphical unit that we will be working with. A real-world scene has infinite resolution, but any digital image that represents that scene has a finite resolution (by necessity, since our host operating system doesn't have infinite memory or infinite storage). The digital image is made up of a two-dimensional array of pixels (or color values) that were sampled from the real-world scene at a regular interval. The XNA Framework's graphics APIs provide functions for us to access the array of individual pixels that make up a texture. We will be using those arrays to see what pixels have been drawn to the screen and manipulate them to create entirely new images.

First, we need to create two arrays to store our pixel data—one to store the data that we capture from the screen and one to store the pixel data that we generate. We won't disturb the first array. It's our source data. Any work that we do to generate a new image will be stored in the second array. Since we'll be generating the entire screen image for every frame of animation pixel by pixel, we need to create arrays that are big enough to store all of the pixels that make up the game screen (a total of SCREEN_WIDTH * SCREEN_HEIGHT pixels).

```
// pixel data for the game's last rendered frame
protected Color[] m_colorDataBuffer =
    new Color[SCREEN_WIDTH * SCREEN_HEIGHT];
// array to store our pixel data for our generated images
protected Color[] m_colorDataWorking =
    new Color[SCREEN_WIDTH * SCREEN_HEIGHT];
```

The XNA Framework's graphics APIs don't like to work at the pixel level. They prefer collections of pixel data to be grouped into textures. So we'll create a new Texture2D object that we can stuff our pixel data into just before drawing it to the screen.

```
// texture to stuff our pixel data in before drawing to screen
protected Texture2D m_texWorkingBuffer = null;
```

Now, we're ready to actually capture the screen's pixel data. The XNA Framework API that we need is a member of the GraphicsDevice object, which is a member of the GraphicsDeviceManager object. Rather than type graphics.GraphicsDevice.SomeMethod(...) every time we want to access this object, we'll store a reference to our graphics.GraphicsDevice instance in a local variable to save ourselves some typing.

```
// grab the latest pixels from the game screen's back buffer
// and convert the data to black-and-white
protected void CaptureGameScreen()
{
    // local variable to save some typing
    GraphicsDevice device = graphics.GraphicsDevice;
```

Since we created the texture that we're using to hand our pixel data over to the XNA Framework ourselves, we need to manage it ourselves. Whenever the XNA

Framework alerts us that textures have been reloaded, we'll set the reference to our texture to null, and recreate it just before we need it.

```
if (m_texWorkingBuffer == null)
{
    // we need to manage this texture ourselves, whenever
    // resources are reloaded, we set the member variable
    // to null, then recreate it here, just before use
    m_texWorkingBuffer = new Texture2D(
        device,
        SCREEN_WIDTH, SCREEN_HEIGHT,
        1,
        ResourceUsage.AutoGenerateMipMap,
        SurfaceFormat.Color,
        ResourceManagementMode.Automatic);
}
```

Our custom effect is only invoked when the user is pressing a certain button (the A button on the Xbox 360 Controller or the space bar on the keyboard). The first time we generate our custom image data, we need to capture the pixels from the current game screen. From that point on, the image on the screen will be our own, and capturing the data again would only pollute our source data.

So, we'll maintain a member variable that indicates the state of the Pause button during the previous frame of animation. We know that we're in the paused state now, or our method would not have been called. We just need to see if this is the first custom frame to be drawn since the button was pressed. If so, we'll capture the game screen's pixel data.

```
// we know the game is paused now, but was it
// paused the last time we checked?
if (!m_WasPaused)
{
    // create a texture to capture the back buffer
    Texture2D tex = new Texture2D(
        device,
        SCREEN_WIDTH,
        SCREEN_HEIGHT,
        1,
        ResourceUsage.ResolveTarget, // this is the magic option
        SurfaceFormat.Color,
        ResourceManagementMode.Manual);
    // grab the image, extract the pixels, then free the memory
```

```
device.ResolveBackBuffer(tex);
tex.GetData<Color>(m_colorDataBuffer);
tex.Dispose();
```

Now that we have the source pixel data, we'll make a simple change so that it's obvious that we've entered our paused state. We'll convert the source pixel data into its grayscale equivalent (a black-and-white image). As I mentioned earlier, color data is typically stored as the red, green, and blue components that make up the color. Those components are known as the RGB color space. Without going into too much technical detail, there are other color spaces that are better suited for specific tasks.

RGB is a great model for displaying computer images that are created with colored light (additive mixture). CMYK (cyan, magenta, yellow, key [or black]) is a color space that's better suited for printed images that are created with colored inks (subtractive mixture). There's another color space, known as HSL (hue, saturation, luminance [or lightness]), that makes it easy to convert RGB data to grayscale data accurately. We'll use the HSL color model to convert our captured color data to a black-and-white image.

To convert an HSL color to a grayscale RGB color we simply assign the value of the L component to all three components of our RGB color. Since we're only interested in the L component of the HSL value, we won't bother to calculate the other two. We just need to iterate over the entire pixel data array, converting the RGB values of each pixel to an L value and assigning that L value back to all three components of our original pixel.

```
// convert our pixel data to grayscale
for (int i = 0; i < m_colorDataBuffer.Length; i++)
{
    Color color = m_colorDataBuffer[i]; // current pixel
    // calculate the luminance (3rd component of HSL color)
    int min = Math.Min(Math.Min(color.R, color.G), color.B);
    int max = Math.Max(Math.Max(color.R, color.G), color.B);
    int lum = (min + max) / 2;
    // convert to grayscale in RGB color space
    m_colorDataBuffer[i] =
        new Color((byte)lum, (byte)lum, (byte)lum);
}
```

Now that our pixel array has been converted to grayscale data, we're ready to stuff the pixels into our texture and start using it.

```
// store our grayscale pixel data in our working texture
m_texWorkingBuffer.SetData<Color>(m_colorDataBuffer);
    }
}
```

The Warp Grid

The effect that we'll be applying to our source image is a very simplified warp effect (see Figure 5.2). We'll break the source image into a number of distinct regions whose rectangular bounds are defined by a regular grid. We will similarly divide our destination image into the same number of regions, but the grid that defines our destination regions will be displaced and scaled to form an irregular grid. To generate the destination image, we'll map the pixels that are contained in each cell of the (regular) source grid to the pixels that are contained in the (irregular) destination grid. The result will be a warped image that's roughly analogous to the refraction that you observe when looking at objects that are immersed in the clear water of a swimming pool.

I said that this effect is a "very simplified warp effect" because all of the grid cells in our warp model are represented by regular rectangles. In more sophisticated warp models, the lines that make up each grid rectangle are not aligned vertically

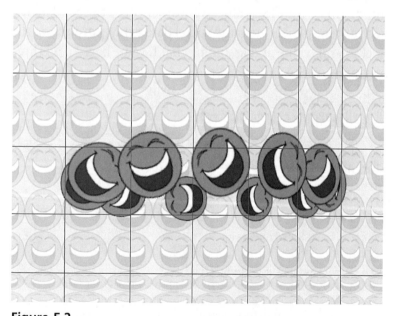

Figure 5.2
The orbiting smileys paused and warping, along with the grid lines that define the boundary of the destination cells.

and horizontally. I simplified this effect so that we can focus on how an effect can be applied, without spending a lot of time laboring over the details of how a specific effect is implemented. This effect strikes a nice balance between complexity of implementation and visual interest.

Another reason for the simplification is that I wanted to show you how the same effect can be achieved using the standard XNA Framework sprite APIs, which use regular rectangles to define sub-image boundaries within texture data. We'll be able to compare and contrast the two implementations of our effect to see how each affects performance and image quality.

Since our source grid is regular (each cell has the same width and height), we don't need to store the location and size of each cell. We can just as easily calculate that information when we need it. The destination grid is a different story, though. The grid cells are irregular (the size and location of cells varies over time, and neighboring cells almost never have the same width and height), but we will ensure that the bounds of each cell are axis-aligned (the lines that make up the cell are vertical or horizontal).

To reduce the complexity of the code, and to share the calculated grid data with both implementations of our warp effect, we'll store values that define the extent of each row and column in a member array. When we work with each grid cell, we'll need to know the rectangle that defines its bounds. These row and column values will make it easy to generate the cell rectangles.

```
// number of rows and columns in our warp grid
protected const int GRID_ROWS = 5;
protected const int GRID_COLS = 7;
// size of an unscaled cell in our warp grid
protected const int ROW_SIZE = SCREEN_HEIGHT / GRID_ROWS;
protected const int COL_SIZE = SCREEN_WIDTH / GRID_COLS;
// X and Y locations of our warped grid columns and rows
protected int[] m_GridWarpX = new int[GRID_COLS + 1];
protected int[] m_GridWarpY = new int[GRID_ROWS + 1];
```

We're now ready to populate our warp grid arrays. Since our generated image will fill the entire game screen, we need to make sure that the bounds of our destination grid extend to the edges of the screen. We'll do that by setting the X component of the first column to zero and the X component of the last column to SCREEN_WIDTH. Similarly, we'll set the Y component of the first row to zero and the Y component of the last row to SCREEN_HEIGHT.

```
// calculate the location and size of cells in our warp grid
protected void CalculateGridWarp()
{
    // first row and column are fixed at image border
    m_GridWarpX[0] = 0;
    m_GridWarpY[0] = 0;
    // last row and column are fixed at image border
    m_GridWarpX[GRID_COLS] = SCREEN_WIDTH;
    m_GridWarpY[GRID_ROWS] = SCREEN_HEIGHT;
```

To vary the height and width of each row, we'll use our old buddy the sine function. We need to generate an angle to feed into the function. Our angle will be 66 degrees per second times the number of seconds that the warp animation has been playing. Since the XNA Framework math APIs prefer to work with radians, we'll also create a couple of variables to store our converted angle and resulting sine value.

```
// calculate the initial rotation angle (66 degrees per second)
float degrees = 66 * (float)m_TotalSecondsPaused;
// temp variables used to store intermediate calculations
double radians;
float val;
```

If we applied the same angle to every row and column, we would still have a regular grid whose location was just shifted by some fixed amount. We need to vary the angle used to calculate the height of each row and the width of each column. I've selected numbers that evenly distribute a full animation cycle (360 degrees) across the entire screen. I just thought those values made for a more interesting animation. These values are arbitrary. I selected them using trial and error. To increase the irregularity of the animation, I could have used a different primary angle for each component of the grid (row and column) or used two different trigonometric functions (sine for one and cosine for the other), or both.

```
// vary cell sizes by offsetting the rotation angle
float dAngleRow = 360.0f / GRID_ROWS;
float dAngleCol = 360.0f / GRID_COLS;
```

We're now ready to calculate the warp grid cell locations. We simply add our angle variance to the primary angle as we move from row to row or column to column. The final location of a row boundary is calculated as the location of the row boundary in a regular grid (row * ROW_SIZE) plus our sine value (which is in the range of −1 to +1) times the half of the height of a regular row (val * ROW_SIZE/2). That means that a row boundary will never be offset more than half of its height above or below its original position. The final location of each column boundary is calculated using a similar method.

```
// calculate row locations
for (int row = 1; row < GRID_ROWS; row++)
{
    radians = MathHelper.ToRadians(degrees + dAngleRow * row);
    val = (float)Math.Sin(radians);
    m_GridWarpY[row] =
        (int)Math.Round(row * ROW_SIZE + val * ROW_SIZE / 2);
}
// calculate column locations
for (int col = 1; col < GRID_COLS; col++)
{
    radians = MathHelper.ToRadians(degrees + dAngleCol * col);
    val = (float)Math.Sin(radians);
    m_GridWarpX[col] =
        (int)Math.Round(col * COL_SIZE + val * COL_SIZE / 2);
    }
}
```

Drawing the Warped Grid (Standard Method)

We now have all the information that we need to describe each cell in our source grid and destination grid. It's time to draw the warped image to the screen. We'll implement the effect using the standard XNA Framework graphics APIs first so that we can focus on the effect. Then we'll implement the effect using our custom pixel-by-pixel code.

To view the warp effect using the standard implementation, the player will press the X button on his Xbox 360 Controller or the X key on his keyboard. To view the warp effect using the custom implementation, the player will press the A button on his Xbox 360 controller or the space bar on the keyboard.

Earlier, we created two arrays to store pixel data—one for the source data and one for our generated data. But, we only created one texture to stuff our pixel data into when calling the XNA Framework APIs. Our custom implementation and our standard implementation use the same Texture2D object to interact with the framework. Our custom implementation will generate new data for every frame of animation and store the results in the texture, but this implementation is only interested in the pixels from the source game screen image. If the player invokes our standard method after viewing the custom method, without returning to the main game's unpaused animation, the texture may be filled with our custom data.

We need to make sure that the texture contains the unmodified, grayscale source image. We could just stuff the pixels from our source array into the texture every time this method is called, but that would be a waste of resources. Instead, we'll just keep track of the state of the paused animation and only reset our texture when we see that the player jumped directly from the custom warp implementation to this one.

```
// use standard XNA methods to draw the warped image
protected void DrawPausedScreenStandard(SpriteBatch batch)
{
    if (m_WasCustomWarp)
    {
        // the player jumped directly from custom to standard warp
        // the working buffer isn't filled with its original data
        // restamp the working buffer with the data from the screen
    m_texWorkingBuffer.SetData<Color>(m_colorDataBuffer);
}
```

To use the standard XNA Framework APIs, we need to work with a source texture rectangle (a cell in the regular source grid) and a destination texture rectangle (the same cell in the irregular destination grid). We'll define those rectangles now and populate them as we move from cell to cell.

```
// source and destination rectangles for our texture data
Rectangle rectSrc = Rectangle.Empty;
Rectangle rectDst = Rectangle.Empty;
```

We'll process each cell in the grid by looping through each row and each column in the grid. For each cell, we'll determine its bounding rectangle by locating the top-most (y1), left-most (x1) pixel, and the bottom-most (y2), right-most (x2) pixel.

```
// for each row in the grid
for (int row = 0; row < GRID_ROWS; row++)
{
    // top and bottom location of the cell
    int y1 = m_GridWarpY[row + 0];
    int y2 = m_GridWarpY[row + 1];
    // for each column in the grid
```

```
    for (int col = 0; col < GRID_COLS; col++)
    {
        // left and right location of the cell
        int x1 = m_GridWarpX[col + 0];
        int x2 = m_GridWarpX[col + 1];
```

To convert those values to a `Rectangle` object, we need to calculate the location (top, left) and the size (width, height) of the current cell. The top and left values are straightforward (y1 and x1). The width of the cell is the difference between the right and left pixel (x2 − x1), and the height of the cell is the difference between the bottom and top pixel (y2 − y1).

```
// destination rectangle, warped screen coordinates
rectDst.X = x1;
rectDst.Y = y1;
rectDst.Width = x2 - x1;
rectDst.Height = y2 - y1;
// source rectangle, unwarped texture coordinates
rectSrc.X = col * COL_SIZE;
rectSrc.Y = row * ROW_SIZE;
rectSrc.Width = COL_SIZE;
rectSrc.Height = ROW_SIZE;
```

Now that we have a rectangle to define the bounds of the source cell and the destination cell, we can call out to the XNA Framework's graphics APIs to draw the cell for us.

```
    // use standard batch draw method
    batch.Draw(
        m_texWorkingBuffer,
        rectDst,
        rectSrc,
        Color.White);
    }
}
```

To help us visualize what this effect is doing, we'll draw the lines that define the warped grid. The grid will only be drawn if the player is pressing the B button on his Xbox 360 Controller or the B key on the keyboard while one of the warp effects is playing. To draw a grid line using the standard framework APIs, we need a source rectangle that encompasses a single pixel (a rectangle with a width and height of one) and a destination rectangle that represents a vertical or horizontal line. To draw the grid lines, we'll iterate through each of the grid rows, drawing a horizontal line, and then each of the columns, drawing a vertical line.

```
// should we show the grid?
if (ShowGrid)
{
    // extract single pixel from texture to draw lines
    rectSrc.X = 1;
    rectSrc.Y = 1;
    rectSrc.Width = 1;
    rectSrc.Height = 1;
    // prepare for drawing horizontal lines
    rectDst.X = 0;
    rectDst.Width = SCREEN_WIDTH;
    rectDst.Height = 1;
    // draw a line between each row of cells
    for (int row = 1; row < GRID_ROWS; row++)
    {
        rectDst.Y = m_GridWarpY[row];
        batch.Draw(
            m_texWorkingBuffer,
            rectDst,
            rectSrc,
            Color.Green);
    }
    // prepare for drawing vertical lines
    rectDst.Y = 0;
    rectDst.Width = 1;
    rectDst.Height = SCREEN_HEIGHT;
    // draw a line between each column of cells
    for (int col = 1; col < GRID_COLS; col++)
    {
        rectDst.X = m_GridWarpX[col];
        batch.Draw(
            m_texWorkingBuffer,
            rectDst,
            rectSrc,
            Color.Green);
    }
}
```

Drawing the Warped Grid (Custom Method)

Now we're ready to implement the same effect by drawing each pixel in the destination image, pixel by pixel. As in the standard implementation, everything starts with knowing the bounds of a cell in the source grid and the bounds of that same cell in the destination grid. If there were no difference in scale between the two cells, we could just copy the pixels from the source array to our working array. But, things are rarely ever that easy.

If the destination cell is larger than the source cell, copying pixels from the source array to the destination array on a one-by-one basis would result in gaps in the image since there aren't enough pixels in the source cell to cover the space that's enclosed by the destination cell. And in the case where the destination cell is smaller than the source cell, pushing pixels over, one by one, would result in overwriting pixels as they compete for space in the compressed area. We need to assign a color to each pixel in our destination cell by interpolating between the pixels that lie on the edges of the source cell.

We know the width of the source cell, and we know the width of the destination cell. When those two values are equal, the first pixel in the destination is the first pixel in the source. Every time we move one pixel to the right in the destination cell, we move one pixel to the right in the source cell to find the proper pixel data. When the two widths are not equal, we need some formula to map a given destination pixel to the equivalent pixel in the source cell.

The basic formula that we will base our calculations on is `SourceCellWidth/ DestinationCellWidth`. When the widths are equal, the value is one. When the destination is larger, the value is less than one. When the destination is smaller, the value is greater than one. This ratio gives us the virtual width of a pixel in the source cell. This number times the number of pixels in the destination cell equals the width of the source cell. So it maps each destination pixel to its corresponding source pixel. In some cases, source pixels will be used more than once, and in some cases source pixels will be skipped altogether. In every case, there will be a color value for every pixel in the destination cell. The height of a pixel in the source cell uses a similar ratio.

```
// draw the warped image, pixel-by-pixel
protected void DrawPausedScreenCustom(SpriteBatch batch)
{
    // for each row in the grid
    for (int row = 0; row < GRID_ROWS; row++)
```

```
  {
      // top and bottom location of the cell
      int y1 = m_GridWarpY[row + 0];
      int y2 = m_GridWarpY[row + 1];
      // sample distance between pixels in source image
      float dy = (float)ROW_SIZE / (float)(y2 - y1);
      // for each column in the grid
      for (int col = 0; col < GRID_COLS; col++)
      {
          // left and right location of the cell
          int x1 = m_GridWarpX[col + 0];
          int x2 = m_GridWarpX[col + 1];
          // sample distance between pixels in source image
          float dx = (float)COL_SIZE / (float)(x2 - x1);
```

At this point, we know the extent of the source and destination rectangles, and we know the virtual width and height of a pixel in the source cell. That's all we need to start copying pixels. When we start copying from a new row (or a new column) of pixels in the source cell, we need to set our pointer into the source data to the top (or left) of the cell. That's our starting point. From there, we simply add the virtual pixel height (or virtual pixel width) to the pointer into the source data every time we move to the next pixel in our destination cell.

Since we're working with fractional numbers, we can't store our source cell indices in integer values. We'll use a float instead, but we need to round those float values to the nearest integer before we can use them as indices into our source color data array.

Conceptually, our pixel data is stored in a two-dimensional array of color values, where the X and Y can be used as indices into the array. In practice, our pixel data is stored in a single-dimensional array, where all of the pixels that make up our screen are stored in a single row in memory. To map X and Y coordinates to this one-dimensional array, we can use a simple formula. Each row of the screen takes up SCREEN_WIDTH pixels in our array. To locate the first pixel of a row in the array, we just multiply the row index by the width of a row (Y * SCREEN_WIDTH). To locate the pixel from a certain column, we just add the column index to the previous calculation (giving us X + (Y * SCREEN_WIDTH)).

```
// set srcY to the top of the source cell
float srcY = row * ROW_SIZE;
// for each row of pixels in the new cell
for (int y = y1; y < y2; y++)
```

```
{
    // set srcX to the left of the source cell
    float srcX = col * COL_SIZE;
    // for each column of pixels in the new cell
    for (int x = x1; x < x2; x++)
    {
        // set pixel in our working buffer
        m_colorDataWorking[x + y * SCREEN_WIDTH] =
            m_colorDataBuffer[
                (int)Math.Round(srcX) +
                (int)Math.Round(srcY) * SCREEN_WIDTH];
```

While we're incrementing our fractional source indices, we need to make sure that we're not overstepping the bounds of the source cell. This can happen in certain fringe cases where rounding errors creep into our calculations. The floats that we're calculating are very close approximations, but they're not perfect.

```
        // increment srcX, checking image bounds
        srcX = Math.Min(srcX + dx, SCREEN_WIDTH - 1);
    }
    // increment srcY, checking image bounds
    srcY = Math.Min(srcY + dy, SCREEN_HEIGHT - 1);
    }
  }
}
```

As with the standard implementation, we'll add the option to draw grid lines to help us visualize what this effect is doing. The grid will only be drawn if the player is pressing the B button on the Xbox 360 Controller or the B key on the keyboard while one of the warp effects is playing. To draw a grid line using our custom implementation, we will just set all of the pixels in a given column (vertical grid line) or row (horizontal grid line) to the same color value.

```
// should we show the grid?
if (ShowGrid)
{
    // draw a line between each row of cells
    for (int row = 1; row < GRID_ROWS; row++)
    {
        int index = m_GridWarpY[row] * SCREEN_WIDTH;
        for (int x = 0; x < SCREEN_WIDTH; x++)
        {
            m_colorDataWorking[index + x] = Color.Red;
```

```
        }
    }
    // temp variable to save some typing
    int lenData = m_colorDataWorking.Length;
    // draw a line between each column of cells
    for (int col = 1; col < GRID_COLS; col++)
    {
        int index = m_GridWarpX[col];
        for (int y = 0; y < lenData; y += SCREEN_WIDTH)
        {
            m_colorDataWorking[index + y] = Color.Red;
        }
    }
}
```

Now that we've populated our destination color data, we're ready to display it on the screen. We'll just stuff our pixel data into our texture and have the XNA Framework's graphics APIs draw the texture for us.

```
    // store our generated pixel data in our working texture
    m_texWorkingBuffer.SetData<Color>(m_colorDataWorking);
    // bounds for the entire image
    Rectangle rectSrc =
        new Rectangle(0, 0, SCREEN_WIDTH, SCREEN_HEIGHT);
    // use standard batch draw method to draw our generated texture
    batch.Draw(m_texWorkingBuffer, Vector2.Zero, rectSrc, Color.White);
}
```

Implementation Differences

The performance of our custom method is much worse than the standard method. The reason is simple. The XNA Framework graphics APIs are tailor-made to work with any available graphics hardware. Our custom implementation does all of its processing on the CPU, where we're constantly fighting low-level issues like CPU cache misses and transferring data across CPU/GPU hardware boundaries.

The quality of the resulting effect in our custom implementation is noticeably worse than the same effect in the standard implementation. It looks fine, and it runs well, but there are certain visual artifacts that appear in our custom effect that aren't there in the standard effect. Figure 5.3 is an enlarged section of the effect in action. The image on the left was generated using the standard

Figure 5.3
Enlarged section of the warp effect in action. The image on the left uses the standard implementation. The image on the right uses the custom implementation.

implementation, and the image on the right was generated using our custom implementation.

Notice the visual artifacts around the curved parts of the sprite in the image on the right—near the edge of the face, the eyes, and the smile. Our pixel selection was based on a simplified "best guess." The XNA Framework's graphics APIs rely on hardware acceleration. Hardware graphics processors do a much better job of approximating the destination pixel colors because they use an algorithm known as bilinear filtering to interpolate between the color values of the surrounding source pixels at a sub-pixel level. We just grabbed the color that was stored in the closest source pixel.

The point of this chapter wasn't to teach you how to write a warp effect. It was to show you how you can create textures by populating pixel data from your code. It doesn't make much sense to base an entire game off of software rendering, but procedural textures are a powerful tool in your overall design strategy. In addition to creating "old skool" demo effects like the warp effect seen here, you can create realistic textures like wood, smoke, and fire for your 3D games. And rendering your game screen to a texture allows you to create interactive environment maps for objects like race cars and armor-clad heroes.

Full-Screen Mode

When the game is running under Windows, you can switch between full-screen and windowed mode by pressing the left trigger on your game pad or the Z key on your keyboard. As long as you hold the button down, the game will be in full-screen mode. As soon as you release the button, you'll return to windowed mode. On the Xbox 360 game console, the game will always run in full-screen mode.

To support this feature, we need to determine when the player has selected full-screen mode. The following code, added to our main game class, does just that.

This property will return true only when the requested screen mode does not match the current screen mode.

```
// player requested full screen mode?
public bool ToggleFullScreen
{
    get
    {
      bool pressed =
        PadState.Triggers.Left > 0 ||
        KeyState.IsKeyDown(Keys.Z);
      return
        (pressed && !graphics.IsFullScreen) ||
        (!pressed && graphics.IsFullScreen);
    }
}
```

To actually toggle between full-screen and windowed mode, we'll add the following code to the game's Update method. When the ToggleFullScreen property returns true, we will toggle the IsFullScreen property of our GraphicsDevice Manager instance and ask it to apply our change.

```
#if !XBOX360
        // toggle between full-screen and windowed mode when
        // the game is running under windows
        if (ToggleFullScreen)
        {
          graphics.ToggleFullScreen();
          // could also do this
          // graphics.IsFullScreen = !graphics.IsFullScreen;
          // graphics.ApplyChanges();
        }
#endif
```

Summary

In this chapter, you learned how to combine multiple sprite effects to create more interesting sprite animations. You also learned how to capture pixel data from your game's back buffer, manipulate it using code, and draw it back to the screen. You also learned how procedural textures can be used in games and some of the caveats to look for when generating images on the fly.

Review Questions

1. List some ways that this example uses the sine and cosine functions to animate sprites.

2. How was our game screen converted to a black-and-white image after it was captured?

3. In the custom implementation of the warp effect, how are pixels mapped from the source image to the destination image?

4. What was the purpose of the `m_texWorkingBuffer` member variable in our example game?

5. What are some of the limitations of generating images in software? What are some of the benefits?

Exercises

EXERCISE 1. Tweak the values that drive the `CalculateGridWarp` method. Find several settings that you like and several settings that you don't like. Describe what makes one set of values seem more appealing than another. How are the settings affecting what you see on the screen?

EXERCISE 2. Google for an article on the HSL color space and create a two-column chart that compares and contrasts the HSL color space to the RGB color space. Focus on how you might use HSL in games or other image processing applications. Explain why RGB is the dominant color space for game programming.

EXERCISE 3. Modify the code in this example so that smileys that are further from the player are drawn with a darker tint than smileys that are closer to the player.

EXERCISE 4. Modify the code in this example to replace the scrolling background with a warp effect on those same tiles during the normal (unpaused) animation.

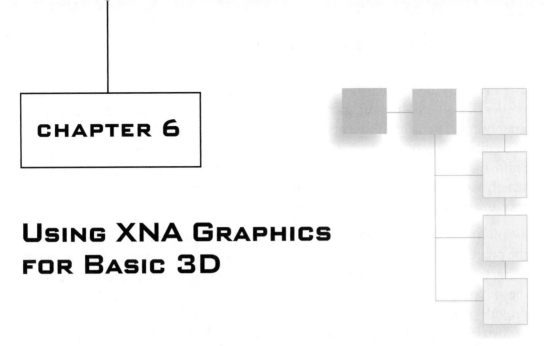

CHAPTER 6

Using XNA Graphics for Basic 3D

Before Carmack and Abrash became instantly recognizable names in the game development community, names like Bresenham and Wu commanded immense respect. For decades, computer graphics research and game development have been separate areas of study, due in large part to the fact that consumer devices just hadn't progressed to the point where graphics theory could practically be applied in real-time games. Game developers have always kept a watchful eye on the work that the research community is doing, spending a great deal of time trying to approximate the researchers' results (a.k.a. "faking it") in games.

Specialized 3D graphics hardware has allowed more and more of that theory to become reality. Most new PC motherboards have integrated graphics chips with 3D hardware support built right in. For the serious gamer, feature-rich graphics cards have dropped in price, become easier to install and configure, and have seen an exponential growth in their processing power and data throughput. This coupling of the greater adoption rates in consumer devices with the rich feature sets of modern graphics cards means that you have more power to bring your gaming visions to life.

In this chapter, we will take a look at how XNA makes taking advantage of 3D hardware acceleration easier for game developers. We'll create a simple game project that loads a 3D model from disk (using the Content Pipeline), manipulates it within a virtual world, renders the world to the screen, and allows the player to move around in this virtual world using his controller or keyboard.

The focus for this chapter is to explain how you can use the XNA Framework to render 3D objects in your game. The purpose of XNA is to make game programming easier. I don't want to pollute that notion by bombarding you with page after page of mathematical equations. You don't need to be an artist, animator, or math wizard to write 3D games. It definitely helps, but it's not strictly required. Most of the hairy details of 3D programming are abstracted into easy-to-use XNA Framework classes.

I want to make sure that you understand the basic concepts behind 3D space and the process of translating your raw 3D data into on-screen images, but we're not going to cover every detail of the underlying process or discuss in any great detail the dozens of different ways that you can perform the same tasks. I'll try to provide an overview of other methods, but the text and code for this chapter will be focused on using the most intuitive APIs so that you can begin working in this fascinating medium a little faster.

In this chapter, you will learn how to:

- Understand the basic concepts behind 3D graphics programming

- Load a 3D model

- View 3D objects within a virtual world from any location, at any angle

- Manipulate 3D objects within a virtual world

- Leverage the BasicEffect class to use vertex and pixel shaders in your game

- Understand the basic concepts behind shaders in XNA

- Write your own vertex and pixel shaders to use in your game

3D Basics

In the early days of 3D graphics in games, graphics hardware was strictly 2D. Graphics cards were just dumb interfaces to the monitor. You could set any pixel on the screen to any (available) color that you wanted, but you had to determine the color of each pixel in that grid on your own. Rendering 3D objects to the screen required custom software, and all the heavy lifting was done by the CPU.

Note

Some games, like *The Bard's Tale*, used a set of fixed-angle wall images to make the player feel like he was navigating a dungeon maze or city streets. Later, games like *Castle Wolfenstein* and *Doom* allowed the player to view those same walls from any angle, but the maps were still locked to a 2D playing field (*Doom*'s rendering engine is commonly referred to as "2.5D" since the data is 2D with height data, but the player believes that he is navigating a 3D world). Other games, like *Decent* and *Ultima Underworld*, used true 3D engines where players could look around the game world in any direction.

For all of these early games, the color of every pixel on the screen was determined by specialized software that the game developers wrote. There was no 3D hardware acceleration for personal computers at that time.

Objects

Objects in a 3D world are represented using meshes. A *mesh* is a collection of points in 3D space that provide a rough approximation of the surface of the object. Objects in 3D space can be moved, rotated, or scaled by simply moving, rotating, or scaling all of the points that define the object by the same amount.

If we were to just draw the individual points to the screen, our rendering wouldn't be very realistic. Those points define the bounds of the object's surface, but to actually draw the surface we need to fill in the space that lies between them. If we were to simply fill in the empty space that lies between all of those dots once they've been drawn to the screen, we would have (at best) a silhouette that represents the object's profile as viewed from a particular angle. That's not exactly what we want either. We need a way to group the points into some polygonal shape that we can easily fill.

Early software renderers gathered the points of a mesh into groups of triangles or groups of rectangles. Generally, triangles were favored because they are guaranteed to be flat surfaces (any three points in 3D space are coplanar, or exist within the same, flat surface). By grouping the points into triangles, and then filling in those triangles as we draw them to the screen, we can create a more realistic representation of our 3D object (see Figure 6.1).

Figure 6.1
A 3D model of a teapot, rendered as a collection of points, a collection of triangles, and a collection of filled triangles.

So, points are grouped to form triangles, and that collection of triangles provides a reasonable approximation of the surface of our 3D object. The colors that we choose to fill those triangles with will greatly influence the overall appearance and realism of our final scene.

Shading Models

I want to take a little time here to discuss the various techniques that can be used to draw your three-dimensional objects on the screen. Most of these techniques were born out of necessity, when 3D hardware was non-existent and the processing power of consumer-grade CPUs was a fraction of what it is today. But, many of these styles of rendering have made a comeback as gaming has spilled into other non-traditional, low-powered platforms like cell phones, PDAs, digital camera LCDs, and the web. And many of these older shading models form the basis of the graphics engines that drive games that have elected to go with a more "retro" style, as well as those that have moved away from the trend of ultra-realism into the emerging field of non-photorealistic rendering (NPR), opting for wildly stylized environments.

Wireframe

Since the processing of 3D objects in early games was handled by the CPU, the amount of work that you could perform during each frame was limited by the speed of the processor on which you were running. The first 3D games were only able to represent 3D objects as simple lines on the screen that outlined the basic shape of the object. This type of 3D drawing is known as *wireframe* rendering.

Flat Shading

As processors became more powerful, programmers were able to do more work in the same amount of time. The next evolution in shading models was known as *flat shading*. As each triangle is drawn in a flat-shading model, the direction in which the triangle faces is compared to the position of one or more imaginary light sources. If the triangle is facing the light source, it is filled with a brighter color. If the triangle faces away from the light, it is filled with a darker color.

Gouraud Shading

Flat-shaded models represent the shape, size, and surface detail fairly well, but they're not very realistic. Flat shading compares virtual light sources once per triangle. So the entire triangle is affected by a light source in the same way. To provide more realism, the pixels that make up a triangle need to vary in color across the surface of the triangle. An easy way to accomplish this task is to compare the orientation of the three, individual points of the triangle to the light source, then interpolate between those three colors as each pixel of the triangle is drawn. This is known as *Gouraud shading*.

Texture Mapping

For even more realism, decals can be applied to the mesh in a process known as *texture mapping*. Each of the three points that make up a triangle is assigned a value known as a texture coordinate. A *texture coordinate* is simply an index into a texture (a bitmap), specifying the column and row (commonly referred to as U and V) of a pixel within the texture. In much the same way that Gouraud shading interpolates between three color values, texture mapping interpolates between these three texture coordinates, selecting the color of each pixel in the triangle based on the color of the appropriate pixel in the texture.

Environment Mapping

While texture maps can be static, like decals that are stuck to our mesh, we can vary the texture coordinates of the points of the triangle over time to change the image that's projected onto the triangle. Environment mapping is a shading technique that does just that.

Environment mapping creates the illusion of shininess by having triangles reflect their surroundings. Texture coordinates are calculated (every time the object is drawn) that map a special texture to each of the three points of the triangle. This special texture is known as an *environment map* (or a *cube map*). This texture contains a rendering of the world, as seen from the mesh's perspective, from six angles, each 90 degrees from its neighbors. The result is an object that appears to reflect the surrounding environment.

Non-Photorealistic Rendering (NPR)

The goal of 3D graphics has long been to render the most realistic worlds possible, given the current state of consumer hardware. But, there's another branch of shading that takes the opposite approach. Known as *non-photorealistic rendering* (NPR) in graphics circles, this method of shading encompasses countless individual styles.

Figure 6.2
A 3D model of a teapot, rendered as Gouraud shaded, environment mapped, and 'toon shaded.

The goal of NPR is to render stylized objects, rather than realistic objects. There's been a lot of impressive research in this area. 3D worlds are rendered to look like artwork, rather than photographs. Water colors, colored pencils, charcoal sketches, impressionist paintings, cartoons, and many more styles can be represented (see Figure 6.2).

Composite Effects

Shading models are not mutually exclusive. Various techniques can be combined to achieve beautiful composite effects. For example, a racing car in your game may be red, shiny, and have a dozen sponsor logos. The base color for each triangle would be calculated based on the triangle's orientation to virtual light sources using Gouraud shading. A texture map would be applied to the triangle to affix the sponsor logos as decals. And, an environment map would be applied to the triangle to reflect the surrounding environment.

The results of each of these calculations can be blended together using a weighted average. The end result is a very realistic-looking mesh, with relatively few sample points of data.

Ultra-Realism (Global Illumination and Cinema-Quality Rendering)

I've mentioned several of the most common in-game shading models, but there are many more shading models that are widely used in 3D computer animation packages and computer graphics research. The most realistic rendering engines attempt to model the way that light is scattered in an environment, reflecting, refracting, and changing in hue and brightness.

Those models require many more calculations than can be performed in the constraints of a real-time game. That's why there's such a difference in the quality of the animations that are produced for cinema and games. As hardware becomes more advanced, we're able to use more of those complex techniques (or "fake" them more effectively). The goal of the game programmer has been, and will continue to be, devising short cuts and trickery to produce similar results in less processing time.

Hardware

As I mentioned earlier, the work done by early 3D rendering engines in games was done on the CPU. The quality of the generated images in your game is directly related to the processing time that you are able to budget for graphics processing. Faster processors and clever rendering techniques make software rendering more realistic, but there's still a lot of data that has to be processed. Time that you spend generating animation frames is time that can't be spent on AI, physics, object management, and other game tasks.

There are many common tasks that must be performed when rendering 3D meshes, regardless of what technique you use to shade them. In the past, each game contained its own, home-grown 3D rendering engine. It didn't take long for specialized APIs to emerge. Games began targeting these APIs, greatly reducing development time and maintenance costs. The most famous of these APIs are OpenGL and DirectX (the XNA Framework is based on DirectX). In time, consumer graphics card manufacturers began providing specialized hardware to efficiently process 3D data, and that hardware was driven by the standard 3D APIs. By building your game on OpenGL or DirectX, you automatically gained a performance boost whenever your game ran on a properly configured PC (using the latest versions of the drivers and APIs).

Fixed-Function Pipelines

Early 3D APIs provided a set of predefined algorithms to process 3D data, known as the *fixed-function pipeline*. The programmer would pass his data through this graphics pipeline to convert textures and 3D mesh data into 2D images on the screen. While the set of operations that could be performed was fixed, the graphics APIs exposed configurable options (in the form of global state variables) so that the programmer could generate many different effects using the same data. Creating custom effects required processing data on the CPU, bypassing many of the benefits of hardware acceleration.

Shaders

The latest generation of video cards provide specialized processing units built right in. These mini CPUs are known as *GPUs (graphics processing units),* and they are able to run specialized code known as *shaders.* Processing 3D mesh data on the graphics card frees up the CPU to perform other tasks, and processing the data on the same hardware where it's stored greatly reduces the amount of data that needs to be shuttled from the computer to the graphics card during every screen update.

Early shader languages resembled assembly language, where cryptic mnemonics map to actual instructions on the GPU, one to one. The XNA Framework supports a high level shader language (known as HLSL), which allows you to take advantage of your graphics card's GPU using an easier-to-understand, C-like language. Shaders currently come in two varieties, vertex shaders and pixel shaders. We will discuss each of these a little later in this chapter.

Note

A third shader type, the geometry shader, is available in the latest DirectX APIs, but the current XNA Framework doesn't support them yet. Support for DirectX 10, which implies support for geometry shaders, has been cited by the XNA team as a goal for a future release of XNA. No details and no date have been provided, though.

Putting It All Together

The 3D APIs that are included with the XNA Framework are built upon DirectX technologies. DirectX provides much-needed hardware abstraction as well as a standard interface for processing 3D meshes and rendering them to the screen. The XNA Content Pipeline provides support for some common 3D data file formats, and allows developers to extend that functionality with custom importers and processors that will support their own data file formats.

Game developers can write custom software renders, access 3D hardware acceleration via the fixed-function pipeline (technically, there is no fixed-function pipeline in XNA—the rough equivalent is the `BasicEffect` class), or separate their rendering logic into shaders, which run on the GPU and pre-processing logic that runs on the CPU. The XNA Framework does not provide support for traditional fixed-function pipeline APIs, but you could emulate that functionality using programmable shaders if you needed to do so (for example, when porting existing fixed-function game code to XNA).

Ultimately, you want to load 3D data into memory, manipulate it, and render it to the screen. The rest of this chapter will walk you through that process. But first, we need to better define some of the discrete tasks that must be performed.

Digging a Little Deeper

3D meshes are a collection of points in 3D space that define the surface of the object being modeled in our virtual world. To move, rotate, or scale the object, we must move, rotate, or scale the individual points that make up the mesh. The 3D graphics APIs contained within the XNA Framework provide several classes that make these tasks easier by abstracting the details of the implementations away, allowing us to work with 3D data at a higher conceptual level.

One such construct is the vector. A *vector* is (in the simplest terms) a way to represent a point in your game world. Vectors contain as many coordinates as you have dimensions in your game world. All vectors provide the same functionality and behave the same way, regardless of the number of dimensions that they represent.

Even though 3D programming can seem a little intimidating at first, you live in a 3D world, and you intuitively understand the relationships between objects within your world. We understand that an object may be above or below, in front of or behind, or to the left or right of another object, as seen from our viewpoint.

Notice that I said "from our viewpoint." When those same objects are seen from someone else's perspective, their relative positions may be completely different, but they're still described using the same general terms. Conceptually, manipulating an object in 3D space is very similar to working in 2D space (or even 1D space). Granted, most of us aren't able to fly around like super heroes, so we do tend to think more in two-dimensional terms. But, we are aware of the relationships that exist between objects in three dimensions.

Vectors

As with all programming tasks, we need to develop some way to easily represent real-world objects (and their interactions) within our game. Most of the concepts that you understand in 2D can be directly applied to your 3D games. To make things easier, let's break things down into their most basic components. Don't worry about the math for now. Just follow the progression from 1D to 2D to 3D.

Location in One Dimension

Imagine yourself at the wheel of a car, driving down a straight, narrow road. You can proceed ahead, or turn back, but you must remain on the road. That's the first dimension. It's a straight line, extending infinitely in either direction. To know where you are on this road, you need a point of reference—an *origin*. The point that you pick on the road as your origin is completely arbitrary; it just needs to be a single spot (a common reference) from which we can describe the position of our car to other observers.

Let's say that your home is just off this road, and your mailbox is planted right at the road's edge. We'll use that as our origin. Let's also say that this road runs east and west. Using these bits of information as a reference, I can now describe the position of my car at any point on the road. I can say, "It's 3 miles west of the mailbox," or "It's 20 miles east of the mailbox."

Now, "east" and "west" aren't exactly programming terms, so we'll want to use some other notation that will be easy to code into our game. We can use positive numbers to denote easterly distances from our origin, and negative numbers to denote westerly distances. Assigning positive or negative to represent either direction, like selecting our point of origin, is completely arbitrary. We just need to pick one or the other, and consistently use that definition of direction whenever we describe our car's position.

We now have enough information to describe our car's position on the road to a program. For example, if the car is at +20 (20 miles east of the mailbox), it will need to travel 20 miles to the west (−20) to return home. Notice how easily we can interchange those terms. While we will describe our position as "20 miles east of the mailbox," our program will always refer to that location as "+20," or more specifically as "origin + 20." This concept is illustrated in Figure 6.3.

Since we're talking about a one-dimensional world, our car's location on the road can be represented in our program using a single number (a single coordinate). The sign of the number indicates the direction from the origin (east or west). The number, without sign, represents the distance from the origin. In programming terms, this number is known as a vector. The length of the vector

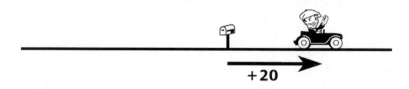

Figure 6.3
Our car 20 miles to the east of the mailbox (+20).

(the absolute value of the number) is the distance from the origin to the car, and the sign of the vector indicates the direction that the car has traveled.

So, vectors represent location as a distance in some direction. In our example, the distance and direction are relative to the origin. Using the origin as the starting point, we travel 20 miles towards the east, and we'll find our car. That's a lot of information, all packed into a single number.

Direction and Orientation

There's a special type of vector, known as a *unit vector* (or a *normal*), which is used to denote direction, ignoring length. This is very handy when you want to move in a certain direction by an arbitrary distance, or you just want to know an object's orientation in the game world.

In the case of our one-dimensional world, rotation is limited to one of two directions, so the unit vector will have one of two values: +1 or −1. In two dimensions, the unit vector is selected from the set of points that make up a circle with a one-unit radius extending from the origin. In three dimensions, the unit vector is selected from the set of points that make up a sphere with a one-unit radius extending from the origin. In all three cases, the length of a unit vector is always one.

Your car can travel some distance, in some direction. If you're only interested in the location of the car, that's all the information that you'll ever need to find it on the road. The location vector is the direction times the distance (or length). The direction that we've discussed up to this point is relative to the origin. We've ignored the direction that the car is facing. We've assumed that the car has been facing in the same direction that it has traveled, but it may very well have gotten to that point by driving in reverse. To determine location, we don't care how the car got there, we just care where it is, relative to our origin.

To draw the car in our game, we will also need to keep track of what direction it is facing. That direction is referred to as the car's *orientation*. Orientation is similar to direction in that it can be represented by a unit vector (a normalized vector)— setting the length to one, retaining the sign. Orientation differs from direction in that orientation represents the direction of the car, relative to the car's current location rather than the direction that the car has traveled, relative to the origin. This concept is illustrated in Figure 6.4.

We represent this in code using −1 to indicate a west-facing car, and +1 to indicate an east-facing car. Those are the only two valid unit vectors in a one-dimensional world (the only two points whose distance from the origin is 1), the

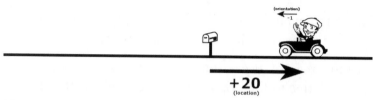

Figure 6.4
The car 20 miles to the east of the mailbox (+20), facing west (−1).

only two valid directions. The XNA Framework provides a class method for vectors to convert a given vector into the unit vector that has the same direction. This method is called normalizing.

It's worth noting that a vector with length zero has no direction. If our car is parked at the mailbox, it's 0 miles from the origin. In that case, its distance from the mailbox is zero, and its direction with respect to the mailbox is undefined. The same is true when normalizing a vector with a length of zero—the direction, with respect to the origin, is impossible to determine (it's meaningless).

Movement

Vectors provide an easy way to represent the location of a car on our road. Normalized vectors can be used to represent the orientation of the car. But, vectors can also be used to describe the movement of the car on the road. By multiplying a unit vector that points in the direction that we want to travel by the distance that we want to travel, we get a vector that describes a change in location. We'll call this new value the movement vector.

For example, we can create a movement vector that represents traveling eleven miles west by multiplying the unit vector that points west (−1) by the number of miles we want to travel (11). To actually move our car, we simply add the car's location vector to the movement vector that we just created. The result of this addition is a vector that represents the car's new location.

```
float origin   = 0;            // location of our mailbox         (  0)
float location = origin + 12;  // 12 miles to the east of the mailbox   (+12)
float movement = -11;          // move 11 miles to the west       (-11)

// the new location (+1)
float newLocation = location + movement;
```

The preceding code snippet moves your car from its current location to its new location in one step. To animate the transition from one location to the next, we need to break this motion into some number of intermediate steps. Luckily, vectors make this task easy for us. To change the magnitude or direction of a vector, we can multiply it by some (real number) value. To double the magnitude of a vector, we can multiply it by 2. To cut the magnitude of a vector in half, we can multiply it by 0.5. To reverse the direction of a vector, we can multiply it by −1.

To smoothly transition our car from one location to the next, we can simply divide the movement vector by the number of steps we want to take. Then we can repeatedly add that smaller vector to the car's location as many times as we have steps. The following pseudo code demonstrates this.

```
float origin    = 0;                    // location of our mailbox              (  0)
float location = origin + 12;           // 12 miles to the east of the mailbox  (+12)
float movement = -12;                   // move 12 miles to the west            (-12)
float steps = 4;                        // number of intermediate steps
float dMove = movement / steps;         // movement vector for each step (-3)

// repeat loop logic once for each step
for(float i = 0; i < steps; i += 1)
{
    // move the car
    location = location + dMove;

    // let some time elapse
    Sleep(250);
}
```

Before the loop, the car is located at +12 (12 miles east of the mailbox). After one iteration, the car is at +9. After two iterations, the car is at +6. After three iterations, the car is at +3. And after the fourth iteration, the car is at the origin. Of course, your game code won't use loops and thread sleeps to animate objects. In an XNA game, the code before the loop would be in an initialization method, where the values for the control variables are initialized whenever some event triggers the animation; and the code within the loop would live in your Update method, which gets called at regular intervals. Your Draw method would render the car to the screen, based on the current location of the car.

In the preceding example, the dMove variable represents the velocity of your car. Velocity is a change in location over time. In this case, the car begins at rest, travels three miles per quarter-second for a full second, and then immediately stops. So movement vectors can be used to represent velocity when they're repeatedly added to an object's current location. That's handy.

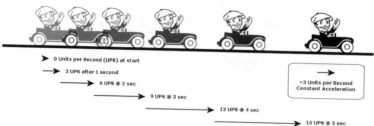

0 Units per Second (UPS) at start

3 UPS after 1 second

6 UPS @ 2 sec

9 UPS @ 3 sec

+3 Units per Second
Constant Acceleration

12 UPS @ 4 sec

15 UPS @ 5 sec

Figure 6.5
The car accelerating from 0 units per second (UPS) to 15 UPS in 5 seconds.

Most cars don't go from 0 to 12 miles per second instantaneously, and then come to a stop equally fast. But, this is our game, and we can do whatever we like. If you would like to add inertia to your movement, you can use another vector. (Man, these vector things are everywhere, aren't they?)

Just as movement is a change in location, and velocity is a change in location that's repeated over time, acceleration is a change in velocity. When the velocity of your car is zero, the car is stationary. In our previous example, we changed the velocity from its current value (zero) to its new value (−3) in one assignment.

A more realistic approach would be to choose an acceleration value, and repeatedly add it to our velocity value until we reach our target velocity. As we're doing this, those intermediate velocities are being added to our car's location on every call to our Update method. When the velocity variable reaches the target speed for the car, we set the acceleration to zero. The result is a more realistic animation where the car speeds up, then travels at a constant velocity. This concept is illustrated in Figure 6.5. To stop the car, we reverse the process by negating our acceleration variable, and waiting for our velocity to reach zero.

Here's a bit of pseudo code that illustrates this concept.

```
public class SimpleCarGame
{
    // control variables to animate our car
    float origin       = 0;            // location of the mailbox
    float location      = origin + 200; // starting location: 200 miles east
    float velocity      = 0;            // start at rest
    float acceleration = 0;            // not accelerating
    // handy constants to drive our simple physics
    const float TARGET_VELOCITY    = -4.0; // 4 MPS to the west
    const float ACCELERATION_GO    = -0.5; // 1/2 MPS to the west
    const float ACCELERATION_STOP =  0.5; // 1/2 MPS to the east
    const float BREAK_AT           = 10.0; // 10 miles east of mailbox
```

```
public void Update(float elapsed)
{
    // speed up or slow down
    velocity += acceleration * elapsed;
    // begin animation?
    if(AnimationWasTriggered)
    {
        acceleration = ACCELERATION_GO; // accelerate
    }

    // are we at our max or min speed?
    if(velocity >= TARGET_VELOCITY)
    {
        velocity = TARGET_VELOCITY; // don't exceed max velocity
        acceleration = 0;           // stop accelerating
    }
    else if(velocity <= 0)
    {
        velocity = 0;               // don't travel backwards
        acceleration = 0;           // stop decelerating
    }

    // move car at current velocity
    location += velocity * elapsed;

    // we've crossed the finish line, start breaking
    if(location <= BREAK_AT)
    {
        acceleration = ACCELERATION_STOP; // decelerate
    }
}

public Draw()
{
    // TODO: draw car at current location
}
}
```

A Note on Vectors

We've discussed four uses for a vector. We can use a vector to define the location of a point in our world (location vector). We can use a vector to define the change in location of a point (movement vector, a.k.a. velocity vector). We can use a vector to define the change in movement of a point (acceleration vector). And, we can use a specialized vector (unit vector, a.k.a. normalized vector) to represent a direction within our world.

A vector is just a handy way to store coordinates. In the case of one-dimensional space, there's just one value to track. We can call it X. This value can represent any point in our 1D world. When we move to 2D space, we'll have two coordinates to keep track of: X and Y. And when we move to 3D space, we'll have three coordinates to keep track of: X, Y, and Z. In all three cases, the coordinates that are contained within a vector hold all the information that we need to define the location of any point in our world.

Regardless of the number of dimensions (the number of coordinates), all vectors behave in the same way. A vector is composed of two components—direction and magnitude (or length). When you add two vectors together, the result is a vector. When you multiply a vector by some scalar value, you change its magnitude and/or direction, but the result is still a vector.

All vectors represent the same data—a location within your world. In the case of a location vector, the direction and length of the vector are relative to the origin of the world. In the case of a movement vector, the direction and length of the vector are relative to a location vector. In the case of an acceleration vector, the direction and length of the vector are relative to a movement vector. In all cases, the coordinates represent a change in coordinate values, relative to another set of coordinate values.

In our one-dimensional world, we're using the float type to store our vectors, but the XNA Framework provides specialized vector classes (technically, they're structures) for our 2D and 3D work. You don't see too many 1D games these days, so there isn't much point in providing specialized classes for 1D vectors. But conceptually, it's all the same, regardless of how many dimensions upon which your game is built.

```
// 1D vector: 14 units to the right of origin
float    pointIn1D = 14.0f;
pointIn1D *= -1.0f; // same distance (14 units), opposite side of origin

// 2D vector: 20 units to the right of, and 16 units above, the origin
Vector2 pointIn2D = new Vector2(20.0f, -16.0f);
pointIn2D *= 0.5f; // half the distance from origin (10, 8)
```

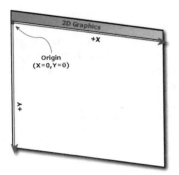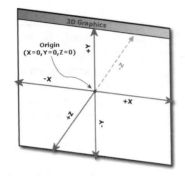

Figure 6.6
A comparison of 2D and 3D coordinate systems in XNA. Note the location of the origin and the direction of the positive and negative axes.

```
// 3D vector: 120 units to the right, 33 units above, and 633 behind origin
Vector3 pointIn3D = new Vector2(120.0f, 33.0f, 633.0f);
pointIn3D /= 3.0f; // one-third the distance from origin (40, 11, 211)
```

Notice in the preceding code snippet that the positive y-axis points down in 2D graphics, and the same axis points up in 3D graphics. So, a point whose Y value is 50 will be below a point whose Y value is 30 for 2D functions. But, a point with a Y of 50 will be above a point with a Y of 30 for 3D functions. In math (using the Cartesian coordinate system), positive Y values are always above negative Y values, irrespective of whether we're modeling two dimensions or three. See Figure 6.6 for a comparison of the 2D and 3D coordinate systems used in XNA.

All of the 3D functions in XNA use a right-handed system. That means that positive Z values are coming toward the player (out of the screen) and negative Z values are moving away from the player (into the screen). Also, vertices are wound (listed) in counter-clockwise order (for culling purposes) in XNA. If you've ever done any 3D work with other (left-handed) APIs, this may seem counterintuitive to you.

Just remember that units of measure, and the use of a right-handed or left-handed coordinate system, are completely arbitrary. The important point is that you're consistent in whichever you choose. Other APIs (including DirectX) allow for flexibility in this area, allowing the programmer to build his game engine upon whichever system he prefers.

The XNA team's decision to pick one coordinate system and stick to it means that all of the samples in the documentation, most of the snippets that you see in the community forums, and nearly all of the third-party XNA content that you find on the web will be consistent. Less confusion is always a good thing.

Note

There's nothing to stop you from representing the 3D worlds of your XNA games in any way you want. In fact, writing your own left-handed APIs might be your best option when porting a large legacy game whose logic relies on assumptions about the handedness of the coordinate system being used. And don't forget that you can convert your old game data into XNA's right-handed system as it's imported through the Content Pipeline, using a custom importer.

Scale and Units of Measure

A common problem that folks who are new to 3D programming run into is a mismatched scale between objects in their virtual world. To avoid this problem, you need to pick a unit of measure for your game and stick to it. The units in your 3D content creation tool are just numbers to help you assign a relative scale to your objects. In the editor, a sphere with a radius of three units is half the size of a sphere with a radius of six units.

If you're designing a race track, you might pick a scale where one unit in the editor is two meters in your virtual world. For a space simulator, one unit may represent a kilometer (or more). For a game based in an anthill, one unit may represent a centimeter (or less). The unit of measure that you use is completely up to you. Just apply it consistently as you create your 3D content.

Matrices

We've learned how to represent the location of a point in 1D, 2D, and 3D using vectors. We've also learned how to use vectors to represent movement and acceleration, as well as direction and orientation. And we saw how to change the scale of a point (with respect to the origin) using simple division and multiplication.

3D objects are just a collection of points. We could move, scale, and translate every one of those points ourselves using what we've learned about vectors (along with some simple trigonometry), but XNA provides an easier way—the Matrix. (It's the question that drives us, Neo.)

The Matrix class (technically it's a structure) represents one or more transformations for our 3D objects. These transformations include (among others) moving (Translation), scaling (Scale), and rotating (RotationX, RotationY, and RotationZ) 3D objects. You can combine the transformations of multiple matrices by simply multiplying them together. For example, the following code generates a matrix that will rotate a 3D object (which is centered at the origin)

45 degrees about the y-axis, and then move the object 30 units to the left of its current location.

```
// rotate, then move
Matrix composite =
    Matrix.CreateRotationY( MathHelper.ToRadians( 45.0f ) ) *
    Matrix.CreateTranslation( new Vector3( -30, 0, 0 ) );
```

The order of multiplication is important. In the preceding example, the object will rotate 45 degrees. In the following (almost identical) code snippet, the object is moved first, and then it's rotated about the y-axis.

```
// move, then rotate
Matrix composite =
    Matrix.CreateTranslation( new Vector3( -30, 0, 0 ) ) *
    Matrix.CreateRotationY( MathHelper.ToRadians( 45.0f ) );
```

Rather than a rotating object, we'll have an object that's orbiting the origin. The orbit path is described by a circle with a radius of 30 units, centered at the origin, contained in the XZ plane. Remember, we're applying the transformation that's described by the Matrix to every point in our 3D object. When those points are centered on the origin, they'll seem to rotate. When they're offset from the origin, they'll seem to orbit.

Similarly, when we scale our 3D objects, we need to make sure that they're centered at the origin. If the object is offset from the origin before the scaling transformation is applied, it will appear to move away from the origin when scaled up and towards the origin when scaled down. In essence, you're scaling the distance from the origin as you scale the object. When the object is centered at the origin, the location remains zero, regardless of the scale that's applied.

In general, you'll want to scale first, then rotate, and then translate.

In the preceding examples, we only rotated about one axis. You can rotate about any of the three major axes or about an arbitrary axis (using the CreateFromAxisAngle method). Rotations are applied per axis, and the order in which you apply your rotations is important. Rotation about the z-axis is commonly referred to as *roll*, rotation about the x-axis is commonly referred to as *pitch*, and rotation about the y-axis is commonly referred to as *yaw*. The Matrix structure exposes a method to apply all three of these rotations in one call—CreateFromYawPitchRoll. As the name implies, rotation is applied about the y-axis, then the x-axis, and then the z-axis.

To apply the transformations of a matrix to a point in 3D space, you'd use code similar to the following.

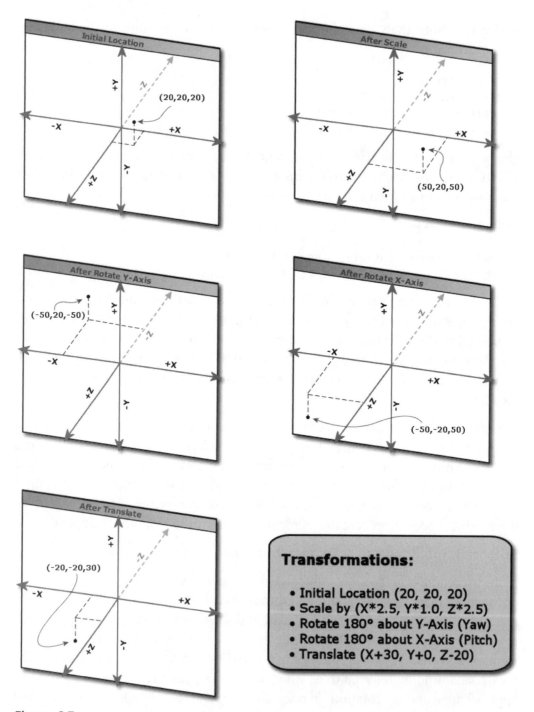

Figure 6.7
A list of the steps that are performed for us in a single call to Vector3.Transform.

```
// scale, rotate, then move
Matrix composite =
    Matrix.CreateScale( new Vector3( 2.5f, 1.0f, 2.5f ) ) *
    Matrix.CreateRotationY( MathHelper.ToRadians( 180.0f ) ) *
    Matrix.CreateRotationX( MathHelper.ToRadians( 180.0f ) ) *
    Matrix.CreateTranslation( new Vector3( 30, 0, -20 ) );

// a point, located at (20, 20, 20)
Vector3 pointIn3D = new Vector.One * 20.0f;

// apply the transformation; new point is at (-20, -20, 30)
Vector3 newPointIn3D = Vector3.Transform( pointIn3D, composite );
```

To see how the point arrived at its new location, let's examine the transformations, step by step. Figure 6.7 shows the location of our point after each stage of the transform.

As I mentioned earlier, we won't be applying matrices to individual points. We'll transform all of the points that make up a 3D object at one time. I just wanted to show you how each point in the object is being processed so that you can understand what the XNA Framework is doing for you.

If you're interested in digging a little deeper into the math behind matrices and other aspects of their inner workings, search the web. It's all very interesting stuff, and knowing what's happening behind the scenes will help you when you run into problems and need to troubleshoot your code. I want to keep things at a higher level here, focusing on what XNA provides the aspiring game developer.

The Example

That's enough overview. Let's write some code.

The example for this chapter is a simple 3D environment that showcases some very basic HLSL shaders and introduces you to the fundamental concepts of 3D programming. At the center of our virtual, cornflower blue world you'll find a rotating teapot surrounded by several orbiting, textured balls—one for each of the custom effects (HLSL shaders) that the example supports. I used 3D Studio Max (version 8) to create the models for this example. The teapot and the sphere are standard 3D primitives in most 3D content creation tools. Just make sure that you can export an FBX file when you're done.

The teapot rotates about all three axes, each with its own rate of rotation. The spheres orbit the teapot in the XZ plane, along a circular path with a radius of 160 units. The spheres complete an orbit every 15.6 seconds. The model file for this example contains one teapot and one sphere. The teapot is located at the origin, and the sphere is offset 160 units along the positive x-axis. Multiple instances of the sphere are created in memory when the game runs.

Each ball that orbits the teapot represents a different effect. Pressing the A button on your controller will cycle through each of the effects, applying the currently selected effect to the teapot.

Loading Media

As with other content, you simply add your FBX file (or any 3D format that is supported by the Content Pipeline, including your own proprietary format if you've written a custom pipeline importer) to your XNA game project, and you're ready to reference it from your code. We'll load the FBX into an instance of the Model class, which will contain references to our teapot and sphere as two instances of the ModelMesh class.

```
// our collection of meshes, loaded from disk
Model m_model = null;
```

I've created a separate class (named MyMesh) to keep the mesh handling code separate from our game logic. It holds a reference to the main Model instance, the name of the mesh within the Model (which was set in our 3D editor), and the currently active shader (an instance of the Effect class). This class exposes one method, Draw, which is responsible for actually rendering the mesh onto the screen. I'll cover the MyMesh class in more detail later in this chapter.

```
// our meshes (a teapot and some balls)
MyMesh m_meshTeapot = null;
MyMesh[] m_meshBall = new MyMesh[(int)EffectType.Count];
```

We'll add code to the main game class's LoadGraphicsContent method to load the 3D content from the hard drive. While we're at it, we'll go ahead and load our environment map, initialize our Effect and MyMesh instances, and initialize our game's camera.

```
/// Load your graphics content.
protected override void LoadGraphicsContent(bool loadAllContent)
{
    if (loadAllContent)
    {
        m_model = content.Load<Model>(@"media\models\example");
```

```
        m_texEnvironmentMap = content.Load<TextureCube>
            (@"media\textures\c_olmForest_16M");
        InitEffects();
        InitMyMeshes();
        m_camera.Location = new Vector3(-725, 600, 590);
        m_camera.LookAt(m_meshTeapot);
    }
    // TODO: Load any ResourceManagementMode.Manual content
}
```

About the Texture

There's only one texture in this example. It's the environment map for the shiny metallic and ceramic surfaces. The environment map that I used in this example was created by Ben Cloward (a talented artist, instructor, and HLSL guru) and placed in the public domain. You can find this, and several of his other environment maps, by visiting www.bencloward.com/CubeMapSets.rar.

You can find Ben's personal blog, as well as samples of his work, by visiting www.bencloward.com.

As with textures in our 2D games, we'll create a member variable to store a reference to the environment map texture, and load it whenever XNA calls our game's LoadGraphicsContent method.

```
// the environment map
TextureCube m_texEnvironmentMap = null;
```

The environment map is made up of six separate images. Conceptually, these images are mapped to the six faces of a cube, and the images are aligned in such a way as to re-create a real-world scene (in this case, a forest) where you can look forward, back, up, down, left, right, or anywhere in between, to see what a viewer at that (fixed) vantage point saw when the picture was taken. When applied to an actual cube that moves with the camera, the image is referred to as a sky box. When it's used to create the illusion of a reflective surface (as we do in this example), it's known as an environment map.

Initializing the Meshes

Each 3D content file is represented by an instance of the Model class. A Model class may contain several meshes. Once the Model class is loaded, we'll use our own class (MyMesh) to keep track of the individual meshes. To reference a particular ModelMesh within a Model class, we'll use its name. Meshes can be named within your 3D content editor. As we create these in-game references to our meshes, we'll go ahead and set their starting location and orientation within the world, and we'll assign the effect that the mesh will use.

```
// init meshes before first use
protected void InitMyMeshes()
{
    // init teapot
    if (m_meshTeapot == null)
    {
        m_meshTeapot = new MyMesh();
        m_meshTeapot.Rotate(0, 180, 0);
    }
    m_meshTeapot.Model = m_model;
    m_meshTeapot.MeshName = "Teapot01";
    SelectEffect(m_CurrentTeapotEffect);
    // init balls (one mesh, multiple instances)
    float angle = 360.0f / (float)(m_meshBall.Length);
    for (int i = 0; i < m_meshBall.Length; i++)
    {
        if (m_meshBall[i] == null)
        {
            m_meshBall[i] = new MyMesh();
            m_meshBall[i].RotateTo(0, i * angle, 0);
        }
        m_meshBall[i].Model = m_model;
        m_meshBall[i].MeshName = "Sphere01";
        m_meshBall[i].Effect = m_effects[i];
    }
}
```

Initializing the Effects

Shader files (*.fx files) are treated like other game resources by the Content Pipeline. Just like images, audio clips, and 3D model files, shaders are processed by the Content Pipeline and stored for later retrieval by the game. Once you've written a shader, you just add it to the project in XNA Game Studio Express, and then you can reference it from your code.

The example code for this chapter uses several different shader files. I store the references to each in an array.

```
// allocate storage for our collection of effects
Effect[] m_effects = new Effect[(int)EffectType.Count];
```

I created several enums to access the array in a type-safe, human-readable way. It may seem like overkill, but I find it easier to read code that references an array using the index WireFrame rather than 2. I could have used integer constants here to get the same readability benefits, but constants aren't type-safe when passed as parameters—they're simply numbers. If I pass the wrong enum to a method, the compiler tells me. If I pass the wrong integer constant to a method, I may not realize the mistake until much later in development.

```
// map friendly names to array indices for our effects
public enum EffectType
{
    Default,
    Points,
    WireFrame,
    //Flat, // not supported (as written) on Xbox 360
    Gouraund,
    Rubber,
    Ceramic,
    Gold,
    Chrome,
    Copper,
    WorldsWorstToonShader,
    // -----
    Count
};
// initial effect for the teapot
EffectType m_CurrentTeapotEffect = EffectType.Gold;
```

I created two methods to help me cycle through all of the available Effect instances. This includes logic to enforce a slight delay between swapping effects.

```
// map our enums to actual effects, apply selected effect to teapot
protected void SelectEffect(EffectType type)
{
    m_CurrentTeapotEffect = type;
    m_meshTeapot.Effect = m_effects[(int)type];
}
// make sure player doesn't change textures too fast
private const double TEXTURE_DELAY = 0.25;
private double m_timeSinceLastSelectNextEffect = TEXTURE_DELAY;
// cycle to next effect
protected void SelectNextEffect()
{
    // if delay has elapsed
    if (m_timeSinceLastSelectNextEffect >= TEXTURE_DELAY)
```

```
    {
        // cycle through all available effects
        if (m_CurrentTeapotEffect == EffectType.Count - 1)
        {
            SelectEffect(EffectType.Default);
        }
        else
        {
            SelectEffect(m_CurrentTeapotEffect + 1);
        }
        // reset delay timer
        m_timeSinceLastSelectNextEffect = 0;
    }
}
```

Now that we've set up member variables to house our effects, it's time to populate
them. The InitEffects method is called from the LoadGraphicsContent method. I
won't list the entire method here. The basic steps are the same for all of the effects
that we use: load the effect from disk, set the parameters that won't change over the
life of the game, and assign (a cloned copy of) the new effect to the proper slot in
our m_effects array.

One notable exception to these common initialization steps is that I don't
actually create an instance of the BasicEffect class. I take advantage of the fact
that one was created for me when the Content Pipeline processed my model. I
just make a copy of that instance and shamelessly use it as my own.

```
// set effect parameters for our materials
protected void InitEffects()
{
    // Default effect—created by content pipeline when mesh
    // is loaded without an attached effect
    BasicEffect basic =
        (BasicEffect)m_model.Meshes[0].MeshParts[0].Effect;
    basic.EnableDefaultLighting();
    basic.CurrentTechnique = basic.Techniques[0];
    m_effects[(int)EffectType.Default] =
        basic.Clone(graphics.GraphicsDevice);
    // Points
    Effect points = content.Load<Effect>(@"media\effects\point");
    points.Parameters["MaterialDiffuseColor"].
        SetValue(Color.White.ToVector4());
    m_effects[(int)EffectType.Points] =
```

```
        points.Clone(graphics.GraphicsDevice);
    // several more effects are loaded and initialized here ...
}
```

Animating the Models

The Update method is responsible for animating our 3D objects. The teapot rotates in place at the origin (0, 0, 0). The balls orbit the teapot.

```
/// game logic such as updating the world
protected override void Update(GameTime gameTime)
{
    // Allows the default game to exit on Xbox 360 and Windows
    if (GamePad.GetState(PlayerIndex.One).Buttons.Back ==
        ButtonState.Pressed)
        this.Exit();
    // time in seconds since last call to update
    float elapsed = (float)gameTime.ElapsedGameTime.TotalSeconds;
    // rotate the teapot mesh
    m_meshTeapot.Rotate(
        17.0f * elapsed,
        9.0f * elapsed,
        7.5f * elapsed);
    // rotate the balls
    foreach (MyMesh ball in m_meshBall)
    {
        ball.Rotate(0, 23.0f * elapsed, 0);
    }
    // process player input, add delay between texture changes
    m_timeSinceLastSelectNextEffect += elapsed;
    ProcessInput(GamePad.GetState(PlayerIndex.One), Keyboard.GetState(),
        elapsed);
    base.Update(gameTime);
}
```

Processing Input

The ProcessInput method processes player input from the Xbox 360 Controller or the keyboard. Since the game only has two functions (toggle the teapot texture and move the camera), and the more complicated of the two is handled by the MyCamera class, there's not much code in this method.

```
// process input from keyboard and game pad
protected void ProcessInput(GamePadState pad1, KeyboardState key1,
```

```
             float elapsed)
{
    // change teapot texture?
    if (pad1.Buttons.A == ButtonState.Pressed ||
        key1.IsKeyDown(Keys.Space))
    {
        SelectNextEffect();
    }
    m_camera.ProcessInput(pad1, key1, elapsed);
}
```

The last thing that our game needs to do is actually render our 3D world to the screen. As with moving the camera, the draw methods in this class delegate the serious code to another, specialized class.

```
/// render game objects
protected override void Draw(GameTime gameTime)
{
    graphics.GraphicsDevice.Clear(Color.CornflowerBlue);
    DrawMeshes();
    base.Draw(gameTime);
}
// draw all meshes
public void DrawMeshes()
{
    // draw teapot
    m_meshTeapot.Draw(graphics.GraphicsDevice, m_camera, m_aspect);
    // draw balls
    foreach (MyMesh ball in m_meshBall)
    {
        ball.Draw(graphics.GraphicsDevice, m_camera, m_aspect);
    }
}
```

The Camera

The camera provides your view into the virtual world. The camera has a location and orientation. The location is represented as a single point within our 3D world. The orientation of the camera is defined by two normalized vectors (length of one unit, only used to determine direction). The first is the up vector; the other is the forward vector. The forward vector points toward whatever you're looking at in the world, and the up vector establishes the roll angle of the camera (whether it's cocked left or right).

```
// location of the camera
MyCamera m_camera = new MyCamera();
```

When we get ready to render our world, we'll also need to know the aspect ratio of the scene. We'll calculate it when we create the member variable, and then use it over and over.

```
// aspect ratio for our game
float m_aspect = (float)SCREEN_WIDTH / (float)SCREEN_HEIGHT;
```

The code that allows us to freely move the camera around in the world is contained within the MyCamera class, which we will discuss in greater detail later in this chapter.

The My3DObject Class

This class provides implementations for the basic properties that all of our game's 3D objects must support. There are two properties, Location and Rotation (orientation); two methods to update the properties with relative values, Move and Rotate; and two methods to update the properties with absolute values, MoveTo and RotateTo.

```
public abstract class My3DObject
{
    // location of this object in the world
    protected Vector3 m_Location = Vector3.Zero;
    public Vector3 Location
    {
        get { return m_Location; }
        set { m_Location = value; }
    }
    // move object, relative to its current location
    public void Move(float x, float y, float z)
    {
        m_Location.X += x;
        m_Location.Y += y;
        m_Location.Z += z;
    }
    // place object in an absolute location within the world
    public void MoveTo(float x, float y, float z)
    {
        m_Location = new Vector3(x, y, z);
    }
```

```
        // rotations (for each axis)
        protected Vector3 m_Rotation = Vector3.Zero;
        public Vector3 Rotation
    {

        get { return m_Rotation; }
        set
        {
            m_Rotation = value;
            RotationUpdated();
        }
    }
    // rotate object, relative to current rotation
    public void Rotate(float pitch, float yaw, float roll)
    {
        m_Rotation.X += pitch;
        m_Rotation.Y += yaw;
        m_Rotation.Z += roll;
        // perform post-processing
        RotationUpdated();
    }
    // set absolute rotation
    public void RotateTo(float pitch, float yaw, float roll)
    {
        m_Rotation = new Vector3(pitch, yaw, roll);
        // perform post-processing
        RotationUpdated();
    }
}
```

This class also provides a virtual method that subclasses can use as a sort of in-game event to take action whenever a specific My3DObject's Rotate property is updated. This method is named RotationUpdated. To perform some task whenever the object rotates, just override this method and insert your custom logic. That's what the MyCamera class does to convert the Euler angles from the rotation into an equivalent Quaternion. We'll discuss the camera in more detail in just a bit.

```
        // pseudo event, child classes can override to receive notification
        public virtual void RotationUpdated()
        {
            // override this method to handle rotation events
        }
    }
```

The MyMesh Class

The MyMesh class is derived from the My3DObject base class. In addition to the properties and methods that are inherited from the base class, this class includes properties and methods to help us manage the 3D models that we load from disk.

Models and Meshes

The XNA Framework's Model class represents a 3D content file that you load from the hard drive. The Model class holds references to all of the 3D objects within the model file, each represented by instances of the ModelMesh class. Among other properties, the ModelMesh class exposes the name of the mesh and the effect that should be applied to it. Our class (MyMesh) exposes these bits of data via the Model, MeshName, and Effect properties.

```
// simple helper to encapsulate tedious mesh tasks
public class MyMesh : My3DObject
{
    // parent model for this mesh
    protected Model m_Model = null;
    public Model Model
    {
        get { return m_Model; }
        set { m_Model = value; }
    }
    // name of this mesh, within the model
    protected string m_MeshName = "";
    public string MeshName
    {
        get { return m_MeshName; }
        set { m_MeshName = value; }
    }
    // the active shader effect for this mesh
    protected Effect m_Effect = null;
    public Effect Effect
    {
        get { return m_Effect; }
        set { m_Effect = value; }
    }
```

The MyMesh class also provides a method to render itself to the screen. The Draw method was intended to be fairly generic, so it contains some code that isn't terribly useful for the simple example we're writing for this chapter. But, it should handle some of the more complex scenes that we throw its way.

Rendering 3D Objects

The first task of the Draw method is to preserve the transforms that are stored in the model file. This will ensure that each mesh is located within your game world in the same relative position and scale as it was in your 3D content editor.

```
// draw this mesh to the screen
public void Draw(GraphicsDevice device, MyCamera camera, float aspect)
{
    // copy parent transforms
    Matrix[] transforms = new Matrix[Model.Bones.Count];
    Model.CopyAbsoluteBoneTransformsTo(transforms);
```

Model.Bones.Count in the preceding snippet tells us how many bones are in the current mesh. Bones are used for more advanced animation techniques than we will cover in this chapter. Our teapot and sphere each only have one bone.

In more complicated models (like a human), your models would be articulated into several parts, each bound to a bone which can be positioned and rotated on its own. This code should handle those more complex models, but the animations that we apply in this example will still be the simple rotations that you see for our primitive models.

The next task that the Draw method handles for us is to apply our selected effect to every part of the mesh that's about to be rendered. Remember that MeshName and Effect are the names of properties of our custom class.

```
// get a reference to the mesh to save some typing
ModelMesh mesh = Model.Meshes[MeshName];
// make sure all our mesh parts are using the current effect
foreach (ModelMeshPart part in mesh.MeshParts)
{
    part.Effect = Effect;
}
```

Once the effect has been applied to our mesh, we need to apply the transforms. We'll combine transforms using the overloaded multiplication operator of the Matrix structure. We won't actually transform the individual points of the mesh ourselves, we'll just prepare the Matrix that will be used to transform them. All of the real work will happen on the GPU.

```
// rotate and transform mesh
float x = MathHelper.ToRadians(Rotation.X);
float y = MathHelper.ToRadians(Rotation.Y);
float z = MathHelper.ToRadians(Rotation.Z);
// matrix to translate this mesh from model
// space to world space
Matrix world =
    transforms[mesh.ParentBone.Index] *
    Matrix.CreateRotationY(y) *
    Matrix.CreateRotationX(x) *
    Matrix.CreateRotationZ(z) *
    Matrix.CreateTranslation(Location);
```

Using Effects

We now have enough information to draw our mesh. The XNA Framework's Effect class is our liaison to the GPU. It encapsulates the HLSL shader logic that will be used to render our mesh. That logic is driven by the parameters that we specify.

In the case of our custom effects, I've included parameters named WorldTransform, WorldViewProjection, and CameraPosition (among others). If the current effect is an instance of BasicEffect (XNA's default effect that you can use when you don't want to write your own HLSL logic), we'll configure similar parameters by setting the public Projection, View, and World properties that the BasicEffect class exposes to us.

```
// set effect parameters
if (Effect is BasicEffect)
{
    // effect is a basic (or default XNA) effect
    BasicEffect basic = (BasicEffect)Effect;
    basic.Projection = camera.ProjectionMatrix;
    basic.View = camera.ViewMatrix;
    basic.World = world;
}
else
{
    // effect is one of our custom effects
    Effect.Parameters["WorldTransform"]
        .SetValue(world);
    Effect.Parameters["WorldViewProjection"]
```

```
            .SetValue(
                world *
                camera.ViewMatrix *
                camera.ProjectionMatrix);
        Effect.Parameters["CameraPosition"]
            .SetValue(camera.Location);
}
```

Transform Contexts

When working with 3D data, there are several contexts that make each stage of processing the data a little easier to work with. Let's take a moment to discuss them.

Model space (a.k.a. object space) is the context that the 3D content editor uses when you're editing data. You may have several models in your game (each represented by a different 3D content file). When working with the model file, it's easier to design your objects centered at the origin. When you bring that model into your game, it needs to be able to move around within your virtual world.

World space is the context that your game uses to place 3D objects within the scene. A model that was centered at the origin in your 3D editor will need to be placed in its proper location, relative to other game objects in the world. After the transforms that move and orient your model within your virtual world have been applied, the model is in world space. Your game's virtual world exists only in the computer's memory. How does all of this raw data ultimately become an image on your screen?

When you view the objects that inhabit your world, you're typically looking at a subset of the objects. The objects that appear on the screen are defined by a virtual camera that's placed in the world. This camera can be located anywhere within the world, it can be pointed in any direction, and it can be oriented however you like (upside down, upright, tilted left or right). This context for your 3D objects is referred to as *view space* (a.k.a., camera space or eye space).

Now you have a camera at some point in your virtual world. It's looking in some direction, and it's oriented a certain way. What does it see? Can you view any 3D objects that are in front of you—whether they're a millimeter away or a light-year away from the camera? Can you view objects that are to the extreme left or right of the camera (but are still "in front of" it, in the strictest sense)? To provide fine-grained control over which objects get drawn, we'll use yet another context—projection space. This context defines what's commonly described as a view frustrum.

In simple terms, a frustrum is a pyramid whose top has been chopped off. The apex of the pyramid is located at the same point in space as the camera, and the center of the rectangular base of the pyramid is pointed wherever the camera is looking. The top of the frustrum is known as the *near plane*. The base of the frustrum is known as the *far plane*. Objects that lie outside of the frustrum will not be rendered to the screen. This clipping region is further defined by the camera's field of view (similar to using wide-angle, fisheye, and normal lenses in a real-world camera) and the aspect ratio of the screen.

The final context is screen space. Unlike the other contexts (which work with points in three dimensions), screen space is where the 3D coordinates of your mesh are mapped to 2D locations on your screen using the projection matrix.

Wrapping Up the Draw Method

If you mix basic effects and custom effects in your game, you will need to be mindful of state changes for one that may affect the other.

```
// reset fill mode; otherwise basic effect will get
// confused whenever our custom "wireframe" effect runs
device.RenderState.FillMode = FillMode.Solid;
```

Now that all of our effect parameters have been configured, we're ready to hand our mesh off to the GPU for processing.

```
    //draw the mesh using the effect options, set above
    mesh.Draw();
  }
}
```

N o t e

One of the effects that I included early in the development of this project was a simple flat shading shader. The simple technique that I used doesn't appear to be supported by the Xbox 360 shader assembler, so I commented out that effect in the game's code. The on-screen results weren't all that impressive, so I had no qualms about removing the effect from the example. Feel free to poke around the source code to reactivate the effect and run it under Windows. Once XNA adds support for geometry shaders, this shader has some potential as the basis for an interesting "retro" look and feel.

The MyCamera Class

The `MyCamera` class is derived from the `My3DObject` base class. In addition to the properties and methods that are inherited from the base class, this class includes code to handle locating and orienting a camera within our virtual world. It also exposes properties that contain all the data that we need to generate the matrices that drive the rendering process.

In the interest of space, I won't provide a complete listing here. Please review the code on the CD-ROM that came with this book. You can see how this class is used by looking at the code for the classes that reference it.

My goal for the `MyCamera` class was to create a plug-able camera class where the programmer could easily switch between a free-moving camera, a third-person camera that follows the player, a camera that orbits a point, or any other camera that implements a specific interface. Unfortunately, I didn't have time to bring that vision to life. If there's much interest, I'll get my thoughts written out in an article and source code on my website. My contact information is listed at the front of this book.

Note

When I first implemented `MyCamera`, I based my logic on rotations using Euler angles (the rotations about the x-, y-, and z-axes that we've discussed). Since I was developing a camera with unrestricted movement (six degrees of freedom), I quickly ran into issues with an irritating quirk known as Gimbal lock.

I rewrote the rotation code, basing it on `Quaternions`. `Quaternions` are an alternative to matrices for representing rotations and orientations of 3D objects. I don't have the time, space, or mathematical expertise to explain the inner workings of `Quaternions` here, and you don't need to understand the theory behind `Quaternions` to use them in your game. They're supported by the XNA Framework, and they're easily converted to the more familiar `Matrix` type.

High Level Shader Language (HLSL)

Shaders are programs that run on the graphics-processing unit (GPU) of your 3D video card. In the early days of shader programming, you had to write your code in a cryptic language, reminiscent of an assembler. These days, we have a better alternative. Microsoft's High Level Shader Language (HLSL) is a C-like language that you can use to write vertex and pixel shaders for use with your DirectX and XNA games. Every vertex of every 3D object that you see in your game passes through these shaders as it makes its way to your screen.

Your game passes vertex data, texture data, and parameterized values to your shader program via the `Effect` class. Vertices are then handed to the vertex shader for processing, one by one. When the vertex shader is done processing a vertex, the return value from the vertex shader is passed on to a pixel shader (if you've specified one). The pixel shader processes this data and returns a color, which is applied to a pixel in the frame buffer (destined for the screen).

Techniques and Passes

A shader file can host multiple technique blocks. The technique is the entry point into the effect. Techniques contain one or more pass blocks. Passes contain zero or more render state settings, at least one vertex shader declaration, and zero or more pixel shader declarations.

```
technique TheOnlyTechnique
{
    // your techniques may have multiple passes,
```

```
// this particular example just has one
pass SinglePass
{
    // don't hide back faces, the teapot has gaps
    // that will show through
    CULLMODE = None;

    // render this model as a solid (opaque) body
    FILLMODE  = Solid;

    // process model with our shaders
    VertexShader = compile vs_2_0 MainVS();
    PixelShader  = compile ps_2_0 MainPS();
}
}
```

In the preceding shader snippet, we have a vertex shader whose entry point is named MainVS, and a pixel shader whose entry point is MainPS. If we didn't want to provide a custom pixel shader, we could have used the following statement in its place. This will cause the GPU to invoke the default pixel shader to process the per-vertex data that is generated by our vertex shader.

```
PixelShader   = NULL;
```

Vertex Shaders

Vertex shaders process mesh data, one vertex (3D point) at a time. The main job of any vertex shader is to transform a point in our mesh from object space (its representation in memory) to screen space (an X, Y coordinate on the display). In other words, the vertex shader is charged with determining where a particular point on our 3D mesh should be drawn on the 2D screen. This process is repeated for every point in the mesh, and the end result is an image on the screen that represents the mesh scaled, rotated, and translated, based on its position, relative to the camera.

In addition to mesh data, vertex shaders have access to the camera position, vertex normal data, the world transformation, the view projection, the location of any light sources, and any number of other programmer-defined and language-defined variables that might prove useful when performing its task.

The vertex shader is called once per vertex. That means that for each triangle, the vertex shader will be called three times, and it will return a screen coordinate each time. Someone needs to fill in the gaps between those three points. That's where pixel shaders come in. For every pixel that lies within those three points on the screen, a pixel shader is called. This process is known as *rasterization*.

BadToon Vertex Shader

We'll take a look at the code for the badtoon.fx shader to get a better idea of how shaders work. We'll be using the following variables within our shader. We'll go ahead and initialize all of the variables that aren't bound to registers with default values, just in case the calling game forgets to set them.

```
// camera and lighting info
float3 CameraPosition : CAMERAPOSITION;
float3 LightDirection = { 0.57f, -0.57f, 0.57f};
float4 LightColor     = { 1, 1, 1, 1};

// color of our teapot
float4 MaterialDiffuseColor    = { 1.00, 0.80, 0.10, 1.00 };
float4 MaterialSpecularColor   = { 1.00, 0.90, 0.40, 1.00 };
int    MaterialSpecularPower   = 2;
float  MaterialSpecularFalloff = 0.33;

// transformations
float4x4 WorldViewProjection : WORLDVIEWPROJECTION;
float4x3 WorldTransform : WORLD;
```

Notice that three of the variable declarations in the preceding listing end with a colon and a token. These tokens are called semantics, and they provide a way to easily map your variables to the input and output hardware registers of the GPU. For example, the CameraPosition variable contains the location of the camera.

The output of BadToon's vertex shader is the ScreenPosition (required), the diffuse color of the vertex, and the specular color of the vertex. When we declare our vertex shader, this structure will be listed as its output. When we declare our pixel shader, this structure will be listed as its input.

```
// vertex shader output is stored in this struct,
// then passed to pixel shader
struct VertexOutput
{
    float4 ScreenPosition      : POSITION;
    float4 DiffuseVertexColor  : COLOR0;
    float4 SpecularVertexColor : COLOR1;
};
```

Here's the main body of our vertex shader. Notice that the return value is the structure that we just defined, and that the first statement in the shader initializes the return value to a known, good state. As with the earlier variable declarations and the VertexOutput structure member declarations, our vertex shader accepts two parameters that are marked with register semantics.

```
// calculate screen location and colors of this vertex
VertexOutput MainVS(
    float3 ModelPosition : POSITION,
    float3 ModelNormal   : NORMAL )
{
    VertexOutput OutputData = (VertexOutput)0;
```

Before we can do anything with our vertex data, we need to translate it into view space. As mentioned earlier in this chapter, this involves transforming the vertex from model to world space, and then from world to view space. The resulting vertex location is stored in the ScreenPosition member of our output structure.

```
// transform the position and normal from model space to world space
float3 WorldPosition =
    mul(float4(ModelPosition, 1), (float4x3)WorldTransform);
float3 WorldNormal =
    normalize(mul(ModelNormal, (float3x3)WorldTransform));

// determine "look at" vector (the direction that the camera is facing)
float3 LookAt = normalize(WorldPosition - CameraPosition);

OutputData.ScreenPosition =
    mul( float4( ModelPosition.xyz, 1 ), WorldViewProjection );
```

Now that we've transformed the vertex, it's time to calculate its diffuse and specular color values. Remember, we've already initialized our ambient color value, and it doesn't change from vertex to vertex.

```
OutputData.DiffuseVertexColor = MaterialDiffuseColor;
OutputData.SpecularVertexColor =
        CalcSpecularColor (WorldNormal, LightDirection, LookAt);
```

Since the objective for this shader is a simple cartoon effect, we'll only be using three colors to draw it. The main color for the mesh will be the diffuse color (MaterialDiffuseColor). To create a solid-colored object, we'll use the same diffuse color for every vertex. We'll go ahead and calculate the specular color just like we do for the other shaders in this chapter's example, and let the pixel shader clamp the resulting color for us.

The third color in the BadToon shader is the black edge that surrounds the edge of the mesh. In a real toon shader, we would actually compute where the edges of our mesh are (with respect to the viewer). I wanted to keep the code simple, and I wanted everything to run in one pass. So, I cheated. If the normal for the current vertex is pointing away from the camera, I set the alpha component (the opacity) of the diffuse color to zero. That's my way of telling the pixel shader that he's working on a pixel that's near the edge of the mesh.

```
// angle between vertex normal and look at
 if( max(0 , dot(WorldNormal,-LookAt)) <= 0.30 )
 {
     OutputData.DiffuseVertexColor.a = 0;
 }

   return OutputData;
}
```

Here's the block of code that calculates the specular component of the current vertex's color. It's actually the same code that we use in the other shader effect files for this chapter's example. The pixel shader is responsible for taking the value that's generated here and deciding what color to paint the resulting pixel.

```
// calculate specular component of this vertex's color
float4 CalcSpecularColor(
    float3 ViewNormal, float3 LightDirection, float3 LookAt)
{
    float3 ReflectedLight = normalize( reflect(LightDirection,ViewNormal) );
    return
        MaterialSpecularColor *
        LightColor *
        pow( saturate(dot(ReflectedLight, -LookAt) ),
            MaterialSpecularPower);
}
```

Swizzles and Indices

HLSL provides several flexible ways to access the components of colors, vectors, and matrices in your shader code. Let's define a float4, and take a look at some of the ways that you can assign data to its four components.

```
// define a float4 structure
float4 MyColor;
```

All of the following are equivalent assignments.

```
// omit component specifier
MyColor = 1.0f;
```

```
// specify all components (rgba)
MyColor.rgba = 1.0f;
// specify all components (xyzw)
MyColor.xyzw = 1.0f;
```

```
// specify each component separately (rgba)
MyColor.r = 1.0f;
MyColor.g = 1.0f;
MyColor.b = 1.0f;
MyColor.a = 1.0f;
```

```
// specify each component separately (xyzw)
MyColor.x = 1.0f;
MyColor.y = 1.0f;
MyColor.z = 1.0f;
MyColor.w = 1.0f;
```

```
// specify each component by index
MyColor[0] = 1.0f;
MyColor[1] = 1.0f;
MyColor[2] = 1.0f;
MyColor[3] = 1.0f;
```

```
// mixed component specifiers, random order
MyColor.br = 1.0f;
MyColor.ga = 1.0f;
```

When using swizzles to reference components in source data, we have even more flexibility.

```
// define a float4 structure
float4 MyColor1 = { 0.9, 0.6, 0.3, 0.0 };
float4 MyColor2;
// result = { 0.9, 0.9, 0.9, 0.9 }
MyColor2.rgba = MyColor1.rrrr;
// result = { 0.6, 0.9, 0.0, 0.3 }
MyColor2 = MyColor1.grab;
```

If you omit any components in the source list, the last component referenced by the source is repeated in the destination.

```
// result = { 0.0, 0.9, 0.9, 0.9 }
MyColor2.rgba = MyColor1.arrr; // pirate's favorite color
// result = { 0.0, 0.9, 0.6, 0.6 }
MyColor2 = MyColor1.arg; // your response to the previous pun
// result = { 0.0, 0.0, 0.0, 0.0 }
MyColor2 = MyColor1.wwww;
MyColor2 = MyColor1.aa;
MyColor2 = MyColor1.w;
```

While you can use the xyzw and rgba notations interchangeably, you cannot mix the two within the same statement. The following is not valid HLSL code.

```
// bad swizzles, invalid HLSL
MyColor.xray = 1.0f;
MyColor.wag  = 1.0f;
```

Pixel Shaders

The pixel shader is responsible for calculating the color of a specific pixel on the screen. The color and texture data that was calculated for each vertex is used to fill in the surface of each triangle using a process known as *linear interpolation*. If one of the three vertices is white and another is red, then the line that connects those two points will start with a red pixel and end with a white pixel. Every pixel in between will have some shade between those two colors. Similarly, texture coordinates will be interpolated so that each pixel on the screen that lies between the two drawn points will map to a pixel in the source texture (known as a *texel*) that lies between the texture coordinates that were mapped to the two vertices.

By the time the pixel shader is invoked, the location of the pixel on the screen has already been determined. It can't read from or write to neighboring pixels. Its sole purpose is to select the colors for the pixels that make up the surface of a 3D face (a triangle) to create an overall visual style for the 3D object (the mesh).

We're about to discuss diffuse and ambient lighting. That's a good illustration of what a pixel shader does. Figure 6.8 shows the triangles that make up a sphere, the same sphere as drawn with a solid color for each triangle, and the sphere with ambient and diffuse lighting calculations applied. The pixel shader selected the color of each individual pixel in the final image such that the surface of each triangle appears smoother than it actually is.

Figure 6.8
A sphere drawn as a wireframe mesh, as a flat-shaded mesh, and smoothed with diffuse and ambient lighting calculations.

Notice how the profile (the silhouette) of the sphere is the same in each rendering. We're not changing the actual shape of the 3D object or adding any more vertices to increase the detail, but it sure seems that way to the player.

Note

There are ways to affect neighboring pixels in a pixel shader, but they involve rendering to a texture, processing the texture after the first pass is done, and then drawing the texture on the screen by applying the texture to two triangles that are arranged so that they completely fill the viewable area. There are many interesting effects that use this technique, making it look like the pixel shader is bypassing the single-pixel restriction.

BadToon Pixel Shader

When we wrapped up the vertex shader for the BadToon effect, I mentioned that the pixel shader is ultimately responsible for determining which of the three cartoon colors will be assigned to the current pixel. Those three values are declared as the first three lines of the pixel shader.

```
float4 MainPS(VertexOutput InputData): COLOR
{
    // define edge color
    float4 pixelColor = {0,0,0,1};
    float4 diffuseColor = {InputData.DiffuseVertexColor.rgb,1};
    float4 specularColor = {InputData.SpecularVertexColor.rgb,1};
```

We start out by assuming the pixel is near the edge of the mesh, setting pixel-Color to black. Next, we check the alpha value of the interpolated diffuse color. When an edge was detected in our vertex shader, we set the alpha value to 0. As we move further from the edge vertex, the alpha gradually returns to 1. When it crosses the 0.33 mark, we'll no longer consider this pixel near an edge, and we'll assume that the pixel will be painted with the diffuse color.

```
if(InputData.DiffuseVertexColor.a >= 0.33)
{
    pixelColor.rgb = diffuseColor.rgb;
```

Remember that we calculated the specular color normally. That means that it has a bright center that falls off as you move away. We don't want any smooth gradients in this shader—the final pixel must be one of three colors. We'll compare the calculated color of the specular component to a threshhold (MaterialSpecularFalloff, which is 0.33 by default). If the specular color is more intense than this value, we'll replace the current value of pixelColor with our constant, toon-friendly specular color.

```
if( specularColor.r >= MaterialSpecularColor.r * MaterialSpecularFalloff &&
    specularColor.g >= MaterialSpecularColor.g * MaterialSpecularFalloff &&
    specularColor.b >= MaterialSpecularColor.b * MaterialSpecularFalloff )
    {
      pixelColor.rgb = MaterialSpecularColor.rgb;
    }
    }

    return pixelColor;
}
```

Geometry Shaders

Since XNA doesn't yet support them, we won't cover geometry shaders at all in this chapter. But, they are worth mentioning. A geometry shader works with the groups of vertices that make up a single face on the mesh (a triangle in most cases). The output of a geometry shader is geometry, which then flows through the other shaders. Working at the vertex or pixel level is ideal for most cases, but those tasks are working with blinders on—completely unaware of the data that came before or will come next.

There are some cases where knowing about sibling vertices is desirable. Toon rendering and various flat-shaded effects use per-face normals, something that would be easy to calculate in a geometry shader. Some games render meshes that are farther away using fewer faces, since the level of detail on those objects is less important than objects that are closer to the viewer. As objects move closer to the viewer, a geometry shader can break large faces into a collection of smaller faces (a process known as *tessellation*).

Shader IDEs

Do yourself a favor and download one of the free shader IDEs from NVidia (FX Composer) or ATI (Render Monkey). Each download includes great example shaders, and they provide real-time previews of your shader code using reference models. Being able to test your changes immediately means that you'll be able to experiment more. I personally prefer FX Composer, but both are excellent tools.

http://ati.amd.com/developer/rendermonkey/index.html

http://developer.nvidia.com/object/fx_composer_home.html

Lighting

Drawing solid-colored triangles makes for a boring and flat 3D environment. Adding textures improves the realism of your 3D scenes, but your world will still feel sterile. Players may not be able to pinpoint what's wrong on a conscious level, but they will sense that something just doesn't feel right. Lighting is one of the most important factors in creating immersive 3D games. By varying the intensity of the colors and textures that are mapped to your 3D objects, they will appear to have more depth and will seem more realistic.

Types of Lights

Conceptually, lighting is pretty simple. You'll have to think back to your high school trigonometry classes, but the math used in lighting calculations is pretty straightforward. In the next few paragraphs, we'll talk about some of the most common methods of representing real-world light sources, and we'll take a look at how several simple lighting models can be combined to create more complex composite effects.

Spotlights

Spotlights are located at some point in the world, and they shine in a certain direction. Light emanates from the source towards a target, expanding in a cone-shaped volume, covering a progressively wider area as it gets farther from its point of origin. Examples of spotlights include flashlights, spotlights, headlights, floodlights, and streetlights. Surfaces near the center of the cone of light are affected by the light more than surfaces near its edge—see Figure 6.9.

Point Lights

Point lights are located at some point in the world, and they shine in all directions. Light emanates from the source, expanding in a sphere-shaped volume, covering a progressively larger area as it gets farther from its point of origin. Examples of point lights include fireflies and light bulbs, as well as candles and other open flames. Surfaces that face the light source are affected by the light more than surfaces that face away from it—see Figure 6.9.

Directional Lights

Directional lights don't have a set location. The light in this lighting model comes from a fixed direction rather than a specific point in space. Rays from this lighting model hit every surface in your virtual world from the same angle, regardless of the surface's location within the world. The best real-world example of this type of light is our Sun.

You might think of the Sun as a point light since it emits light from a point in space, in all directions. If you were creating a simulation of our solar system, a point light would be an ideal choice. But here on Earth, the Sun is so far away that its light appears to be coming from the same direction, regardless of where you stand. In this lighting model, the light source is considered to be infinitely far away. Surfaces that face the light source are affected by the light more than surfaces that face away from it—see Figure 6.9.

More Complex Lighting Methods

There are many different lighting models, and each has its own benefits and shortcomings. In general, the more realistic lighting techniques require more processing power. More time spent processing each triangle means that fewer triangles can be drawn in a given span of time. Fewer triangles equates to less complex representations of your game objects, which translates to less detailed 3D meshes. That's not always a bad thing, though.

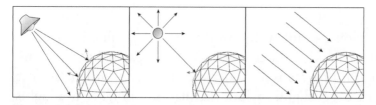

Figure 6.9
The effect of spotlights, point lights, and directional lights on surfaces based on the angle of the surface's normal and the direction from which the light hits the surface.

If you can represent an object with fewer data points, and yet achieve a higher level of realism using the same (or a nominally larger) portion of your processing budget, it's worth the trade. I won't cover the fancier lighting models here. There's plenty of information on the web if you want dig a little deeper into this topic.

Lighting Components

The overall effect that light has on objects can be broken down into three basic components. By combining these three factors in different ways, you can approximate real-world lighting in your virtual environments. There are more realistic lighting models that account for the complex interactions between objects and light (the reflection, refraction, and absorption of light as it bounces from object to object before finally reaching your eyes), but our focus in this text will be on making our games "real enough."

Ambient Light

Few real-world scenes are totally void of any light. In bright sunlight, you can clearly see objects that are in the shade. In a dimly lit room, you can still see a good bit of detail on objects that aren't near a light source. This effect is known as *ambient light.*

Ambient light is applied to a 3D object by allowing the raw surface colors of the mesh to have a greater influence on the final appearance of the image on the screen. When the ambient value is zero, the object will appear as a black silhouette. When the ambient value is maxed out, the surface colors of the mesh will dominate the final image (tinted with the ambient color value), and the mesh will appear to be self-illuminating, especially when surrounded by darker objects. Ambient light is applied uniformly, completely ignoring surface normals.

Diffuse Light

Light travels from a light source in a straight line until it hits a surface and gets reflected. Surfaces that are facing the light source will receive more light, and they will appear brighter than surfaces that are facing away from the light source. This effect is known as *diffuse lighting.* The intensity with which diffused light affects a surface is dependent on the angle between the surface normal and the light source.

Specular Light

When light hits a curved surface, it is scattered in many different directions. Some of that light is reflected toward your eyes, and that portion of the surface shines very brightly. This effect is known as a *specular highlight*. The effect is highly localized, and it's dependent on the angles between the light source, the surface normals, and the location of your eye (the camera). Only when the light from the light source is reflected toward your eye will you see this intense highlight on the surface.

Combining the Three

Figure 6.10 shows how these three components of light change the appearance of your 3D objects. From left to right, top to bottom, the first frame shows a teapot with only ambient lighting applied. The next frame adds diffuse lighting, revealing the curvature of the mesh's surface. In the third frame, I've disabled the diffuse component and added in the specular highlights. And in the last frame, all three components have been blended together to create the final effect.

Lights don't have to be white. They can be any color. The three lighting components that we've talked about can be based on different colors, each blended with the surface color of the mesh using weighted averages.

Figure 6.10
Ambient light, diffuse light, and specular highlights are combined to create more realistic 3D scenes.

Figure 6.11
A wireframe sphere, a smooth-shaded sphere, and a texture-mapped sphere.

There are some lighting techniques that project textures onto the surfaces of your mesh to create effects like sunshine streaming in through stained glass. In that scenario, the surface color of the mesh, the color of the ambient lighting, the color of the diffuse lighting, the color of the specular highlights, the colors of any applied mesh textures, and the colors of the texture map that are projected from the light source are combined to create the final effect.

Texture Mapping

Textures are applied to meshes like decals. The vertices of the mesh serve as anchor points for pixels in the source image. As with lighting calculations, these texture coordinates are sampled on a per-vertex basis, and then linearly interpolated as the pixel shader processes each pixel that makes up the triangle. This concept is illustrated in Figure 6.11.

Texture maps are primarily used to store color data, but there are other techniques that encode custom data within the red, green, and blue values of the texture. We'll briefly discuss some of the most popular techniques that employ this device.

Bump Mapping

Rather than interpolating vertex data, smoothly transitioning from vertex to vertex, a pixel shader can use data that's encoded within a texture to perturb the normal data that it's processing, resulting in slight variations in the lighting calculations that make the surface appear to be bumpy. This technique is known as *bump mapping*, and you'll find an illustration of it in Figure 6.12.

Again, notice how the silhouette of the sphere is the same in each rendering. We haven't added a single new vertex to our mesh, but the shadows and highlights of the resulting image show incredible detail.

Figure 6.12
A wireframe sphere, a smooth-shaded sphere, and a bump-mapped sphere.

Figure 6.13
A wireframe sphere, a smooth-shaded sphere, and a sphere with a procedurally generated texture that mimics the grain of wood.

Procedural Textures

There's no law that says that a pixel shader has to work with actual textures. In fact, the diffuse lighting technique that we discussed earlier didn't use a texture. You could write a pixel shader that returns a constant value every time it's called (a simple example of self-illumination), or you could write a pixel shader that returns random values (raw colors for a stylized effect, grayscale for a TV static effect, or clamped to a certain range and combined with diffuse shading to produce a grainy film effect).

Procedural textures use custom algorithms to determine the color of each pixel in a virtual texture. Materials that are commonly generated using this technique include marble, fire, wood, and clouds. Using the texture coordinates that would normally point to a texel in a texture, the pixel shader calculates color values using some function. You'll find an example of a procedural wood texture in Figure 6.13.

Many implementations of this technique use random data that's encoded into the red, green, and blue values of a texture that the application passes into the shader. Using random values results in textures that seem more natural, devoid of the patterns or regular gradients that are typically associated with sterile, computer-generated images.

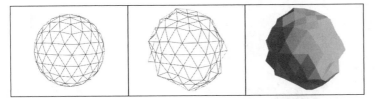

Figure 6.14
A wireframe sphere alongside the same sphere after a displacement map has been applied.

Normal Mapping

There's a pixel-shading technique known as *normal mapping* that is similar to bump mapping in that it tries to approximate the look of a high-resolution mesh using fewer vertices. Unlike bump mapping, which uses encoded texture data to perturb normal data as the pixel shader performs lighting calculations, normal mapping uses the encoded data as the actual surface normal at that point.

The normal map is generated from a high-resolution 3D object. More vertices mean more vertex normals. We could just use the high-resolution mesh in our game, but all the extra vertices would take too much time to process (remember, we need to render screens 30, 60, or more times every second). If we use the low-resolution mesh, we'll be better able to render it in the allotted time, but we lose all the surface detail that made the high-resolution version so appealing in the first place.

The solution is to store all that high-res vertex normal data in a texture (called a *normal map*). That way, we can use the high-resolution surface normal data in our lighting calculations and use the low-resolution mesh for our 3D calculations. As with the other pixel-shading techniques that we've discussed, we're not actually adding any more vertices to our in-game mesh. The edges of the mesh (the silhouette) will seem rough when compared to the detail of the rendered surface. Overall, the effect is very nice, though.

Displacement Mapping

The pixel shader isn't the only one who has access to texture data. And, as we just saw in our discussions on normal mapping, bump mapping, and procedural textures, texture data doesn't have to be used to store color values. Vertex shaders can use values that are encoded within a texture to change the location of the vertices that it processes. This technique of perturbing vertex positions is known as *displacement mapping*. Figure 6.14 shows a simple example of this technique in action.

Let's consider a more practical application of this technique. To represent a rectangular surface in 3D, you'll typically split the rectangle into two triangles.

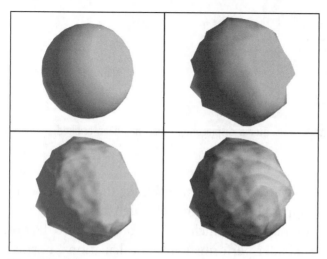

Figure 6.15
Progression of a sphere: diffuse lighting, displacement map, bump map, and procedural texture.

Since there's not much surface detail to the rectangle (it's flat), these two triangles are all you need.

If we were to repeatedly split each triangle of this mesh into two triangles, we'd have more and more vertices in our mesh, but it's still just a rectangle. The player wouldn't see any difference in the on-screen image, even though we're doing a lot more work to generate it. This is a simple example of a process known as *tessellation*.

Here's where the displacement map comes in. Rather than storing color data in a displacement map, the red, green, and blue values of the texture are used to store the X, Y, and Z components of vectors, which are added to the 3D position of the vertex in a vertex shader. The result is no longer a rectangle; it's a 3D mesh with depth. Since the mesh is procedurally generated, you can dynamically determine how many triangles are generated, using more triangles when the object is close to the viewer and fewer when it's farther away (a concept known as *level of detail* or *LOD*).

Combining Effects

Many of the amazing effects that you see in games today are actually built up from techniques like those we've just discussed. By combing several simple shader effects, you can create more realistic (or more stylized) environments for your players. Figure 6.15 shows a wooden nugget that was created by blending several effects.

Summary

We've covered a lot of material in this chapter. I've tried to keep a balance between the extremes of a high-level overview with no practical application and a low-level, exhaustive study of the inner workings of 3D hardware, the Direct3D APIs, and the math involved in converting 3D data in memory to 2D images on the screen.

I wanted to make sure that you understood the basic concepts behind the topics covered so that you will recognize the terminology and be able to piece things together a little easier as you learn more about 3D game programming from other sources. I wish I could have gone into more detail in several areas, but entire books have been written on Direct3D, vertex and pixel shaders, texturing and lighting, and general 3D programming. You don't have to master all of the topics that we've discussed in this chapter to start writing 3D games in XNA. The XNA Framework does a great job of abstracting many of the implementation details away.

On the other hand, I believe it's worth your time to deepen your knowledge in this area of game programming. While the days of crafting your own code to tediously convert points in 3D space to points on the screen are largely behind us, you can benefit greatly by understanding what the graphics hardware and the shaders are doing under the covers. Once you master the basic ideas found in this chapter, I highly recommend that you take the time to read one of those dusty 3D books lying on your bookshelf or Google for some old 3D tutorials that don't use HLSL.

In this chapter, we learned how to load a 3D model from the hard disk, move it around in our virtual world, and apply shader effects to change its appearance. We learned how the GPU can be used to offload many rendering chores, freeing up the CPU to handle other game-related tasks. We learned that the XNA Framework supports 3D content and shader scripts much like any other game resource, as far as the IDE and Content Pipeline are concerned, providing the same, familiar tools and interfaces for all.

Review Questions

1. List at least five ways that vectors can be used to represent attributes of objects in a 3D game.

2. Define the following contexts for 3D data: model space, world space, view space, and screen space. What role does each play?

3. What is HLSL? What XNA Framework class encapsulates HLSL? Can you write a 3D game in XNA without using HLSL?

4. Your 3D game will create and manage the matrices that drive the conversion of in-memory data to on-screen images. Where are those matrices actually applied? Who's responsible for processing all of that 3D data, point by point?

5. How does lighting work to make (otherwise) flat-shaded models more visually interesting? Name some lighting models and explain how they differ from each other.

Exercises

EXERCISE 1. This example doesn't modify the scale of any of the objects in the scene. Add code to reduce the scale of all of the orbiting spheres by 30% or so. Don't apply this scaling factor to the sphere that uses the same effect as the one that's currently assigned to the teapot mesh. This will draw the player's attention to that sphere, and provide a little more visual interest.

EXERCISE 2. The spheres currently orbit around the teapot in the XZ plane (they orbit about the y-axis). Modify the code so to that the plane of their orbit rotates about the x-axis. As written, the My3DObject class always applies rotations in the order y-axis, x-axis, z-axis. So you shouldn't have to change the code in that class to support this new animation.

EXERCISE 3. Create your own 3D object (perhaps a cube?), or download a model from the web that's been placed in the public domain. If needed, convert the model into an XNA-friendly format. Load this model into the scene and allow the player to move it around the XZ plane using the DPad on his controller. Apply the same texture to this new object that's currently applied to the teapot.

EXERCISE 4. Read the article entitled, "How to: Draw Points, Lines, and Other 3D Primitives" in the XNA Framework documentation that was installed with XNA Game Studio Express. Use the information in that article to draw a white grid on the XZ plane that extends twice as far as the orbit radius of the spheres.

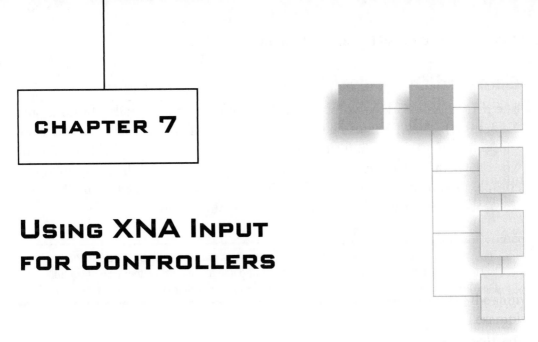

CHAPTER 7

USING XNA INPUT FOR CONTROLLERS

Games are useless unless the player can interact with them. In fact, there's a special name for a game that doesn't accept input—it's called a screen saver.

The XNA Framework provides support for three categories of user input devices: the Xbox 360 Controller, the keyboard, and the mouse. This chapter, and the two that follow, describes the differences between each, and presents code and design guidelines to help you use player input in your game to maximum effect. In this chapter, we will develop a simple game project that graphically shows the state of all the buttons of the Xbox 360 Controller and turns the rumble motors on and off to give the player tactile feedback.

In this chapter, you will learn how to:

- Process input from the Xbox 360 Controller (on Windows and the Xbox 360 game console)

- Use the vibration motors of the controller to present tactile feedback to the player

- Manage many in-game objects, each with independent states

- Break large game tasks into smaller, more manageable tasks

GamePad Overview

The XNA Framework has support for 14 digital buttons, 4 analog buttons, and 2 vibration motors when using the Xbox 360 Controller. The media button is not supported. Up to four actively connected controllers are supported, and the Xbox 360 Controller is supported on both the Windows and the Xbox 360 game console platforms. The number and variety of input sources on an Xbox 360 Controller make it the ideal input device for your games.

Note

The only type of controller that is supported by the XNA Framework is the Xbox 360 Controller. If you're writing a Windows game, and you want your game to support another type of controller (like the Microsoft Sidewinder Controller), you will need to access that controller via some other API.

Polling

Input from the controller is collected by the XNA Framework via polling. During every frame of your game, you will ask the controller what the current state of its buttons is. This state information is wrapped in an XNA Framework structure known as the GamePadState, and it represents a snapshot of the state of all the controller's buttons at the time the request was made. This state information can be saved from frame to frame (so that you can determine which buttons were pressed or released since the last frame), and you can pass the state as a parameter to your methods (so that you don't need to poll the controller repeatedly, running the risk of retrieving conflicting information).

If you've done any Windows programming in the past, you've dealt with event-driven programming. Polling may seem inefficient by comparison, and you might think that it would be easy to miss player input between GetState calls. But, you need to keep in mind that your game is running at 15, 30, 60, or more frames per second. When you're gathering input data 60 times a second, it's not very likely that a player can press and release a button between any two polling requests. If you want to test this out, run the example that we develop in this chapter and try to press and release a button without the screen registering your action.

Note

Per the XNA Framework documentation, the state of a controller is undefined when the controller is disconnected. The API will allow you to poll for the state of a disconnected controller, and there is a boolean property in the GamePadState structure that indicates whether the controller is connected or not. All of the other controller state information is unreliable, and should not be trusted. You may want to automatically pause your game whenever there are no controllers connected.

GamePadState information is retrieved using the GetState member of the GamePad class. Only four Xbox 360 Controllers are supported, and each must be polled separately. The following code shows how you would get the state of the controller used by player one.

```
// Poll the current controller state for player one
GamePadState padState1 = GamePad.GetState(PlayerIndex.One);
```

Digital Buttons

The Xbox 360 Controller has 14 (accessible) digital buttons. The 10 most obvious digital buttons are the A, B, X, Y, Start, Back, left shoulder, and right shoulder buttons. The four directions of the DPad are actually four separate digital buttons (one for each direction), and the left and right thumbsticks can be pressed, each behaving as a digital button. Digital buttons have only two states—pressed and released—so they can be represented with Boolean values in your code. The following code demonstrates how you would see if player one is pressing the A button on his controller.

```
// Poll the current controller state for player one
GamePadState padState1 = GamePad.GetState(PlayerIndex.One);

// make sure the controller is connected
if (padState1.IsConnected)
{
    if (padState1.Buttons.A == ButtonState.Pressed)
    {
        // player one is pressing the A button
    }
}
```

Analog Buttons

Unlike their digital siblings, analog buttons can report a range of values. The Xbox 360 Controller has two triggers on the back side of the controller. The state of each trigger is represented by a float, ranging from 0.0f (not pressed) to 1.0f (fully pressed). The controller also sports two directional thumbsticks. Each thumbstick has an x- and a y-axis. Each axis is represented by a float ranging from −1.0f to 1.0f. For the x-axis, −1.0f indicates that the player is pressing the stick fully to the left, 1.0f indicates that the player is pressing the stick fully to the right, and 0.0f indicates that the stick is not being used at all. Similarly for the y-axis, −1.0f represents down, 1.0f represents up, and 0.0f represents no action.

The following code demonstrates how you would see if player one is using the left thumbstick on his controller.

```
// Poll the current controller state for player one
GamePadState padState1 = GamePad.GetState(PlayerIndex.One);

// make sure the controller is connected
if (padState1.IsConnected)
{
    if (padState1.ThumbSticks.Left.X != 0.0f)
    {
        // player one is directing the left thumbstick to the left or right
    }
    if (padState1.ThumbSticks.Left.Y != 0.0f)
    {
        // player one is directing the left thumbstick up or down
    }
}
```

When processing analog input from the thumbsticks, there's a concept known as *dead zone processing* that you should be aware of. There are minor variances in manufacturing from controller to controller; and over time, movable parts can wear with use. When at rest, thumbsticks will almost always be slightly off center. To account for this, the GetState method automatically disregards values that are below a certain threshold. That threshold is known as the dead zone. If the dead zone weren't taken into account, you would see what's commonly referred to as "drift" in your game—phantom user actions, like moving left even though you're not pressing any buttons.

The overloaded version of the GetState API provides three methods of dead zone processing, each represented by a member of the GamePadDeadZone enumeration.

- **IndependentAxes**—The X and Y components of the thumbstick position are processed against the dead zone independently. This is the default behavior of the API if you don't identify a specific dead zone processing method. For most applications, this is the best, general-purpose processing mode.

- **Circular**—The X and Y components of the thumbstick position are combined before processing the dead zone. In some applications, this will provide better control.

- **None**—The raw values reported by the controller are returned to your game, and you can process the dead zone using your own logic.

Vibration

It's amazing how adding simple little details to a game can make it so much more immersive. Vibration effects are an effective way to draw your player into the experience. When his car hits a wall, or a grenade explodes just a few feet away, or he's just fallen to his death from a high-rise apartment complex, shake the controller to provide tactile feedback.

The Xbox 360 Controller has two vibration motors. The left is a low-frequency rumble motor, and the right is a high-frequency rumble motor. Each motor can be activated independently of the other. And each motor supports varying speeds. You can turn the motors on and off, and adjust their speeds, using the SetVibration method of the GamePad class. The following snippet demonstrates how you would enable the vibration motors.

```
// Poll the current controller state for player one
GamePadState padState1 = GamePad.GetState(PlayerIndex.One);

// make sure the controller is connected
if (padState1.IsConnected)
{
    if (padState1.Buttons.A == ButtonState.Pressed)
    {
        // shake the controller if the A button is pressed
        GamePad.SetVibration(PlayerIndex.One, 1.0f, 1.0f);
    }
    else
    {
        // otherwise, disable the motors
        GamePad.SetVibration(PlayerIndex.One, 0f, 0f);
    }
}
```

Note

The preceding example simply set each motor to its maximum speed, but you can create all sorts of effects by combining various motor speeds and varying the settings over time. Imagine enabling and disabling the motors in rapid succession to simulate riding over a gravel road or firing a machine gun. Or think about using the low-frequency motor to provide constant, pulsing ambient feedback when the player enters a room filled with humming alien technology.

Wrapper Class

It's a good idea to wrap the GamePad and GamePadState functionalities within your own custom helper class. That way, you can make global changes to how your game processes input by changing one source code file. Imagine that you've written a game that uses the controller. This game has several types of levels—each programmed as a separate C# class and each accessing the controller via the XNA Framework's GamePad class. After play testing, you decide to provide an option so that the player can reverse the controls for looking up and down (a common option in most first-person shooter games).

Without the wrapper class, you'll need to edit and test every class that directly accesses the controller APIs. With the wrapper class, you edit one source code file, and the change is inherited by all your custom C# game classes that use it. Of course, you'll also want to provide a way to temporarily return to your default controller mappings for menus, but there is great benefit in centralizing your controller logic.

Let's consider another scenario. Imagine that you've written your game solely for the Xbox 360 game console. When you're done writing it, you decide that you would also like to release it as a Windows game. Not every Windows gamer will have an Xbox 360 Controller connected to his PC, so you decide to add keyboard support. Touching every game screen that accepts controller input will be a pain. You don't want to punish the Windows gamers with Xbox 360 Controllers by simply replacing your controller logic with keyboard logic, so you'll need to make sure that your game logic gracefully combines input from both sources. If you're using a wrapper class, you can intercept keyboard input, map it to controller input, and inject phantom button presses into the controller state that your game uses. In fact, we will develop such a beast in a later chapter.

If you do decide to write your own custom wrapper to gather user input, you should be aware of the fact that the GamePadState structure contains a handy little member named PacketNumber that will let you know if the controller state has changed since the last time you polled it. Many times, there will be relatively long spans where the player is pressing the same button or combination of buttons. In a racing game, the player may be on a straightaway, pressing the accelerator all the way in. In a first-person shooter, the player may be crouched in a corner, waiting to snipe one of his buddies. On a pause screen, the player has likely put the controller down and isn't pressing anything.

The Example

We will develop a simple "game" that exercises each of the features of the controller. Each digital button will be represented on the screen with a graphic, and when the player presses a button, its graphic will change to reflect the change in state. The screen will also contain "slider" images where the state of each of the analog buttons will be presented. In addition to the button images, there will be a small viewport where a ship flies around on a sheet of graph paper. As the player uses any of the directional controls to move left or right, the ship will rotate. When the player presses the triggers or uses any of the directional controls to move up or down, the ship will move.

Figure 7.1 shows a screenshot of the final game.

The Source Images

I created two graphics for each digital button, one for each state (pressed and released). To lay out the screen, I played around with the images in a paint program, moving them around until I was happy with the rough design. Figures 7.2, 7.3, and 7.4 show the source graphics. I divided the collection of images into three files, but this separation is fairly arbitrary.

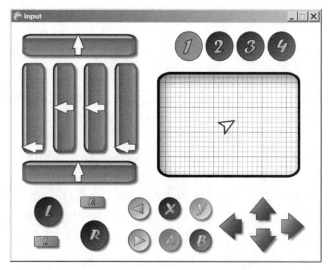

Figure 7.1
A screenshot of the example game that we will develop in this chapter.

Figure 7.2
The sprites that represent the pressed and released states for each of the 14 digital buttons.

Figure 7.3
The sprites for the sliders to show the state of the six analog buttons, as well as the sprites that show which controller ports are active.

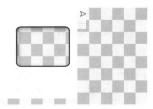

Figure 7.4
The background sprite that will be layered on top of the scrolling grid. The game screen is 640 × 480, but the image is 1024 × 512 (dimensions as powers of 2).

The first source image, shown in Figure 7.2, is named "buttons," and it contains the pressed and released graphics for each of the 14 digital buttons.

The second image, shown in Figure 7.3, is named "analog," and it contains the slider bars and arrows that I use to render the states of the analog buttons. It also contains the images that I use to indicate which of the four Xbox 360 Controllers are currently connected. Rather than having eight separate images of the controller connection states (four controllers, each with two states), I decided to build a composite image at runtime by layering the images that you see here. The actual source image is transparent, but I've added a simple checkerboard pattern so that you can see how the individual components of the image line up with each other.

The final image, shown in Figure 7.4, is named "background," and it contains the graph paper graphic that is tiled across the entire game screen, as well as the ship, and the 640-by-480-pixel background image, which includes the viewport (complete with drop shadow). The actual source image is transparent, but I've added a simple checkerboard pattern so that you can see how the individual components of the image line up with each other.

The ButtonSprite Class

The individual graphics are lined up in the source image so that I can render each of the button state graphics to the same X and Y coordinates on the screen. When it's time to draw the button on the screen, I select the appropriate graphic based on the current state of the button it represents. I wanted to be able to easily move the buttons around on the screen in case I decided to change my layout, so I created a simple C# class to represent the on-screen button.

For each button, I need references to two Texture2D objects—one for the pressed state and one for the released state. Since my source images contain multiple graphics, I can use the same texture for many of the buttons, but I'll still need some way to remember where the individual graphics are within the larger source image. To keep track of their locations, I'll use a Rectangle for each state.

```
private Texture2D m_TextureNormal;
public Texture2D TextureNormal
{
    get { return m_TextureNormal; }
    set { m_TextureNormal = value; }
}

private Rectangle m_RectNormal = Rectangle.Empty;
public Rectangle RectNormal
{
    get { return m_RectNormal; }
    set { m_RectNormal = value; }
}

private Texture2D m_TexturePressed;
public Texture2D TexturePressed
{
    get { return m_TexturePressed; }
    set { m_TexturePressed = value; }
}

private Rectangle m_RectPressed = Rectangle.Empty;
public Rectangle RectPressed
```

```
{
    get { return m_RectPressed; }
    set { m_RectPressed = value; }
}
```

I also need to know where to draw the button on the screen. To store the X and Y coordinates, I'll use a Vector2D structure.

```
public Vector2 Location = Vector2.Zero;
```

Using this basic class, I can place the ButtonSprite anywhere on the screen, and not worry about the details of how it's rendered. Each ButtonSprite will be rendered the same way—using code similar to that found in the following snippet.

```
// bat is an XNA SpriteBatch class, btn is our custom ButtonSprite class
bat.Draw(btn.TexturePressed, btn.Location, btn.RectPressed, Color.White);
```

Note

Rather than writing new classes to support the other (non-digital) buttons, I reuse the properties of this class. Where I deviate from the obvious functionality, I've included comments in the source code. For example, the left trigger is an analog control that has no "pressed" state. The TextureNormal and RectNormal properties of the ButtonSprite are used to define the texture and bounds of the vertical slider graphic. Since there is no pressed state, I use the RectPressed structure to denote the bounds of the "usable" area of the slider—the subset of the graphic that excludes the rounded edges, the transparent areas, and the drop shadow. This inner rectangle is used to place and constrain the vertical bar arrow graphic.

Draw Methods

The final game screen that you see is made up of many independent components. I've broken the task of rendering all of these components into separate, specialized drawing methods.

- DrawButton renders a graphic based on a digital button's state (pressed or released).

- DrawHBar renders a slider bar and its arrow to reflect the state of one of the thumbstick's x-axis values.

- DrawVBar renders a slider bar and its arrow to reflect the state of one of triggers or one of the thumbstick's y-axis values. Since triggers have a range of values from zero to one, and thumbsticks report values between negative one and positive one, this method assumes that the vertical bar represents a trigger. By passing it a value of –1 for the optional min para-meter, the bar can represent the full range of a thumbstick.

- DrawGraph fills the screen with the graph paper tile, rendered relative to the ship's current location. The results of this render step will be overlayed with the background image and the graph paper will show through the viewport. You could save some processing by only rendering the part of the paper that will be visible through the viewport, but filling the entire screen means that you can move your viewport to another part of the screen in your graphics editor without editing the rendering code.

- DrawCursor draws the ship, at its current rotation.

For details on the implementation of these methods, keep reading. They're described in greater detail in the section entitled, "Drawing the Game." You can also find the full source code for this game on the CD-ROM that came with the book.

Update( )

The Update method of this game includes logic to poll the controllers and update the ship's location based on the player's input. The ship itself doesn't actually move on the screen. The paper texture below the ship moves to show the relative direction and speed of the ship.

The Update method is where the code that tracks the state of each of the controller buttons is housed. And this is also where the vibration motors on the controller are set to rumble as long as the A button is pressed on the controller.

While the state of each of the four controllers is polled, only the controller in port one can affect the state of the button images on the screen. The other controller states are only used to detect when those controllers are added or removed, updating the port connection indicator images.

```
/// run logic such as updating the world
protected override void Update(GameTime gameTime)
{
    // capture pad state once per frame
    m_pad1 = GamePad.GetState(PlayerIndex.One);
    m_pad2 = GamePad.GetState(PlayerIndex.Two);
    m_pad3 = GamePad.GetState(PlayerIndex.Three);
    m_pad4 = GamePad.GetState(PlayerIndex.Four);
```

```
// only process input from player one, and only if
// the controller is connected
if (m_pad1.IsConnected)
{
    // combine states to rotate left, true if any are pressed
    bool bLeft = m_pad1.DPad.Left == ButtonState.Pressed;
    bLeft |= m_pad1.ThumbSticks.Left.X < 0;
    bLeft |= m_pad1.ThumbSticks.Right.X < 0;
    if (bLeft) { m_angle -= 5.0f; }

    // combine states to rotate right, true if any are pressed
    bool bRight = m_pad1.DPad.Right == ButtonState.Pressed;
    bRight |= m_pad1.ThumbSticks.Left.X > 0;
    bRight |= m_pad1.ThumbSticks.Right.X > 0;
    if (bRight) { m_angle += 5.0f; }

    // distance to travel per frame, split into X and Y
    float dx = (float)Math.Cos(m_angle * ToRadians);
    float dy = (float)Math.Sin(m_angle * ToRadians);

    // check button states to determine thrust
    float fMove = 0.0f; // assume no movement

    // is the player moving the ship?
    if (m_pad1.ThumbSticks.Left.Y != 0.0f)
    {
        fMove = m_pad1.ThumbSticks.Left.Y;
    }
    else if (m_pad1.ThumbSticks.Right.Y != 0.0f)
    {
        fMove = m_pad1.ThumbSticks.Right.Y;
    }
    else if (m_pad1.Triggers.Right != 0.0f)
    {
        fMove = m_pad1.Triggers.Right;
    }
    else if (m_pad1.Triggers.Left != 0.0f)
    {
        fMove = -m_pad1.Triggers.Left;
    }
    else if (m_pad1.DPad.Up == ButtonState.Pressed)
    {
        // treat as max thumbstick Y
```

```
                fMove = 1.0f;
            }
        else if (m_pad1.DPad.Down == ButtonState.Pressed)
        {
            // treat as min thumbstick Y
            fMove = -1.0f;
        }

        // ship's thrust is relative to analog button states
        m_GraphOrigin.X -= dx * fMove;
        m_GraphOrigin.Y -= dy * fMove;

        // make sure that 0 <= graph origin x <= 50
        while (m_GraphOrigin.X < 0.0f)
        {
            m_GraphOrigin.X += 50.0f;
        }
        while (m_GraphOrigin.X > 50.0f)
        {
            m_GraphOrigin.X -= 50.0f;
        }

        // make sure that 0 <= graph origin y <= 50
        while (m_GraphOrigin.Y < 0.0f)
        {
            m_GraphOrigin.Y += 50.0f;
        }
        while (m_GraphOrigin.Y > 50.0f)
        {
            m_GraphOrigin.Y -= 50.0f;
        }

        // shake the controller while the A button is pressed
        if (m_pad1.Buttons.A == ButtonState.Pressed)
        {
            GamePad.SetVibration(PlayerIndex.One, 1.0f, 1.0f);
        }
        else
        {
            GamePad.SetVibration(PlayerIndex.One, 0f, 0f);
        }
    }
    base.Update(gameTime);
}
```

Drawing the Game

The standard Draw method of this game includes logic to build the screen, piece by piece. First, the graph paper is drawn via a call to DrawGraph. Then, the background image is rendered over the graph tiles so that they can show through the viewport. Then, all of the digital and analog buttons are drawn, along with the four controller connection states, via a call to DrawButtons (note the plural version). And finally, the ship is drawn via a call to DrawCursor.

DrawGraph

The DrawGraph method is very similar to the logic that you see in Chapter 8, "Using XNA Input for Keyboards." A small image is tiled to form an array of images that cover the screen.

Covering the screen is a bit of overkill in this example, since most of the graph is obscured by the rest of the interface. But, by covering the entire screen, we can change the size or location of the window in the interface (that lets the graph show through) without worrying whether there will be any visible gaps in the tiles.

```
// render the graph paper
private void DrawGraph(SpriteBatch batch)
{
    // a single graph tile is only 50-by-50, so repeat
    // it as many times as needed to cover the entire
    // game screen. since the paper is overlaid with the
    // background image, we don't need to worry too much
    // about the edges.

    // temp variable for tiling
    Vector2 vSquare = new Vector2();

    // round to nearest pixel
    float oy = (float)Math.Round(m_GraphOrigin.Y);
    float ox = (float)Math.Round(m_GraphOrigin.X);

    for (float y = oy; y < SCREEN_HEIGHT; y += 50.0f)
    {
        // row by row
        vSquare.Y = y;
        for (float x = ox; x < SCREEN_WIDTH; x += 50.0f)
        {
            // column by column
```

```
            vSquare.X = x;
            batch.Draw(m_texBackground, vSquare,
                m_rectGraph, Color.White);
        }
    }
}
```

DrawVBar and DrawHBar

The DrawVBar and DrawHBar methods are very similar, so I'll list the more general of the two. The value of an analog button is translated to a percentage (0.0f - 1.0f) of the button's full range, and that adjusted value is used to map the analog state to an on-screen pixel. A graphic that represents the button's full range of values is drawn, and an arrow is overlaid to show the current value.

```
// overload for DrawVBar, with default min
private void DrawVBar(SpriteBatch batch, ButtonSprite btn,
    float value)
{
    DrawVBar(batch, btn, value, -1.0f);
}

// draw the bar and the arrow
private void DrawVBar(SpriteBatch batch, ButtonSprite btn,
    float value, float min)
{
    // determine the X of the arrow
    // NOTE: btn.RectNormal describes the bounds of the image
    // btn.RectPressed describes the bounds of the bar itself
    m_btnVBarArrow.Location.X =
        btn.Location.X +
        btn.RectPressed.X +
        btn.RectPressed.Width / 2 -
        m_btnVBarArrow.RectNormal.Width / 2;

    if (min < 0.0f)
    {
        // value is between -1.0f and 1.0f. offset value
        // so that value is between 0.0f and 2.0f
        value += 1.0f;
        // then scale so that value is
        // between 0.0f and 1.0f
        value /= 2.0f;
    }
```

```
    // since value is now between 0 and 1, we can treat it
    // like a percentage. so, Y becomes value percent of
    // Height. NOTE: need to invert value since Y values
    // increase as you move down the screen. (see line with
    // "// bottommost" comment)
    m_btnVBarArrow.Location.Y =
        btn.Location.Y + btn.RectPressed.Y +    // topmost pixel
        btn.RectPressed.Height -                 // bottommost
        btn.RectPressed.Height * value -        // scaled value
        m_btnVBarArrow.RectNormal.Height / 2; // arrow midpoint

    // draw bar
    batch.Draw(btn.TextureNormal, btn.Location,
        btn.RectNormal, Color.White);
    // draw arrow
    DrawButton(batch, m_btnVBarArrow, false);
}
```

DrawPort

The DrawPort method calls out to the DrawButton method to draw a green (if active) or gray (if inactive) button, and then overlays a number image to indicate the state and number of the port.

```
// draw the active port indicators
private void DrawPort(SpriteBatch batch, ButtonSprite btn,
    int index, bool active)
{
    // gray (inactive) or green (active) circle
    DrawButton(batch, btn, active);
    // port number
    batch.Draw(btn.TextureNormal, btn.Location,
        m_rectPortNum[index], Color.White);
}
```

DrawButton

The DrawButton method is used by nearly all of the other draw methods. It uses the data that's contained within our ButtonSprite class to draw an image at the proper location, with the proper dimensions, and (with the help of the pressed parameter) in the proper color.

```
// draw the button at its current location in its current state
```

```
private void DrawButton(SpriteBatch batch, ButtonSprite btn,
    bool pressed)
{
    if (pressed)
    {
        batch.Draw(btn.TexturePressed, btn.Location,
            btn.RectPressed, Color.White);
    }
    else
    {
        batch.Draw(btn.TextureNormal, btn.Location,
            btn.RectNormal, Color.White);
    }
}
```

LoadGraphicsContent( )

The standard LoadGraphicsContent method of this game includes the logic to
load the three source images and to define the location of each graphic with the
images. When you view the source code, you'll notice that whenever possible,
many buttons will share the same Texture2D object. That way, we're not loading
the same image into memory over and over.

```
/// Load your graphics content.
protected override void LoadGraphicsContent(bool loadAllContent)
{
    if (loadAllContent)
    {
        // local temp variables
        Texture2D texTemp;
        Rectangle recTemp;

        // initialize our sprite batch here
        m_batch = new SpriteBatch(graphics.GraphicsDevice);

        // background, cursor, and graph textures
        m_texBackground =
            content.Load<Texture2D>(@"media\background");

        // button textures
        texTemp = content.Load<Texture2D>(@"media\buttons");

        // init A
```

```
        m_btnA.TextureNormal = texTemp;
        m_btnA.RectNormal =
            new Rectangle(0, 64, 64, 64);
        m_btnA.TexturePressed = texTemp;
        m_btnA.RectPressed =
            new Rectangle(128, 64, 64, 64);

        // init B
        m_btnB.TextureNormal = texTemp;
        m_btnB.RectNormal =
            new Rectangle(64, 64, 64, 64);
        m_btnB.TexturePressed = texTemp;
        m_btnB.RectPressed =
            new Rectangle(192, 64, 64, 64);

        // init X
        m_btnX.TextureNormal = texTemp;
        m_btnX.RectNormal =
            new Rectangle(0, 128, 64, 64);
        m_btnX.TexturePressed = texTemp;
        m_btnX.RectPressed =
            new Rectangle(128, 128, 64, 64);

        // NOTE: listing edited to conserve space
        //          see accompanying CD for full listing

        // layout the UI
        PositionButtons();
    }
}
```

Once all the images have been loaded and the bounds of the button graphics have been defined, LoadGraphicsContent makes a call to PositionButtons to define where each of the buttons will be drawn on the screen.

Ideally, groups of buttons would be positioned relative to each other so that they can be moved as a single unit (e.g., A, B, X, Y as a group, the DPad arrows as a group). But in the interest of brevity and clarity, I just hard-coded the X and Y values for each button. If you wanted to change this code so that the buttons were positioned relative to each other, or you wanted to devise some way to load the button locations from an XML or INI file, the PositionButtons method is where you would inject your changes.

```
public void PositionButtons()
{
    // horizontal analog bars
    m_btnHBarLThumb.Location.X = 15;
    m_btnHBarLThumb.Location.Y = 15;

    m_btnHBarRThumb.Location.X = 15;
    m_btnHBarRThumb.Location.Y = 271;

    // vertical analog bars
    m_btnVBarLTrigger.Location.X = 15;
    m_btnVBarLTrigger.Location.Y = 79;

    m_btnVBarLThumb.Location.X = 79;
    m_btnVBarLThumb.Location.Y = 79;

    m_btnVBarRThumb.Location.X = 143;
    m_btnVBarRThumb.Location.Y = 79;

    m_btnVBarRTrigger.Location.X = 207;
    m_btnVBarRTrigger.Location.Y = 79;

    // Left Thumbstick button
    m_btnLThumb.Location.X = 47;
    m_btnLThumb.Location.Y = 351;

    // Left Shoulder button
    m_btnShoulderLeft.Location.X = 47;
    m_btnShoulderLeft.Location.Y = 431;

    // NOTE: listing edited to conserve space
    //       see accompanying CD for full listing
}
```

Summary

In this section, you learned how to capture and process player input from an Xbox 360 Controller. You learned how to use this data to update objects in your game world. You saw how large tasks can be broken down into a series of smaller, more manageable tasks. You learned how to send feedback to the user through the controller using the vibration motors. You learned about dead zone processing and what support XNA Framework includes to manage dead zones. And we discussed the importance of wrapping the standard GamePad APIs within your own centralized, custom class.

Review Questions

Think about what you've read in this chapter (and the included source code) to answer the following questions.

1. What is a thumbstick "dead zone"? How can you avoid "drift" in your games?

2. What are some reasons that you should write your own wrapper class for the GamePad APIs?

3. Can you use a standard Xbox 360 Controller on your PC? Can you use another PC joystick, like the Microsoft Sidewinder?

4. Does the XNA Framework provide support for novel input devices like light guns? If so, how? If not, why?

5. How many vibration motors does an Xbox 360 Controller have? How do they differ from each other?

Exercises

EXERCISE 1. Modify this code so that the maximum speed of the ship is double what it is now.

EXERCISE 2. Expand this example so that input from any attached Xbox 360 Controller will be reflected on the screen.

EXERCISE 3. Modify this code so that the controller starts vibrating when the player presses the A button, and continues to vibrate until the player presses the B button.

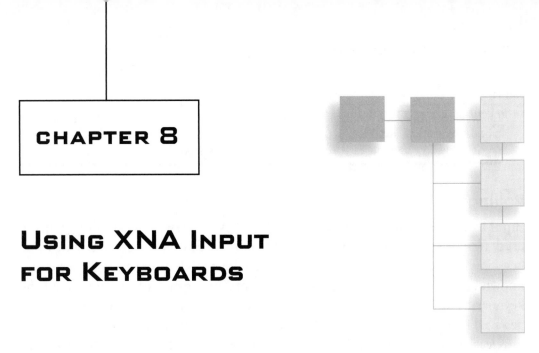

CHAPTER 8

Using XNA Input for Keyboards

In this chapter, we will cover another of the input devices supported by the XNA Framework. We will develop a simple game project that processes player input from the keyboard.

In this chapter, you will learn how to:

- Process input from the keyboard (on Windows and the Xbox 360 game console)

- Manage several in-game objects, each with independent states

- Break large game tasks into smaller, more manageable tasks

Keyboard Overview

Believe it or not, your Xbox 360 game console does provide out-of-the-box support for a standard USB keyboard. While the keyboard isn't supported for playing commercial Xbox 360 games, it can be used for data entry in place of the on-screen virtual keyboard. However, you *can* use a USB keyboard on your Xbox 360 game console with the games that you create in XNA Game Studio Express. On the Windows platform, any keyboard that's supported by the operating system should be supported by the XNA Framework.

The XNA Framework supports more than 100 digital keys when using a standard USB keyboard. As far as this API is concerned, there are no analog buttons on a keyboard. Individual keys have one of two states—pressed or released.

Note

For Windows games, keyboard support is practically a must-have feature, but you should also provide support for the Xbox 360 Controller for those players who own one. The controller provides the best user interface experience for most game scenarios.

Polling

Input from the keyboard is collected by the XNA Framework via polling. During every frame of your game, you will ask the keyboard what the current state of its keys is. This state information is wrapped in an XNA Framework structure known as the KeyboardState, and it represents a snapshot of the state of all the keyboard's buttons at the time the request was made. This state information can be saved from frame to frame (so that you can determine which keys were pressed or released since the last frame), and you can pass the state as a parameter to your methods (so that you don't need to poll the keyboard repeatedly, running the risk of retrieving conflicting information).

If you've done any Windows programming in the past, you've dealt with event-driven programming. Polling may seem inefficient by comparison, and you might think that it would be easy to miss player input between GetState calls. But, you need to keep in mind that your game is running at 15, 30, 60, or more frames per second. When you're gathering input data 60 times a second, it's not very likely that a player can press and release a key between any two polling requests. If you want to test this out, run the example that we develop in this chapter and try to press and release the fire button (the space bar) without the game registering your action. If you do test this out, don't forget to account for the delay between shots that was coded into the game logic.

KeyboardState information is retrieved using the GetState member of the Keyboard class. The following code shows how you would get the current state of the keyboard.

```
// Poll the keyboard state
KeyboardState keyState = Keyboard.GetState();
```

Digital Buttons

Keyboards have 100+ keys, each treated as a digital button. The following code snippet shows how you would determine if the player is pressing the up key on his keyboard.

```
// Poll the keyboard state
KeyboardState keyState = Keyboard.GetState();
if (keyState.IsKeyDown(Keys.Up))
{
    // Up key is being pressed
}
```

To see if a particular key is being pressed, you call the IsKeyDown method of the KeyboardState structure, passing in a member of the Keys enumeration. In most cases, checking for pressed keys one by one is just fine for your game logic, but KeyboardState has another handy method that will let you retrieve a complete list of the currently pressed keys in a single call—GetPressedKeys. GetPressedKeys returns an array of Keys that you can loop through. If the length of this array is zero, then you know that no keys are currently being pressed.

As with the controller input, it's probably a good idea to wrap the Keyboard and KeyboardState functionality within your own custom helper class. That way, you can make global changes to how your game processes input by changing one source code file. Without the wrapper class, you'll need to edit and test every class that directly accesses the keyboard APIs.

Note

If you've ever done any Windows programming, you're aware that the Windows API treats certain keys as special keys. Within the XNA Framework, all keys are peers and are treated equally.

The Example

Now, let's develop a simple "game" that accepts player input from the keyboard. In our new game, as in the example from Chapter 7, the player will control a ship that flies around a sheet of graph paper. The player will use the up and down keys for thrust, and he will use the left and right keys to turn the ship. As in the previous example, the ship will actually remain in the same position on the screen while the game world moves. For our new game, we will add weapons to the ship, allowing the player to fire bullets whenever he presses the space bar. The game will exit when the player presses the Escape key.

Figure 8.1 is a screenshot of the final game.

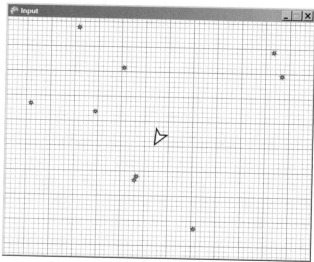

Figure 8.1
The final game.

Figure 8.2
The source image.

The Source Image

The graphics for this game are contained in a single image file. The source image is named game.png, and it contains the graph tile, the ship, and the bullet graphics. The actual source image is transparent, but I've added a simple checkerboard pattern to the figure so that you can see how the individual components of the image line up with each other (see Figure 8.2).

The Bullets

The bullets in this game are very simple objects. They're rendered on the screen, traveling in a fixed direction, at a fixed rate, and they never collide with any other objects. Since we're basically just interested in what to draw and where to draw it, I made the decision to use a structure and manage the bullets in the main game's logic. In a real game, I might have chosen to write a more robust class that provides support for different types of projectiles, but this is an example on how to use the keyboard, and I wanted to keep the example as simple as possible.

In addition to moving along a fixed trajectory, the bullets also rotate as they move. So there are three basic bits of information that we need to track for each bullet—current location, current velocity, and angle of rotation.

To make managing the bullets simple, I store them in an array of Bullets. There are a fixed number of bullets. If the player attempts to shoot a bullet when all the bullets in the array are being used, the shot fails. Once a bullet leaves the viewable area of our game, it is marked inactive and can be reused the next time the player presses the fire button. The number of bullets is dictated by the BULLET_MAX constant.

Well, that's enough information to define our structure and declare our array. Here's the Bullet structure.

```
public struct Bullet
{
    // active = on-screen, not active = available to reuse
    public bool Active;
    // current location on the screen
    public Vector2 Location;
    // delta X and delta Y for this bullet
    public Vector2 Motion;
    // current image rotation angle (spinning bullets)
    public float Angle;
}
```

And here's the code (within the main game class) to allocate the array of bullets.

```
// max num active bullets
const int BULLET_MAX = 75;
// array to track bullets
Bullet[] m_Bullets = new Bullet[BULLET_MAX];
```

Whenever a player fires a shot, there is a delay before he can fire another. This delay is measured in game frames, and it is managed by the main game class.

```
// frames to wait between shots
const int BULLET_DELAY = 9;
// number of frames until next shot can be fired
int m_nBulletCountDown = 0;
```

Once a bullet has been successfully fired, the countdown starts by setting the m_nBulletCountDown member variable equal to BULLET_DELAY. Every time the game's Update method is called, this value is decremented. Shots may only be fired when this variable equals zero.

LoadGraphicsContent()

This example is much simpler than the previous one. The LoadGraphicsContent method only contains two custom lines of code—one to initialize our SpriteBatch and one to load our single game source image.

```
// the only game texture
Texture2D m_texGame;
// the only sprite batch
SpriteBatch m_batch;
/// Load graphics
protected override void LoadGraphicsContent(bool loadAllContent)
{
    if (loadAllContent)
    {
        m_batch = new SpriteBatch(graphics.GraphicsDevice);
        m_texGame = content.Load<Texture2D>(@"media\game");
    }
}
```

Since we only have three game objects, the bounds of the individual graphics for those objects are defined within the main game class as hard-coded member initializers.

```
// individual game images
Rectangle m_rectShip = new Rectangle(1, 1, 62, 62);
Rectangle m_rectBullet = new Rectangle(65, 1, 62, 62);
Rectangle m_rectGraph = new Rectangle(0, 64, 50, 50);
```

Update( )

The standard Update method of this game includes logic to poll the keyboard and perform one of four actions, based on the player's input—turn the ship, move the ship, fire a bullet, or exit the game.

```
protected override void Update(GameTime gameTime)
{
    // get keyboard state once per frame
    KeyboardState keyState = Keyboard.GetState();
```

```
    // exit the game?
    if (keyState.IsKeyDown(Keys.Escape))
    {
        this.Exit();
    }


    // turn the ship?
    if (keyState.IsKeyDown(Keys.Left))
    {
        TurnShip(-DELTA_ROTATE);
    }
    if (keyState.IsKeyDown(Keys.Right))
    {
        TurnShip(DELTA_ROTATE);
    }


    // move the ship?
    float fMove = 0.0f;
    if (keyState.IsKeyDown(Keys.Down))
    {
        fMove = DELTA_MOVE;
    }
    if (keyState.IsKeyDown(Keys.Up))
    {
        fMove = -DELTA_MOVE;
    }
    MoveShip(fMove);


    // fire delay
    if (m_nBulletCountDown > 0)
    {
        m_nBulletCountDown--;
    }


    // fire bullet?
    if (keyState.IsKeyDown(Keys.Space))
    {
        Shoot();
    }
    base.Update(gameTime);
}
```

Rotating the Ship

To rotate the ship on the screen, we just pass the angle of rotation to the Draw method. The m_angle member variable stores the current angle, and this is where it gets updated.

```
// rotate the ship
private void TurnShip(float delta)
{
    m_angle += delta;
}
```

Moving the Ship

The ship doesn't actually move within this game world. The ship sits still, and the world moves around it. Moving the world involves moving the grid and any active, on-screen bullets.

Our grid is a 50-by-50 sprite that is tiled on the screen. To make sure that the entire screen is filled, and that we don't have to draw any more than one extra row or column of sprites, we need to make sure that the top-left tile is located between (−50,−50) and (0,0).

```
// move the ship (actually, move the world while
// the ship stands still)
private void MoveShip(float delta)
{
    // distance to travel per frame, split into X and Y
    float dx = delta * (float)Math.Cos(m_angle * ToRadians);
    float dy = delta * (float)Math.Sin(m_angle * ToRadians);
    // update graph
    m_GraphOrigin.X += dx;
    m_GraphOrigin.Y += dy;
    // make sure x is between -50 and 0
    while (m_GraphOrigin.X < -50)
    {
        m_GraphOrigin.X += 50.0f;
    }
    while (m_GraphOrigin.X > 0)
    {
        m_GraphOrigin.X -= 50.0f;
    }
    // make sure y is between -50 and 0
    while (m_GraphOrigin.Y < -50)
```

```
    {
        m_GraphOrigin.Y += 50.0f;
    }
    while (m_GraphOrigin.Y > 0)
    {
        m_GraphOrigin.Y -= 50.0f;
    }
    UpdateBullets(dx, dy);
}
```

Updating the Bullets

For every active (on-screen) bullet, we need to make sure it hasn't left the screen, then update its position and update its location. The following code does just that.

```
// update location of any active bullets
private void UpdateBullets(float dxShip, float dyShip)
{
    // for every bullet ...
    for (int i = 0; i < m_Bullets.Length; i++)
    {
        // only update active bullets
        if (m_Bullets[i].Active)
        {
            // see if the bullet has left the screen
            bool bDead = false;
            bDead = m_Bullets[i].Location.X < -64;
            bDead |= m_Bullets[i].Location.X > SCREEN_WIDTH + 64;
            bDead |= m_Bullets[i].Location.Y < -64;
            bDead |= m_Bullets[i].Location.Y > SCREEN_HEIGHT + 64;
            if (bDead)
            {
                // bullet is off-screen, mark for reuse
                m_Bullets[i].Active = false;
            }
            else
            {
                // move the bullet. since the ship is
                // stationary and the background moves,
                // be sure to account to recent ship
                // movements
                m_Bullets[i].Location.X += dxShip +
                    m_Bullets[i].Motion.X;
```

```
                    m_Bullets[i].Location.Y += dyShip +
                        m_Bullets[i].Motion.Y;
                    // rotate the bullet
                    m_Bullets[i].Angle += 20.0f;
                }
            }
        }
    }
```

Firing a New Bullet

Bullets are stored in a fixed-size array. Each bullet has a property (Active) that lets us know whether it is already on the screen. If there's at least one inactive bullet in the array, and enough frames have passed since the last time a bullet was fired, this method will launch a new bullet from the ship and send it off in whatever direction the ship is facing at the time.

```
// try to create a new on-screen bullet
private void Shoot()
{
    // make sure we don't inject too many bullets at once
    if (m_nBulletCountDown == 0)
    {
        // scan list of bullets for an available slot
        for (int i = 0; i < m_Bullets.Length; i++)
        {
            // can't use a bullet that's already on-screen
            if (!m_Bullets[i].Active)
            {
                // start at the center of the screen
                m_Bullets[i].Location = m_CenterScreen;

                // calc distance to travel per frame,
                // split into X and Y
                float dx = 3.0f *
                    (float)Math.Cos(m_angle * ToRadians);
                float dy = 3.0f *
                    (float)Math.Sin(m_angle * ToRadians);
                // set bullet into motion
                m_Bullets[i].Motion = new Vector2(dx, dy);
                // init rotation
                m_Bullets[i].Angle = 0.0f;
                // mark as active so we stop ignoring it
```

```
            m_Bullets[i].Active = true;
            // reset delay counter
            m_nBulletCountDown = BULLET_DELAY;
            // we're done, so exit the loop
            break;
        }
    }
  }
}
```

Draw()

The standard Draw method of this game includes logic to build the screen, piece by piece. First, the graph paper is drawn via a call to DrawBackground. Then, all active bullets are drawn via a call to DrawBullets. And finally, the ship is drawn via a call to DrawShip.

```
/// This is called when the game should draw itself.
protected override void Draw(GameTime gameTime)
{
    // start with a clean slate
    graphics.GraphicsDevice.Clear(Color.CornflowerBlue);
    // start drawing our images
    m_batch.Begin();
    // draw game objects
    DrawBackground(m_batch);
    DrawBullets(m_batch);
    DrawShip(m_batch);
    // let batch know that we're done
    m_batch.End();
    base.Draw(gameTime);
}
```

Drawing the Grid

To fill the screen with our graph paper background, we just draw our single tile over and over again to the right and down from the origin. The call to MoveShip ensured that the first tile was placed properly, but tracking the world's origin with a floating point value means that our graph paper tiles may not be centered on the nearest pixel. To keep the background from appearing "wavy," we'll round the origin to the nearest pixel before we start drawing our tiles.

```
// fill screen with graph tile, offset by ship movement
private void DrawBackground(SpriteBatch batch)
```

```
    {
        // round to nearest whole pixel
        float ox = (float)Math.Round(m_GraphOrigin.X);
        float oy = (float)Math.Round(m_GraphOrigin.Y);
        // temp variable used by batch.Draw()
        Vector2 v = Vector2.Zero;
        for (float y = oy; y < SCREEN_HEIGHT; y += 50)
        {
            // row by row
            v.Y = y;
            for (float x = ox; x < SCREEN_WIDTH; x += 50)
            {
                // column by column
                v.X = x;
                batch.Draw(m_texGame, v, m_rectGraph, Color.White);
            }
        }
    }
}
```

Drawing the Ship

All of the real work has already been done by the time this method is called. We just need to draw the ship sprite at the proper location, with the proper rotation.

```
// render the ship, rotated
private void DrawShip(SpriteBatch batch)
{
    batch.Draw(
        m_texGame,                      // ship texture
        m_CenterScreen,                 // ship x, y
        m_rectShip,                     // ship source rect
        Color.White,                    // no tint
        (float)(m_angle * ToRadians),   // ship rotation
        m_CenterShip,                   // center of ship
        1.0f,                           // don't scale
        SpriteEffects.None,             // no effect
        0.0f);                          // topmost layer
}
```

Drawing the Bullets

As with the ship sprite, most of the work has already been done for us by the time we get to this point. We just need to draw the active bullets at their proper location, with their proper rotation.

```
// render each active bullet
private void DrawBullets(SpriteBatch batch)
{
    // scan entire list of bullets
    foreach (Bullet b in m_Bullets)
    {
        // only draw active bullets
        if (b.Active)
        {
            double angle = b.Angle * ToRadians;
            batch.Draw(
                m_texGame,              // bullet texture
                b.Location,             // bullet x, y
                m_rectBullet,           // bullet source rect
                Color.White,            // no tint
                (float)(angle),         // bullet rotation
                m_CenterBullet,         // center of bullet
                1.0f,                   // don't scale
                SpriteEffects.None,     // no effect
                0.0f);                  // topmost layer
        }
    }
}
```

A Quick Note on Math

I didn't really cover this in the last chapter, but there's a line or two in the source code that probably merits some discussion. You may have noticed the following two lines in the MoveShip method (and similar code in the Update method of the game source code in the previous chapter).

```
// distance to travel per frame, split into X and Y
float dx = delta * (float)Math.Cos(m_angle * ToRadians);
float dy = delta * (float)Math.Sin(m_angle * ToRadians);
```

The XNA Framework provides support for many of the basic math functions that you find yourself using again and again when programming games. Two such functions are Sin and Cos (sine and cosine). Without going into too much detail, just know that Sin and Cos are easy ways for you to move an object in a given direction by translating the direction of movement into X and Y components.

Let's examine the first of those two assignments in more detail. The variable name is dx, which is shorthand for "delta x" or "change in x." The variable delta is the magnitude of the change, or the velocity in our case—when delta is twice as big, our ship moves twice as fast. The m_angle variable is a member variable that holds the ship's current angle of rotation, expressed in degrees. ToRadians is just a handy constant to help us convert our angle from degrees to radians—most people feel more comfortable with expressing angles (like the rotation of our ship) in degrees, whereas most math functions express angles in radians. Once the angle has been converted to radians, it is then passed to the Cos method so that the X component of the direction can be determined.

When m_angle is 0.0f, the ship is moving due right and there should be no change in the Y component of its location. In that case, Cos returns 1.0f and Sin returns 0.0f. When m_angle is 90.0f, the ship is moving straight up, and there should be no change in the X component of its location. In that case, Sin returns 1.0f and Cos returns 0.0f. If we were to sweep every angle between 0 and 360, and plot the value of Cos as X and plot the value of Sin as Y, we would have a circle with a radius of 1.0f. When we multiply those results by our velocity, we have a ship that's traveling in the direction we want, covering the distance we expect.

Summary

In this chapter, you learned how to capture and process player input from a keyboard. You learned how to use this data to update objects in your game world. You saw how large tasks can be broken down into a series of smaller, more manageable tasks. We talked about some of the simple match functions that are provided by the Math class, and we discussed the importance of wrapping the standard keyboard APIs within your own centralized, custom class.

Review Questions

Think about what you've read in this chapter (and the included source code) to answer the following questions.

1. Does the Keyboard class provide any mechanisms for checking the pressed state of keys other than querying individual keys using IsKeyDown?

2. Does the Xbox 360 game console support USB keyboards? Explain.

3. How many analog buttons does the XNA Framework support when processing keyboard input?

4. How might you determine how long a player has been pressing a button?

Exercises

EXERCISE 1. Currently, the bullets move at twice the maximum speed of the ship. Modify this code so that bullets move three times the maximum speed of the ship. If you're feeling especially adventurous, make the speed of a bullet a function of how long the fire button was pressed—the longer the player presses the space bar, the faster the bullet travels (up to some maximum velocity).

EXERCISE 2. Create a new bullet type. Allow the player to fire this new bullet by pressing the left Shift key (Keys.LeftShift) on the keyboard. Be sure to use a different bullet velocity than the current bullet. Use the same graphic as the current bullet, but tint it red using the overloaded Draw method of the SpriteBatch class. To keep track of two types of bullets, you can create a separate array for each (of type Bullet[]), or you can add a property to the Bullet class that indicates which kind of projectile it represents, and store all bullets in the same array.

EXERCISE 3. Add code to limit the amount of time the player can maintain thrusters. As the player approaches this limit, make the ship flash between a red tint and its normal color. If the thrusters overheat, don't allow the player to move again until they've had a chance to cool off.

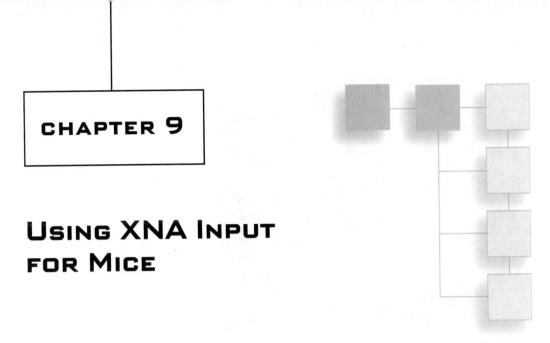

CHAPTER 9

Using XNA Input for Mice

In this chapter, we will cover yet another input device supported by the XNA Framework. We will develop a simple game project that processes player input from the mouse.

In this chapter, you will learn how to:

- Process input from the mouse (Windows only)

- Manage several in-game objects, each with independent states

Overview

The XNA Framework includes support for any standard mouse that Windows supports. The mouse is only available to your Windows games. There is no support for the mouse on the Xbox 360 game console.

In this chapter, we will develop a simple "game" project that demonstrates the basic functionality of the XNA Framework APIs that support the mouse. The application that we develop will display a grid of blue blocks. Whenever the mouse moves over a block, it becomes white. Whenever the mouse moves away from the block, it slowly fades back to its default color (blue). If the player clicks on one of the blocks, the block's color becomes white and stays white until the user clicks on the block again.

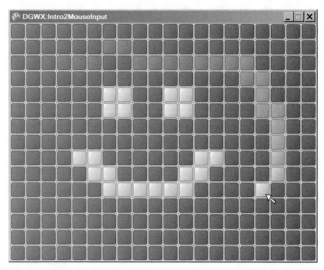

Figure 9.1
A screenshot of the game that we develop in this chapter.

Figure 9.1 shows the example game in action. I've clicked some cells to create a smiley face, and I moved the cursor around the top and down the right to demonstrate the fading cell effect.

Polling

Input from the mouse is collected by the XNA Framework via polling. During every frame of your game, you will ask the mouse what the current state of its buttons is and where it is located on the screen. This state information is wrapped in an XNA Framework structure known as the MouseState, and it represents a snapshot of the state of all the mouse's buttons and its on-screen location at the time the request was made. This state information can be saved from frame to frame (so that you can determine which buttons were pressed or released since the last frame), and you can pass the state as a parameter to your methods (so that you don't need to poll the mouse repeatedly, running the risk of retrieving conflicting information).

If you've done any Windows programming in the past, you've dealt with event-driven programming. Polling may seem inefficient by comparison, and you might think that it would be easy to miss player input between GetState calls. But, you need to keep in mind that your game is running at 15, 30, 60, or more frames per second. When you're gathering input data 60 times a second, it's not very likely that a player can press and release a button between any two polling requests. If you want to test this out, run the example that we develop in this chapter and try to press and release the left mouse button without the game registering your action.

Mouse state information is retrieved using the GetState member of the Mouse class. The following code shows how you would get the current state of the mouse.

```
// Poll the mouse state
MouseState mouseState = Mouse.GetState();
```

The Buttons

In addition to the left, right, and center buttons that are common to most mice, the XNA Framework also provides support for some of the more modern mouse features. For example, many mice provide back and forward buttons that help you easily navigate visited web pages. These buttons are accessed in the XNA Framework using the XButton1 and XButton2 members of the MouseState class.

Most modern mice also provide a scroll wheel to help you scroll within content that's just too big to fit on a single screen. This feature is exposed by the XNA Framework as the ScrollWheelValue member of the MouseState class. Under the Windows APIs, scroll wheel values are typically returned as a relative value (the amount changed since the last time the device reported an update). In the XNA Framework, this value represents a cumulative change, over the lifetime of the game.

The Example

Processing mouse input is fairly straightforward, so this example is pretty simple. All input processing is handled by the Update method. The current mouse location is stored in the CursorPosition member variable so that it can be used by the Draw method. Button presses are recorded in the BlockState struct for each block on the screen.

The BlockState Struct

The code for the BlockState struct follows:

```
// simple struct to track the state of each block
public struct BlockState
```

```
{
    public bool IsSelected;
    public double EffectAge;
}
```

The IsSelected boolean is used to indicate whether this block should remain white, rather than fading back to blue. The EffectAge double value is the number of seconds to pass before this block is fully idle (blue). Between the active and idle states, the block gradually fades from white to blue.

Determining the Grid Size

Our game runs with a resolution of 640 horizontal pixels and 480 vertical pixels. Our grid will be 20 cells wide and 15 cells tall. That means that each cell will be 32 pixels wide and 32 pixels tall.

```
// width and height of screen, in pixels
const int SCREEN_WIDTH = 640;
const int SCREEN_HEIGHT = 480;

// width and height of grid, in cells
private const int GRID_WIDTH = 20;
private const int GRID_HEIGHT = 15;

// width and height of cell, in pixels
private const int CELL_WIDTH = SCREEN_WIDTH / GRID_WIDTH;
private const int CELL_HEIGHT = SCREEN_HEIGHT / GRID_HEIGHT;
```

Using this information, we can create an array to hold our instances of the BlockState structure (one for each cell on the screen).

```
// array containing the state of every block in the grid
private BlockState[,] BlockStates =
    new BlockState[GRID_WIDTH, GRID_HEIGHT];
```

Processing Input

We need to track the location of the mouse from frame to frame (to highlight the cells that the cursor passes over), and we need to know when the player has clicked the mouse button (to toggle the IsSelected flag for the clicked cell).

To make sure that we don't register a click more than once, we'll keep track of the state of the mouse button from the previous frame. Whenever the state from the previous frame doesn't match the state of the current frame, the player has pressed or released the button.

```
// remember the last button state we saw, so we don't repeat it
ButtonState LastMouseButtonState = ButtonState.Released;

/// game logic such as updating the world
protected override void Update(GameTime gameTime)
{
    // Allows the default game to exit on Xbox 360 and Windows
    if (GamePad.GetState(PlayerIndex.One).Buttons.Back ==
        ButtonState.Pressed)
        this.Exit();

    // we'll work with the elapsed seconds since the last update
    double elapsed = gameTime.ElapsedGameTime.TotalSeconds;

    // get the mouse state, and record its current location
    MouseState mouse1 = Mouse.GetState();
    CursorPosition.X = mouse1.X;
    CursorPosition.Y = mouse1.Y;

    // which grid cell is this mouse over now?
    int gx = (int)Math.Floor(CursorPosition.X / CELL_WIDTH);
    int gy = (int)Math.Floor(CursorPosition.Y / CELL_HEIGHT);
```

We need to iterate over the entire grid, updating the EffectAge for any cells that have recently been passed over. While we're at it, we'll also update the cell that's currently under the cursor.

```
for (int y = 0; y < GRID_HEIGHT; y++) // for each row
{
    for (int x = 0; x < GRID_WIDTH; x++) // for each column
    {
        // if the current cell is under the mouse
        if (gx == x && gy == y)
        {
            // start the fade effect
            BlockStates[x, y].EffectAge = EFFECT_DURATION;

            // if the player clicks, toggle the IsSelected flag
            if (mouse1.LeftButton == ButtonState.Pressed)
```

```
                {
                    // don't toggle more than once for a single click
                    if (mouse1.LeftButton != LastMouseButtonState)
                    {
                        BlockStates[x, y].IsSelected =
                            !BlockStates[x, y].IsSelected;
                    }
                }
            }
            else
            {
                // this cell not under mouse, just update fade state
                BlockStates[x, y].EffectAge -= elapsed;
                if (BlockStates[x, y].EffectAge < 0)
                {
                    BlockStates[x, y].EffectAge = 0;
                }
            }
        }
    }
}
```

Lastly, we need to remember the current mouse button state so that the next frame won't process it again.

```
    // remember the last click state so we don't process it again
    LastMouseButtonState = mouse1.LeftButton;

    base.Update(gameTime);
}
```

The Draw Method

The main `Draw` method delegates game rendering tasks to the helper methods.

```
/// render game objects
protected override void Draw(GameTime gameTime)
{
    graphics.GraphicsDevice.Clear(Color.White);

    // draw the game components
    batch.Begin();
    DrawGrid(batch);
    DrawBlocks(batch);
    DrawCursor(batch);
```

```
    batch.End();

    base.Draw(gameTime);
}
```

Drawing the Grid Lines

There's a small gap between each cell in the grid. We'll decorate that gap with a grid of blue lines.

```
// fill the screen with a grid of blue lines
private void DrawGrid(SpriteBatch batch)
{
    // horizontal and vertical line rectangles
    Rectangle horizontal = new Rectangle(0, 0, SCREEN_WIDTH, 1);
    Rectangle vertical = new Rectangle(0, 0, 1, SCREEN_HEIGHT);

    // draw horizontal lines
    for (int y = 0; y < GRID_HEIGHT; y++)
    {
        horizontal.Y = y * 32;
        batch.Draw(
            Texture,
            horizontal,
            PixelRect,
            Color.CornflowerBlue);
    }

    // draw vertical lines
    for (int x = 0; x < GRID_WIDTH; x++)
    {
        vertical.X = x * 32;
        batch.Draw(Texture, vertical, PixelRect, Color.CornflowerBlue);
    }
}
```

Drawing the Blocks

Since there are three basic states for a block (idle, active, and fading), there are three paths in the DrawBlocks method, each with its own call to batch.Draw(). The states are processed in the following order: active (IsSelected == true), fading (state.EffectAge > 0), and idle (IsSelected == false && state.EffectAge = 0).

```
if (state.IsSelected)
{
    // is selected, draw as fully-highlighted
    batch.Draw(Texture, pos, BlockRect, ColorActiveBlock);
}
else if (state.EffectAge > 0)
{
    // ------------------------------------------------------
    // this block of code is detailed in the next section
    // ------------------------------------------------------
}
else
{
    // block is idle, draw as fully-idle
    batch.Draw(Texture, pos, BlockRect, ColorIdleBlock);
}
```

Fading Blocks

To fade from one color to another, we'll need to split the starting and ending colors into their primary components: red, green, and blue. To calculate a color in between these two extremes, we'll use a process known as *linear interpolation*. Linear interpolation is an easy way of gradually transitioning from one value to another. The basic formula for linear interpolation looks something like this:

```
result = value1 + (value2 - value1) * weight
```

In this formula, value1 is our starting value, value2 is our target value, and weight is a number between 0.0 and 1.0 that represents the progress of the transition. When weight is 0.0, result is value1, and when weight is 1.0, result is value2.

The XNA Framework provides a utility class called MathHelper, which includes a method that we can use for linear interpolation. This method is called Lerp. Interpolation works with discrete values, but we want to transition between colors, which are a more complex type. To make our transition, we'll need to interpolate each of the color components separately.

```
// start with fully idle and fully highlighted colors
vColorA = ColorActiveBlock.ToVector3();
vColorI = ColorIdleBlock.ToVector3();
```

The ToVector3() method of the Color class converts the RGB (red, green, blue) values of the color to a Vector4 value, with XYZ components. The reason we need to convert the color components to vectors is that the Color class is read-only. Once you create a new Color, you cannot change the values of its members. Once we have our colors as vectors, we can easily interpolate the XYZ components of each using the block's EffectAge to calculate the progress of the transition.

```
// perform linear interpolation (Lerp) between the two
vColor.X = MathHelper.Lerp(vColorI.X, vColorA.X,
    (float)(state.EffectAge / EFFECT_DURATION));
vColor.Y = MathHelper.Lerp(vColorI.Y, vColorA.Y,
    (float)(state.EffectAge / EFFECT_DURATION));
vColor.Z = MathHelper.Lerp(vColorI.Z, vColorA.Z,
    (float)(state.EffectAge / EFFECT_DURATION));
```

Now that we have our new transitional color as a vector, it's a trivial task to convert it back to a Color object and render our block.

```
// use the interpolated color
Color col = new Color(vColor);

// actually draw the block
batch.Draw(Texture, pos, BlockRect, col);
```

Drawing the Cursor

The DrawCursor method is very simple. We just need to draw our arrow sprite wherever the mouse cursor is located within the game screen.

```
// current location of the mouse
private Vector2 CursorPosition = Vector2.Zero;

// draw the mouse cursor at its current location
private void DrawCursor(SpriteBatch batch)
{
    batch.Draw(Texture, CursorPosition, ArrowRect, Color.White);
}
```

That's basically all there is to this example. As I said earlier, processing mouse input is fairly straightforward.

Summary

In this chapter, you learned how to process input from a standard mouse connected to a Windows PC. You also learned how to manage several game objects simultaneously.

Review Questions

Think about what you've read in this chapter (and the included source code) to answer the following questions.

1. What types of mice does the Xbox 360 support?

2. What does `MathHelper.Lerp` do?

3. There's only one `BlockState` struct, but there are hundreds of independent blocks on the screen at once, each with its own state information. How does that single structure become hundreds of in-game objects?

4. Other than the left and right mouse buttons, what mouse buttons are supported by the XNA Framework?

5. How is the fading block effect implemented in this example?

Exercises

EXERCISE 1. Modify this example so that when a block is selected (by left-clicking on it), it is tinted green (rather than the current white tint) so that it stands out from the surrounding blocks that are highlighted when the mouse moves over them.

EXERCISE 2. Modify this example so that the user can toggle the state of multiple blocks by "dragging" the mouse across the grid. Be sure to keep track of when the mouse enters and leaves a particular cell so that the same block isn't toggled more than once as the mouse moves over it.

EXERCISE 3. Modify this example so that the grid can scroll when the player uses his mouse's scroll wheel. Implement your change in such a way that any rows of blocks that exit the grid appear in the opposite row so that no existing cell states are lost.

EXERCISE 4. The player can move his mouse fast enough that some blocks are bypassed as the cursor moves past them. Implement logic that fills in these gaps, in a straight line, between the last two blocks that were highlighted.

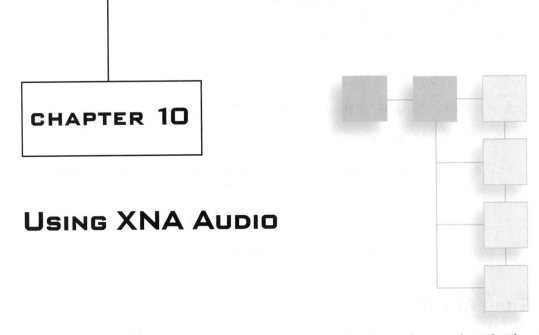

CHAPTER 10

USING XNA AUDIO

Audio is one of those areas of game development that is often neglected. The Cross-Platform Audio Creation Tool (XACT) is a powerful authoring environment for creating interactive audio content from simple wave files. I won't be able to cover XACT exhaustively because there's just so much that this tool is capable of doing.

XACT is NOT a tool that was developed specifically for XNA and Game Studio Express. It's a part of the DirectX SDK. As such, there may be features of XACT that aren't directly accessible to your XNA game. As the XNA platform matures and community feedback drives its new features, you'll find that the gap between what XNA supports and what XACT provides will narrow greatly.

In this chapter, we will cover the basics of using XACT to convert your wave files into a format that the XNA Framework understands, and we will create a simple example that plays those sounds on Windows and the Xbox 360 game console.

Note

> While you can bypass XACT and the XNA Framework's Audio APIs in your Windows games by using other APIs, XACT and the `Microsoft.Xna.Framework.Audio` namespace are your only options for playing music and sounds within your XNA titles on the Xbox 360 game console.

In this chapter, you will learn how to:

- Use XACT to convert standard audio content into XNA-friendly media

- Use XACT to logically group sounds

- Use XACT to distort, loop, and combine simple sounds to make more complex sounds

- Use the XACT Auditioning Utility to make your workflow more efficient

- Manipulate in-game sounds independently or in groups

The XACT UI

The Microsoft Cross-Platform Audio Creation Tool is the only way to get audio into your XNA games for the Xbox 360 and Windows platforms. You can create your content as uncompressed wave files in another content creation tool or bring in files from a third-party sound library.

In addition to converting your audio content into a format that's compatible with the XNA Framework's APIs, XACT lets you create variations of your content so that you can use a smaller number of source sounds to create a wide variety of in-game audio effects. XACT also allows you to expose internal properties for your cue objects so that you can manipulate them at runtime.

This tool is capable of doing a lot more than we can cover in this chapter, and it's well worth the time investment to scan the web and read up on how audiophiles are using XACT to enhance the immersive experience of their XNA games.

You can think of XACT as a tool for audio designers, much like Photoshop is a tool for graphic designers. In practice, most hobbyists are programmer, artist, audio designer, and level designer for their projects, all rolled into one. Everyone who reads this chapter will be able to import sounds into their XNA games. Few of us will be able to use XACT to its fullest, the way an experienced audio designer can.

Wave Bank

The Wave Bank contains your collection of source audio files. Add your uncompressed wave files here and they become a part of your project. Drag your wave content to the Sound Bank to create the sounds that you can access from your game. You can set several properties on the individual files in your Wave Bank, including the compression settings for your game media. A single XACT project can contain multiple Wave Banks. Each Wave Bank is represented by its own XWB file.

Sound Bank

The Sound Bank is the staging area for your game sounds. It represents a collection of sounds and cues that your game can access. There is no actual sound data contained within a Sound Bank—that data lives in the Wave Bank. The Sound Bank is the place where you define how your sounds will be played. A single XACT project can contain multiple Sound Banks. Each Sound Bank is represented by its own XSB file.

Sounds

Sounds define how waves are played. They posses certain properties, like volume and pitch, which can be configured within the XACT user interface. Sounds are made up of one or more tracks.

Tracks

Tracks provide a way to logically group wave events. The simplest, and only event that is automatically added when you create a new sound, is the Play Wave event. Events expose properties that let you change the way that sounds are played. In our example, we'll use the `Play` event to vary the pitch and volume of our laser sound each time it is played.

Cues

Cues are the interface to sounds that the programmer uses to play sounds within his XNA game. Cues are composed of one or more sounds. XNA programmers kick off cues whenever certain game events occur. Some examples of cues in games are gunshots, footsteps, squealing tires, or (as in our example's case) laser fire.

It may seem like there's a little too much abstraction going on here. One or more waves map to a sound. One or more sounds map to a cue. Why not just have the programmer use sounds and skip the cues? Beyond the obvious XNA Audio API restrictions, cues provide a convenient layer that gives the audio designer more flexibility to compose complex sounds from simpler sounds. The programmer references these composite sounds via a cue. If the audio designer decides to completely redesign a cue, the code isn't affected. It's still the same logical audio cue, no matter how it was composed.

Categories

Categories provide a way to logically organize related resources into collections of related sounds where settings for all sounds within the group can be manipulated with a single update. A good example of categories in action is having separate groups for your music and your game sounds. That way, you can provide an option for the player to set the volume of each, independently. Another good use of categories is to group related enemy gunfire or dialog so that no more than a certain number of cues will be played simultaneously, reducing the chance that your sounds will be so busy that they distract from the game play.

RPC Presets

Runtime Parameter Controls (RPCs) allow your program to vary sounds using variables. For a good illustration of the usefulness of RPCs, consider the engine sound in a racing game. As the player accelerates and changes gears, the volume and pitch of the engine sound should change. The programmer could tweak the volume and pitch settings within his code, but XACT provides a better way.

The audio designer can create a variable within XACT called RPM. Using a graphical UI, the audio designer can then define how the volume and pitch of the engine sound should vary, based on the value of the RPM variable. Now, the programmer can update a single variable to change the way the engine sound is played back within the game. This is a very logical division of labor where the audio designer is able to use his expertise to create great sounds for the game, and the programmer is able to easily use these dynamic sounds by tying them to internal game state variables.

Variables

Variables are the interface to RPCs that programmers can use to change the way that sounds are played. The audio designer defines the relationship between various settings and XACT variables, then the programmer updates those variables from within the game at runtime.

DSP Effect Path Presets

Digital Signal Processing (DSP) Effect Path Presets provide a way for the audio designer to apply DSPs to his sounds within the XACT project. XACT ships with a reverb DSP that makes it seem as though your sounds were recorded in different environments. The presets for the reverb DSP include bathroom, stone room, stadium, and several others. You can use these presets as they are defined, or you can use them as a starting point for your own custom reverb effects.

Compression

XACT uses uncompressed audio source files, but you may want to save some space in your game by compressing your sound data. In XACT, create a new compression preset by right-clicking on the Compression Presets folder in your XACT project. Settings are applied at the wave file level. Within XACT, you can drag a wave from your Wave Bank onto your new Compression Preset to associate the two. To verify that your wave has been assigned to the preset, select the wave by clicking on it. The Compression Preset property for that wave should reflect your selection. You can tweak your Windows and Xbox 360 properties independently to favor smaller file sizes or better quality.

The XACT Auditioning Utility

Sometimes it's a hassle to rebuild your game project just to listen to a simple change that you've made to the sounds in your XACT project. The XACT Auditioning Utility provides a means to let you play back your modified sounds within the XACT user interface. Just launch this utility alongside the XACT designer, and you will be able to play back your sounds within XACT. This makes life a lot easier if you use XACT as a true design tool, rather than just as a conversion utility.

Playing Sounds in Your XNA Game

Okay. You're able to compose great effects using XACT, and you're able to play them back using the auditioning utility. But we're here to write games. The following text will help you get your new content into your XNA game.

The Content Pipeline

The XACT utility is capable of generating your XWB, XSB, and other content files on its own, but XNA provides another path for importing data from your XACT project into your game. The standard XNA Content Pipeline supports XACT project files. You can just import your XAP file, along with any wave files on which it depends, into your project and the Content Pipeline will automatically build the XACT project for you whenever you build your game project.

AudioEngine Object

The AudioEngine object is the heart of audio support for your XNA game. You create a new AudioEngine object by referencing the XGS file that was produced when your XACT project was built. This is the object that manages the references to the Sound Banks and Wave Banks of your XACT project.

WaveBank Object

The WaveBank object represents the collection of wave objects in your XACT project.

SoundBank Object

The SoundBank object represents the collection of sound and cue objects in your XACT project. This is the object that you will keep coming back to when you want to play sounds and get references to your cue objects.

Cue Object

The Cue object represents an instance of a cue from your XACT project. XNA game programmers use Cue objects to play sounds whenever specific game events occur (like a gunshot, footsteps, or a slamming door). Cues may be made up of more than one sound. Whenever a cue is played, all of the sounds for that cue are played, using the settings and effects that were configured in the XACT project.

Note

Whenever possible, favor SoundBank.PlayCue("Name") over SoundBank.GetCue ("Name"). The way that the SoundBank class is implemented, the sound that's associated with a Cue is released when the garbage collector disposes of an unreferenced Cue object.

When you use the PlayCue method, you needn't worry about the inner workings of the audio framework—everything is handled for you. When you manage your own Cue objects, your code will need to keep a reference to the Cue until you no longer need the sound that's associated with it.

Walk Through

The following paragraphs provide step-by-step instructions for taking sound content from uncompressed wave files on your hard drive to in-game sound effects and music.

Creating the XACT Project

Open XACT by clicking on your Start button in Windows. Select App Programs > Microsoft XNA Game Studio Express > Tools > Microsoft Cross-Platform Audio Creation Tool (XACT). When you initially open XACT, you will be greeted by a new, blank project, as shown in Figure 10.1.

The next step is to create our Wave Bank and Sound Bank for the XACT project. Right-click on each of those project folders within the tool and add one new bank for each. Two new MDI (Multiple Document Interface) child windows will open within the tool. To make things easier to work with, click on the Window menu, then select Tile Horizontally. Your project should now look something like Figure 10.2.

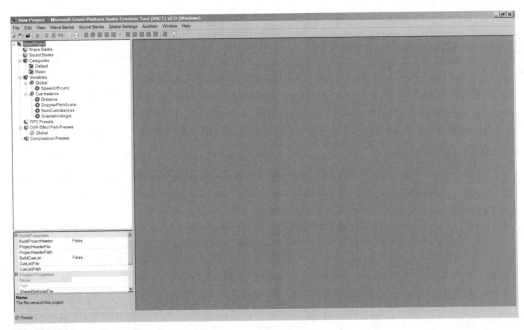

Figure 10.1
A new, blank XACT project.

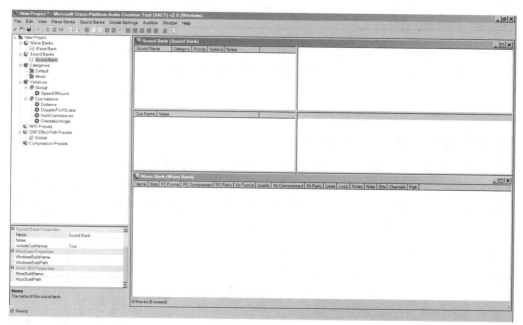

Figure 10.2
The XACT project, with new Wave Bank and Sound Bank windows.

Now we're ready to add wave files to our XACT project. You could just drag your wave files from a Windows Explorer window into the Wave Bank pane in your project. The project would then reference those wave files from wherever they are stored on your PC. There's just one problem with that. Once we're done creating and tweaking our XACT project, we will need to copy the project file (the *.xap file) and all of our source wave files into our Game Studio Express game project's directory so that the Content Pipeline will be able to find them. It would make a lot of sense to go ahead and save our XACT project now and copy our wave files into a common directory. I named my XACT project "example.xap," and I copied my three source wave files into the same directory as my new XACT project.

Note

XACT is not an audio content creation tool. You will need to have some existing wave file content before you go any further. I've included the source wave files on the CD along with the source code for this chapter.

There are several sound libraries out there, and there are many commercial sound editors that you can purchase. One of the most popular sound editors is Sony's Sound Forge (formerly from Sonic Foundry). In keeping with my long-standing tradition of using less-popular or unknown brands, my audio editor of choice is the one found in ULead's Media Studio Pro suite of audio editing, video editing, and DVD authoring tools.

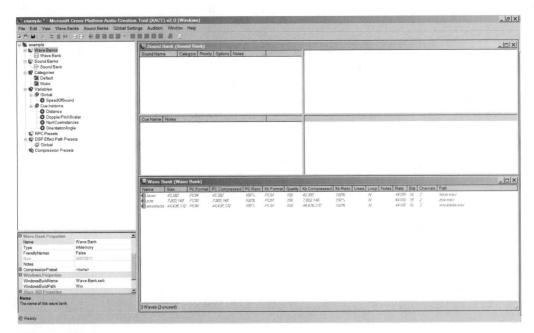

Figure 10.3
The XACT project, with three wave files.

The three files that I've added are ensalada.wav (a really corny song that a good friend's band produced), laser.wav (a sound effect that I created myself by distorting a recording of myself whistling), and zoe.wav (a story that my eldest girl made up for me when she was three years old). I'll use ensalada.wav as my background music, zoe.wav as my game's primary sound, and laser.wav as a sound that will be triggered whenever the user presses a certain button.

Drag your source files into the XACT project and drop them into the Wave Bank pane. Your project should now look something like Figure 10.3.

Items in the Wave Bank are the raw source files. They're not quite ready for use in our game. Drag each wave from the Wave Bank to the Sound Bank and drop them in the panel that's labeled Cue Name. Your XACT project should now look something like Figure 10.4.

We could stop right here and our sounds would be ready for use in our game project, but I want to tweak some of the settings before we go too much further. First, let's compress our game sounds by adding a new Compression Preset. Right-click the Compression Presets folder within your XACT project, then click New Compression Preset. We'll just accept the defaults for now, but you can tweak the compression settings by editing the properties of your new preset

Figure 10.4
The XACT project, with three sounds and cues.

within the XACT interface. The new preset won't have any effect on our project until we bind it to our wave files in the Wave Bank. The easiest way to do this is to drag each wave from the Wave Bank onto the new Compression Preset node.

Next, we need to determine which sounds are background music and which are game-related sounds. This chapter's code will allow the user to adjust the volume of the music and the game sounds independently. By default, your XACT project contains two ready-to-use categories—Default and Music. All new sounds are bound to the Default category when they're first created in the project. So, we just need to assign our background music sound to the Music category. The easiest way is to just drag the sound from the Sound Bank onto the Music category.

Note

I said that there are two pre-configured categories. There are actually three. The third is called Global, and changes to that Category affect both the Music and Default categories. Music and Default are sub-categories of Global.

While we're at it, it would be nice if the background music were to loop indefinitely. Select the music sound in the Sound Bank, then select the Play Wave event, which should be to the right of your selected sound, located under the Track 1 node. Set the LoopEvent property to Infinite.

I would like the laser sound to vary by volume and pitch whenever it is played within the game to make the sound seem less "canned" and repetitive. Select the laser sound within the Sound Bank, then set its VolumeVariation and PitchVariation properties to True. Expand each of those properties by clicking on the plus sign next to the property name, then set the RangeMinimum and RangeMaximum to –9.0 and 9.0, respectively. We just have two more changes before we'll be ready to start writing some code.

Running our XACT project through the Content Pipeline will generate several files. The first file is named after our project. The other two files that are generated are related to our Sound Bank and Wave Bank settings. Since we can have multiple Sound Bank panes and multiple Wave Bank panes within the same project, the tool can't just name them after the project. Click on the Wave Bank node under the Wave Banks folder in the tree that's displayed in the top-left pane of the XACT user interface. Set both the WindowsBuildName and the XboxBuild-Name properties to "example.xwb". Similarly set the same two properties on the Sound Bank node under the Sound Banks folder to "example.xsb".

Note

> If you would like to change the name of the XGS file that your XACT project generates, you can edit the WindowsGlobalSettingsFile and XboxGlobalSettingsFile properties for the root node of the XACT project. In practice, you probably won't need to change these properties, but they're there if you need them.

That's it. Now we're ready to write some code!

Adding Content to Your Game Project

Create a new Windows Game project or a new Xbox 360 Game project within XNA Game Studio Express. Add the following member variable declarations near the top of your Game1 class.

```
// our sound objects
AudioEngine audio;
WaveBank wave;
SoundBank sound;
```

In your game class' `Initialize()` method, add the following code to initialize the sound objects and kick off the background music.

```
// initialize our sound objects
audio = new AudioEngine("example.xgs");
wave = new WaveBank(audio, "example.xwb");
sound = new SoundBank(audio, "example.xsb");
// start playing our background music
sound.PlayCue("ensalada");
```

Then add the following line to your game's `Update()` method to make sure that the internal Audio APIs get a chance to perform regular internal processing.

```
// allow the Audio APIs to do their magic
audio.Update();
```

Next, we need to add our sound data and our XACT project files to our Game Studio Express project. Right-click on your project within the Solution Explorer, then select Add/Existing Item . . . Browse to the directory where your XACT project and wave files are located and select them. You may need to change the Files of Type dropdown on the browse dialog to All Files (*.*), since wave files and XAP files aren't normally associated with Visual Studio.

At this point you can run your game and hear the music looping over and over while you stare at that beautiful `CornflowerBlue` screen. Feel free to do so now. I'll wait. . . . Done? Good.

Note

If you're wondering about the lyrics, they roughly translate to, "Where is the library? What time is it? This is very important! Make yourself at home. Where is my beer? You have my beer! What a fat dog!"

Clearly, the song writer wasn't a localization expert, and he probably didn't make it too far past his first-year Spanish class, but it is an entertaining song, nevertheless.

Playing Sounds in Your Game

Rather than list the code twice (once here, and once at the end of the chapter), I'll just list the most relevant bits for now. To dig a little deeper into the topic of audio programming in XNA, read the entire source code listing at the end of this chapter, read the XNA Framework documentation on audio programming, and search Google to see what your peers are doing with XACT and the XNA Framework Audio APIs.

Whenever the player presses the A button on his controller or the space bar on his keyboard, play the laser sound using code similar to the following in your game's Update() method.

```
sound.PlayCue("laser");
```

Whenever the player moves his left thumbstick up or down, we want to increase or decrease the volume of the background music. Whenever he moves his right thumbstick up or down, we want to increase or decrease the volume of the game sounds (in this example, the laser and the little girl's story).

To do this, we'll need to keep a reference to the two sound groups (or categories) that we set up in our XACT project earlier. The objects that represent those two groups expose a Volume property as a float value where 0.0f is no sound and 1.0f is the highest sound level that you configured for each sound in the group when you created your XACT project. To manipulate an AudioCategory, you'll need to use code similar to the following.

```
// declare a reference as a member variable
AudioCategory catMusic;

// on init, get a reference to the object
catMusic = audio.GetCategory("Music");
// as needed, update the object in your code
catMusic.SetVolume(m_MusicVolume);
```

For the final game sound (the little girl's story), the player will be able to pause and resume the story by pressing the B button on the controller or the Enter key on the keyboard. Unlike the laser and the background music, this will require a reference to the Cue object. Without the reference, the audio engine will play the sound from start to finish, and we won't be able to control its playing state. We will add code similar to the following to our Game1 class.

```
// keep a reference to Zoe's story as a member variable so
// that we can pause and resume it
Cue story;

// get a reference to Zoe's story in your init method
story = sound.GetCue("zoe");

// pause and resume the story in your update method
if (story.IsPaused)
```

```
{
    // resume a prepared and paused cue
    story.Resume();
}
else if (story.IsPlaying)
{
    // pause a prepared and playing cue
    story.Pause();
}
```

Since the story cue is in the same group (AudioCategory) as the laser cue, changes to the volume of our Default category will affect both.

Summary

In this chapter, you learned how to use the XACT utility to use simple sounds to create interesting and varied audio for your games. You also learned how to take that new content and incorporate it into your XNA game projects. We discussed the Auditioning Utility, which greatly improves the workflow of tweaking and testing game sounds. And we developed a simple example game that contains three of the most common uses of sound in your game.

Review Questions

Think about what you've read in this chapter (and the included source code) to answer the following questions.

1. XACT is a simple utility that programmers use to convert wave files into a format that can be used in their XNA games. True or False? Explain.

2. How can you use XACT to create a variety of sounds from a single source wave file?

3. How many sounds can a cue reference in an XACT project? How many waves can an XNA project contain?

4. In the context of an XACT project, what is a category?

5. Which object is the workhorse of the XNA Framework Audio APIs? Which object is your liaison for playing sounds and retrieving references to Cue objects?

Exercises

EXERCISE 1. In a real game project, you'll likely have many more sounds than you see in this chapter's example, but most of those sounds will fall into one of the three categories that we've covered here—looping background music, play-and-forget sounds (like the laser), and sounds that you will want to manipulate based on various game states.

Think about how your favorite game uses audio. Whether it's a racing title, WWII first-person shooter, or a fantasy MMORPG, the objects within the game each have their own sounds. Notice how music and ambient sound effects are used to set the mood for the action that's taking place on the screen. And notice how the game manages those categories of sounds via menu options and player actions.

EXERCISE 2. Add a DSP effect to your XACT project that makes the little girl's story sound like she's reciting it in an auditorium. Remember to associate the story with the new effect by dragging it from the Sound Bank to the Microsoft Reverb node that you created. You can then audition the cue within XACT or rebuild your game to see how this DSP affects the original sound.

Special Thanks

I would like to thank Eric McGinty for letting me use a track from one of his albums. He's a great musician and a great friend. You can hear more of his band's music on their website, http://www.averyellis.com. If you live near the Birmingham area, you can book his band for your special events. Who knows, your money may go towards some much-needed Spanish lessons.

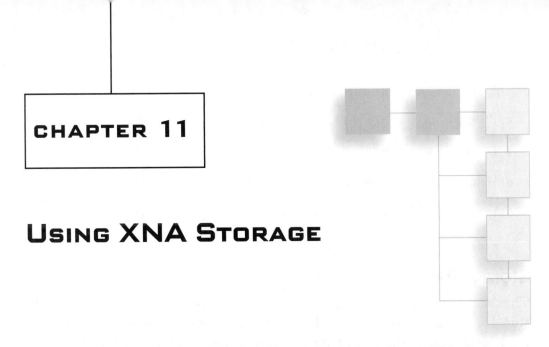

CHAPTER 11

USING XNA STORAGE

Most of the games that you play take longer to complete than a single sitting. For those games, the player is offered a chance to save his progress and return to the game whenever it's convenient for him to do so. In the XNA Framework, the preferred way to save game data is the Storage APIs.

If you knew where you wanted to save your data, you could just use the standard .NET Framework's System.IO APIs. On Windows, that's not such a big deal. The user-writable regions of the hard drive are clearly defined. But what path would you use for your Xbox games? There is no C:\Documents and Settings path on the Xbox 360. The Storage APIs are the only supported way to save game data to the hard drive or memory cards of an Xbox 360 game console.

The Storage APIs provide a unified means to create, read, write, and delete data files for your game on both the Windows and Xbox 360 platforms. If you've ever used the System.IO classes to access files in Windows, you'll find the code in this chapter to be very familiar. The Storage APIs use the standard file classes that you would use in a non-XNA application. The biggest difference is that the Storage APIs manage the location of those files for you.

In this chapter, you will learn how to:

- Prompt Xbox 360 players for a storage device

- Load and save your game data

- Determine the path where your game has been installed

- Simultaneously manage the state of multiple game objects

StorageDevice

The StorageDevice class represents a media device where user data may be stored. This class provides a couple of methods to prompt the player to select an available device. In the case of Windows, no prompt is presented to the player. The device is automatically mapped to the Documents and Settings folder for the current Windows user. In the case of the Xbox 360 game console, the player is prompted with a dashboard tab that lets him select the hard drive or a removable memory unit. Once a device has been selected, the game can call the OpenContainer method of the StorageDevice object to get a reference to a StorageContainer object.

Prompting the Player

There are two methods of prompting the player to select a storage device. The first method is named ShowStorageDeviceGuide. This blocking method returns a reference to a StorageContainer object. Calling it from your game's main thread will lock your game. It's safe to call from a secondary thread, but for single-threaded games you must use the second method.

The second method is BeginShowStorageDeviceGuide. This method provides an asynchronous way to prompt the player. It immediately returns a reference to an IAsyncResult object, which you can use to tell when the player has made his selection. In the meantime, your game loop continues processing its Update and Draw events. Once the IAsyncResult object's IsCompleted property returns true, you know that the data is ready to be saved. Call the EndShowStorageDeviceGuide method of the StorageDevice object to retrieve a reference to the StorageContainer object.

Note

Much like the Highlander, when it comes to the storage device guide on the Xbox 360, there can be only one. Attempts to launch the guide when it is already on-screen will result in an `InvalidOperationException`.

Unfortunately, this same exception can also occur if you call `BeginShowStorage DeviceGuide` immediately after calling `EndShowStorageDeviceGuide`, since the dialog may still be dismissing itself. To play it safe, try not to open a new guide for at least a few seconds after closing the old one.

Device State Properties

The `StorageDevice` class exposes several useful bits of information about the device it represents. The `IsConnected` property allows you to determine whether a removable storage device (like the memory unit) is still attached to the console. The `TotalSpace` property reports the capacity (in bytes) of the referenced device and the `FreeSpace` property reports the amount of free space (in bytes) that are available for your save game data.

StorageContainer

The `StorageContainer` class represents a logical collection of game data files. This is the class that provides you with the path to save your data. Once you have this path, you can use the .NET Framework's standard file management classes to create, read, write, delete, or rename files within that path.

Note

There's one important Xbox 360 caveat to note when using the Storage APIs. Any changes that you make to files located in the path provided by the `StorageContainer` object are not actually committed until the `StorageContainer` has been disposed of. To dispose of this object, call its `Dispose` method.

The reason for the different behavior on the Xbox 360 platform is that save game devices are mounted by the host operating system. You never have direct access to the storage devices. Your code is sandboxed so that it cannot affect data that has been saved for other titles. (Yep. That's right. You can't write an XNA game to hack *Halo* to give your save game infinite lives.)

Player Profiles

Within your title's save game storage container, data is stored within a player profile. If you specify a `PlayerIndex` when displaying the storage device guide, that index maps to a subdirectory of the save game area—Player1, Player2, Player3, or Player4. If you don't specify a PlayerIndex, then the default profile is used—AllPlayers.

TitleLocation

There are basically two categories of locations where files are stored for your XNA game—user storage, where the save games are stored; and title storage, where your game's executable and data are stored. We've already discussed user storage. The StorageContainer has a static property called TitleLocation that provides a path to your game's root directory. Since it's a static method, you don't need to bother prompting the player with the storage device guide. For example, you can determine the location of a shader file with code similar to the following:

```
string filename = StorageContainer.TitleLocation + @"shaders\shader1.fx";
```

Note

Certain directories may be restricted to normal users on the Windows file system. If your game has been installed in the Program Files directory, some players may get an exception when attempting to access files that live in the TitleLocation directory. This shouldn't be a concern for your Xbox 360 games.

Enumerating Files

Since the path that's returned by the StorageContainer object can be treated like a normal Windows path, you can get a list of files within that directory by using the Directory.GetFiles API of the .NET Framework. This might be useful if you allow the player to name his own files or if you allow the user to snapshot data with a certain hot key and you append an auto-incremented number to the end of each snapshot's filename.

In general, it's better if you manage the names of the files yourself, and then store player-generated names within those files. For example, many commercial games allow the player to save his game into one of several predetermined "slots."

The Example

In the example code for this chapter, we'll develop a simple drawing program. The player can use his controller or keyboard to move a cursor around the screen.

Whenever the player presses the A button on the controller (or the space bar on the keyboard), an image of a daisy will appear under the cursor. Using these flower stamps, the player can draw whatever he likes on the screen. Also on the screen are two buttons. These buttons will allow the player to save artwork to a storage device, and retrieve it later.

There's not really too much to say about the drawing and player input code. It's very similar to the examples that we've already covered. There's a single texture for the game, and portions of that texture are drawn to the screen to create the final image.

The data for this game is very simple. There's a single list containing a collection of Vector2 objects. Whenever the player presses the action button, the current location of the cursor is added to the list. Every time the Draw method of our game is called, the code iterates through the list of locations, drawing a flower image centered on each recorded location.

Whenever the player presses the Save button, the current list of stamp locations is saved to the storage device. Whenever the player presses the Load button, the current list of stamp locations is replaced with the data from our save game file. The code that actually handles loading and saving our game data is contained within the GameStorage class, exposed as static methods—Load and Save.

The GameData Class

The GameData class contains the list of flower stamps that the player has placed on the screen. This class is marked with the Serializable attribute so that we can use the .NET Framework's XML serialization functionality to handle the persisting of our game data to and from storage. In a real game, this data structure would be more complex, but the basic principles are the same.

```
// mark our game data as serializable so that we can easily
// persist its contents as an XML data file
[Serializable]
public class GameData
{
    // the list of the player's stamp coordinates
    public List<Vector2> Stamps = new List<Vector2>();
}
```

The GameStorage Class

The GameStorage class handles the details of reading and writing game data files. It exposes two static methods (one for loading game data and one for saving game data) and one static property (that returns the name of our game).

The GameName property is a read-only property that uses reflection to retrieve the title of our game. This property could just return a hard-coded string and avoid reflection, but using reflection means that there's one less detail to maintain in our code. If we decide to change the name of our game, we need only update its AssemblyTitleAttribute.

Reflection gets a bad rap in performance circles, but it's a very handy tool, when used properly. Consider the number of frames that will be drawn during this game's lifetime. Thousands? Millions? And how many times will this reflection-based property be called? Once per save or load—an immeasurably small percentage of the overall runtime.

```
public class GameStorage
{
    // get the title of this game from its assembly info
    public static string GameName
    {
        get
        {
            // get a reference to this assembly
            Assembly asm = Assembly.GetExecutingAssembly();

            // grab a reference to the title attribute
            AssemblyTitleAttribute ata =
                (AssemblyTitleAttribute)asm.GetCustomAttributes(
                typeof(AssemblyTitleAttribute), false)[0];

            // return the title of the assembly. you can change this
            // by editing the AssemblyInfo.cs class within your game
            // project.
            return ata.Title;
        }
    }
```

The Save and Load methods handle writing to and reading from our save game data (respectively). This code is very straightforward. Once you have a reference to a StorageDevice object, files are processed just as they would be in any other (non-XNA game) application. We simply open a `FileStream`, let the `XmlSerializer` work its magic, and then close the stream. Getting a reference to the `StorageDevice` is a little more complicated.

```
// save game data to a storage device
public static void Save(StorageDevice device, GameData data,
     string name)
{
    // get a container reference (hard drive or memory card)
    StorageContainer container = device.OpenContainer(GameName);

    // build the filename for the save game
    string filename = Path.Combine(container.Path, name + ".xml");

    // open the file and write our game data
    FileStream stream = File.Open(filename, FileMode.Create);
    XmlSerializer serializer = new XmlSerializer(typeof(GameData));
    serializer.Serialize(stream, data);
    stream.Close();

    // dispose of the container. data isn't truly saved until
    // you make this call. if you forget to call dispose, your
    // game will have issues if you try to load or save again.
    container.Dispose();
}

    // load game data from a storage device
    public static GameData Load(StorageDevice device, string name)
    {
        // return a new game data object on failure
        GameData data = new GameData();

        // get a container reference (hard drive or memory card)
        StorageContainer container = device.OpenContainer(GameName);

        // build the filename for the save game
        string filename = Path.Combine(container.Path, name + ".xml");

        // only attempt a load if we know the file is actually there
        if (File.Exists(filename))
        {
            // open the file and read our game data
            FileStream stream = File.Open(filename, FileMode.Open);
```

```
        XmlSerializer serializer = new XmlSerializer(typeof(GameData));
        data = (GameData)serializer.Deserialize(stream);
        stream.Close();
    }

    // dispose of the container. if you forget to call dispose,
    // your game will have issues if you try to load or save again.
    container.Dispose();

    // return the game data object
    return data;
    }
}
```

Processing Player Input

The Update method delegates most of its tasks to the ProcessInput method, which is responsible for processing player input, allowing the player to place new stamps, clearing the screen, and loading or saving their artwork.

```
/// game logic such as updating the world
protected override void Update(GameTime gameTime)
{
    // Allows the default game to exit on Xbox 360 and Windows
    if (GamePad.GetState(PlayerIndex.One).Buttons.Back ==
        ButtonState.Pressed)
        this.Exit();

    // get a reference to the input states, and processes them
    GamePadState pad1 = GamePad.GetState(PlayerIndex.One);
    KeyboardState key1 = Keyboard.GetState();
    ProcessInput(pad1, key1);

    base.Update(gameTime);
}
```

The ProcessInput method is where most of the update tasks are carried out. Its first task is to see if the player is moving the cursor. The player can move the cursor using his controller or keyboard.

```
protected void ProcessInput(GamePadState pad1,KeyboardState key1)
{
    // is the player moving left or right?
    if (pad1.ThumbSticks.Left.X < 0)
```

```
        {
            m_cursor.X += pad1.ThumbSticks.Left.X * 3.0f;
        }
        else if (key1.IsKeyDown(Keys.Left))
        {
            m_cursor.X -= 3.0f;
        }
        else if (pad1.ThumbSticks.Left.X > 0)
        {
            m_cursor.X += pad1.ThumbSticks.Left.X * 3.0f;
        }
        else if (key1.IsKeyDown(Keys.Right))
        {
            m_cursor.X += 3.0f;
        }

        // is the player moving up or down?
        if (pad1.ThumbSticks.Left.Y < 0)
        {
            m_cursor.Y -= pad1.ThumbSticks.Left.Y * 3.0f;
        }
        else if (key1.IsKeyDown(Keys.Down))
        {
            m_cursor.Y += 3.0f;
        }
        else if (pad1.ThumbSticks.Left.Y > 0 )
        {
            m_cursor.Y -= pad1.ThumbSticks.Left.Y * 3.0f;
        }
        else if (key1.IsKeyDown(Keys.Up))
        {
            m_cursor.Y -= 3.0f;
        }
```

Next, the ProcessInput method checks to see if the player is requesting to clear the canvas and start creating a new masterpiece.

```
// is the player pressing the clear button?
if (pad1.Buttons.Start == ButtonState.Pressed ||
    key1.IsKeyDown(Keys.Enter))
{
    // clear our list of stamps
    m_data.Stamps.Clear();
}
```

The last task for the ProcessInput method is to handle action button presses. If the cursor is over the Load or Save buttons, a Boolean is set to indicate that a load or save is pending. The player must release the button to initiate the load or save operation. If the cursor is not over one of these buttons, then a new stamp will be added to the screen at the cursor's current location.

```
// is the player pressing the action button?
if (pad1.Buttons.A == ButtonState.Pressed ||
    key1.IsKeyDown(Keys.Space))
{
    // only register a save or load if there's not
    // a save or load currently in progress
    if (m_resultStorage == null)
    {
        // clear the button press states
        m_pressedSave = false;
        m_pressedLoad = false;

        // is player pressing the save button?
        if (InRect(m_cursor, m_rectSave, m_posButtonSave))
        {
            m_pressedSave = true;
        }
        // is player pressing the load button?
        else if (InRect(m_cursor, m_rectLoad, m_posButtonLoad))
        {
            m_pressedLoad = true;
        }
        // add a new stamp to our list
        else if (!m_data.Stamps.Contains(m_cursor))
        {
            m_data.Stamps.Add(m_cursor);
        }
    }
}
```

If the Load or Save button is highlighted, and the user has released the action button without moving the cursor away from the on-screen buttons, then the load or save operation will be kicked off by telling the XNA Framework's Storage APIs to show the display guide. Remember, for Windows games, the storage guide won't actually be shown, but the code for both platforms looks exactly the same.

```
// the player isn't pressing the action button
else
{
    // there is no load or save in progress
    if (m_resultStorage == null)
    {
        // the player just released the action button
        if (m_pressedLoad || m_pressedSave)
        {
            // show the storage guide on Xbox, has no
            // effect on Windows
            m_resultStorage = StorageDevice
                .BeginShowStorageDeviceGuide(null, null);
        }
    }
}
```

At this point, we know that none of the controller or keyboard buttons that we're interested in are being pressed. Now, we'll just see if we've previously requested that the storage guide be shown, and if the user has selected his save game location.

```
// there is a load or save in progress
else
{
    // has the player selected a device?
    if (m_resultStorage.IsCompleted)
    {
        // get a reference to the selected device
        m_storage = StorageDevice
            .EndShowStorageDeviceGuide(m_resultStorage);

        // save was requested, save our data
        if (m_pressedSave)
        {
            GameStorage.Save(m_storage, m_data, "test01");
        }
        // load was requested, load our data
        else if (m_pressedLoad)
        {
            m_data = GameStorage.Load(m_storage, "test01");
        }

        // reset up our load / save state data
```

```
                    m_storage = null;
                    m_resultStorage = null;
                    m_pressedSave = false;
                    m_pressedLoad = false;
                }
            }
        }
    }
```

Managing Asynchronous States

Since this game is single-threaded, we need to use the asynchronous version of the method that prompts the player to select a storage device. While we're waiting for the player to select a device, the game's Update and Draw methods are still being called. We need to manage some state information to let us know when a save or load has been initiated, when the player has actually selected a storage device, and when the save or load process is complete.

When the player is pressing the action button and the cursor is over the Load or the Save button, a Boolean member variable is set to true. The Draw method takes advantage of this information to highlight the button as long as it's being pressed. If the player moves the cursor away from the on-screen button before releasing the action button, the Boolean is reset, and no load or save occurs.

When the player releases the pressed action button over the Load or the Save button, that's our cue to kick off a load or save. The first step is to prompt the player to select a storage device. This is done by calling the StorageDevice.BeginShow-StorageDeviceGuide method. That method returns a reference to an IAsyncResult object, which we can use to tell when the device has been selected.

Once the IsComplete property of the IAsyncResult object is set to true, it's time to dismiss the guide and get a reference to the selected StorageDevice object. This is done by calling the StorageDevice.EndShowStorageDeviceGuide method. That method returns a reference to the selected StorageDevice object, which we can then pass to our GameStorage.Load or GameStorage.Save method.

Drawing Game Data

The Draw method is responsible for drawing any of the flowers that the player has stamped on the screen, and for highlighting the Load or Save button whenever the player selects it.

```
/// render game objects
protected override void Draw(GameTime gameTime)
{
    graphics.GraphicsDevice.Clear(Color.CornflowerBlue);

    m_batch.Begin();

    // draw all of the stamps that the player has made
    DrawStamps();

    // if the player is pressing the save button, highlight it
    if (m_pressedSave)
    {
        m_batch.Draw(
            m_Texture, m_posButtonSave, m_rectSave, Color.Goldenrod);
    }
    // draw the normal save button
    else
    {
        m_batch.Draw(
            m_Texture, m_posButtonSave, m_rectSave, Color.White);
    }

    // if the player is pressing the load button, highlight it
    if (m_pressedLoad)
    {
        m_batch.Draw(
            m_Texture, m_posButtonLoad, m_rectLoad, Color.Goldenrod);
    }
    // draw the normal load button
    else
    {
        m_batch.Draw(
            m_Texture, m_posButtonLoad, m_rectLoad, Color.White);
    }

    // draw the cursor
    m_batch.Draw(m_Texture, m_cursor, m_rectArrow, Color.White);

    m_batch.End();

    base.Draw(gameTime);
}
```

The DrawStamps method draws every flower that the player has placed on the screen.

```
// used to calc the center of the stamp
private Vector2 m_StampOffset = Vector2.Zero;
protected void DrawStamps()
{
    // center the stamp on the cursor location
    m_StampOffset.X = 0 - m_rectStamp.Width / 2;
    m_StampOffset.Y = 0 - m_rectStamp.Height / 2;

    // draw each stamp in our list
    foreach (Vector2 pos in m_data.Stamps)
    {
        m_batch.Draw(
            m_Texture, pos + m_StampOffset, m_rectStamp, Color.White);
    }
}
```

Summary

In this chapter, you learned how to prompt Xbox 360 players to select a storage device using the storage device guide. You learned how to load and save simple game data using XML serialization. You learned how to determine the install path of your game. And you learned how to manage files within your save game storage area.

See the Storage Overview section of the XNA Framework documentation for a step-by-step walk through of some of the most common save game file IO tasks.

Review Questions

Think about what you've read in this chapter (and the included source code) to answer the following questions.

1. What two basic categories of storage are available to an XNA game?

2. Why should an XNA game developer favor the XNA Framework Storage APIs over the standard .NET Framework APIs?

3. Save game data is committed to the storage device when the Close method of the FileStream object is called. True or False? Explain.

4. Why doesn't the example code for this chapter use the simpler ShowStorageDeviceGuide rather than the asynchronous version of that method?

5. How can you tell how much space is free on the selected storage device?

Exercises

EXERCISE 1. The code in this example does not do any bounds checking for the player's cursor. The player can move the cursor off the screen and stamp flowers that will never be seen. Also, it's confusing to the player when the cursor disappears. Add code to the Update method that forces the cursor to remain within the bounds of the screen.

EXERCISE 2. If you're feeling especially adventurous, store the elapsed game time whenever you add new stamps to the list. Offer the player an option to play back his artwork as an animation. To play back the player's brush strokes, reset some internal counter and only draw those stamps that have an earlier timestamp than your counter. As your counter progresses, you'll render more and more stamps from the list, until your counter exceeds the age of the oldest stamp in your list.

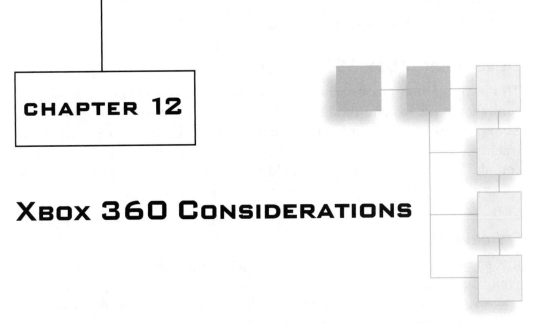

CHAPTER 12

XBOX 360 CONSIDERATIONS

One of the most exciting aspects of XNA Game Studio Express is its support for developing games for the Xbox 360 game console. While the XNA Framework makes developing games for Windows and Xbox 360 nearly seamless, there are some differences between the two platforms that developers will need to handle in their code. This chapter will detail some of the biggest factors that need to be considered when developing games for the Xbox 360 game console.

In this chapter, you will learn how to:

- Join the XNA Creators Club so that you can create Xbox games

- Configure your Xbox 360 and your development PC

- Build, deploy, and run games on your Xbox 360 game console

- Configure your firewall to allow communication between your console and PC

- Provide a meaningful name and description for your game within the XNA Game Launcher

Developing Xbox 360 Games

This section details many of the most common differences between developing games for Windows and the Xbox 360 game console. We'll cover some of the Xbox 360 features in a little greater detail. Later chapters also include notes whenever platform-specific code is required to support the Xbox 360 game console. In general, though, you should be able to design your game to run on either platform with very few (and in most cases, no) changes.

Framework APIs

If you want your game to run on the Xbox 360 game console, then you need to avoid platform-specific code. Don't use Windows-specific classes like `Form`, `Control`, or `EventArgs`. Don't make calls to native APIs. Don't use XNA Framework APIs, like `Texture2D.FromFile()` or `Mouse.GetState()`, that are clearly labeled as Windows-only in the documentation. There are some situations where this might be advantageous (for example, when writing a level editor for your game), but in most cases, it's better if you just avoid conflicts in the first place.

If your design requires support for Windows-specific or Xbox-specific APIs, be sure to isolate that code using the "`#if XBOX360`" compiler constant, or by providing separate Windows and Xbox 360 game libraries with identical interfaces.

```
#if XBOX360
// insert Xbox 360-specific code here ...
#endif
```

Player Input

The Xbox 360 game console supports the Xbox 360 controller and any standard USB keyboard, but it does not support the mouse. Always support the controller, regardless of which platform you're targeting. Never use the mouse if there's even a slight chance that you may want to support the Xbox 360 game console in the future. Only support the keyboard as an option, allowing the player to revert to the controller.

Note

You can use the `KAGamePad` component that we develop in Chapter 19, "Keyboard-Aware Game Pad," to emulate the controller using the keyboard.

Screen Layout

When designing games on your PC, your monitor will display every pixel that you render. When you take that same game to the Xbox 360 game console, though, you'll find that the outer edge of your game's display is either obscured or distorted. Television sets can only reliably display the innermost 80%–90% of the game screen's buffer. This area of the screen is known as the "title safe" region. All commercial Xbox and Xbox 360 games are required to adhere to this restriction before they are certified for release by the Xbox team.

This same problem is encountered when authoring DVD menus. To make your layout planning easier, you should use a paint program that supports layers, and add a layer with two thin rectangles—one sized to 80% of the target resolution, and one sized to 90% of the target resolution. Make sure that any critical data (like the score, remaining lives, and other HUD data) falls within the smaller of the two rectangles. Remember that your game screen may be automatically scaled to fit the screen, so you'll want to test your game on a standard television screen to make sure that your text is visible and legible. If possible, test your final game on more than one TV.

Storage

The total size of your Xbox 360 game, including all code, media, game data, and other resources, should not exceed 2GB. Any save game data should not exceed 52MB.

Filenames on the Xbox 360 file system must not exceed 40 characters. To be safe, only use ASCII characters in the filename. The file system supports other characters, but there's no point in using them without good reason. If you forget about this rule and violate the Xbox 360 naming conventions, you will likely encounter problems when deploying your project. Fix the offending filename, close the Visual C# 2005 Express IDE, and then open your solution again. This will reset the incremental build data and force a full deployment to the game console, which should overwrite the erroneous file(s).

For a more detailed description of storage on the Xbox 360 game console, see Chapter 11, "Using XNA Storage."

Firewall Issues

If your router or your PC is running a firewall, you may encounter issues when deploying your games to the Xbox 360. If you're just using the standard Windows firewall, it should have been automatically configured for you when you installed XNA Game Studio Express. If you're using third-party firewall software, you may need to configure it manually. Make sure that your development PC and your Xbox 360 game console are on the same subnet of your network. Then make sure that your development PC's firewall is configured to allow the following:

- xnatrans.exe as a client and as a server

- incoming UPD on port 3825

- incoming UPD on port 3835

- incoming UPD on port 1000

- incoming TCP on port 1001

In addition to supporting communication between your development PC and your Xbox 360 game console, you also need to make sure that your Xbox 360 is able to connect to the Internet for the Xbox Live service. If you've been playing Xbox Live games, then you're already good to go. If you're having problems connecting to the Xbox Live service, be sure that your network router's firewall is configured to allow the following:

- incoming and outgoing UPD on port 88

- incoming and outgoing UPD on port 3074

- incoming and outgoing TCP on port 3074

Threading

Threads are the mechanism by which you can run multiple processes concurrently. Unless you explicitly write code to support threading, your main game logic will run on a single thread, on a single processor—each block of code running to completion before the next begins.

Your game has several tasks that must be completed every time the Update method is called. Many times, those tasks are independent of each other. If there's no need for one block of code to wait for the results of another block of code, your game logic may be able to take advantage of a multi-threaded design.

For details on Xbox 360 threading topics and the Xbox 360 CPU architecture, see Chapter 25, "Threading in XNA."

When moving from a Windows-based threading model to the Xbox 360, it's important to remember that the Xbox 360 Common Language Runtime (CLR) is based on the Compact Framework CLR, whereas Windows uses the full CLR. These two flavors of the runtime were written with drastically different design goals. The Compact Framework was designed for devices with limited resources like PDAs, handheld devices, and set-top devices.

Two of the most notable differences in threading between the two versions of the CLR are that the Xbox 360 CLR does not support parameterized thread starts, and you cannot alter the culture settings for a running thread on the Xbox 360. You will see work-around code for these differences in Chapter 27, "Embedded Resources and Localization," and Chapter 25, "Threading in XNA."

Deployment

Once properly configured, deploying your Xbox 360 game to your game console is as easy as debugging a Windows game locally. Your game (and any relevant content) is copied to your console and launched automatically. Updates to Xbox 360 games are made incrementally. With each successive deployment, only the modified bits are copied to the console. There may be rare instances where the system gets a little confused during this process. To force a full deployment, close the Visual C# 2005 Express IDE and open your solution again. This will reset the project's incremental build state data and force a full deployment of your game to the console.

Deployment of Xbox 360 games is covered in more detail later in this chapter. The documentation that was installed along with the XNA Framework also includes a detailed section on Xbox 360 deployment. Search for "Deploying an Xbox 360 Game" within the XNA documentation to read more on this topic.

Joining the XNA Content Creators Club

To deploy games to your Xbox 360 game console, you must have an active Xbox Live account, and you need to be a member of the XNA Content Creators Club. At the time of this writing, membership in the club costs around 100 dollars a year. You can purchase a membership from your Xbox 360 console by visiting the Xbox Live Marketplace.

Power up your Xbox 360, and bring up the dashboard. (If you're playing a game, press and release the media button on the center of your controller to access the dashboard.)

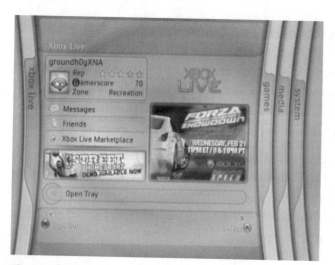

Figure 12.1
The Xbox Live tab.

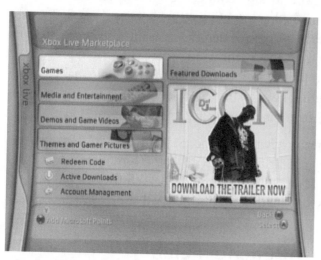

Figure 12.2
Xbox Live Marketplace.

From the Xbox Live tab, select Xbox Live Marketplace, as shown in Figure 12.1.

Select Games (see Figure 12.2).

Select the Game Downloads by Genre option (see Figure 12.3).

Select Other (see Figure 12.4).

Figure 12.3
Games on Xbox Live Marketplace.

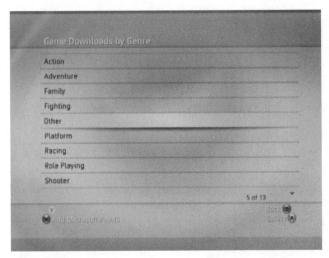

Figure 12.4
Games, grouped by genre.

Select XNA Creators Club (see Figure 12.5).

Follow the prompts to purchase your membership. After you've successfully purchased your subscription to the club, you may need to follow these steps again to return to the Content Creators Club section of the Xbox Live Marketplace and select XNA Game Launcher (see Figure 12.6). A special Xbox 360

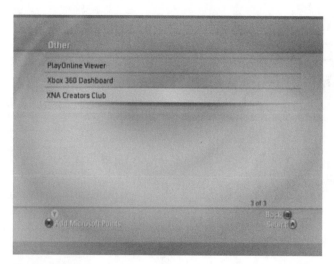

Figure 12.5
Select XNA Content Creators Club.

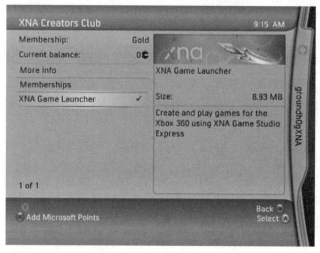

Figure 12.6
The XNA Game Launcher.

"game," called the XNA Game Launcher, will be installed on your console's hard drive. This is the application that will host the XNA games that you create.

The XNA Game Launcher is considered "unrated" content. If you have established parental controls on your Xbox 360, you may need to temporarily enable the "allow all games" setting before the launcher appears in the Xbox Live

Marketplace. Once you've installed the launcher, you can return your settings to their original values. If parental controls are enabled, you may need to enter your pass code whenever you start the launcher.

Configuring Your PC and Xbox 360

Before you can connect your development PC to your Xbox 360 game console, you will need to configure both.

Power up your Xbox 360 and bring up the dashboard. (If you're playing a game, press and release the media button on the center of your controller to access the dashboard.)

From the Games tab, select Demos and More (see Figure 12.7).

Select XNA Game Launcher (see Figure 12.8).

Select Launch (see Figure 12.9).

The XNA Game Launcher is now running on your Xbox 360. From here, you configure the connection to your development PC, connect to your development PC for the deployment and debugging of your XNA games, or play games that you have already deployed to your Xbox 360 (does not require a connection to your development PC).

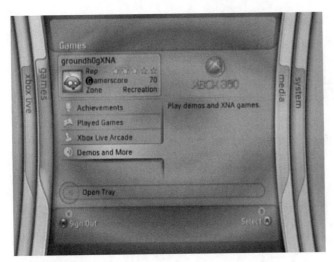

Figure 12.7
The Games tab of the Xbox 360 dashboard.

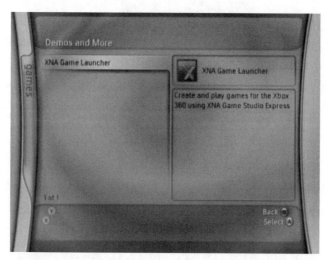

Figure 12.8
List of downloaded games on your Xbox 360.

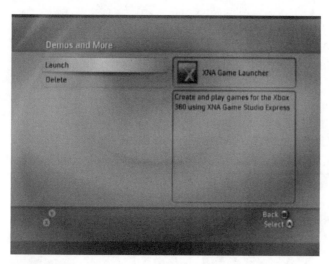

Figure 12.9
Ready to run the XNA Game Launcher.

Select Settings (see Figure 12.10).

Select Generate Connection Key (see Figure 12.11).

You now have a secure connection key that you can use to allow your Xbox 360 to communicate with your development PC. Don't accept the key just yet; this is

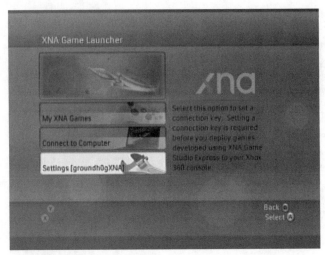

Figure 12.10
Settings for XNA Game Launcher.

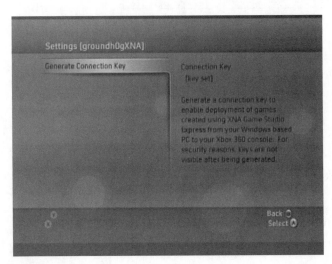

Figure 12.11
Our new connection key.

the only time that you will be able to see it. For security reasons, the keys are not retrievable once they've been accepted. You'll need to enter this key into XNA Game Studio Express.

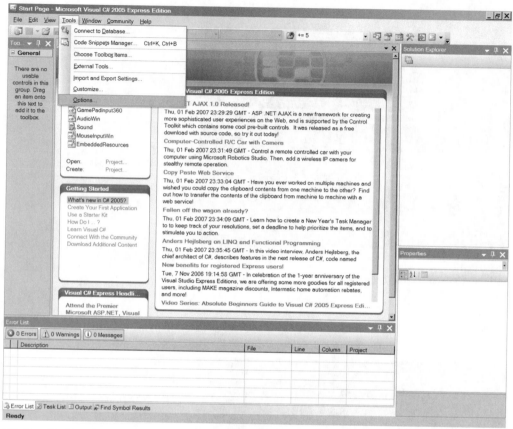

Figure 12.12
Options menu item in the IDE.

Within the Visual C# 2005 Express Edition IDE, select Options from the Tools menu (see Figure 12.12).

Select the Xbox 360 node from the XNA Game Studio folder in the Options tree view. If you don't see that option, make sure that the Show All Settings checkbox has been checked.

Click the Add button, and enter the name of your console along with its connection key (see Figure 12.13).

Click OK on that dialog, then return to your Xbox 360 game console and accept the new connection key. You are now ready to run your games on your Xbox 360!

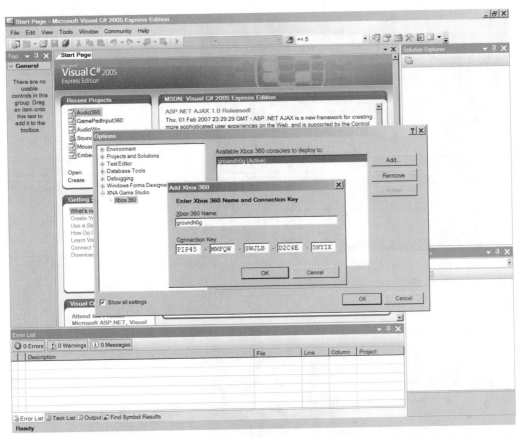

Figure 12.13
Entering the connection key.

Deploying Xbox 360 Games

Deploying and debugging a game on your Xbox 360 game console is as easy as debugging on your PC. The same debugger features like watches, breakpoints, and the Immediate Window commands are available when debugging Xbox 360 games. You just run your game within the Visual C# 2005 Express Edition IDE as you would your Windows game. Before you can connect to your Xbox 360, you'll need to make sure that it's listening for your connection.

Power up your Xbox 360, and bring up the dashboard. (If you're playing a game, press and release the media button on the center of your controller to access the dashboard.)

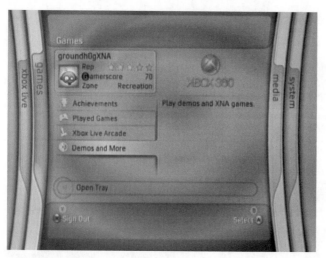

Figure 12.14
The Games tab of the Xbox 360 dashboard.

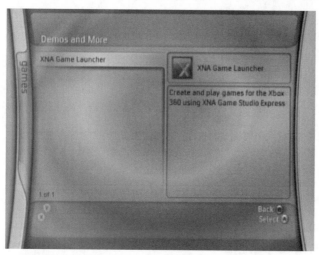

Figure 12.15
List of downloaded games on your Xbox 360.

From the Games tab, select Demos and More (see Figure 12.14).

Select XNA Game Launcher (see Figure 12.15).

Select Launch (see Figure 12.16).

Select Connect to Computer (see Figure 12.17).

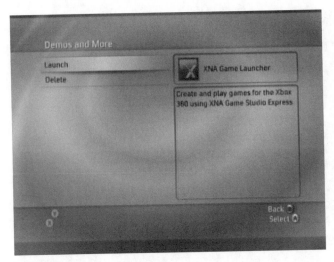

Figure 12.16
Ready to run the XNA Game Launcher.

Figure 12.17
Select Connect to Computer.

Your console is now waiting for your development PC to initiate a connection (see Figure 12.18).

Start debugging your Xbox 360 game project, and the IDE will automatically connect to the console, deploy your project, and launch your game on the console.

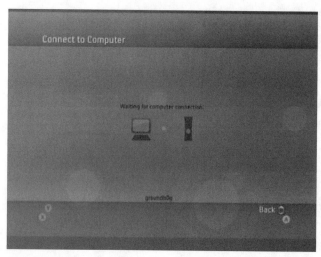

Figure 12.18
Waiting to connect.

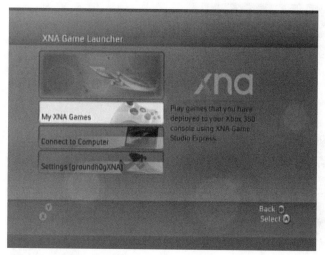

Figure 12.19
Play previously deployed games.

Running Existing Games

Once you've successfully deployed and run a game on your Xbox 360, it is stored on the hard drive of the console. You can now run your game without using your development tools or your PC. From the XNA Game Launcher, select My XNA Games (see Figure 12.19).

A list of previously deployed games appears. Select the game that you want to run. In this case, I'll select the example from Chapter 7, "Using XNA Input for Controllers" (see Figure 12.20).

A housekeeping screen appears. You have the option of playing or deleting the game. Select Play Game (see Figure 12.21).

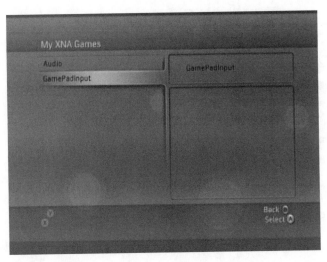

Figure 12.20
Choosing a game.

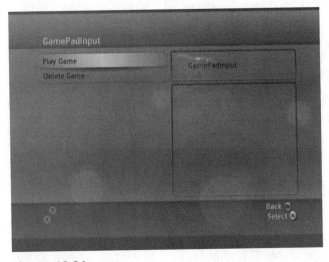

Figure 12.21
Housekeeping.

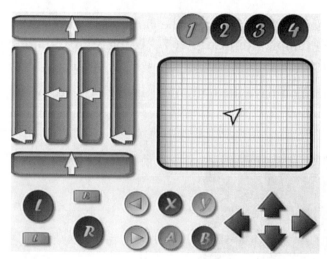

Figure 12.22
The game running without a connection to the PC.

The game starts running, without the need for your development PC. This is a great way to show off your creations when your friends come over.

Performance Tuning

There's a performance monitor tool that ships with XNA Game Studio Express called the XNA Framework Remote Performance Monitor for Xbox 360. For a more detailed description of this tool, see Chapter 29, "Optimization," found later in this book.

Naming Your Games

Within each of the XNA game projects that you create, you'll find a file named AssemblyInfo.cs. It's located in the Solution Explorer under the Properties folder. There are two lines that dictate the title and description of your game under the XNA Game Launcher on your Xbox 360 game console.

```
[assembly: AssemblyTitle("My Game's Title")]
[assembly: AssemblyDescription("A description of my game.")]
```

The AssemblyTitle attribute contains the name of your game as displayed within the XNA Game Launcher. The AssemblyDescription attribute contains the descriptive text that's displayed when you select your game within the launcher.

Summary

In this chapter, you learned how to configure your development PC and your Xbox 360 game console for XNA game development. You learned about some of the caveats when developing for a gaming console. You also learned how to design your games so that they can run on Windows and the Xbox 360 with little or no modifications.

Review Questions

Think about what you've read in this chapter to answer the following questions.

1. What is the "title safe" region for a television set? What are some considerations regarding this region that must be addressed when designing your game?

2. What are some limitations of developing for the Xbox 360 gaming console? What are some benefits?

3. What is the XNA Content Creators Club?

4. How do you change the name and description of your game that are displayed in the XNA Game Launcher?

5. How long can a save game filename be? How big can a save game be?

Exercises

EXERCISE 1. Create a new, unmodified Xbox 360 game and run it on your Xbox 360. If you're having trouble, refer to the instructions in the "Deploying Xbox 360 Games" section, found earlier in this chapter.

EXERCISE 2. Launch the game that you ran in the first exercise without using your development PC. Your game should be listed in the "My XNA Games" section of the XNA Game Launcher on your Xbox. If you're having trouble, refer to the instructions in the "Running Existing Games" section, found earlier in this chapter.

EXERCISE 3. Set a breakpoint in the `Update` method of the game that you created in the first exercise, then run the game from the debugger. When the breakpoint is hit, notice how you can inspect member variables and perform the other debugging tasks that you would perform when debugging a Windows game.

EXERCISE 4. Create a new Spacewar Xbox 360 Starter Kit project and run it on your Xbox 360.

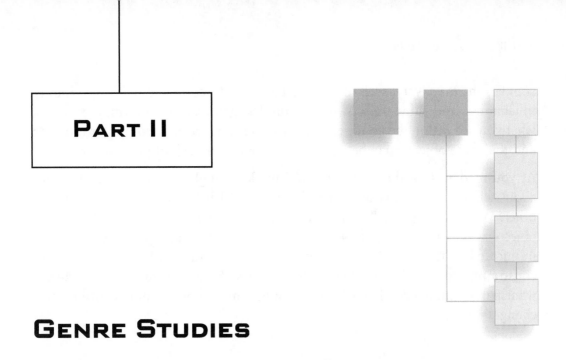

PART II

GENRE STUDIES

In this section, we will dissect several popular categories of games. The goal of this section is not to make you an expert in any of the genres discussed—there is just too much information to cover here. Entire books can be written on any one of these games. The goal of this section is to make you look at the games that you play a little differently—as a developer, rather than as a player.

As you play your favorite commercial games, try to see past the overall game. Try to imagine the individual parts that make up the whole. Writing a commercial-quality game can be an overwhelming task, but creating any single component of that same game is relatively easy. To become a better game programmer, you need to view games the way a director views a movie, an animator views a cartoon, or an architect views a skyscraper. When designing your own games, it's important to keep the big picture in mind so that your virtual world is cohesive and believable, but you also need to break your design down to its most basic components before you can implement it.

Look for Common Themes

At the highest level, every game that you play has the same basic components. There's a simulated, virtual world, and there are objects in that world that interact with the player or with each other. In the most complex games, that simulation may very well be a virtual world, complete with geography, inhabitants, and game objects. In the simplest games, the world may simply be what you see within the confines of your television screen or computer monitor, and the game objects may be a paddle and ball or a deck of playing cards.

As you read each of these chapters and work through the example code, think about what components make up the game and how they interact with each other. What is the game "world"? What are the objects in this world? How do objects affect each other? How are player stats tracked and how are they communicated to the player? How does the player interact with the world? What constraints are placed on the player? What parts of the game play do you like and what parts would you change? How would you go about implementing those changes?

Don't Fear Ignorance

For any game programming project that you undertake, don't let the fear of doing something wrong keep you from implementing your ideas. There is no "right" or "wrong" way to write a game. Experiment. Try new things. Chances are good that the folks who play your game will never see the code that you write. If it works, it works. There have been many popular commercial games that ship with sub-par code. Under the pressures of a looming deadline, developers have to triage their remaining tasks. Revisiting code that works will always be assigned a lower priority than fixing actual bugs.

When you try to bring your ideas to life and you fail, regroup and try again. After thousands of failed experiments, Thomas Edison is frequently quoted as saying, "I have not failed. I've just found 10,000 ways that won't work." In the process of implementing the previous version, you've gained valuable knowledge for your next attempt.

That's not to say that you should completely disregard the design and planning process or that you shouldn't study what others have done in your game's genre. While I don't believe there's a "right" or "wrong" way to program a game, there are clearly standards and best practices that have been developed by those programmers who've come before you. Learn from their work. Build on it. Make it better. Make it yours.

Success Isn't Final

In the not so distant future, you'll look back at the code that you're writing today (as a novice game developer) and wonder what the heck you were thinking. The more you code, the more you learn. Even revisiting a project that you've completed will give you invaluable insight into its inner workings. I have several game projects that I've written from scratch several times. That's no way to finish a project, but it's a great way to develop your design skills. If you're just starting out as a game programmer, trust me, you're not writing groundbreaking code. Don't be afraid to scrap your work, and approach the same tasks from a new angle. The new version will most likely be more stable, more robust, easier to maintain, and generally better designed.

Game Programming Heresy

I'm about to say something here that will likely get my game programmer membership card revoked—don't optimize your code. There. I said it. Phew! It feels good to get that out in the open.

As a game programmer, you have an innate desire to pick things apart and understand how they work. You love to solve problems. You especially love to solve problems that none of your peers have been able to solve. Performance optimization is the holy grail of your breed. Making your code smaller and faster is very rewarding work. So, why in the heck would I tell you not to optimize your code?

Code optimizations that are introduced early in your project are likely to be thrown out as your game evolves. Even with proper planning and a great high-level design, you'll often find that the details of your implementation tend to deviate from the design as the project progresses. It's better to get your game completely fleshed out than to spend time optimizing code that you'll likely revise or throw out later. Given the choice of "slightly faster but harder to maintain" and "slightly slower but easier to read and understand," choose the more readable code.

Optimized code is generally more complex than unoptimized code. That increased complexity means

- You're more likely to introduce subtle, hard-to-find bugs.

- It will be harder to add new features to your optimized code.

- Future optimizations will be much harder to implement.

- Optimizations in related code will be much harder to implement.

No rule is absolute, and "Thou Shalt Not Optimize" is no exception. There will be times that you need to optimize your code. If your game's frame rate drops to a minute per frame, that's a bad thing and it must be addressed. But be aware of the pitfalls of optimization before you go down that path. For those times when your code actually does need a performance boost, I've included a section later in this book to help you focus your performance tuning efforts.

Goals for This Section

The motivation for this section isn't to provide you with an exhaustive study of each genre. I just want you to look at the games that you play a little differently. I want you to be able to dissect your favorite games and understand what basic building blocks make them up and how those parts work together to create the whole. I want you to experiment and try to write programs that you think are beyond your ability—by breaking games down into smaller components that you feel more confident in writing. When you learn how to assemble these well-understood parts into a larger project, you'll have a working game.

The examples in this section of the book have limited error checking and have been stripped of many of the bells and whistles that you typically see in most commercial games. I intentionally left out features like audio and menuing systems so that I could focus on the mechanics of the genre, and show you how the objects in your code work together to form the overall game.

I try to cover code modularity and code reuse as it applies to the example being discussed, but I don't explore those (very noble and good) principles as far as I would in an actual game project. For example, you will find that there's not a lot of data-driven design to these examples. For an actual game project, I would never hard-code references to media or other resources. Again, the focus of this section is very narrow, and such generalized code would only distract from the topic being discussed.

The Code

Each of the samples in this book starts from the generic XNA game project. I do all of my development under Windows, keeping a focus on compatibility with Xbox 360. When I'm done, I create a new Xbox 360 solution and project, and then I include the existing files from the Windows project in the new Xbox 360 project. That means there's just one copy of the source to manage, and changes on one platform are reflected in the other the next time I rebuild the executables for either platform. Solution and project files for both platforms have the same name, with a "Win" suffix for Windows projects and a "360" suffix for Xbox 360 projects.

This section assumes that you have a basic understanding of the Visual Studio IDE and how the XNA Framework supports graphics and player input. It also assumes that you know how to write, build, and deploy simple programs. If you're not confident in these fundamental areas of game development, please take time to review the introductory content found earlier in this book.

The full source code for each of the examples in this book is included on the accompanying CD-ROM. Before you can build the projects on the CD, you must configure your PC as described in earlier chapters of this book.

Overview of Chapters

The following paragraphs provide an overview of this section's contents.

Chapter 13: Arcade

In Chapter 13, you will develop a game based on the arcade classic, *Pong*, which supports two players. This is just about as simple as it gets when it comes to real-time interactive games, so it's a great starting point for folks who don't have any game programming experience or just want to see the XNA way of doing things.

Chapter 14: Brick Breaker

In Chapter 14, you will develop a game based on the arcade classics, *Arkanoid* and *Breakout*. It may not look it, but this game is very similar in design to the game in the preceding chapter. There are a few more bells and whistles, but the underlying game mechanics are nearly identical. When you're done, keep the example code from this chapter handy. We'll be developing a level editor for the game in Chapter 24, "Brick Breaker Level Editor."

Chapter 15: Puzzle Games

In Chapter 15, you will develop a game based one of my favorite puzzle game titles, *Tetris Attack* (based on *Panel De Pon*, and revisited as *Pokemon Puzzle League*). Puzzle games are one of those rare genres that cross gender and age boundaries, appealing to casual and hardcore gamers alike. While the data structures and logic behind puzzle games are a little more complex than those found in the retro arcade examples found in the first two chapters of this section, they're still relatively simple (in the greater realm of game programming). In fact, *Tetris* clones are often used as the "Hello, World" of game programming, serving as the introduction to game development for most programmers.

Chapter 16: Top-Down Scroller

In Chapter 16, you will develop a game based on the many top-down scrolling shooter games like *Xevious*, *1942*, *Galaga*, and *Raiden*, which supports two players. Players shoot enemy ships and collect power-ups that improve their weapons, shields, health, and score. While the code for this game is a little more complicated than the games in the first two chapters of this section, the basic concepts are the same, and you'll be able to build on your knowledge from the earlier games as you work through this chapter.

Chapter 17: Card Games—Solitaire

In Chapter 17, you will develop a game based on the popular Solitaire card game. For this game, we will build reusable data structures and logic for representing, shuffling, drawing, and animating playing cards.

Chapter 18: Board Games—Reversi

In Chapter 18, you will develop a game based on the popular Reversi and Othello board games. This game supports two players, and it provides a computer opponent for folks like me who don't have any human friends to play with. Three variants of the computer opponent are implemented, and the base game code is written so that you can easily add more. The first AI randomly selects a move from all the available, legal moves—fast, but stupid. The second AI is a basic implementation of the MinMax algorithm—more thoughtful, but slower. The third AI is based on the second, but implements the standard AlphaBeta pruning for the MinMax routine—smart and (relatively) fast.

CHAPTER 13

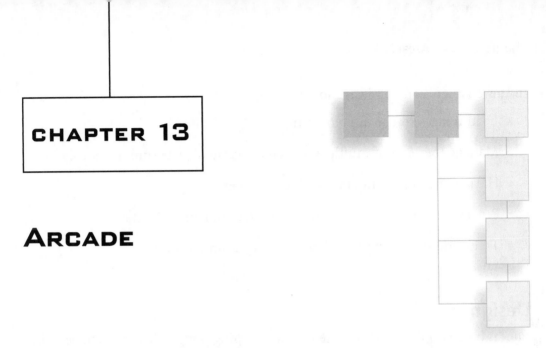

ARCADE

The arcade genre includes the early "coin-op" video games of the 1970s and 1980s, where the action generally takes place on a single screen. These games were easy to learn, but difficult to master. Graphics and other media were generally minimal due to the constraints of the hardware of the day, but these seemingly simple games had an addictive quality that hooked their players, draining their time and their pockets. With the explosion in popularity of cell phones and PDAs, many of these "retro" arcade titles are finding new life. With a design that favors game play over today's epic cut scenes and rich story lines, these games are well-suited for the minimal hardware specs of most handheld devices.

Some of the more popular examples of this category of games are *Space Invaders*, *Galaga*, *Pac-Man*, *Dig Dug*, *Centipede*, *Arkanoid*, and *Pong*.

In this chapter, we will develop a *Pong*-like game. *Pong* was released by Atari near the end of 1972. While it wasn't technically the first arcade game, it was certainly the first game to gain widespread popularity, and it is arguably the game that launched the genre of arcade games. *Pong* was later released as a home video game console. Again, Atari wasn't the first to enter this new area of gaming, but their *Pong* console was the first to popularize the idea of home video game consoles, and their success kicked off the consumer market for video games that we see today.

In this chapter, you will learn how to:

- Load images to use in your game

- Manage the state of multiple on-screen game objects simultaneously

- Have game objects interact with each other

- Process user input to manipulate the state of game objects

- Track and display a player's score using a bitmap font

Design

Pong is based on the sport of table tennis (or "ping pong"). The game mechanics are very simple. Players control virtual paddles by moving them up and down. The ball travels in a straight line. If the ball hits the upper or lower bounds of the screen or one of the players' paddles, it ricochets back onto the play field. If the player is unable to deflect the ball before it touches his side of the screen, a point is awarded to his opponent. To make the game more interesting, the ball will travel a little faster after it touches one of the player's paddles, picking up speed with each volley.

The game will feature a heads up display (HUD) to let the players quickly see the current score. To keep things simple in this example, there will be no menu, no special screen for pausing the game, and no end-game graphics. Whenever a player reaches 10 points, the game resets itself to its initial state and game play continues.

Architecture

The paragraphs that follow describe how the objects on the screen were implemented in the code for this game.

The World

For this game, the screen bounds are the world bounds. In many of the example games that we develop later, the screen is merely a view into a much larger world. That's not the case here. All of the objects that exist in this world are on the screen, so we only need to keep track of the game objects.

Game Objects—The Ball

Within our game world, there is a ball. The ball has a fixed size. It follows a linear path, at a constant speed, until it encounters some obstacle. We will need to keep track of the ball's position, and its direction of movement. Since the design calls for the ball to move a little faster with each volley, we will also need to keep track of the ball's current velocity. Here's a simple C# class to represent the ball. You'll find the descriptions for the members of this class after the listing.

```csharp
class Ball
{
    protected float m_X;
    public float X
    {
        get { return m_X;  }
        set { m_X = value;  }
    }

    protected float m_Y;
    public float Y
    {
        get { return m_Y;  }
        set { m_Y = value;  }
    }

    protected float m_Width;
    public float Width
    {
        get { return m_Width;  }
        set { m_Width = value;  }
    }

    protected float m_Height;
    public float Height
    {
        get { return m_Height;  }
        set { m_Height = value;  }
    }

    protected float m_DX;
    public float DX
    {
        get { return m_DX;  }
```

```
        set { m_DX = value; }
    }

    protected float m_DY;
    public float DY
    {
        get { return m_DY;   }
        set { m_DY = value;  }
    }

    public Rectangle Rect
    {
        get { return new Rectangle( X, Y, Width, Height ); }
    }

    private object m_Visual = null;
    public object Visual
    {
        get { return m_Visual;   }
        set { m_Visual = value;  }
    }
}
```

To keep things simple and to fit the retro style, the ball in this game is a simple square. This ball has a size, represented by the Width and Height properties, and the ball has a location, represented by the X and Y properties. The direction and velocity of the ball are tracked using the DX and DY properties (delta-X and delta-Y). The sprite texture for the ball can be stored in the Visual property.

The location (X and Y) and size (Width and Height) of the ball are used to tell the game where to draw the square that represents the ball, and how large that square should be.

The DX and DY properties describe the direction and velocity of the ball. The ball is moving to the left if DX is negative, and it's moving to the right if DX is positive. The ball is moving down if DY is positive, and it's moving up if DY is negative. While the direction of the ball is determined by the signs of DX and DY, the speed is determined by the magnitude of those numbers. The larger the number, the faster the ball is traveling. The magnitude is proportionate, so that a ball with twice the DX of another is traveling twice as fast.

The Visual property is provided as a convenience so that the game can associate a texture to the ball object generically, without forcing the ball to know what a texture is. By declaring Visual as an object, the part of our application that is responsible for drawing the ball can store any data that it needs in that field. Today, that data is a Texture2D object; but by abstracting the rendering from the game object, major changes to the render code won't affect the game logic. For example, if we later decide to render the game in 3D, we can associate a mesh object to the Visual property without changing the way a ball moves or interacts with its environment.

We now have enough information to get started with a prototype of our game by drawing our ball on the screen and letting it bounce around. Once we have stubbed out the basic ball mechanics, we can go back and add in the paddles, the user input, and the scoring.

Drawing the Ball

To render our ball, we'll need a texture. I've created a simple, pure-white texture in a paint program that we can use for the ball. We'll load in the texture and assign it to the Visual property of the ball. We'll also define the starting position of the ball, its size, and its direction and speed.

```
// helper to render our game objects
SpriteBatch m_batch = null;

// the ball
Ball m_ball;
Texture2D m_textureBall;

public void InitGameObjects()
{
    // create an instance of our ball
    m_ball = new Ball();

    // set the size of the ball
    m_ball.Width = 15.0f;
    m_ball.Height = 15.0f;

    // place the ball at the center of the screen
    m_ball.X = SCREEN_WIDTH / 2 - m_ball.Width / 2;
    m_ball.Y = SCREEN_HEIGHT / 2 - m_ball.Height / 2;

    // set a speed and direction for the ball
    m_ball.DX = 5.0f;
```

```
    m_ball.DY = 4.0f;
}

protected override void LoadGraphicsContent(bool loadAllContent)
{
    if (loadAllContent)
    {
        // load images from disk
        LoadGameGraphics();
        // init sprite helper
        m_batch = new SpriteBatch(graphics.GraphicsDevice);
    }
}

protected void LoadGameGraphics()
{
    // load the texture for the ball
    m_textureBall = content.Load<Texture2D>("media\\ball");
    // assign the texture to the ball
    m_ball.Visual = m_textureBall;
}
```

Here's the code to actually render the ball to the screen.

```
public void Render()
{
    // black background
    graphics.GraphicsDevice.Clear(Color.Black);

    // render the white ball
    m_batch.Begin();
    m_batch.Draw((Texture2D)m_ball.Visual, m_ball.Rect, Color.White);
    m_batch.End();
}
```

Moving the Ball

At this point, we have a ball located at the center of the screen. To animate the ball, we will need to update its location every time the game's Update method is called, using the DX and DY properties of the ball. As we move the ball around, we will also need to make sure that it never leaves the screen.

```
protected override void Update(GameTime gameTime)
{
    // update the ball's location on the screen
    MoveBall();

    base.Update(gameTime);
}
```

If any part of the ball leaves the top or bottom side of the screen, the vertical direction and speed will be reversed, while the horizontal direction and speed remain unchanged. If any part of the ball leaves the left or right side of the screen, a point will be awarded to the scoring player, and the ball will be placed back in play traveling at its initial horizontal and vertical speed, in a random vertical direction. For now, though, there are no paddles, so we'll just let the ball bounce back onto the play field if it hits the left or right side of the screen.

```
private void MoveBall()
{
    // actually move the ball
    m_ball.X += m_ball.DX;
    m_ball.Y += m_ball.DY;

    // did ball touch top or bottom side?
    if (m_ball.Y <= 0 ||
        m_ball.Y >= SCREEN_HEIGHT - m_ball.Height)
    {
        // reverse vertical direction
        m_ball.DY *= -1;
    }

    // did ball touch left or right side?
    if (m_ball.X <= 0 ||
        m_ball.X >= SCREEN_WIDTH - m_ball.Width)
    {
        // reverse horizontal direction
        m_ball.DX *= -1;
    }
}
```

So, we now have a ball that freely bounces around the screen. Figure 13.1 is a time-lapse snapshot of the ball in motion.

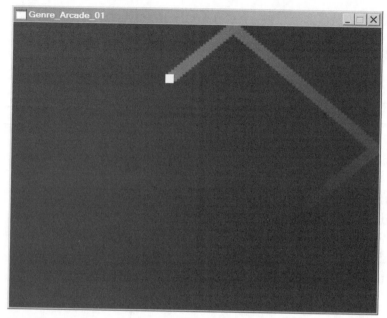

Figure 13.1
A time-lapsed image showing the ball bouncing off a wall.

Game Objects—The Paddles

In addition to the ball, there are also two player-controlled paddles. Paddles have a location in the world, and they have a constant size. The next change that we'll make to our code is to render the paddles and have them deflect the ball. We can hook up the user interaction in the next step. Here's a simple C# class to represent a paddle.

```
class Paddle
{
    protected float m_X;
    public float X
    {
        get { return m_X;  }
        set { m_X = value;  }
    }

    protected float m_Y;
    public float Y
    {
        get { return m_Y;  }
```

```
        set { m_Y = value;  }
    }

    protected float m_Width;
    public float Width
    {
        get { return m_Width;   }
        set { m_Width = value;  }
    }

    protected float m_Height;
    public float Height
    {
        get { return m_Height;   }
        set { m_Height = value;  }
    }

    public Rectangle Rect
    {
        get { return new Rectangle( X, Y, Width, Height ); }
    }

    private object m_Visual = null;
    public object Visual
    {
        get { return m_Visual;   }
        set { m_Visual = value;  }
    }
}
```

You may have noticed that the Ball and the Paddle classes have a lot of code in common. They both have an X, Y, Width, Height, and Visual property. Whenever you see patterns of duplicate code like this in your projects, it's usually a good indication that it's time to refactor your design so that your game objects can share the common bits. For now, we'll just focus on getting our paddles working, but we need to make a mental note to come back to this code when we're done so that we can trim this redundant code.

Drawing the Paddles

To render the paddles, we'll need a texture. I've created another simple, pure-white texture in a paint program that we can use. We'll load in the texture and assign it to the Visual property of each paddle. We'll also go ahead and define the starting position of the paddles and their size. Since we haven't actually added any code to allow the user to interact with the paddle, the paddles will just sit idle on the screen, but we will be able to observe the ball interacting with them. Add the following member variables to the Game1 class.

```
// the paddles
Paddle m_paddle1;
Paddle m_paddle2;
Texture2D m_texturePaddle;
```

Add the following code to the end of the InitGameObjects method of our game class to create the paddles and place them in their initial positions.

```
// create 2 instances of our paddle
m_paddle1 = new Paddle();
m_paddle2 = new Paddle();

// set the size of the paddles
m_paddle1.Width = 15.0f;
m_paddle1.Height = 100.0f;
m_paddle2.Width = 15.0f;
m_paddle2.Height = 100.0f;

// place the paddles at either end of the screen
m_paddle1.X = 30;
m_paddle1.Y = SCREEN_HEIGHT / 2 - m_paddle1.Height / 2;
m_paddle2.X = SCREEN_WIDTH - 30 - m_paddle2.Width;
m_paddle2.Y = SCREEN_HEIGHT / 2 - m_paddle1.Height / 2;
```

Add the following code to the end of the LoadGameGraphics method of our game class to load the paddle image from disk.

```
// load the texture for the paddles
m_texturePaddle = content.Load<Texture2D>(@"media\paddle");
m_paddle1.Visual = m_texturePaddle;
m_paddle2.Visual = m_texturePaddle;
```

Replace the Render method with the following code, which now handles the paddles and the ball.

```
public void Render()
{
```

```
// black background
graphics.GraphicsDevice.Clear(Color.Black);

// render the white ball and paddles
m_batch.Begin();
m_batch.Draw((Texture2D)m_ball.Visual, m_ball.Rect, Color.White);
m_batch.Draw((Texture2D)m_paddle1.Visual, m_paddle1.Rect, Color.White);
m_batch.Draw((Texture2D)m_paddle2.Visual, m_paddle2.Rect, Color.White);
m_batch.End();
}
```

Solid Paddles

If you run the game now, you'll see the paddles on the screen, along with the bouncing ball. The ball just passes through the paddles because we haven't updated the MoveBall logic to account for them. Let's do that now. Replace your MoveBall method with the following code.

```
private void MoveBall()
{
    // actually move the ball
    m_ball.X += m_ball.DX;
    m_ball.Y += m_ball.DY;

    // did ball touch top or bottom side?
    if (m_ball.Y <= 0 ||
    m_ball.Y >= SCREEN_HEIGHT - m_ball.Height)
    {
    // reverse vertical direction
    m_ball.DY *= -1;
    }

    // did ball touch left or right side?
    if (m_ball.X <= 0 ||
    m_ball.X >= SCREEN_WIDTH - m_ball.Width)
    {
    // reverse horizontal direction
    m_ball.DX *= -1;
    }

    // did ball hit a paddle?
    if (CollisionOccurred())
    {
```

```
        // reverse horizontal direction
        m_ball.DX *= -1;
        }
    }
```

In the final game, the ball should never hit the paddle from the rear. But we haven't written the code to update the score yet, so our ball just bounces around the screen. Ultimately, I'd like for this code to support a "doubles" mode, where up to four players can compete. When that happens, the ball may be deflected from one player's paddle to his teammate's paddle. In that scenario, the ball should just pass through the teammate's paddle. So, we can go ahead and add that logic now. The rule is simple—ignore a collision between the ball and paddle if the ball is moving away from the defending player's goal.

```
private bool CollisionOccurred()
{
    // assume no collision
    bool retval = false;

    // heading towards player one
    if (m_ball.DX < 0)
    {
        Rectangle b = m_ball.Rect;
        Rectangle p = m_paddle1.Rect;
        retval =
            b.Left < p.Right &&
            b.Right > p.Left &&
            b.Top < p.Bottom &&
            b.Bottom > p.Top;
    }
    // heading towards player two
    else // m_ball.DX > 0
    {
        Rectangle b = m_ball.Rect;
        Rectangle p = m_paddle2.Rect;
        retval =
            b.Left < p.Right &&
            b.Right > p.Left &&
            b.Top < p.Bottom &&
            b.Bottom > p.Top;
    }

    return retval;
}
```

The collision code may seem a little cryptic, but it's easier to understand if you read it backwards.

- If the ball is to the right of the paddle, there's no collision.

- If the ball is to the left of the paddle, there's no collision.

- If the ball is below the paddle, there's no collision.

- If the ball is above the paddle, there's no collision.

- Otherwise, there's a collision.

Cleaning Up the Code

Another thing that you may have noticed about the collision logic is that we have introduced some more redundant code into our game. It's probably a good idea to refactor this code as well. In fact, collision detection is something that we'll be doing quite a lot of as we develop more games, so this might be a good candidate for a common, shared utility class that we can reuse in future games. This is probably a good time to take a break from developing the game and clean up the code a little.

Remember the duplicate properties that exist between the Ball and Paddle classes? Let's create a common game object class to house those properties, then derive the Ball and Paddle from the new class. The code for the GameObject class follows.

```
class GameObject
{
    protected float m_X;
    public float X
    {
        get { return m_X;  }
        set { m_X = value;  }
    }

    protected float m_Y;
    public float Y
    {
        get { return m_Y;  }
        set { m_Y = value;  }
    }
```

```
    protected float m_Width;
    public float Width
    {
        get { return m_Width;  }
        set { m_Width = value;  }
    }

    protected float m_Height;
    public float Height
    {
        get { return m_Height;  }
        set { m_Height = value;  }
    }

    public Rectangle Rect
    {
        get { return new Rectangle( X, Y, Width, Height ); }
    }

    private object m_Visual = null;
    public object Visual
    {
        get { return m_Visual;  }
        set { m_Visual = value;  }
    }
}
```

Now we can derive our `Ball` and `Paddle` classes from this base class, as in the following code.

```
class Ball : GameObject
{
    protected float m_DX;
    public float DX
    {
        get { return m_DX;  }
        set { m_DX = value;  }
    }

    protected float m_DY;
    public float DY
    {
        get { return m_DY;  }
```

```
        set { m_DY = value;  }
    }
}

class Paddle : GameObject
{
}
```

Notice how much smaller the new code is. If fact, the Paddle class currently has no extra code. The GameObject class contains every property that the Paddle needs. Now that these two objects share the same code base, the code is easier to maintain, since any changes that we make to the base class will be propagated to the derived classes.

As for the collision code, we need to make sure that there's not already an API in the Framework that does the task that we're attempting to do before we invest time in designing our own. In general, using the Framework is preferable to writing your own routines because the provided code is field-tested by the XNA Framework user base, and the XNA Framework has been specifically optimized for game development (especially true on the Xbox 360 platform).

A quick search of the Framework documentation leads us to the BoundingBox class, which would meet our needs just fine, so I won't bother refactoring our collision class into a reusable utility class. I just want to make sure that you understand the process of refactoring—identify redundant code, make it more generic and reusable, and replace the duplicate code with calls to your generic method (or class).

Back to Work

Now we can get back to programming the game. At this point, the ball is bouncing around the screen, and the paddles deflect the ball when there's a head-on collision (see Figure 13.2). The paddles still don't move. We need to update the paddles' positions based on the state of the controllers.

Every time the game's Update method is called, we need to check the state of the input devices to see if the player is trying to move his paddle. If so, we'll update the paddle's Y property, taking care not to let the paddle leave the screen.

```
// how much to move paddle each frame
private const float PADDLE_STRIDE = 10.0f;
```

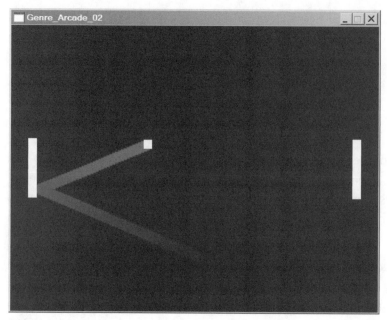

Figure 13.2
A time-lapsed image showing the ball bouncing off a paddle.

```
// actually move the paddles
private void MovePaddles()
{
    // define bounds for the paddles
    float MIN_Y = 0.0f;
    float MAX_Y = SCREEN_HEIGHT - m_paddle1.Height;

    // get player input
    GamePadState pad1 = GamePad.GetState(PlayerIndex.One);
    GamePadState pad2 = GamePad.GetState(PlayerIndex.Two);
    KeyboardState keyb = Keyboard.GetState();

    // check the controller, PLAYER ONE
    bool PlayerUp   = pad1.DPad.Up == ButtonState.Pressed;
    bool PlayerDown = pad1.DPad.Down == ButtonState.Pressed;

    // also check the keyboard, PLAYER ONE
    PlayerUp   |= keyb.IsKeyDown(Keys.W);
    PlayerDown |= keyb.IsKeyDown(Keys.S);

    // move the paddle
```

```
if (PlayerUp)
{
    m_paddle1.Y -= PADDLE_STRIDE;
    if (m_paddle1.Y < MIN_Y)
    {
        m_paddle1.Y = MIN_Y;
    }
}
else if (PlayerDown)
{
    m_paddle1.Y + = PADDLE_STRIDE;
    if (m_paddle1.Y > MAX_Y)
    {
        m_paddle1.Y = MAX_Y;
    }
}

// check the controller, PLAYER TWO
PlayerUp = pad2.DPad.Up == ButtonState.Pressed;
PlayerDown = pad2.DPad.Down == ButtonState.Pressed;

// also check the keyboard, PLAYER TWO
PlayerUp |= keyb.IsKeyDown(Keys.Up);
PlayerDown |= keyb.IsKeyDown(Keys.Down);

// move the paddle
if (PlayerUp)
{
    m_paddle2.Y -= PADDLE_STRIDE;
    if (m_paddle2.Y < MIN_Y)
    {
        m_paddle2.Y = MIN_Y;
    }
}
else if (PlayerDown)
{
    m_paddle2.Y + = PADDLE_STRIDE;
    if (m_paddle2.Y > MAX_Y)
    {
        m_paddle2.Y = MAX_Y;
    }
}
}
```

Notice that this code checks both the controller and the keyboard. While the keyboard is not the ideal input device for a two-player game, supporting the keyboard means that you can test your game even when your controller isn't handy. I've selected keys for each player that are at opposite ends of the keyboard, but things will still be pretty cramped. The "W" and "S" keys are equivalent to player one's gamepad's DPad up and down, respectively. Likewise, the cursor keys "up" and "down" represent the DPad up and down for player two's controller.

Also notice that the code checks for input from the controller, then input from the keyboard. The overloaded "or equals" operator will return true if either the controller or the keyboard (or both) indicates movement. The code to have the keyboard emulate a controller is definitely something that we'll want to use in the future, and we'll want it to handle more than just up and down on the controller's DPad. This is a great candidate for a reusable utility class, and we will develop such a component later in the book.

To hook our new `MovePaddles` method into the game, we need only call it from the `UpdateMethod`. The updated listing for the `UpdateMethod` follows.

```
protected override void Update(GameTime gameTime)
{
    // update the ball's location on the screen
    MoveBall();
    // update the paddles' locations on the screen
    MovePaddles();

    base.Update(gameTime);
}
```

We now have a playable game. The paddles move, and the ball reacts to its environment as expected. We still need some way to keep and display the score, and there are a few more bells and whistles that were mentioned in the design that we haven't gotten around to implementing yet. So let's go ahead and wrap up this project.

Keeping Score

We'll need to add a couple of member variables to our class to track each player's score.

```
public int m_Score1 = 0;
public int m_Score2 = 0;
```

Up until this point, the ball has happily bounced from wall to wall. Now it's time to pay special attention to the left and right bounds of the screen. Whenever the ball collides with the left or right walls, we will increment the score for the player who's defending the opposite goal. If you'll recall, the code that handles collisions between the ball and its environment is the MoveBall method. The following is an excerpt from that method as it exists now.

```
// did ball touch left or right side?
if (m_ball.X <= 0 ||
    m_ball.X >= SCREEN_WIDTH - m_ball.Width)
{
    // reverse horizontal direction
    m_ball.DX *= -1;
}
```

As things currently stand, we're just reversing the DX of the ball when it collides with a vertical wall. We'll need to add some code to increment the proper player's score. To make things easier, let's separate the code that checks the left and right bounds into two blocks of code so that we can tell which player scored the point.

```
// did ball touch the left side?
if (m_ball.X <= 0 )
{
    // increment player 2's score
    m_Score2++;

    // reduce speed, reverse direction
    m_ball.DX = 5.0f;
}

// did ball touch the right side?
if (m_ball.X >= SCREEN_WIDTH - m_ball.Width)
{
    // increment player 1's score
    m_Score1++;

    // reduce speed, reverse direction
    m_ball.DX = -5.0f;
}
```

We're tracking the score now, but it doesn't do any good to keep score if the players can't see it. We need to display the score on the game screen so that the players can taunt each other properly.

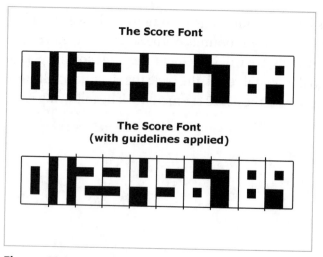

Figure 13.3
The simple number font image, used in this game to display scores.

In an XNA game, there is no built-in font support. The games that you play on game consoles and in arcades typically don't have system support for drawing text to the screen. Each of the text characters that you see in those games has been drawn by an artist and rendered onto the game screen just like our ball, paddles, or any other texture. If you've done a lot of programming in Windows, this may seem strange to you. For a more detailed discussion of this topic, see the chapters on bitmap game fonts, Chapters 20, "Game Font Maker Utility," and 21, "Game Font Library."

I've created a simple graphic to fit with our retro theme that contains the numbers zero through nine. Whenever we need to display a number on the screen, we'll just render the portion of the image that corresponds to the desired character. Figure 13.3 shows the font as it exists on disk, and a version with guidelines that may help you see the individual numbers a little easier.

We'll load the texture into a member variable, just like we did with our paddle and ball.

```
// load the texture for the score
m_textureNumbers =
    content.Load<Texture2D>(@"media\numbers");
```

With the paddle and ball textures, we rendered the entire image whenever we wanted to display our game object. In this case, we only want to render a small subset of the texture. The subset of the image that we're interested in varies, based on the number that we want to draw. So we need some way to subdivide the image into smaller parts, and we need to know which part maps to which digit. Knowing that each character in the image is 45 pixels wide, that the image is 75 pixels tall, and that there are 10 digits stored within the image, we can map out each character with code like the following.

```
// map the digits in the image to actual numbers
m_ScoreRect = new Rectangle[10];
for (int i = 0; i < 10; i++)
{
    m_ScoreRect[i] = new Rectangle(
        i * 45, 0, // X, Y
        45, 75 );  // Width, Height
}
```

The code to actually draw the score on the game screen follows.

```
// draw the score at the specified location
public void DrawScore(float x, float y, int score)
{
    m_batch.Draw((Texture2D)m_textureNumbers,
        new Vector2(x, y),
        m_ScoreRect[score % 10],
        Color.Gray);
}
```

One Last Feature

At this point, we have a fairly playable game. There was one more feature that we mentioned in our design that I would like to cover before we bring this chapter to a close, though. Whenever the ball bounces off a paddle, we'll make it move a little faster. And when the ball touches a goal, we will return it to its initial speed.

We added code to check for ball-to-paddle collisions earlier in this chapter. That section of the code is the ideal place to add our logic to quicken the game pace. Whenever a player successfully defends her goal, we will increase the speed of the ball by 15%.

```
// did ball hit the paddle from the front?
if (CollisionOccurred())
{
    // reverse horizontal direction
    m_ball.DX *= -1;
```

```
    // increase the speed a little.
    m_ball.DX *= 1.15f;
}
```

Once a goal has been touched, and a point awarded, the ball needs to return to its initial speed. We're already checking for an out-of-bounds condition in the MoveBall method, and that's where we are tracking the players' scores. It seems like a good place to add our new logic. Since the code for each player is so similar, I'll just list the snippet that handles player one's scoring.

```
// did ball touch the right side?
if (m_ball.X >= SCREEN_WIDTH - m_ball.Width)
{
    // increment player 1's score
    m_Score1++;

    // reduce speed, reverse direction
    m_ball.DX = -5.0f;
}
```

Figure 13.4 is a screen shot of the final game, which includes all the features that we've discussed in this chapter.

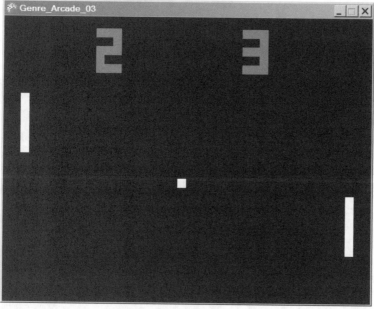

Figure 13.4
The final game in all its glory. Clearly, I'm player two.

Note

This game is very simple. They don't get too much easier than this. Because it's so simple, I've placed most of the game logic in the main file. In a real game, you will need to divide your code among several specialized classes rather than a single, monolithic class. We did that to some degree in this project with the `Ball` and `Paddle` classes and their parent class, `GameObject`. But as you develop larger games and you have to manage more (and more complex) game objects, and more game states, and more object states, a single file just won't cut it.

Summary

In this chapter, you learned how to incorporate the basic elements that you learned about in the earlier chapters to create an interactive game. Even the most basic, simple ideas can make fun and addictive games, drawing players into the experience.

You also learned that by breaking a large programming task down into a collection of smaller, more manageable tasks, you can take your game from concept to screen. All of this happens by combining the most basic building blocks of graphics and user input concepts to manage game objects in your virtual world and allowing the user to interact with them (and each other).

Review Questions

Think about what you've read in this chapter (and the included source code) to answer the following questions.

1. How can you ensure that one sprite renders "on top of" another sprite?

2. How can you dynamically change the color of a sprite while your game is running?

3. How can you allow a player to use any attached input device to play your game?

4. How do you track changes to multiple game objects at the same time?

5. How do you draw text to a game screen?

Exercises

EXERCISE 1. After 10 volleys without a score, have the ball blink by toggling its color between red and white every 250 milliseconds. Be sure to disable the blink once one of the players finally scores a goal.

EXERCISE 2. Add support for a third and fourth player. Reuse the existing Paddle class, and place the new players 30 pixels farther from their respective goals than the existing players. Be sure that your new code ignores collisions when the ball is traveling away from the defender's goal so that teammates don't have to worry about getting in each other's way.

EXERCISE 3. There's a bug in this game where the ball could travel fast enough to pass over the paddle without ever touching it. Fix this bug. One solution might be to detect when the absolute value of the DX of the ball is greater than the Width of the ball. If the ball is traveling faster than this threshold, check for a collision at the location that lies exactly between the ball's new position and its old position, where it was in the previously rendered frame.

Note

Technically, in Exercise 3 you could just check for the case where the ball's delta-X is greater than the ball's width plus the paddle's width, since a ball that travels its own width (or less) every frame will occupy all the space between those two locations. Stated another way, a 15-pixel-wide ball will occupy no more than 30 unique horizontal pixels in two frames. If the ball is traveling 15 horizontal pixels per frame, then those 30 pixels will be contiguous and nothing can fit between them without causing a collision. Only when the gap between the ball's two locations is wide enough for a paddle to fit inside will you need to check for a collision.

EXERCISE 4. This exercise uses what you've learned in this chapter along with Chapter 10, "Using XNA Audio." Locate the ding.wav sound file in your Windows media directory. Convert it to a format that can be used by the XNA Framework. Play that sound whenever the ball collides with a paddle.

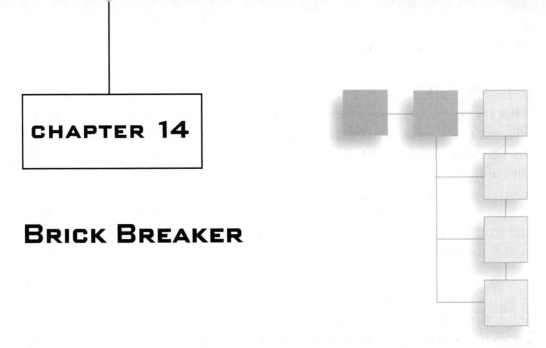

CHAPTER 14

BRICK BREAKER

There were several *Pong*-inspired games that came out between the mid-1970s and the mid-1980s. Among the most popular of these were Atari's *Breakout* (1976) and Taito's *Arkanoid* (1986). In these games, the player controls a paddle that he uses to deflect a moving ball in an attempt to eliminate some number of bricks that occupy the playing field. I pumped more than my fair share of quarters into *Arkanoid* during high school and college. Its collection of power-ups and variety of level designs made it quite an addictive game.

In this chapter, we will develop a simple game, inspired by these popular titles. The game that we develop will be driven by level data that is stored in an external file. Along the way, we'll also develop a Windows application to create and edit our level data. The level editor is described in detail in Chapter 24, "Brick Breaker Level Editor."

In this chapter, you will learn how to:

- Manage multiple on-screen game objects at the same time

- Load level data from a file

- Detect collisions between multiple sprites

- Update the game state as the player progresses from level to level

- Track the player's score and high score

The Design

This example has many more active objects to manage than our first game. Players control a paddle that they use to deflect a constantly moving ball. The ball moves freely about the playable area of the game screen, bouncing off the walls and colliding with any number of bricks. The bricks remember how many times they've been hit, changing colors as they become weaker, and removing themselves from the game once they've taken as much abuse as they can stand. Along the way, the HUD (heads-up display) reports the player's score, along with other useful statistics.

It may seem like a lot to manage for only our second game, but there's no single element to this example that even the most casual hobbyist developer couldn't implement. The trick to working on larger projects is breaking them down into smaller, more manageable components. Each self-contained component is highly specialized, making it easy to write. By combining these components together, you can create a moderately complex game that's fun to play. Figure 14.1 shows a screenshot of the game that we will develop in this chapter.

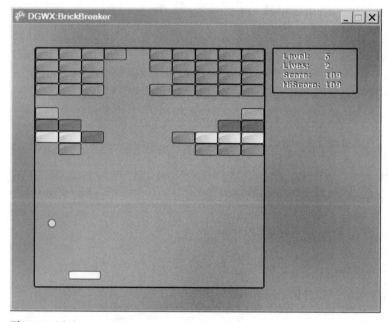

Figure 14.1
A screen shot of the final game.

Reusable Components

This example uses a couple of components that we will develop in later chapters. I won't spend a lot of time discussing their implementation, since the other chapters explain how they work in so much detail. For now, you can treat them as a black box, flip ahead a few chapters to get a better understanding of how they work, or just take a peek at the source code and verbose comments of the controls. (The controls weren't linked to this example's project as game libraries; their source files were included directly into the project.)

If you feel like this is too much information to take in right now, you can skip this overview of the components. You don't need to know how they work to use them for this game. That's the beauty of writing reusable components. Complex tasks are encapsulated behind simple interfaces. We'll get into how the components work soon enough. For now, it's enough to focus on the design of the game that we're about to write.

The GameFont Class

The GameFont class provides a simple way for your games to draw text to the screen. The GameFontUtility program (which we develop in Chapter 20, "Game Font Maker Utility") converts Windows TrueType fonts into PNG images using the options that you specify. Those images contain a subset of Unicode characters, packed tightly together. At runtime, the GameFont class treats each character that is embedded within the image as a separate sprite. Those sprites are arranged on the screen to form readable text when you call the DrawString method.

To use this component, we create an instance of the class, initialize the instance with a source image, and then call the methods on the instance whenever we need to draw text to the screen or measure the extents of the text that we want to draw. The following code snippet illustrates the basic usage of the GameFont class.

```
// -- typically stored as member variables of our game class --
// bitmap game font and texture
GameFont  font = null;
Texture2D fontTexture = null;
// -- typically called from the game's LoadGraphicsContent method --
// initialize our game font
fontTexture = content.Load<Texture2D>(@"media\Verdana8Bold");
font = GameFont.FromTexture2D(fontTexture);
// -- typically called from the game's Draw method --
```

```
// draw some text to the screen
font.DrawString(batch, "Hello, World!", 100, 250, Color.White);
```

The PixelPerfectHelper Class

The `PixelPerfectHelper` class (developed and described in Chapter 28, "Pixel-Perfect Collision Detection") contains a collection of static methods that make detecting collisions between 2D sprites easier. Since the methods are static (they're marked with C#'s "static" keyword), we never actually create an instance of this class. We invoke the methods of this class using the class name.

To perform pixel-perfect collision detection between two sprites, we need to compare the individual pixels of each to see if they overlap. If any pixel in one sprite occupies the same space on the screen as any pixel in another sprite, a collision has occurred. As you might imagine, comparing the location of every pixel in each sprite against every pixel in all of the other sprites in the game can lead to millions of comparisons. That's quite a CPU-intensive task. Luckily, there are some logical rules that we can apply to shortcut this process, saving valuable processing time.

As soon as we see that any two pixels occupy the same on-screen space, we can stop comparing pixels. It doesn't matter if 2 pixels or 2,000 pixels are touching—a collision is a collision. Scanning the rest of the pixels in the two sprites is a waste of time.

If the bounding rectangles of two sprites don't overlap, the pixels that make up those sprites will never overlap, and they cannot possibly collide with each other. We can determine whether two rectangles overlap a lot faster than we can scan the pixels that make up the two sprites. If the rectangles do overlap, we still have to check the individual pixels. But, we save a lot of time by avoiding the fruitless searches that are triggered in the vast majority of comparisons.

Due to the low-level inner workings of graphics cards, graphics card drivers, and graphics APIs, it's not a good idea to inspect the pixel data of our game textures every time we want to check for a collision. The `PixelPerfectHelper` class provides methods to extract this data into arrays of boolean values, based on the opacity (transparency) of the source pixels. These boolean arrays are used in the comparisons, making the process much faster.

Collision detection requires several independent pieces of information to perform its comparisons. We need to know the location, the dimensions, and the opacity data of each sprite. The `PixelPerfectHelper` class provides an interface that you can implement in your custom sprite classes, exposing the relevant data as members of a single object. This interface is called `IPixelPerfectSprite`. The sprites in this chapter's example game will implement this interface.

Using the `PixelPerfectHelper` class to detect collision requires a little preparation. We need to initialize each of our sprite classes with a texture, a texture rectangle (the location and dimensions of the sprite image within the larger game image), an on-screen location, and opacity data. Once those key properties have been initialized, we can carry out our normal game tasks, updating the location of our sprites and checking for sprite-to-sprite collisions as needed. The following code snippet demonstrates the basic usage of the `PixelPerfectHelper` class.

```
// -- typically stored as member variables of our game class --
// sprites for paddle and ball
protected PaddleSprite m_spritePaddle = new PaddleSprite();
protected BallSprite   m_spriteBall   = new BallSprite();
// -- typically called when the game is initialized --
// texture rectangles for our sprites
m_spritePaddle.TextureRect = new Rectangle(4, 481, 56, 14);
m_spriteBall.TextureRect   = new Rectangle(65, 481, 14, 14);
// center paddle and ball
m_spritePaddle.Location = new Vector2(217, 415);
m_spriteBall.Location   = new Vector2(233, 401);
// -- typically called from the game's LoadGraphicsContent method --
// load the sprite textures
m_spritePaddle.TextureData = content.Load<Texture2D>(@"media\sprite1");
m_spriteBall.TextureData   = content.Load<Texture2D>(@"media\sprite2");
// extract the opaque data from the sprite images
m_spritePaddle.OpaqueData =
    PixelPerfectHelper.GetOpaqueData(m_spritePaddle);
m_spriteBall.OpaqueData   =
    PixelPerfectHelper.GetOpaqueData(m_spriteBall);
// -- typically called from the game's Update method --
// update sprite locations
UpdateBallSprite();
UpdatePaddleSprite();
// check for collision
bool collision =
    PixelPerfectHelper.DetectCollision(m_spriteBall, m_spritePaddle);
```

The Brick Class

As far as the game is concerned, the Brick class is basically only responsible for two pieces of information—its location on the screen and how many more times the player has to hit the brick before it is destroyed. The Brick class provides two other members that the level editor uses. These members include a boolean property named Changed that lets the editor know if this brick has been edited, and an overridden ToString method that the editor uses to serialize an instance of the Brick class to disk. We'll cover the editor-specific code later in the book when we talk about the level editor for this game.

The brick's coordinates are stored as separate integer values. You may be asking yourself why I didn't use a Vector2 object. The reason is that Vector2 is an XNA Framework construct, and it shouldn't be used in our (Windows-based) editor. There are equivalent structures in the Windows-specific Framework, but those might violate the design requirement that we be XNA-friendly. To avoid platform-specific code, I decided to use plain old integers.

```
public class Brick
{
    // editor-specific Changed property omitted for this listing
    // editor-specific ToString method omitted for this listing
    // the left-most coordinate of the brick
    protected int m_X = 0;
    public int X
    {
        get { return m_X; }
        set
        {
            Changed |= (m_X == value);
            m_X = value;
        }
    }
    // the top-most coordinate of the brick
    protected int m_Y = 0;
    public int Y
    {
        get { return m_Y; }
        set
        {
            Changed |= (m_Y == value);
            m_Y = value;
        }
    }
}
```

The last few members support the HitsToClear counter for the brick. This value is used by the Tint property of the BrickSprite class to report the color of the brick. When this counter reaches zero, the brick has been destroyed and the sprite that represents the brick is removed from the screen.

```
// number of times this brick must be hit to disappear
protected int m_HitsToClear = 1;
public int HitsToClear
{
    get { return m_HitsToClear; }
    set
    {
        Changed |= (m_HitsToClear == value);
        m_HitsToClear = value;
    }
}
// ball hit brick, register the hit
public void RegisterHit()
{
    if (HitsToClear > 0)
    {
        HitsToClear--;
        Changed = true;
    }
}
// simple property to save some typing
public bool Active
{
    get { return HitsToClear > 0; }
}
}
```

The BrickSprite Class

The BrickSprite class is a sprite wrapper for the Brick object. The code in this class could just have easily been placed in the Brick class, but that would mean that the Brick class would have to link to, and know about, the XNA Framework. If that were the case, then the level editor would also have to link to, and know about, the XNA Framework. By separating the sprite functions from the brick data, we can reuse the brick data in both applications.

The BrickSprite class maintains a list of colors that are exposed by the Tint property. Colors are selected according to the strength of the brick (the number of times the player has to hit the brick before it's destroyed). The BrickSprite maintains a reference to a copy of the Brick instance, which it represents. The copy of the brick is made so that the original brick isn't changed as the game is played, allowing the brick to be reused when the player plays the same level again.

The BrickSprite class implements the IPixelPerfectSprite interface, exposing members that the PixelPerfectHelper class can use to detect collisions between sprites. The IPixelPerfectSprite interface and the PixelPerfectHelper class are described in detail in Chapter 28.

```
public class BrickSprite : IPixelPerfectSprite
{
    #region IPixelPerfectSprite Members
    // The IPixelPerfectSprite members have been omitted for this listing
    #endregion
    // create references for each of our brick colors
    public static readonly Color[] m_Tint =
    {
        new Color(255,128,128), // 1 hit
        new Color(128,255,128), // 2 hits
        new Color(128,128,255), // 3 hits
        new Color(255,128,255), // 4 hits
        new Color(255,255,128), // 5 hits
        new Color(255,194,129), // 6 hits
        new Color(192,192,192), // 7 hits
        new Color(255,192,192), // 8 hits
        new Color(192,255,255), // 9 hits
    };
    // the color of the brick, based on the remaining number of hits
    public Color Tint
    {
        get { return m_Tint[m_Brick.HitsToClear - 1]; }
        set { }
    }
    // the instance of the Brick class to which this sprite is associated
    protected Brick m_Brick = null;
    public Brick Brick
    {
        get { return m_Brick; }
        set
```

```
    {
        // make a copy of the brick; preserving the original
        // brick data so that it can be reused if this level
        // is played again
        m_Brick = new Brick();
        m_Brick.X = value.X;
        m_Brick.Y = value.Y;
        m_Brick.HitsToClear = value.HitsToClear;
        m_Brick.Changed = false;
        // update the sprite location, based on brick location
        m_Location.X = Game1.PlayableRect.Left + m_Brick.X;
        m_Location.Y = Game1.PlayableRect.Top  + m_Brick.Y;
    }
  }
}
```

The BallSprite Class

The BallSprite class manages the location, direction, and speed of the on-screen ball. Whenever the ball strikes a wall, this class will make the appropriate changes to the ball's properties to keep it in the playing field. These calculations are done in the Update method of the BallSprite class, which is called from the main game class and returns a boolean.

The BallSprite class implements the IPixelPerfectSprite interface, exposing members that the PixelPerfectHelper class can use to detect collisions between sprites. The IPixelPerfectSprite interface and the PixelPerfectHelper class are described in detail in Chapter 28.

```
public class BallSprite : IPixelPerfectSprite
{
    #region IPixelPerfectSprite Members
    // The IPixelPerfectSprite members have been omitted for this listing
    #endregion
```

The Movement property exposes a Vector2 instance that holds the change in location for the sprite, expressed as pixels per second. There's also a helper method that allows the caller to set this property without creating a new Vector2 instance.

```
// the change in location, in pixels per second
protected Vector2 m_Movement = Vector2.Zero;
public Vector2 Movement
```

```
{
    get { return m_Movement; }
    set { m_Movement = value; }
}
// simple helper to assign a movement vector without having
// to create a new Vector2 object
public void SetMovement(float dx, float dy)
{
    m_Movement.X = dx;
    m_Movement.Y = dy;
}
```

The BallSprite's Update method is responsible for animating the ball, and making sure that it stays on the playing field. Normally, the Update method returns true, but it returns false when the ball leaves the playing field by moving past the paddle and striking the bottom wall. That's the signal to the main game class that the player has failed to keep the ball in play. At that point the game will reset the ball's properties and decrement the player's life count.

```
// update the location of the sprite, check for wall collisions
public bool Update(double elapsed)
{
    // is ball still in playing field?
    bool InBounds = true;
    // update the ball's location
    float seconds = (float)elapsed;
    m_Location += seconds * m_Movement;
    // did ball leave playing field to the left?
    if (m_Location.X < Game1.PlayableRect.Left)
    {
        // bring ball back into field, reverse X movement
        m_Location.X = Game1.PlayableRect.Left;
        m_Movement.X *= -1;
    }
    // did ball leave playing field to the right?
    else if (m_Location.X >
        Game1.PlayableRect.Right - TextureRect.Width)
    {
        // bring ball back into field, reverse X movement
        m_Location.X = Game1.PlayableRect.Right - TextureRect.Width;
        m_Movement.X *= -1;
    }
    // did ball leave playing field at the top?
```

```
if (m_Location.Y < Game1.PlayableRect.Top)
{
    // bring ball back into field, reverse Y movement
    m_Location.Y = Game1.PlayableRect.Top;
    m_Movement.Y *= -1;
}
// did ball leave playing field at the bottom?
else if (m_Location.Y >
    Game1.PlayableRect.Bottom - TextureRect.Height)
{
    // tell the main game class that the player messed up
    InBounds = false;
}
// return game state: true = ok, false = oops
return InBounds;
}
}
```

The PaddleSprite Class

The PaddleSprite class has no meaningful internal logic. It's only purpose in life is maintaining the properties that the PixelPerfectHelper needs to handle collision detection. All of the real work for the paddle happens in the main game class.

The PaddleSprite class implements the IPixelPerfectSprite interface, exposing members that the PixelPerfectHelper class can use to detect collisions between sprites. The IPixelPerfectSprite interface and the PixelPerfectHelper class are described in detail in Chapter 28.

The LevelManager Class

The LevelManager class is a helper class that contains several static members. This class manages the collection of levels for the game, and it loads level data from project files that were created by our level editor. The collection of levels is stored in a generics-based List. The game requests level data by calling the GetLevel method, specifying a level number.

Note

The List class is a strongly typed, growable array that's built into the standard .NET Framework APIs. It's based on the generics technology of the 2.0 version of .NET. See the section entitled "Use Strongly-Typed Collections" in Chapter 20, "Optimization," for a description and example of the benefits of using generics-based collections in your game code.

The GetLevel method allows the game to request levels that are greater than
the number of levels that are stored in the collection. As the game progresses, the
level keeps increasing. When the level number exceeds the number of items in the
collection, the index wraps back around to the first element in the collection.
The levels repeat, but the game will continue as long as the player has at least one
life left.

```
public class LevelManager
{
    // the collection of levels for the game
    protected static List<LevelData> m_Levels = new List<LevelData>();
    // read-only count of levels
    public static int LevelCount
    {
        get { return m_Levels.Count; }
    }
    // get LevelData, based on game level
    // repeat when we reach the end of the list
    public static LevelData GetLevel(int number)
    {
        return m_Levels[Math.Abs(number) % m_Levels.Count];
    }
}
```

The project file that contains the levels for the game is opened and read in by the
LoadProject method. The data file is a simple text file. Each line in the data file
represents a level in the game. Each line contains a list of integer values, separated with
the pipe symbol. The first two numbers represent the width and height of a brick for
the level. The remaining numbers are arranged in groups of three values that describe
the X and Y location of each brick on the screen, and the number of times the player
must hit the brick before it is destroyed. The following listing includes the first part of
several lines from the game project file that our example uses.

```
40|20|0|0|1|40|0|1|80|0|1|120|0|1|160|0|1|200|0|1|240|0|1|280|0|1|...
40|20|0|0|1|0|20|1|0|40|2|0|60|2|0|80|2|0|100|1|0|120|1|40|120|1|...
40|20|0|0|1|0|20|1|240|120|1|280|120|1|320|120|1|360|120|1|...
40|20|27|150|1|89|179|1|128|110|1|68|119|1|139|150|1|200|190|1|...
```

The first line in the preceding listing begins with 40|20|0|0|1|40|0|1. The level
that's described by those numbers has bricks that are 40 pixels wide and 20 pixels
tall. The first two bricks are located at (0,0) and (40,0). Both bricks can be
destroyed with just a single hit. Brick coordinates are relative to the top, left pixel
of the playable area of the game screen.

Notice the last line of level data in the listing. The locations of the bricks in that level seem more random and irregular than the bricks in the previous lines. When creating that level, I turned off the level editor's snap-to-grid feature and placed the bricks on the playable area in random positions. The game has no concept of a regular grid. Each brick is positioned independently on the screen. The snap-to-grid feature is just there to help you create levels with regular brick patterns.

Note

Even though the data file supports levels with varying brick sizes, our example game and level editor only support 40 × 20 bricks.

The LevelManager class doesn't know how to parse a line of level data from the file, so he just passes the line of text along to an overloaded constructor for the LevelData class. This new LevelData instance is added to the collection of levels, and it is immediately available for use in the game.

```
// load level data from a game project file
public static void LoadProject(string filename)
{
    // check for null filename
    if (filename == null) { return; }
    // prepend the app's path
    string path = StorageContainer.TitleLocation + "\\" + filename;
    // if the file exists, process it
    if (File.Exists(path))
    {
        try
        {
            // local variable to read file, line-by-line
            string line = null;
            // clear any existing level data from our
            // in-memory collection
            m_Levels.Clear();
            // open the file
            StreamReader reader =
                new StreamReader(
                    new FileStream(path, FileMode.Open));
            // for every line in the file, read it in,
            // create a level from the data, and add the
            // newly created level to our collection
            while ((line = reader.ReadLine()) != null)
```

```
            {
                m_Levels.Add(new LevelData(line));
            }
            // after reading all the lines, close the file
            reader.Close();
        }
        catch { }
    }
  }
}
```

The LevelData Class

The LevelData class maintains the collection of bricks for the level. The bricks are stored internally in a generics-based List of Brick objects that is exposed to calling classes via the Bricks property.

```
public class LevelData
{
    // editor-specific properties omitted for this listing:
    //    Changed, HalfWidth, HalfHeight
    // editor-specific methods omitted for this listing:
    //    ToString, FindBrick, AddBrick, DeleteBrick
    // the collection of bricks for this level
    protected List<Brick> m_Bricks = new List<Brick>();
    public List<Brick> Bricks
    {
        get { return m_Bricks; }
    }
```

There are two constructors for the LevelData class. The default constructor creates an empty level whose bricks are 40 pixels wide and 20 pixels tall. The second constructor accepts a string that describes the level, as described in the earlier paragraphs on the LevelManager class.

```
// accept defaults: bricks are 40x20, no bricks in the level
// this might be useful for creating levels from code
public LevelData() : base()
{
}
// overload used to deserialize level data from a file
public LevelData(string data)
    : base()
```

```
{
    // the first two tokens are the width and height
    string[] tokens = data.Split("|".ToCharArray());
    if (tokens.Length > 1)
    {
        BrickWidth = int.Parse(tokens[0]);
        BrickHeight = int.Parse(tokens[1]);
    }
    // the remaining tokens are brick triplets
    // skip first two tokens, we've already extracted them
    int index = 2;
    // as long as more tokens remain, process them
    while (index < tokens.Length)
    {
        // brick data is stored as a triplet:
        // Width, Height, and NumHitsToClear
        if (index + 2 < tokens.Length)
        {
            Brick brick = AddBrick(
                int.Parse(tokens[index + 0]),
                int.Parse(tokens[index + 1]),
                int.Parse(tokens[index + 2]));
            brick.Changed = false;
        }
        // move on to the next three tokens
        index += 3;
    }
    // reset the changed flag
    Changed = false;
    }
}
```

When the editor-specific properties are stripped from this listing, there's not much left. In our game, the LevelData class is just a glorified container for Brick objects. We'll cover the other functions of the LevelData class when we discuss the level editor in Chapter 24.

The Game

The main logic for our example is contained in the Game1 class. This class coordinates the efforts of the other classes, processes player input, manages the game state, and draws game objects to the screen.

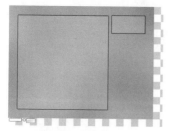

Figure 14.2
The source texture for the game, cropped to eliminate unused space. Notice the paddle, ball, and brick sprites, just below the background sprite.

Graphics

All of the sprites for this game are contained within a single texture. The 1024 × 512 texture includes the images for the background, paddle, ball, and brick sprites. The source texture is shown in Figure 14.2.

The game may have many bricks, but it has just one brick sprite image, which is shared by all instances of the BrickSprite class. Rather than initializing each sprite with a reference to the source texture every time the texture is reloaded, the Game1 class exposes a static property that the game sprites use to reference their texture data.

```
// the one and only sprite batch
protected SpriteBatch m_batch = null;
// main game texture
protected static Texture2D m_GameTexture = null;
public static Texture2D GameTexture
{
    get { return m_GameTexture; }
}
```

The game sprites also refer to the Game1 class for their texture rectangles. Since the texture rectangles don't change as the game progresses, we don't really save any work by placing them in a common location, but the texture rectangles are closely tied to the texture. It makes sense to manage it all in one place in the code. In addition to the texture rectangles, the bounds of the playable area are stored here. The PlayableRect doesn't have anything to do with texture coordinates; it's used to keep the ball confined to the playable area.

```
// boundary rectangles
public static readonly Rectangle BackgroundRect =
    new Rectangle(0, 0, SCREEN_WIDTH, SCREEN_HEIGHT);
```

```
public static readonly Rectangle PlayableRect =
    new Rectangle(40, 40, 400, 400);
// texture rectangles
public static readonly Rectangle BallRect =
    new Rectangle(65, 481, 14, 14);
public static readonly Rectangle PaddleRect =
    new Rectangle(4, 481, 56, 14);
public static readonly Rectangle BrickRect =
    new Rectangle(80, 481, 40, 20);
```

The last bit of relevant sprite data that we store in member variables is the sprite instances, themselves. There is only one instance of the ball and paddle sprites, but we can have many brick sprites in a single level. The ball and paddle sprite instances are stored in simple member variables. The brick sprite instances are stored in a generics-based List. When a new level is requested, this List is cleared, and then populated with the brick data for the level.

```
// sprites for paddle and ball
protected PaddleSprite m_spritePaddle = new PaddleSprite();
protected BallSprite   m_spriteBall   = new BallSprite();
// brick sprites for current level
protected List<BrickSprite> m_Bricks = new List<BrickSprite>();
```

The Game1 class is responsible for loading the game's texture data whenever the LoadGraphicsContent method is called (i.e., when the game starts up and when a windowed game is dragged from one monitor to another on a multi-monitor PC). In this method, we will load our main game texture, initialize our (one and only) SpriteBatch object, extract our pixel-perfect collision data for each of our collidable game sprites, and initialize our game font. We'll discuss the GameFont and PixelPerfectHelper classes in more detail a little later in this chapter. The listing for our game's LoadGraphicsContent method follows.

```
// shared opaque data, used by pixel-perfect
// 2d collision detection helper
public static bool[,] BrickOpaqueData  = null;
public static bool[,] PaddleOpaqueData = null;
public static bool[,] BallOpaqueData   = null;
/// Load your graphics content.
protected override void LoadGraphicsContent(bool loadAllContent)
{
    if (loadAllContent)
    {
```

```
        // initialize our sprite batch
        m_batch = new SpriteBatch(graphics.GraphicsDevice);

        // load the main game texture
        m_GameTexture =
            content.Load<Texture2D>(@"media\brickbreaker");
        // extract the opaque data from the sprite images
        PaddleOpaqueData =
            PixelPerfectHelper.GetOpaqueData(m_spritePaddle);
        BallOpaqueData =
            PixelPerfectHelper.GetOpaqueData(m_spriteBall);
        BrickOpaqueData =
            PixelPerfectHelper.GetOpaqueData(new BrickSprite());
        // initialize our game font
        m_GameFontTexture =
            content.Load<Texture2D>(@"media\Verdana8Bold");
        m_GameFont = GameFont.FromTexture2D(m_GameFontTexture);
    }
    // TODO: Load any ResourceManagementMode.Manual content
}
```

Initializing Game State

The InitializeGame method resets the game's state data, preparing the Game1
class for a new game. The player is given three new lives, his score is set back to
zero, the level counter is reset to zero (the first level in a game project), and the
brick data for the level is reloaded (from an in-memory copy of the level). This
method is called when the game first starts and whenever the player fails to keep
the ball in play for the third time.

```
// reset state variables, restart level 0
protected void InitializeGame()
{
    Level = 0;
    Lives = 3;
    Score = 0;
    InitializeLevel();
}
```

The InitializeLevel method requests the first level from the LevelManager class,
re-creates the BrickSprite instances for the level, and then resets the paddle and
ball sprites. This method is called from the InitializeLevel method and from the

Update method (where player input and collision detection are processed). The BrickSprite class maintains a reference to the Brick object that it represents.

As each BrickSprite instance is created, a copy of the Brick that it represents is assigned to the sprite, rather than a reference to the actual object. This is done so that we do not modify the original Brick data, which may be reused many times over the lifetime of the game.

```
// reset level state variables
protected void InitializeLevel()
{
    // get level data
    LevelData level = LevelManager.GetLevel(Level);
    // clear existing bricks, repopulate our collection
    // with those stored in the current level data
    m_Bricks.Clear();
    foreach (Brick brick in level.Bricks)
    {
        // copy the data so that it's available when the
        // level is replayed
        BrickSprite sprite = new BrickSprite();
        sprite.Brick = brick;
        m_Bricks.Add(sprite);
    }
    // reset paddle and ball
    InitializePaddle();
}
```

The InitializePaddle method places the paddle at the horizontal center of the playable area of the game, places the ball at the center of the paddle, and then selects a new random direction for the ball to travel. The speed of the ball is also reset during this process.

```
// center paddle and ball, reset ball speed
protected void InitializePaddle()
{
    // center paddle and ball
    m_spritePaddle.Location = new Vector2(217, 415);
    m_spriteBall.Location = new Vector2(233, 401);
    // set initial speed and direction of ball
    m_spriteBall.Movement =
        new Vector2(m_rand.Next(120) - 60, -90);
}
```

Managing the Game's State

The Update method is responsible for coordinating the efforts of all the game's objects, based on the player's input. The Update method is called several times per second, and with each call, he delegates tasks to other, specialized methods. The first part of this method was generated for us by Visual Studio when the project was created. It shuts the game down when the player presses the Back button on the game pad.

```
/// game logic such as updating the world
protected override void Update(GameTime gameTime)
{
    // Allows the default game to exit on Xbox 360 and Windows
    if (GamePad.GetState(PlayerIndex.One).Buttons.Back ==
        ButtonState.Pressed)
        this.Exit();
```

Since the time between calls to the Update method can vary, changes in the state of objects are scaled according to the amount of time that has elapsed since they were last updated. To keep things simple, references to movement will be stored in pixels per second. That way we can simply multiply our target values by the number of seconds that have elapsed (typically some small fraction) to scale our movement from frame to frame. If the ball is moving at 40 pixels per second, and a quarter of a second has elapsed since the last update, the ball will only move 10 pixels from its most recent position (40 * 0.25 = 10).

```
// total elapsed seconds since last frame
double elapsed = gameTime.ElapsedGameTime.TotalSeconds;
```

At this point, we need to poll the state of the game pad to see if the player is trying to move the paddle. We'll delegate the implementation details to a helper method named ProcessInput.

```
// process player input from keyboard and game pad
ProcessInput(elapsed);
```

Next, we need to update the position of the ball, and then check to see if it's touching any other active game objects at its new position. The Update method of the BallSprite class will manage ball-to-wall collisions, but we need to check for ball-to-paddle and ball-to-brick collisions ourselves. Sounds like another job for some helper functions.

```
// have the ball update itself; returns true as long as
// the ball is still in play
```

```
if (m_spriteBall.Update(elapsed))
{
    CheckForBallBrickCollision(elapsed);
    CheckForBallPaddleCollision(elapsed);
}
```

As long as the ball is still in play, the Update method of the BallSprite class will return true. As soon as it returns false, we know that the player has failed to keep the ball in play, and we need to take action. When we see that the ball has left the playable area, we'll take one of the player's lives away. If the player was on his last life, we'll restart the game by calling the InitializeGame method. Otherwise, we'll just reset the ball and paddle states via a call to the InitializePaddle method.

```
else
{
    // out of bounds! subtract a life
    Lives--;
    // check for game over condition
    if (Lives <= 0)
    {
        // out of lives, restart game
        InitializeGame();
    }
    else
    {
        // still have a life left, reset paddle and ball
        InitializePaddle();
    }
}
```

After the call to the CheckForBallBrickCollision method, a brick may have been destroyed. If that was the last brick on the screen, we need to know about it so that we can take the player to the next game level.

```
    // no active bricks? start new level
    if (!ScreenHasBricks())
    {
        Level++;
        InitializeLevel();
    }
    base.Update(gameTime);
}
```

Clearing the Level

The ScreenHasBricks method checks to see if there are any active bricks left on the current level. If there's not at least one brick left in the playable area, this level has been cleared, and it's time to move on to the next level. The method iterates through each brick in the current level, checking its Active property.

The Active property for a brick that has been destroyed will be false. If the brick still has some life left in it, this property will be true. Once we find the first active brick in the collection, we can stop looking. As long as any one brick remains on the level, the level isn't clear, and the ScreenHasBricks method returns true.

```
// see if there are any bricks on the screen
protected bool ScreenHasBricks()
{
    bool foundBrick = false;
    // scan for active bricks
    foreach (BrickSprite sprite in m_Bricks)
    {
        foundBrick |= sprite.Active;
        // found at least one, stop searching
        if (foundBrick) { break; }
    }

    return foundBrick;
}
```

Processing Player Input

For this game, it would be nice to allow the player to use the game pad or the keyboard to interact with the game. We will poll both devices and integrate the resulting inputs into our logic.

```
// process the player's input from game pad and keyboard
protected void ProcessInput(double elapsed)
{
    // grab keyboard and game pad states
    GamePadState  pad1 = GamePad.GetState(PlayerIndex.One);
    KeyboardState key1 = Keyboard.GetState();
```

The only object that the player has any direct control over is the paddle. The player moves the paddle by moving the left thumbstick on the game pad, or by pressing a direction key on the keyboard. The thumbstick allows a range of inputs, but the keyboard is a digital device (on or off, pressed or released). When the player is using the game pad, we will vary the change in the paddle's location by noting how far the player has moved the thumbstick (a range from −1 to +1, and everything in between). We will treat input from the keyboard the same as the extreme values of the thumbstick (the discreet values −1 and +1).

```
// temp variables to calc new location for paddle
Vector2 loc = m_spritePaddle.Location;
float dx = 0.0f;
// calc dx for paddle, based on input
if (pad1.ThumbSticks.Left.X != 0.0f)
{
    dx = pad1.ThumbSticks.Left.X;
}
else if (key1.IsKeyDown(Keys.Left))
{
    dx = -1.0f;
}
else if (key1.IsKeyDown(Keys.Right))
{
    dx = 1.0f;
}
```

As I mentioned earlier, we need to scale the movement of our game objects by the amount of time that has elapsed since the last update. In the case of our paddle, which has a maximum velocity of 255 pixels per second, the maximum change in horizontal location is multiplied by the number of elapsed seconds (255.0f * elapsed). We will further scale that value by the intensity of the player's input (stored in the local variable, dx).

```
// apply dx to location
loc.X += (float)(255.0f * dx * elapsed);
```

After moving the paddle, we need to make sure that it hasn't left the playable area. We will check its new position against the bounds of the playable area (recorded in the PlayableRect structure). If the paddle has strayed too far, we'll bring it back.

```
// stay within playable bounds
if (loc.X < PlayableRect.Left)
{
    loc.X = PlayableRect.Left;
}
```

```
else if (loc.X > PlayableRect.Right -
    m_spritePaddle.TextureRect.Width)
{
    loc.X = PlayableRect.Right - m_spritePaddle.TextureRect.Width;
}
```

Now that we know the paddle's new position, we can let the game sprite that wraps the paddle handle the rest. We'll just store the new location in a property on the PaddleSprite, and then go about the rest of our updating business.

```
    // actually update the paddle's location
    m_spritePaddle.Location = loc;
}
```

Detecting Collisions

One of the most important tasks in this game is detecting collisions between the ball and the other game objects. The BallSprite class handles collisions between the ball and the borders of the playable area, and it manages the speed and direction of the ball; but the game class is responsible for detecting collisions between the ball and paddle as well as collisions between the ball and bricks.

We'll be using the PixelPerfectHelper class to detect collisions between our game objects. This class is described in detail in Chapter 28. By having our game objects implement the IPixelPerfectSprite interface, we can treat them as objects of that type. That interface exposes all the information that we'll need to perform collision detection between our sprites.

When the ball collides with the paddle, we'll reverse its vertical direction and set its horizontal direction based on the ball's distance from the center of the paddle. By doing so, we give the player more control over the ball, allowing him to aim the ball at specific bricks by positioning the paddle just before impact.

```
// did the ball collide with the paddle?
protected void CheckForBallPaddleCollision(double elapsed)
{
    // calculate the horizontal center of the ball
    float ballCenterX =
        m_spriteBall.Location.X +
        m_spriteBall.TextureRect.Width / 2;
```

There will be times when the ball is moving so fast that it has partially passed through the paddle by the time we detect the collision. Since the time between calls to the Update method is variable, and we use the elapsed time to scale the movement of our ball, there may be rare cases where the ball doesn't move far enough on the update just after a collision to prevent registering a second collision. To account for this fringe case, we'll only process collisions with the paddle if the ball is moving towards the bottom of the screen (when m_spriteBall.Movement.Y > 0).

```
// only register paddle collision when ball is moving down
bool collision =
    m_spriteBall.Movement.Y > 0&& PixelPerfectHelper
    .DetectCollision(m_spriteBall, m_spritePaddle);
```

As I mentioned earlier, the angle that the ball leaves the paddle after a collision is a function of the distance from the center of the paddle to the ball's center. When the ball is at the center of the paddle, it will move straight up after the collision (a horizontal speed of zero, since the distance between the centers of the paddle and the ball is zero). When the ball is at the left or right edge of the paddle, it will cover slightly more horizontal pixels per second than the width of the paddle (2.5 times half of the paddle's width, when the distance between centers is half of the paddle's width).

The value 2.5 is a number that I came up with using trial and error. It's a good horizontal speed that still allows the user to retain control of the ball as the pace of the game quickens.

```
// did ball collide with paddle?
if (collision)
{
    // simple deflection where movement.x is a function
    // of the ball's distance from the center of the paddle
    float paddleCenterX =
        m_spritePaddle.Location.X +
        m_spritePaddle.TextureRect.Width / 2;
    float dx = (ballCenterX - paddleCenterX) * 2.5f;
```

Every time the player is able to return the ball to the playing field, the vertical speed of the ball is increased by some small amount. To keep things sane, the maximum vertical velocity of the ball is capped at 380 pixels per second. Again, the values for the speed increase per volley (10%) and the maximum vertical velocity of the ball (380 pps) were chosen using trial and error. They're completely arbitrary.

```
// reverse direction, and increase speed by 10%;
// not too fast, though
float dy = Math.Max(
    -1.1f * m_spriteBall.Movement.Y,
    -380.0f);
```

Once we've calculated the new vertical and horizontal movement values, we need to update them in our `BallSprite` instance. The `BallSprite` class is responsible for the movement of the ball. We just give it the desired values and let it worry about the details.

```
// update the ball's movement vector with our calculations
m_spriteBall.SetMovement(dx, dy);
```

The majority of a player's score comes from destroying bricks. We'll also reward the player for keeping the ball in play by adding one point to his score every time he saves the ball from oblivion.

```
        // increment score slightly for each volley
        Score += 1;
    }
}
```

At this point, we have the ball bouncing off the walls of the playable area, and we're able to respond when the ball comes into contact with the player's paddle. Now we need to take care of the case where the ball strikes a brick. The code that handles ball-to-brick collisions is very similar to the code that handles ball-to-paddle collisions. We'll start by calculating the position of the center of the ball.

```
// did the ball collide with any bricks?
protected void CheckForBallBrickCollision(double elapsed)
{
    // calculate the center of the ball
    Vector2 ballCenter = Vector2.Zero;
    ballCenter.X =
        m_spriteBall.Location.X +
        m_spriteBall.TextureRect.Width / 2;
    ballCenter.Y =
        m_spriteBall.Location.Y +
        m_spriteBall.TextureRect.Height / 2;
```

We were able to check for collisions with the paddle in a single `if` statement, but there are typically many bricks on each game level. We'll use the same basic logic to check for collisions, but we need to perform that check for every brick that's still in the playable area. Checking for a collision between dozens of sprites, pixel by pixel, may sound like a lot of work for a routine that has to run dozens of times a second. It is.

Fortunately, the PixelPerfectHelper class doesn't have to compare every pixel of every sprite. It breaks the collision detection task into two stages. The first stage checks to see if the bounds of two given sprites overlap. If they don't, there's no need to scan for collisions at the pixel level. The pixels of two sprites cannot be touching if their texture rectangles don't overlap. The second stage is more CPU-intensive, but it's not called that often. The ball spends most of its time traveling through empty space, where collision detection doesn't get past the first stage.

```
// check for collision with each brick
foreach (BrickSprite brickSprite in m_Bricks)
{
    // only check active bricks (drawn bricks)
    bool collision =
        brickSprite.Active && PixelPerfectHelper
        .DetectCollision(m_spriteBall, brickSprite);
    // did ball collide with an ACTIVE brick?
    if (collision)
    {
```

At this point, we know that the ball has collided with a brick. We even know which brick the ball is touching. We'll just gather some useful information into a few local variables so that we can perform some simple calculations to decide what action to take. We'll record the current movement vectors of the ball, as well as the bounds of the brick with which the ball just collided.

```
// local variables to save some typing
float dx = m_spriteBall.Movement.X;
float dy = m_spriteBall.Movement.Y;
// local variables to save some typing
float ballWidth  = m_spriteBall.TextureRect.Width;
float brickLeft   = brickSprite.Location.X;
float brickWidth  = brickSprite.TextureRect.Width;
float brickRight  = brickLeft + brickWidth;
```

Whenever the ball hits a surface, it responds by changing its direction. It bounces off of the object with which it collided. To calculate the new movement vectors, we need to determine the direction from which the ball struck the brick. There are four basic places that a ball will strike a brick—the left or right of the brick, the top or bottom of the brick, or one of the four corners of the brick.

To determine which category our collision falls into, we'll compare the location of the ball's center to the bounds of the brick that was struck. If the center of the ball is located between the top and bottom boundaries of the brick, the ball probably struck the brick from one of its sides. If the center of the ball is located between the left and right boundaries of the brick, the ball probably struck the brick from the top or the bottom. If the center of the ball isn't within either of these boundaries, it probably struck the brick on one of its corners.

In my original implementation, I used these states to determine the new direction of the ball. If the ball struck a side, I reversed the X component of the movement vector. If it struck the top or bottom, I reversed the Y component. If it struck a corner, I reversed both. In general, this approach worked well, but it fell apart as the ball started moving faster or struck a brick's corner from an awkward angle.

As the ball moves faster and faster, there are cases where the ball can move so many pixels in a single update that it passes most of the way through a brick before the collision is detected. If the next update comes faster than the last, the ball may not cover enough distance to escape the brick, triggering another collision and another "about face." In the blink of an eye, the ball will escape its trap or the brick will be destroyed (by registering multiple, back-to-back hits). In some of these cases, the ball may appear to pass through a brick after registering the strike.

To account for this, and to correct some other visual anomalies at higher ball speeds, I settled on the following logic. The left and right bounds of the brick are checked separately, and the ball moves away from the surface that was struck. If the ball didn't hit one of the sides, the vertical direction is reversed (assuming the ball hit the brick on the top, bottom, or one of the corners). Regardless of the adjusted direction, the ball follows its new trajectory using the same scale of movement that was used for the most recent update (i.e., the distance is multiplied by the same elapsed time value).

```
// from which direction did ball hit?
if (ballCenter.X < brickLeft)
{
    // struck brick from left
    dx = -Math.Max(Math.Abs(dx), ballWidth / 2);
}
else if (ballCenter.X > brickRight)
```

```
{
    // struck brick from right
    dx = Math.Max(Math.Abs(dx), ballWidth / 2);
}
else
{
    // hit broad side of brick
    dy = -dy;
}
// update the ball's location and movement
m_spriteBall.Movement = new Vector2(dx, dy);
// back track to avoid multiple hits when the ball is
// traveling at max (or near max) velocity
m_spriteBall.Update(elapsed);
```

We can now handle the last couple of post-collision tasks. We'll add a few points to the player's score for striking the brick, and we'll make sure that the brick knows that it's been hit so that it can decrement the HitsToClear counter, possibly marking itself inactive.

```
            // add some points for each brick cleared
            Score += 5;
            // notify the brick that it has been hit
            brickSprite.Brick.RegisterHit();
        }
    }
}
```

Note
_____

> While the current game and level editor don't support this feature as is, this would be a good place to add logic that awards different points for selected categories of bricks. You could add a new property to the Brick class that contains a bonus point value that is awarded when the brick is cleared. When new bricks are added to a level within the editor, they can contain the default score (5 in our case), and the level designer can assign a different bonus value for any brick in the editor. The value for each brick could be saved into our data file and read back in when the game loads the level. As things exist now, the score per brick is hard-coded.

_____

Drawing Game Objects

The Draw method is regularly called from the main game loop. It wraps several helper drawing methods in a common sprite batch. We'll cover each of these methods in the following paragraphs.

```
/// render game objects
protected override void Draw(GameTime gameTime)
{
    graphics.GraphicsDevice.Clear(Color.CornflowerBlue);
    m_batch.Begin();

    // draw game objects
    DrawBackground(m_batch);
    DrawBricks(m_batch);
    DrawPaddle(m_batch);
    DrawBall(m_batch);
    // draw HUD, with simple "dropshadow"
    DrawHUD(m_batch, 473, 43, Color.Black);
    DrawHUD(m_batch, 472, 44, Color.White);

    m_batch.End();
    base.Draw(gameTime);
}
```

Our background is drawn from a single image whose width and height are the same as our game screen. Since the background image covers the game screen, we see that the call to the GraphicsDevice's Clear method from the game's Draw method wasn't really necessary. That line was added by Visual Studio when our game project was created.

```
// draw the background
protected void DrawBackground(SpriteBatch batch)
{
    batch.Draw(
        GameTexture,
        BackgroundRect,
        BackgroundRect,
        Color.White);
}
```

The paddle, ball, and bricks are all wrapped in classes that support a common interface (IPixelPerfectSprite) that the collision detection routines use. We'll take advantage of that fact to eliminate some redundant code and save some typing by adding a simple helper method to draw sprites that implement the interface.

```
// generic helper to draw any game sprite
protected void DrawSprite(
    SpriteBatch batch, IPixelPerfectSprite sprite)
```

```
{
    if (sprite.Active)
    {
        batch.Draw(
            sprite.TextureData,
            sprite.Location,
            sprite.TextureRect,
            sprite.Tint);
    }
}
```

Using the DrawSprite method, the code for drawing the ball, paddle, and bricks becomes incredibly simple.

```
// draw the paddle in its current location
protected void DrawPaddle(SpriteBatch batch)
{
    DrawSprite(batch, m_spritePaddle);
}
// draw the ball in its current location
protected void DrawBall(SpriteBatch batch)
{
    DrawSprite(batch, m_spriteBall);
}
// draw all active bricks
protected void DrawBricks(SpriteBatch batch)
{
    foreach (BrickSprite sprite in m_Bricks)
    {
        DrawSprite(batch, sprite);
    }
}
```

Only one drawing task remains. We need to print a simple heads-up display to let the player know how many lives he has left, what his current score is, what his highest score is, and what level he's currently on. This functionality is wrapped in the DrawHUD method, and it relies heavily on the GameFont component that we develop in Chapter 21, "Game Font Library."

```
// draw important heads-up-display data
protected void DrawHUD(SpriteBatch batch, int x, int y, Color tint)
{
    int locX = x;
```

```
int locY = y;
int maxWidth = 0;
Vector2 size = Vector2.Zero;
```

The HUD is made up of two columns of text. The first column contains the labels that describe the data displayed, and the second column contains the actual data. Two local variables (locX and locY) are used to position text on the screen. As each row of text in a column is drawn, the locY variable is incremented by an amount equal to the height of the font so that the next line of text will be drawn just below the previous line. As each label is drawn, its width (in pixels) is recorded so that the data in the second column can be aligned just to the right of the widest label in the first column.

```
// draw labels in first column
string[] data = { "Level:", "Lives:", "Score:", "HiScore:" };
foreach (string text in data)
{
    size = m_GameFont.DrawString(batch, text, locX, locY, tint);
    locY += m_GameFont.FontHeight;
    maxWidth = Math.Max((int)(size.X + 0.5f), maxWidth);
}
// set location to start of second column
locX += maxWidth + 7;
locY = y;
// draw data in second column
data = new string[]
    { LevelString, LivesString, ScoreString, HiScoreString };
foreach (string text in data)
{
    m_GameFont.DrawString(batch, text, locX, locY, tint);
    locY += m_GameFont.FontHeight;
}
}
```

The LevelString, LivesString, ScoreString, and HiScoreString member variables contain string representations of numeric data that is tracked over the lifetime of the game. The numeric data is maintained by member properties, and those properties update their string counterparts only when the data that they manage changes. By reducing the number of updates to the string data, we're able to save valuable processor time. They're all very similar in function, so I'll just list one here (the Lives property).

```
// number of lives remaining
protected int m_Lives = 3;
protected string LivesString = "3";
public int Lives
{
    get { return m_Lives; }
    set
    {
        if (m_Lives != value)
        {
            m_Lives = value;
            LivesString = m_Lives.ToString("0");
        }
    }
}
```

Summary

In this chapter, you learned how to manage multiple on-screen game objects, detecting collisions between each. You managed the state of your game objects (location, strength, color), as well as the state of the game (level number, high score, remaining lives). You learned how to load data from your own proprietary file format, and how to create in-memory objects from that data that your game can use. And you saw examples of sharing common game object state via static member variables and methods.

Review Questions

1. What is the maximum velocity (in pixels) of the paddle? The ball?

2. What XNA Framework API does the game use to load texture data?

3. What XNA Framework API does the game use to locate its level data?

4. What .NET Framework API does the game use to load level data?

5. Which class is responsible for loading level data from disk? Which class is responsible for converting data from a line of text in the file to usable, in-memory game levels?

6. In the current implementation of this game, how many bricks can exist in a single level? What's the maximum number of bricks that can exist in a level that is considered playable? How did you determine these numbers?

Exercises

EXERCISE 1. Increase the range of values for the X component of the `m_spriteBall.Movement` property by tweaking the constant that is used to calculate the new horizontal speed of the ball in the `CheckForBallPaddleCollision` method.

EXERCISE 2. Increase the initial speed of the ball as a function of the level number so that the level of difficulty increases each time the player visits the same level data.

EXERCISE 3. There's a bug in this code where the ball can destroy multiple bricks when it passes a vertical arrangement of bricks, regardless of their hits-to-clear setting. This occurs when the ball's horizontal velocity is at or near zero and the ball passes the column of bricks just to the left or right. In this case, the ball is never deflected, and multiple hits are registered as the ball passes over the brick.

Add code to the `CheckForBallBrickCollision` method that detects and corrects this condition. One solution might involve reversing the ball's vertical movement vector. Another might involve moving the ball a few pixels to one side so that future collisions on the same path aren't registered. Yet another may rely on the existing logic, performing comparisons against different values (i.e., comparing the closest side of the ball to the closest side of the brick, rather than using the center of the ball). Study the problem, devise a solution, and implement it.

EXERCISE 4. Modify this game to allow levels to vary the size of a brick. You can retain the current restriction that all bricks within a single level have the same size, but your new game should allow each level to specify its own brick dimensions. Remember to provide a sprite texture for each size, or create a generic brick that can be scaled to any size.

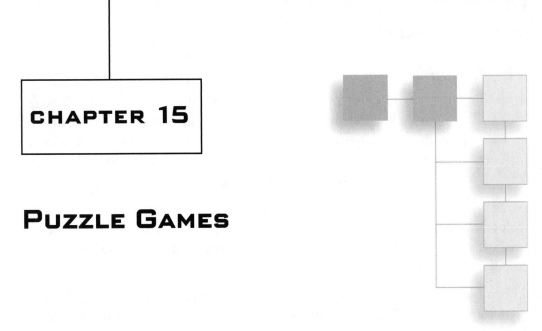

CHAPTER 15

PUZZLE GAMES

Most game genres have a fairly narrow demographic to which they appeal. Typically, that demographic is young males. Puzzle games are one of those rare categories of games that cross gender and age barriers. Their simple, yet addictive game play seduces the casual gamer and the hard-core gamer alike. They even appeal to many people who wouldn't consider themselves "gamers" at all. With a focus on problem solving, and having their roots in logic and math, puzzle games prove that simple games can be fun, even without a multi-million-dollar development budget or a big-name intellectual property license.

By far, the most popular title in this genre is *Tetris,* created by Russian mathematician Alexey Pajitnov (Pazhitnov) in 1985. *Tetris,* and the many clones and variants that it has inspired, has found its way onto nearly every platform imaginable. Most recently, puzzle games have found new life on cell phones and PDAs, introducing many people who may otherwise never have been exposed to their addictive game play. And a new generation of puzzle games, like PopCap Games' *Bejeweled,* are doing their part to entice new players with this genre's broad appeal.

In this chapter, you will learn how to:

- Simultaneously manage the state of multiple on-screen game objects

- Add simple, yet effective animations and visual effects to your game

- Track and display a player's score using a bitmap font

The Design

In this chapter, we will develop a simplified clone of one of my favorite puzzle games. The action takes place on a 9-by-15 grid of square blocks (or cells, as I call them in the code). These blocks rest on top of each other. Every eight seconds, a new row of blocks appears at the bottom of the grid. When the grid fills up, and there is no more room to add a new row, the game is over.

Your goal is to clear these blocks by lining up three or more blocks of the same color horizontally or vertically. You score five points for each block that you clear. If you clear more than one color with a single swap, a combo multiplier is applied to your score.

When blocks are removed from the grid, any blocks that were resting on top of the cleared blocks fall down to occupy any empty spaces. To move blocks, the game has a cursor that's two blocks wide and one block tall. Whenever you press the A button on your game pad, or the space bar on the keyboard, the two blocks that are under the cursor are swapped. To move the cursor, you can use the left thumbstick or DPad on your Xbox 360 Controller or the cursor keys on your keyboard. Figure 15.1 shows a screen shot of the final game.

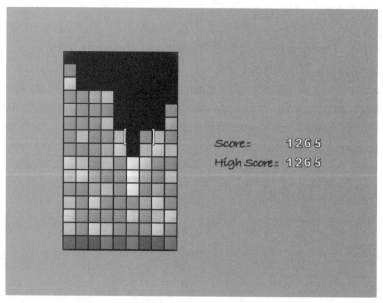

Figure 15.1
A screen shot of the final game.

The Architecture

To be honest, I completely underestimated the complexity of this chapter's code. I've written dozens of puzzle clones in my time as a hobbyist game programmer, and I once developed a *Tetris* clone for a classroom that I was teaching as a fun Friday-afternoon, last-day project in about two hours. In fact, *Tetris* is generally cited as the "Hello, world!" of game programming by many beginning game programming tutorials that you find on the web because it's about as simple a game as you can write (technically speaking). So, when I approached the code for this chapter, I didn't put much thought into my implementation.

When I got to the end of the project, I realized that my code was a giant, monolithic mess. I refactored the code into the classes that you see here before writing this text, but it goes to show how important good design and planning are to ANY game. Never short-change the planning phase of your game's development.

GameBoard Properties

The GameBoard class represents the grid of blocks. While the game play of this version of the game is static, several of the following public properties allow you to configure the game at runtime, so the game dynamics can change as the player progresses through the game.

- CurrentState—the current state of the game (GameState.Playing, GameState.GameOver)

- Score—the score for the current game

- HighScore—the best score seen so far

- BaseScore—the score awarded for each cleared cell

- BoardWidth—the width (in blocks) of the grid

- BoardHeight—the height (in blocks) of the grid

- BoardTopLeft—the location of the top, left pixel of the grid

- NewGameRowCount—the number of rows that a player starts with when a new game begins

- **SecondsBeforeNewRow**—the number of seconds before a new row is added to the bottom of the grid

- **CursorPulseInSeconds**—the number of seconds it takes for the cursor to complete an animation cycle

There will be a more detailed discussion of how the GameBoard class processes data internally later in this chapter. These are just the properties and methods that are exposed to other classes.

GameBoard Methods

The GameBoard class exposes the following public methods.

InitCells

The InitCells method creates and populates the array of blocks that the game uses. This method is called from the GameBoard class' constructor, and whenever the BoardWidth or BoardHeight properties are set.

```
// index into color array for each cell on the board
private Cell[,] m_Cells;

private void InitCells()
{
    // init array
    m_Cells = new Cell[BoardWidth, BoardHeight];

    // assign new cell to each element
    for (int y = 0; y < BoardHeight; y++)
    {
        for (int x = 0; x < BoardWidth; x++)
        {
            m_Cells[x, y] = new Cell();
        }
    }

    // clear the game board
    Clear();
}
```

Draw

The Draw method (and its helper methods) renders the grid, the cursor, and the scores for the game.

```
// the main Draw method
public void Draw(SpriteBatch batch)
{
    // no matter what we draw, it will have a background
    DrawBoardBackground(batch);
    switch (CurrentState)
    {
        // player is actively playing the game
        case GameState.Playing:
            DrawActiveGameBoard(batch);
            DrawCursor(batch);
            break;

        // the game is paused or over
        // case GameState.Paused:
        case GameState.GameOver:
            DrawInactiveGameBoard(batch);
            break;
    }
}
```

LoadMedia

The LoadMedia method reloads texture data for the Cell and NumberSprite classes, it loads the text that's used in the heads-up display, and it sets the locations for that text.

```
// load game textures
public void LoadMedia(ContentManager content)
{
    // cells and cursor
    Cell.Texture = content.Load<Texture2D>(@"media\cell");
    Cell.TextureRectCell = new Rectangle(1, 33, CELL_SIZE, CELL_SIZE);
    Cell.TextureRectCursorLeft = new Rectangle(0, 0, 5, 28);
    Cell.TextureRectCursorRight = new Rectangle(32, 0, 5, 28);

    // numbers for score
    NumberSprite.Texture = content.Load<Texture2D>(@"media\numbers");
```

```
    // miscellaneous text
    m_TextureText = content.Load<Texture2D>(@"media\text");

    // vertical center of game board, for locations of scores
    int BoardCenterY = (BoardHeight * (CELL_SIZE + CELL_PADDING)) / 2;

    // set locations for score labels
    m_ScoreLabelLoc.X = BoardTopLeft.X + BoardWidth * (CELL_SIZE +
        CELL_PADDING) + 64;
    m_ScoreLabelLoc.Y = BoardTopLeft.Y + BoardCenterY-
        m_ScoreRect.Height - 8;
    m_HighScoreLabelLoc.X = m_ScoreLabelLoc.X;
    m_HighScoreLabelLoc.Y = BoardTopLeft.Y + BoardCenterY + 8;

    // set locations for score values
    m_HighScoreValueLoc.X = m_HighScoreLabelLoc.X +
        m_HighScoreRect.Width + 8;
    m_HighScoreValueLoc.Y = m_HighScoreLabelLoc.Y;
    m_ScoreValueLoc.X = m_HighScoreValueLoc.X;
    m_ScoreValueLoc.Y = m_ScoreLabelLoc.Y;
}
```

Update

The Update method processes player input and updates the state of each block in the grid.

```
// update the scrolling rows and the pulsing cursor
public void Update(double elapsed)
{
    // process player input
    CheckButtons(elapsed);

    // only update the counters if the game is active
    if (CurrentState == GameState.Playing)
    {
        // scrolling row counter
        m_SecondsSinceLastRow += elapsed;
        if (m_SecondsSinceLastRow > m_SecondsBeforeNewRow)
        {
            // time for a new row
            NewRow(1);
```

```
    }

    // pulsing cursor counter
    m_CursorAge += elapsed;
    while (m_CursorAge > CursorPulseInSeconds)
    {
        // try to keep counter between 0 and max seconds
        // not entirely necessary since the math functions
        // will handle angles greater than 360 degrees,
        // but I like to do it.
        m_CursorAge -= CursorPulseInSeconds;
    }
}

// eliminate vertical gaps in the cells
Gravity();

// have each cell update itself
foreach (Cell cell in m_Cells)
{
    cell.Update(elapsed);
}

// animate "game over" text
m_GameOverHover += elapsed;
}
```

CheckButtons

The CheckButtons method is responsible for merging keyboard and controller inputs for the keys and buttons in which we are interested. The real work is done by the ProcessButton method. This method's job is to coordinate and delegate.

```
// the (virtual) buttons that we're actually interested in
private enum GameButton
{
    Up,
    Down,
    Left,
    Right,
    Fire,
    Pause,
    // ------------
```

```
        Count
    };

    // process player input
    private void CheckButtons(double elapsed)
    {
        // poll the current states
        GamePadState pad1 = GamePad.GetState(PlayerIndex.One);
        KeyboardState key1 = Keyboard.GetState();

        // helper to merge keyboard and gamepad inputs
        bool pressed = false;

        // UP Button
        pressed = key1.IsKeyDown(Keys.Up);
        pressed |= pad1.DPad.Up == ButtonState.Pressed;
        pressed |= pad1.ThumbSticks.Left.Y > 0;
        ProcessButton(GameButton.Up, pressed, elapsed);

        // DOWN Button
        pressed = key1.IsKeyDown(Keys.Down);
        pressed |= pad1.DPad.Down == ButtonState.Pressed;
        pressed |= pad1.ThumbSticks.Left.Y < 0;
        ProcessButton(GameButton.Down, pressed, elapsed);

        // LEFT Button
        pressed = key1.IsKeyDown(Keys.Left);
        pressed |= pad1.DPad.Left == ButtonState.Pressed;
        pressed |= pad1.ThumbSticks.Left.X < 0;
        ProcessButton(GameButton.Left, pressed, elapsed);

        // RIGHT Button
        pressed = key1.IsKeyDown(Keys.Right);
        pressed |= pad1.DPad.Right == ButtonState.Pressed;
        pressed |= pad1.ThumbSticks.Left.X > 0;
        ProcessButton(GameButton.Right, pressed, elapsed);

        // FIRE Button
        pressed = key1.IsKeyDown(Keys.Space);
        pressed |= pad1.Buttons.A == ButtonState.Pressed;
        ProcessButton(GameButton.Fire, pressed, elapsed);
    }
```

ProcessButton

The ProcessButton method is responsible for processing player input, one button at a time. It simulates repeated presses for buttons that are held down, it tracks how long each button has been pressed, and it calls out to the appropriate methods when key game events occur. By processing each button, one by one, we're able to reuse a lot of code that we would otherwise have cut and pasted.

```
// track how long each button has been held down
private double[] ButtonPressDuration =
    new double[(int)GameButton.Count];

// rate at which to repeat presses when button is held down
private const double BUTTON_REPEAT_RATE = 0.2;

// eliminate redundant button press code by generalizing it here
private void ProcessButton(GameButton button, bool pressed,
    double elapsed)
{
    if (pressed)
    {
        // manage button repeats by tracking how long
        // this button has been pressed
        ButtonPressDuration[(int)button] += elapsed;

        // if the repeat rate has been exceeded, treat
        // this as a new button press
        if (ButtonPressDuration[(int)button] > BUTTON_REPEAT_RATE)
        {
            ButtonPressDuration[(int)button] = elapsed;
        }

        // button was just pressed or has repeated
        if (ButtonPressDuration[(int)button] == elapsed)
        {
            switch (button)
            {
                case GameButton.Up:
                    MoveCursor(CursorDirection.Up);
                    break;
                case GameButton.Down:
                    MoveCursor(CursorDirection.Down);
                    break;
```

```
                    case GameButton.Left:
                        MoveCursor(CursorDirection.Left);
                        break;
                    case GameButton.Right:
                        MoveCursor(CursorDirection.Right);
                        break;
                    case GameButton.Fire:
                        if (CurrentState == GameState.GameOver)
                        {
                            // start a new game
                            Clear();
                            CenterCursor();
                            CurrentState = GameState.Playing;
                        }
                        else
                        {
                            // swap the currently-selected cells
                            SwapCells();
                        }
                        break;
                }
            }
        }
        else
        {
            // button was released, reset counter
            ButtonPressDuration[(int)button] = 0;
        }
    }
}
```

CenterCursor

The CenterCursor method moves the game cursor to the center of the grid.

```
// the current cursor position, or index into the cells array
private Vector2 m_CursorPosition = Vector2.Zero;
public Vector2 CursorPosition
{
    get { return m_CursorPosition; }
    set { m_CursorPosition = value; }
}


// center the cursor on the game board
```

```
public void CenterCursor()
{
    m_CursorPosition.X = (float)Math.Round(BoardWidth / 2.0) - 1;
    m_CursorPosition.Y = (float)Math.Floor(BoardHeight / 2.0);
}
```

MoveCursor

The MoveCursor method moves the cursor some distance, relative to its current location.

```
// handy "constants" for the MoveCursor method
public struct CursorDirection
{
    public static readonly Vector2 Left = new Vector2(-1,0);
    public static readonly Vector2 Right = new Vector2(1, 0);
    public static readonly Vector2 Up = new Vector2(0, -1);
    public static readonly Vector2 Down = new Vector2(0, 1);
};

// move the cursor
public void MoveCursor(Vector2 delta)
{
    CursorPosition += delta;

    // check horizontal bounds
    if (CursorPosition.X < 0)
    {
        m_CursorPosition.X = 0;
    }
    else if (CursorPosition.X > BoardWidth - 2)
    {
        // width minus two since cursor is two cells wide
        m_CursorPosition.X = BoardWidth - 2;
    }

    // check vertical bounds
    if (CursorPosition.Y < 0)
    {
        m_CursorPosition.Y = 0;
    }
    else if (CursorPosition.Y > BoardHeight - 2)
    {
```

```
        // height minus two since last row is not playable
        m_CursorPosition.Y = BoardHeight - 2;
    }
}
```

Clear

The Clear method clears all grid cells, then adds NewGameRowCount new rows to the bottom of the game board.

```
// reset game to initial state
public void Clear()
{
    // fill board with empty cells
    for (int y = 0; y < BoardHeight; y++) // for each row
    {
        for (int x = 0; x < BoardWidth; x++) // for each column
        {
            // empty the cell
            m_Cells[x, y].Reset();
        }
    }

    // create NewGameRowCount rows now that board is clear
    for (int i = 0; i < NewGameRowCount; i++)
    {
        NewRow(1);
    }

    // center the cursor on the game board
    CenterCursor();

    // reset the score
    Score = 0;
}
```

NewRow

The NewRow method immediately adds some number of new rows to the bottom of the grid.

```
// add a new row to the board, moving existing rows up
public bool NewRow(int numRows)
```

```csharp
{
    // handy temp variable to note last row
    int LastRow = BoardHeight - 1;

    // repeat add operation numRows times
    for (int row = 0; row < numRows; row++)
    {
        // scan top row to see if there is room for a new row
        for (int x = 0; x < BoardWidth; x++)
        {
            if (m_Cells[x, 0].ColorIndex !=
                CellColors.EmptyCellColorIndex)
            {
                // nope. game over!
                CurrentState = GameState.GameOver;
                return false;
            }
        }

        // move all rows up one
        for (int y = 0; y < LastRow; y++) // for each (but last) row
        {
            for (int x = 0; x < BoardWidth; x++) // for each column
            {
                // copy next row to the current row
                m_Cells[x, y].Copy( m_Cells[x, y + 1]);
            }
        }

        // fill last row with new random cells
        for (int x = 0; x < BoardWidth; x++)
        {
            // pick a new cell color from our array, randomly
            m_Cells[x, LastRow].Reset();
            m_Cells[x, LastRow].ColorIndex = CellColors.RandomIndex();

            // if this cell matches the previous cell, try again
            if (x > 0)
            {
                int cell1 = m_Cells[x - 1, LastRow].ColorIndex;
                while (m_Cells[x, LastRow].ColorIndex == cell1)
                {
                    m_Cells[x, LastRow].ColorIndex =
```

```
                            CellColors.RandomIndex();
                    }
                }
            }

        // move cursor up a row
        MoveCursor(CursorDirection.Up);
    }

    // reset vertical offset
    m_SecondsSinceLastRow = 0.0f;

    // see if there are any matches
    ScanForMatches();

    // success
    return true;
}
```

Cell Properties

The Cell class represents a single block. The Cell class exposes the following public properties:

- **Texture**—the source texture that contains the brick image, marked as static so that all bricks share the same texture rather than each having its own reference

- **TextureRectXXX**—the coordinates of the sprite image within the larger texture, used for brick images and the animated cursor

- **ColorIndex**—the index into the CellColors.Normal and CellColors.Dark arrays

- **IsClearing**—true when this block has been marked to be removed from the grid

- **ClearDuration**—number of seconds to flash before actually removing this block from the grid

- **m_ClearAge**—number of seconds that this block has been clearing (not technically a property)

- **ClearFlashRate**—number of seconds between color changes for a flashing block

- **IsFalling**—true when this block is actively falling to the next row

- **FallRate**—number of seconds it takes for a falling block to travel a single row

- **FallAge**—number of seconds that this brick has been falling

In addition to these properties, the Cell class exposes public, static properties for the texture (Texture) and texture rectangles (TextureRectCell, Texture-RectCursorLeft, and TextureRectCursorRight). Marking these properties as static means that a single reference to the texture and its rectangles is stored for all Cell instances. That way, we don't have to worry about assigning a texture to each instance whenever the XNA Framework tells us to reload our textures.

Cell Methods

The Cell class exposes the following methods.

Copy

The Copy method configures a block, using the state information from another block.

```
// copy another cell's state to this cell
public void Copy(Cell cell)
{
    // copy public properties
    ColorIndex = cell.ColorIndex;
    IsClearing = cell.IsClearing;
    IsFalling = cell.IsFalling;

    // also need to copy state data since Cell.Copy() may have
    // been called from GameBoard.NewRow() and resetting these
    // values will make the gravity animation seem choppy
    m_ClearAge = cell.m_ClearAge;
    m_FallAge = cell.m_FallAge;
}
```

Reset

The Reset method resets a block's state as if it were a new instance (empty, not falling, not clearing).

```
// initialize this cell (empty, not falling, not clearing)
public void Reset()
{
    ColorIndex = CellColors.EmptyCellColorIndex;
    IsClearing = false;
    IsFalling = false;
}
```

Draw

The Draw method renders a block to the screen, taking into account falling, clearing, or new row (dark) states.

```
// draw this cell
public void Draw(SpriteBatch batch, Vector2 location,
    Rectangle texRect, bool dark)
{
    // don't bother drawing empty cells
    if (ColorIndex != CellColors.EmptyCellColorIndex)
    {
        // if cell is falling, proportionally offset towards next row
        if (IsFalling)
        {
            location.Y += (float)Math.Round((CELL_SIZE + CELL_PADDING) *
                (FallAge / FallRate));
        }

        // assume this is a normal cell
        Color tint = CellColors.Normal[ColorIndex];

        // flash clearing cells
        if (IsClearing)
        {
            // toggle color every time ClearFlashRate seconds pass by
            bool flash = (int)(m_ClearAge / ClearFlashRate) % 2 == 1;
            if (flash)
            {
                tint = Color.White;
```

```
                }
            }
            else if (dark)
            {
                // draw (unplayable) cells on the bottom row a little darker
                tint = CellColors.Dark[ColorIndex];
            }

            // actually draw the cell
            batch.Draw(
                Texture,
                location,
                texRect,
                tint);
        }
    }
}

// draw full cell in specified color, used by game over screen
public void Draw(SpriteBatch batch, Vector2 location, int color )
{
    batch.Draw(
        Texture,
        location,
        TextureRectCell,
        CellColors.Normal[color]);
}
```

DrawCursor

The DrawCursor method renders the cursor to the screen, based on its location within the grid. While not strictly a block function, the cursor is related to the block closely enough that it didn't merit its own class. This method is called from the GameBoard class.

```
// draw the cursor around the currently selected cells
public static void DrawCursor(SpriteBatch batch, Vector2 BoardTopLeft,
    Vector2 CursorPosition,double pulse)
{
    // create local copy of position to tweak, pulsing the X component
    Vector2 position = CursorPosition;

    // convert X index to screen coordinate
```

```
        position.X *= (CELL_SIZE + CELL_PADDING);
        // move cursor just to left of cell
        position.X -= TextureRectCursorLeft.Width;
        // pulse cursor
        position.X += (float)Math.Cos(2 * MathHelper.Pi * pulse);

        // round to the nearest pixel
        position.X = (int)Math.Round(position.X);
        position.Y = (int)Math.Round(position.Y);

        // draw left cursor
        batch.Draw(
            Texture,
            BoardTopLeft + position,
            TextureRectCursorLeft,
            Color.White);

        // reset X index
        position.X = CursorPosition.X + 2;
        // convert X index to screen coordinate
        position.X *= (CELL_SIZE + CELL_PADDING);
        // pulse cursor
        position.X -= (float)Math.Cos(2 * MathHelper.Pi * pulse) +
            CELL_PADDING;

        // round to the nearest pixel
        position.X = (int)Math.Round(position.X);
        position.Y = (int)Math.Round(position.Y);

        // draw right cursor
        batch.Draw(
            Texture,
            BoardTopLeft + position,
            TextureRectCursorRight,
            Color.White);
    }
```

Update

The Update method updates a block's state, based on the number of seconds that have elapsed since an animated state (like falling or clearing) began.

```
// update cell state, based on elapsed time (in seconds)
```

```
public void Update(double elapsed)
{
    // update clearing state
    if (IsClearing)
    {
        m_ClearAge += elapsed;
        if (m_ClearAge > ClearDuration)
        {
            // we're done, this cell is officially gone
            IsClearing = false;
            IsFalling = false;
            ColorIndex = CellColors.EmptyCellColorIndex;
        }
    }

    // update falling state
    if (IsFalling)
    {
        // falling is managed by GameBoard, just update the age here
        m_FallAge += elapsed;
    }
}
```

CellColors

The CellColors class is a simple helper class that manages the unique colors with which a block may be drawn. This class provides a method to generate a new random color from the pool of unique colors. It also provides a darker version of each normal block color.

The darker colors are used when rendering the bottom row of the grid. The last row is not playable, and the dark blocks provide a simple visual reminder. You fill the CellColors.Normal array with as many colors as you like. The CellColor class declares the Dark color array as static, and assigns its value from a static method (InitDarkCellColors), which automatically fills the Dark array with darker versions of the colors that you specified in the Normal array.

```
class CellColors
{
    // the normal game cell colors
    public static readonly Color[] Normal =
    {
```

```
            Color.Black,            // Empty Cell
            Color.DarkOrange,       // Orange
            Color.LawnGreen,        // Green
            Color.CornflowerBlue,   // Blue
            Color.Orchid,           // Purple
            Color.OrangeRed,        // Red
            Color.Gold,             // Yellow
    };

    public const int EmptyCellColorIndex = 0;

    // while a row is being added, it's only partially visible so that
    // the player can see what's coming up and he can plan a few
    // moves ahead. draw this preview row in a darker shade to set it
    // apart and let the player know that the row isn't playable just
    // yet. Rather than specifying another set of colors, we'll just
    // generate our darker shades from the list of "real" colors.
    public static Color[] Dark = InitDarkCellColors();

    // since this method is marked static, and it's being assigned
    // to a static member variable, you don't need to do anything to
    // make sure that this parallel array is initialized properly.
    // once this class is loaded from its assembly, this method will
    // be triggered, and the results will be stored in Dark[].
    private static Color[] InitDarkCellColors()
    {
        Dark = new Color[Normal.Length];
        for (int i = 0; i < Normal.Length; i++)
        {
            Dark[i] = new Color(
                (byte)(Normal[i].R / 2),
                (byte)(Normal[i].G / 2),
                (byte)(Normal[i].B / 2));
        }
        return Dark;
    }

    // helper to generate random numbers
    private static Random m_rand = new Random();

    // get the next random color index
    public static int RandomIndex()
        {
```

```
        return m_rand.Next(Normal.Length - 1) + 1;
    }
}
```

NumberSprite

Rather than using a full-blown font rendering class, this class is a simple helper that draws numbers on the screen. We'll use this class to render our scores. `NumberSprite` exposes a public, long property called `Value`. This is the number that will be rendered. Like the `Cell` class, the `NumberSprite` class stores its texture and texture rectangle data in a static variable so that it's accessible from all instances of the class. This texture must have a special layout. The `NumberSprite` class assumes that there are ten evenly spaced, single-digit numbers in the texture on a single row, in order from zero to nine. The `Draw()` method of this class renders each digit of `Value`, one by one.

One method of converting a long value into a series of human-readable bitmaps would be to repeatedly divide the number by 10, and use the remainder as an index into our list of digit bitmaps. This process would be pretty quick, but it would return the individual digits in reverse order. We'll be using another method for the code in this chapter.

Whenever the `Value` property is updated, the new value is compared to the existing value. If the value is changing, then we update the internal value (m_Value) and use the APIs in the .NET Framework to create the array of text characters that represent this number. Whenever we're ready to draw the number, we'll refer to this array of characters rather than the number. Each character can be converted to an index into our array of bitmaps by subtracting the '0' character literal. By caching the character array, we don't need to calculate it every time the number is drawn (every frame of the game). We only need to generate the character array when the value actually changes.

```
class NumberSprite
{
    // texture is shared across all instances (static)
    private static Texture2D m_Texture;
    private static Rectangle[] TextureRects = new Rectangle[10];
    public static Texture2D Texture
    {
        get { return m_Texture; }
        set
```

```
        {
            // set texture
            m_Texture = value;

            // texture is 10 evenly spaced numbers
            int widthChar = Texture.Width / 10;
            int heightChar = Texture.Height;
            for (int i = 0; i < 10; i++)
            {
                TextureRects[i] = new Rectangle(
                    i * widthChar,
                    0,
                    widthChar,
                    heightChar );
            }
        }
    }


// cache a copy of the last value to save some CPU cycles
private char[] m_ValueAsText = "0".ToCharArray();
private long m_Value = 0;
public long Value
{
    get { return m_Value; }
    set
    {
        if (m_Value != value)
        {
            m_Value = value;
            m_ValueAsText = value.ToString().ToCharArray();
        }
    }
}


// actually draw the number (using default White tint)
public void Draw(SpriteBatch batch, Vector2 position)
{
    Draw(batch, position, Color.White);
}


// actually draw the number
public void Draw(SpriteBatch batch, Vector2 position, Color tint)
{
```

```
    // draw the number, char-by-char, from cache
    for (int i = 0; i < m_ValueAsText.Length; i++)
    {
        int c = m_ValueAsText[i] -'0';
        batch.Draw(Texture, position, TextureRects[c], tint);
        position.X += TextureRects[c].Width;
    }
  }
}
```

Putting It All Together

Now that we've covered the rules of the game, and the basic division of labor across the game classes, we need to dive a little deeper into the details of the implementation.

Moving Blocks—GameBoard.SwapCells()

The SwapCells method swaps the contents of the two grid cells that are under the game cursor. There are a few cases where a swap cannot occur. You cannot move a block that is in the process of clearing, so the SwapCells method does nothing if either of the blocks has its IsClearing flag set. You cannot move a block that is in the process of falling, so the SwapCells method does nothing if either of the blocks has its IsFalling flag set. You cannot move a block into a cell that is about to be occupied by a falling block, so the SwapCells method does nothing if either cell has a falling block immediately above the cursor.

N o t e

Technically, the logic on the third condition is a little flawed since there is a fringe case where you may be swapping a valid block with an empty cell and the move would actually be moving a block out of the way of a falling block. This would be a legal move, but the SwapCells method would not allow it. In practice, this hasn't been an issue. Feel free to fix the logic if you like. I'm leaving the "bug" as is, since handling that fringe case would make the code more complex, and my goal is to illustrate the handling of the other 99.99% of valid game states.

If a block is moved over an empty cell, it needs to fall. So, the SwapCells method calls the Gravity method whenever a successful swap occurs. Since moving blocks can trigger a match, the SwapCells method also makes a call to the ScanForMatches method if any blocks were actually moved.

```
// swap the two cells that lie beneath the cursor
private void SwapCells()
```

```
{
    // temp variables to save some typing
    int x = (int)CursorPosition.X;
    int y = (int)CursorPosition.Y;

    // can't swap a cell that's being cleared ...
    bool OkToSwap = !m_Cells[x, y].IsClearing;
    OkToSwap&= !m_Cells[x + 1, y].IsClearing;

    // ... or falling ...
    OkToSwap&= !m_Cells[x, y].IsFalling;
    OkToSwap&= !m_Cells[x + 1, y].IsFalling;

    // ... or has a falling cell above it ...
    OkToSwap&= !(y > 0&& m_Cells[x, y - 1].IsFalling);
    OkToSwap&= !(y > 0&& m_Cells[x + 1, y - 1].IsFalling);

    // if conditions are met, swap it
    if (OkToSwap)
    {
        // swap cells that lie beneath the cursor
        Cell swap = m_Cells[x + 1, y];
        m_Cells[x + 1, y] = m_Cells[x, y];
        m_Cells[x, y] = swap;

        // check gravity right away so that player can't swap
        // a cell over an empty cell for a match.
        Gravity();

        // check for matches after a valid swap
        ScanForMatches();
    }
}
```

Falling Blocks—GameBoard.Gravity()

The Gravity method is responsible for making sure that we don't have any blocks hovering in mid-air. Whenever a block is removed from the grid, any blocks that were resting on it fall down to occupy the empty grid cells. Blocks don't just immediately pop from row to row; they appear to slowly fall into place. This is done by offsetting the Y location of the Cell texture over time as it's rendered.

Once the block has fallen far enough, it is actually moved to the next row, and the process begins again if the block is hovering over another empty grid cell.

```
// remove vertical gaps between cells
private void Gravity()
{
    // when a cell is done falling, it may trigger a match
    bool CheckForMatches = false;

    // scan each column
    for (int x = 0; x < BoardWidth; x++)
    {
        // scan reach row, from the 3rd-to-last row to the first.
        // cells on the last row can't fall, they're not even playable.
        // cells on the 2nd-to-last row can't fall, they're resting
        // on the last row.
        for (int y = BoardHeight - 3; y >= 0; y--)
        {
            // a handy temp variable to save some typing
            Cell cell1 = m_Cells[x, y + 0];

            // See if cell has fallen far enough to merit moving to
            // the next row
            if (cell1.FallAge >= cell1.FallRate)
            {
                // mark cell as done falling
                cell1.IsFalling = false;

                // when a cell is done falling, it may trigger a match
                CheckForMatches = true;

                // actually move the cell to the next row
                m_Cells[x, y + 1].Copy(cell1);
                m_Cells[x, y + 0].Reset();

                // process this row again, just to make sure we're not
                // triggering any false hits - since we set the
                // IsFalling flag to false, this cell is technically
                // available for a match, but it may not be completely
                // done falling. add two since we've already moved the
                // cell down a row
                y += 2;
            }
```

```
                    // is cell falling?
                    if (cell1.ColorIndex != CellColors.EmptyCellColorIndex)
                    {
                        // a handy temp variable to save some typing.
                        // cell immediately below the cell we're processing
                        Cell cell2 = m_Cells[x, y + 1];

                        // can fall if the cell bellow is empty ...
                        bool flag = cell2.ColorIndex ==
                            CellColors.EmptyCellColorIndex;

                        // ... or falling
                        flag |= cell2.IsFalling;

                        // but don't set a cell to fall if it's already
                        // falling since it will reset its state
                        // information (FallingAge, ...)
                        flag &= !cell1.IsFalling;

                        // ok, flag to fall if conditions are met
                        if (flag)
                        {
                            cell1.IsFalling = true;
                        }
                    }
                }
            }
        }

    if (CheckForMatches)
    {
        ScanForMatches();
    }
}
```

Since falling blocks change the state of the grid, we need to scan for matches any time a block comes to rest. The Gravity method looks for this condition, and triggers a scan for matches whenever it occurs.

Matching Cells—GameBoard.ScanForMatches

Whenever the state of the grid changes, a check for matching blocks is triggered. There are three basic ways that this state can be updated, and therefore three ways a scan for matches will be triggered: swapping blocks, falling blocks coming to rest, and adding a new row of blocks. Scanning for matched blocks is the responsibility of the ScanForMatches method.

The scan for matches happens in three passes. The first pass looks for three or more neighboring blocks on the same row.

```
private void ScanForMatches()
{
    // temp variables to save some typing
    bool valid = false;
    int cell1, cell2, cell3;

    // PASS ONE - Scan Horizontal
    for (int y = 0; y < BoardHeight - 1; y++) // for each row
    {
        for (int x = 2; x < BoardWidth; x++) // for each column
        {
            // grab the ColorIndex for the next 3 cells
            cell1 = m_Cells[x - 2, y].ColorIndex;
            cell2 = m_Cells[x - 1, y].ColorIndex;
            cell3 = m_Cells[x - 0, y].ColorIndex;

            // can't match if a cell is empty ...
            valid = cell1 != CellColors.EmptyCellColorIndex;

            // ... or is already being cleared ...
            valid &= !m_Cells[x - 2, y].IsClearing;
            valid &= !m_Cells[x - 1, y].IsClearing;
            valid &= !m_Cells[x - 0, y].IsClearing;

            // ... or is falling
            valid &= !m_Cells[x - 2, y].IsFalling;
            valid &= !m_Cells[x - 1, y].IsFalling;
            valid &= !m_Cells[x - 0, y].IsFalling;

            // if the conditions are met, mark the cells as
            // "to be cleared", and scan for more matches
            if (valid && cell1 == cell2 && cell2 == cell3)
            {
                m_Cells[x - 2, y].ColorIndex = -cell1;
                m_Cells[x - 1, y].ColorIndex = -cell1;
                m_Cells[x - 0, y].ColorIndex = -cell1;
```

```
                        x++;
                        while (x < BoardWidth &&
                            cell1 == m_Cells[x, y].ColorIndex)
                        {
                            m_Cells[x++, y].ColorIndex = -cell1;
                        }
                    }
                }
            }
```

Pass two looks for three or more neighboring blocks in the same column. During these first two passes, matches are marked by negating the ColorIndex of the matched blocks. The reason that we don't set the IsClearing flag for these blocks is that clearing blocks cannot be matched to their like-colored neighbors.

```
// PASS TWO - Scan Vertical
// in this pass, we need to check for the absolute value
// of the ColorIndex since we marked matched cells with
// a negative sign
for (int x = 0; x < BoardWidth; x++) // for each column
{
    for (int y = 2; y < BoardHeight - 1; y++) // for each row
    {
        // grab the ColorIndex for the next 3 cells
        cell1 = Math.Abs(m_Cells[x, y - 2].ColorIndex);
        cell2 = Math.Abs(m_Cells[x, y - 1].ColorIndex);
        cell3 = Math.Abs(m_Cells[x, y - 0].ColorIndex);

        // can't match if a cell is empty ...
        valid = cell1 != CellColors.EmptyCellColorIndex;

        // ... or is alredy being cleared ...
        valid &= !m_Cells[x, y - 2].IsClearing;
        valid &= !m_Cells[x, y - 1].IsClearing;
        valid &= !m_Cells[x, y - 0].IsClearing;

        // ... or is falling
        valid &= !m_Cells[x, y - 2].IsFalling;
        valid &= !m_Cells[x, y - 1].IsFalling;
        valid &= !m_Cells[x, y - 0].IsFalling;

        // if the conditions are met, mark the cells as
        // "to be cleared", and scan for more matches
```

```
        if (valid && cell1 == cell2 && cell2 == cell3)
        {
            m_Cells[x, y - 2].ColorIndex = -cell1;
            m_Cells[x, y - 1].ColorIndex = -cell1;
            m_Cells[x, y - 0].ColorIndex = -cell1;
            y++;
            while (y < BoardHeight - 1 &&
                cell1 == Math.Abs(m_Cells[x, y].ColorIndex))
            {
                m_Cells[x, y++].ColorIndex = -cell1;
            }
        }
    }
}
```

In the third (and final) pass, any color indices that are less than zero are actually flagged as IsClearing, and their ColorIndex is negated again (to restore it to its original state). This third pass is also responsible for calculating how much to add to the score.

```
// PASS THREE - Scan for Marked Matches
// the reason we do this in a separate pass is that immediately
// flagging a horizontal match would make those same cells
// unavailable for a vertical match

// track the number of unique colors matched
List<int> matchedColors = new List<int>();

// score this round of matches separately
long points = 0;

// scan for cells that have been flagged as matched
for (int y = 0; y < BoardHeight - 1; y++) // for each row
{
    for (int x = 0; x < BoardWidth; x++) // for each column
    {
        // negative color indices are matches
        if (m_Cells[x, y].ColorIndex < 0)
        {
            // reset color index so that it's valid, then
            // actually mark this cell as clearing
            int color = m_Cells[x, y].ColorIndex;
            m_Cells[x, y].ColorIndex = -color;
```

```
                m_Cells[x, y].IsClearing = true;

                // if this is a newly visited index, remember it
                if (!matchedColors.Contains(color))
                {
                    matchedColors.Add(color);
                }

                // update the local score
                points += BaseScore;
            }
        }
    }

    // multiply new score by the number of unique colors as
    // a simple combo bonus, then add it to the real score
    Score += points * matchedColors.Count;
}
```

Scoring

The player scores a set number of points (determined by the `GameBoard.BaseScore` property) for each block that he clears. If he's able to clear more than one color with a single swap or gravity event, then a combo bonus is awarded. The combo bonus is the number of unique colors involved in the match times the typical score that would be awarded for clearing the same number of blocks.

This makes the game more interesting because more advanced players can focus on scoring more points, whereas a new player might struggle just to clear the blocks fast enough to avoid a gruesome demise. There are more scoring options that you could implement to increase this game's replay-ability, and one of the exercises at the end of this chapter mentions one such option.

Summary

In this chapter, you learned how to manage the state of dozens of independent blocks. You processed player input from the keyboard and the game pad to manipulate the location of those blocks. And you provided simple, yet effective visual cues to the player to let him know when blocks were clearing, falling, or being added to the game grid. You also implemented a simple heads-up display to relay the current and high score to the player.

Review Questions

Think about what you've read in this chapter (and the included source code) to answer the following questions.

1. How do the blocks in this game appear to move independently of each other, even though there's only one game loop, only one `Cell.Draw` method, and only one `Cell.Update` method?

2. How does this game merge keyboard and game pad input so that the player can seamlessly use either to move the blocks?

3. How do the blocks in this game appear to slowly fall into place rather than simply "popping" from one row to the next?

4. How do the `Cell` and `NumberSprite` classes share textures and texture rectangle data across all instances?

Exercises

EXERCISE 1. To make the game a little more exciting, add some visual effects that activate when any of the top three rows are occupied. Add any or all of the following effects:

- Make the cursor pulse faster

- Flash or pulse the background color

- Make all of the blocks on the board "vibrate" by adding a random value between −1 and 1 to the X and Y location of each block whenever it's rendered

EXERCISE 2. Implement levels for this game. Whenever the player clears some predetermined number of blocks, increase the level number. Make any or all of the following changes when the player progresses to a new game level.

- Add a `NumberSprite` and corresponding label to let the player know what level he's on

- Change the background color

- Increase the `BaseScore` property

342 Chapter 15 ■ Puzzle Games

- Decrease the SecondsBeforeNewRow property

- Add one or more rows as the level changes

EXERCISE 3. The commercial game that inspired this chapter includes a compelling game play feature that this example lacks—chains. Whenever a falling block comes to rest, there's a chance that it will trigger another match with its new neighbors. In the original game, this resulted in a chain multiplier (similar to the combo multiplier that was implemented in this example). Add code that checks for a match just after a block comes to rest in the GameBoard.Gravity method. As long as any blocks are clearing or falling, keep track of the number of chains that the player has achieved, and multiply the local score by the chain count. Whenever all blocks in the grid are idle, reset the chain count.

EXERCISE 4. The original game had special types of blocks. Some of these blocks were larger than a single grid cell. One type of block could only be cleared when normal blocks were cleared next to it. Add a special block type to this example. Implement the block type that I mentioned here, or come up with your own.

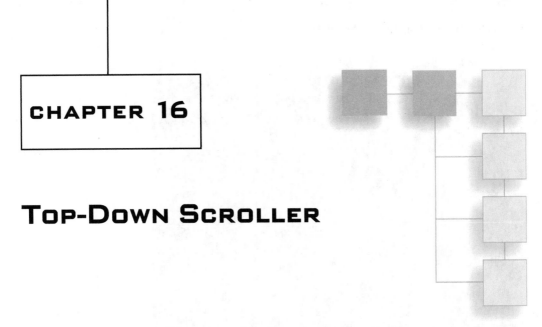

CHAPTER 16

Top-Down Scroller

In this chapter, we will develop a top-down scrolling shooter game. Two of the most popular games in this genre are *Xevious* (Namco, 1982) and *Raiden* (Seibu Kaihatsu, 1990). In these games, players pilot fighter jets and destroy enemy aircraft and ground vehicles. During the game, certain enemies will drop bonus items that increase the player's weapon systems or score. The end of game levels are typically marked with bosses (large, powerful opponents that the player must defeat before proceeding to the next level). To keep things simple, our game, shown in Figure 16.1, won't include some of the features found in these titles, like ground troops, bosses, or the ability to scar the terrain, but our game will capture the essence of the vertical scroller's game play.

In this chapter, you will learn how to:

- Load images to use in your game

- Manage the state of multiple on-screen game objects simultaneously

- Have game objects interact with each other

- Process user input to manipulate the state of game objects

- Track and display a player's score using a bitmap font

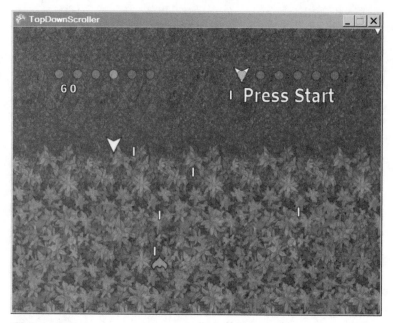

Figure 16.1
The example game for this chapter.

The Design

The game that we will develop in this chapter will have one enemy type, a fighter jet. The action will take place over a terrain that is randomly generated from tile images that include grass, gravel, stones, and trees. When destroyed, enemy aircraft will drop bonus items that the player can collect to increase his health, shields, weapons system, or score. For variety, the enemy fighters will follow one of six randomly selected paths.

Players

Players are restricted to the bottom two-thirds of the screen. Points are awarded for each downed enemy and score bonus (the blue star) collected. If the player is struck by an enemy bullet or collides with an enemy aircraft, he takes damage. Players start with three health points and three shield points. When the player takes a hit, a point is subtracted from his shield, if any shield points are available. If the player has no shield points, a point is subtracted from his health. If the player takes damage when he has no shield points and no health points, the game is over. The player gains health points and shield points by collecting the red and green bonus objects, respectively.

Player jets fire bullets. There is a preset delay between each round fired, but that delay is reduced whenever the player collects a weapons upgrade (the yellow star). If enough weapon system power-ups are collected, the delay between shots becomes zero and the player's fighter jet emits a continuous stream of bullets (reminiscent of those old-school vertical scrollers).

Enemies

There is only one type of enemy in this example, but that enemy appears with enough frequency and variety to keep the game play interesting. Enemy aircraft follow one of six predetermined paths. While moving along their chosen paths, the enemy fighters fire bullets towards the players at regular intervals. Unlike the player, a single shot will destroy an enemy. Once destroyed, the enemy drops a bonus which either player may collect.

Terrain

In most top-down scrollers, the terrain is made up of a predetermined set of tiles (small images placed side by side to form the overall landscape). To keep things simple in our example, the terrain will be randomly generated from a selection of tiles which transition between grass, trees, gravel, and stones. This method of terrain generation gives us an interesting backdrop for our game's action, but frees us from actually having to design game levels.

I was able to find some great, public-domain landscape tile images from an artist named Danc. Many thanks to Danc and other artists like him. His tiles allow for a lot more variety than the simple transitions that you'll see in our terrain. Be sure to check out his complete tile set on his blog:

http://www.lostgarden.com/2006/02/250-free-handdrawn-textures.html.

For simplicity, our game's terrain will consist of large patches of similar terrain, with transitions to and from grass tiles. By always returning to the "home base" of grass tiles, we don't need to account for smooth transitions between each of the different tile types. Ultimately, that means fewer tiles to store, load, and manage (see Figure 16.2).

Figure 16.2
The one and only texture for our game.

The Architecture

The code for this project is split into the following logical groups.

ScrollingBackground

The ScrollingBackground class manages the terrain. It randomly selects runs of tiles and smoothly transitions between each. When available, this class will draw variations of the selected tiles, side by side. That reduces the appearance of patterns in the tiles, and makes for a more natural-looking landscape. Each of the tiles in our background is 128 pixels by 128 pixels, so a grid of tiles that's five tiles wide and four tiles tall will cover our game screen, which is only 640 pixels by 480 pixels. We'll need an extra row at the top of the screen so that we can move the tiles down a little with each frame of the game to create the illusion that the player is traveling forward.

```
// tile sets fall into three categories:
//    Fill - tiles that are one type
//    ToGrass - tiles whose top half is grass
//    FromGrass - tiles whose bottom half is grass
protected List<Rectangle[]> m_FillTiles = new List<Rectangle[]>();
protected List<Rectangle[]> m_ToGrassTiles = new List<Rectangle[]>();
protected List<Rectangle[]> m_FromGrassTiles = new List<Rectangle[]>();

// initialize texture rects and fill tile array with grass tiles
public void InitTiles()
{
```

```
// init texture rects for the tiles
InitTilesHelper.InitFillTiles(m_FillTiles);
InitTilesHelper.InitToGrassTiles(m_ToGrassTiles);
InitTilesHelper.InitFromGrassTiles(m_FromGrassTiles);

// fill screen with grass
RowsOfCurrentTypeRemaining = 6;
CurrentType = 0;
NextRow();
NextRow();
NextRow();
NextRow();
NextRow();
NextRow();
}
```

To keep things simple, we'll always transition from and to grass tiles from other tile types. That way, we can keep the number of transitional tiles small, and the game logic will be simpler. Whenever a new set of tiles is selected, we'll randomly select a minimum and maximum number of rows of that type to display before returning to the grass tiles. That will make the terrain a little more interesting by varying the look of the landscape as we fly overhead.

```
// minimum number of rows that a tile type will be shown
protected int m_MinTypeLength = 5;
public int MinTypeLength
{
    get { return m_MinTypeLength; }
    set { m_MinTypeLength = value; }
}

// maximum number of rows that a tile type will be shown
protected int m_MaxTypeLength = 20;
public int MaxTypeLength
{
    get { return m_MaxTypeLength; }
    set { m_MaxTypeLength = value; }
}

// speed at which new rows are introduced (in seconds)
protected double m_RowsPerSecond = 0.75;
public double RowsPerSecond
{
```

```csharp
        get { return m_RowsPerSecond; }
        set { m_RowsPerSecond = value; }
    }

    // our "in-between" tile, all tiles transition from and to this type
    protected const int GRASS_TILE = 0;

    // how many rows of the current type remain?
    protected int RowsOfCurrentTypeRemaining = 0;

    // start with grass tiles
    protected int CurrentType = GRASS_TILE;

    // helper member to generate random numbers
    Random m_rand = new Random();

    // introduce a new row of tiles
    protected void NextRow()
    {
        // will ultimately point to the textures for the next row's tiles
        Rectangle[] sourceRects;

        // is it time to pick a new tile type?
        if (RowsOfCurrentTypeRemaining == 0)
        {
            // randomly pick the next tile type
            int nextType = m_rand.Next(m_FillTiles.Count - 1) + 1;
            if (Game1.GameOver || CurrentType != GRASS_TILE)
            {
                // if the game is over or the current tile isn't grass,
                // the next tile type should be grass
                nextType = GRASS_TILE;
            }

            if (!Game1.GameOver)
            {
                // how many rows of this new type will we display?
                RowsOfCurrentTypeRemaining = MinTypeLength +
                    m_rand.Next(MaxTypeLength - MinTypeLength);
            }

            if (CurrentType == GRASS_TILE)
            {
```

```
            // we're transitioning away from grass tiles
            sourceRects = m_FromGrassTiles[nextType];
        }
        else
        {
            // we're transitioning to grass tiles
            sourceRects = m_ToGrassTiles[CurrentType];
        }
        CurrentType = nextType;
    }
    else
    {
        // it's not time for a new tile, create next from
        // the existing tiles
        sourceRects = m_FillTiles[CurrentType];
    }

    // our "first row" index moves through the tile rects array
    // that way, we don't need to keep moving the existing tiles
    // in the array as they move down the screen, we just point
    // to a new "first row".
    FirstRowIndex = (FirstRowIndex + 1) % 6;

    // fill the new row with our new tiles
    for (int x = 0; x < 5; x++)
    {
        m_TileRects[x, FirstRowIndex] =
            // randomly select a tile from the available source tiles
            sourceRects[m_rand.Next(sourceRects.Length)];
    }

    // decrement the "rows remaining" count
    RowsOfCurrentTypeRemaining -= 1;

    // if we're done with this tile type, get ready for a new type
    if (RowsOfCurrentTypeRemaining < 0)
    {
        RowsOfCurrentTypeRemaining = 0;
    }
}

// time in seconds spent on the current row, when this
// value exceeds RowsPerSecond, it's time for a new row
```

```
protected double TimeSpentOnCurrentRow = 0;

// keep track of how long we've been on the current row,
// generate a new row when it's time
public void Update(double elapsed)
{
    TimeSpentOnCurrentRow += elapsed;
    if (TimeSpentOnCurrentRow >= RowsPerSecond)
    {
        TimeSpentOnCurrentRow -= RowsPerSecond;
        NextRow();
    }
}
```

If we actually moved the tiles down as they enter and exit the screen, we would be constantly moving tiles around in our internal data structure. To avoid that, we'll keep track of the row index within our grid that represents the top-most row of tiles that will be drawn. Then we can move through our array, row by row, looping back to the actual first row of the array (the one with an index of zero) whenever we increment our row pointer beyond the last row of the array.

```
// helper to save a little typing
public static readonly Rectangle EmptyRect = Rectangle.Empty;

// index into m_TileRects array, first row
protected int FirstRowIndex = 0;

// the tiles that are currently on the screen
protected Rectangle[,] m_TileRects = new Rectangle[5,6]
{
    {EmptyRect, EmptyRect, EmptyRect, EmptyRect, EmptyRect, EmptyRect },
    {EmptyRect, EmptyRect, EmptyRect, EmptyRect, EmptyRect, EmptyRect },
    {EmptyRect, EmptyRect, EmptyRect, EmptyRect, EmptyRect, EmptyRect },
    {EmptyRect, EmptyRect, EmptyRect, EmptyRect, EmptyRect, EmptyRect },
    {EmptyRect, EmptyRect, EmptyRect, EmptyRect, EmptyRect, EmptyRect },
};
```

Since we keep incrementing our row index as we add new rows, we will need to draw our rows in reverse order. Why? The top row on the screen is represented by our "first row" index. The previously added row is the one just before that row, and the second-most previous row lies two rows above the first row. As we progress backward in our array, each row represents the tiles that were added just before the row below. When we draw those rows on the screen, though, we want earlier rows to appear below later rows. So, we need to render the rows in reverse order.

```
// draw all the tiles
public void Draw(SpriteBatch batch)
{
    // position to draw each tile
    Vector2 pos = Vector2.Zero;

    // offset from top, based on time the
    // current row has been on the screen
    double dy = (TimeSpentOnCurrentRow / RowsPerSecond) * 128.0 - 256.0;

    // for each row of tiles
    for (int y = 0; y < 6; y++)
    {
        // y location of this row, in pixels
        pos.Y = (float)((6 - y) * 128.0 + dy);

        // index into m_TileRects array for this row
        int row = (FirstRowIndex + y) % 6;

        // for each column of tiles
        for (int x = 0; x < 5; x++)
        {
            // x location of this tile, in pixels
            pos.X = x * 128;

            // actually draw the current tile
            batch.Draw(Game1.Texture, pos,
                m_TileRects[x, row], Color.White);
        }
    }
}
```

InitTilesHelper

The InitTilesHelper is a simple helper class that tells the ScrollingBackground where to find each terrain tile in the master game texture.

```
// simple helper class to note where each
// tile lives in the master game texture
```

```
public class InitTilesHelper
{
    public static void InitFillTiles(List<Rectangle[]> list)
    {
        list.Clear();
        list.Add(m_GrassRects);
        list.Add(m_TreeRects);
        list.Add(m_RockRects);
        list.Add(m_StoneRects);
    }

    public static void InitToGrassTiles(List<Rectangle[]> list)
    {
        list.Clear();
        list.Add(m_GrassRects); // cheat, same tiles
        list.Add(m_TreeRectsToGrass);
        list.Add(m_RockRectsToGrass);
        list.Add(m_StoneRectsToGrass);
    }

    public static void InitFromGrassTiles(List<Rectangle[]> list)
    {
        list.Clear();
        list.Add(m_GrassRects); // cheat, same tiles
        list.Add(m_TreeRectsFromGrass);
        list.Add(m_RockRectsFromGrass);
        list.Add(m_StoneRectsFromGrass);
    }

    private static Rectangle[] m_GrassRects =
    {
        new Rectangle(000,000,128,128),
        new Rectangle(128,000,128,128),
        new Rectangle(256,000,128,128),
        new Rectangle(384,000,128,128),
    };

    private static Rectangle[] m_TreeRects =
    {
        new Rectangle(000,128,128,128),
        new Rectangle(128,128,128,128),
        new Rectangle(256,128,128,128),
        new Rectangle(384,128,128,128),
```

```
    new Rectangle(512,128,128,128),
    new Rectangle(640,128,128,128),
    new Rectangle(768,128,128,128),
};

private static Rectangle[] m_TreeRectsToGrass =
{
    new Rectangle(512,000,128,128),
};

private static Rectangle[] m_TreeRectsFromGrass =
{
    new Rectangle(256,256,128,128),
};

private static Rectangle[] m_RockRects =
{
    new Rectangle(000,256,128,128),
    new Rectangle(128,256,128,128),
};

private static Rectangle[] m_RockRectsToGrass =
{
    new Rectangle(640,000,128,128),
    new Rectangle(768,000,128,128),
};

private static Rectangle[] m_RockRectsFromGrass =
{
    new Rectangle(384,256,128,128),
    new Rectangle(256,384,128,128),
};

private static Rectangle[] m_StoneRects =
{
    new Rectangle(000,384,128,128),
    new Rectangle(128,384,128,128),
};

private static Rectangle[] m_StoneRectsToGrass =
{
    new Rectangle(896,000,128,128),
};
```

```
    private static Rectangle[] m_StoneRectsFromGrass =
    {
        new Rectangle(384,384,128,128),
    };
}
```

GameSprite

Player ships, enemy ships, bullets, bonus stars, and splats are represented in code by subclasses of the GameSprite class. This class is just a simple wrapper for the most common state data that you need to maintain when managing your on-screen game objects.

Among others, the properties of this class include the location, source texture, texture rectangle, and color of the sprite. Grouping these properties into a single object makes life a lot easier when you want to pass sprites between methods or store them in an array. Also included within this class is the logic to restrict the sprite's movement. For example, the player is restricted to the bottom two-thirds of the screen.

```
// define the bounds of the game sprite instance,
// Rectangle.Empty indicates no bounds checking
protected Rectangle m_ScreenBounds = Rectangle.Empty;
public Rectangle ScreenBounds
{
    get { return m_ScreenBounds; }
    set { m_ScreenBounds = value; }
}

// get and set the on-screen location of the game sprite
protected Vector2 m_Location = Vector2.Zero;
public Vector2 Location
{
    get { return m_Location; }
    set
    {
        // account for ScreenBounds, if any
        m_Location = value;
        if (ScreenBounds != Rectangle.Empty)
        {
            if (m_Location.X < ScreenBounds.Left)
```

```
            {
                m_Location.X = ScreenBounds.Left;
            }
            else if (
                m_Location.X + TextureRect.Width > ScreenBounds.Right)
            {
                m_Location.X = ScreenBounds.Right - TextureRect.Width;
            }
            if (m_Location.Y < ScreenBounds.Top)
            {
                m_Location.Y = ScreenBounds.Top;
            }
            else if (
                m_Location.Y + TextureRect.Height > ScreenBounds.Bottom)
            {
                m_Location.Y = ScreenBounds.Bottom - TextureRect.Height;
            }
        }
    }
}

// the texture rectangle for this sprite's image
protected Rectangle m_TextureRect = Rectangle.Empty;
public Rectangle TextureRect
{
    get { return m_TextureRect; }
    set { m_TextureRect = value; }
}

// the tint for this sprite
protected Color m_Color = Color.White;
public Color Color
{
    get { return m_Color; }
    set { m_Color = value; }
}

// indicates whether this sprite is on the screen or not
protected bool m_IsActive = false;
public bool IsActive
{
    get { return m_IsActive; }
    set { m_IsActive = value; }
```

```
}

// velocity of this sprite
protected double m_MovePixelsPerSecond = 100;
public double MovePixelsPerSecond
{
    get { return m_MovePixelsPerSecond; }
    set { m_MovePixelsPerSecond = value; }
}

// helper for sprites to generate random numbers
protected static Random m_rand = new Random();
```

GameSprite instances are responsible for updating and drawing themselves. They keep track of their age so that they can manage their internal state data (like delays between shots, when to stop drawing themselves, and so on).

```
protected double TotalElapsed = 0;
public virtual void Update(double elapsed)
{
    TotalElapsed += elapsed;
}

// draw this sprite on the screen, if it's active
public virtual void Draw(SpriteBatch batch)
{
    if (IsActive)
    {
        batch.Draw(Game1.Texture, Location, TextureRect, Color);
    }
}
```

Shared Data

Since all sprites in this game use the same texture, I created a static property to expose the texture that's stored in the Game1 class. All GameSprite instances refer to the same source texture. Each has its own texture rectangle (which defines the location of the sprite's pixels within the larger texture), but all GameSprite instances share a single reference to the one and only game texture.

```
// point back to the one and only game texture
public Texture2D TextureData
{
```

```
    get { return Game1.Texture; }
    set { }
}
```

Each sprite is responsible for maintaining its own opacity data as well. Since the opacity data is different for each category of sprite, sharing a common reference isn't an option. There can be dozens of sprites on the screen at the same time. Storing that data within the base class (GameSprite) or within the host game (Game1) means that there's only one copy, but we need a separate copy of that data for each subclass of the GameSprite base class.

Of course, it doesn't make much sense to duplicate the opacity data across every instance either. Storing that data as a member variable with each instance means that every instance of a subclass (like Bullet) will need to maintain its own copy.

The happy medium here was to create an abstract property on the base class (GameSprite), which returns the value of a static member variable that is contained in each subclass. Each subclass (like Bullet, Enemy, or Bonus) is then required (by the compiler) to manage its own copy of the data, but all instances of the same subclass share a single data reference.

```
// declare this property abstract so that
// the derived game sprites can store their
// own pixel-perfect data as a static member
// (shared across instances of the same class)
// if we declare the static member here, it's
// shared across all subclasses, if we declare
// the member here as non-static, there will be
// a copy of the data (and a call to the helper)
// for each instance of a game sprite (hundreds)
public abstract bool[,] OpaqueData
{
    get;
    set;
}
```

NumberSprite

This isn't the first time we've used the NumberSprite class in an example. The NumberSprite class is the lazy man's bitmap font. It provides a simple way to store and render our player scores.

HUD

Current player scores, high scores, shield indicators, health indicators, and the "press start" prompt are all managed by the HUD (heads-up display) class.

```
public class HUD
{
    // texture rectangles for the HUD (heads-up display) components
    protected static Rectangle m_RectPressStart =
        new Rectangle(544, 320, 160, 32);
    protected static Rectangle m_RectHealth =
        new Rectangle(672, 288, 32, 32);
    protected static Rectangle m_RectShield = m_RectHealth;

    // flash between score and "press start" if player's game is over
    protected bool FlashState = true;
    protected double TotalElapsed = 0;
    protected double m_PromptFlashInterval = 1.5;
    public double PromptFlashInterval
    {
        get { return m_PromptFlashInterval; }
        set { m_PromptFlashInterval = value; }
    }

    // update the flash state of the "press start" prompt
    public void Update(double elapsed)
    {
        TotalElapsed += elapsed;
        if (TotalElapsed > PromptFlashInterval)
        {
            TotalElapsed = 0;
            FlashState = !FlashState;
        }
    }

    // actually draw the HUD
    public void Draw(SpriteBatch batch, Player player)
    {
        // top, left of the three health lights
        Vector2 locHealthHUD = player.HudPosition;

        // top, left of the three shield lights
        Vector2 locShieldHUD = player.HudPosition;
```

```
locShieldHUD.X += 3 * 32;

// top, left of the score text and "press start" prompt
Vector2 locPressStart = player.HudPosition;
locPressStart.X += 16;
locPressStart.Y += 32;

if (FlashState && !player.IsActive)
{
    // alternate between score and prompt,
    // as long as player's game is over
    batch.Draw(Game1.Texture, locPressStart,
        m_RectPressStart, Color.White);
}
else
{
    // if player is active, draw his score every time
    player.NumberSprite.Draw(batch, locPressStart);
}

// render the health and shield lights
for (int i = 0; i < 3; i++)
{
    // render the shield lights
    if (player.Shield > i && player.IsActive)
    {
        // active! draw green light
        batch.Draw(Game1.Texture, locShieldHUD,
            m_RectShield, Color.PaleGreen);
    }
    else
    {
        // inactive, draw dim light
        batch.Draw(Game1.Texture, locShieldHUD,
            m_RectShield, Color.LightSlateGray);
    }

    // render the health lights
    if (player.Health > i && player.IsActive)
    {
        // active! draw red light
        batch.Draw(Game1.Texture, locHealthHUD,
            m_RectHealth, Color.LightCoral);
```

```
                    }
                    else
                    {
                        // inactive, draw dim light
                        batch.Draw(Game1.Texture, locHealthHUD,
                            m_RectHealth, Color.LightSlateGray);
                    }

                    // move to the next light's location
                    locShieldHUD.X += 32;
                    locHealthHUD.X += 32;
                }
            }
        }
```

GameObjectManager

Rather than creating game objects when they're needed, and destroying them when we're done, this class manages a pool of objects that can be activated and deactivated as needed. This means that we can create fewer objects, and (in theory), our game should be less demanding of the CLR Garbage Collector.

This class is also responsible for updating and rendering every game object, as well as handling the collision checks for us. I won't list the entire class here. Please see the complete source on the CD-ROM that came with this book.

```
// update all game objects, check for collisions
public static void Update(double elapsed)
{
    // update all game objects
    UpdateBullets(elapsed);
    UpdateBonuses(elapsed);
    UpdateEnemies(elapsed);
    UpdateSplats(elapsed);

    // check for collisions
    CheckForHitEnemies();
    CheckForHitBonuses(Game1.m_PlayerOne);
    CheckForHitBonuses(Game1.m_PlayerTwo);
    CheckForHitPlayer(Game1.m_PlayerOne);
    CheckForHitPlayer(Game1.m_PlayerTwo);
}
```

```
// draw all active game objects
public static void Draw(SpriteBatch batch)
{
    DrawBullets(batch);
    DrawBonuses(batch);
    DrawEnemies(batch);
    DrawSplats(batch);
}
```

PixelPerfectHelper

I cover the PixelPerfectHelper class in more detail in Chapter 28, "Pixel-Perfect Collision Detection." This class provides several static methods that detect collisions between sprites for you with pixel-perfect accuracy by comparing the opaque pixels of each sprite's texture data.

Player Input

Player one can use the keyboard or a controller. Player two must use a controller. Players avoid enemy bullets, destroy enemy fighters, and collect power-ups to increase their score and prolong the game.

The code that handles player input is contained within the ProcessInput method. ProcessInput has three overloads: one to process GamePadState, one to process KeyboardState, and a third to manage the other two. The third overload is responsible for actually collecting the input data and handing it off to the other two overloaded methods for processing.

```
public void ProcessInput(double elapsed)
{
    GamePadState pad1 = GamePad.GetState(PlayerIndex.One);
    GamePadState pad2 = GamePad.GetState(PlayerIndex.Two);
    KeyboardState key = Keyboard.GetState();
    ProcessInput(elapsed, m_PlayerOne, pad1);
    ProcessInput(elapsed, m_PlayerOne, key);
    ProcessInput(elapsed, m_PlayerTwo, pad2);
}
```

Controller Input

There are two overloaded versions of the ProcessInput method. The first, described here, processes input from the controller. The other, described in the

next section, processes keyboard input. This method is responsible for starting a
new game, moving the player's ship, and firing bullets from the player's ship.

```
// handle game pad input
public void ProcessInput(double elapsed, Player player, GamePadState pad)
{
    if (!player.IsActive && pad.Buttons.Start == ButtonState.Pressed)
    {
        // start or join the game
        player.Init();
        player.IsActive = true;
    }
    else if (player.IsActive)
    {
        // change in location
        Vector2 delta = Vector2.Zero;

        // moving left or right?
        if (pad.ThumbSticks.Left.X < 0)
        {
            delta.X = (float)(-player.MovePixelsPerSecond * elapsed);
        }
        else if (pad.ThumbSticks.Left.X > 0)
        {
            delta.X = (float)(player.MovePixelsPerSecond * elapsed);
        }

        // moving up or down?
        if (pad.ThumbSticks.Left.Y > 0)
        {
            delta.Y = (float)(-player.MovePixelsPerSecond * elapsed);
        }
        else if (pad.ThumbSticks.Left.Y < 0)
        {
            delta.Y = (float)(player.MovePixelsPerSecond * elapsed);
        }

        // actually move the player
        player.Location += delta;

        // if the player is pressing the action
        // button, try to fire a bullet
        if (pad.Buttons.A == ButtonState.Pressed && player.Fire())
```

```
        {
            GameObjectManager.AddBullet(player, true);
        }
    }
}
```

Keyboard Input

This is the other overloaded `ProcessInput` method. Like its controller-based counterpart, this method is responsible for starting a new game, moving the player's ship, and firing bullets from the player's ship.

```
// handle player input from the keyboard
public void ProcessInput(double elapsed, Player player, KeyboardState key)
{
    if (!player.IsActive && key.IsKeyDown(Keys.Enter))
    {
        // start or join the game
        player.Init();
        player.IsActive = true;
    }
    else if (player.IsActive)
    {
        // change in location
        Vector2 delta = Vector2.Zero;

        // moving left or right?
        if (key.IsKeyDown(Keys.Left))
        {
            delta.X = (float)(-player.MovePixelsPerSecond * elapsed);
        }
        else if (key.IsKeyDown(Keys.Right))
        {
            delta.X = (float)(player.MovePixelsPerSecond * elapsed);
        }

        // moving up or down?
        if (key.IsKeyDown(Keys.Up))
        {
            delta.Y = (float)(-player.MovePixelsPerSecond * elapsed);
        }
        else if (key.IsKeyDown(Keys.Down))
        {
```

```
            delta.Y = (float)(player.MovePixelsPerSecond * elapsed);
        }

        // actually move the player
        player.Location += delta;

        // if the player is pressing the action
        // button, try to fire a bullet
        if (key.IsKeyDown(Keys.Space) && player.Fire())
        {
            GameObjectManager.AddBullet(player, true);
        }
    }
}
}
```

Summary

In this chapter, you learned how to load and manage multiple on-screen sprites. You also learned how to manage the state of player-controlled objects. And you learned how to detect collisions between those sprites and take some action whenever a collision occurs. You also saw how to use simple, tiled graphics to create an interesting backdrop on which your game action can play out.

Review Questions

Think about what you've read in this chapter (and the included source code) to answer the following questions.

1. This example covers the basic features of its genre that make similar games fun to play. What features are missing from this example? Discuss the changes that you would implement to make this game more enjoyable. Explain your decisions.

2. How does this game provide support for both keyboards and game pads?

3. How are game objects managed within this game? Where do new objects come from? How are unused game objects removed from the screen?

4. How is the scrolling background implemented in this example? What design decisions were made to simplify the code required to generate and animate this game's terrain?

5. How many instances of the game texture are in memory at any one time? How many instances of each game object's opacity data are in memory at any one time? How many instances of each game object's location data are in memory at any one time?

Exercises

EXERCISE 1. Give the player a visual cue so that he can more quickly determine which path an enemy ship is following. Tint each ship according to its path. Use at least three different colors (the six enemy paths are actually derived from three mirrored paths).

EXERCISE 2. This game is begging for some audio. If you need to, review Chapter 10, "Using XNA Audio." Play the laser sound effect from that chapter whenever the player or enemy fires a shot. Find some sounds on the web to play when a ship is destroyed, and when a player collects a bonus star.

If you're having trouble locating suitable sounds, pick two from your C:\Windows\media directory on your Windows XP-based development PC. The chimes.wav sounds might be a good candidate for collecting bonus stars, and recycle.wav might sound good as a destroyed ship sound.

EXERCISE 3. Use more of the tiles from Danc's collection to create more elaborate transitions between tile types. Rather than transitioning from one tile set to another in a single row, spread the transition over multiple rows so that the edges between terrain zones aren't a straight line.

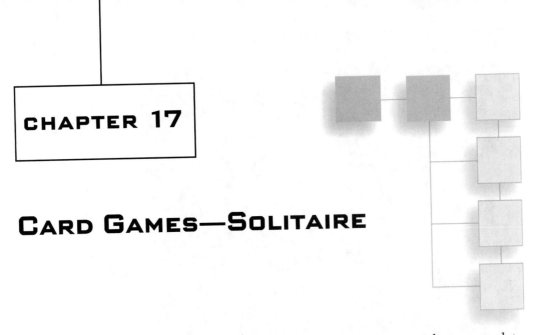

CHAPTER 17

CARD GAMES—SOLITAIRE

Before the invention of the computer and the television, people managed to entertain themselves with puzzle games, board games, and card games. There are literally hundreds of different card games, and each can be a great source of inspiration for your new computer game. My personal favorite is poker, due mainly to the social and competitive aspects of that game. My poker buddies and I will talk about a great hand weeks after it's been played. I would love to have used the game of poker for the example in this book, but I didn't have time to do it justice. To keep things simple, we'll cover another immensely popular card game—Solitaire.

Solitaire is a single-player game (assuming, of course, that you don't count other people looking over your shoulder and criticizing your moves as participating in the game). The origin of Solitaire isn't certain. It was popular in England centuries ago, when it went by the name "Patience." Some early British texts refer to a French variation of Patience, so many believe that Solitaire may have originated in France. Game historians have pretty much eliminated Japan as the country of origin for this game since it wasn't originally entitled "Super Happy Fun Solo Card Supreme."

Figure 17.1 shows the Solitaire game we will develop in this chapter.

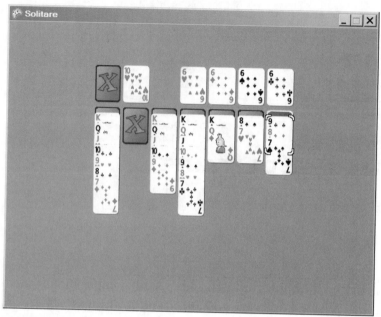

Figure 17.1
Our version of Solitaire.

In this chapter, you will learn how to:

- Logically group related tasks into game objects that represent real-world objects

- Manage the state of multiple on-screen game objects simultaneously

- Process user input to manipulate the state of game objects

Game Rules

Solitaire lacks the social interaction of other card games, but it has a simple rule set and an element of strategy that make its game play rather addictive. Solitaire is played using a standard deck of 52 playing cards. The cards are shuffled, and then dealt into seven stacks. The first stack is dealt one card, face up. Then the remaining stacks each receive one card, face down. The deal continues, starting with the second stack, which receives one card, face up. And the remaining stacks (save the first) are each dealt a card, face down. This continues until each stack has a single, face-up card and as many as six face-down cards under the top card. I'll refer to each of the face-up cards in these seven stacks as the start of the "chute," and the face-down cards as the "stack stock."

Once the chutes have been dealt, the remaining cards are placed, face down, into a single pile of cards known as the "stockpile." The cards in this pile may be moved, one at a time, into a pile next to the stockpile known as the "waste" pile. When the stockpile is empty, all of the cards in the waste pile are placed back into the stockpile, face down. The player can use cards in the waste pile, as well as any face-up cards in any of the seven chutes. If a face-up card is moved from one chute to another, and the move exposes a face-down card, that card is turned up and becomes the new start of the chute. As face-up cards are added to a chute, they're arranged in a cascade so that the player can see the rank and suit of each card in the chute.

A card can only be placed into a chute if its rank is one less than the lowest card in the chute and it has the opposite suit color of the lowest card in the chute. If any of the seven chutes is empty, then a king may be moved to that chute. When moving cards between chutes, groups of cards may be moved in a single turn as long as none of the other rules are violated. For example, if you have chute with cards ranked seven to two, and a chute with cards ranked king to eight, you can move all of the face-up cards from the first chute to the second (assuming that the suits of the eight and seven have opposite colors).

There are four other card piles in Solitaire, one for each suit. I refer to these as the "home" piles. Cards may be placed into a home pile if their rank is one greater than the top card in the pile. The first card that may be added to a home pile is the ace of that suit. The game is over when all four home piles have a king as their top card (implying that all of the other game piles are empty), or when there are no more legal moves.

Card Images

Game graphics are important. Player expectations are high, and first impressions really matter. My focus for the examples in this book is to create games that demonstrate the concepts of the chapter that contains them, but I have made an attempt to apply basic user interface design principles so that the examples are visually interesting. After several failed attempts to create my own halfway-decent card images, I found a great set of card images on the web that an artist had placed into the public domain. There are other card images out there, but I liked Nicu Buculei's work the best. They're very clean and very modern. His playing card images can be found on the openclipart.org website. Before I could use Nicu's playing card images in this chapter's example, I needed to scale his original artwork down to half its normal size. (So don't judge the quality of Nicu's work based solely on the version of the images that you find in the sample.)

Converting the Source Artwork

The images in Nicu's collection are distributed as 64 separate files (52 cards, 2 jokers, and 10 card backs). There are four variations on his playing card theme, so the grand total comes to 256 files. Those images are distributed in the SVG format (an xml-based vector format popular in many open-source and commercial graphics tools). Since XNA doesn't support SVG, we'll need to convert them to a format that XNA can use. Also, dealing with 256 separate textures in our code would be inefficient, and managing and maintaining those textures would be cumbersome. We'll need to create a single image for each card set (4 card sets as 4 textures, with 64 images arranged on each texture). While I could have done this work by hand using my image editing software, I decided to write a custom Windows tool to automatically generate the composite image (as a PNG) from all of the source images (see Figure 17.2). I won't go into detail on how the tool was created, but the source for the tool is included along with the example code for this chapter.

To resize the source images and convert them to PNG files, I used the batch conversion tool that came with my graphics editor. I also created an image for the cursor that indicates which chute the player is currently manipulating. From that point, I used my custom tool to create the master PNG image from all those source images. Writing the tool was a great investment. During the development of this chapter's example code, I had to tweak the master image several times. Using the tool saved me time during the design phase, and provided consistent results for each of the resulting textures by eliminating my opportunities to introduce errors into the layout.

The Architecture

This chapter's example code tries to mimic an actual physical game. There is an object for each card in the deck. Cards are grouped together into a collection known as CardContainer. The main card container is the deck where cards are shuffled and from which they are dealt. Other card containers are used to represent the various piles of cards that lie on the table when you play a real game of Solitaire.

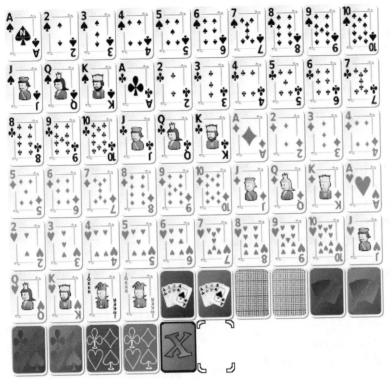

Figure 17.2
The composite game image, as created by the custom tool.

CardBack Class

This class manages a list of texture rectangles that point into the game's main texture. These rectangles contain the images that are displayed on the back of the cards. The player can change the look of the card backs by pressing the Page Up or Page Down buttons on the keyboard, or by using the shoulder buttons on the controller.

```
public static class CardBack
{
    // list of all available card backs
    private static List<Rectangle> m_TextureRects = new List<Rectangle>();
    public static void ClearTextureRects() { m_TextureRects.Clear(); }
    public static void AddTextureRect(Rectangle rect)
        { m_TextureRects.Add(rect); }
```

```
    // which card back image is active?
    private static int m_BackIndex = 0;
    public static int BackIndex
    {
        get { return m_BackIndex; }
        set { m_BackIndex = value; }
    }


    // select the next image
    public static void NextCardBack()
    {
        BackIndex += 1;
        if (BackIndex >= m_TextureRects.Count)
        {
            BackIndex = 0;
        }
    }


    // select the previous image
    public static void PreviousCardBack()
    {
        BackIndex -= 1;
        if (BackIndex < 0)
        {
            BackIndex = m_TextureRects.Count - 1;
        }
    }


    // useful for card back animations, unused in this game
    public static void Update(double elapsed)
    {
    }


    // actually draw the card back
    public static void Draw(SpriteBatch batch, Vector2 position)
    {
        batch.Draw(GameLogic.Texture, position,
            m_TextureRects[BackIndex], Color.White);
    }
}
```

Card Class

The Card class contains the property information for a single playing card. This information includes the texture rectangle into the main game texture for this card instance, the card's suit, the card's rank, and whether the card is face up (player can see the card face) or face down (player isn't allowed to see the card face). In addition to this instance data, the Card class also manages several static properties and methods for the game. These static members are responsible for performing routine tasks like drawing "empty" cards (placeholders when no card instance is specified), drawing the jokers, and drawing an animated cursor around cards that the player has selected.

```
public class Card
{
    // the texture rect for this card instance
    protected Rectangle m_TextureRect;
    public Rectangle TextureRect
    {
        get { return m_TextureRect; }
        set { m_TextureRect = value; }
    }

    // the graphic to display when container holds no cards
    protected static Rectangle m_TextureRectEmpty;
    public static Rectangle TextureRectEmpty
    {
        get { return m_TextureRectEmpty; }
        set { m_TextureRectEmpty = value; }
    }

    // texture rect for the red joker (not used in this game)
    protected static Rectangle m_TextureRectRedJoker;
    public static Rectangle TextureRectRedJoker
    {
        get { return m_TextureRectRedJoker; }
        set { m_TextureRectRedJoker = value; }
    }

    // texture rect for the black joker (not used in this game)
    protected static Rectangle m_TextureRectBlackJoker;
    public static Rectangle TextureRectBlackJoker
    {
```

```
        get { return m_TextureRectBlackJoker; }
        set { m_TextureRectBlackJoker = value; }
    }


    // top left of cursor
    protected static Rectangle m_TextureRectCursorNW;
    public static Rectangle TextureRectCursorNW
    {
        get { return m_TextureRectCursorNW; }
        set { m_TextureRectCursorNW = value; }
    }


    // top right of cursor
    protected static Rectangle m_TextureRectCursorNE;
    public static Rectangle TextureRectCursorNE
    {
        get { return m_TextureRectCursorNE; }
        set { m_TextureRectCursorNE = value; }
    }


    // bottom right of cursor
    protected static Rectangle m_TextureRectCursorSE;
    public static Rectangle TextureRectCursorSE
    {
        get { return m_TextureRectCursorSE; }
        set { m_TextureRectCursorSE = value; }
    }


    // bottom left of cursor
    protected static Rectangle m_TextureRectCursorSW;
    public static Rectangle TextureRectCursorSW
    {
        get { return m_TextureRectCursorSW; }
        set { m_TextureRectCursorSW = value; }
    }


    // the size of a single card
    protected static Vector2 m_CardSize = new Vector2(47, 64);
    public static Vector2 CardSize
    {
        get { return m_CardSize; }
        set { m_CardSize = value; }
    }
```

```csharp
// display the chutes so that you can read each card
protected static Vector2 m_CascadeOffset = new Vector2(0, 18);
public static Vector2 CascadeOffset
{
    get { return m_CascadeOffset; }
    set { m_CascadeOffset = value; }
}

// the face values of the standard cards
public enum RANKS
{
    Ace,
    Deuce,
    Three,
    Four,
    Five,
    Six,
    Seven,
    Eight,
    Nine,
    Ten,
    Jack,
    Queen,
    King,
    Joker,
}

// the rank of this card instance
protected RANKS m_Rank;
public RANKS Rank
{
    get { return m_Rank; }
    set { m_Rank = value; }
}

// the suits of the standard cards
public enum SUITS
{
    Spade,
    Club,
    Diamond,
    Heart,
```

```
    }

    // the suit of this card instance
    protected SUITS m_Suit;
    public SUITS Suit
    {
        get { return m_Suit; }
        set { m_Suit = value; }
    }

    // true when this card instance has a suit of heart or diamond
    // useful for Solitare's game rules
    public bool IsRedCard
    {
        get { return Suit == SUITS.Diamond || Suit == SUITS.Heart; }
    }

    // can the player see this card?
    protected bool m_IsFaceUp = false;
    public bool IsFaceUp
    {
        get { return m_IsFaceUp; }
        set { m_IsFaceUp = value; }
    }

    // useful for card-level animations, unused for this game
    public void Update(double elapsed)
    {
    }

    // draw this card, normal
    public void Draw(SpriteBatch batch, Vector2 position)
    {
        Draw(batch, position, false);
    }

    // draw this card, optionally highlighted as "selected"
    public void Draw(SpriteBatch batch,Vector2 position,bool isSelected)
    {
        if (IsFaceUp)
        {
            if (isSelected)
            {
```

```
                 // face up and selected, highlight in yellow
                 batch.Draw(GameLogic.Texture, position,
                     TextureRect, Color.Goldenrod);
            }
        else
            {
                 // face up and not selected, draw normally
                 batch.Draw(GameLogic.Texture, position, TextureRect,
Color.White);
            }
        }
    else
        {
            // not face up, draw the back of the card
            CardBack.Draw(batch, position);
        }
    }

    // draw the "no card here" placeholder image
    public static void DrawNoCard(SpriteBatch batch, Vector2 position)
    {
        batch.Draw(GameLogic.Texture, position, TextureRectEmpty,
Color.White);
    }

    // helpful const for loading and drawing the card cursor
    public const int CURSOR_SIZE = 12;

    // draw a pulsing cursor around the card
    public static void DrawCursor(SpriteBatch batch,
        Vector2 position, double cycle)
    {
        // pulsing effect is based on simple Sin function
        float delta = (int)Math.Round(Math.Sin(cycle * 4) * 2.0f - 3.0f);

        // location of the four cursor images, plus pulsing offset
        Vector2 vNW = position + new Vector2(delta, delta);
        position.X += CardSize.X - CURSOR_SIZE;
        Vector2 vNE = position + new Vector2(-delta, delta);
        position.Y += CardSize.Y - CURSOR_SIZE;
        Vector2 vSE = position + new Vector2(-delta, -delta);
        position.X -= CardSize.X - CURSOR_SIZE;
        Vector2 vSW = position + new Vector2(delta, -delta);
```

```
        // actually draw the cursor
        batch.Draw(GameLogic.Texture, vNW, TextureRectCursorNW, Color.White);
        batch.Draw(GameLogic.Texture, vNE, TextureRectCursorNE, Color.White);
        batch.Draw(GameLogic.Texture, vSE, TextureRectCursorSE, Color.White);
        batch.Draw(GameLogic.Texture, vSW, TextureRectCursorSW, Color.White);
    }
}
```

The card rank and suit is stored as an enum. More often than not, I convert the enum to an int before making comparisons, but the enums are handy for debugging, they provide automatic (compile-time) range checks, and they make the code a little more readable in cases like the following code snippet:

```
if(card.Rank == Card.RANKS.Ace) ...
```

CardContainer Class

Card containers represent the individual piles of cards on your table when you play a real game of Solitaire. Each CardContainer contains a collection of zero or more cards (all face up or all face down), handles the animations for its own cards, and supports a "cascade" rendering mode where all the cards in the collection are drawn with a small offset so that the player can see the rank and suit of each.

The main CardContainer instance is the deck, where all cards are created, shuffled, and then distributed to the other containers. When the player starts a new game (using the Start button on the controller or the Enter key on the keyboard), all subordinate containers return their cards to the deck. The other containers that are used by this game are the four home piles, the stockpile, the waste pile, the seven chute piles, and the seven stack stockpiles. These instances of the CardContainer class are stored as members of the GameLogic class.

```
// all 52 cards are created once in this container.
// shuffling happens here. this container is never
// rendered. cards are distributed to the other
// containers from here, and returned back whenever
// the game is reset.
CardContainer m_Deck = new CardContainer(0,0);

// the solitare "stock" pile
CardContainer m_Stock = new CardContainer(150, 70);
```

```
// the solitare "waste" pile
CardContainer m_Waste = new CardContainer(200, 70);

// the four solitare "home" piles
CardContainer m_HomeHeart = new CardContainer(300, 70);
CardContainer m_HomeDiamond = new CardContainer(350, 70);
CardContainer m_HomeSpade = new CardContainer(400, 70);
CardContainer m_HomeClub = new CardContainer(450, 70);

// the seven "chute" and "stack stock" piles
CardContainer[] m_StackStock = new CardContainer[7];
CardContainer[] m_StackChute = new CardContainer[7];
```

The `CardContainer` class has several helpful properties and methods to make inspecting and managing the card collections easier. For example, `TopCard`, `SecondCard`, and `BottomCard` provide access to the most commonly accessed card indices. And the `DrawCard()` method removes the top card from the collection and returns it to the calling method.

```
public class CardContainer
{
    // no default constructor, init with position
    public CardContainer(float x, float y) : this(new Vector2(x, y)) { }
    public CardContainer(Vector2 position)
    {
        Position = position;
    }

    // list of all cards in this container
    protected List<Card> m_Cards = new List<Card>();

    // empty this container
    public void ClearCards() { m_Cards.Clear(); }

    // receive a new card into this container
    public void AcceptCard(Card card)
    {
        if (card != null)
        {
            m_Cards.Add(card);
        }
    }
}
```

```csharp
// receive all cards from another container, empty the donor
public void AcceptAllCards(CardContainer container)
{
    if (container != null)
    {
        foreach (Card card in container.m_Cards)
        {
            AcceptCard(card);
        }
        container.ClearCards();
    }
}


// the top card in this pile of cards
public Card TopCard
{
    get
    {
        Card card = null;
        if (m_Cards.Count > 0)
        {
            card = m_Cards[m_Cards.Count-1];
        }
        return card;
    }
}


// the second card in this pile of cards
public Card SecondCard
{
    get
    {
        Card card = null;
        if (m_Cards.Count > 1)
        {
            card = m_Cards[m_Cards.Count - 2];
        }
        return card;
    }
}


// the bottom card in this pile of cards
```

```
public Card BottomCard
{
    get
    {
        Card card = null;
        if (m_Cards.Count > 0)
        {
            card = m_Cards[0];
        }
        return card;
    }
}

// retrieve a specific card from this container
public Card GetCard(int index)
{
    Card card = null;
    if (m_Cards.Count > 0&& index >= 0&& index < m_Cards.Count)
    {
        card = m_Cards[index];
    }
    return card;
}

// how many cards do we have?
public int CardCount
{
    get { return m_Cards.Count; }
}

// remove the top card from this container
public Card DrawCard()
{
    Card card = TopCard;
    if (card != null)
    {
        m_Cards.Remove(card);
    }
    return card;
}
```

The CardContainer class also contains the logic for shuffling the cards that it contains. The Shuffle() method performs its magic by iterating through the collection of cards, one card at a time, swapping the current card with another, randomly selected card. While any container could shuffle its contents, the only container in this game that actually calls the Shuffle() method is the main deck. Using this scheme, it would be fairly straightforward to create a multi-deck game, like Blackjack.

```
// helper for shuffling the cards in this container
protected Random m_rand = new Random();

// randomize the order of cards in this container
public void Shuffle(int repeat)
{
    // shuffle the deck "repeat" times
    if (repeat > 0 && m_Cards.Count > 0)
    {
        // helpers for shuffling
        Card swap;
        int card1;
        int card2;

        for (int i = 0; i < m_Cards.Count * repeat; i++)
        {
            // randomly pick two cards, then swap them
            card1 = m_rand.Next(m_Cards.Count);
            card2 = m_rand.Next(m_Cards.Count);
            swap = m_Cards[card1];
            m_Cards[card1] = m_Cards[card2];
            m_Cards[card2] = swap;
        }

        // mark all the cards in this container as face down
        Orient(false);
    }
}

// randomize the order of cards in this container
public void Shuffle()
{
    Shuffle(1);
}
// mark all cards in this container as face up or face down
public void Orient(bool faceUp)
```

```
{
    foreach (Card card in m_Cards)
    {
        card.IsFaceUp = faceUp;
    }
}

// reverse the order of the cards in this container
// useful for stock and waste piles
public void Reverse()
{
    m_Cards.Reverse();
}
```

Animating cards between containers is managed using the MoveTowards and MoveStartingWith properties of the CardContainer class. Whenever these properties contain valid values, the hosting card container is in the process of moving one or more cards from itself to another container. From the time this move is initiated, the selected cards are moved towards their new home, until MOVE_DURATION seconds have elapsed, at which time the cards are actually transferred to their new CardContainer home.

```
// duration of moving cards, in seconds
protected const float MOVE_DURATION = 0.5f;

// number of seconds into current animation
protected double m_MoveProgress = 0;

// where are the cards heading?
protected CardContainer m_MoveTowards = null;
public CardContainer MoveTowards
{
    get { return m_MoveTowards; }
    set
    {
        m_MoveTowards = value;
        m_MoveProgress = 0;
    }
}

// for the chutes, may be moving more than one card
protected int m_MoveStartingWith = -1;
public int MoveStartingWith
```

```
    {
        get { return m_MoveStartingWith; }
        set { m_MoveStartingWith = value; }
    }

    // the position of this container on the screen
    protected Vector2 m_Position = Vector2.Zero;
    public Vector2 Position
    {
        get { return m_Position; }
        set { m_Position = value; }
    }

    // update, useful for card animations
    public bool Update(double elapsed)
    {
        bool animating = false;
        if (MoveTowards != null)
        {
            // we're in the middle of an animation
            m_MoveProgress += elapsed;
            if (m_MoveProgress > MOVE_DURATION)
            {
                // the animation is done, actually move the cards now
                if (MoveStartingWith >= 0)
                {
                    // moving multiple cards
                    int count = m_Cards.Count - MoveStartingWith;
                    for (int i = 0; i < count; i++)
                    {
                        Card card = GetCard(MoveStartingWith);
                        MoveTowards.AcceptCard(card);
                        m_Cards.Remove(card);
                    }

                    // reset animation variables
                    MoveTowards = null;
                    MoveStartingWith = -1;
                    m_MoveProgress = 0;
                }
                else
                {
                    // only moving one card
```

```
                MoveTowards.AcceptCard(DrawCard());

                // reset animation variables
                MoveTowards = null;
                MoveStartingWith = -1;
                m_MoveProgress = 0;
            }
        }
        else
        {
            // not done animating yet; ignore player input until we are
            animating = true;
        }
    }
    return animating;
}


// draw a non-chute container
public void Draw(SpriteBatch batch, bool isChute)
{
    Draw(batch, isChute, false);
}


// draw this container
public void Draw(SpriteBatch batch, bool isChute,bool isSelected)
{
    Vector2 position = this.Position;

    // unless this is a "chute," draw the empty container image
    // if there are cards in this container, they will overdraw this image
    if (!isChute)
    {
        Card.DrawNoCard(batch, position);
    }

    // if animating, how far are we?
    Vector2 progress =
        new Vector2((float)m_MoveProgress / MOVE_DURATION,
        (float)m_MoveProgress / MOVE_DURATION);

    if (m_Cards.Count > 0)
    {
        // we do have cards, draw them
```

```
        if (isChute)
        {
            // "chute" piles arrange the cards so that the player
            // can see each of the cards that they contain.

            if (MoveTowards == null)
            {
                // we're not in an animation, just draw the cards
                for (int i = 0; i < m_Cards.Count; i++)
                {
                    m_Cards[i].Draw(batch, position,isSelected );
                    position += Card.CascadeOffset;
                }
            }
            else
            {
                // we are in an animation
                if (MoveStartingWith < 0)
                {
                    MoveStartingWith = CardCount;
                }
                if (MoveStartingWith >= m_Cards.Count)
                {
                    MoveStartingWith = m_Cards.Count - 1;
                }

                // draw the stationary cards ...
                for (int i = 0; i < MoveStartingWith; i++)
                {
                    m_Cards[i].Draw(batch, position, isSelected);
                    position += Card.CascadeOffset;
                }

                // ... then draw the moving cards
                position += (MoveTowards.Position - this.Position) * progress;
                for (int i = MoveStartingWith; i < m_Cards.Count; i++)
                {
                    m_Cards[i].Draw(batch, position, isSelected);
                    position += Card.CascadeOffset;
                }
            }
        }
        else
```

```
        {
            // this isn't a "chute" pile
            if (MoveTowards == null)
            {
                // we're not in an animation, just draw the top card
                if (TopCard != null)
                {
                    TopCard.Draw(batch, position, isSelected);
                }
            }
            else
            {
                // we are in an animation
                if (SecondCard != null)
                {
                    // if there's a second card, draw it
                    SecondCard.Draw(batch, position, isSelected);
                }
                if (TopCard != null)
                {
                    // if there's a top card, draw it (moving)
                    position +=
                        (MoveTowards.Position - this.Position) * progress;
                    TopCard.Draw(batch, position, isSelected);
                }
            }
        }
    }
}
```

GameLogic Class

The GameLogic class manages all of the game's objects and enforces the game rules. While all player input is processed in the Game1 class, that class delegates all of the real work back to this class.

The GameLogic class uses what it knows about the size of the game texture and the size of individual cards to determine the location of each card when the main texture is loaded. The logic for this is contained in the FillMainDeck() method. This class is also responsible for managing visual feedback that's presented to the player when he moves the cursor from chute to chute, and when he selects the cards in a chute.

```
// called once, after the GameLogic object is created
public void Init()
{
    ClearDecks();
    FillMainDeck();
}


// empty all containers, including the main deck
public void ClearDecks()
{
    m_Deck.ClearCards();
    m_Stock.ClearCards();
    m_Waste.ClearCards();
    m_HomeHeart.ClearCards();
    m_HomeDiamond.ClearCards();
    m_HomeSpade.ClearCards();
    m_HomeClub.ClearCards();

    if (m_StackStock[0] == null)
    {
        // the chutes haven't been created yet, do it now
        for (int i = 0; i < m_StackStock.Length; i++)
        {
            m_StackStock[i] = new CardContainer(150 + i * 50, 140);
            m_StackChute[i] = new CardContainer(150 + i * 50, 150);
        }
    }
    else
    {
        // empty the existing chutes
        for (int i = 0; i < m_StackStock.Length; i++)
        {
            m_StackStock[i].ClearCards();
            m_StackChute[i].ClearCards();
        }
    }
}

// populate the main deck
public void FillMainDeck()
```

```
{
    if (Texture == null)
    {
        // the texture MUST be loaded before this method is called
        // this method inspects the texture to determine the locations
        // of each card, card back, and the cursor images
        throw new Exception(
            "Card.Texture must be set before SolitareGame.Init is called.");
    }

    // helper variables to save some typing
    int w = Texture.Width;
    int h = Texture.Height;
    float dx = Card.CardSize.X;
    float dy = Card.CardSize.Y;

    // current position in the texture
    float x = 0;
    float y = 0;

    // for each suit
    for (int suit = 0; suit < 4; suit++)
    {
        // for each rank
        for (int rank = 0; rank < 13; rank++)
        {
            // create and configure a new card instance
            Card card = new Card();
            card.TextureRect =
                new Rectangle((int)x, (int)y, (int)dx, (int)dy);
            card.IsFaceUp = false;
            card.Rank = (Card.RANKS)rank;
            card.Suit = (Card.SUITS)suit;

            // add the new card to the deck
            m_Deck.AcceptCard(card);

            // determine where the next card image will be
            x += dx;
            if (x > w || x + dx > w)
            {
                y += dy;
                x = 0;
```

```
                }
            }
        }

        // beyond the 52 standard cards, there are 14 other "card" images
        for (int back = -2; back < 12; back++)
        {
            if (back == -2)
            {
                // the black joker image
                Card.TextureRectBlackJoker =
                    new Rectangle((int)x, (int)y, (int)dx, (int)dy);
            }
            else if (back == -1)
            {
                // the red joker image
                Card.TextureRectRedJoker =
                    new Rectangle((int)x, (int)y, (int)dx, (int)dy);
            }
            else if (back == 10)
            {
                // the "no card here" image
                Card.TextureRectEmpty =
                    new Rectangle((int)x, (int)y, (int)dx, (int)dy);
            }
            else if (back == 11)
            {
                // the card cursor, split into four separate images
                int cw = Card.CURSOR_SIZE;
                int ch = Card.CURSOR_SIZE;
                Card.TextureRectCursorNW = new Rectangle((int)x, (int)y, cw, ch);
                Card.TextureRectCursorNE =
                    new Rectangle((int)x + (int)dx - Card.CURSOR_SIZE,
                    (int)y, cw, ch);
                Card.TextureRectCursorSE =
                    new Rectangle((int)x + (int)dx - Card.CURSOR_SIZE,
                    (int)y + (int)dy - Card.CURSOR_SIZE, cw, ch);
                Card.TextureRectCursorSW =
                    new Rectangle((int)x, (int)y + (int)dy - Card.CURSOR_SIZE,
                    cw, ch);
            }
            else
            {
```

```
            // one of the 10 card back images
            CardBack.AddTextureRect(
                new Rectangle((int)x, (int)y, (int)dx, (int)dy));
        }

        // determine the location of the next card image
        x += dx;
        if (x > w || x + dx > w)
        {
            y += dy;
            x = 0;
        }
    }
}


// used to animate the cursor
protected double m_CursorCycle = 0;

// index to the currently-selected chute
protected int m_Cursor = 0;
public int Cursor
{
    get { return m_Cursor; }
    set
    {
        // enforce upper array bounds
        if (value > m_StackStock.Length - 1)
        {
            value = m_StackStock.Length - 1;
        }

        // enforce lower array bounds
        if (value < 0)
        {
            value = 0;
        }

        // set value
        m_Cursor = value;
    }
}

// index of the "selected" cute
```

```
protected int m_Selected = -1;
public int Selected
{
    get { return m_Selected; }
    set
    {
        // enforce cute array bounds
        if (value >= 0 && value < m_StackChute.Length &&
            m_StackChute[value].TopCard != null)
        {
            m_Selected = value;
        }
        else
        {
            m_Selected = -1;
        }
    }
}


// select a chute, or move waste card to chute
public void Select()
{
    // default case is to just select a chute
    bool doSelect = true;

    // helper variables to save some typing
    Card waste = m_Waste.TopCard;
    Card chute = m_StackChute[Cursor].TopCard;

    if (waste != null && chute != null)
    {
        // see if waste card can be moved to the current chute
        int rankWaste = (int)waste.Rank;
        int rankChute = (int)chute.Rank;
        if (rankWaste == rankChute - 1 && waste.IsRedCard != chute.IsRedCard)
        {
            m_Waste.MoveTowards = m_StackChute[Cursor];
            doSelect = false;
        }
    }
    else if (waste != null&& chute == null&& waste.Rank == Card.RANKS.King)
    {
        // move king from waste to chute
```

```
            m_Waste.MoveTowards = m_StackChute[Cursor];
            doSelect = false;
        }

        // nothing else seems to have worked, just select the current chute
        if (doSelect)
        {
            Selected = Cursor;
        }
    }

// prep the board for a new game
public void NewGame()
{
    Reset();
    m_Deck.Shuffle(3);
    DealChutes();
}

// move all cards back to the main deck
public void Reset()
{
    m_Deck.AcceptAllCards(m_Stock);
    m_Deck.AcceptAllCards(m_Waste);
    m_Deck.AcceptAllCards(m_HomeHeart);
    m_Deck.AcceptAllCards(m_HomeDiamond);
    m_Deck.AcceptAllCards(m_HomeSpade);
    m_Deck.AcceptAllCards(m_HomeClub);
    for (int i = 0; i < m_StackStock.Length; i++)
    {
        m_Deck.AcceptAllCards(m_StackStock[i]);
        m_Deck.AcceptAllCards(m_StackChute[i]);
    }
    m_Deck.Orient(false);
}

// deal the cards out of the deck for a new game
public void DealChutes()
{
    // helper variable to save some typing
    Card card;

    // deal cards to the chutes
```

```
    for (int iChute = 0; iChute < m_StackChute.Length; iChute++)
    {
        card = m_Deck.DrawCard();
        card.IsFaceUp = true;
        m_StackChute[iChute].AcceptCard(card);
        for (int iStock = iChute + 1; iStock < m_StackStock.Length; iStock++)
        {
            card = m_Deck.DrawCard();
            card.IsFaceUp = false;
            m_StackStock[iStock].AcceptCard(card);
        }
    }


    // put the remaining cards into the stock pile
    m_Stock.AcceptAllCards(m_Deck);
}

// move the top stock card to the waste pile
public void DrawCardFromStock()
{
    Card card = m_Stock.TopCard;
    if (card != null)
    {
        // typical scenario, just move the card
        card.IsFaceUp = true;
        m_Stock.MoveTowards = m_Waste;
    }
    else
    {
        // the stock pile has no cards, move waste cards back over
        m_Stock.AcceptAllCards(m_Waste);

        // waste cards are face up, flip them back over
        m_Stock.Orient(false);

        // waste cards are in reverse order from the stock pile
        m_Stock.Reverse();

        // now we can draw the top card from the stock pile
        card = m_Stock.TopCard;
        if (card != null)
        {
            card.IsFaceUp = true;
```

```
                m_Stock.MoveTowards = m_Waste;
            }
        }
}


// move card(s) from one chute to another
public void MoveCards()
{
    if (Selected >= 0 && Selected != Cursor)
    {
        // player is trying to move card(s) between chutes, validate

        // helper variables to save some typing
        CardContainer moveTo = m_StackChute[Cursor];
        CardContainer moveFrom = m_StackChute[Selected];
        if (moveTo.TopCard == null && moveFrom.BottomCard.Rank ==
            Card.RANKS.King)
        {
            // player is moving a king to an empty chute
            moveFrom.MoveTowards = moveTo;
            moveFrom.MoveStartingWith = 0;
            Selected = -1;
        }
        else if (moveTo.TopCard != null)
        {
            // player is moving non-king card(s) between chutes

            // get the rank and suit color of the "bottom" card
            // (the top card in a chute container is the "bottom"
            // card, as viewed on the screen - it sits on top of
            // the other cards)
            int rankTo = (int)moveTo.TopCard.Rank;
            bool redTo = moveTo.TopCard.IsRedCard;

            // scan the source chute for the (only) card that
            // satisfies the moving rules of the game
            for (int i = 0; i < moveFrom.CardCount; i++)
            {
                // the current card
                Card card = moveFrom.GetCard(i);
                if ((int)card.Rank == rankTo - 1 && card.IsRedCard != redTo)
                {
                    // we have a match! stop looking.
```

```
                              moveFrom.MoveTowards = moveTo;
                              moveFrom.MoveStartingWith = i;
                              Selected = -1;
                              break;
                          }
                    }
               }

           if (Selected >= 0)
           {
               // this wasn't a valid move, or the player was
               // de-selecting the currently selected chute
               Selected = Cursor;
           }
      }
}


// try to move the top card in the waste pile home or
// try to move the last card in the current chute home
public void GoHome()
{
    // see if top waste card can move home
    CardContainer home = FindHome(m_Waste.TopCard);
    if (home!=null)
    {
        m_Waste.MoveTowards = home;
    }
    else
    {
        // waste card failed, see if current chute has a card
        home = FindHome(m_StackChute[Cursor].TopCard);
        if (home != null)
        {
            m_StackChute[Cursor].MoveTowards = home;
        }
    }
}

// given a card, see if any of the home piles will accept it
protected CardContainer FindHome(Card cardToMove)
{
    // the home that will allow the card
    CardContainer home = null;
```

```
if (cardToMove != null)
{
    // determine potential home, based on suit
    switch (cardToMove.Suit)
    {
        case Card.SUITS.Spade:
            home = m_HomeSpade;
            break;
        case Card.SUITS.Club:
            home = m_HomeClub;
            break;
        case Card.SUITS.Diamond:
            home = m_HomeDiamond;
            break;
        case Card.SUITS.Heart:
            home = m_HomeHeart;
            break;
    }

    // the top card in the selected home pile
    Card cardToHost = home.TopCard;

    // the rank of the card that is moving
    int rankMove = (int)cardToMove.Rank;

    if (cardToHost != null)
    {
        // see if the cards have the proper ranks
        int rankHost = (int)cardToHost.Rank;
        if (rankHost != rankMove - 1)
        {
            home = null;
        }
    }
    else
    {
        // player may be trying to move an ace home
        if (rankMove != (int)Card.RANKS.Ace)
        {
            home = null;
        }
    }
}
```

```
        // return our findings
        return home;
    }


// update each container (for moving card animations),
// animate cursor pulse
public bool Update(double elapsed)
{
    // as long as any deck is animating a card, we need to
    // ignore player input
    bool animating = false;

    // update each container, noting whether it was animating
    animating |= m_Deck.Update(elapsed);
    animating |= m_Stock.Update(elapsed);
    animating |= m_Waste.Update(elapsed);
    animating |= m_HomeHeart.Update(elapsed);
    animating |= m_HomeDiamond.Update(elapsed);
    animating |= m_HomeSpade.Update(elapsed);
    animating |= m_HomeClub.Update(elapsed);
    for (int i = 0; i < m_StackStock.Length; i++)
    {
        animating |= m_StackStock[i].Update(elapsed);
        animating |= m_StackChute[i].Update(elapsed);

        // if a chute is empty, and its stock isn't, deal the
        // top card to the chute
        if (m_StackChute[i].TopCard == null&&
            m_StackStock[i].TopCard != null&&
            m_StackStock[i].MoveTowards == null)
        {
            m_StackStock[i].TopCard.IsFaceUp = true;
            m_StackStock[i].MoveTowards = m_StackChute[i];
            animating = true;
        }
    }
    // update cursor pulse
    m_CursorCycle += elapsed;

    // return our findings
    return animating;
}
```

```
// render the cards to the screen
public void Draw(SpriteBatch batch)
{
    // draw the home piles
    m_HomeHeart.Draw(batch, false);
    m_HomeDiamond.Draw(batch, false);
    m_HomeSpade.Draw(batch, false);
    m_HomeClub.Draw(batch, false);

    // draw the chutes
    for (int i = m_StackStock.Length-1; i >= 0; i-)
    {
        m_StackStock[i].Draw(batch, false);
        m_StackChute[i].Draw(batch, true, Selected == i);
        if (i == Cursor)
        {
            Card.DrawCursor(batch, m_StackChute[i].Position, m_CursorCycle);
        }
    }

    // draw the waste and stock piles
    m_Waste.Draw(batch, false);
    m_Stock.Draw(batch, false);
}
```

Be warned that to keep the code simple, this game is a little stricter than most Solitaire implementations. For example, you can't move a card out of a home pile once it's been placed there, there is no option to deal three cards to the waste pile like you'd find in most Solitaire games, and there is no "undo move" option. A good strategy for this implementation is to keep all of the cards in the chutes until you're ready to start filling in the home piles.

Game1 Class

The Game1 class is the default game implementation that's automatically generated when you create a new game project. To that base, I just added a little "glue" code to bind the other classes together. This class acts as a liaison to the GameLogic class, where all the real work is done.

All player input is handled in the Game1 class. The game supports player input from the keyboard and the Xbox 360 Controller. To keep button presses from repeating with every game frame, there is a simple input delay built into the Update() method. To keep the card animation logic simple, only one group of cards is allowed to be moving at any time. This is accomplished by disabling player input whenever the Update() method detects that any of the containers has an animation in progress.

```
/// game logic such as updating the world
protected override void Update(GameTime gameTime)
{
    // Allows the default game to exit on Xbox 360 and Windows
    if (GamePad.GetState(PlayerIndex.One).Buttons.Back == ButtonState.Pressed)
        this.Exit();

    // record the elapsed time (in seconds)
    double elapsed = gameTime.ElapsedGameTime.TotalSeconds;

    // used for simple button delay logic
    m_LastButtonPress += elapsed;

    // process player input
    ProcessButtons();

    // update card containers
    if (m_logic.Update(elapsed))
    {
        // at least one deck is animating, block player input
        m_LastButtonPress = 0;
    }

    base.Update(gameTime);
}

// button repeat delay (in seconds)
public const double BUTTON_DELAY = 0.25;

// don't register repeat button presses on
// every frame, limit to once every
// BUTTON_DELAY seconds as long as a button
// is pressed.
protected double m_LastButtonPress = BUTTON_DELAY;

// actually process player input
```

```
protected void ProcessButtons()
{
    // support for keyboard and first game pad
    KeyboardState key1 = Keyboard.GetState();
    GamePadState pad1 = GamePad.GetState(PlayerIndex.One);

    // if no buttons are being pressed, reset the delay timer
    if (NoButtonsPressed(key1, pad1))
    {
        m_LastButtonPress = BUTTON_DELAY;
    }
    else if (m_LastButtonPress > BUTTON_DELAY)
    {
        // keep delay active as long as any registered button is pressed
        bool pressed = true;
        if (key1.IsKeyDown(Keys.Enter) ||
            pad1.Buttons.Start == ButtonState.Pressed)
        {
            // start a new game
            m_logic.NewGame();
        }
        else if (key1.IsKeyDown(Keys.Tab) ||
            pad1.Buttons.Y == ButtonState.Pressed)
        {
            // move card from stock to waste pile
            m_logic.DrawCardFromStock();
        }
        else if (key1.IsKeyDown(Keys.Left) ||
            pad1.DPad.Left == ButtonState.Pressed ||
            pad1.ThumbSticks.Left.X < 0)
        {
            // move cursor left
            m_logic.Cursor -= 1;
        }
        else if (key1.IsKeyDown(Keys.Right) ||
            pad1.DPad.Right == ButtonState.Pressed ||
            pad1.ThumbSticks.Left.X > 0)
        {
            // move cursor right
            m_logic.Cursor += 1;
        }
        else if (key1.IsKeyDown(Keys.LeftControl) ||
            pad1.Buttons.B == ButtonState.Pressed)
```

```
        {
            // try to move a card into home pile
            m_logic.GoHome();
        }
        else if (key1.IsKeyDown(Keys.Space) ||
            pad1.Buttons.A == ButtonState.Pressed)
        {
            if (m_logic.Selected == m_logic.Cursor)
            {
                // deselect selected cards
                m_logic.Selected = -1;
            }
            else if (m_logic.Selected >= 0)
            {
                // try to move cards between chutes
                m_logic.MoveCards();
            }
            else
            {
                // select the current chute, or move a
                // card from the waste pile to this chute
                m_logic.Select();
            }
        }
        else if (key1.IsKeyDown(Keys.PageUp) ||
            pad1.Buttons.LeftShoulder == ButtonState.Pressed)
        {
            // select previous card back image
            CardBack.PreviousCardBack();
        }
        else if (key1.IsKeyDown(Keys.PageDown) ||
            pad1.Buttons.RightShoulder == ButtonState.Pressed)
        {
            // select next card back image
            CardBack.NextCardBack();
        }
        else if (key1.IsKeyDown(Keys.Home) ||
            pad1.Triggers.Left > 0)
        {
            // select previous game texture
            PreviousImage();
        }
        else if (key1.IsKeyDown(Keys.End) ||
```

```
            pad1.Triggers.Right > 0)
        {
            // select next game texture
            NextImage();
        }
        else
        {
            // no buttons that we care about were pressed,
            // reset the button delay variables
            pressed = false;
        }

        if (pressed)
        {
            // start countdown for next button repeat
            m_LastButtonPress = 0;
        }
    }
}

/// render game objects
protected override void Draw(GameTime gameTime)
{
    // clear the screen
    graphics.GraphicsDevice.Clear(Color.CornflowerBlue);

    // draw all the game objects
    m_batch.Begin();
    m_logic.Draw(m_batch);
    m_batch.End();

    base.Draw(gameTime);
}
```

Summary

In this chapter, you learned how to develop a basic framework for card games. You learned how to logically separate related tasks into separate classes, and how to manage the interactions between those classes. We also discussed some of the issues involved in using artwork from a third party.

Review Questions

1. How are individual cards represented in the code?

2. How are cards grouped?

3. How are cards animated from group to group?

4. How might you implement a multi-deck card game (like Blackjack) using similar code?

5. List some considerations when importing artwork from third parties.

Exercises

EXERCISE 1. There's a bug in this game where moving cards may be rendered behind static cards. This occurs because each CardContainer is rendered in turn. To correct this behavior, you'll need to make sure that moving cards are rendered after all the static cards have been rendered, or you will need to temporarily change the Z-order for any moving cards so that they are drawn on top of the static cards. Since the game was designed so that only one group of cards is moving at any one time, you should be able to keep your new logic fairly simple by drawing the (only) container with moving cards last.

EXERCISE 2. Write a routine that applies the rules of the game to each of the card containers to determine if there are any valid moves left. You can discount the moving a King-based chute from one empty stack store to another empty stack store, since the player wouldn't progress any closer to their goal with that move. If there are no more valid moves left, display a "game over" graphic.

EXERCISE 3. Use the logic that you created in EXERCISE 2 to provide an optional "hint" mode for the player. Highlight any valid moves that you discovered so that the player may select one.

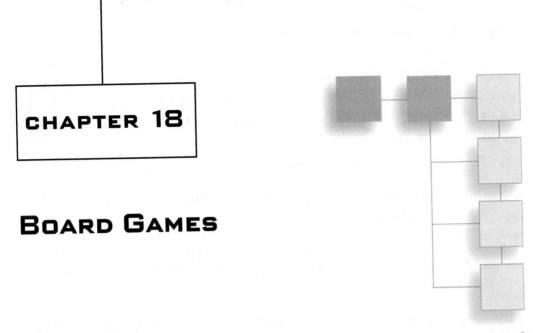

CHAPTER 18

BOARD GAMES

Board games are another of those categories of games that have mass appeal, and many of the most popular board games have been around so long that copyright issues are no longer a concern, so they can be a great source of inspiration for your original titles.

In this chapter, you will learn how to:

- Implement simple computer opponents to enhance single-player game play

- Simultaneously manage the state of multiple on-screen game objects

- Add simple, yet effective animations and visual effects to your game

- Use threading to keep animations going while processing background tasks

- Track and display a player's score using a bitmap font

The Design

In this chapter, we will develop a simple version of a popular board game that originated in England around 1880. Reversi gained wide-spread popularity in England towards the end of the 19th century, and it experienced a resurgence in popularity in the 1970s, when it was refined into its modern incarnation and banded with a new moniker—Othello.

In our version of the game, the action takes place on a 12-by-12 grid. Each player starts with two pieces, placed in the center of the grid. One point is awarded for each piece a player has on the grid. Players must place their piece on the board according to the following rules:

- The grid cell into which the piece is placed must be empty.

- The grid cell into which the piece is placed must be adjacent to one of the opponent's pieces.

- The player's new piece, along with an existing piece, must "surround" at least one piece of the opponent, in a straight line (horizontally, vertically, or diagonally).

Players take turns placing pieces on the board in an attempt to capture their opponent's pieces and maximize the number of grid cells that are occupied by their own pieces. When there is no legal move for a player, he forfeits his turn and play passes to his opponent. If neither player can make a legal move (as is the case when the grid is full), the game is over. The player with the most pieces on the board wins.

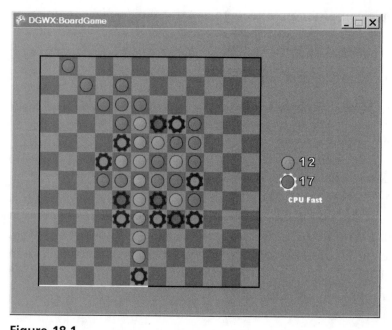

Figure 18.1
A screen shot of the game that we will develop in this chapter. The CPU opponent is considering his options, and has evaluated just over half of the possible moves.

The Architecture

The basic design for this game is fairly simple. The game grid starts out empty and is gradually filled, one piece at a time. As pieces are added to the grid, we need to make sure that the additions satisfy the game rules. The basic components to handle these tasks are detailed in the following text.

The GameBoard

The GameBoard class contains a two-dimensional array of GamePiece objects. The dimensions of this array are determined by the GridWidth and GridHeight member variables. The GameBoard class is also responsible for making sure that any moves that are made by a player (human or CPU) conform to the rules of the game. This is done by determining the complete list of valid moves (stored in the ValidMoves array) whenever a game turn begins. Only moves in this list are allowed.

Determining Valid Moves

The UpdateListOfValidMoves method creates a list of all the grid cell locations where the current player may legally place his new game piece. New pieces may only be placed on the game board if they meet the three requirements of the game rules: the cell is empty, the cell is adjacent to an opponent's piece, and the new piece (along with an existing piece) will surround at least one of the opponent's pieces.

```
// list of valid moves for this player and board
public List<Point> ValidMoves = new List<Point>();
public void UpdateListOfValidMoves()
{
    // off-grid, start with invalid cursor position
    m_Cursor = -Vector2.One;

    // clear current valid moves
    Vector2 position = Vector2.Zero;
    ValidMoves.Clear();

    // don't bother scanning if no one's playing
    if (CurrentPlayer == Player.None) return;

    // reset scores
    int score1 = 0;
    int score2 = 0;
```

```
for (int y = 0; y < GridHeight; y++) // for each row
{
    position.Y = y;
    for (int x = 0; x < GridWidth; x++) // for each column
    {
        position.X = x;
        if (Grid[x, y].Owner == Player.None)
        {
            // rules for valid move: 1) empty cell, 2) next to
            // opponent's piece, 3) scan straight-line reveals
            // piece owned by current player
            if (Scan(position, CursorDirection.North) ||
                Scan(position, CursorDirection.NorthEast) ||
                Scan(position, CursorDirection.East) ||
                Scan(position, CursorDirection.SouthEast) ||
                Scan(position, CursorDirection.South) ||
                Scan(position, CursorDirection.SouthWest) ||
                Scan(position, CursorDirection.West) ||
                Scan(position, CursorDirection.NorthWest))
            {
                ValidMoves.Add(new Point(x, y));
            }
        }
        else if (Grid[x, y].Owner == Player.One)
        {
            score1++;
        }
        else
        {
            score2++;
        }
    }
}

// if there's at least one valid move, locate the cursor on
// the first valid move in the list
if (ValidMoves.Count > 0)
{
    MoveCursorTo(ValidMoves[0]);
}

// update the NumberSprites with the new scores
m_ScoreOne.Value = score1;
m_ScoreTwo.Value = score2;
}
```

The first two rules are easy enough to check, but the `UpdateListOfValidMoves` method relies on the (first overloaded) `Scan` method to look for cells that satisfy the third rule. This version of the `Scan` method just examines the pieces that occupy the game board, without changing any state information.

```
// scan without marking
private bool Scan(Vector2 position, Vector2 direction)
{
    return Scan(position, direction, false);
}
```

Relative Cell Locations

To make the code a little easier to follow, directions are expressed as instances of the `Vector2` structure, which contain a value that can be added to a cell location to determine its neighbor. By doing this, our code can refer to the relative location of [−1,+1] as `SouthWest`, making the logic easier to follow.

```
// simple "constants" for scanning grid cells
public sealed class CursorDirection
{
    public static readonly Vector2 North     = new Vector2(  0, -1);
    public static readonly Vector2 NorthEast  = new Vector2(  1, -1);
    public static readonly Vector2 East       = new Vector2(  1,  0);
    public static readonly Vector2 SouthEast   = new Vector2(  1,  1);
    public static readonly Vector2 South      = new Vector2(  0,  1);
    public static readonly Vector2 SouthWest  = new Vector2( -1,  1);
    public static readonly Vector2 West       = new Vector2( -1,  0);
    public static readonly Vector2 NorthWest  = new Vector2( -1, -1);
}
```

Navigating the List of Valid Moves

The two overloaded `MakeMove` methods and the two `MoveCursorTo` methods serve as the gatekeepers to the `ValidMoves` array and prevent players from selecting invalid moves. The `NextValidMove` and `PreviousValidMove` methods help the game logic use gamepad events from the player to select moves from the list of valid moves.

```
// move cursor to the next valid move
public void NextValidMove()
{
    Point current = new Point((int)m_Cursor.X, (int)m_Cursor.Y);
    int index = ValidMoves.IndexOf(current);
```

```
        index++;
        if (index >= ValidMoves.Count) index = 0;
        MoveCursorTo(index);
}


// move cursor to the previous valid move
public void PreviousValidMove()
{
    Point current = new Point((int)m_Cursor.X, (int)m_Cursor.Y);
    int index = ValidMoves.IndexOf(current);
    index--;
    if (index < 0) index = ValidMoves.Count - 1;
    MoveCursorTo(index);
}


// the current cursor location in grid units
private Vector2 m_Cursor = Vector2.Zero;

// move cursor to specified location
public void MoveCursorTo(Point location)
{
    m_Cursor = new Vector2(location.X, location.Y);
}


// move cursor to location indicated by index into ValidMoves array
public void MoveCursorTo(int index)
{
    if (index >= 0 && index < ValidMoves.Count)
    {
        m_Cursor =
            new Vector2(ValidMoves[index].X, ValidMoves[index].Y);
    }
}
```

The MakeMove and Scan Methods

The MakeMove method actually commits the selected move to the current game
board. This method assumes that the game rules were enforced when the list of
valid moves was determined. Capturing opponent pieces in any direction is
enough to satisfy the game rules, but this method will scan the game board in all
eight directions to make sure that the current player claims all of the opponent's
pieces to which he is entitled.

```csharp
// commit currently selected cell as player's move
public void MakeMove()
{
    Point current = new Point((int)m_Cursor.X, (int)m_Cursor.Y);
    int index = ValidMoves.IndexOf(current);
    MakeMove(index);
}

// select a move from the ValidMove list, useful for CPU players
public void MakeMove(int index)
{
    if (index >= 0 && index < ValidMoves.Count)
    {
        Point move = ValidMoves[index];
        Vector2 position = new Vector2(move.X,move.Y);

        // mark current cell as belonging to the current player
        Grid[move.X, move.Y].Owner = CurrentPlayer;

        // scan each direction, if valid, claim it
        if (Scan(position, CursorDirection.North))
        {
            Scan(position, CursorDirection.North, true);
        }
        if (Scan(position, CursorDirection.NorthEast))
        {
            Scan(position, CursorDirection.NorthEast, true);
        }
        if (Scan(position, CursorDirection.East))
        {
            Scan(position, CursorDirection.East, true);
        }
        if (Scan(position, CursorDirection.SouthEast))
        {
            Scan(position, CursorDirection.SouthEast, true);
        }
        if (Scan(position, CursorDirection.South))
        {
            Scan(position, CursorDirection.South, true);
        }
        if (Scan(position, CursorDirection.SouthWest))
        {
            Scan(position, CursorDirection.SouthWest, true);
```

```
        }
        if (Scan(position, CursorDirection.West))
        {
            Scan(position, CursorDirection.West, true);
        }
        if (Scan(position, CursorDirection.NorthWest))
        {
            Scan(position, CursorDirection.NorthWest, true);
        }

        // move has been committed, switch players
        ToggleCurrentPlayer();
    }
}
```

The Scan Method

Once a move has been committed, the MakeMove method uses the second overloaded Scan method to claim the opponent's captured game pieces for the current player.

```
// scan, possibly committing move to game state
private bool Scan(Vector2 position, Vector2 direction, bool mark)
{
    // assume caller verified that first cell is empty
    // move to next cell in scan ...
    Player other = OtherPlayer();
    position += direction;
    int count = 0;

    // ... and start matching opponent cells
    while (InBounds(position) && GetPiece(position).Owner == other)
    {
        if (mark)
        {
            Grid[(int)position.X,(int)position.Y].Owner = CurrentPlayer;
        }
        count++;
        position += direction;
    }

    // return result as boolean
    return
```

```
            count > 0 &&
            InBounds(position) &&
            GetPiece(position).Owner == CurrentPlayer;
    }

    // is the specified cell within the grid?
    private bool InBounds(Vector2 position)
    {
        return
            position.X >= 0 &&
            position.X < GridWidth &&
            position.Y >= 0 &&
            position.Y < GridHeight;
    }

    // get a game piece, given a vector (rather than [x,y])
    public GamePiece GetPiece(Vector2 position)
    {
        return Grid[(int)position.X, (int)position.Y];
    }
}
```

The Score Method

The Score method is used by the Evaluate method, which is called from the AI of the various computer opponents to determine the state of the potential game boards that are being examined. The score that this method calculates is also stored in the corresponding NumberSprite instance for each player, which is used by the heads-up display logic to render the current scores to the screen.

```
// get the score for the specified player
// rather than store the scores in member variables and try
// to keep them in sync with the display, pull Value from
// the NumberSprite directly
public int Score(Player player)
{
    long score = 0;
    switch (player)
    {
        case Player.One:
            score = m_ScoreOne.Value;
            break;
        case Player.Two:
```

```
                score = m_ScoreTwo.Value;
                break;
        }
        return (int)score;
}
```

The ToggleCurrentPlayer Method

The ToggleCurrentPlayer method is used to switch players after a valid move has been committed to the game board. It is also used by the AI of the various computer opponents to toggle between the two players as potential game boards are being evaluated. In the former case, the CpuMoveHasBeenStarted flag is set to false when the player is toggled, alerting the CPU opponent (if any) that his turn is ready to begin.

```
// switch between Player.One and Player.Two
public void ToggleCurrentPlayer()
{
    // toggle player, then regenerate list of valid moves
    CurrentPlayer = OtherPlayer();
    UpdateListOfValidMoves();

    // if there aren't any valid moves ...
    if (ValidMoves.Count == 0)
    {
        // ... switch back to the original player
        CurrentPlayer = OtherPlayer();
        UpdateListOfValidMoves();

        // if there still aren't any valid moves, the game is over
        if (ValidMoves.Count == 0)
        {
            State = GameState.GameOver;
        }
    }

    // if this player is a CPU player, note that it's ready
    // to kick off its AI processing thread
    CpuMoveHasBeenStarted = false;
}
```

In addition to managing the GamePiece objects and enforcing the game rules, the GameBoards class also manages the three artificial intelligence variants that are supported by this game (described in more detail later).

The DrawGrid Method

The DrawGrid method renders the game grid in a checkerboard pattern.

```
// draw the game board
private void DrawGrid(SpriteBatch batch)
{
    // big rect, draw grid border
    Rectangle borderRect = new Rectangle(
        (int)TopLeft.X - 2,
        (int)TopLeft.Y - 2,
        GridWidth * 32 + 4,
        GridHeight * 32 + 4);
    batch.Draw(Texture, borderRect, PixelRect, Color.Black);

    // size of a single grid cell
    Rectangle cellRect = new Rectangle(0, 0, 32, 32);

    // alternating colors for grid cells
    Color[] colors = {
        Color.CornflowerBlue,
        Color.RoyalBlue,
        };

    for (int y = 0; y < GridHeight; y++) // for each row
    {
        cellRect.Y = y * 32 + (int)TopLeft.Y;
        for (int x = 0; x < GridWidth; x++) // for each column
        {
            cellRect.X = x * 32 + (int)TopLeft.X;
            batch.Draw(
                Texture,
                cellRect,
                PixelRect,
                colors[(x + y) % 2]);
        }
    }
}
```

The DrawCursor Method

The DrawCursor method renders a rotating gear icon for every possible legal move for the current player in dark blue. If the current player is human, the cursor for the currently selected move is rendered as a spinning white gear.

```csharp
// render valid move hints in blue, and current selection in white
private void DrawCursor(SpriteBatch batch)
{
    Point current = Point.Zero;
    Vector2 position = Vector2.Zero;
    Vector2 center = new Vector2(16, 16);

    for (int y = 0; y < GridHeight; y++) // for each row
    {
        current.Y = y;
        position.Y =
            TopLeft.Y + // top of the grid
            y * 32 +    // grid position of this cell
            center.Y;   // plus rotation offset

        for (int x = 0; x < GridWidth; x++) // for each column
        {
            current.X = x;
            position.X =
                TopLeft.X + // left of the grid
                x * 32 +    // grid position of this cell
                center.X;   // plus rotation offset

            // highlight this cell if it's selected by human player
            bool highlight = current.X == m_Cursor.X;
            highlight &= current.Y == m_Cursor.Y;
            highlight &= CurrentPlayerType() == PlayerType.Human;

            if (highlight)
            {
                batch.Draw(
                    Texture,            // cursor texture
                    position,           // cursor x, y
                    CursorRect,         // cursor source rect
                    Color.White,        // color
                    (float)m_EffectAge, // cursor rotation
                    center,             // center of cursor
                    1.0f,               // don't scale
                    SpriteEffects.None, // no effect
                    0.0f);              // topmost layer
            }
            else if(ValidMoves.Contains(current))
            {
```

```
        batch.Draw(
            Texture,            // cursor texture
            position,           // cursor x, y
            CursorRect,         // cursor source rect
            Color.Navy,         // color
            (float)m_EffectAge, // cursor rotation
            center,             // center of cursor
            1.0f,               // don't scale
            SpriteEffects.None, // no effect
            0.0f);              // topmost layer
    }
}
}
}
```

The DrawPieces Method

The DrawPieces method renders every piece on the game grid.

```
// draw any existing game pieces
private void DrawPieces(SpriteBatch batch)
{
    Vector2 position = Vector2.Zero;
    for (int y = 0; y < GridHeight; y++) // for each row
    {
        position.Y = TopLeft.Y + y * 32;
        for (int x = 0; x < GridWidth; x++) // for each column
        {
            position.X = TopLeft.X + x * 32;
            Grid[x, y].Draw(batch, position);
        }
    }
}
```

The DrawHUD Method

The DrawHUD method renders the player scores, along with a visual indicator to
denote the current player.

```
// score for player one and player two
NumberSprite m_ScoreOne = new NumberSprite();
NumberSprite m_ScoreTwo = new NumberSprite();
```

```
// extra pieces for HUD
GamePiece m_PieceOne = new GamePiece(Player.One);
GamePiece m_PieceTwo = new GamePiece(Player.Two);

// render the heads up display
private void DrawHUD(SpriteBatch batch)
{
    Vector2 position = Vector2.Zero;
    Vector2 center = new Vector2(16, 16);

    position.X =
        TopLeft.X +      // left of grid
        GridWidth * 32 + // right of grid
        2 +              // plus border
        32;              // plus some space
    position.Y =
        TopLeft.Y +      // top of grid
        GridWidth * 16 - // middle of grid
        32;              // minus one row (since HUD takes up two rows)

    // draw gear around player one's HUD piece?
    if (State == GameState.Playing && CurrentPlayer == Player.One)
    {
        position += center - Vector2.One;
        batch.Draw(
            Texture,             // cursor texture
            position,            // cursor x, y
            CursorRect,          // cursor source rect
            Color.White,         // color
            (float)m_EffectAge,  // cursor rotation
            center,              // center of cursor
            1.0f,                // don't scale
            SpriteEffects.None,  // no effect
            0.0f);               // topmost layer
        position -= center - Vector2.One;
    }
    // draw player one's HUD piece?
    batch.Draw(
        Texture,
        position,
        GamePiece.PieceRect,
        GamePiece.Colors[1]);
```

```
// draw gear around player two's HUD piece?
position.Y += 32;
if (State == GameState.Playing && CurrentPlayer == Player.Two)
{
    position += center;
    batch.Draw(
        Texture,             // cursor texture
        position,            // cursor x, y
        CursorRect,          // cursor source rect
        Color.White,         // color
        (float)m_EffectAge,  // cursor rotation
        center,              // center of cursor
        1.0f,                // don't scale
        SpriteEffects.None,  // no effect
        0.0f);               // topmost layer
    position -= center;
}
// draw player two's HUD piece?
batch.Draw(
    Texture,
    position,
    GamePiece.PieceRect,
    GamePiece.Colors[2]);

// draw scores
position.Y -= 26;
position.X += 32;
m_ScoreOne.Draw(batch, position);
position.Y += 32;
m_ScoreTwo.Draw(batch, position);

if (PlayerTypeRect != Rectangle.Empty)
{
    position.X -= 16;
    position.Y += 32;
    batch.Draw(Texture, position, PlayerTypeRect, Color.White);
}
}
```

The DrawProgress Method

The DrawProgress method renders a progress bar that represents the state of completion of the currently selected AI. This lets the human player (if any) know that his CPU opponent is still thinking, and that the game is not "locked up." It's important to provide feedback to your players when you're performing long-running tasks.

```
// if CPU player is working, show progress on screen
private void DrawProgress(SpriteBatch batch)
{
    if (State == GameState.Playing)
    {
        // assume zero progress
        double progress = 0;

        // grab progress from current CPU player, if any
        ArtificialIntelligence ai = CurrentAI;
        if (ai != null)
        {
            progress = ai.Status;
        }

        // actually draw progress bar
        Rectangle rect = new Rectangle(
            (int)TopLeft.X,
            (int)TopLeft.Y + GridHeight * 32,
            (int)Math.Round(progress * (GridWidth * 32)),
            2);
        batch.Draw(Texture, rect, PixelRect, Color.White);
    }
}
```

The GamePiece

The GamePiece class holds only one important piece of data—its owner (to which a reference is stored in the GamePiece.Owner property). GamePiece objects are responsible for rendering themselves in the appropriate color, but don't really perform any other noteworthy tasks.

```
public struct GamePiece
{
    // simple copy constructor
    public GamePiece(Player owner)
    {
        Owner = owner;
    }
```

```
// texture rectangle
public static readonly Rectangle PieceRect =
    new Rectangle(0, 0, 32, 32);

// color, based on owner
public static readonly Color[] Colors = {
    Color.TransparentWhite,
    Color.Goldenrod,
    Color.OrangeRed,
};

// owner of this piece
public Player Owner;

// update this piece
public void Update(double elapsed)
{
}

// render this piece at the specified position
public void Draw(SpriteBatch batch,Vector2 position)
{
    if (Owner == Player.None) return;
    batch.Draw(
        GameBoard.Texture,
        position,
        PieceRect,
        Colors[(int)Owner]);
}
}
```

NumberSprite

Rather than using a full-blown font rendering class, this class is a simple helper that draws numbers on the screen. We'll use this class to render our scores. NumberSprite exposes a public, long property called Value. This is the number that will be rendered. The NumberSprite class stores its texture and texture rectangle data in a static variable so that it's accessible from all instances of the class. This texture must have a special layout. The NumberSprite class assumes that there are 10 evenly spaced, single-digit numbers in the texture on a single row, in order from zero to nine. The Draw() method of this class renders each digit of Value, one by one.

```
class NumberSprite
{
    // texture is shared across all instances (static)
    private static Texture2D m_Texture;
    private static Rectangle[] TextureRects = new Rectangle[10];
    public static Texture2D Texture
    {
        get { return m_Texture; }
        set
        {
            // set texture
            m_Texture = value;

            // texture is 10 evenly spaced numbers
            int widthChar = Texture.Width / 10;
            int heightChar = Texture.Height;
            for (int i = 0; i < 10; i++)
            {
                TextureRects[i] = new Rectangle(
                    i * widthChar,
                    0,
                    widthChar,
                    heightChar );
            }
        }
    }

    // actually draw the number (using default White tint)
    public void Draw(SpriteBatch batch, Vector2 position)
    {
        Draw(batch, position, Color.White);
    }

    // actually draw the number
    public void Draw(SpriteBatch batch, Vector2 position, Color tint)
    {
        // draw the number, char by char, from cache
        for (int i = 0; i < m_ValueAsText.Length; i++)
        {
            int c = m_ValueAsText[i] - '0';
            batch.Draw(Texture, position, TextureRects[c], tint);
            position.X += TextureRects[c].Width;
        }
    }
```

Whenever the `Value` property is updated, the new value is compared to the existing value. If the value is changing, then we update the internal value (m_Value) and use the APIs in the .NET Framework to create the array of text characters that represent this number. Whenever we're ready to draw the number, we'll refer to this array of characters rather than the number. Each character can be converted to an index into our array of bitmaps by subtracting the '0' character literal. By caching the character array, we don't need to calculate it every time the number is drawn (every frame of the game). We only need to generate the character array when the value actually changes.

```
// cache a copy of the last value to save some CPU cycles
private char[] m_ValueAsText = "0".ToCharArray();
private long m_Value = 0;
public long Value
{
    get { return m_Value; }
    set
    {
        if (m_Value != value)
        {
            m_Value = value;
            m_ValueAsText = value.ToString().ToCharArray();
        }
    }
}
```

The User Interface

This game uses threads to keep the animations running smoothly, even when the processor is busy calculating the next move for a computer opponent. While the CPU is busy planning its next move, human input is blocked.

The HUD (Heads-Up Display)

The game displays a spinning gear in every cell of the grid that would be a valid move for the current player. The game allows for either a human or computer opponent as player two. If the current player is human, one of the gears is highlighted, representing the currently selected move. If the current player is a CPU opponent, no gears are highlighted and a simple progress meter is displayed at the bottom of the grid to let player one (always human) know how the AI is

Table 18.1 Player Input

Keyboard	Game Pad	Description
Left	Left	Highlight previous valid move
Right	Right	Highlight next valid move
Space	A	Make the currently highlighted move
Page Up	Left Shoulder	Lower CPU difficulty or allow human as player two
Page Down	Right Shoulder	Raise CPU difficulty or allow human as player two
Enter	Start	Restart the game

progressing. If the input for player two is being managed by AI, the level of difficulty of the CPU player is noted in the HUD as well. The HUD logic also indicates the current player by rendering a spinning gear next to their stats in the HUD, and it displays the current score for each player.

Player Input

The game supports both the keyboard and the game pad. If there are two human players, they can take turns on the keyboard or on a single controller. If there is a controller active on port two, then each player can use his own controller. As mentioned earlier, human input is blocked while the AI is processing. This keeps thread synchronization simple by preventing the creation of multiple, concurrent AI threads.

The list of buttons and their functions are shown in Table 18.1

There is a delay of a quarter of a second between each button press. This makes handling repeating button presses easier. Rather than tracking each button's pressed and released state from frame to frame, the delay serves as a global repeat rate. The biggest drawback to this method of processing player input is that it doesn't allow for button combinations. Considering the type of game that we're writing, that's not such a big issue, though. And the savings in code complexity far outweigh any potential loss in player input design options.

Artificial Intelligence

To make things a little more interesting, this game supports two players. The second player can be human, but the game also provides four CPU opponents that the player can challenge. These computer opponents are processed on a separate thread so that the game animations can continue uninterrupted.

The Base Class

The base class for the CPU opponent (ArtificialIntelligence) manages the creation of worker threads, handles thread synchronization tasks, and provides a single interface to the GameBoard class for all the CPU opponents that we will develop. While the AI is processing game data to decide which move to make, human inputs are ignored. This makes thread synchronization easier by ensuring that only one AI thread is active at any one time.

The GameBoard class is responsible for populating the list of valid moves whenever a new turn begins. The derived AIs are responsible for determining which move they would like to make from that list, and they're responsible for reporting their progress back to the GameBoard class (for use in the DrawHUD method) by updating their Status property as they churn through all possible moves. The Status property is a double value, where 0.0 represents 0% completion and 1.0 represents 100% completion. Generally speaking, the derived class can assume that it's running exclusively, since the base class is handling all the threading tasks.

```
public abstract class ArtificialIntelligence
{
    // a default constructor
    public ArtificialIntelligence()
    {
    }

    // constructor with depth initialization
    public ArtificialIntelligence(int depth)
    {
        Depth = depth;
    }

    // used by UI to render progress bar
    protected double m_Status = 0;
    public double Status
    {
        get { return m_Status; }
    }

    // used by GameBoard to know when the AI is done taking its turn
    protected bool m_Done = true;
    public bool Done
```

```
    {
        get { return m_Done; }
    }

    // the move that the AI selected, as an index into
    // GameBoard.ValidMoves[]
    protected int m_Move = 0;
    public int Move
    {
        get { return m_Move; }
    }

    // number of levels to recurse when searching all possible board combos
    protected int m_Depth = 4;
    public int Depth
    {
        get { return m_Depth; }
        set { m_Depth = value; }
    }

    // handy member to generate random values
    protected Random m_rand = new Random();

    // the public interface to other classes, kicks off threaded
    // task, then returns to caller. caller polls AI.Done to see
    // if threaded task is done
    public void SelectMove(GameBoard board)
    {
        m_Done = false;
        m_Move = 0;
        m_Status = 0;
        SelectMoveParams param = new SelectMoveParams();
        param.Board = board;
        param.Depth = Depth;
        Thread task = new Thread(SelectMoveTask);
        task.Start(param);
    }

    // parameters for the threaded task
    public struct SelectMoveParams
    {
        public int Depth;
        public GameBoard Board;
    }
```

```
// the method that is actually called when threading starts
protected void SelectMoveTask(object obj)
{
    SelectMoveParams param = (SelectMoveParams)obj;
    m_Move = SelectMoveRecursive(param.Board, param.Depth);
    m_Status = 1;
    m_Done = true;
}

// helper method to generate a simple heuristic for a given GameBoard
// add 1 for each piece owned by Player.One, subtract 1 for each piece
// owned by Player.Two. Larger sums favor Player.One, smaller sums
// favor Player.Two.
protected int Evaluate(GameBoard board)
{
    return board.Score(Player.One) - board.Score(Player.Two);
}

// this method must be implemented by any actual AIs that derive
// from this base class. the threaded method calls this method,
// which only exists in derived classes. that way, this base
// class can handle the nitty-gritty threading and synchronization
// tasks, and leave the actual AI processing to the derived classes.
protected abstract int SelectMoveRecursive(GameBoard board, int depth);
}
```

RandomAI

This is about as simple a CPU opponent as we could create. The "easy" opponent (RandomAI) randomly selects a single move for the list of valid moves. The only AI that would be easier than this would be one that selects the first valid move every time, but that would be really boring. Every now and then, this CPU opponent may get lucky and select a great move. But, over time, this AI should be fairly easy to beat.

```
class RandomAI : ArtificialIntelligence
{
    // constructor with depth initializer
    public RandomAI(int depth) : base(depth) { }

    // as simple as AI gets -- random selection
    protected override int SelectMoveRecursive(GameBoard board, int depth)
    {
```

```
    // randomly select a move from the list of valid moves
    return m_rand.Next(board.ValidMoves.Count);
  }
}
```

EasyAI

Another strategy that we can use is to pick the best move for the current turn. We can make each valid move on a copy of the current game board and see which one improves our score the most. While this makes for a more challenging opponent than the random AI, it's a very short-sighted strategy. In this game, there are many times when a move that gains you many pieces in a single turn will lead to a move where your opponent can reclaim even more pieces on the next turn.

```
class EasyAI: ArtificialIntelligence
{
    // constructor with depth initializer
    public EasyAI(int depth) : base(depth) { }

    // called by base class from separate thread
    protected override int SelectMoveRecursive(GameBoard board, int depth)
    {
        // assume first move is the best
        int move = 0;

        // best score, based on player
        if (board.CurrentPlayer == Player.One)
        {
            move = FindBestMove(board, true, int.MinValue);
        }
        else if (board.CurrentPlayer == Player.Two)
        {
            move = FindBestMove(board, false, int.MaxValue);
        }

        // return selected move
        return move;
    }
}
```

```
protected int FindBestMove(GameBoard board, bool isPlayerOne, int score)
{
    // assume first move is the best
    int move = 0;

    // scan valid moves, looking for best score
    for (int index = 0; index < board.ValidMoves.Count; index++)
    {
        // create copy of current board to play with
        GameBoard board2 = new GameBoard(board);

        // make the next valid move
        board2.MakeMove(index);

        // what's the score?
        int val = Evaluate(board2);

        // best score for player one is positive,
        // best score for player two is negative
        if (isPlayerOne)
        {
            if (val > score)
            {
                score = val;
                move = index;
            }
        }
        else
        {
            if (val < score)
            {
                score = val;
                move = index;
            }
        }
    }

    // report findings to the caller
    return move;
}
}
```

MinMaxAI

Reversi falls into a category of games known as "zero sum games with perfect information." That means that when one player wins, the other loses (a zero sum game). It also means that you can inspect the game board at any time during the game and know who's winning at that instant and know all of the moves that are legal for the current turn (perfect information). There is no chance element to this game. Other games in this category are checkers, chess, connect four, and tic-tac-toe. Games like these are ideal candidates for creating virtual opponents using an algorithm known as Min/Max.

The Min/Max algorithm attempts to minimize its opponent's score while maximizing its own. It does this by recursively examining all the possible moves, counter moves, counter-counter moves, etc. This is similar to what the grand-masters of checkers and chess do. To win at this type of game against a veteran player, you need to think several moves ahead of the current turn. "If I move here, and he moves there, I can move here and win!"

Where a human player relies on experience, skill, and instinct, the computer player uses simple brute force—playing out every possible scenario to see how it turns out. Even though computers are great at processing large sets of data like this, and they're able to consider more moves faster than any human can, there are limits. As you examine these potential moves further into the future, the number of combinations grows exponentially.

If we assume that there are an average of eight legal moves in a turn (and eight legal counter moves, and eight legal counter-counter moves, ...), then you would have "8 to the power of the recursion depth" GameBoard objects to create, manipulate, and examine. So if we wanted to examine 12 moves into the future, we'd have to look at just under 69 billion game boards and decide which move (from the initial eight valid moves) would likely lead to the best end result.

Of course, most games last longer than 12 moves. But we can't just keep looking further ahead. Just looking one more move ahead in our hypothetical scenario would require examining another 480 billion game boards. Your PC just isn't big enough or fast enough to process that kind of data before the player gets bored and shuts your game off. Clearly, we'll need to make a decision long before we see how the game ends.

Since we're selecting our move before we know for certain that it will lead to our victory, there's always a chance that we're choosing a short-term gain that will ultimately lead to our opponent's victory. We can't just blindly select the move that yields the highest score for us. That's too short-sighted a strategy. The way that the Min/Max algorithm handles this problem is by selecting the move that leads to the highest score for us, while simultaneously limiting the gains made by our opponent. It's not perfect, but it's a solid strategy. The more future moves that you can examine, the better your decisions for the current move will be.

Clearly you can't dictate what move your opponent will make, but you can safely assume that he will make the best possible move that he can. If he doesn't, then you'll have an even better set of moves to pick from on the next turn. With each recursive call, the AI will assume the role of the new player and pick the best move for that player every time.

Pseudo code for the Min/Max algorithm follows:

```
Begin Max Method
     If RecursionDepth is Zero Then
          Return Score
     End If
     For Each Valid Move
          Make Move
          NewScore = Min( RecursionDepth - 1)
          If NewScore > Score Then
               Score = NewScore
          End If
          Undo Move
     End For
     Return Score
End Max Method

Begin Min Method
     If RecursionDepth is Zero Then
          Return Score
     End If
     For Each Valid Move
          Make Move
          NewScore = Max( RecursionDepth - 1)
          If NewScore < Score Then
               Score = NewScore
          End If
          Undo Move
     End For
     Return Score
End Min Method
```

The complete listing for this class can be found on the CD-ROM that came with the book.

AlphaBetaAI

The Min/Max algorithm does a wonderful job, and the deeper we allow it to search, the better it is at picking great moves. We can optimize our implementation as much as we like, but the sheer number of game board combinations that we have to examine dwarfs any potential performance boosts that we may come up with. To really speed things up, we need to limit the amount of data that the algorithm needs to examine. Well, it just so happens that there is a way to safely ignore many of those game board combinations.

The Min and Max methods exchange the same dialog, over and over—"If I move here, where will you move?" Max will always pick the best move for player one and Min will always pick the best move for player two. So, what is "the best move"? The best move is the one that presents the worst options for your opponent. If you choose a move for which your opponent has a brilliant counter-move, there's a good chance that he'll take it. So the strategy that Min/Max uses is to choose a move such that the best counter-move is as undesirable as possible.

For each possible move, Max will ask Min what his best counter move would be. Max then selects his move based on the worst of the counter-moves that Min reported. Understanding this exchange is essential in limiting the number of game boards that we need to process.

If Max is looking for Min's worst counter-move, then Min can stop evaluating game boards as soon as he realizes that the current list of valid counter-moves contains a move that's better than a counter-move that he's already reported to Max. Why? Because Min will chose a counter-move that's at least as good as the counter-move he's currently evaluating (that is, after all, his goal). There's no reason for Min to find the best counter-move if Max is sure to throw the results out anyway. That, in a nutshell, is the logic behind the Alpha/Beta algorithm.

The following is a bit of pseudo code that demonstrates the basic Alpha/Beta algorithm. Notice how similar it is to the Min/Max algorithm.

```
Begin Max Method
    If RecursionDepth is Zero Then
        Return Score
```

```
        End If
        For Each Valid Move
            Make Move
            NewScore = Min( RecursionDepth - 1)
            If NewScore >= Beta Then
                Return Beta
            End If
            If NewScore > Alpha Then
                Alpha = NewScore
            End If
            Undo Move
        End For
        Return Alpha
End Max Method

Begin Min Method
    If RecursionDepth is Zero Then
        Return Score
    End If
    For Each Valid Move
        Make Move
        NewScore = Max( RecursionDepth - 1)
        If NewScore <= Alpha Then
            Return Alpha
        End If
        If NewScore < Beta Then
            Beta = NewScore
        End If
        Undo Move
    End For
    Return Beta
End Min Method
```

The complete listing for this class can be found on the CD-ROM that came with the book. While Alpha/Beta produces roughly the same results as Min/Max for a given recursion depth, it does so much faster. That means that you could increase the recursion depth for Alpha/Beta until it takes as long to run as the unmodified Min/Max algorithm and make better decisions with the same amount of processing time. For this chapter's example, I kept the recursion depths for these two AIs the same so that you get comparable decisions to the CPU Hard opponent (which uses a vanilla Min/Max implementation), in much less time.

Summary

In this chapter you learned how to implement simple computer opponents to enhance single-player game play. You saw how adding simple animations and other user interface niceties can make plain game designs more appealing. You also learned how to handle player input by adapting to the available input hardware. This chapter even included a little threading code to keep the animations running while the AI was busy deciding what move to make.

The example code for this chapter is by no means fully optimized. It's just an illustration of how you might go about implementing AI in your game. For more information on threading, read Chapter 25, "Threading in XNA."

Review Questions

Think about what you've read in this chapter (and the included source code) to answer the following questions.

1. How does the game ensure that players can only make legal moves?

2. How does the game keep the animations running smoothly, even when a computer opponent is busy processing game board data?

3. What are the differences between the three AI implementations?

4. Why does the game disable player input while the artificial intelligence is processing?

5. The implementation for the RandomAI class is very simple. Why do you think it's threaded just like its CPU-intensive siblings?

Exercises

EXERCISE 1. Modify this example so that the player can change the recursion depth of the selected AI to make the game easier or harder to suit their taste.

EXERCISE 2. As written, the Min/Max routine will always make the same move for any given game board. In many cases, there may be more than one move that will yield the same end result. Since Min/Max is evaluating every possible game board anyway, keep track of all moves that yield the same result and randomly pick a move from this list of "best" moves. That little bit of variety will make the computer opponent more interesting.

EXERCISE 3. Implement an "undo" feature for this game to allow the human player to reconsider his last move. Since every game board state is completely independent of every other game board state, this should be as easy as remembering the state of the board before the last human turn.

EXERCISE 4. Min/Max is by far the most popular implementation for AI to tackle this type of game. Come up with an original, novel AI subclass. Don't worry if it's not as strong a player as the existing AIs—just make something original. Experiment with more complex heuristics than simply comparing scores. For example, you might weigh piece placement so that grid cells on the edge of the board are more valuable than grid cells in the center (assumes that edge pieces are less likely to be recaptured). Be creative.

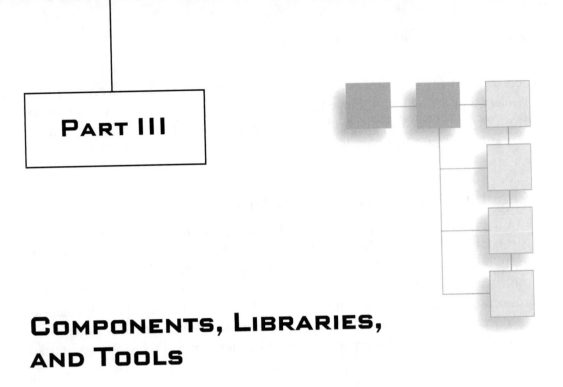

PART III

COMPONENTS, LIBRARIES, AND TOOLS

Game development extends beyond the bits that you see on the screen. No matter how great your content creation tools are, there will be times when you need to write custom tools to manage your game data. And there are many blocks of code that you'll write as you develop games that you will find yourself referencing again and again.

Writing tools, reusable libraries, and drop-in components is one of my favorite aspects of game programming. Eliminating redundancy, automating tasks, and providing intuitive interfaces for games and tools are usually smaller-scale projects where you can be very creative, produce a product in a relatively short time period, and enjoy the fruits of your labor quicker than would normally be possible in an actual game project.

Overview of Chapters

The following paragraphs provide an overview of this section's contents.

Chapter 19: Keyboard-Aware Game Pad

In Chapter 19, we develop a reusable component that emulates the Xbox 360 Controller using the keyboard. This configurable component is a drop-in replacement for the standard controller APIs. It merges input from any controllers that are actually plugged in so that the player can transition seamlessly from keyboard to controller and back. The game never knows where player input is coming from; it just handles it as if the player is using a controller.

Chapter 20: Game Font Maker Utility

In Chapter 20, we develop a Windows-based tool to create bitmap fonts for our games. The XNA Game Studio 1.0 Refresh includes support for bitmap game fonts, but it's still handy to understand how things work "under the covers." The tool processes the selected TrueType font, accounting for the specified font options, generating an image that contains the characters and other information, encoded within the image. This image is then loaded in your XNA game where you use the game font library developed in the next chapter to position and draw in-game text.

Chapter 21: Game Font Library

In Chapter 21, we develop an XNA game library that uses the bitmap fonts that were generated by the tool from the previous chapter to render text within our XNA games. This library provides methods to draw text in any color, at any location, and it provides methods to measure strings before they're drawn so that you can perform text justification and animated effects.

Chapter 22: Particle System

In Chapter 22, we develop a simple, reusable XNA game library to create, manage, and draw particles within our games. This particle system can be used to create a variety of in-game visual effects. The code for this chapter is far from optimized, but it provides a good overview of how particle systems work, and should be a good inspiration for you as you develop your own.

Chapter 23: Virtual Keyboard

In Chapter 23, we develop a reusable XNA game library to display an on-screen keyboard that the player can use to enter textual data using his controller. This component also accepts keyboard input, seamlessly integrating player inputs from either device. This is useful for providing a means for players to enter user names for high scores, name player characters, and label save game files.

Chapter 24: Brick Breaker Level Editor

In Chapter 24, we develop a level editor for the game that we wrote in Chapter 14, "Brick Breaker." This tool is written as a Windows application, and it demonstrates some of the most common user interface topics that should be considered when developing a tool for your team (or your players).

CHAPTER 19

KEYBOARD-AWARE GAME PAD

The mouse, keyboard, and game pads are very different devices, each requiring specialized code. There are times when it would be nice to play a game without hooking up a controller. But you don't want to write code to support multiple devices every time you start a game project. Besides, some of the Windows gamers who want to play your game may not have an Xbox 360 Controller hooked up to their PC. And there are many times (especially if you're doing your development on a laptop) when it may not be convenient to carry a controller around. Wouldn't it be nice to emulate a controller using your keyboard? You could just map some keyboard keys to the game pad buttons and play test your game without ever taking your hands off the keyboard.

In this chapter, we'll develop a reusable, keyboard-aware replacement for the standard game pad classes. In addition to mapping keyboard keys to controller buttons, our new component will also relay the states of any actual Xbox 360 Controllers that are connected. And since the Xbox 360 game console and the XNA Framework both support a keyboard device, we should be able to use the same code on the Windows or Xbox 360 platforms.

In this chapter, you will learn how to:

- Intercept input states and modify them before the game has a chance to see them

- Provide abstractions that allow you to utilize multiple devices with minimal impact to your game code

- Use .NET Framework collection classes to manage your game objects

Caveats and Pitfalls

Of course, a keyboard isn't an Xbox 360 Controller. So there are some caveats to note when using this new component. The actual Xbox 360 Controller supports several analog buttons. Since keyboard keys are digital (pressed or not pressed), we'll need to map the analog buttons to their extremes when updating their state. In essence, the keyboard-emulated thumbsticks and triggers will behave like the directional pad on the real controller. One of the following constants is reported to the calling code whenever a (always digital) key press is mapped to an analog game pad button.

```
// extreme values for the analog game pad buttons
public const float TRIGGER_MAX = 1.00f;
public const float TRIGGER_MIN = 0.00f;
public const float THUMBSTICK_MAX = 1.00f;
public const float THUMBSTICK_MIN = -1.00f;
```

The players who are using the keyboard are playing in a physically constrained space—it's not the best device to have four players use at the same time. To keep our design simple, we'll restrict our new component to support no more than two players. And since the keyboard is so cramped, we'll only provide support for one of the analog thumbsticks (the left one) when two players are using the keyboard. Figure 19.1 shows which keyboard keys map to the Xbox 360 game pad buttons in a two-player configuration.

Wish List

In the interest of brevity and simplicity, I'm purposefully limiting the scope of this component. The following features are food for thought. As you work through this chapter's text and source code, think about how you might implement these features.

Disable Keyboard Emulation—Since most console games support virtual keyboards (on-screen keyboards that the player manipulates using his controller), and since it's not a good practice to require devices that not all of your

Figure 19.1
A diagram that shows which keyboard keys are used when simultaneously emulating two game pads.

players will have (while the Xbox 360 game console supports a keyboard, it's not realistic to expect every Xbox 360 gamer to have a keyboard plugged into their console), there will be times when you want to disable keyboard emulation. It would be nice to provide such a feature.

Configurable Game Pad Indices—It would also be nice if we didn't limit which controllers can support keyboard emulation. The component would make use of reasonable defaults (`PlayerIndex.One` and `PlayerIndex.Two`), but it would allow the hosting game to change those settings so that any two of the four controllers may be emulated.

Getting Started

This component was designed to mimic the functionality of the standard game pad classes of the XNA Framework, and it was written so that you can easily swap between the standard game pad APIs and the keyboard-aware game pad APIs by simply changing your declarations. In the vast majority of cases, you will not need to change your game's input processing logic.

This library provides a keyboard-aware replacement for each of the standard game pad APIs. If you've written a game that only accepts input from the Xbox 360 Controller, you can tweak your member declarations and method parameters to reference instances of the classes that we will develop in this chapter, and your game will support the keyboard as an alternate controller "for free."

Note

Writing a replacement class for each of the standard game pad classes may seem like overkill, but the standard game pad APIs use classes that expose read-only properties, and those classes are typically declared as `static` or `sealed`, preventing us from subclassing them.

The KAGamePad Class

The `KAGamePad` class is a drop-in replacement for the standard `GamePad` class that takes into account the state of any keyboard keys that are mapped to the specified controller.

```
// a drop-in replacement for the GamePad class
// which maps keyboard keys to gamepad buttons
public class KAGamePad
{
    // private constructor to prevent caller from
    // creating their own instances
    protected KAGamePad() { }

    // get the state of the virtual gamepad
    public static KAGamePadState GetState(PlayerIndex player)
    {
        // create the gamepad state instance
        KAGamePadState state =
            new KAGamePadState(GamePad.GetState(player));

        // append the state of mapped keyboard keys (if any)
        KeyMapHelper.ProcessKeyboardInput(player, state);

        // return the composite state
        return state;
    }

    // pass through for querying the underlying gamepad
    public static GamePadCapabilities GetCapabilities(PlayerIndex index)
    {
        return GamePad.GetCapabilities(index);
    }

    // pass through for controlling the rumble
    // motors of the underlying gamepad
    public static bool SetVibration(
```

```
        PlayerIndex index, float left, float right)
    {
        return GamePad.SetVibration(index, left, right);
    }
}
```

The KAGamePadButtons Class

The KAGamePadButtons class is a drop-in replacement for the standard Game-PadButtons class.

```
// a drop-in replacement for the GamePadButtons class
public class KAGamePadButtons
{
    // public members to represent the state of each
    // of the buttons on a standard Xbox 360 game pad
    public ButtonState A;
    public ButtonState B;
    public ButtonState Back;
    public ButtonState LeftShoulder;
    public ButtonState LeftStick;
    public ButtonState RightShoulder;
    public ButtonState RightStick;
    public ButtonState Start;
    public ButtonState X;
    public ButtonState Y;

    // overridden Equals method; are the current and
    // specified instances the same?
    public override bool Equals(object obj)
    {
        bool same = false;

        if (obj != null && obj is KAGamePadButtons)
        {
            same =
                KAGamePadButtons.AreSame(this, (KAGamePadButtons)obj);
        }

        return same;
    }

    // overridden "not equals" operator
```

```
public static bool operator !=
    (KAGamePadButtons state1, KAGamePadButtons state2)
{
    return !KAGamePadButtons.AreSame(state1, state2);
}

// overridden "equals" operator
public static bool operator ==
    (KAGamePadButtons state1, KAGamePadButtons state2)
{
    return KAGamePadButtons.AreSame(state1, state2);
}

// overridden GetHashCode method
public override int GetHashCode()
{
    return base.GetHashCode();
}

// are the two specified instances the same?
public static bool AreSame(
    KAGamePadButtons state1, KAGamePadButtons state2)
{
    return
        state1.A == state2.A &&
        state1.B == state2.B &&
        state1.Back == state2.Back &&
        state1.LeftShoulder == state2.LeftShoulder &&
        state1.LeftStick == state2.LeftStick &&
        state1.RightShoulder == state2.RightShoulder &&
        state1.RightStick == state2.RightStick &&
        state1.Start == state2.Start &&
        state1.X == state2.X &&
        state1.Y == state2.Y;
}

// a string representation of this instance
public override string ToString()
{
    return
        A.ToString() +
        B.ToString() +
        Back.ToString() +
```

```
            LeftShoulder.ToString() +
            LeftStick.ToString() +
            RightShoulder.ToString() +
            RightStick.ToString() +
            Start.ToString() +
            X.ToString() +
            Y.ToString();
    }
}
```

The KAGamePadDPad Class

The KAGamePadDPad class is a drop-in replacement for the standard GamePadDPad class.

```
// a drop-in replacement for the GamePadDPad class
public class KAGamePadDPad
{
    // public members to represent the state of each of the
    // directional buttons on a standard Xbox 360 game pad
    public ButtonState Down;
    public ButtonState Left;
    public ButtonState Right;
    public ButtonState Up;

    // overridden Equals method; are the current and
    // specified instances the same?
    public override bool Equals(object obj)
    {
        bool same = false;

        if (obj != null && obj is KAGamePadDPad)
        {
            same = KAGamePadDPad.AreSame(this, (KAGamePadDPad)obj);
        }

        return same;
    }

    // overridden "not equals" operator
    public static bool operator !=
        (KAGamePadDPad state1, KAGamePadDPad state2)
    {
```

```
            return !KAGamePadDPad.AreSame(state1, state2);
    }


    // overridden "equals" operator
    public static bool operator ==
        (KAGamePadDPad state1, KAGamePadDPad state2)
    {
        return KAGamePadDPad.AreSame(state1, state2);
    }


    // overridden GetHashCode method
    public override int GetHashCode()
    {
        return base.GetHashCode();
    }


    // are the two specified instances the same?
    public static bool AreSame(KAGamePadDPad state1, KAGamePadDPad state2)
    {
        return
            state1.Down == state2.Down &&
            state1.Left == state2.Left &&
            state1.Right == state2.Right &&
            state1.Up == state2.Up;
    }


    // a string representation of this instance
    public override string ToString()
    {
        return
            Down.ToString() +
            Left.ToString() +
            Right.ToString() +
            Up.ToString();
    }
}
```

The KAGamePadThumbsticks Class

The KAGamePadThumbsticks class is a drop-in replacement for the standard GamePadThumbsticks class.

```
// a drop-in replacement for the GamePadThumbsticks class
```

```
public class KAGamePadThumbSticks
{
    // public members to represent the state of each of the
    // thumbsticks on a standard Xbox 360 game pad
    public Vector2 Left;
    public Vector2 Right;

    // overridden "not equals" operator
    public static bool operator !=
        (KAGamePadThumbSticks state1, KAGamePadThumbSticks state2)
    {
        return !AreSame(state1, state2);
    }

    // overridden "equals" operator
    public static bool operator ==
        (KAGamePadThumbSticks state1, KAGamePadThumbSticks state2)
    {
        return AreSame(state1, state2);
    }

    // overridden Equals method; are the current and
    // specified instances the same?
    public override bool Equals(object obj)
    {
        bool same = false;

        if (obj != null && obj is KAGamePadThumbSticks)
        {
            same = AreSame(this, (KAGamePadThumbSticks)obj);
        }

        return same;
    }

    // are the two specified instances the same?
    public static bool AreSame(
        KAGamePadThumbSticks state1, KAGamePadThumbSticks state2)
    {
        return
            state1.Left == state2.Left &&
            state1.Right == state2.Right;
    }
```

```
    // overridden GetHashCode method
    public override int GetHashCode()
    {
        return base.GetHashCode();
    }


    // a string representation of this instance
    public override string ToString()
    {
        return
            Left.ToString() +
            Right.ToString();
    }
}
```

The KAGamePadTriggers Class

The KAGamePadTriggers class is a drop-in replacement for the standard Game-
PadTriggers class.

```
// a drop-in replacement for the GamePadTriggers class
public class KAGamePadTriggers
{
    // public members to represent the state of each of the
    // triggers on a standard Xbox 360 game pad
    public float Left;
    public float Right;

    // overridden "not equals" operator
    public static bool operator !=
        (KAGamePadTriggers state1, KAGamePadTriggers state2)
    {
        return !AreSame(state1, state2);
    }

    // overridden "equals" operator
    public static bool operator ==
        (KAGamePadTriggers state1, KAGamePadTriggers state2)
    {
        return AreSame(state1, state2);
    }
```

```
// overridden Equals method; are the current and
// specified instances the same?
public override bool Equals(object obj)
{
    bool same = false;

    if (obj != null && obj is KAGamePadTriggers)
    {
        same = AreSame(this, (KAGamePadTriggers)obj);
    }

    return same;
}

// are the two specified instances the same?
public static bool AreSame(KAGamePad Triggers
    state1, KAGamePadTriggers state2)
{
    return
        state1.Left == state2.Left &&
        state1.Right == state2.Right;
}

// overridden GetHashCode method
public override int GetHashCode()
{
    return base.GetHashCode();
}

// a string representation of this instance
public override string ToString()
{
    return
        Left.ToString() +
        Right.ToString();
}
}
```

The KAGamePadState Class

The KAGamePadState class is a drop-in replacement for the standard GamePadState class. In addition to the functionality provided by the standard class, this class exposes a property (the IsIdle property) to let you know when the game pad is sitting idle (no buttons are being pressed).

```csharp
// a drop-in replacement for the GamePadState class
public class KAGamePadState
{
    // the current state of the digital buttons
    protected KAGamePadButtons m_Buttons = new KAGamePadButtons();
    public KAGamePadButtons Buttons
    {
        get { return m_Buttons; }
    }

    // the current state of the directional buttons
    protected KAGamePadDPad m_DPad = new KAGamePadDPad();
    public KAGamePadDPad DPad
    {
        get { return m_DPad; }
    }

    // the current state of the thumbsticks
    protected KAGamePadThumbSticks m_ThumbSticks =
        new KAGamePadThumbSticks();
    public KAGamePadThumbSticks ThumbSticks
    {
        get { return m_ThumbSticks; }
    }

    // the current state of the triggers
    protected KAGamePadTriggers m_Triggers = new KAGamePadTriggers();
    public KAGamePadTriggers Triggers
    {
        get { return m_Triggers; }
    }

    // is this virtual gamepad connected?
    protected bool m_IsConnected = false;
    public bool IsConnected
    {
        get { return m_IsConnected; }
        set { m_IsConnected = value; }
    }
```

```csharp
// the packet number for the current state, parallels the
// PacketNumber of the standard GamePadState class
protected static int m_PacketNumberMaster = 0;
protected int m_PacketNumber = 0;
public int PacketNumber
{
    get { return m_PacketNumber; }
}

// don't allow callers to create their own
// instances of this class
private KAGamePadState() { }

// create an instance of our gamepad state object, using an
// instance of the standard gamepad state object
public KAGamePadState(GamePadState state)
{
    m_IsConnected = state.IsConnected;

    if (IsConnected)
    {
        m_Buttons.A = state.Buttons.A;
        m_Buttons.B = state.Buttons.B;
        m_Buttons.Back = state.Buttons.Back;
        m_Buttons.LeftShoulder = state.Buttons.LeftShoulder;
        m_Buttons.LeftStick = state.Buttons.LeftStick;
        m_Buttons.RightShoulder = state.Buttons.RightShoulder;
        m_Buttons.RightStick = state.Buttons.RightStick;
        m_Buttons.Start = state.Buttons.Start;
        m_Buttons.X = state.Buttons.X;
        m_Buttons.Y = state.Buttons.Y;

        m_DPad.Down = state.DPad.Down;
        m_DPad.Left = state.DPad.Left;
        m_DPad.Right = state.DPad.Right;
        m_DPad.Up = state.DPad.Up;

        m_ThumbSticks.Left = state.ThumbSticks.Left;
        m_ThumbSticks.Right = state.ThumbSticks.Right;

        m_Triggers.Left = state.Triggers.Left;
        m_Triggers.Right = state.Triggers.Right;
```

```csharp
                m_PacketNumber = m_PacketNumberMaster++;
        }
    }


    // overridden "not equals" operator
    public static bool operator !=
        (KAGamePadState state1, KAGamePadState state2)
    {
        return !AreSame(state1, state2);
    }


    // overridden "equals" operator
    public static bool operator ==
        (KAGamePadState state1, KAGamePadState state2)
    {
        return AreSame(state1, state2);
    }


    // overridden Equals method; are the current and
    // specified instances the same?
    public override bool Equals(object obj)
    {
        bool same = false;

        if (obj != null && obj is KAGamePadState)
        {
            same = AreSame(this, (KAGamePadState)obj);
        }

        return same;
    }


    // overridden GetHashCode method
    public override int GetHashCode()
    {
        return base.GetHashCode();
    }


    // are the two specified instances the same?
    public static bool AreSame(KAGamePadState state1, KAGamePadState state2)
    {
        return
            state1.Buttons == state2.Buttons &&
```

```
            state1.DPad == state2.DPad &&
            state1.IsConnected == state2.IsConnected &&
            state1.ThumbSticks == state2.ThumbSticks &&
            state1.Triggers == state2.Triggers;
    }

    // a string representation of this instance
    public override string ToString()
    {
        return
            Buttons.ToString() +
            DPad.ToString() +
            IsConnected.ToString() +
            ThumbSticks.ToString() +
            Triggers.ToString();
    }

    // true when no gamepad buttons are being pressed
    public bool IsIdle
    {
        get { return this.ToString() == m_IdleState; }
    }

    // create a string representation of the default
    // instance of the KAGamePadState class
    protected static readonly string m_IdleState =
        new KAGamePadState().ToString();
}
```

The KeyMap Class

The KeyMap class manages a list of keyboard-to-game pad mappings for each player, and it uses that data to combine inputs from the keyboard and any attached controllers to provide the state of each virtual controller.

There are no mapped keys for PlayerIndex.Three or PlayerIndex.Four in this implementation, so the state of the physical game pads for those players is passed back to the caller, as is. The same is true of any unmapped buttons for the game pads that are used by PlayerIndex.One and PlayerIndex.Two.

```
// used by the KeyMapHelper to map keyboard keys to
// gamepad buttons for a given player
public class KeyMap
```

```
{
    // store the list of button-to-key mappings
    protected Dictionary<PadButtons, Keys> m_KeyMap =
        new Dictionary<PadButtons, Keys>();

    // default, empty constructor
    public KeyMap() { }

    // does this instance of the KeyMap class contain
    // any keyboard mappings? In the case of Player.Three
    // and Player.Four, the answer is always "no" (false).
    public bool HasMappings
    {
        get { return m_KeyMap.Count > 0; }
    }

    // map a keyboard key to a game pad button
    public void AddMapping(PadButtons button, Keys key)
    {
        m_KeyMap.Add(button,key);
    }

    // given a game pad button, return the keyboard
    // key to which it maps (if any). in the case of
    // PlayerIndex.Three and PlayerIndex.Four, this
    // method will always return a zero (Keys.None).
    public Keys GetKey(PadButtons button)
    {
        Keys key = Keys.None;

        if (m_KeyMap.ContainsKey(button))
        {
            key = m_KeyMap[button];
        }
        return key;
    }

    // get the state of a mapped digital button
    public ButtonState GetButtonState(
        KeyboardState keyState,
        ButtonState btnState,
        PadButtons button)
    {
```

```
    // is the mapped key pressed?
    bool keyPressed = keyState.IsKeyDown(GetKey(button));
    // is the actual gamepad button pressed?
    bool btnPressed = (btnState == ButtonState.Pressed);

    // if either is pressed, treat the virtual button as
    // pressed; otherwise, report the state as released
    return keyPressed || btnPressed ?
        ButtonState.Pressed :
        ButtonState.Released;
}

// get the state of a mapped trigger
public float GetTriggerState(
    KeyboardState keyState,
    float btnState,
    PadButtons button)
{
    // if the trigger on the controller isn't
    // being used, check the keyboard
    if (btnState == 0.0f)
    {
        // since the keyboard is digital, and the
        // trigger is analog, map pressed keys to
        // the extreme trigger value
        if (keyState.IsKeyDown(GetKey(button)))
        {
            btnState = KeyMapHelper.TRIGGER_MAX;
        }
    }
    return btnState;
}

// get the state of a mapped thumbstick
public float GetStickState(
    KeyboardState keyState,
    float btnState,
    PadButtons btnMin,
    PadButtons btnMax)
{
    // if the thumbstick on the controller isn't
    // being used, check the keyboard
    if (btnState == 0.0f)
```

```
        {
            // since the keyboard is digital, and the
            // thumbstick is analog, map pressed keys
            // to one of the extreme thumbstick values
            if (keyState.IsKeyDown(GetKey(btnMin)))
            {
                btnState = KeyMapHelper.THUMBSTICK_MIN;
            }
            else if (keyState.IsKeyDown(GetKey(btnMax)))
            {
                btnState = KeyMapHelper.THUMBSTICK_MAX;
            }
        }
        return btnState;
    }
}
```

The collection of key mappings is indexed by the game pad buttons that they represent. By indexing the collection by game pad buttons, we're able to use the same key to represent several buttons simultaneously. So the up key on your keyboard can emulate the player pressing up on the left thumbstick, up on the right thumbstick, and up on the DPad, all at the same time.

In most scenarios, you'll map keys to buttons one by one. But mapping a single key to multiple buttons makes it easier for us to cram more functionality into the tight constraints of the keyboard, and should make retrofitting existing code easier (for many games, the DPad and the left thumbstick provide the same functionality).

Note

Of course, this means that you can't represent the same game pad button with more than one keyboard key—at least not for the same player. A single key can be mapped to one button for each player, so you can control two players with the same keyboard key, but that's probably not very useful. It's interesting, but not useful.

The KeyMapHelper Class

The KeyMapHelper class is responsible for associating instances of the KeyMap class with specific players. Players are mapped to key mappings within a generics-based Dictionary collection.

```
// collection of key mappings, indexed by player
protected static Dictionary<PlayerIndex, KeyMap> m_KeyMaps = null;
```

```
protected static Dictionary<PlayerIndex, KeyMap> KeyMaps
{
    get
    {
        if (m_KeyMaps == null)
        {
            UseDefaultMappings();
        }
        return m_KeyMaps;
    }
}

// reserve space in the list to map
// keys for players one and two
protected static void InitKeyMaps()
{
    // initialize the list
    KeyMapHelper.m_KeyMaps = new Dictionary<PlayerIndex, KeyMap>();

    // populate the list with empty mappings
    KeyMapHelper.m_KeyMaps.Add(PlayerIndex.One, new KeyMap());
    KeyMapHelper.m_KeyMaps.Add(PlayerIndex.Two, new KeyMap());
}

// does the specified player have any keyboard mappings?
public static bool HasMappings(PlayerIndex player)
{
    bool hasMappings = false;

    if (player == PlayerIndex.One || player == PlayerIndex.Two)
    {
        hasMappings = KeyMapHelper.KeyMaps[player].HasMappings;
    }

    return hasMappings;
}
```

Merging Inputs

The KeyMapHelper class is also responsible for collecting the current state of the keyboard and game pads, merging those inputs in a non-destructive way whenever state info is requested by the game.

```csharp
// true if there is an active, physical gamepad or there are
// mapped keyboard keys for the specified player; assumes that
// there is an attached keyboard
public static bool IsConnected(PlayerIndex player)
{
    bool isConnected = GamePad.GetState(player).IsConnected;

    if (player == PlayerIndex.One || player == PlayerIndex.Two)
    {
        isConnected |= KeyMapHelper.KeyMaps[player].HasMappings;
    }

    return isConnected;
}


// augment state data from the physical game pad (if any) with
// mapped keyboard state data (if any)
public static void ProcessKeyboardInput(
    PlayerIndex player, KAGamePadState state)
{
    // set the connection state for the virtual controller
    state.IsConnected = KeyMapHelper.IsConnected(player);

    // if the specified player has keyboard mappings, process them
    if (HasMappings(player))
    {
        // get the current state of the keyboard
        KeyboardState keyState = Keyboard.GetState();

        // get the key mappings (if any) for the specified player
        KeyMap mapper = KeyMapHelper.KeyMaps[player];

        // update digital button state data
        state.Buttons.A = mapper.GetButtonState(
            keyState,
            state.Buttons.A,
            PadButtons.A);
        state.Buttons.B = mapper.GetButtonState(
            keyState,
            state.Buttons.B,
            PadButtons.B);
        state.Buttons.Back = mapper.GetButtonState(
            keyState,
```

```
        state.Buttons.Back,
        PadButtons.Back);

    // NOTE: similar code omitted from this listing
    // to save space. see CD for complete listing

    // update thumbstick state data (right)
    stick = state.ThumbSticks.Right;
    stick.X = mapper.GetStickState(
        keyState,
        stick.X,
        PadButtons.ThumbRightLeft,
        PadButtons.ThumbRightRight);
    stick.Y = mapper.GetStickState(
        keyState,
        stick.Y,
        PadButtons.ThumbRightDown,
        PadButtons.ThumbRightUp);
    state.ThumbSticks.Right = stick;
    }
}
```

Key Mapping Files

The KeyMapHelper class also provides a mechanism for loading and parsing text files that contain key mapping data. These data files contain lines of text that are parsed into entries in the specified player's KeyMap instance. The "button=key" strings in this file represent the members of the Codetopia.Input.PadButtons and Microsoft.Xna.Framework.Input.Keys enumerations. An example key mapping file follows.

```
##############################
PlayerOne
##############################

// colored buttons
A=V
B=G

// left thumbstick
ThumbLeft=X
ThumbLeftDown=S
ThumbLeftLeft=A
```

```
ThumbLeftRight=D
ThumbLeftUp=W

// system buttons
Start=LeftControl
Back=LeftShift


############################
PlayerTwo
############################

// colored buttons
A=NumPad5
B=NumPad6

// left thumbstick
ThumbLeft=End
ThumbLeftDown=Down
ThumbLeftLeft=Left
ThumbLeftRight=Right
ThumbLeftUp=Up

// system buttons
Start=RightControl
Back=RightShift
```

Your game imports these mappings by calling the `ProcessMappingFile` method. That method calls out to an overloaded version of itself which supports recursion. Recursion allows the parsing logic to support an "`#include`" token. That token imports the contents of another mapping file, allowing you to reuse the same key mappings across multiple files.

An example mapping file where this feature was put to use follows. The game for this chapter only references this mapping file. Using the "`#include`" functionality means that we can easily change the keyboard mappings without recompiling the game.

```
// handy way to swap key mappings without rebuilding the
// game. still need to restart the game, but don't have
// to recompile. Just edit this file, exit, and restart.

//#include KeyMappings\SinglePlayer.txt
#include KeyMappings\TwoPlayers.txt
```

The listing for the main `ProcessMappingFile` method follows. It calls out to its recursive sibling, passing a zero to indicate that this is the first call in the chain, and then verifies that mapping data was actually read in. If there was a problem reading the data, the default mapping values are used as a failsafe measure.

```
// read keyboard mappings from a data file
public static void ProcessMappingFile(string filename)
{
    // try to process the file
    KeyMapHelper.ProcessMappingFile(filename, 0);

    // if the mappings failed, just use our hard-coded defaults
    if (KeyMapHelper.KeyMaps.Count == 0)
    {
        KeyMapHelper.UseDefaultMappings();
    }
}
```

The listing for the recursive `ProcessMappingFile` method follows.

```
// read keyboard mappings from a data file
protected static void ProcessMappingFile(string filename, int depth)
{
    // check for null filename
    if (filename == null) { return; }

    // prepend the app's path
    string path = StorageContainer.TitleLocation + "\\" + filename;

    // if the file exists, process it
    if (File.Exists(path))
    {
        try
        {
            // local variable to read file, line-by-line
            string line = null;

            // open the file
            StreamReader reader =
                new StreamReader(
                    new FileStream(path, FileMode.Open));

            // if this is the first call in the chain, initialize
```

```
                        // our key mapping data, clearing any existing mappings
                        if (depth == 0)
                        {
                            KeyMapHelper.InitKeyMaps();
                        }

                        // always need a valid player, assume player one, just
                        // in case the data file forgot to specify a player
                        PlayerIndex player = PlayerIndex.One;

                        // for every line in the file, read it in and process it
                        while ((line = reader.ReadLine()) != null)
                        {
                            KeyMapHelper
                                .ProcessMappingLine(ref player, line, depth);
                        }

                        // after reading all the lines, close the file
                        reader.Close();
                    }
                catch { }
            }
}
```

The `ProcessMappingLine` method parses each line of text, looking for the tokens that it recognizes. Beyond mapping buttons to keys, the file parsing logic also allows you to specify to which player the next group of key mappings applies. Currently, only `PlayerOne` and `PlayerTwo` are supported.

This same parsing logic also allows you to include other mapping files within the current file as if their content had been typed into in the current file, and it allows you to decorate your mapping files with descriptive comments. Comment lines start with the "//" or "#" tokens.

```
// process a single line of data from a mapping file
protected static void ProcessMappingLine(
    ref PlayerIndex player, string line,int depth)
{
    // trim leading and trailing whitespace from the line
    line = line.Trim();

    // convert to lowercase for case-insensitive comparisons
    string lower = line.ToLower();
```

```csharp
if (lower.StartsWith("#include"))
{
    // process the specified file as if its contents had
    // been embedded within the current file
    string include =
        line.Substring("#include".Length).Trim();
    KeyMapHelper.ProcessMappingFile(include, depth + 1);
}
else if (
    line.StartsWith("#") ||
    line.StartsWith("//") ||
    line.Length == 0)
{
    // ignore line, it's blank or a comment
}
else if (lower.StartsWith("playerone"))
{
    // start applying mappings for PlayerIndex.One
    player = PlayerIndex.One;
}
else if (lower.StartsWith("playertwo"))
{
    // start applying mappings for PlayerIndex.Two
    player = PlayerIndex.Two;
}
else
{
    // actual mapping line is in the form " button=key"
    int index = line.IndexOf("=");
    if (index > 0)
    {
        // extract key and button names
        string btnName = line.Substring(0, index).Trim();
        string keyName = line.Substring(index + 1).Trim();

        // assume failure (we don't recognize the names)
        Keys key = UNKNOWN_KEY;
        PadButtons button = UNKNOWN_BUTTON;

        try
        {
            if (Enum.IsDefined(typeof(Keys), keyName))
            {
```

```
                    // the string to the left of the equals
                    // sign should be the name of a valid
                    // member of the Keys enumeration
                    key = (Keys)Enum.Parse(
                        typeof(Keys), keyName, true);
                }
                if (Enum.IsDefined(typeof(PadButtons), btnName))
                {
                    // the string to the right of the equals
                    // sign should be the name of a valid
                    // member of the PadButtons enumeration
                    button = (PadButtons)Enum.Parse(
                        typeof(PadButtons), btnName, true);
                }
            }
            catch { }

            if (key != UNKNOWN_KEY && button != UNKNOWN_BUTTON)
            {
                // looks valid, go ahead and apply the
                // mapping between the button and the key
                KeyMapHelper.KeyMaps[player]
                    .AddMapping(button, key);
            }
        }
    }
}
```

The ProcessMappingLine method is also used by the UseDefaultMappings method to easily create in-memory key mappings from human-readable data within the source code.

```
// clear the current mappings and use our hard-coded defaults
public static void UseDefaultMappings()
{
    // clear any existing mappings
    KeyMapHelper.InitKeyMaps();

    // keep track of which player's keys are being mapped
    PlayerIndex player = PlayerIndex.One;

    // map defaults for player one
    ProcessMappingLine(ref player, "PlayerOne", 0);
```

```
ProcessMappingLine(ref player, "X=F", 0);
ProcessMappingLine(ref player, "Y=T", 0);
// NOTE: similar code omitted from this listing
// to save space. see CD for complete listing
ProcessMappingLine(ref player, "ThumbLeftUp=S", 0);
ProcessMappingLine(ref player, "ThumbLeftRight=D", 0);

// map defaults for player two
ProcessMappingLine(ref player, "PlayerTwo", 0);
ProcessMappingLine(ref player, "X=NumPad4", 0);
ProcessMappingLine(ref player, "Y=NumPad8", 0);
// NOTE: similar code omitted from this listing
// to save space. see CD for complete listing
ProcessMappingLine(ref player, "ThumbLeftDown=Down", 0);
ProcessMappingLine(ref player, "ThumbLeftRight=Right", 0);
    }
}
```

The Example Game

To demonstrate our new keyboard-aware game pad library, I converted the example game from Chapter 7 to use these new classes. Functionally, it's identical to the original example, but it now supports keyboard inputs as well as input from the game pad.

I won't list the source for the game here, since we covered it in Chapter 7. Compare the source for that chapter to the source for this chapter (found on the accompanying CD-ROM) to see what changed.

Summary

In this chapter, you learned what's involved in capturing user input from physical devices and manipulating that data before the game ever sees it. By providing this layer of abstraction, your game code can focus on a single (virtual) input source, and you can report input data to the game that isn't necessarily being generated by the player.

As an added benefit, having a single point of access for your input devices makes incorporating any future, new input devices trivial, requiring little or no change to the game code itself.

Review Questions

Think about what you've read in this chapter (and the included source code) to answer the following questions.

1. Why doesn't this component support the full range of analog button states when using keyboard emulation?

2. Why does this component not support four simultaneous keyboard-emulated players?

3. I don't plan on ever being without my game pad. How does this abstraction benefit me if I never use the keyboard to play the games that I create?

4. For this control, we intercept keyboard input and make the game believe that the player is using an actual game pad. This might be useful in other scenarios. For example, we could receive commands from another game over a network and translate those commands to changes in our virtual game pad's button states. Can you think of other ways that the relaying or replaying button states might be useful?

Exercises

EXERCISE 1. Choose a feature from the "Wish List" section at the beginning of this chapter and implement it. The easier of the two is the ability to temporarily disable keyboard support. As you implement your feature, keep your users in mind—the player and the game developer. The component needs to be transparent to the player, and the interface that you present to the developer needs to be simple and intuitive. Be sure to document your code.

EXERCISE 2. Implement a cheat system where a keyboard-based player can enable and disable a "rapid fire" mode, which will repeatedly cycle the pressed state of a virtual game pad button from pressed to not pressed and back. Provide a function key for each of the four game pad buttons (A, B, X, and Y) that enables and disables the cheat mode for each button, independently.

EXERCISE 3. Take the code you wrote for Exercise 2 and provide two "rapid fire" modes. In the first mode, the pressed state of the virtual button is cycled as long as the player is pressing the appropriate mapped keyboard key. In the second mode, the pressed state is cycled without the player having to touch the mapped key at all—as long as the mode is enabled, the virtual button is repeatedly being pressed and released by your code. Provide a way for the player to switch between these three cheat modes: repeatedly fire while a virtual button is pressed, continuous fire (ignoring the button state), and disable the cheat altogether. Be sure to provide some way for the programmer to configure the delay between these phantom button presses.

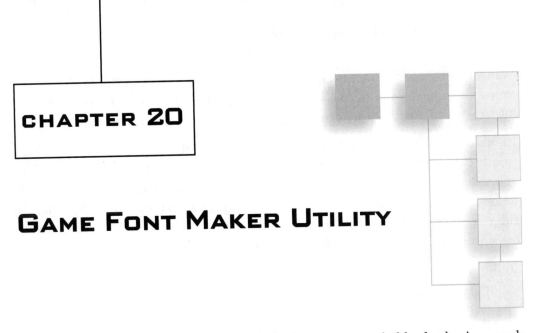

CHAPTER 20

GAME FONT MAKER UTILITY

When programming applications for Windows, you probably don't give much thought to the inner workings of how text is rendered to the screen. Unless you write custom controls or your application supports printing to the printer, you can usually get by just fine without knowing how each pixel of the text in your selected font is drawn.

In the realm of game programming, things aren't quite that easy. Games typically draw their text on screen as sprites, where each printable character has been rendered to a texture at design time. At runtime, these images are displayed in sequence to build words and sentences. In fact, on most dedicated game consoles, there is no system support for runtime fonts. All the text you see on a game console is comprised of pre-rendered character images. This method of drawing text provides the designer with an incredible level of control. Text rendered on one machine will look exactly the same on another, just as any picture rendered on each would look the same.

Of course the down side to the lack of system fonts on game consoles is that there are no options when it comes to drawing text. If you're interested in designing games that will run on Windows and the Xbox 360 game console, you must render your game's text using bitmap fonts.

There are definitely times when you will want to design some of your game fonts by hand, but there are countless free and cheap (and not-so-cheap) fonts available on the web. The variety and quality of many TrueType fonts (TTFs) will more than meet your needs. Wouldn't it be nice to convert those fonts into bitmaps so that your game can make use of them?

In this chapter, we will develop a Unicode-aware tool to convert TrueType fonts to a texture that we can then render to the screen like any other texture. This generated image will contain various control points, encoded throughout, to denote the location, size, and Unicode mapping for each encoded character. In the next chapter, we will develop a component that will render strings to the screen using the fonts generated by this tool.

In this chapter, you will learn how to:

- Measure text extents

- Render text to an in-memory bitmap

- Manipulate a bitmap, pixel by pixel

- Parse command line input and act on it

- Read a text file

- Save an image file

What Is Unicode?

Computers deal with numbers. Written characters like letters, numbers, and symbols are stored on the computer using some numeric encoding where the number stored is actually an index into a table of characters in some encoding scheme. For example, if you have been coding for a while, you're probably familiar with ASCII (American Standard Code for Information Interchange, pronounced "ask key"), which is an encoding scheme for the English alphabet.

Devices that use ASCII encoding recognize the integer value 65 as the capital letter A, 66 as capital B, 67 as capital C, and so on. ASCII uses seven bits per character, so ASCII encoding can only represent 128 unique characters, many of which are non-printable. That's fine if you speak and write in English and if you only have need for the symbols that appear in the ASCII table. But we live in a big world, with many distinct languages, and many specialized fields of study and business that each has its own technical symbols and notations. There's no way to cram all the world's characters into a 128-character table.

There are hundreds of standard encoding schemes, each specialized for its own language, technical notations, business application, or platform. Each of these schemes is generally ignorant of the others. Often different schemes will map the same character to different numbers or map the same number to different characters. Unicode attempts to unify these disparate schemes by providing a unique number for every character, regardless of platform, program, or language.

Using Unicode in Games

What does all this have to do with programming XNA games? The C# language represents all strings internally using Unicode. That means C# (and therefore XNA) pretty much supports all the world's languages. For Windows applications, that's a powerful tool. Displaying text in various languages is basically the same as displaying text in English. As long as the proper fonts are installed, your Unicode characters should display just fine.

Since our Xbox 360 games won't have access to the system font support of Windows, we're forced to use bitmap fonts. But our text is still stored internally as Unicode. It would be nice to have some simple way to map those language-agnostic characters to their pre-rendered bitmap counterparts, and then be able to render them to the screen using a simple function call within our game. That's where the tools that we'll develop in this chapter and the next chapter come in.

Limitations, Caveats, and Notes

I've tried to limit the scope of this tool so that we can cover the implementation in some detail. There are several features that would be worth adding, but I've excluded them for the sake of brevity. One such feature is the ability to replace infrequently used glyphs with your own custom graphics. For example, you could map the tilde (the "~" character) to a picture of the A button from the Xbox 360 Controller. Then you could print "Press the ~ button to continue" and see the embedded graphic on screen. As the code is written now, you'll need to display that message in three parts—the text before, the image, and the text after. Of course, you could just tweak the bitmap font in a paint program after you've built it using this tool, but where's the fun in that?

Since I am an English speaker, all my talk on multi-language support is purely theoretical. There may very well be scenarios where this tool falls short. Localization is a complex subject that rarely gets the attention it deserves—and this chapter won't be any exception. This tool is being provided for educational purposes. If you need something more powerful, search the web. There are several bitmap font generators out there. Most don't support Unicode, but a few do.

Fonts, like any other creative work, are intellectual property. Make sure that you're not violating any copyright laws before you start shipping copies of your bitmap fonts around the web. For hobbyist and education purposes, you're probably safe. Just be sure to dot your i's and cross your t's if you decide to create a commercial title.

The fonts generated by this tool aren't terribly large, but you may want to experiment with running them through an image optimizer to reduce the size. Just make sure that the character encodings aren't altered in any way. A change in a single pixel can drastically affect the ability of the program to determine which glyph belongs to which Unicode character.

Getting Started

We need to create a texture (an image file) based on a Windows TrueType font. This image will need to support transparency so that text can be rendered over existing game objects. We will also need some way to know where each character has been drawn in this texture. The interface for the user will be a console application where he can specify options at the command prompt. The bitmap font will have a fixed font size, determined by the user when he creates it.

Open up Visual C# 2005 Express Edition and create a new Console Application project. Console applications differ from Windows applications and game titles in that they are typically task-oriented. They take input from the command line and process it until completion. Once its task is complete, the console application terminates.

To keep things easy, we'll break the code for our tool into two basic parts—parse the user's input and generate the bitmap font. The user interface is contained in one file (Program.cs), and the image generation code is contained in another (FontMaker.cs). Let's create the user interface first.

The User Interface

The user interface is made up of four basic parts—collecting and parsing user input, merging default values with the user's input, generating the bitmap font, and providing feedback to the user. Figure 20.1 shows what the finished utility looks like.

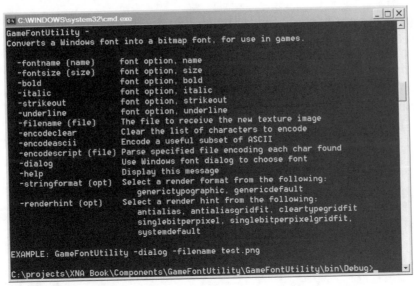

Figure 20.1
A screen shot of our new command-line tool in action.

Processing User Input

To make things easy on the users, we'll go ahead and define reasonable defaults for all of the options that they can specify so that when they omit an option, we can act as if they actually specified our default. These defaults are stored as member variables of the application. Whenever the user specifies an option on the command line, that value will override our default.

The default font will be Courier New, 10 point, with no font styles applied. The default output file will be "font.png." By default the ASCII characters from Space ("") to Tilde ("~") will be encoded, along with the copyright symbol ("©"), the registered trademark symbol ("®"), the left-pointing double angle ("«"), and the right-pointing double angle ("»"). The default rendering hint will be Anti-AliasGridFit, and the default string format will be GenericTypographic. Most of these options are pretty clear. The two that you might have questions about are the rendering hint and the string format. We'll discuss those in more detail when we work on the image generation code.

When parsing the command line, we'll convert a leading "/" to a "-" so that the application supports both, but we need only check one. We'll also convert command-line options to upper case before processing them so that options are not case sensitive. And we will provide several shortcut options that all map to the same function so that the user can be verbose when writing scripts (as in

"-underline") or save himself some typing when entering values by hand (as in "-u"). The ParseOptions method handles all processing of the user's input.

There are two command-line options that are worth taking a closer look at. The "-dialog" option will present the user with a standard Windows font dialog so that he can specify the font name, size, and styles rather than typing each on the command line. The following is a snippet from the source that demonstrates this functionality.

```
case "-FONTDIALOG":
case "-DIALOG":
case "-DLG":
    FontDialog dlg = new FontDialog();
    if (DialogResult.OK == dlg.ShowDialog())
    {
        Font f = dlg.Font;
        m_Bold = f.Bold;
        m_Italic = f.Italic;
        m_Strikeout = f.Strikeout;
        m_Underline = f.Underline;
        m_FontSize = f.Size;
        m_FontName = f.Name;
    }
    break;
```

The other noteworthy command-line argument is the "-script" option. This option allows the user to specify a Unicode text file that contains all the characters that he's interested in encoding in his bitmap font. This is especially useful if you already have localized voice scripts or string tables for your game. The application will identify every unique character within the file and configure the bitmap font generator to capture only those glyphs.

Image Generation

The class that actually takes a Windows TTF font and generates a bitmap game font is named FontMaker. This class is responsible for managing a list of characters to encode, for tracking any user-specified rendering options, and for laying out and encoding the glyphs on the image in a way that minimizes the final size of the image.

The list of glyphs that should be encoded is stored in a Dictionary collection class. The key to this collection is the character itself, and the value stored is a Rectangle structure that defines the location and size of the glyph on the final image.

```
// collection of char / rectangle pairs,
// defines glyph boundries
private Dictionary<char, Rectangle> m_GlyphBounds =
    new Dictionary<char, Rectangle>();
```

There are four methods that the FontMaker class exposes to the caller to manage this list of glyphs. ClearCharsToEncode will empty the list of tracked glyphs. AddCharToEncode will add a single character to the list of glyphs. AddCharsToEncode accepts two characters as parameters, and it will populate the list of glyphs with every character between the two specified characters, inclusive. And DefaultCharsToEncode will populate the list of glyphs with a predetermined list of characters of interest. Today, the only supported default character list is ASCII; but as I mentioned earlier, Unicode characters can be listed using the "-script" option from the command line of this tool.

Limiting the Game Font Image Size

When glyphs are initially added to the list, the location and size of the glyph are filled with zeros. Later, when the individual glyphs are processed, the width and height values are populated with the width and height of each character in the specified font. Once all the glyph sizes have been recorded, the location of each glyph is determined as they are arranged on the final image.

```
// temp rect variable used throughout method
Rectangle r = Rectangle.Empty;

// get sorted list of chars to capture
char[] keys = new char[m_GlyphBounds.Count];
m_GlyphBounds.Keys.CopyTo(keys, 0);
Array.Sort(keys);

// dummy graphics objs to get font data ...
Bitmap bmp = new Bitmap(10, 10, m_pixfmt);
Graphics g = Graphics.FromImage(bmp);
g.TextRenderingHint = RenderHint;

// ... in graphics units
float ffLineSpacing = font.FontFamily
    .GetLineSpacing(font.Style);
float ffAscent = font.FontFamily
    .GetCellAscent(font.Style);
float ffDescent = font.FontFamily
    .GetCellDescent(font.Style);
```

```
float ffHeight = font.FontFamily
    .GetEmHeight(font.Style);

// ... in pixels
int height = font.Height;
float ascent =
    height * ffAscent / ffLineSpacing;

// get width of each char in font
SizeF glyphSize;
foreach (char c in keys)
{
    // measure characters
    glyphSize = g.MeasureString("" + c, font,
        0xFFFFFF, RenderFormat);
    // get the current glyph bounds
    r = m_GlyphBounds[c];

    // update the glyph's width and height
    r.Width = (int)Math.Ceiling(glyphSize.Width);
    r.Height = height;

    // record the current glyph bounds
    m_GlyphBounds[c] = r;
}
```

This class tries to minimize the size of the final image by attempting to fit the glyphs on a 128-by-128 image. If that fails, the image height is doubled (so that the image is 128-by-256) and the process begins again. For reasons that are specific to the internal workings of DirectX and the graphics hardware, the routine that arranges the glyphs only uses image widths and heights that are a power of two (128, 256, 512, ...). This routine tries to keep the width and height equal (a square image), but favors height over width when only one of the bounds needs to be expanded.

```
// Try to fit the glyphs onto the smallest possible
// image. Start with a 128 x 128 image, and expand
// those bounds until we can make the glyphs fit.
int wout = 128;
int hout = 128;

// when the glyphs fit the image, match is true
bool match = false;
while (!match)
```

```
{
    // start at top, left. y equals 1 since the first
    // row of pixels (where y == 0) for every row of
    // glyphs is reserved to mark the start, end, and
    // character value of the glyph. x = 1 since the
    // height and ascent of the font are encoded in
    // the first column of the first row of glyphs.
    int x = 1;
    int y = 1;

    // assume success
    match = true;

    // step through each glyph
    foreach (char c in keys)
    {
        // get width and height of next glyph
        r = m_GlyphBounds[c];

        // is glyph too wide for this row?
        if (x + r.Width < wout)
        {
            // glyph fits, record new x and y
            r.Y = y;
            r.X = x;
            m_GlyphBounds[c] = r;

            // get ready for the next glyph
            x += r.Width;
        }
        else
        {
            // glyph is too wide, try the next row
            x = 0;
            y += height + 1;

            // did we run out of rows?
            if (y + height > hout)
            {
                // note failure and exit for loop
                match = false;
                break;
            }
```

```
                    // is glyph too wide for this new row?
                    if (x + r.Width < hout)
                    {
                        // glyph fits, record new x and y
                        r.Y = y;
                        r.X = x;
                        m_GlyphBounds[c] = r;

                        // get ready for the next glyph
                        x += r.Width;
                    }
                    else
                    {
                        // note failure and exit for loop
                        match = false;
                        break;
                    }
                }
            }

            // did we run out of space? expand the image
            if (!match)
            {
                // try to keep the image square, and sized
                // as a power of two.
                if (wout == hout)
                {
                    // double the height if the image is
                    // already square.
                    hout = hout << 1;
                }
                else
                {
                    // otherwise, double the width to make
                    // the image square.
                    wout = wout << 1;
                }
            }
        }

// free old resources
g.Dispose();
bmp.Dispose();
```

```
// create new resources
bmp = new Bitmap(wout, hout, m_pixfmt);
g = Graphics.FromImage(bmp);
g.TextRenderingHint = RenderHint;

// define our transparent pixel, clear image
Color transparent = Color.FromArgb(0x00, Color.White);
for (int y = 0; y < bmp.Height; y++)
{
    for (int x = 0; x < bmp.Width; x++)
    {
        bmp.SetPixel(x, y, transparent);
    }
}
```

Encoding Font Data onto the Image

Unicode character values are encoded on the image using the first row of pixels above each row of glyphs. Whenever a pixel is encountered that isn't fully transparent, the font decoder notes the start of a new glyph and records the character to which the glyph belongs. The Unicode character is encoded in the last two bytes of the four-byte pixel color (the green and blue color values).

The top, left pixel of the image and the pixel just below the top, left pixel hold what's commonly referred to as a "magic number" (the hex value 0xC0DE), which acts as a simple (though certainly not fool-proof) way to distinguish this image as a game font, versus some generic texture.

```
// set the first magic number (0xC0DE) for the
// new image, and note the height of the font.
// the magic number helps us distinguish this
// image file (which contains font data) from
// generic images
bmp.SetPixel(0, 0,
    Color.FromArgb(0xC0, 0xDE,
        (height    >> 8) & 0xFF,
        (height    >> 0) & 0xFF
    ));

// set the second magic number (0xC0DE) for the
// new image, and note the ascent of the font.
// the ascent is the distance from the top of a
```

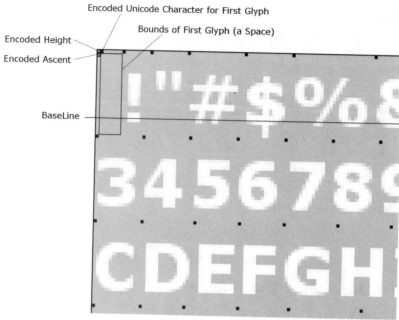

Figure 20.2
Part of a game font that was generated using our new tool.

```
// glyph to its baseline. knowing this value
// helps us to render fonts side-by-side,
// aligned by their baseline.
int fontAscent = (int)ascent;
bmp.SetPixel(0, 1,
    Color.FromArgb(0xC0, 0xDE,
        (fontAscent >> 8) & 0xFF,
        (fontAscent >> 0) & 0xFF));
```

In addition to the magic numbers, the top, left pixel contains the height of the font, and the pixel just below that contains the ascent of the game font. The height and ascent for a given font are constant. Every character within the font has the same height, and uses the same baseline. Figure 20.2 shows part of an actual game font that was generated using this tool.

Space Invaders

In my initial testing, I noticed that some glyphs in some fonts don't always live within the constraints that Windows reports. In those cases, I noticed that there were stray pixels on some of the glyphs when they were rendered. This was hard to

Joker

Figure 20.3
An extreme example of kerning.

spot when viewing the game font source image because the offending characters were sorted so that they sat next to the neighboring glyph that they were invading.

These visual artifacts are due to a feature of TrueType fonts known as *kerning*. Figure 20.3 is a great example of this effect. The text you see was rendered in my paint program, using the Monotype Corsiva TrueType font.

As you can see, the letter k invades the space reserved for the letter e. While this makes for beautiful documents and flyers, it makes our job a lot more difficult when rendering game text. This tool does not support kerning. It would be fairly easy to modify the code to allow for the glyphs that make up characters to extend beyond the bounds that define where you place them (and their neighbors), but true kerning support is more involved than that. So, by design, this tool does not support kerning.

To resolve this issue, I create a little bitmap for each glyph based on its reported bounds. I render each glyph to its own small bitmap, and render the small bitmap to the large, master image. This enforces proper clipping of each glyph. I'm sure there's a more efficient way to accomplish this task, but this was the most straightforward approach, and it was the easiest to explain.

```
// now that we've made sure everything fits, it's
// time to stamp them onto our new image
foreach (char c in keys)
{
    // get location and size of next glyph
    r = m_GlyphBounds[c];

    // this is inefficient, but need to make sure
    // that glyphs don't invade each other's space
    // creating a tiny Bitmap for each glyph rather
    // than just drawing the image on the master
    // Bitmap ensures there's no overlap between
    // characters
    Bitmap bmpGlyph =
        new Bitmap(r.Width, height, m_pixfmt);
    Graphics gGlyph = Graphics.FromImage(bmpGlyph);
    gGlyph.TextRenderingHint = RenderHint;
```

```
    // clear the tiny Bitmap
    for (int yc = 0; yc < height; yc++)
    {
        for (int xc = 0; xc < r.Width; xc++)
        {
            bmpGlyph.SetPixel(xc, yc, transaprent);
        }
    }

    // draw the glyph onto the tiny Bitmap
    gGlyph.DrawString("" + c, font,
        Brushes.White, 0, 0, RenderFormat);
    gGlyph.Flush(System.Drawing.Drawing2D.
        FlushIntention.Sync);

    // draw the new glyph onto the master Bitmap
    g.DrawImage(bmpGlyph, r.X, r.Y);
    g.Flush(System.Drawing.Drawing2D.FlushIntention.Sync);

    // go ahead and mark the next glyph as the end
    // of row. if it's not the last glyph on the row,
    // the next glyph will overwrite this value. by
    // assuming failure and marking it now, we don't
    // need to have special logic to handle an end-of-
    // row condition.
    if (r.X + r.Width < bmp.Width)
    {
        bmp.SetPixel(r.X + r.Width, r.Y - 1, m_EndOfRow);
    }

    // mark the start of the glyph and encode its
    // char value
    bmp.SetPixel(r.X, r.Y - 1,
        Color.FromArgb(0xFF,
            0x00,
            (c & 0xFF00) >> 8,
            c & 0xFF));
}
```

Spatial-Case Code

I had to special case the logic that encodes the space character. Since no pixels are actually rendered when drawing a Space, the system seems to report its width as zero. I would imagine the same is true for like-minded characters (like the Tab key), but I never actually tested it. The easy way to accommodate zero-width characters is to search and replace them with a space. Most will need to be treated specially by your code anyway. But a better approach may be to handle any character that reports its width as zero in the same way that I handled the Space—wrap it in two characters that you know have a non-zero width and measure the difference. The code snippet that handles the Space key follows.

```
if (c == ' ')
{
    // MeasureString returns 0 for ' ' when
    // using StringFormat.GenericTypographic
    SizeF asa = g.MeasureString("a a", font,
        0xFFFFFF, RenderFormat);
    SizeF aa = g.MeasureString("aa", font,
        0xFFFFFF, RenderFormat);

    // the difference between the widths of
    // "a a" and "aa" should be the typical
    // width of a space in the current font
    glyphSize = asa - aa;
}
else
{
    // measure non-space characters
    glyphSize = g.MeasureString("" + c, font,
        0xFFFFFF, RenderFormat);
}
```

Those Other Two Options

I promised to cover the two options that I glossed over earlier, so I guess I had better make good on my promise before we close this chapter.

I have provided support for each of the TextRenderingHints that Windows supports. In general, I don't suggest using anything other than the default (AntiAliasGridFit). There are three basic categories of TextRenderingHint, each with a normal and "grid fit" option. The three basic categories are

- **SingleBitPerPixel**—This option ignores aliasing issues altogether. No attempt is made to reduce the jaggedness of the rendered font.

- **AntiAlias**—This option attempts to smooth the edges of the font so that they don't appear jagged. This smoothing is done by varying the alpha component of the affected pixels to make them less intense, thereby blending into their background. Since the XNA Framework supports tinting sprites as they're rendered, our white text (with its alpha data) can easily be rendered in any color we choose.

- **ClearType**—This option also attempts to smooth the edges of the font so that they don't appear jagged. This smoothing is done by varying the blue and red tints of fringe pixels to take advantage of the physical characteristics of certain monitors. Since the pixel colors are modified rather than the alpha component of those colors, this rendering hint is practically useless for our purposes. I highly recommend that you avoid using this rendering hint for your game fonts.

The GridFit option for each of those render hints ensures that an "A" always looks the same, regardless of where you render it on the screen. Without the GridFit option, individual characters may be rendered slightly differently as you draw strings in a Windows application. This actually makes for a better user experience for desktop applications. Windows is able to determine how a particular character should look, based on its relation to other text, with sub-pixel accuracy. The GridFit option tells Windows to align the character with the closest whole pixel, ignoring this sub-pixel mumbo-jumbo.

For our bitmap game fonts, it makes more sense to have consistent glyphs. Since our glyphs are statically rendered, and since we don't know where the character will be drawn on the screen ahead of time, we need to make sure that an "A" always looks like an "A" regardless of its position on the screen.

As for the GenericTypographic string format, there's really only one option for our purposes. GenericTypographic provides the most accurate measurement of the individual glyphs. There may be some anomalies when using GenericDefault. So again, I'm going to recommend against changing the defaults provided by this utility. The options are there, and you can play with them to see what kind of results you get, but the most useful configuration is a rendering hint of AntiAliasGridFit and a string format of GenericTypographic.

Summary

In this chapter, you learned what's involved in rendering anti-aliased text to an in-memory bitmap. You learned how to encode useful data into an image, and save that image for use in your game. You learned about character encoding schemes, and how they affect your game. And you learned precious little about localization issues and how to create game fonts that can be used to display localized text in your game.

In the next chapter, we will write an XNA class that reads in the bitmap fonts that were generated using this tool. That new class will also provide methods for rendering text to your game screen and calculating the space that your text will occupy.

Review Questions

Think about what you've read in this chapter (and the included source code) to answer the following questions.

1. Why can't Xbox 360 games use TrueType fonts?

2. Why would anyone want to use Unicode text in their game?

3. If I'm not concerned about localization, do I have to use bitmap game fonts? Explain.

4. What is the difference between the various text rendering hint options? Which is best for general use?

5. The width and height of a glyph is clearly something that I need to draw strings that are relative to each other. But what is font ascent? Why would I ever need to know where the baseline of my font is?

Exercises

EXERCISE 1. Add a command-line option that allows the user to specify a range of Unicode characters to encode. If the user types "-range 0020-007E", the ASCII characters from Space (" ") to the Tilde ("~") will be encoded. If the user omits the second character (as in "-range 00DF"), just add the single character ("β" in this case). Don't forget that the FontMaker class already has support for adding a range of characters. So your task for this exercise is limited to parsing this new input to determine the start and end of the range, then pass those two characters (or the single character) off to the existing method.

EXERCISE 2. Generate a bitmap font of your choice using the default ASCII characters. Open the resulting image file in a paint program and edit the Tilde character glyph to be a smiley face. Be sure to use a paint program that supports transparent PNG files (like Photoshop or Paint Shop Pro). After completing the next chapter, try out your newly modified font by displaying the string "Have a nice day! ~". If your paint program supports layers, you may want to temporarily add a solid black background behind your font data while you work so that you can see your edits more easily. Just remember to delete it before you save the bitmap font back out to disk.

CHAPTER 21

GAME FONT LIBRARY

In the last chapter, we took an arbitrary TrueType font and created an image file that can be used in our game. This image was encoded with special markers that define the bounds of bitmap glyphs for each encoded character, the height of the glyphs, the ascent of the glyphs, and a list of the Unicode characters that were actually included in the encoding process.

The program that we developed in Chapter 20 used Windows-specific features to render individual characters and to generate the resulting image file. For design-time and compile-time tasks, that's fine. After all, our development environment is a Windows-only application. But we can't rely on Windows-specific APIs if we want our games to work on the Xbox 360 game console.

In this chapter, we will develop an XNA game library that will use the bitmap font image files that are created by the tool from the last chapter. The code in this new library is responsible for loading the image, decoding the data, and rendering arbitrary text using the decoded glyphs. This library will be built on XNA Framework APIs so that it will run, without change, on Windows and Xbox 360. Figure 21.1 shows a screen shot of the example game that we will develop in this chapter.

In this chapter, you will learn how to:

- Process a Texture2D object, pixel by pixel

- Decode data that's been embedded within an image

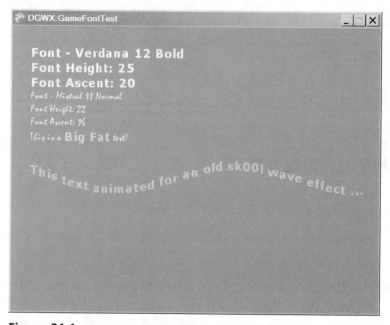

Figure 21.1
A screen shot of the example that we will develop in this chapter to demonstrate drawing text within our games.

- Manage a list of Unicode characters and their associated glyphs

- Render text to the screen by drawing glyphs from a bitmap font texture

- Use this new library to render text using multiple fonts

- Use this new library to create animated text effects

GameFont Class

The GameFont class represents a bitmap font in our game. It provides several useful properties that describe the font, as well as methods to measure text and draw text to the screen.

FontHeight

The FontHeight property is a read-only property that holds the height, in pixels, for the glyphs in the current font.

FontAscent

The FontAscent property is a read-only property that holds the ascent for the current font. The ascent is the distance from the top of a glyph to its baseline, measured in pixels. We will discuss font ascent in more detail later in this chapter.

Texture

The Texture property contains a reference to the in-memory image that contains our encoded bitmap font data. This property is set when you first create an instance of the GameFont object, but it can also be set by your game code. That might be useful when the ContentManager alerts you that the texture has been reloaded. In that case, there's no need to decode the texture again. You just need to update the texture reference in the GameFont class.

ErrorMessages

During the decoding process, a list of warnings and errors is maintained in the ErrorMessages property. This property exposes an array of strings, with each element containing a separate warning or error. The decoding process could just as easily have thrown an exception when it ran into problems, but this method of reporting errors allows the decoding process to continue (assuming that it's able to do so).

These messages can be inspected in the debugger, displayed to the screen (assuming that enough glyphs were successfully decoded), or used within simple error handling logic.

After the decoding process is complete, future errors will generate actual exceptions. The ErrorMessages property retains this history of the decoding process for the lifetime of the GameFont object.

```
// useful in debugger to see why the font didn't initialize
private List<string> _messages = new List<string>();
public string[] ErrorMessages
{
    get { return _messages.ToArray(); }
}
protected void AddMessage(string msg)
{
    _messages.Add(msg);
}
```

Extracting Glyphs from the Texture

Instances of the GameFont class are created using the static FromTexture2D method, which accepts the bitmap font texture as its only parameter and returns the new instance of the GameFont object. Assuming the texture that was passed into this method is a valid bitmap font (i.e., it was created using the Game-FontUtility that we wrote in the previous chapter), then the FromTexture2D method will attempt to extract the encoded glyphs from the texture using the ExtractGlyphDescriptors method.

```
// given a texture with encoded glyphs, return a BitmapFont object
public static GameFont FromTexture2D(Texture2D texture)
{
    // new instance placeholder
    GameFont font = null;

    // first, make sure it's a valid texture
    if (texture == null)
    {
        throw new GameFontException("Texture2D cannot be null.");
    }
    else
    {
        // try to extract the glyphs from the texture
        font = new GameFont();
        font.Texture = texture;
        font.ExtractGlyphDescriptors();
    }

    // return the fruits of our labor
    return font;
}
```

The ExtractGlyphDescriptors method scans the bitmap font texture, pixel by pixel, looking for encoded glyph data. The first two pixels that this method will inspect are the left-most pixels of the first two rows of pixels. These two pixels should contain our "magic number," encoded in the alpha and red channels of the pixel color. A magic number is just a value that helps us quickly determine whether or not this image was created using our bitmap font generation tool.

Also encoded in these first two pixels are the height and the ascent of the font glyphs. If the magic number is there, then the height and ascent of the bitmap font are extracted from the pixel data (they're stored in the green and blue channels of the pixel color), and the method continues scanning the image, looking for glyph markers.

Glyph markers are pixels that are encoded with a Unicode character. If the alpha component of the pixel is 0xFF, then the pixel is a glyph marker and the green and blue components of the pixel contain the Unicode character that the glyph represents.

Once a glyph marker is encountered, the method calculates the width of the current glyph by scanning ahead until it discovers another glyph marker or the end of the current row of pixels is reached. At this point, we have enough data to define our glyph's bounds.

The texture rectangle for the glyph is located just below its glyph marker, its width extends just to the left of the next glyph marker, and it shares the same height as all the other glyphs in the texture (the glyph height is encoded in the first pixel of the texture). Now that we know the current Unicode character and the texture rectangle that contains its glyph, we need to store this decoded information in some structure for later retrieval.

```
// interpret the encoded data to determine the individual
// glyph boundries
protected void ExtractGlyphDescriptors()
{
    // save some typing
    int w = Texture.Width;
    int h = Texture.Height;

    // grab the pixels of the texture so we can inspect them
    uint[] data = new uint[w * h];
    Texture.GetData<uint>(data);

    // check for magic numbers
    bool valid = w > 0 && h > 1;
    valid = valid && ((data[0] & MAGIC_MASK) == MAGIC_NUMBER);
    valid = valid && ((data[w] & MAGIC_MASK) == MAGIC_NUMBER);

    // is this a valid font texture
    if (valid)
    {
        // record the height and ascent of this font
        _fontHeight = (int)(data[0] & CHAR_MASK);
        _fontAscent = (int)(data[w] & CHAR_MASK);
```

```
// scan the image for our glyph markers
for (int y = 0; y < h; y += _fontHeight + 1)
{
    // we encode the height and ascent in the first column of
    // the first row, so it cannot be a valid glyph. skip it.
    int nFirstColumn = (y == 0 ? 1 : 0);

    // if there's no glyph marker here (in the first column),
    // there's no point in looking at the rest of the row
    if ((data[y * w + nFirstColumn] & ROW_COLUMN_MASK) ==
        ROW_COLUMN_MASK)
    {
        // found a marker, scan the row for glyphs
        for (int x = nFirstColumn; x < w; x++)
        {
            // is this a glyph?
            if ((data[y * w + x] & ROW_COLUMN_MASK) ==
                ROW_COLUMN_MASK)
            {
                // yes. record the details and ...
                char key = (char)(data[y * w + x] & CHAR_MASK);
                int top = y + 1;
                int left = x;
                int width = 1;

                // ... keep scanning to determine the width
                while ((x + width < w - 1) &&
                    ((data[y * w + x + width] & ROW_COLUMN_MASK)
                    != ROW_COLUMN_MASK))
                {
                    width++;
                }

                // record this glyph in our master list
                AddGlyph(key, left, top, width, _fontHeight);

                // make sure the scan catches the next glyph
                x += width - 1;
            }
        }
    }
}
```

```
        else
        {
            // this may be a texture, but it's no gamefont!
            AddMessage("ERROR: Invalid texture. Bad MAGIC_NUMBER.");
        }
    }

    // a collection of glyph descriptors, indexed by unicode char
    private Dictionary<char, GlyphDescriptor> _descriptors =
        new Dictionary<char, GlyphDescriptor>();

    // add glyph to our list of recognized characters
    // top, left, right, and bottom define the texture coordinates
    protected void AddGlyph(char key,
        int left, int top, int width, int height)
    {
        // make sure we haven't already seen this character
        if (!_descriptors.ContainsKey(key))
        {
            // perform some simple validation
            if (left < 0 || top < 0 || width < 1 || height < 1)
            {
                // texture bounds specified can't be drawn
                AddMessage(string.Format(
                    "WARNING: Invalid glyph bounds. [{0},{1},{2},{3}]",
                    left, top, width, height));
            }
            else
            {
                // looks good. add it to our list.
                _descriptors.Add(
                    key,
                    new GlyphDescriptor(left, top, width, height));
            }
        }
    }
```

GlyphDescriptor Class

The GlyphDescriptor class is a read-only collection of properties that define the bounds of a given glyph. These bounds define the subset of the main bitmap font texture that contains the glyph. The values of these properties are initialized in the constructor, and cannot be changed once they've been set.

Instances of this class are paired with the Unicode character that they represent using a generics-based `Dictionary` object where the Unicode character is the key, and the `GlyphDescriptor` instance is the value. Currently, the `GlyphDescriptor` object only contains the texture rectangle for the glyph, but other relevant data can easily be added without breaking any existing code.

So, why are we doing all of this? When the `ExtractGlyphDescriptors` method is finished scanning the texture, the `GameFont` class contains a list of all of the encoded Unicode characters and the texture rectangles that define the glyphs for those characters. This makes it easy to map a single character in a string to a sprite that can be drawn on the screen. Repeat that lookup-and-draw process for each character in the string, and you have text on the game screen.

```
// simple class to store individual glyph bounds
public class GlyphDescriptor
{
    // left bounds of glyph
    public int Left { get { return Rect.Left; } }

    // top bounds of glyph
    public int Top { get { return Rect.Top; } }

    // width of glyph bounds
    public int Width { get { return Rect.Width; } }

    // height of glyph bounds
    public int Height { get { return Rect.Height; } }

    // most APIs will want a Rect to define bounds
    private Rectangle _rect = new Rectangle();
    protected Rectangle Rect { get { return _rect; } }
    public Rectangle GetRectangle() { return Rect; }

    // only way to set properties is via the constructor
    public GlyphDescriptor(int left, int top, int width, int height)
    {
        _rect = new Rectangle(left, top, width, height);
    }
}
```

Extracting Glyphs, Revisited

Earlier, I said that the `ExtractGlyphDescriptors` method scans the entire texture, pixel by pixel. That's not quite true. If there are any glyphs in the texture, then the first few encoded Unicode characters are contained in the texture's first row of pixels.

The extractor will scan that first row, recording any glyphs that it discovers, until it reaches the end of the row or a special marker (called `INVALID_CHAR` in the code). This special marker is encoded just like any other Unicode character. Its value is '\xFFFF'.

The pixel that contains this special end-of-encoded-data marker defines the place where the next glyph would have started, but was too wide to fit within the remaining pixels on the current row. The remaining pixels on the current row can safely be ignored.

Not every row in the texture contains encoded Unicode characters. Each row of glyphs is topped with a single row of pixels that contain the character encodings and define the bounds of the glyph. These encoded rows are never drawn to the screen; they're just there to mark the place where one glyph ends and another begins.

Only rows that contain character encodings need to be processed by our decoding logic. When we reach the end of an encoded row, we can skip past the current row of glyph images (we know that every glyph in our font is `FontHeight` pixels tall).

Glyphs will always be aligned to the left of the texture. If the first pixel on an encoded row doesn't contain a glyph marker, we can stop searching that row. In the worst-case scenario of a texture that is absolutely packed full of glyphs, we should only have to scan as many rows of pixels as we have rows of glyphs (texture height / glyph height). The entire process happens very quickly.

Drawing Text

Now that we have loaded our bitmap font texture, and the `GameFont` class has extracted the encoded characters and their associated glyphs from the texture, we're ready to start drawing text to the screen. The `GameFont` class provides a method that does just that.

Given a string and a position on the screen, `GameFont`'s `DrawString` method will render the text, character by character. `DrawString` takes an optional `Color` parameter so that you can draw strings in different colors, using the same glyphs. It also takes an optional boolean parameter, which tells the method whether it should actually render the text to the screen, or just report how much space the text would have taken if it had been drawn.

We'll cover that last option a little later.

Once we have a list of valid characters and their associated glyphs, actually drawing the text is as easy as drawing any other sprite. Since the collection of texture rectangles for our glyphs is keyed on the Unicode character that they represent, the first thing that we need to do is break the text (a string) that was passed to DrawString into an array of characters.

As we loop through this array of characters, we'll make sure the character is one that was actually encoded in our bitmap font texture (i.e., the character is a valid key in our collection). If it's a character that we recognize, we draw its glyph to the screen.

Whenever we draw a glyph, we'll add its width to a running total so that we can report the size of the entire string to the calling method. Since all characters in our font have the same height, there's no need to keep a similar running total for the glyph heights—the DrawString method only prints single lines of text.

If we encounter a character in the string that wasn't encoded in our bitmap font texture, we don't draw anything, and we don't add anything to our running total for the width. That way, the total width that we report is the actual width, in pixels, of the text on the screen.

```
// draw each character of the string and return the width
// and height drawn
public Vector2 DrawString(SpriteBatch batch, string text,
    int x, int y, Color color, bool draw)
{
    // keep track of what's been drawn
    Vector2 v2 = Vector2.Zero;

    // make sure the glyph texture is still there
    if (_texture != null)
    {
        // init return value, assume at least one char was drawn
        v2.Y = _fontHeight;
        v2.X = 0.0f;
```

```csharp
        // the location to draw the next character
        Vector2 dest = Vector2.Zero;
        dest.X = x;
        dest.Y = y;

        // break string into characters and process each
        foreach (char c in text.ToCharArray())
        {
            // make sure this is a recognized glyph
            if (_descriptors.ContainsKey(c))
            {
                // don't actually draw glyph if we're just measuring
                if (draw)
                {
                    batch.Draw(
                        _texture,
                        dest,
                        _descriptors[c].GetRectangle(),
                        color);
                }
                // increment next location and total width
                dest.X += _descriptors[c].Width;
                v2.X += _descriptors[c].Width;
            }
        }
    }

    // return the bounds of the rendered string
    return v2;
}

// overload to draw text in specified color
public Vector2 DrawString(SpriteBatch batch, string text,
    int x, int y, Color color)
{
    return DrawString(batch, text, x, y, color, true);
}

// overload to draw white text (default color)
public Vector2 DrawString(SpriteBatch batch, string text, int x, int y)
{
    return DrawString(batch, text, x, y, Color.White, true);
}
```

Measuring Text

The last optional parameter in the DrawString method is a boolean that tells us whether we should actually render the text or not. To save ourselves some typing, the GameFont class also provides a MeasureString method which takes a single parameter—the text you want to draw.

Determining the size of rendered text is useful for those times when you want to know how much space the text will occupy on the screen before you actually draw it. For example, you may want to render the text inside a box. In that case, you can call MeasureString, draw a box that's a little bigger than the string, then render the text on top of the box.

For another example, you may want to render text that's centered within a certain part of the screen, or text that's right-justified. In those cases, you can call MeasureString to determine the dimensions of the rendered text, and then adjust the destination of your text before actually drawing it.

If you just want to render multiple lines of text, you don't need to call Measure-String. Since MeasureString and DrawString return the same information, you can use the results of the previous call to DrawString to determine the location of the next row of text. In fact, there's an even easier way to handle this simple scenario by taking advantage of the fact that all glyphs in our GameFont have the same height.

To render multiple rows of text, simply call the DrawString method once for each line of text, adding GameFont.Height to the Y component of the location each time so that each new line appears just below the last.

Since MeasureString and DrawString perform practically identical functions (the only difference is whether the glyphs are rendered or not), MeasureString simply calls out to DrawString, telling it not to draw anything.

```
// go through the motion of drawing the string, without actually
// rendering it to the batch. other than blitting the pixels to
// the screen, these two methods do pretty much the same tasks,
// so why not combine them?
public Vector2 MeasureString(string text)
{
    return DrawString(null, text, 0, 0, Color.White, false);
}


// useful overload for character-based animated effects
public Vector2 MeasureString(char c)
```

```
{
    return DrawString(null, c, 0, 0, Color.White, false);
}
```

Animating Text

Another area where measuring text comes in handy is when animating individual characters for interesting text effects. Imagine opening credits for your game where text appears on the screen, then explodes after a few seconds, sending letters flying off in random directions. Or, imagine on-screen text being formed as individual characters fall into place.

In the example code for this chapter, I've included a simple example of this concept where a string is rendered along an animated sine wave. To make developing your own custom animated character effects easier, the GameFont class provides overridden versions of each of the DrawString methods that accept a single Unicode character rather than a string.

```
// useful overload for character-based animated effects
public Vector2 DrawString(SpriteBatch batch, char c,
    int x, int y, Color color, bool draw)
{
    // report size of glyph, if valid
    Vector2 v2 = Vector2.Zero;

    // make sure we have a valid texture
    if (_texture != null)
    {
        // make sure this is a valid glyph
        if (_descriptors.ContainsKey(c))
        {
            // don't draw if we're just measuring
            if (draw)
            {
                batch.Draw(
                    _texture,
                    new Vector2(x,y),
                    _descriptors[c].GetRectangle(),
                    color);
            }
            // glyph was valid, return its measurements
            v2.Y = _fontHeight;
```

```
            v2.X = _descriptors[c].Width;
        }
    }
    return v2;
}


// useful overload for character-based animated effects
public Vector2 DrawString(SpriteBatch batch,
    char c, int x, int y, Color color)
{
    return DrawString(batch, c, x, y, color, true);
}


// useful overload for character-based animated effects
public Vector2 DrawString(SpriteBatch batch, char c, int x, int y)
{
    return DrawString(batch, c, x, y, Color.White, true);
}
```

Font Ascent

Encoded within the bitmap font texture is the ascent of the font. The ascent is the distance, in pixels, from the top of the glyph to its baseline. Imagine writing text on a sheet of ruled paper. The blue, pre-printed lines on that sheet are the baseline for your handwritten text. The distance from the highest point of the tallest character that you write to the blue line on the page is the ascent of your handwriting. (Conversely, the distance from the pre-printed line on the page to the lowest point of your text is known as the descent.)

You're probably thinking, "Thanks for the lesson in fonts, but how does this help me write games?" Well, I'm getting to that. Geez, you're so impatient.

If you've loaded multiple bitmap fonts, and you render a string using two or more different fonts (or different sizes of the same font), side by side, the text won't look right when the glyphs are aligned along their tops.

We're used to seeing text aligned to a common baseline. But, the DrawString expects a "top, left" position, not a "baseline, left" position. To properly align text from multiple fonts, we'll need to pick a virtual baseline on the screen, and subtract the ascent of each font from the baseline before drawing the string.

GameFontException Class

The GameFontException class is a subclass of the standard Exception class. It adds no new functionality to its parent. I just wanted to provide a unique exception type so that games that use the GameFont class can add error handling logic that's tailored to the specific errors that the GameFont class generates. There's nothing to see here. Move along.

```
// nothing special here, just wanted a unique class so that
// calling program can handle GameFont-specific exceptions
class GameFontException : Exception
{
    public GameFontException() : base() { }
    public GameFontException(string msg) : base(msg) { }
    public GameFontException(string msg, Exception inner) :
        base(msg, inner) { }
}
```

The Example

The example game for this chapter demonstrates how you can easily draw text in your game using an arbitrary font. The game loads two bitmap fonts, one based on the Mistral (11 point) TrueType font and the other based on Verdana (12 point, bold). Each font is contained within its own GameFont instance.

Once the fonts are loaded and initialized, the game renders some simple information about each font in the top, left corner of the screen. Each font's name, height, and ascent are drawn using the GameFont that the data represents.

Just below this font data, a line of text is drawn using both fonts, aligned along their baselines, as described earlier in this chapter. And below this WYSIWYG-like string is a simple example of animated text where a string is drawn using a simple sine function whose input is updated over time.

Summary

In this chapter, you learned how to access and process the pixel data of a texture. You learned how to map the individual Unicode characters of a string to the glyphs (little pictures of letters) that they represent and draw those glyphs on the screen to form words.

You also learned how to handle more complex tasks like rendering multiple lines of text, justifying text, drawing text from one font within text from another font, and performing simple animated text effects.

Review Questions

Think about what you've read in this chapter (and the included source code) to answer the following questions.

1. Name two ways to determine how much space a string will occupy on the screen before you actually render it using the GameFont class.

2. What method of the Texture2D class would you use to inspect the individual pixels of an image?

3. How many textures can a GameFont reference at the same time?

4. What is the INVALID_CHAR constant found in the GameFont code? What does it do?

5. What is the purpose of the GameFontException class? Why not just throw a normal Exception?

Exercises

EXERCISE 1. Every time a string is passed to the DrawString method, it generates an array of characters. Even when you're rendering static text, you're updating the screen 30, 60, or more times every second. There's not much point in converting the same string to a character array thousands of times.

Cache the result of the conversion, along with the original string, in the GameFont class. If future calls to DrawString are using the same (cached) string, don't bother creating the character array; just use the same one that you used on the last call. If the caller passes in a new string, generate the new character array and replace your cached values with these new values.

EXERCISE 2. Once you have generated a bitmap font, open the resulting image file in a paint program and edit the tilde glyph (the "~" character) to be a smiley face. Be sure to use a paint program that supports transparent PNG files (like Photoshop or Paint Shop Pro). Using this newly modified font, display the string "Have a nice day! ~".

EXERCISE 3. Create a `DrawStringEx` method that allows the user to specify a scale (as a float parameter) for his text. Be sure to multiply your running totals by this scale so that the characters still line up properly, and be sure that your reported width and height for the string take into account the new scale.

EXERCISE 4. Extend the `DrawStringEx` method from the previous exercise to allow the user to specify an angle of rotation for his text. You will need to calculate the position of each new character by multiplying the (possibly scaled) width of the previously rendered glyph by the cosine of the angle for the X component of the new location, and the sine of the angle for the Y component of the new location.

You will also need to make sure that the size of the text that you report back to the caller accounts for the fact that rotated text takes up more space than text that isn't rotated. Perhaps the simplest way to calculate this on-screen size is to note where the top, left and bottom, left pixels of the first glyph are drawn and where the top, right and bottom, right pixels of the last glyph are drawn.

These four points define a (possibly rotated) rectangle in which all the rendered glyphs are contained. You can calculate the on-screen size by finding the highest, lowest, leftmost, and rightmost points of those four. The result will be the smallest non-rotated rectangle that contains all of the glyphs that were just drawn.

Since the calling code is probably using the reported width to determine where to draw the next string, you should still just return the (possibly scaled) running width total and simple glyph height as you always have. That way, the calling routine can determine the location for the next substring by applying the same trigonometric formulas that you did on a per-glyph basis.

Report the actual on-screen size via a new property. Name this new property `UpdatedRect`. Be sure to modify the original `DrawString` methods so that this new property gets updated regardless of which method the caller uses. When no glyphs are drawn, set this property to an empty rectangle.

EXERCISE 5. The first exercise for this chapter sounds like a reasonable optimization, but there's a major flaw in its logic. When implementing optimizations, you need to consider how users will be calling your code. A typical scenario for the `GameFont` class would be a game that wants to render several strings to the screen during every update.

For example, the game may render a countdown timer, the health for player one, the health for player two, the score for player one, the score for player two, and a high score, with every update to the screen. In this scenario, the cached data will be overwritten with every call to DrawString. That's certainly not what we wanted to happen.

This story has two morals. The first is, "Don't fix it if it ain't broke." The other is, "Profile your 'optimizations' to make sure that they're doing what you think they're doing."

Think about other optimizations that can be made to this library. What are some benefits of your new approach? What are some limitations? Are you sure?

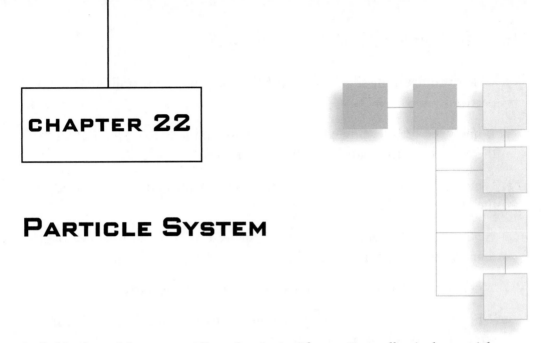

CHAPTER 22

PARTICLE SYSTEM

Individual particles are usually rather insignificant. But collectively, particles can be used to great effect, with minimal resource consumption. Particles are created and managed by an object known as an emitter. The emitter spawns new particles from its current location, configuring each with a location, velocity, lifetime, and other properties. Once they leave the emitter, particles are pretty much independent objects. Particles may be affected by global forces like gravity and wind, and they may vary their color or opacity over time (for example a burning ember may fade to nothing).

In this chapter, you will learn how to:

- Manage thousands of simple game objects simultaneously

- Limit the resources that these objects consume

- Add simple effects to your game to make it more immersive

Particle systems are used in a wide variety of game genres for a wide variety of in-game effects.

- When your race car scrapes against a guard rail, the sparks are particles.

- When you're snowboarding down a mountain, the snow wash from your board is made up of particles.

- When you fire a missile from your fighter jet, the vapor trail is made up of particles.

- When your 12th-level mage summons enough mana to cast a healing spell, the aura that surrounds her contains particles.

- When you clear a row in your favorite puzzle game and the blocks explode, the falling pieces are particles.

- When you shoot out a window in a first-person shooter, the shards of glass that fall to the ground are particles.

- When a comet flies by your starship, its tail contains particles.

- When you throw a smoke grenade onto the battle field, the resulting smoke screen is made up of particles.

- When you walk past a fountain in your favorite MMORPG, the water jets are made up of particles.

In this chapter, we will create the simple 2D particle system shown in Figure 22.1. The example code that we will develop is by no means a complete implementation,

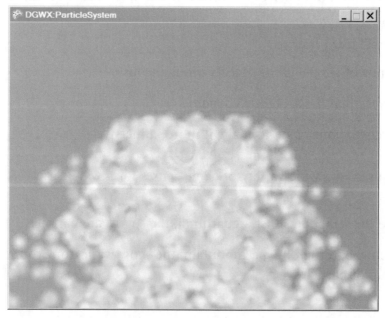

Figure 22.1
The particle effect demo game, with gravity turned on.

but it should provide a good base for you to build on, and it will effectively demonstrate the basic features of a 2D particle system. Many of the concepts that you learn here will apply to 3D particle systems as well. Some particle systems account for collisions between particles and other game objects but rarely include checks for collisions between particles. In the interest of simplicity, the code that we develop in this chapter doesn't include any non-particle game objects, so we won't add collision checking to our system.

The Architecture

The particle effect is made up of a few, specialized classes. These classes work together to manage the state of individual particles, then render the results to the screen. This example is designed around the XNA Framework's 2D graphics APIs, but most of the principles that we'll discuss in this chapter are also applicable in a 3D particle system.

The Particle

The particle is the basic building block of any particle system. Particles appear on the screen as a single point or a 2D graphic. Minimally, particles have a location and velocity. Our particles will also include properties for color, age, lifetime, rotation, opacity, scale, and depth. The Particle class has only two methods: Update and Draw. The following list describes each of the parameters and methods of this class.

- Age—The number of (cumulative) seconds that this particle has been active.

- Color—The tint with which to draw this sprite.

- Depth—The Z-Order of this sprite, expressed as a float between 0.0f and 1.0f.

- IsActive—The current state of this particle. Particles are created once, and placed in a pool. When a particle is marked as inactive, it's available to be spawned as a new on-screen particle.

- Lifetime—The maximum number of (cumulative) seconds that this particle may remain active.

- Movement—The distance that this particle will travel in a single second, assuming no outside force (like gravity) is affecting it.

- **Opacity**—The current transparency of this particle. (Not implemented in this example.)

- **Location**—The current location (screen coordinates) of this particle.

- **Rotation**—The current rotation of this particle, expressed in radians.

- **Scale**—The scale of this particle, where 1.0f is the actual size of the source texture.

- **Draw()**—Draw this particle using its current properties.

- **Update()**—Move the sprite, and update its age.

The Particle2D class is basically just a warehouse for the properties that the Emitter2D class uses to manage each particle. I won't list the code for the properties here, but I will list the Update and Draw methods.

```
// update position (based on m_Movement) and age
public void Update(float elapsed)
{
    // only update active particles
    if (IsActive)
    {
        // move the particle
        m_Position += m_Movement * elapsed;

        // check for expired particles
        if (LifeTime != 0.0f) // 0.0f == never dies
        {
            Age += elapsed;
            if (Age > LifeTime)
            {
                IsActive = false;
            }
        }
    }
}

// render the particle
public void Draw(SpriteBatch batch, Texture2D texture,
    Rectangle clipRect)
{
```

```
// only draw active particles
if (IsActive)
{
    batch.Draw(
        texture,
        Position,
        clipRect,
        new Color(Color),
        Rotation,
        Vector2.Zero,
        Scale,
        SpriteEffects.None,
        Depth);
}
}
```

As you can see from the preceding listing, the particle implementation is (intentionally) quite simple. Particle systems are meant to be lightweight, requiring very little CPU time and memory for each particle.

The Emitter

The emitter is responsible for managing individual particles, spawning new particles and reclaiming expired particles. The emitter is initialized with a maximum number of particles to manage. Particles are created once, and placed in a pool of inactive particles, ready to be spawned. Whenever a new particle is needed, it's moved from the inactive pool, initialized with new property values, and placed in a pool of active particles. With each call to the emitter's Update method, the particle's Update method is called for each particle object in the active pool.

Note

There are a couple of reasons why particles are implemented as a pooled resource, rather than creating them as they're needed. The first reason is to reduce the overhead of creating and destroying the objects that represent each particle. There is a performance penalty for allocating, initializing, and releasing thousands or millions of in-memory objects. By creating the objects once, and then placing them in a pool, we eliminate two of those three tasks.

The second reason that particles are implemented as a pooled resource is that they're basically just eye candy. They're not essential to the game play. By limiting our particles to a fixed number, we can be sure that we won't create so many particles that their processing and memory usage affects more critical areas of the game logic.

The emitter also contains the ranges of values that each of the particle's properties should be initialized to. By initializing properties from a range of values (rather than simply assigning a single, static value to each new particle) particles seem to act more independently. To help us track these ranges, I've created a simple, templated class that will contain the minimum and maximum values for a given property, and generate a random value for us that lies within that range. This class is called RangedValue, and we will discuss it in more detail later in this chapter.

The emitter also manages a list of global particle forces, like gravity and wind. These global forces are derived from a common base class called a modifier, which we will also discuss later in this chapter.

The following list describes each of the parameters and methods of the Emitter2D class.

- **Active**—When false, active particles will continue to be updated and drawn, but new particles will not be spawned.

- **Enabled**—When false, all processing is paused. Active particles will not be updated, and nothing will be drawn.

- **EmitterRect**—Emitters have a width and height so that particles can be spawned from within a rectangle, rather than from a single point.

- **EmitterBoundsRect**—In addition to a particle's Lifetime property, we can reclaim particles when they leave the screen (or when they leave the EmitterBoundsRect).

- **Position**—It's a pain to update a rectangle when all you wanted to do was move the emitter to a new location, so this helper allows you to just specify a new X and Y to change the EmitterRect.

- **ParticlesPerUpdate**—This is the number of new particles to emit with each call to Update. If there aren't enough particles in the inactive pool to satisfy this request, the number of particles actually spawned will be less than this value.

- **MaxParticles**—This is the maximum number of particles that the emitter will ever actively manage. By placing an upper limit, we can make sure that our emitter isn't stealing resources that could be better used for other parts of our game.

- **ParticleLifetime**—The number of seconds that a single particle may be active before being reclaimed.

- **RangeColor**—The range of colors from which a new particle will have its Color property initialized.

- **RangeMovement**—The range of velocities from which a new particle will have its Movement property initialized.

- **Texture**—The texture of the sprite that represents a particle.

- **TextureRect**—The source rectangle, within the Texture, for all particles.

- **AddModifier()**—Add a modifier (like gravity) to this emitter.

- **ClearModifiers()**—Clear the list of modifiers for this emitter.

- **RemoveModifier()**—Remove a specific modifier from this emitter.

- **Draw()**—Draw all active particles.

- **Update()**—Spawn new particles, update all active particles, apply any global modifiers (like gravity) to all active particles, and reclaim any inactive particles for later use.

As with the Particle2D class, the Emitter2D class has many configurable properties. And, as with the description of the particle class, I won't list the code for all those properties here.

The Update method manages the active particles that it owns, reclaiming spent particles and spawning new particles as needed.

```
// manage active particles, spawn new particles if it's time to do so
public virtual void Update(float elapsed)
{
    // only update if enabled
    if (Enabled)
    {
        // temp variables to save typing
        bool outOfBounds;
        int parX, parY;
        for (int i = 0; i < m_ActiveParticles.Count;i++ )
        {
            Particle2D particle = m_ActiveParticles[i];
```

When a particle leaves the area of the screen that's defined by the `Emitter-BoundsRect` property, it becomes inactive.

```
// when particle leaves emitter bounds, mark inactive
parX = (int)Math.Round(particle.Position.X);
parY = (int)Math.Round(particle.Position.Y);
outOfBounds = parX < EmitterBoundsRect.Right;
outOfBounds &=
    parX + TextureRect.Width > EmitterBoundsRect.Left;
outOfBounds &=
    parY < EmitterBoundsRect.Bottom;
outOfBounds &=
    parY + TextureRect.Height > EmitterBoundsRect.Top;
if (outOfBounds) particle.IsActive = false;
```

If the current particle is (still) active, any attached modifiers will be allowed to process it before it is asked to update itself.

```
// process active particles, clean up inactive particles
if (particle.IsActive)
{
    // allow active modifiers to update particle
    foreach (Modifier2D modifier in m_Modifiers)
    {
        if (modifier.Enabled)
        {
            // tell the modifier to update this particle
            modifier.Update(particle, elapsed);
        }
    }
    // tell particle to update itself
    particle.Update(elapsed);
}
```

If the current particle has been marked as inactive, it will be reclaimed for later use.

```
    else
    {
        // move particle to inactive list for later reuse
        m_InactiveParticles.Add(particle);
        m_ActiveParticles.RemoveAt(i);
        i--;
    }
}
```

Now that all of the active particles have been updated, and newly inactive particles have been reclaimed, it's time to spawn new particles.

```
// try to generate ParticlesPerUpdate new particles
for (long i = 0; Active && i < ParticlesPerUpdate; i++)
{
    if (m_InactiveParticles.Count > 0 )
    {
        // reset particle add it to pool of active particles
        Particle2D particle = m_InactiveParticles[0];
        particle.Position = m_EmitterRV2.RandomValue();
        particle.Movement = m_RangeMovement.RandomValue();
        particle.Color = m_RangeColor.RandomValue();
        particle.IsActive = true;
        particle.LifeTime = m_ParticleLifetime;
        m_InactiveParticles.Remove(particle);
        m_ActiveParticles.Add(particle);
    }
```

If we've run out of particles in our inactive pool, there's no need to keep trying to spawn new particles. We'll just exit the loop. Maybe there will be some more particles to play with during the next frame.

```
        else
        {
            // no more particles in our inactive pool
            break;
        }
    }
}
```

The Draw method of the Emitter2D class simply iterates through the list of active particles, asking each to draw itself.

```
// render the active particles
public virtual void Draw(SpriteBatch batch)
{
    // only draw particles when emitter is enabled
    if (Enabled)
    {
        foreach (Particle2D particle in m_ActiveParticles)
        {
            // ask the particle to draw itself
```

```
                particle.Draw(batch, Texture, TextureRect);
            }
        }
    }
```

Modifiers

Left to their own devices, particles will move at a constant rate, in a fixed direction. Particles maintain their own position data (the Position property) and velocity data (the Movement property). Whenever the Update method is called on a particle, it modifies its own position using the simple formula, "Position = Position + Movement." That's fine if you're simulating a frictionless, gravity-free environment. In most scenarios, that's not the case.

It doesn't make much sense to implement global changes like gravity and wind at the particle level. Gravity affects every particle. The emitter manages a list of helper objects that can make global changes to particles. These helper objects are derived from the Modifier2D base class. You can think of modifiers as a kind of plug-in. A simple gravity modifier would update particles using a formula similar to particle.Movement.Y = particle.Movement.Y + Gravity. Modifiers are typically very simple, but they can be combined with other simple modifiers to achieve great composite effects.

```
// update a particle based on custom code
// used by emitter
public abstract class Modifier2D
{
    // only update active modifiers
    protected bool m_Enabled = true;
    public bool Enabled
    {
        get { return m_Enabled; }
        set { m_Enabled = value; }
    }

    // custom code goes here, in derived class
    // called for each particle, every frame, by emitter, if enabled
    public abstract void Update(Particle2D particle, float elapsed);
}
```

While this chapter's code includes implementations for simple gravity and wind modifiers, modifiers can perform more complex tasks. You might change the particles' colors to create a pulsing or fading effect. Or you might change the particles' size or rotation to create interesting falling leaves or snow. Or you might create a single-point gravity effect so that particles are pulled into a black hole or whirlpool.

Note

We could just as easily have implemented these effects in the `Emitter2D` class, but using modifiers allows us to add new effects without changing the core emitter class every time. Coding and maintenance are easier since the effect classes are self-contained, and debugging is easier because the emitter implementation isn't constantly changing.

Of course, there may be a performance penalty for calling the modifier's `Update` method once for every particle. If we find that to be the case, we could consider breaking the modifier updates into a separate pass, processing particles before or after the emitter is done with its update pass.

In that scenario, modifiers no longer work on a single particle at a time—they're called once per update, and they process all the active particles in a loop (saving thousands of calls to the modifier's `Update` method). This method might introduce other performance issues, though (like cache misses). So, you'll want to profile your code before and after to see if your "optimizations" are doing what you think they should.

The listings for the two modifier classes from this demo game (gravity and wind) follow.

```
// pull particle down (or up), accounting for current momentum
public class Modifier2DGravity : Modifier2D
{
    protected float m_Gravity = 200.0f;

    public Modifier2DGravity() { }
    public Modifier2DGravity(float gravity)
    {
        m_Gravity = gravity;
    }

    // called for each particle, every frame, by emitter, if enabled
    public override void Update(Particle2D particle, float elapsed)
    {
        Vector2 v2 = particle.Movement;
        v2.Y += m_Gravity * elapsed;
        particle.Movement = v2;
    }
}
```

```
// blow particle to left or right, accounting for current momentum
public class Modifier2DWind : Modifier2D
{
    protected float m_Wind = 200.0f;

    public Modifier2DWind() { }
    public Modifier2DWind(float wind)
    {
        m_Wind = wind;
    }


    // called for each particle, every frame, by emitter, if enabled
    public override void Update(Particle2D particle, float elapsed)
    {
        Vector2 v2 = particle.Movement;
        v2.X += m_Wind * elapsed;
        particle.Movement = v2;
    }
}
```

Ranged Values

The RangedValue class contains two properties (Min and Max) that store the minimum and maximum values for this range, and a method (RandomValue) to generate a value within this range. The class also contains another property (Value) that returns the result of the last call to the RandomValue method. This is the first time that we'll be using a feature of the C# programming language known as generics. *Generics* allow you to define a single class that performs a common set of tasks, then change the type of data that the class uses. For example, we can define a simplified RangedValue class that just holds our Min and Max values using the following code:

```
public class RangedValue<T>
{
    // the min value
    protected T m_Min;
    public T Min
    {
        get { return m_Min; }
        set { m_Min = value; }
    }
    // the max value
```

```
    protected T m_Max;
    public T Max
    {
        get { return m_Max; }
        set { m_Max = value; }
    }
}
```

To use this class for a ranged integer, a ranged string, and a ranged `Color`, we could then add code similar to the following to our game:

```
RangedValue<int>    IntRange;
RangedValue<string> StringRange;
RangedValue<Color>  ColorRange;
```

Before generics, we had two basic options. The first option was to implement each of these variations as a separate class, possibly implementing a common interface in each specialized class (or deriving each from a common base class) so that we could pass the object among methods generically. The second option was to implement the `RangedValue` class so that the `Min` and `Max` properties used `System.Object` as their data type, but would require runtime casting, and performance would suffer if we used the class extensively. While the first option is better in terms of performance, maintaining multiple classes is a pain. If you make a change to one of the classes, you need to remember to make the same change to the other classes.

Under the covers, the compiler is basically doing the work of the first option for us when we use generics by creating separate, specialized classes, each based on our template. This gives us the performance benefits of using the data types that we're actually interested in using, while limiting the amount of code that's involved (versus writing everything by hand). Of course, generics have some restrictions, and that's why the preceding example is simplified.

Storing type-specific data is the easy part. Converting random values (which are stored as integers or floating-point values) to types that cannot be known at compile time is harder. For that reason, we do have to implement type-specific classes, but generics still save us from duplicating more code than we have to.

The actual `RangedValue` class source code listing follows.

```
// simple class to hold min / max values and generate random values
// within those bounds. base class uses generics (templates)
public abstract class RangedValue<T>
```

```
{
    // default constructor, .NET type-specific initial values
    public RangedValue()
    {
    }

    // constructor to specify min and max
    public RangedValue(T min, T max)
    {
        Min = min;
        Max = max;
    }

    // the min value
    protected T m_Min;
    public T Min
    {
        get { return m_Min; }
        set { m_Min = value; }
    }

    // the max value
    protected T m_Max;
    public T Max
    {
        get { return m_Max; }
        set { m_Max = value; }
    }

    // random number generator
    protected Random m_rand = new Random();

    // generate a random value between min and max, inclusive
    public abstract T RandomValue();

    // get the last random value
    protected T m_Value;
    public T Value
    {
        get { return m_Value; }
        set { m_Value = value; }
    }
}
```

The source code listings for three of the `RangedValue`-derived classes—`RangedInt`, `RangedDouble`, and `RangedVector4` (also used for ranges of color)—are listed here:

```
// type-specific subclass
public class RangedInt : RangedValue<int>
{
    public RangedInt() : base() { }
    public RangedInt(int min, int max) : base(min, max) { }

    // generate a random value between min and max, inclusive
    public override int RandomValue()
    {
        // linear interpolation between min and max based on random number
        Value = (int)MathHelper.Lerp(
            (float)Min,
            (float)Max,
            (float)m_rand.NextDouble());
        return Value;

    }
}


// type-specific subclass
public class RangedDouble : RangedValue<double>
{
    public RangedDouble() : base() { }
    public RangedDouble(double min, double max) : base(min, max) { }

    // generate a random value between min and max, inclusive
    public override double RandomValue()
    {
        // linear interpolation between min and max based on random number
        Value = (double)MathHelper.Lerp(
            (float)Min,
            (float)Max,
            (float)m_rand.NextDouble());
        return Value;

    }
}

// type-specific subclass
```

```csharp
public class RangedVector4 : RangedValue<Vector4>
{
    public RangedVector4() : base() { }
    public RangedVector4(Vector4 min, Vector4 max) : base(min, max) { }

    // generate a random value between min and max, inclusive
    public override Vector4 RandomValue()
    {
        // linear interpolation between min and max based on random number
        m_Value.X = (float)MathHelper.Lerp(
            (float)Min.X,
            (float)Max.X,
            (float)m_rand.NextDouble());
        m_Value.Y = (float)MathHelper.Lerp(
            (float)Min.Y,
            (float)Max.Y,
            (float)m_rand.NextDouble());
        m_Value.Z = (float)MathHelper.Lerp(
            (float)Min.Z,
            (float)Max.Z,
            (float)m_rand.NextDouble());
        m_Value.W = (float)MathHelper.Lerp(
            (float)Min.W,
            (float)Max.W,
            (float)m_rand.NextDouble());
        return Value;
    }

    // determine min and max values from colors
    public static RangedVector4 FromColors(Color min, Color max)
    {
        Vector4 v4Min = Vector4.Zero;
        v4Min.X = (float)min.R / (float)byte.MaxValue;
        v4Min.Y = (float)min.G / (float)byte.MaxValue;
        v4Min.Z = (float)min.B / (float)byte.MaxValue;
        v4Min.W = (float)min.A / (float)byte.MaxValue;

        Vector4 v4Max = Vector4.Zero;
        v4Max.X = (float)max.R / (float)byte.MaxValue;
        v4Max.Y = (float)max.G / (float)byte.MaxValue;
        v4Max.Z = (float)max.B / (float)byte.MaxValue;
        v4Max.W = (float)max.A / (float)byte.MaxValue;
```

```
        RangedVector4 rv4 = new RangedVector4();
        rv4.Min = v4Min;
        rv4.Max = v4Max;

        return rv4;
    }
}
```

The Example Game

The example game that we'll use to try out our new particle system has just one `Emitter2D` instance, with two generic `Modifier2D` instances (`Modifier2DGravity` and `Modifier2DWind`) attached to it. Both modifiers will affect all active particles with an acceleration of 200 pixels per second (pps)—gravity pulling the particles down at 200 pps, and wind blowing the particles to the right at 200 pps.

```
// a 2d particle emitter
Emitter2D m_emitter;

// two example particle modifiers
private static readonly Modifier2D m_ModGravity =
    new Modifier2DGravity(200.0f);
private static readonly Modifier2D m_ModWind =
    new Modifier2DWind(200.0f);
```

The emitter will spawn no more than 20 new particles per frame, and no more than 15,000 particles will be active at any one time. Particles will be spawned from a single point on the screen (rather than a rectangular area), but the player will be able to move the emitter around the screen using his controller. New particles will be tinted yellow, orange, or some shade between those two extremes.

```
/// perform any initialization before game starts
protected override void Initialize()
{
    // ... [some code omitted to shorten listing] ...

    // init our emitter
    m_emitter = new Emitter2D();
    m_emitter.ParticlesPerUpdate = 20;
    m_emitter.MaxParticles = 15000;
    m_emitter.EmitterRect = new Rectangle(200, 200, 0, 0);
    m_emitter.RangeColor =
```

```
              RangedVector4.FromColors(Color.Orange, Color.Yellow);

    // add our modifiers to the emitter
    m_emitter.AddModifier(m_ModGravity);
    m_emitter.AddModifier(m_ModWind);

    // disable the modifiers for now
    m_ModGravity.Enabled = false;
    m_ModWind.Enabled = false;

    base.Initialize();
}
```

To make sure that we don't process the same button press more than once, we need to keep track of the state of the buttons that we're interested in from frame to frame.

```
// remember pressed state between frames. without this, the
// action for the button would be triggered on every frame.
private bool m_ButtonA = false;
private bool m_ButtonB = false;
private bool m_ButtonX = false;
private bool m_ButtonY = false;
```

The player can move the emitter around the screen using the left thumbstick or the cursor keys on his keyboard.

```
// handy constants to move the emitter around
private static readonly Vector2 MOVE_LEFT = new Vector2(-5, 0);
private static readonly Vector2 MOVE_RIGHT = new Vector2(5, 0);
private static readonly Vector2 MOVE_UP = new Vector2(0, -5);
private static readonly Vector2 MOVE_DOWN = new Vector2(0, 5);

/// game logic such as updating the world
protected override void Update(GameTime gameTime)
{
    // Allows the default game to exit on Xbox 360 and Windows
    if (GamePad.GetState(PlayerIndex.One).Buttons.Back ==
        ButtonState.Pressed)
        this.Exit();

    // support for game pad and keyboard
    GamePadState pad1 = GamePad.GetState(PlayerIndex.One);
    KeyboardState key1 = Keyboard.GetState();
```

```
    // move emitter left or right
    if (pad1.ThumbSticks.Left.X < -0.10 || key1.IsKeyDown(Keys.Left))
    {
        m_emitter.Position += MOVE_LEFT;
    }
    else if (pad1.ThumbSticks.Left.X > 0.10 ||
        key1.IsKeyDown(Keys.Right))
    {
        m_emitter.Position += MOVE_RIGHT;
    }

    // move emitter up or down
    if (pad1.ThumbSticks.Left.Y > 0.10 || key1.IsKeyDown(Keys.Up))
    {
        m_emitter.Position += MOVE_UP;
    }
    else if (pad1.ThumbSticks.Left.Y < -0.10 ||
        key1.IsKeyDown(Keys.Down))
    {
        m_emitter.Position += MOVE_DOWN;
    }
```

Whenever the player presses the A button, the gravity modifier will be toggled between enabled and disabled. Whenever he presses the B button, the wind modifier will be toggled between enabled and disabled.

```
// enable / disable gravity
bool buttonPressed = (pad1.Buttons.A == ButtonState.Pressed);
buttonPressed |= key1.IsKeyDown(Keys.A);
if (buttonPressed && !m_ButtonA)
{
    m_ModGravity.Enabled = !m_ModGravity.Enabled;
}
m_ButtonA = buttonPressed;

// enable / disable wind
buttonPressed = (pad1.Buttons.B == ButtonState.Pressed);
buttonPressed |= key1.IsKeyDown(Keys.B);
if (buttonPressed && !m_ButtonB)
{
    m_ModWind.Enabled = !m_ModWind.Enabled;
}
m_ButtonB = buttonPressed;
```

When the player presses the X button, the emitter will be toggled between enabled and disabled. When the emitter is disabled, new particles will not be spawned, but any existing, active particles will continue to be updated. Whenever he presses the Y button, the emitter will be toggled between active and inactive. When the emitter is inactive, none of the particles that are owned by the emitter are updated or drawn.

```
// enable / disable emitter
buttonPressed = (pad1.Buttons.X == ButtonState.Pressed);
buttonPressed |= key1.IsKeyDown(Keys.X);
if (buttonPressed && !m_ButtonX)
{
    m_emitter.Enabled = !m_emitter.Enabled;
}
m_ButtonX = buttonPressed;

// mark emitter as active / inactive
buttonPressed = (pad1.Buttons.Y == ButtonState.Pressed);
buttonPressed |= key1.IsKeyDown(Keys.Y);
if (buttonPressed && !m_ButtonY)
{
    m_emitter.Active = !m_emitter.Active;
}
m_ButtonY = buttonPressed;
```

When the Update method is called on the Emitter2D class, it calls the Update method for every active Particle2D instance that it owns and each attached Modifier2D instance.

```
// tell the emitter to update its state
m_emitter.Update((float)gameTime.ElapsedGameTime.TotalSeconds);

    base.Update(gameTime);
}
```

When the Draw method is called on the Emitter2D class, it calls the Draw method for every active Particle2D instance that it owns. Particles are ultimately responsible for drawing themselves.

```
/// render game objects
protected override void Draw(GameTime gameTime)
{
    graphics.GraphicsDevice.Clear(Color.CornflowerBlue);
```

```
// tell the emitter to draw the particles
m_batch.Begin();
m_emitter.Draw(m_batch);
m_batch.End();

base.Draw(gameTime);
}
```

Summary

In this chapter, you learned how to manage tens of thousands of simple game objects at the same time, with minimal resource usage. You also learned how particles are used in a wide variety of games as a simple way to make the environment more immersive.

This example is by no means fully optimized. It's just an illustration of how you might go about implementing particles in your game. If you found this example interesting, be sure to read Chapter 25, "Threading in XNA." That chapter takes the code from this chapter and makes it multi-threaded so that you can take advantage of multi-processor or multi-core CPUs (like the Xbox 360 CPU and most new Intel-based and AMD-based PCs).

Review Questions

Think about what you've read in this chapter (and the included source code) to answer the following questions.

1. How do the particles seem to move independently of each other even though there's only one game loop, one `Particle2D.Update` method, and one `Particle2D.Draw` method?

2. What mechanism did we implement to make global changes across all particles?

3. What is the `RangedValue` class? How is it useful for this chapter's example code?

4. Using everything you've read about this chapter's particle system implementation, how might you go about simulating a fire using particles?

5. List some examples of particles (or effects that you think may have been created using particles) in games that you have actually played. If those effects were omitted, would the game play suffer? Would the game be less immersive?

Exercises

EXERCISE 1. Create a new particle image and swap out the image in this sample. Be creative. Create a leaf, a snowflake, or a smiley face. Instantiate an emitter for these particles that is located at the top-left of the screen with a width equal to the screen's width and a height of zero. Set the `RangeMovement` property of the emitter to `new RangedVector2( Vector2.Zero, Vector2.Zero )` so that the particles enter the simulation at rest, then fall as gravity takes hold of them.

EXERCISE 2. Modify this sample so that the emitter supports more than one particle image and randomly selects one image from the available images when spawning a new image. Rework the code you modified in the first exercise so that you can see a snowfall or autumn day with more variety.

EXERCISE 3. Create a new modifier that attracts particles toward a single point on the screen. Instantiate an emitter with an `EmitterRect` that encompasses the entire screen so that particles can appear anywhere on the screen, then move toward this point.

EXERCISE 4. Create a simple fireworks game that fires an exploding rocket whenever the player presses the A button on his controller. As the rocket travels up, leave a thin trail of small, orange particles. When the rocket reaches a certain altitude, change the behavior of the emitter to release several hundred brightly colored particles in a single burst. Make sure that all of these particles are affected by gravity.

CHAPTER 23

VIRTUAL KEYBOARD

As your game designs become more complex, the way in which you interact with your players will become more complex. Mapping game actions to button presses is clearly the most intuitive and the simplest interface that you can provide to your players. Simple is good. Intuitive is good. Our goal as game designers should always be to keep our interface to the player as simple and as intuitive as possible. Remember, XNA Game Studio Express isn't just a tool for creating Windows games. One of its most exciting features is its support for developing Xbox 360 games.

Console programming has its own restrictions and rewards. Arguably, the biggest reward of console development is the consistency between devices—a true "write once, run everywhere" experience. One of the biggest restrictions of console development is the user interface. The game pad is ideally suited for playing games, but it's a horrible input device for more involved tasks like word processing and graphic design.

For more complex interactions, you can present the player with a series of menus from which he can select options or trigger actions. While menus are a more complex form of interacting with the player, most players understand that their interaction with a game changes when they're presented with a menu. A certain button may have triggered a jump animation for their character outside of the menu, but that same button performs a different action when pressed in the context of a menu screen.

When saving games, we can present the player with predetermined save game slots, providing menu options for each. When recording a high score, we can present the player with a simple interface to enter his initials by manipulating three letters using his thumbstick and save his selection by pressing the A button. For games with some level of character development, we can provide simple customizations using random name generators, possibly driven by player selections.

Try as you may, there will come a time when your design requires console players to enter text in your game. In this chapter, we will develop a virtual keyboard component that you can use in your games to allow the player to enter textual data via their Xbox 360 Controller or a physical keyboard. To demonstrate this new component, we'll develop a simple game where a player-entered phrase bounces around the game screen. The player can edit this text by pressing the X button on the game pad or the space bar on the keyboard. The game text is edited using the game pad or keyboard, and the player can elect to commit or cancel his changes.

In this chapter, you will learn how to:

- Display a virtual keyboard component over your active game

- Intercept game input and process it in your component

- Allow the player to enter and edit textual data using a virtual keyboard

- Report changes from the component back to the game

The Design

Of course, our virtual keyboard needs to allow the player to enter text via the game pad or keyboard. But, it also needs to allow the player to edit existing text easily, without needlessly deleting and reentering text at the end of the data to fix errors within the data. So the virtual keyboard will support the concept of a cursor, where the player can navigate within existing text. The text that the player is editing will be displayed just above the key images, and a simple, blinking line will indicate the current position of the text cursor. The player will use the left and right shoulder buttons on his game pad to move the text cursor.

The virtual keyboard will allow the player to enter alphanumeric text, as well as symbols and accented characters. The virtual keyboard only displays one set of characters at a time. The player can cycle through each available set of characters

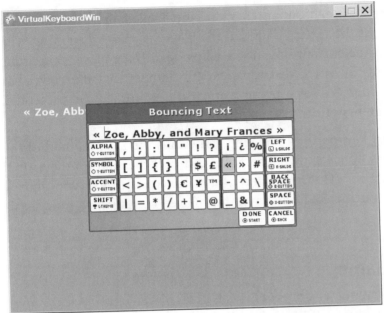

Figure 23.1
A screen shot of the example game that we will develop in this chapter. The text is animated behind the virtual keyboard as edits are being made.

using the Y button on his game pad, and he can press the left thumbstick to toggle between upper- and lowercase versions of the current character set.

The player will use the left thumbstick to select characters, the A button to insert the currently selected character, and the B button to delete the character that sits just to the left of the text cursor. The X button can be used to insert a space. Pressing the Start button will commit the changes to the game, and pressing the Back button will cancel the changes.

Every function that is accessible via one of the mapped game pad buttons will also be available as an on-screen virtual keyboard button. A screen shot of the example "game" that we will develop in this chapter is shown in Figure 23.1.

Since the VirtualKeyboard class is a reusable component, we can use it to prompt the player for many different inputs. The player can use the same virtual keyboard to name his in-game persona, enter a password, or name a save game data file. To make it clear to the player what data the game is requesting, the VirtualKeyboard class exposes a property, called Caption, that allows the game to get and set the text that is displayed in the title bar of the virtual keyboard when it is drawn on the screen. In this way, the caption doubles as a prompt.

The `VirtualKeyboard` class exposes another property, called `Text`, which allows the game to get and set the textual data that the player is currently editing. The `Text` property reflects the current state of the edited text. If the player cancels his edit, the most recently accepted text replaces any changes that the player has made. If the `Text` property is set programmatically, it is immediately accepted, and the previous contents of the property are forgotten.

To display the virtual keyboard, the hosting game calls the `Show` method of the `VirtualKeyboard` class. Once shown, the game can poll the state of the virtual keyboard by checking its `Visible` property, or it can register its own callback method, which will be invoked whenever the player commits or cancels his changes.

The Example Game

The example game is about as simple as it gets. The player-editable text moves around the screen, bouncing off the walls that define the screen boundaries. The text is drawn using the `GameFont` class that we developed in Chapter 21, "Game Font Library." The location of the text is tracked via a `Vector2` member variable, and the velocity of the moving text is stored in another `Vector2` object. In addition to these members, the `Game1` class also maintains a reference to the game's (one and only) sprite batch, and a reference to our `VirtualKeyboard` instance.

```
// the one and only sprite batch
protected SpriteBatch m_batch = null;
// bitmap font for our bouncing text
protected GameFont m_font = null;
// virtual keyboard to edit bouncing text
protected VirtualKeyboard m_VirtualKeyboard = new VirtualKeyboard();
// location and speed of the bouncing text
protected Vector2 m_TextLocation = new Vector2(20.0f, 20.0f);
protected Vector2 m_TextVelocity = new Vector2(83.0f, 67.0f);
```

Initializing the Game State

When the game starts up, the `VirtualKeyboard`'s `Text` and `Caption` properties are set to their initial values. The location of the virtual keyboard is also initialized, placing it at the center of the screen.

```
/// perform any initialization before game starts
protected override void Initialize()
```

```
{
    // initialize the virtual keyboard
    m_VirtualKeyboard.Text = "Press space bar, or X on GamPad.";
    m_VirtualKeyboard.Caption = "Bouncing Text";
    m_VirtualKeyboard.CenterIn(
        new Rectangle(0, 0, SCREEN_WIDTH, SCREEN_HEIGHT));
    base.Initialize();
}
```

Managing Media Dependencies

The VirtualKeyboard class needs a source texture to draw its background and keys. It also relies heavily on the GameFont class (which we developed in Chapter 21) to draw the keys that represent the current character set and the currently edited text. These media dependencies are satisfied in the LoadGraphicsContent method of the Game1 class.

```
/// Load your graphics content.
protected override void LoadGraphicsContent(bool loadAllContent)
{
    if (loadAllContent)
    {
        // initialize the sprite batch
        m_batch = new SpriteBatch(graphics.GraphicsDevice);

        // load the texture for the virtual keyboard dialog
        m_VirtualKeyboard.Texture =
            content.Load<Texture2D>(@"media\virtualkeyboard");
        // create our bitmap font, share it with the virtual keyboard
        m_font = GameFont.FromTexture2D(
            content.Load<Texture2D>(@"media\font"));
        m_VirtualKeyboard.Font = m_font;
    }
    // TODO: Load any ResourceManagementMode.Manual content
}
```

Drawing the Text

Our animated text is drawn by the game's DrawText method, passing in the current text and the current on-screen position of the text to the DrawString method of the GameFont class. The DrawText method is called from the game's Draw method.

```
// draw the bouncing text at its current location
protected void DrawText(SpriteBatch batch)
{
    m_font.DrawString(
        batch,
        m_VirtualKeyboard.Text,
        (int)(m_TextLocation.X + 0.5f),
        (int)(m_TextLocation.Y + 0.5f));
}
```

Animating the Text

The task of actually moving the text is handled by the UpdateText method, which is called from the game's Update method. In this method, we update the current location of the text by adding the movement vector to the location vector, scaled by the number of seconds that have elapsed since the last update was processed.

```
// animate the bouncing text
protected void UpdateText(double elapsed)
{
    // move bouncing text along current trajectory
    m_TextLocation += (float)elapsed * m_TextVelocity;
```

Once the location has been updated, we need to make sure that no part of the text has left the screen. If the text has crept out of bounds, we will reverse the direction of the movement vector component that violated its parole, and we'll pull the text back into view.

```
    // check bounds (left)
    if (m_TextLocation.X < 0)
    {
        m_TextLocation.X = 0;
        m_TextVelocity.X *= -1;
    }
    // check bounds (top)
    if (m_TextLocation.Y < 0)
    {
        m_TextLocation.Y = 0;
        m_TextVelocity.Y *= -1;
    }
    // check bounds (right)
```

```
    if (m_TextLocation.X > SCREEN_WIDTH - m_VirtualKeyboard.TextSize.X)
    {
        m_TextLocation.X = SCREEN_WIDTH - m_VirtualKeyboard.TextSize.X;
        m_TextVelocity.X *= -1;
    }
    // check bounds (bottom)
    if (m_TextLocation.Y > SCREEN_HEIGHT - m_VirtualKeyboard.TextSize.Y)
    {
        m_TextLocation.Y = SCREEN_HEIGHT - m_VirtualKeyboard.TextSize.Y;
        m_TextVelocity.Y *= -1;
    }
}
```

Processing Player Input

As long as the virtual keyboard isn't being used, the game will handle certain player actions by itself. When the virtual keyboard is active, the game will defer input processing to the component. We need to pay special attention to the cases where the same button is mapped to actions in both the game and the component. Two such overlapping responsibilities exist in our example game.

The first dual-function button is the Back button. When the virtual keyboard is active, the Back button cancels the current edit and hides the virtual keyboard. When the virtual keyboard isn't active, the Back button exits the game. If we don't account for this duality, the game will exit as soon as the player cancels an edit. It's very likely that the Back button will still be pressed when the next call to Update occurs, a small fraction of a second after the edit has been canceled. When the game sees that the virtual keyboard is no longer visible, and that the Back button is pressed, the game will shut down.

One way to handle this is for the game to ignore Back button presses until it processes at least one update where the button is not pressed and the virtual keyboard is not visible. We'll track this condition in the m_IgnoreExit member variable.

```
// avoid exiting the game when the player cancels an edit
protected bool m_IgnoreExit = false;
/// game logic such as updating the world
protected override void Update(GameTime gameTime)
{
```

```
// get state of pad in slot one
GamePadState pad1 = GamePad.GetState(PlayerIndex.One);
KeyboardState key1 = Keyboard.GetState();
// is the player requesting that we exit?
bool isExit =
    pad1.Buttons.Back == ButtonState.Pressed ||
    key1.IsKeyDown(Keys.Escape);
// make sure we're not capturing an "exit game" just after
// a "cancel edit" since they use the same button presses
if (!isExit)
{
    // exit button isn't being pressed now, ignore next exit
    // request if the virtual keyboard is currently visible
    m_IgnoreExit = m_VirtualKeyboard.Visible;
}
else if (!m_IgnoreExit)
{
    // exit button is being pressed now, and it has been
    // released since the virtual keyboard was last visible
    this.Exit();
}
```

The other dual-function button is the X button. When the virtual keyboard is active, the X button inserts a space into the editable text. When the virtual keyboard isn't active, the X button displays the virtual keyboard. We'll handle this conflict a little differently. Rather than remembering the previous state of the X button, we'll just blindly request that the virtual keyboard show itself. The VirtualKeyboard will be responsible for knowing its own state, and treat calls to its Show method differently, based on its Visible property.

Typically, the last button to be pressed when the virtual keyboard closes will either be the Start button (to accept changes) or the Back button (to reject changes). Since the player doesn't use the X button to close the virtual keyboard, we don't need to worry about processing stray X presses like we did with the Back button.

```
// player requested virtual keyboard?
if (pad1.Buttons.X == ButtonState.Pressed ||
    key1.IsKeyDown(Keys.Space))
{
    m_VirtualKeyboard.Show();
}
```

Our game is done processing player input at this stage. We just need to tell our animated text to update itself, and then we can hand off processing to the virtual keyboard.

```
// calculate the number of seconds since the last update
double elapsed = gameTime.ElapsedGameTime.TotalSeconds;
// animate our bouncing text
UpdateText(elapsed);
// allow the virtual keyboard to process player input
m_VirtualKeyboard.Update(elapsed);
base.Update(gameTime);
}
```

The VirtualKeyboard Class

As mentioned earlier, the VirtualKeyboard class exposes several useful properties that the hosting game can access. Among these are the location of the virtual keyboard on the screen (Location), the caption of the dialog (Caption), the text that's being edited (Text), and the visibility of the virtual keyboard (Visible). These properties are fairly straightforward, so I won't list the complete source here. You can find the full source code for this chapter on the CD that accompanies this book.

Source Media

The VirtualKeyboard class uses a single texture to generate the interface that you see on the screen. The silhouette of the dialog is formed by one sprite, and the keys and text edit area are formed by a second sprite. Two more sprites are contained in this texture. The first is a small, empty button. The other is a large, empty button. The small button is used to highlight the character keys on the virtual keyboard. The large button is currently unused. The source texture is shown in Figure 23.2.

The source texture is loaded into memory by the main game class whenever its LoadGraphicsContent method is invoked by the XNA Framework. That method assigns the texture to the Texture property of the VirtualKeyboard class. The boundaries of the sprite images are defined using several static readonly Rectangle member variables and each is hard-coded with its location and size data. Again, this is all pretty basic stuff, so I won't list the complete source here. You can find the full source code for this chapter on the CD that accompanies this book.

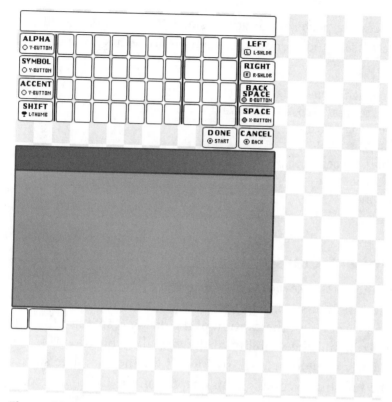

Figure 23.2
The source texture that contains the sprites that are used by the `VirtualKeyboard` class.

Character Sets

The virtual keyboard contains several fixed-function buttons. These are the large buttons that occupy the outer edges of the dialog on the virtual keyboard, and they do not change. The small buttons that line the interior of the dialog are the individual, selectable characters. The characters that occupy these buttons change as the user switches between character sets, or toggles the case of the current character set.

The grid that houses these buttons can easily be represented by a two-dimensional array of characters. That's exactly how we'll represent these character sets in our code, and we'll group these sets into a larger array so that the individual characters can easily be accessed using an index that represents the character set.

```
// virtual keyboard indices
protected const int VKB_ALPHAL = 0; // Alphabet (lower)
protected const int VKB_ALPHAU = 1; // Alphabet (upper)
```

```
protected const int VKB_SYMBOL = 2; // Symbols
protected const int VKB_ACCNTL = 3; // Accents  (lower)
protected const int VKB_ACCNTU = 4; // Accents  (upper)
// currently selected virtual keyboard
protected int m_CurrentVKB = VKB_ALPHAL;
public int CurrentVKB
{
    get { return m_CurrentVKB; }
    set { m_CurrentVKB = value; }
}
// chars for each virtual keyboard
protected static readonly char[][][] m_CharGrids =
{
    // Alphabet - lower case
    new char[][] {
        "abcdefg123".ToCharArray(),
        "hijklmn456".ToCharArray(),
        "opqrstu789".ToCharArray(),
        "vwxyz-@_0.".ToCharArray(),
    },
    // Alphabet - upper case
    new char[][] {
        "ABCDEFG123".ToCharArray(),
        "HIJKLMN456".ToCharArray(),
        "OPQRSTU789".ToCharArray(),
        "VWXYZ-@_0.".ToCharArray(),
    },
    // Symbols
    new char[][] {
        ",;:'\"!?¡¿%".ToCharArray(),
        "[]{}´$£« »#".ToCharArray(),
        "<>() ¥™-^\\".ToCharArray(),
        "|=*/+-@_&." .ToCharArray(),
    },
    // Accents - lower case
    new char[][] {
        "àáâãäåñœæβ".ToCharArray(),
        "èéêëþçýÿ °°".ToCharArray(),
        "ìíîïùúûüµζ".ToCharArray(),
        "òóôõöō©_× .".ToCharArray(),
    },
    // Accents - upper case
    new char[][] {
```

```
        "ÀÁÂÃÄÅÑŒÆβ".ToCharArray(),
        "ÈÉÊËÞÇÝŸ°°".ToCharArray(),
        "ÌÍÎÏÙÚÛÜMΞ".ToCharArray(),
        "ÒÓÔÕÖŌ®_×.".ToCharArray(),
    },
};
```

Character Placement

We want to draw each character on the virtual keyboard so that it is centered within its button on the screen. Since the size of the letters that adorn the virtual keyboard buttons varies according to the character being displayed, we need to calculate the on-screen position of each letter such that it is centered within its host button. Rather than performing this calculation every time we draw the virtual keyboard, we'll calculate the locations for every letter of every character set at one time, and store the results in an array of Vector2 objects that will be used by our drawing methods.

While we're at it, we'll create a similar array to store the locations of the buttons on which the letters are drawn so that we don't have to calculate them while we're drawing. Since the location of the character buttons is independent of the character set being shown, we don't need to index this array by the currently selected character set (CurrentVKB). These locations will be used to draw the small button sprite, highlighting the currently selected character button.

```
// virtual keyboard character button counts
protected const int COUNT_VKBS = 5;   // number of character sets
protected const int COUNT_ROWS = 4;   // number of character rows
protected const int COUNT_COLS = 10; // number of character per row
// top, left location of each character button
protected static Vector2[,] m_CharButtonLoc =
    new Vector2[COUNT_ROWS, COUNT_COLS];
// location from top, left of button for each character
protected Vector2[, ,] m_CharLoc =
    new Vector2[COUNT_VKBS, COUNT_ROWS, COUNT_COLS];
// calculate the position of each glyph, centered in its own button
protected void UpdateCharLocations()
{
    // for each set of virtual keyboard characters
    for (int vkb = 0; vkb < COUNT_VKBS; vkb++)
    {
```

```
// for each row
for (int row = 0; row < COUNT_ROWS; row++)
{
    // track top, left for each button
    int btnLocX = 30;
    int btnLocY = 33 + 30 * row;
    // for each column
    for (int col = 0; col < COUNT_COLS; col++)
    {
        // button locations aren't indexed by vkb,
        // only calculate these values on the first
        // pass of the outer loop.
        if (vkb == 0)
        {
            // calculate button location
            btnLocX += (col == 7 ? 27 : 25);
            m_CharButtonLoc[row,col].X = btnLocX;
            m_CharButtonLoc[row,col].Y = btnLocY;
        }
        // calculate character location, within the button
        Vector2 size =
            Font.MeasureString(m_CharGrids[vkb][row][col]);
        m_CharLoc[vkb,row,col].X =
            m_RectButtonSmall.Width / 2 - size.X / 2;
        m_CharLoc[vkb,row,col].Y =
            m_RectButtonSmall.Height / 2 - size.Y / 2;
    }
}
```

Navigating the Virtual Keyboard

Our virtual keyboard is made up of a grid of buttons. The small buttons in the center of the grid map to characters that may be inserted into the text that is being edited. The outer edge of the grid contains the buttons that perform some fixed function. The player navigates this grid using his left thumbstick. The currently selected button is represented as a Vector2 object whose X and Y components indicate the column and row of the button. The grid of buttons is 12 buttons wide (columns 0 through 11) and 5 buttons tall (rows 0 through 4). The last row contains only two buttons, which occupy columns 10 and 11.

```
// selected character button
protected Vector2 m_SelectedCharButton = new Vector2(1, 0);
// move the button cursor within the virtual keyboard
protected void ChangeSelectedCharButton(int dx, int dy)
{
    // update location
    m_SelectedCharButton.X += dx;
    m_SelectedCharButton.Y += dy;
    // check bounds
    m_SelectedCharButton.X = Math.Max(m_SelectedCharButton.X, 0);
    m_SelectedCharButton.X = Math.Min(m_SelectedCharButton.X, 11);
    m_SelectedCharButton.Y = Math.Max(m_SelectedCharButton.Y, 0);
    m_SelectedCharButton.Y = Math.Min(m_SelectedCharButton.Y, 4);
    // last row is special case; two large buttons
    if (m_SelectedCharButton.Y == 4)
    {
        m_SelectedCharButton.X = Math.Max(m_SelectedCharButton.X, 10);
    }
}
```

The `VirtualKeyboard` exposes a property named `SelectedChar`, which serves two purposes. When the currently selected button is an insertable character, the value of this property is the character to which the button refers. When the currently selected button is one of the fixed-function buttons, the value of this property is `'\0'`.

```
// if selected button is a character, return it
public char SelectedChar
{
    get
    {
        // assume failure
        char selected = '\0';
        // get indices into virtual keyboard char array
        int col = (int)m_SelectedCharButton.X - 1;
        int row = (int)m_SelectedCharButton.Y;
        // check bounds of indices
        if (col >= 0 && col < COUNT_COLS &&
            row >= 0 && row < COUNT_ROWS)
        {
            // extract selected character
            selected = m_CharGrids[CurrentVKB][row][col];
        }
```

```
        // return our findings
        return selected;
    }
}
```

Editing the Text

The position of the text cursor is represented by an integer whose value is used as the index into the string that we are editing. For that reason, the value that is stored in our cursor cannot be less than zero or greater than the length of the string.

```
// cursor (as index into Text characters)
protected int m_Cursor = 0;
public int Cursor
{
    get { return m_Cursor; }
    set
    {
        m_Cursor = value;
        m_Cursor = Math.Max(0, m_Cursor);
        m_Cursor = Math.Min(Text.Length, m_Cursor);
    }
}
```

The InsertChar method inserts a character into the string. The character value ultimately comes from the SelectedChar property, which is set to '\0' when the currently selected virtual keyboard button is one of the fixed-function buttons. For that reason, we need to ignore calls to this method when the value of the character that was passed in is '\0'.

```
// insert a character at the current cursor position
protected void InsertChar(char c)
{
    if (c != '\0')
    {
        Text = Text.Insert(Cursor, c.ToString());
        Cursor++;
    }
}
```

The BackSpace method deletes the character that lies just to the left of the text cursor. Since there are no characters to the left of the first character, we need to make sure that the `Cursor` property isn't zero before we attempt to remove a character.

```
// delete the character just before the current cursor position
protected void BackSpace()
{
    if (Cursor > 0)
    {
        Text = Text.Remove(Cursor - 1, 1);
        Cursor--;
    }
}
```

Updates

If we blindly added the selected character to the text whenever we detected that the A button was pressed, the string would fill with that character in the blink of an eye. We could register each button press only once by tracking the previous state of the button between each call to the `Update` method, but our component will mimic the function of a real keyboard by repeating the selected character at regular intervals for as long as the button is pressed.

To regulate the rate at which button presses are repeated, we'll keep track of the last time a button press was processed. Whenever the time that has elapsed since the last button press was registered is greater than our delay, we'll register the button press again and reset the counter.

```
// enforce delay before repeating a button press
protected double m_TimeSinceLastProcessInput = ProcessInputDelay;
protected const double ProcessInputDelay = 0.2;
```

Similarly, we need to monitor the time that elapses between showing and hiding our text cursor. If we didn't keep track of this value, our cursor would toggle between visible and hidden on each call to the `Update` method, appearing as an irritating, flickering line.

```
// the blinking cursor for the text editor
protected bool m_CursorBlink = true;
protected const double CursorBlinkRate = 0.75;
protected double m_CursorBlinkCounter = 0;
```

The main game class calls the `Update` method, passing in the number of seconds that have elapsed since the last time `Update` was called. If the game doesn't pass in the state of the game pad or keyboard, our Update method will collect that data and hand it off to its slightly beefier sibling.

```
// gather player input, and call the overloaded Update
public void Update(double elapsed)
{
    // don't update if the dialog isn't visible
    if (Visible)
    {
        Update(elapsed,
            GamePad.GetState(PlayerIndex.One),
            Keyboard.GetState());
    }
}
```

In this overloaded version of the Update method, the delay counters are incremented, the visibility of the text cursor is conditionally toggled, and a call is made to the ProcessInput method that handles all the dirty little details of input processing. While we handle the blinking cursor within the Update method, we can't process the player input delay just yet. We only want to reset our delay counter when the player has performed some valid action. If we wind up ignoring their input (e.g., they press a button that we don't support), a delay would only serve to irritate them.

```
// update state and process player input
public void Update(double elapsed,
    GamePadState pad1, KeyboardState key1)
{
    // don't update if the dialog isn't visible
    if (Visible)
    {
        // increment repeat delay counter
        m_TimeSinceLastProcessInput += elapsed;
        // increment cursor flash counter, toggle blink
        m_CursorBlinkCounter += elapsed;
        if (m_CursorBlinkCounter >= CursorBlinkRate)
        {
            m_CursorBlinkCounter = 0;
            m_CursorBlink = !m_CursorBlink;
        }
        // process player input
        ProcessInput(pad1, key1);
    }
}
```

Processing Player Input

The next method is a total hack. It's easy to tell when no keys are being pressed on the (physical) keyboard. There's a property of the KeyboardState object that contains a list of all the keys that are currently being pressed. In the case where no keys are being pressed, the length of that collection is zero. There is no such property on the GamePadState object.

To detect the case where no buttons are being pressed on the game pad, we could check each button, one by one. That would be the most reliable method, and it would certainly conform to the documented specifications of the XNA Framework APIs. But, I wanted something simpler. So, the NonePressed method takes advantage of the fact that all objects in .NET derive from the common base class System.Object.

The System.Object class has a method called ToString that all .NET objects support (in one way or another). In the case of our GamePadState instance, the strings that are returned by that method return a known value when no buttons are being pressed. This method compares those known values against the current state of the game pad to determine when no keys are being pressed.

If the behavior of the GamePadState class ever changes (not altogether unlikely), this method will need to be rewritten. I just wanted to show you a novel approach to the problem, and remind you that there's always more than one way to perform a given task.

```
// simple method to determine when no game pad buttons are pressed
protected bool NonePressed(GamePadState pad1)
{
    return
        pad1.Buttons.ToString() == "{Buttons:None}" &&
        pad1.DPad.ToString() == "{DPad:None}" &&
        pad1.Triggers.ToString() == "{Left:0 Right:0}" &&
        pad1.ThumbSticks.ToString() ==
            "{Left:{X:0 Y:0} Right:{X:0 Y:0}}";
}
```

If no keyboard keys or game pad buttons are being pressed, we can safely reset our repeat delay counter. The next button press will be intentional.

```
// process player input
protected void ProcessInput(GamePadState pad1, KeyboardState key1)
{
    // forego delay if no keys are pressed
    if (NonePressed(pad1) && key1.GetPressedKeys().Length == 0)
```

```
    {
        m_TimeSinceLastProcessInput = ProcessInputDelay;
    }
```

If the repeat delay hasn't been satisfied, don't process any player input. If enough time has elapsed, we'll capture certain important states before we start processing the player's input. When we're done processing the input, we will compare the new values in these state variables against our snapshot of the same data to see if anything has changed. If nothing has changed, there's no need to reset the repeat delay counter.

```
// don't repeat same press on every frame, delay between repeats
if (m_TimeSinceLastProcessInput >= ProcessInputDelay)
{
    // capture state before updates to detect changes
    Vector2 prevSelectedKey = m_SelectedCharButton;
    string prevText = Text;
    int prevCursor = Cursor;
    bool prevShiftPressed = ShiftPressed;
    int prevVKB = CurrentVKB;
    // process input from game pad and keyboard
    ProcessInput(pad1);
    ProcessInput(key1);
    // detect changes
    bool changed =
        (prevSelectedKey    != m_SelectedCharButton) ||
        (prevText           != Text)              ||
        (prevCursor         != Cursor)            ||
        (prevShiftPressed   != ShiftPressed)      ||
        (prevVKB            != CurrentVKB);
    // state changed
    if (changed)
    {
        // reset button delay
        m_TimeSinceLastProcessInput = 0;
        // reset cursor blink
        m_CursorBlink = true;
        m_CursorBlinkCounter = 0;
    }
}
}
```

Now we can actually put our GamePadState data to use. The first thing we'll check is whether the player is using the left thumbstick to navigate the virtual keyboard's button grid. We'll track the change in grid selection using the variables dx and dy. Those variables are initialized to zero, based on the assumption that the player isn't using the thumbstick. When we're done checking the thumbstick state, we'll call out to the ChangeSelectedCharButton method, passing the (possibly unchanged) values that are stored in dx and dy.

```
// process player input from the game pad
protected void ProcessInput(GamePadState pad1)
{
    // change in selected virtual keyboard button
    int dx = 0;
    int dy = 0;
    // select button to the left or right
    if (pad1.ThumbSticks.Left.X < 0)
    {
        dx = -1;
    }
    else if (pad1.ThumbSticks.Left.X > 0)
    {
        dx = 1;
    }
    // select button up or down
    if (pad1.ThumbSticks.Left.Y > 0)
    {
        dy = -1;
    }
    else if (pad1.ThumbSticks.Left.Y < 0)
    {
        dy = 1;
    }
    // actually change the selected button
    ChangeSelectedCharButton(dx, dy);
```

Next, we'll process the shortcut button for toggling the shifted state of the virtual keyboard.

```
// shift shortcut
if (pad1.Buttons.LeftStick == ButtonState.Pressed)
{
    ShiftPressed = !ShiftPressed;
}
```

The next game pad state that we'll check is that of the A button. This is the generic action button, and its function is dependent on its location in the button grid. Most of the buttons on our virtual keyboard are used to insert a single character into the text that the player is editing, so we'll check that case first.

```
// press the selected virtual keyboard button
if (pad1.Buttons.A == ButtonState.Pressed)
{
    if (SelectedChar != '\0')
    {
        // selected button is a character, add to text
        InsertChar(SelectedChar);
    }
```

The bottom row of our grid has only two buttons. It's a special case that we can check with very little code. If the Done or Cancel buttons are currently selected, we'll call their corresponding methods, ending the need to process any more input data.

```
else if (m_SelectedCharButton.Y == 4)
{
    if (m_SelectedCharButton.X == 10)
    {
        // selected done button
        Done();
        return;
    }
    else if (m_SelectedCharButton.X == 11)
    {
        // selected cancel button
        Cancel();
        return;
    }
}
```

At this point, the only buttons that remain are in the first and last column. These are all fixed-function buttons. The first column contains buttons that change the currently selected character set. It's easy enough to map those buttons to character sets (or VKBs as they're referred to in the source code). While it may not seem like toggling the ShiftPressed property is actually changing the selected character set, we will use that property later in this method to do just that.

```
else if (m_SelectedCharButton.X == 0)
{
    // button in first column
    switch ((int)m_SelectedCharButton.Y)
```

```
    {
        case 0: // Alpha
            CurrentVKB = VKB_ALPHAL;
            break;
        case 1: // Symbol
            CurrentVKB = VKB_SYMBOL;
            break;
        case 2: // Accent
            CurrentVKB = VKB_ACCNTL;
            break;
        case 3: // Shift
            ShiftPressed = !ShiftPressed;
            break;
    }
}
```

Now we can process the fixed-function buttons that live in the last column of our button grid. The function of each button is mapped to the appropriate member method in the following code snippet.

```
else if (m_SelectedCharButton.X == 11)
{
    // button in last column
    switch ((int)m_SelectedCharButton.Y)
    {
        case 0: // Left
            Cursor--;
            break;
        case 1: // Right
            Cursor++;
            break;
        case 2: // Back Space
            BackSpace();
            break;
        case 3: // Space
            InsertChar(' ');
            break;
    }
}
```

That's it for the action button (the A button). Now we need to check the game pad buttons that are mapped directly to member methods. That's what this next block of code does.

```
// process shortcut game pad buttons
if (pad1.Buttons.LeftShoulder = = ButtonState.Pressed)
{
    Cursor--; // Left
}
else if (pad1.Buttons.RightShoulder = = ButtonState.Pressed)
{
    Cursor+ +; // Right
}
if (pad1.Buttons.Start = = ButtonState.Pressed)
{
    Done(); // Done
    return;
}
else if (pad1.Buttons.Back = = ButtonState.Pressed)
{
    Cancel(); // Cancel
    return;
}
else if (pad1.Buttons.B = = ButtonState.Pressed)
{
    // Back Space
    BackSpace();
}
else if (pad1.Buttons.X = = ButtonState.Pressed)
{
    // Space
    InsertChar(' ');
}
```

The Y button is used to cycle through each of the available character sets. Since the ShiftPressed member property determines the case of the characters, we can ignore the case of the selected character set. In this code block, I just pick the lowercase version of each set.

```
else if (pad1.Buttons.Y = = ButtonState.Pressed)
{
    // toggle character mappings (alpha, symbol, accent)
    switch (CurrentVKB)
    {
        case VKB_ACCNTL:
        case VKB_ACCNTU:
            CurrentVKB = VKB_ALPHAL;
            break;
```

```
        case VKB_SYMBOL:
            CurrentVKB = VKB_ACCNTL;
            break;
        case VKB_ALPHAL:
        case VKB_ALPHAU:
            CurrentVKB = VKB_SYMBOL;
            break;
    }
}
```

We're at the end of our game pad processing logic. It's finally time to apply that ShiftPressed property that you've been hearing so much about. In the case of the character set that contains only symbols, text case is irrelevant. For the other two character sets, we need to make sure that the shift state is properly applied. The following code snippet performs that task for us.

```
// preserve shift state
if (CurrentVKB == VKB_ACCNTL || CurrentVKB == VKB_ACCNTU)
{
    CurrentVKB = (ShiftPressed ? VKB_ACCNTU : VKB_ACCNTL);
}
else if (CurrentVKB == VKB_ALPHAL || CurrentVKB == VKB_ALPHAU)
{
    CurrentVKB = (ShiftPressed ? VKB_ALPHAU : VKB_ALPHAL);
}
}
```

Supporting the (Physical) Keyboard

Virtual keyboards should never punish players who have real keyboards attached. We need to process input from the (physical) keyboard, and apply those inputs to our edited text. Unfortunately, the XNA Framework isn't going to provide much help in this area. We have a lot of work to do when mapping KeyboardState keys to usable characters within our component.

To make things easier, I decided to create a simple jagged array to map ranges of KeyboardState keys to their Unicode character equivalents. That way, we don't have to account for every key mapping individually, in code. Each array in this collection contains at least four values. In order, they are the first and last KeyboardState keys in the range that we're interested in mapping, the first Unicode character to which the first key in the range maps, and a flag to indicate whether the characters being mapped are shifted or not.

For those cases where a range of keys doesn't map cleanly to a range of Unicode characters, the array also contains the list of Unicode characters to which each key in the range (which are specified by the first two array elements) maps.

```
// map Input.Keys to chars, by range
// an array of an array of int -- first four int values are always
// { starting Keys enum, ending Keys enum, first char, shift flag }
// inner array may also have a list of chars to map the Key enum
protected int[][] m_KeyMap = {
    new int[] {(int)Keys.A,           (int)Keys.Z,          'a', 0},
    new int[] {(int)Keys.A,           (int)Keys.Z,          'A', 1},
    new int[] {(int)Keys.NumPad0,     (int)Keys.NumPad9, '0', 0},
    new int[] {(int)Keys.D0,          (int)Keys.D9,         '0', 0},
    new int[] {(int)Keys.D0,          (int)Keys.D9,         '0', 1,
        ')', '!', '@', '#', '$', '%', '^', '&', '*', '(', },
    new int[] {(int)Keys.OemSemicolon, (int)Keys.OemTilde, ';', 0,
        ';', '=', ',', '-', '.', '/', '`', },
    new int[] {(int)Keys.OemSemicolon, (int)Keys.OemTilde, ';', 1,
        ':', '+', '<', '_', '>', '?', '\0', },
    new int[] {(int)Keys.OemOpenBrackets, (int)Keys.OemQuotes, ';', 0,
        '[', '\\', ']', '\'', 'z', '\\', },
    new int[] {(int)Keys.OemOpenBrackets, (int)Keys.OemQuotes, ';', 1,
        '{', '|', '}', '"', 'Z', '|', },
    new int[] {(int)Keys.OemBackslash, (int)Keys.OemBackslash, ';', 0,
        '\\', },
    new int[] {(int)Keys.OemBackslash, (int)Keys.OemBackslash, ';', 1,
        '|', },
};
```

The overloaded ProcessInput method that accepts a KeyboardState as its only parameter uses the data in the m_KeyMap array to actually perform the mapping. It begins by getting the list of pressed keys from the KeyboardState instance and checking the state of the shift keys on the (physical) keyboard.

```
// process player input from the keyboard
protected void ProcessInput(KeyboardState key1)
{
    // get a list of pressed keys
    Keys[] keys = key1.GetPressedKeys();
    // get the state of the shift key
    bool shift =
        key1.IsKeyDown(Keys.LeftShift) ||
        key1.IsKeyDown(Keys.RightShift);
```

The method then iterates over every key that was reported as being pressed, attempting to map the pressed key to a valid Unicode character. Each entry in the m_KeyMap array is compared against the pressed key to determine whether it lies within the range of keys that are handled by the mapping entry.

```
// process each pressed key
foreach (Keys key in keys)
{
    // map pressed key and shift state to int values
    int keyInt = (int)key;
    int shiftInt = (shift ? 1 : 0);
    // keep track of selected char (if any)
    char c = '\0';
    // see if this key is listed in our char map
    foreach (int[] map in m_KeyMap)
    {
        if (
            shiftInt == map[3] &&
            keyInt >= map[0] &&
            keyInt <= map[1])
        {
            // is in map, standard entry
            if (map.Length == 4)
            {
                c = (char)(map[2] + (keyInt - map[0]));
            }
            // is in map, with list of chars to map
            else
            {
                c = (char)(map[4 + (keyInt - map[0])]);
            }
            // stop looking, we mapped it
            break;
        }
    }
```

If our attempts at mapping the key press to a Unicode character failed, we'll see if the pressed key was one of the special cases where individual keys are directly associated with one of the VirtualKeyboard's method.

```
// if we didn't identify the key in our mapping,
// see if it's another key that we're interested in
if (c == '\0')
{
```

```
switch (key)
{
    case Keys.Space:
        c = ' ';
        break;
    case Keys.Enter:
        Done();
        return;
    case Keys.Escape:
        Cancel();
        return;
    case Keys.End:
        Cursor = Text.Length;
        break;
    case Keys.Home:
        Cursor = 0;
        break;
    case Keys.Left:
        Cursor--;
        break;
    case Keys.Right:
        Cursor+ +;
        break;
    case Keys.Back:
        BackSpace();
        break;
    }
}
```

At this point, we have a valid Unicode character, or our local character variable has a value of '\0'. Either way, we can just hand the value off to the InsertChar method for processing.

```
        // add char to text, if we mapped one
        InsertChar(c);
    }
}
```

Drawing the Virtual Keyboard

The VirtualKeyboard's Draw method is called from the main game class every time its own Draw method is called. We'll only draw our virtual keyboard when the Visible property is true.

```
// draw the virtual keyboard
public void Draw(SpriteBatch batch)
{
    // only draw when visible
    if (Visible)
    {
        DrawVirtualKeyboard(batch);
    }
}
```

The virtual keyboard is drawn in several stages, building the final image that you see by layering sprites on top of each other. The sprite that contains the button grid is embedded in the source texture without reserving (empty) space for the dialog caption. To account for this, we need to draw that sprite slightly offset from the top of our dialog. This offset is stored in a local variable named btnOffset.

The first three layers of sprites are the dialog, the empty button grid, and the (highlighted) currently selected button. Highlighting the selected button requires enough code that I pulled it out into its own method, which we'll cover as soon as we're done discussing this method.

```
// draw the virtual keyboard
protected void DrawVirtualKeyboard(SpriteBatch batch)
{
    // offset to account for dialog caption
    Vector2 btnOffset = new Vector2(0, 32);
    // draw background and keys
    batch.Draw(Texture, Location, m_RectBackground, Color.White);
    batch.Draw(Texture, Location + btnOffset, m_RectButtons,
        Color.White);
    HiliteSelectedButton(batch);
```

Next, we draw the caption text, centered in the caption area of our dialog. To make it stand out from the other text, we'll add a little drop shadow by drawing the caption text twice. Once with a black tint, offset one pixel down and one pixel to the right, and again, with a white tint at the calculated location.

```
// draw caption
Vector2 size = Font.MeasureString(Caption);
float x = Location.X + m_RectCaption.Left +
    m_RectCaption.Width / 2 - size.X / 2;
float y = Location.Y + m_RectCaption.Top +
```

```
            m_RectCaption.Height / 2 - size.Y / 2;
Font.DrawString(
        batch, Caption, (int)x + 1, (int)y + 1, Color.Black);
Font.DrawString(
        batch, Caption, (int)x, (int)y, Color.White);
```

Using a similar calculation to center our string, we'll draw the text that's being edited in the middle of the edit portion of our dialog. And to let the player know where the cursor is located within the text, we'll draw a simple line. We'll only draw the cursor when m_CursorBlink is true. The m_CursorBlink member variable is toggled every CursorBlinkRate seconds, and it is set to true whenever the player modifies the text or moves the cursor.

```
// draw text
x = Location.X + m_RectText.Left;
y = Location.Y + m_RectText.Top +
    m_RectText.Height / 2 - Font.FontHeight / 2;
Font.DrawString(batch, Text, (int)x, (int)y, Color.Black);
// draw cursor
if (m_CursorBlink)
{
    y = Location.Y + m_RectCursor.Top + 35;
    x += Font.MeasureString(Text.Substring(0, Cursor)).X;
    batch.Draw(
        Texture, new Vector2(x, y), m_RectCursor, Color.Navy);
}
```

The last thing we need to do is fill in all of those small, empty buttons in the middle of our button grid with the Unicode characters that comprise the currently selected character set. This is where all those calculations that we did in the UpdateCharLocations method are put to use.

```
            // draw button text
            Vector2 loc = Vector2.Zero;
            for (int row = 0; row < 4; row++)
            {
                for (int col = 0; col < 10; col++)
                {
                    // calc location
                    loc = Location + btnOffset +
                        m_CharButtonLoc[row,col] +
                        m_CharLoc[CurrentVKB,row,col];
                    // draw character
```

```
            m_Font.DrawString(
                batch,
                m_CharGrids[CurrentVKB][row][col],
                (int)loc.X,
                (int)loc.Y,
                Color.Black);
        }
    }
}
```

The shift state of the virtual keyboard is used to select alternate character sets when both an uppercase version and a lowercase version of the Unicode characters are provided. But, we'll also use that information to determine whether we should highlight the Shift button on our virtual keyboard.

```
// state of the shift modifier for characters
protected bool m_ShiftPressed = false;
public bool ShiftPressed
{
    get { return m_ShiftPressed; }
    set { m_ShiftPressed = value; }
}
```

Our virtual keyboard buttons come in two sizes. The small buttons in our button grid are grouped in the center of the grid, and they have no embedded text or images. The large buttons line the outer edges of the grid, and they do have embedded text and images.

We will highlight the small buttons using the small, blank button that sits at the bottom of our source texture. That sprite can safely be drawn over the existing button grid since it won't be obscuring any existing text or image data. The large buttons are a different story, though.

We don't want to cover the text or image data that decorates the large buttons in our button grid, so we can't use the large, blank button from our source texture. To highlight those buttons, we'll select the source texture rectangle that encloses the button that we're interested in, and render that as a sprite with the highlighting tint applied.

The Shift button is our wild card here, though. It reflects the state of the ShiftPressed property by highlighting the Shift button in a shade of gold, regardless of what button is actually selected on our button grid. When the Shift button is actually selected by the player, it takes on the green tint that any other selected button would show.

```
// highlight the selected virtual keyboard button
protected void HiliteSelectedButton(SpriteBatch batch)
{
    // offset to account for dialog caption
    Vector2 btnOffset = new Vector2(0, 32);
    // texture rect and screen location for button
    Rectangle rect = Rectangle.Empty;
    Vector2 loc = Vector2.Zero;
    // indicate shift state
    if (ShiftPressed)
    {
        rect = m_RectButtonLarge;
        rect.X = 3;
        rect.Y = 33 + 30 * 3;
        loc.X = Location.X + rect.X + btnOffset.X;
        loc.Y = Location.Y + rect.Y + btnOffset.Y;
        batch.Draw(Texture, loc, rect, Color.PaleGoldenrod);
    }
}
```

The on-screen location (Vector2 loc) and size of the sprite (Rectangle rect) are assigned values based on the currently selected button. Once set, we just need to render the given sprite at the given location with our green tint. It's at this point that the Shift button may be overdrawn with a green-tinted version of itself.

It doesn't matter whether the selected button is one of the small buttons or one of the large buttons. The drawing code doesn't care. Those details are accounted for in the local variables, loc and rect.

```
// small button is active?
if (SelectedChar != '\0')
{
    rect = m_RectButtonSmall;
    loc = Location + btnOffset +
        m_CharButtonLoc[
            (int)m_SelectedCharButton.Y,
            (int)m_SelectedCharButton.X - 1];
}
// large button is active?
else
{
    // first or last column
    rect = m_RectButtonLarge;
    rect.X = (m_SelectedCharButton.X == 0 ? 3 : 309);
    rect.Y = 33 + 30 * (int)m_SelectedCharButton.Y;
```

```
            // Done button is special case
            if (m_SelectedCharButton.Y == 4 && m_SelectedCharButton.X == 10)
            {
                rect.X = 259;
            }
            loc.X = Location.X + rect.X + btnOffset.X;
            loc.Y = Location.Y + rect.Y + btnOffset.Y;
        }
        // draw the highlighted button
        batch.Draw(Texture, loc, rect, Color.LightGreen);
    }
```

Showing and Hiding the Virtual Keyboard

We're almost done! The last bit of code that we need to cover is the methods that are used to show and hide the dialog that houses our virtual keyboard. There are two overloaded versions of the Show method. One accepts a callback delegate, which the virtual keyboard will call when the dialog is closed. And the other takes no parameters (assuming that the caller will be repeatedly checking the Visible property in their Update logic to see when the player has finished editing the text).

```
// show the virtual keyboard dialog
public void Show()
{
    Show(null);
}
```

When the virtual keyboard is first shown, it performs several tasks. It starts the button repeat delay counter, selects the first valid Unicode character in the button grid, places the cursor at the end of the text that's being edited, and stores a copy of the text that can be recalled if the player decides not to commit his changes. This is also the place that the callback is registered, if the caller passed one in.

```
// store copy of text without edits (in case player decides to cancel)
protected string m_OriginalText = "";
// show the virtual keyboard dialog, register callback (delegate)
public void Show(InputCompleteEvent callback)
{
    // don't reset dialog if it's already visible
    if (!Visible)
    {
```

```
        // make visible
        Visible = true;
        // reset state variables
        m_TimeSinceLastProcessInput = 0;
        m_SelectedCharButton = new Vector2(1, 0);
        Cursor = Text.Length;
        // remember original text (in case player decides to cancel)
        m_OriginalText = Text;
        // register callback delegate
        m_Callback = callback;
    }
}
```

You can think of the callback method as a simple event. If the caller would prefer to be notified when the player closes the dialog, rather than constantly checking the Visible property, they can pass in the address of a method that matches the signature of the InputCompleteEvent delegate.

```
// delegate to notify host when we're done editing
public delegate void InputCompleteEvent(string text);
protected InputCompleteEvent m_Callback = null;
protected void OnInputComplete()
{
    if (m_Callback != null)
    {
        m_Callback(Text);
    }
}
```

There are two ways that the player can close the dialog on which the virtual keyboard is housed. The first is when he accepts the edits by pressing the Start button on the game pad, by pressing the Enter key on the (physical) keyboard, or by selecting the Done button on the virtual keyboard. The second is when he rejects his edits by pressing the Back button on the game pad, by pressing the Escape key on the (physical) keyboard, or by selecting the Cancel button on the virtual keyboard.

```
// we're done editing, notify host
protected void Done()
{
    Visible = false;
    OnInputComplete();
}
```

```
// edit canceled, reset text and notify host
protected void Cancel()
{
    Text = m_OriginalText;
    Visible = false;
    OnInputComplete();
}
```

Summary

In this chapter, you learned how to display a virtual keyboard component over your active game and use it to collect somewhat complex input from the player. You also learned about some of the issues that are involved with ferrying input from context to context. You saw how complex mappings (like mapping keyboard keys to Unicode characters or mapping character sets to your virtual keyboard states) can be made easier using arrays and data-driven code. You also saw how delegates can be used in your game to create games with more of an event-driven model.

Review Questions

1. How is the text in the game animated? How does the game logic accurately know when the text strikes one of the edges of the screen even though the length of the text can change while the game is running?

2. What is the purpose of a virtual keyboard? When should you use one? Why would you avoid using one?

3. How are the buttons with the Unicode characters drawn? How are the fixed-function buttons drawn?

4. What is the m_KeyMap member variable used for? How is it structured? How is it actually used?

5. The VirtualKeyboard class uses the Back button to cancel edits, and the Game1 class uses the same button to exit the game. How does the code handle this duality of function? How does each class know when to process that button press and when to ignore it?

Exercises

EXERCISE 1. The existing code and source texture only allow for a blue dialog. Use your favorite image editor to convert the background image to grayscale. Then add a property to the `VirtualKeyboard` class called `DialogColor`. Use this color as the tint whenever you draw the background sprite.

EXERCISE 2. Modify this code to add an "uppercase" character set for symbols. When the shift mode is set, swap in your new character set just as you would for the Accents set or the Alpha set. Since symbols don't have case, select some other characters. One of the Windings fonts might be nice. Whatever characters you decide to use, be sure your game font includes the new characters. You may need to create a new bitmap font image using the utility that we developed in an earlier chapter.

EXERCISE 3. There's a nasty visual glitch in this control that really should be fixed. Whenever the player enters text that extends beyond the width of the dialog, the drawn text ignores the boundaries and spills onto the game surface, with new characters eventually exiting the viewable screen altogether. Devise a fix and implement it. One simple fix would be to restrict the length of edited text. A more complex solution might involve rendering only the substring of the edited text that will fit into the edit window.

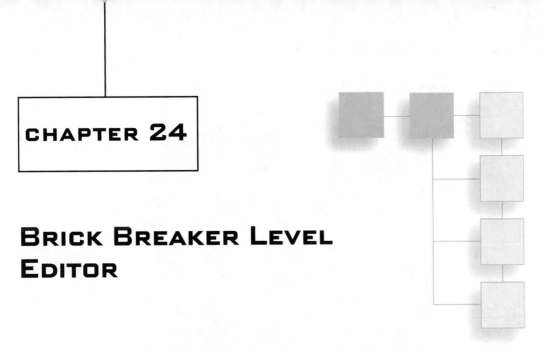

CHAPTER 24

BRICK BREAKER LEVEL EDITOR

When working on a game, you'll use a variety of tools beyond your compiler. You (or some of your more creative teammates) will spend a lot of time in digital content creation tools like 3D modelers, paint programs, audio editors, and video editors. Today, there are more affordable (or free) third-party content creation tools than ever before. And thanks to increased competition, the quality of these tools rivals the quality of many of their high-priced counterparts that are used in most large development studios. But, no matter how feature-rich these tools become, there will be times when you will need to create your own game-specific tools.

In this chapter, we will develop a Windows-based application (using Visual C# 2005 Express Edition) to create and edit game levels for the Brick Breaker game that we developed in Chapter 14.

In this chapter, you will learn how to:

- Use Visual C# 2005 Express Edition to write GUI Windows applications to support game development

- Take advantage of existing Visual Studio and .NET Framework features to benefit usability with little or no extra code

- Reuse the same classes in the editor and the XNA game by avoiding platform-specific code

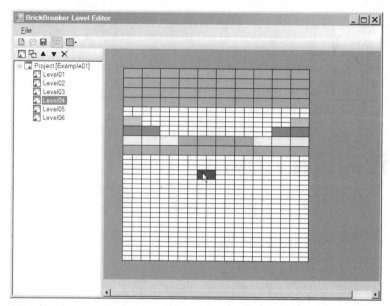

Figure 24.1
A screen shot of the editor that we will develop in this chapter.

- Use standard Windows controls to save coding time and provide the polished and professional user interface elements that today's users have come to expect

- Create new user controls when the standard controls don't meet your needs

- Implement simple fool-proofing measures to help prevent accidental loss of data

The Design

Our editor will provide a simple, intuitive interface for creating and editing game levels for our Brick Breaker game (see Figure 24.1). To reduce redundant code, the editor will use the same core classes that the game uses to represent bricks and level data. The tool will use some common user interface elements to make it feel more like a commercial application, without spending too much time on those "frilly" dressings.

User Expectations

The personal computing market has exploded in recent years. That increase in the number of computer users has spurred an equally impressive increase in the number and variety of commercial software applications that are available today. Over this same time, standards in user interface design have evolved and user expectations have risen.

Many disparate applications share a core set of common, basic user interface elements. Users have come to expect features like toolbars, standardized keyboard shortcuts, minimal fool-proofing measures (like prompting to save changes before closing a program or prompting before overwriting existing data), and consistent interfaces to the most common tasks (like printing a document, selecting a color, or opening a file).

Unless you plan on distributing the tools that you develop to your end-users, you shouldn't waste too much time adding bells and whistles. But, there are a few, minimal user interface elements that you can add to your tools that will help reduce the users' workload, increase their workflow, and provide some measure of protection against lost data. The majority of those simple UI features can be integrated into your applications with little or no extra code, thanks to the tools, components, and libraries that Visual Studio provides.

RAD (Rapid Application Development) in Visual Studio

Visual Studio provides common user controls like toolbars, menus, tree views, tooltips, and system dialogs that help you logically present your data and expose intuitive interfaces for each of your tool's tasks. Using the familiar document-view model, you can easily present large sets of data to the user, allowing him to manipulate the view of that data to focus on areas of interest, or see the state of the entire data set at a glance.

Our tool will present a view of our game data that a level designer can manipulate via a simple point-and-click interface. The level designer can edit any level in the project by selecting it from a tree view docked to the left of the client area. The selected level appears in the client area, where the level designer can add, edit, or remove bricks by clicking them with the mouse. Where screen real estate is limited, the application automatically presents scroll bars for the user to zero in on specific areas of the level.

Tasks are represented as menu options, toolbar buttons, and (right-click) context menus. In general, the same task can be accessed multiple ways. For example, the user can save a project using the File > Save menu option, the save icon on the toolbar, or by pressing Crtl+S on the keyboard.

At first glance, it may seem strange to provide multiple paths to the same function, but different users are able to perform tasks more efficiently using the mouse, the keyboard, or some combination of the two. The programming model for Windows applications in Visual Studio makes it easy to hook several events to the same task, so there's no extra work for us; and the increased flexibility of our tool will translate to increased efficiency for a variety of user types.

Inspiration versus Creeping Scope

User interface standards have evolved over time. The interfaces of early Windows applications seem primitive by today's standards, even though the developers of that era were following the de facto design standards of their day. If you want your users to feel comfortable with your tool, you'll want to mimic the interfaces of the most popular applications of today. The most widely used programs are popular for a reason.

As with game programming, we need to avoid getting distracted by shiny objects. Establish functional goals when planning and designing your programs. During the implementation, try like heck to stick to the design. If you see a feature that would be nice, but is not strictly necessary, add it to a list of future enhancements. Functionality should always be priority one.

Note

I'm the chief sinner in this area. I enjoy interface design and tools programming as much as I enjoy game programming. UI work frequently gets my game projects off track, and I finish fewer projects because of it. Do as I say, not as I do.

Designing the Editor

Create a new Windows Application project, and name it `BrickBreakerEditor`. The IDE generates a stub application for us, which is just a blank form. As with the other Visual Studio project types, we can run the application right now, without making any changes, and all of the plumbing is there to display this blank form to the user (see Figure 24.2). It doesn't do anything useful right now, but there's a lot of code behind just creating, displaying, and managing a window.

Naming Classes

The default names for new controls and forms leave a lot to be desired. With names like `Form1`, `Form2`, and `Form3`, it's easy to get confused as to which form

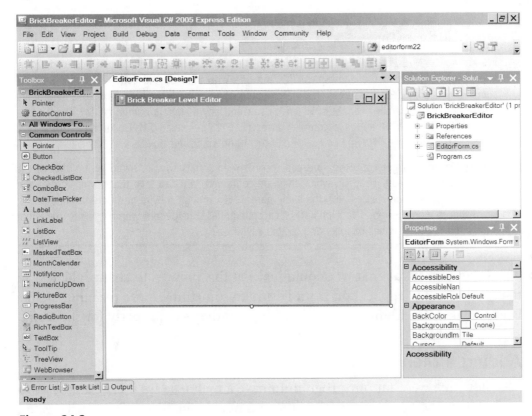

Figure 24.2
The default Windows application.

performs what tasks. Right-click the form (Form1.cs) in the solution, and then select Rename. Type EditorForm.cs and press Enter. You will likely be prompted with a message box that reads, "You are renaming a file. Would you also like to perform a rename in this project of all references to the code element 'Form1'?" Click Yes.

Note

Be careful when renaming controls and forms not to select the same name as the namespace (by default, the namespace is the same as the solution name). The Visual Studio designer often prefixes added controls with its namespace. If your form has the same name as its namespace, the IDE may get confused and look for your control as a member of the form rather than as a member of the namespace. This will result in a compile-time error.

Consider the case where you have a solution named MyEditor. The IDE automatically assigns a default namespace of MyEditor. If you then rename your form to MyEditor, it's fully qualified name becomes MyEditor.MyEditor. Next, you add a new control named MyControl, whose fully qualified name is MyEditor.MyControl. When you add the control to the form, the designer injects the fully qualified name into the code for the form—`this.myControl1 = new MyEditor.MyControl();`.

We know that `MyEditor` in this case refers to the namespace, and the Visual Studio designer knows that it refers to the namespace (it's the one who injected the code, after all). But, the compiler gets confused. It assumes that statements that begin with the class name of the form are referencing static member variables. When it can't find any members named `MyControl` in the class `MyEditor`, it generates a compiler error (`The type name 'MyControl' does not exist in the type 'MyEditor.MyEditor'`) and stops the build.

If the compiler can get confused, you can too. To keep things simple, avoid giving classes the same name as the namespace in which they are contained. You can take that a step further and avoid naming any two classes with the same name, even though they're in different namespaces. Namespaces were designed to eliminate such ambiguities, but people weren't. Write code that makes the fewest number of folks as possible say "Huh?"

Another minor tweak that we should make at this point is to change the text in the title bar of the application from Form1 to something more meaningful, like Brick Breaker Level Editor. Type that title into the Text property for the form.

Adding a Menu

We know that we want our program to have a menu, so we'll drag a `MenuStrip` control from the Toolbox and drop it on our new, blank form. Then we'll create a new top-level menu item named `&File`, and then add menu items under that root item for `&New`, `&Open`, `&Close`, `&Save`, `Save &As`, and `E&xit`. The ampersand (the "&" character) prefixes the keyboard shortcut that you would like to use for the menu item. In this case, pressing and releasing Alt, F, and X while the program is running will cause the editor to shutdown.

Note

Why? The `File` menu item has an ampersand just before the "F," and the `Exit` menu item has an ampersand just before the "x." Pressing the Alt key opens the main menu in a state that allows the user to navigate the menu items using his keyboard.

Figure 24.3 shows what your form should look like after you've created these menu items.

Adding a Toolbar

Our editor will also have a toolbar to make editing functions easily accessible to the level designer. Drag a `ToolStrip` control from the Toolbox and drop it on our

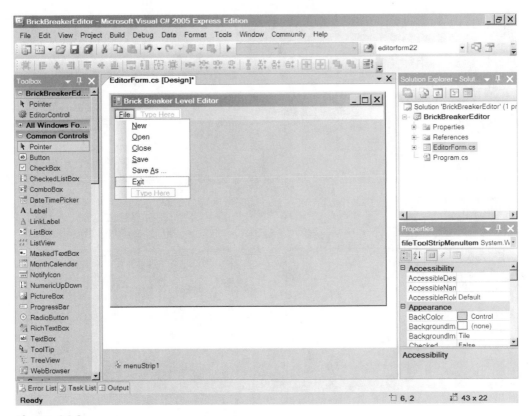

Figure 24.3
Our new menu.

form. Add three new buttons for the New, Open, and Save functions. Add a separator, and then a new button for toggling the "snap to grid" mode for our editor. And finally, add a new button that the level designer can use to select the "number of hits to clear" for any new bricks that are added to the level.

The last two buttons on the toolbar are special button types. The "snap to grid" button is a toggle button, and the "number of hits to clear" button is a dropdown list button. Select the grid button and set its CheckOnClick property to True. Then set its Checked property to True. Add nine menu items under the "number of hits to clear" dropdown button, named "1 Hit" to "9 Hits." When you're done, your form should look something like Figure 24.4.

Next, we'll add some images to our toolbar so that the player can easily tell what function each button performs. For each button, select an image by editing its Image property. The images that I used are in the media subdirectory under the

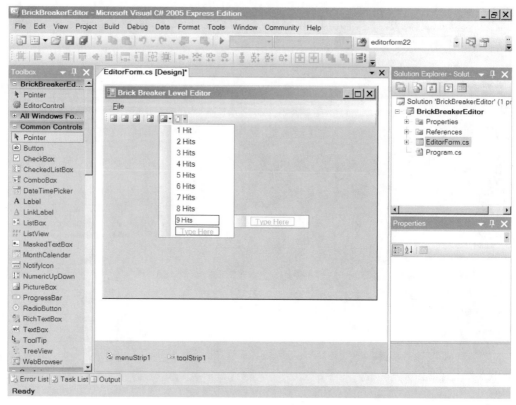

Figure 24.4
Our new toolbar.

project for the editor. When you're done, your form should look something like Figure 24.5. By adding simple, colored squares to the menu items, the user can quickly identify and select the option that he's looking for.

User-Defined Workspace

The client area of our application will contain a control to select a level to edit and another to actually handle level-editing tasks. To allow the user to resize his workspace, we'll use a standard control known as a SplitContainer. The SplitContainer control provides two panels, separated by a draggable splitter that the user can move to allocate more screen real estate for one control or the other. Drag the SplitContainer from the Toolbox and drop it on our form. Your form should now be split into two distinct areas, as illustrated by Figure 24.6.

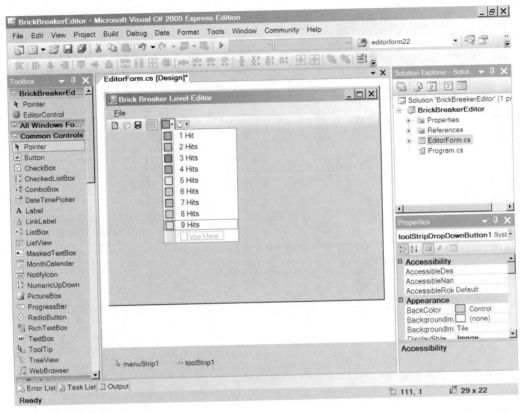

Figure 24.5
Toolbar with button images.

Selecting Levels within the Project

Mimicking the document model of Visual Studio, our editor is project-based. A project contains one or more game levels. To help the level designer manage those levels, we'll add a TreeView control from the Toolbox. Drag a TreeView control from the Toolbox and drop it on the area of the SplitContainer that's labeled Panel1. Set the Dock property of the new control to Fill. To see how the control will look at runtime, add a root node named Project and two child nodes named Level01 and Level02. Your form should now look something like Figure 24.7.

Unlike toolbar items and menu items, nodes in the TreeView control get their images from a control known as an ImageList. Drag an ImageList control from the Toolbox and drop it on the form. You can add images to the ImageList control by editing its Images property. Add an image for the project node and

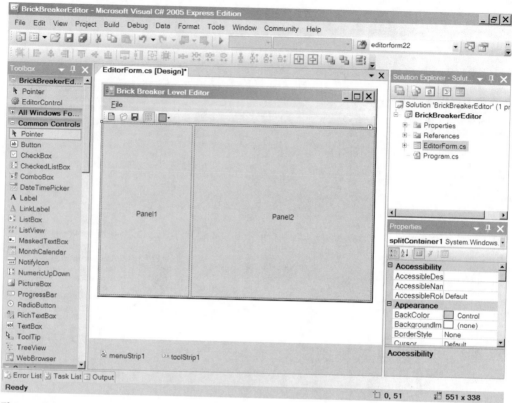

Figure 24.6
The `SplitContainer` control—two panels, separated by a small, draggable gap.

another for the level nodes. The images that I used are in the media subdirectory under the project for the editor.

Assign the new `ImageList` control to the `TreeView` control's `ImageList` property. By default, all of the nodes in the tree are assigned the first image in the list. We need to correct that. Edit the `TreeView` control's `Nodes` property. For each node, select the appropriate image for its `ImageIndex` and `SelectedImageIndex` property. When you're done, your form should look something like Figure 24.8.

The nodes and images that you see in the Visual Studio designer are there solely for our benefit. We'll need to assign those same settings when the application is running, since we'll be adding and removing nodes dynamically.

Actually Editing Level Data

We're almost done designing our level editor. The last thing that we need to add is the control that the user will use to actually edit level data. Up to this point,

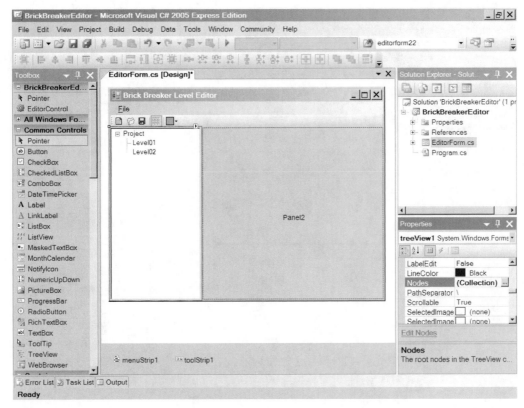

Figure 24.7
The `TreeView` control, used to select levels for editing.

we've dragged and dropped the standard controls that are provided by Visual Studio. Obviously, there is no standard control that will edit our proprietary game data. So, we'll need to write one.

To add a custom control to our project, right-click on the project node within the Solution Explorer, and then select Add > User Control. Name the new control `EditorControl` and click OK. A new, blank control will appear in the designer (as illustrated by Figure 24.9). We won't write any code for the new control just yet, but let's set the `BackColor` property for our control to `ControlDark` so that we can easily see it when we drop it on our form.

Go ahead and close the designer for the control to return to the designer for the editor. The user should be able to scroll around within the editor control if the level data is larger than the client area of our editor. To implement this, we'll cheat a little.

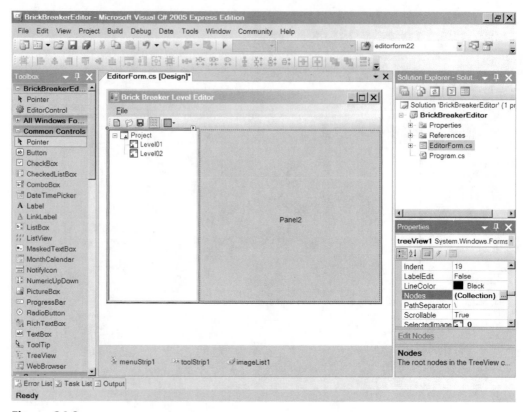

Figure 24.8
The `TreeView` control, with images assigned to the placeholder nodes.

The `Panel2` of our `SplitContainer` has a property named `AutoScroll`. Set this property to `True`, and then build our project by clicking Build > Build Solution from the main menu in Visual Studio.

Building the project generated executable code for our new, blank control. The IDE also added our new control (named `EditorControl`) to the Toolbox under a section labeled "BrickBreakerEditor Components." You can see our new control in the Toolbox in Figure 24.10.

Drag this control from the Toolbox and drop it on the area of the `SplitContainer` that's labeled `Panel2`. Set the `Location` property to 0, 0 and the `Size` property to 640, 480. If your designer window isn't large enough to accommodate the new control, you'll see that the panel has automatically added scrollbars to allow you to navigate within the client area. An example of this feature in action is shown in Figure 24.11.

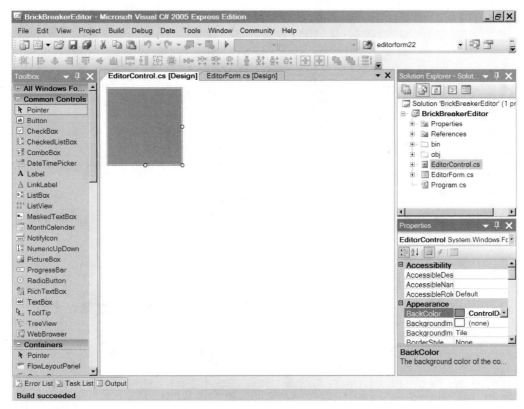

Figure 24.9
Our new, blank user control.

Coding the EditorForm

We now have the shell of our new application. It doesn't do anything useful yet, but it has the same look and feel now as it will have when we're done. You can run it in its current state to see how it behaves. It's really quite amazing that we have a working, empty shell of our new application, and we haven't written a single line of code. That's RAD (Rapid Application Development).

Event-Driven Programming

Unlike XNA games where the main game loop is running full bore, polling input devices, updating game state, and drawing game objects to the screen, standard Windows applications are made up of a collection of highly specialized, disparate methods that spend the majority of their time in an idle state, only springing into action when specific events (like a mouse click or a key press) occur.

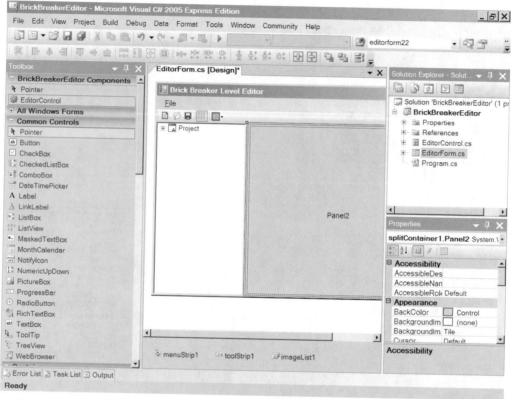

Figure 24.10
Our custom control has been added to the Toolbox.

These event-handling methods are tailored to process specific events, which can come from a variety of sources, including the user and the operating system. Visual Studio makes the job of binding application events to your code easier by generating empty method stubs for each event that you want to handle. If you want to take some action when the user clicks File > Exit in your application, just double-click on the Exit menu item. Visual Studio generates a do-nothing method stub where you can add your own code.

Handling Menu Events

Let's go ahead and hook up our first event. Double-click EditorForm.cs in the Solution Explorer to bring up the form designer. Select the File menu on the form, and then double-click the Exit menu item. Visual Studio will create an empty event handler for the Exit menu item's click event to which you will add code similar to the following.

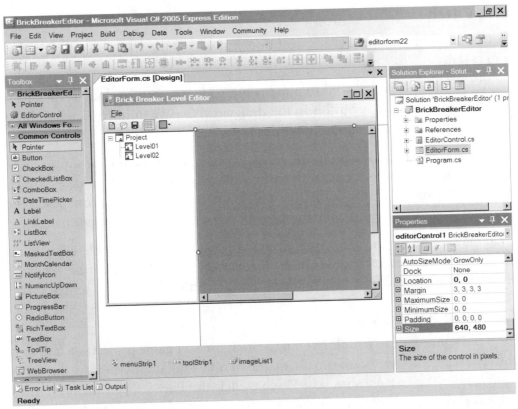

Figure 24.11
Our custom control, dropped onto the form, with scrollbars.

```
private void exitToolStripMenuItem_Click(object sender, EventArgs e)
{
    this.Close();
}
```

Now, when the user selects the File > Exit menu item, the application will exit. Run the program now by pressing F5 or by selecting Debug > Start Debugging from Visual Studio's main menu. When the program appears, click File > Exit, and you'll see that the program shuts down and you're returned to the Visual Studio IDE.

That's it. Visual Studio handles all of the internal plumbing required to tie your code to application events. Visual Studio's drag-and-drop, point-and-click model for Windows application development allows you to focus on your program's functionality, so you're able to get much more done in much less time.

The Catch

You're probably saying, "That's neat, Joe. But what's the catch?" Well, I'm glad you asked.

Hooking an application event to our custom code is as easy as double-clicking a menu item or a toolbar button in the designer. It's easy to introduce duplicate code by implementing similar functions separately.

In the case of the Exit function, we only had one path to the task of shutting the application down. In the case of opening a file, it's much better to have a single method that knows how to read project files, and call that method from our event handlers, than it is to add code to open the file on each independent path.

That may sound obvious, but you'll frequently catch yourself double-clicking an element in the designer and adding logic without first considering whether there's a block of existing code that could be generalized to handle similar tasks.

Opening Projects

Let's add some code to handle opening a Brick Breaker game project—a task that the user can initiate via the main menu or the toolbar. Return to the form designer for the EditorForm class. Double-click the File > Open menu item to generate an empty event handler. Return to the form designer and double-click on the toolbar button that represents the open project task (the open file folder icon) to generate another empty event handler. You should now see the following method stubs, just waiting for you to populate them.

```
private void openToolStripMenuItem_Click(object sender, EventArgs e)
{
}
private void toolStripButton2_Click(object sender, EventArgs e)
{
}
```

We don't want to write the code to load a project file twice. It would also be a bad idea to write it in one method stub, and then copy and paste it into the other. We want to implement this functionality in one place, and then reference that single code block from both event handlers. Let's call the new method OpenProject. Add the following line to both of our event handlers.

```
OpenProject();
```

Now, we just need to implement a method called OpenProject that takes no parameters and returns no results. Within that method, we'll want to prompt the user for the location of the project file. Visual Studio provides a standard dialog control for this purpose.

Return to the form designer for the EditorForm class. Drag an OpenFileDialog from the Toolbox and drop it anywhere on the editor form. While we're at it, we'll also go ahead and drag a SaveFileDialog onto the form as well. Set the Filter property for both of these controls to BrickBreaker Projects|*.bbp|All Files|*.*.

The Filter property is where you establish the filename filters for your common file dialogs. The filter is made up of pairs of tokens, separated by the pipe character ("|"). Each pair contains the description of the filter and the wildcard against which files in the current directory are matched. In this case, there are two filters: BrickBreaker Projects, which only shows the files with a .bbp extention, and All Files, which shows all of the files in the current directory.

Figure 24.12 shows what our form looks like after adding the Open and Save file dialogs. Like the image list control, the common file dialogs won't actually appear on your form. You'll find them in a special area of the designer, just below your form.

We're now ready to write our OpenProject method. The following code snippet contains the implementation for this method. We'll add it just below the two event handlers that we added earlier.

```
// the collection of levels for this project
protected List<LevelData> m_Levels = new List<LevelData>();
// filename of the currently loaded project
protected string m_Filename = null;
// actually open a project file from disk
protected void OpenProject()
{
    // give user a chance to save any unsaved data
    if (!CheckForChanges())
    {
        // prompt user for filename
        if (DialogResult.OK == openFileDialog1.ShowDialog(this))
        {
            try
            {
                // remember the filename, open the file,
                // read the first line
                m_Filename = openFileDialog1.FileName;
```

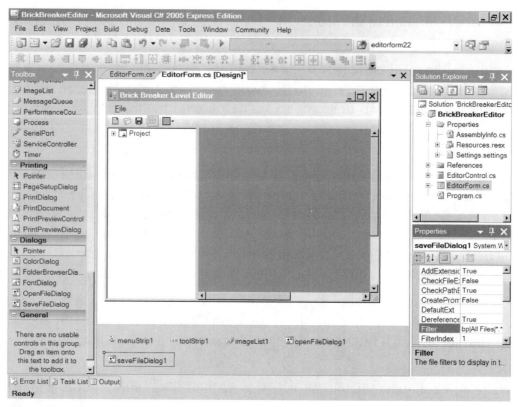

Figure 24.12
Adding the open and save file dialogs.

```
StreamReader reader =
    new StreamReader(
        new FileStream(m_Filename, FileMode.Open));
string line = reader.ReadLine();
// clear any existing level data from our
// in-memory collection
m_Levels.Clear();
// for every line in the file, read it in,
// create a level from the data, and add the
// newly created level to our collection
while (line != null)
{
    m_Levels.Add(new LevelData(line));
    line = reader.ReadLine();
}
// after reading all the lines, close the file
```

```
            reader.Close();
        }
        catch (Exception ex)
        {
            MessageBox.Show(ex.Message + "\n" + ex.StackTrace);
        }
        // rebuild our navigation tree and select the
        // first level, if there is one
        RebuildTree();
        if (m_Levels.Count > 0)
        {
            SelectNode(m_Levels[0]);
        }
    }
}
}
```

Saving Users from Themselves

The preceding code block calls out to a method (CheckForChanges) that determines whether the current project has any unsaved changes. If the current project does have unsaved changes, the user is given a chance to save his changes, discard his changes, or cancel the open project task.

Next, the user is presented with the familiar Windows Open file dialog. If he selects a valid game project file, all of the levels in the current project are discarded, and the levels from the new project are read in from the file, one by one.

```
// give the user a chance to save any changed work
// returns true if the action should be canceled, false otherwise
private bool CheckForChanges()
{
    bool cancel = false;
    foreach (LevelData level in m_Levels)
    {
        // has the current level been edited?
        if (level.Changed)
        {
            // offer the user a chance to save his work
            DialogResult result = MessageBox.Show(
                "The project has changed. Save changes?",
                "Save Changes?",
```

```
                        MessageBoxButtons.YesNoCancel);
                    // he clicked Yes, save the file
                    if (result == DialogResult.Yes)
                    {
                        cancel = !SaveProject(false);
                    }
                    // he clicked Cancel for the current action
                    else if (result == DialogResult.Cancel)
                    {
                        cancel = true;
                    }

                    // stop searching, save applies to all levels
                    // in the project; save one, save all
                    break;
                }
            }
    return cancel;
}
```

Updating the Navigation User Control

Once the new project has been loaded, the TreeView control is updated to reflect
the new project (by calling out to the RebuildTree method).

```
// build the navigation tree, based on the collection of levels
protected void RebuildTree()
{
    // disable redraws while updating tree nodes
    treeView1.BeginUpdate();
    // identify the root, and clear all existing child nodes
    TreeNode root = treeView1.Nodes[0];
    root.Nodes.Clear();
    // add a node to the root for every level in our collection
    int num = 1;
    foreach (LevelData level in m_Levels)
    {
        // name incrementally
        TreeNode node = root.Nodes.Add("Level" + num.ToString("00"));
        // store reference to the level in the tag
        node.Tag = level;
        // set the images for the new node
        node.ImageIndex = 2;
```

```
        node.SelectedImageIndex = 2;
        // increment the name counter
        num++;
    }

    // allow redraws for tree control
    treeView1.EndUpdate();
}
```

And after the `TreeView` has been repopulated, the first level of the new project is selected (by calling out to the `SelectNode` method, specifying the first level in our collection). Selecting the level in the `TreeView` control automatically populates our `EditorControl` with the selected level data.

```
// locate the tree node that refers to the given level
// and select it in our navigation tree control
protected void SelectNode(LevelData level)
{
    // locate root node, clear selection
    TreeNode root = treeView1.Nodes[0];
    treeView1.SelectedNode = null;
    // reset editor control's level data reference
    brickBreakerEditorControl1.LevelData = null;
    // scan the navigation tree, looking for the given level
    foreach (TreeNode node in root.Nodes)
    {
        if (node.Tag == level)
        {
            // simply selecting the node will trigger the
            // selection events on the navigation tree control
            // which will call our handler for AfterSelect
            // and tell the editor control to display the level
            // data for the newly selected node
            treeView1.SelectedNode = node;
            // stop looking, we found it
            break;
        }
    }
}
```

That's all the code that we need for opening a project file. But, during the `CheckForChanges` method, we called out to another method that we haven't covered yet—`SaveProject`.

Saving Projects

The SaveProject method will prompt the user for a filename whenever its saveAs parameter is true (whenever the user clicks the File > Save As menu item) or m_Filename is null (the first time the project is saved). When the saveAs parameter is false, the SaveProject methods works under the assumption that the m_Filename member variable contains the full path to a valid project file (to be created or overwritten).

```
// actually save the project to disk
protected bool SaveProject(bool saveAs)
{
    // report success or failure
    bool saved = false;
    // if this is the first save, prompt the user for a filename
    if (m_Filename == null || saveAs)
    {
        if (DialogResult.OK == saveFileDialog1.ShowDialog(this))
        {
            m_Filename = saveFileDialog1.FileName;
        }
        else
        {
            // user canceled the save as
            return false;
        }
    }
    // if we have a filename, we're ready to save our level data
    if (m_Filename != null)
    {
        try
        {
            // create the file (or truncate it, if it already exists)
            StreamWriter writer =
                new StreamWriter(
                    new FileStream(m_Filename, FileMode.Create));
            // write out each level, and reset its changed flag
            foreach (LevelData level in m_Levels)
            {
                writer.WriteLine(level.ToString());
                level.Changed = false;
            }
            // close the file
```

```
            writer.Flush();
            writer.Close();
            // report success to caller
            saved = true;
        }
        catch (Exception ex)
        {
            MessageBox.Show(ex.Message + "\n" + ex.StackTrace);
        }
    }
    return saved;
}
```

Now that we have a method to save our project files, we can also hook up the events for the File > Save menu item, the File > Save As menu item, and the Save icon on the toolbar. Double-click each of those controls to generate empty event-handler stubs, and then add a call out to the SaveProject method from each.

```
// user requested a save, and wants to be prompted for the filename
private void mnuFileSaveAs_Click(object sender, EventArgs e)
{
    SaveProject(true);
}
// user requested a save, and wants to forego the filename prompt
private void mnuFileSave_Click(object sender, EventArgs e)
{
    SaveProject(false);
}
// user has requested that we save the current project
private void toolSave_Click(object sender, EventArgs e)
{
    SaveProject(false);
}
```

Moving On

I'm not going to cover the rest of the code for the editor here. I think you get the basic idea behind visually designing an application and hooking up event handlers to process application events. I want to move on to how the Editor-Control works, and how you can use custom UserControl-derived classes to encapsulate game-specific logic in a Windows-friendly way that makes your job easier when working in Visual Studio's form designer.

Please be sure to review the source code for this project on the CD-ROM that accompanies this book. That source code contains extensive comments to help you understand how each task is handled, and how each class that makes up the editor project is responsible for its own piece of the puzzle.

Coding the EditorControl

Earlier, we created a do-nothing placeholder for our editor control. Let's take a little time to flesh that control out some more. The EditorControl class provides the interface that the user will use to edit level data. The EditorControl class has no concept of a game project. It is only ever aware of a single level at any one time.

There is only one editor control for the entire application, so each time the user selects a level for editing, the internal data for the editor control is replaced with the data for the newly selected level. Since the LevelData class is a reference type, we don't need to copy its contents into and out of the editor control. We just need to point the control to the new reference. Any changes that the editor control makes to the level are made to the actual level data, in memory.

Swapping Level Data In and Out

When the user clicks on a node in the TreeView on the EditorForm, the handler for the node selection event assigns the level data for that node to the editor control via the public EditorControl.LevelData property. The level data for each node is stored in the node's Tag property. Tag is a common property for most (if not all) visual Windows controls in the .NET Framework APIs. Its data type is System.Object, so it can store any .NET object. In our case, it contains a reference to our LevelData object for that node.

```
// the level data that we're currently editing
protected LevelData m_LevelData = new LevelData();
public LevelData LevelData
{
    get { return m_LevelData; }
    set
    {
        m_LevelData = value;

        // the level changed, redraw our edit window
```

```
        this.Invalidate();
    }
}
```

When there is no level data to edit, the control displays a generic message rather than presenting the typical editable view. Presenting the editable view would be confusing if the user couldn't make any changes. Displaying the message makes it clear that he will need to select a valid level before he can use the editor control.

```
// used when no level is actively being edited
protected Font m_font = new Font(FontFamily.GenericSansSerif, 12.0f);
protected const string
    MSG_NO_LEVEL = "[No data. Select a level to edit.]";
// update our editor window
private void BrickBreakerEditorControl_Paint(
    object sender, PaintEventArgs e)
{
    // local temp variable to save some typing
    Graphics g = e.Graphics;
    // if there is no level selected, draw a generic message
    if (LevelData == null)
    {
        SizeF dimensions = g.MeasureString(MSG_NO_LEVEL, m_font);
        PointF loc = new PointF(
            this.Width / 2.0f - dimensions.Width / 2.0f,
            this.Height / 2.0f - dimensions.Height / 2.0f);
        g.DrawString(
            MSG_NO_LEVEL,
            m_font,
            SystemBrushes.ControlText,
            loc);
    }
    // looks like we have a level to edit, render its current state
    else
    {
        DrawLevelBorder(g);
        DrawLevelGrid(g);
        DrawLevelData(g, LevelData);
        DrawGhostBrick(g, LevelData);
    }
}
```

Adding New Bricks

Users click on the EditorControl's client area to place the individual bricks for the level. As the mouse moves over the surface of the control, a special "ghost brick" is drawn to indicate the exact location where a new brick will be placed when the user clicks the left mouse button, taking into account the checked state of the "snap to grid" button on the toolbar. If a brick cannot be placed in the current location, the ghost brick is not drawn.

```
// create brush for our ghosted brick
protected Brush m_GhostBrush =
    new HatchBrush(
        HatchStyle.Percent30,
        SystemColors.Window,
        SystemColors.ControlText);
// draw "ghosted" brick where the new brick would be located
protected void DrawGhostBrick(Graphics g, LevelData level)
{
    if (m_NewBrickX >= 0 && m_NewBrickY >= 0)
    {
        g.FillRectangle( // fill brick
            m_GhostBrush,
            m_GameRect.Left + m_NewBrickX,
            m_GameRect.Top + m_NewBrickY,
            level.BrickWidth,
            level.BrickHeight);
        g.DrawRectangle( // outline brick
            Pens.Black,
            m_GameRect.Left + m_NewBrickX,
            m_GameRect.Top + m_NewBrickY,
            level.BrickWidth,
            level.BrickHeight);
    }
}
```

Incorporating the Toolbar State

When the user clicks on the editor control to place a brick, the control assigns the value of its NumHitsToClear property to the brick's HitsToClear property. The control's NumHitsToClear is set by the EditorForm class whenever the user selects a new value from the dropdown button on the toolbar.

```
// the HitsToClear value to be used with new bricks
protected int m_NumHitsToClear = 1;
```

```
public int NumHitsToClear
{
    get { return m_NumHitsToClear; }
    set { m_NumHitsToClear = value; }
}
```

Similarly, the EditorForm class is also responsible for managing the state of the EditorControl's DrawGrid property, based on the checked state of the "snap to grid" button on the toolbar.

```
// enable and disable the grid snap feature
protected bool m_DrawGrid = true;
public bool DrawGrid
{
    get { return m_DrawGrid; }
    set { m_DrawGrid = value; this.Invalidate(); }
}
```

Editing Bricks

To edit or delete a brick, the user right-clicks on the brick and a popup menu appears. This menu allows the user to delete the brick, visually edit the brick's HitsToClear property, or cancel the edit. The popup menu is shown in Figure 24.13. Notice how similar it is to the dropdown button on the toolbar, which mirrors its functionality.

To support the popup menu, we'll need to drag a ContextMenu control from the Toolbox and drop it onto the EditorControl in the Visual Studio designer. Then, we can visually edit the popup menu just like we edited the main menu for our editor form. We'll tie events to our event handlers by double-clicking the popup's menu items, just like we did for the main menu.

```
// user requested that we remove the selected brick
private void deleteToolStripMenuItem_Click(object sender, EventArgs e)
{
    LevelData.DeleteBrick(m_ClickedBrick);
    this.Invalidate();
}
// user changed the HitsToClear value for the selected brick
private void toolStripMenuItem_Click(object sender, EventArgs e)
{
    // has a brick been selected?
    if (m_ClickedBrick != null)
```

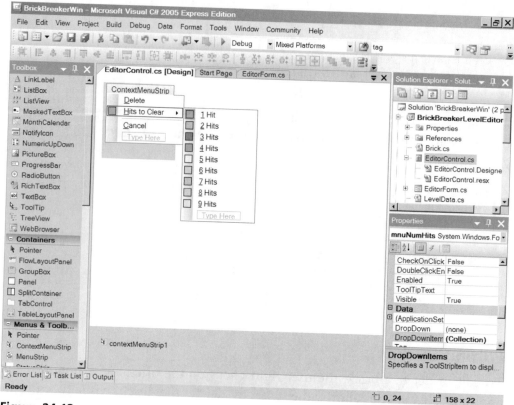

Figure 24.13
The popup menu for our custom user control.

```
    {
        // update brick's HitsToClear with the menu item's value
        ToolStripMenuItem item = (ToolStripMenuItem)sender;
        m_ClickedBrick.HitsToClear = int.Parse(item.Tag.ToString());
        this.Invalidate();
    }
}
```

Just before the popup menu is shown, we'll automatically select the proper menu sub item, based on the brick's HitsToClear property. That way, the popup menu seems to be more context-aware. When you right-click on a red brick, the red icon is already selected in the popup. When you right-click on a yellow brick, the yellow icon is already selected. That makes for a better user experience, and a more professional-looking application.

```
// process mouse clicks
private void BrickBreakerEditorControl_MouseUp(
```

```
    object sender, MouseEventArgs e)
{
    // if we're actually editing a level
    if (LevelData != null)
    {
        // right-clicked an existing brick, show popup menu
        if (m_ClickedBrick != null && e.Button == MouseButtons.Right)
        {
            // get HitsToClear for the selected brick
            string hits = m_ClickedBrick.HitsToClear.ToString();
            // find the corresponding menu item and set the
            // top-level HitsToClear menu's icon to the selected
            // child menu item's icon
            foreach (
                ToolStripMenuItem item in mnuNumHits.DropDownItems)
            {
                if (item.Tag.ToString() == hits)
                {
                    mnuNumHits.Image = item.Image;
                    break;
                }
            }
            // we're ready, show the popup menu
            this.contextMenuStrip1.Show(MousePosition);
        }
        // left-clicked empty space; try to add a new brick; redraw
        if (m_ClickedBrick == null && e.Button == MouseButtons.Left)
        {
            LevelData.AddBrick(
                m_NewBrickX,
                m_NewBrickY,
                NumHitsToClear);
            this.Invalidate();
        }
    }
}
```

Processing Mouse Movement Events

In addition to processing mouse click events, we'll also need to process the events that are generated whenever the mouse moves over the surface of our control. This is done so that the ghosted brick can follow the mouse cursor.

While we're at it, we'll also set a member variable (named `m_ClickedBrick`) to indicate which brick the mouse is currently hovering over. This is useful for knowing which brick is being edited when the popup menu is summoned, and it's handy for quickly determining when the ghost brick should be hidden.

```
// reference to selected brick for context menu (right-click popup)
// and by logic to deny placement over existing bricks
protected Brick m_ClickedBrick = null;
// need to repaint when the mouse moves so that we
// can draw the ghosted brick
private void BrickBreakerEditorControl_MouseMove(
    object sender, MouseEventArgs e)
{
    // if we're actually editing a level
    if (LevelData != null)
    {
        // see if mouse is over an existing brick
        // brick data is zero-based, so we subtract the top, left
        // of the playable area to translate to a 0,0 origin
        m_ClickedBrick =
            LevelData.FindBrick(
            e.X - m_GameRect.Left,
            e.Y - m_GameRect.Top);
        // apply grid settings and bounds checking
        CalcNewBrickXY(e.Location);
    }
}
```

Determining the Exact Location of a New Brick

Here's the logic for determining the exact location where a new brick will be placed. This method takes the "snap to grid" setting into account, makes sure that the new brick won't overlap with any existing bricks, and makes sure that the new brick will be entirely within the bounds of the playable area.

```
// position of new brick, based on grid settings
protected int m_NewBrickX = -1;
protected int m_NewBrickY = -1;

// calc position of new brick, based on grid settings
// called whenever the mouse moves, while over our editor control
protected void CalcNewBrickXY(Point location)
```

```
{
    // make sure mouse is within the playable area and
    // that it's not over an existing brick
    if (m_GameRect.Contains(location) && m_ClickedBrick == null)
    {
        // determine raw top, left for brick
        m_NewBrickX = location.X - m_GameRect.Left;
        m_NewBrickY = location.Y - m_GameRect.Top;
        // snap to grid?
        if (DrawGrid)
        {
            // snap to nearest grid cell's top, left
            m_NewBrickX =
                (m_NewBrickX / LevelData.HalfWidth) *
                LevelData.HalfWidth;
            m_NewBrickY =
                (m_NewBrickY / LevelData.HalfHeight) *
                LevelData.HalfHeight;
        }
        // make sure that the new brick won't extend
        // outside of the playable area
        m_NewBrickX =
            Math.Min(
                m_NewBrickX,
                m_GameRect.Width - LevelData.BrickWidth);
        m_NewBrickY =
            Math.Min(
                m_NewBrickY,
                m_GameRect.Height - LevelData.BrickHeight);
        // since the intended location may have changed (due to
        // grid snap or enforcement of playable bounds), make
        // sure that the new brick isn't about to sit on top of
        // an existing brick
        bool collide =
            LevelData.FindBrick(m_NewBrickX, m_NewBrickY) != null;
        collide |=
            LevelData.FindBrick(
                m_NewBrickX + LevelData.BrickWidth - 1,
                m_NewBrickY) != null;
        collide |=
            LevelData.FindBrick(
                m_NewBrickX,
                m_NewBrickY + LevelData.BrickHeight - 1) != null;
```

```
        collide |=
            LevelData.FindBrick(
                m_NewBrickX + LevelData.BrickWidth - 1,
                m_NewBrickY + LevelData.BrickHeight - 1) != null;
        // did we collide with another brick?
        if (collide)
        {
            // disallow placement of new brick
            m_NewBrickX = -1;
            m_NewBrickY = -1;
        }
        // redraw the editor so that we can see the ghosted brick
        this.Invalidate();
    }
    // mouse is not within the playable area
    else
    {
        // avoid repainting when the mouse moves outside of the
        // playable area or moves within an existing brick;
        // we have to redraw when it first moves into one of these
        // forbidden positions to get rid of the ghosted brick
        if (m_NewBrickX != -1 || m_NewBrickY != -1)
        {
            m_NewBrickX = -1;
            m_NewBrickY = -1;
            this.Invalidate();
        }
    }
}
```

Source Code

Remember, the source code that was listed in this chapter is not complete. Be sure to review the actual source for the level editor, which can be found on the CD-ROM that accompanies this book.

Summary

In this chapter, and the accompanying chapter in which the Brick Breaker game was developed (Chapter 14), you learned how to use the free Visual C# 2005 Express Edition IDE to write professional Windows-based tools to make your game development tasks easier. You learned about the standard controls that are provided within the IDE, and you learned how to create your own, custom user controls for those times when the standard controls don't quite meet your needs.

You saw how to reuse the same classes in your Windows-based applications that you use in your XNA games by avoiding platform-specific code. And you learned how to implement simple fool-proofing measures to help keep users from accidentally losing the game data that they worked so hard to generate.

Review Questions

Think about what you've read in this chapter (and the included source code) to answer the following questions.

1. List some reasons to use the standard Windows controls that Visual C# 2005 Express Edition provides. List some scenarios in which you would want to implement your own, custom user controls.

2. Why is it important to avoid the Windows-only .NET Framework APIs when writing Windows-based tools to support your XNA games?

3. What are some similarities between writing Windows applications and writing XNA games? What are some differences? Explain how each platform processes user input and how each platform presents its graphical interface to the user.

4. How does Visual Studio make programming Windows applications with rich graphical user interfaces easier? Are there any caveats to this ease of use?

5. Why should you provide multiple user interface elements that perform exactly the same task? Are there any issues with doing so?

Exercises

EXERCISE 1. Currently, the EditorControl has no concept of a selected brick, except within the context of the popup menu. Devise a way to allow users to select one or more bricks. A selected brick will need to be drawn in such a way as to distinguish it from bricks that aren't selected.

EXERCISE 2. Building on the first example, allow the user to move selected bricks. Be sure that their new location doesn't violate any of the existing restrictions on new brick placement.

EXERCISE 3. Building on the first example, allow the user to apply changes that are made via the popup menu to groups of selected bricks.

EXERCISE 4. Building on the first example, allow the user to cut, copy, and paste selected bricks. Be sure that the locations of newly pasted bricks don't violate any of the existing restrictions on new brick placement. Use the methods of the System.Windows.Forms.Clipboard class to make this task easier. Serialize your brick data to and from a string when interacting with the clipboard so that the user can paste the serialized data in a text editor or an e-mail.

EXERCISE 5. Store a copy of the Windows-based version of the Brick Breaker game (developed in Chapter 14) alongside the level editor. Provide a toolbar button and a main menu item that allows the user to preview the current project—by playing it. Save the data for the in-memory project into a location where the game expects to find it, and then kick off an instance of the game.

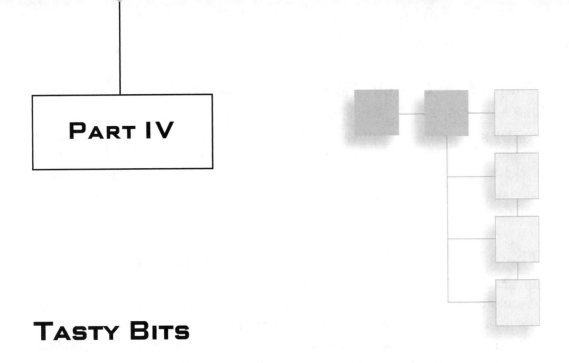

PART IV

TASTY BITS

This section contains the content that interests me as a hobbyist game developer. I hope you'll find it interesting as well. Within this part of the book, you will find code and commentary, tricks and tips, and techniques and tools to help make your game projects a success.

Overview of Chapters

The following paragraphs provide an overview of this section's contents.

Chapter 25: Threading in XNA

In Chapter 25, we take a look at threading in XNA by creating a multithreaded version of the particle system from Chapter 22. This is by no means a fully optimized implementation; it's just here to demonstrate some of the benefits and pitfalls of writing multithreaded code. The example code in this chapter works on Windows and the Xbox 360 game console, and an overview of the Xbox 360 CPU architecture is provided.

Chapter 26: Content Pipeline Extensions

In Chapter 26, we develop a custom Content Pipeline extension to process our bitmap game fonts. Rather than creating an image that we import into our game, this pipeline extension accepts a text file that the game font maker utility (from Chapter 20) generates, which describes the font and its attributes. The image that contains the text characters is generated during the build process, and the new resource is exposed as a GameFont object, rather than as a Texture2D object.

Chapter 27: Embedded Resources and Localization

In Chapter 27, we create a game whose media is embedded within the game executable, rather than as independent files on the file system. As an added bonus, this chapter shows you how to embed text within your resource files, which can be localized for specific markets. Using similar code, your game can dynamically select translated text and media, and it can alter its game play based on culture-specific settings that are selected based on the region encoding of the host platform on which it runs.

Chapter 28: Pixel-Perfect Collision Detection

In Chapter 28, we develop a reusable component that can quickly and easily detect collisions between any two sprites with pixel-perfect accuracy. This component takes into account the opacity of every pixel within the sprites, and includes some simple optimizations to make the collision detection process a little smarter.

Chapter 29: Optimization

In Chapter 29, we cover some common-sense tips and best practices for optimizing your XNA games. You'll learn how to take advantage of (and avoid counteracting) the optimizations that are built into the XNA Framework and the Common Language Runtime which we get "for free," and you'll read about some of the tools that you can use to identify problem code.

Chapter 30: Team Development

In Chapter 30, we discuss some of the tools and processes for working with small and mid-sized teams. Many of the tips and best practices in this chapter are also useful when you're working solo.

Chapter 31: XNA Game Studio Express 1.0 Refresh

In Chapter 31, we explore some of the most notable new features of the latest update to XNA Game Studio Express—the 1.0 Refresh. While it's not as "code heavy" as previous chapters, a good depth of coverage is provided for the topics discussed.

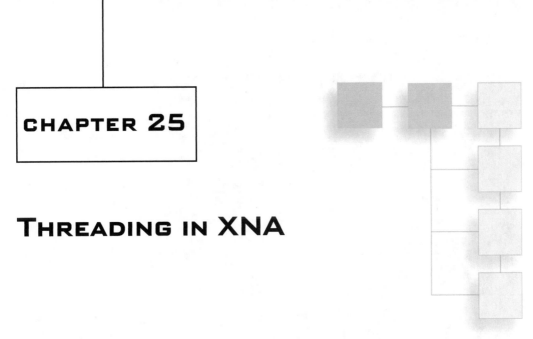

CHAPTER 25

THREADING IN XNA

In this chapter, we will take the particle system that we developed in Chapter 22 and make it multithreaded. Just because this chapter discusses a topic that's closely associated with optimization, don't assume that the code in this chapter is fully optimized. Quite the contrary—this chapter's code is designed to illustrate the proper use of threads in your games, so readability is favored over performance.

In this chapter, you will learn how to:

- Retrofit your existing game code to take advantage of multithreading

- Make good use of threads, and know when not to use them

- Manage concurrent access to data and resource

- Synchronize worker threads and your main game thread

Overview of Threaded Code

A typical C# game runs in a single thread automatically created by the Common Language Runtime (a.k.a., the "main" thread). In a single-threaded program, methods are executed in turn, each blocking until it has completed its given task. Multithreaded programs process data in parallel using some number of tasks that

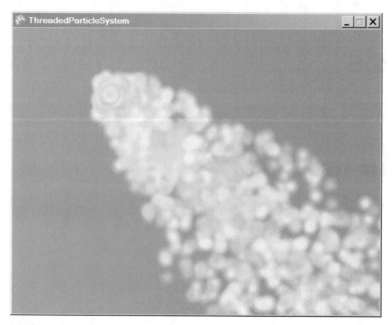

Figure 25.1
The particle effect demo game, with gravity and wind turned on. To the player, this example is indistinguishable from the example in Chapter 22.

each manipulate their own subset of the game data. In many games, there are certain tasks that don't have to be executed in any particular order. For example, updating hundreds (or thousands, or millions) of independent game objects is a problem that's well suited for parallel processing.

On a system with multiple CPUs, these parallel processes, or "threads," truly run at the same time. On a single-processor system (or when multiple threads are attached to the same processor), threads appear to be running at the same time, but the operating system is actually managing the threads for you by letting each run exclusively for some small slice of time before suspending the active thread, saving its current state, and moving on any other waiting threads in a round-robin fashion.

When you have more than one thread tied to a single processor, performance can actually decrease (when compared to a single-threaded implementation of the same set of tasks), so threading isn't a magic bullet that automatically increases your game's performance. As with any optimizing strategy, you'll need to test, tweak, and repeat, ad nauseam. Your assumptions, no matter how well planned, will almost always be disproved once implemented.

Locks and Shared Resources

As long as each thread is processing its own data (or its own subset of shared data), coordinating their efforts is almost as simple as in the single-threaded scenario. When multiple threads need to access the same data, you need to take special care that one thread isn't changing data that another thread is actively using. C# has a built-in language feature, called a *lock,* to help you in this later scenario. The following example illustrates the use of the lock keyword to gain mutually exclusive access to a given resource.

```csharp
// LockExample.cs
using System;
using System.Threading;
class LockExample
{
    // typically, the object that you lock is the actual resource that you're
    // interested in protecting from data corruption, like a collection object,
    // but any shared object will do the trick
    protected object m_objToLock = new object();

    // this task can be executed by one or more simultaneous threads
    public void ThreadedTask()
    {
        // lock will wait until the resource is available, then reserve it
        // for the requesting thread. the resource will be released when
        // the statement block that it encompasses falls out of scope
        lock( m_objToLock )
        {
            // safely access your shared resource here, knowing that you are
            // the only active thread that is modifying the data it contains.

            // try to limit the time that you retain this lock. as long as
            // this thread retains the lock, any other threads that are
            // requesting the same resource will be blocked, sitting idle
        }
    }
    // the application's entry point
    static void Main()
    {
        LockExample theApp = new LockExample();
        Thread thread1 = new Thread(theApp.ThreadedTask);
        thread1.Start();
    }
}
```

Using the `lock` keyword does not automatically make your code thread-safe, unless you use it consistently. Any code blocks that access the shared resource without first locking it are not participating in the lock, and data corruption is a real possibility. For this reason, you should try to limit locks to non-public resources because public objects can be accessed from anywhere, increasing the risk that the calling code forgot to lock the object before using it.

This rule also applies to strings, since string literals are interned by the runtime (for a given string literal, there may only be one instance, shared among all references to that literal from anywhere within the program). Some framework classes (like most of the collection classes) provide an object specifically for locking, named `SyncRoot`.

There are other methods of restricting simultaneous access to protected resources, but the `lock` keyword is by far the cleanest way to handle this in managed code. If you're interested in looking into the other methods, search for "Monitor," "Synchronization Events," and "Mutex" in the C# documentation from within Visual C# 2005 Express.

Other Concurrency Strategies

Another strategy for accessing shared resources from multiple threads is to avoid sharing them in the first place. For example, you can divide a collection of independent game objects into some number of segregated subsets. This is the strategy that we'll take in this chapter's example project. We'll take the code from the particle system that we developed in an earlier chapter and make it multi-threaded by processing the `Update` method in parallel, with each thread handling its own subset of the particles.

Since the particles are independent objects, they're not shared resources. The collection that contains the list of active particles, however, is a shared resource. As long as we don't update the collection from the individual threads, we're safe. So rather than adding and removing particles from the collection as they're created and expire, we'll just mark dead particles as inactive in the worker threads, then process the entire list of "active" particles once the worker threads are done, looking for newly deceased particles.

The threads that we use to split the particle emitter's `Update` method into multiple, concurrent tasks are created and destroyed with each call to the main `Update` method (technically, they're recycled into a pool of threads that the operating system manages for us), so we don't need to worry about concurrency issues once the last thread has terminated. If you want to create threads that live longer than a single game frame, then you'll need to provide some mechanism to let the thread know when it's time to terminate. This might be done by setting a Boolean that the thread polls with each iteration of its main processing loop.

Thread Pools

As I mentioned earlier, this example uses thread pools rather than creating and destroying threads with each frame of the game. If you would like to read more about creating and managing your own threads, search for "threading" in the C# documentation from within Visual C# 2005 Express. For a simple example of creating your own threads, see the section "Locks and Shared Resources," earlier in this chapter, or take a closer look at the source code for the board game that we developed in Chapter 18.

While most of the same logistic caveats apply to the threads that you create yourself as the threads that are managed within a thread pool, using pooled threads saves the overhead of creating and destroying your own threads. The operating system manages a pool of some number of Thread objects. When you request a thread, one of the pooled threads is assigned to you. When your thread completes its task, it's returned to the pool, where it can be reused. If there are no available threads in the pool to service your requests, your request is queued up to be processed as soon as a thread becomes available.

A Quick Note on Threading on the Xbox 360 Game Console

Conceptually, the Xbox 360 game console has six CPUs—three CPUs, each with two cores. That means that you can have six concurrent threads that each run on their own (mostly) dedicated processor. In practice, you won't see the same benefits as six separate CPUs, though. Cores on the same CPU share some resources (like the L1 cache), and only four of the six cores are available to your XNA game (the other two cores are reserved for system use).

Note

The details of the hardware aren't terribly important for this discussion, but these three dual-core processors are actually contained on a single chip. So, when I'm talking about the three "CPUs," I'm actually referring to the three physical cores of the single physical processor. And when I'm talking about the six "cores," I'm actually referring to the six physical hardware threads of the three physical cores of the single physical processor. It can get a little confusing, so I've chosen to discuss the hardware at one level of abstraction less than it actually is. I hope the purists among you can forgive me.

The XNA Framework provides a special method to give you control over where your threads will live on the Xbox 360. This method is not currently available for your Windows game projects, but there are other, Windows-specific methods of setting processor affinity in the standard .NET Framework. The SetProcessor-Affinity method allows you to specify which Xbox 360 core a given thread will execute on. You can change the core on which a software thread is running by calling the SetProcessorAffinity method again, specifying a different core. SetProcessorAffinity should not be used with threads that were created from a thread pool.

The SetProcessorAffinity method accepts a single-element integer array. The integer that you pass to this method represents one of the Xbox 360 cores. Table 25.1 shows the core mappings.

Why Bother with Threading at All?

Threaded code is inherently more error prone and harder to debug. You'll frequently find yourself struggling with hard-to-troubleshoot problems like dead-locks, synchronization issues, and performance numbers that fall far short of your expectations. At this point, you may be asking why anyone would bother with the added complexity of threading at all.

Even if your games don't target the Xbox 360, you should keep in mind that most new PCs are multi-core. If your game is single-threaded, then you can't take advantage of the extra processing resources that may be available to you. Your

Table 25.1 Core Mappings

Index	CPU	Core	Comment
0	1	1	Not available to your game.
1	1	2	Available. Main thread. Your game runs here by default.
2	2	1	Not available to your game.
3	2	2	Available. Parts of the Guide and Dashboard live here.
4	3	1	Available. Xbox Live Marketplace downloads.
5	3	2	Available. Parts of the Guide and Dashboard live here.

single-threaded game will happily live within the constraints of a single processor and leave the other cores idle.

If properly planned, you can implement your game to support threading as an option so that single processor systems aren't bogged down with the overhead of task swapping, but players with better hardware don't feel slighted. Clearly, not all tasks are well suited for parallel processing, so you need to be discerning about where you focus your programming efforts.

Design for Multithreading

If you do decide to implement parallel processing in your game, you need to carefully architect your code so that it actually benefits from threading. Poorly planned multithreading code can actually perform worse than well-designed single-threaded game code.

A Couple of Threading Strategies

A well-implemented multithreaded strategy will limit the number and frequency of interactions between individual threads. If you can segregate tasks into mutually exclusive groups of code, your code will be cleaner and much easier to read, debug, and maintain. For example, a good strategy might include separate threads for

- file I/O tasks like saving games, saving checkpoints, and loading level data
- networking and communication tasks
- physics system calculations
- particle system calculations
- artificial intelligence processing
- updates to game objects that don't interact with each other
- rendering tasks like skinning, bones, and animation
- eye candy like cloth simulation, procedural clouds, and waving grass
- ambient effects like butterflies, cockroaches, and weather effects

Another valid multithreading strategy might involve working on multiple game frames at the same time, each in a slightly different state of readiness. In such a scenario, you might have dedicated threads for processing player input, game object updates, AI, and rendering.

It may seem strange to work three or four frames behind the current action, and you might think that this strategy would result in a large enough delay to be perceived by the user, but remember that for a game that runs at 60 frames per second, four frames fly by at just under seven one-hundredths of a second, and the average time that the user sees any single frame isn't really increased at all. The points at which threads have to share data are well-defined in this scenario, and data flow is generally one way.

A Few Do's and Don'ts

As you develop your own threading strategies for your games, remember not to misuse threads by assigning them tasks that would be better handled "offline" (before runtime). It's silly to perform tasks like compressing textures, converting media or game data, and compacting level data when you could just as easily do that at build time and use the already-processed data when you're ready for it.

Also, try to use a little common sense as you divide your tasks up and assign them to specific processors. More than one thread per core isn't necessarily a bad thing, but more than one processor-intensive task per core is very bad. When balancing threads, try to assign your most intensive tasks to separate cores, then mix in some less-demanding tasks on those same cores—especially threads that work in short bursts or threads that perform blocking tasks like disk I/O.

Since we're on the topic of what not to do in your threaded code, it's a good time to tell you to make sure that your threads exit cleanly. Although Windows provides an API to terminate a thread from outside that thread, threads don't like to be terminated unexpectedly. When you kill a thread, you have no idea what it was doing at the time. Shared data could be in a funky state, or you may have lingering resources that will never be properly released. Similarly, you should avoid suspending threads from the main loop. You just can't know what's going on in there when you try to interrupt a threaded task.

Threads can have names—a simple string that will show up in the Visual Studio IDE when debugging and in some profilers. This can help you quickly determine which thread you're dealing with. If you created the thread yourself, you can set its `Name` property before you call `Start`. If you created your thread from a pool, you can include the name in the data that you pass to the thread, and have it set its own name, using `Thread.CurrentThread.Name`.

Now would be a good time to re-read the section on "Locks and Shared Resources," earlier in this chapter. Pay special attention to the code comments. In a nutshell, you need to limit the number of synchronization points, don't lock resources any longer than absolutely necessary, and (wherever possible) avoid sharing data between threads altogether.

Even with the best planning, there are times when you're introducing synchronization points without even realizing it. In some cases, allocating memory, specifying certain graphic rendering options, or other seemingly innocuous tasks cause the underlying framework to synchronize data access "under the covers." Always profile your code before and after to make sure that you're getting the performance benefits that you expect. If you're not, trash the code and go with a simpler (possibly single-threaded) design.

Waiting for Threads to Complete

Just like your main thread, threads that you spawn will run until they're ready to exit. In your main thread, you typically include logic that exits your main loop when a certain condition is met. The same is true for your threaded code. If the method (the task) that you associate with your thread just processes some data, then returns, the thread terminates once the method returns. If your task processes data in an loop, the thread hangs around until you exit the loop and return from the method.

This chapter's example code shows two methods for alerting the main thread when threaded tasks have completed—polling and wait events. The code for polling is actually commented out, but you can see how it works, side by side with the event-wait version of the code. A more detailed description of each method follows. In some of the following paragraphs, I'll refer to source code from other chapters of the book. Take the time to read that referenced code to see these concepts in action.

Polling

Polling describes the process of waiting for an internal flag in your class to be set. You manage thread synchronization for yourself, constantly checking this flag to see if the worker threads are done. This is a viable option if you need to do some processing in your main thread while your worker threads are still processing data. If you just want to wait until the worker threads are done, and you don't have any work for the main thread that has to be done in parallel, the second method is a much better option. For an example of polling, see the source code that we developed in Chapter 18, "Board Games—Reversi." In that game, the main thread updates the display while AI is processed on a separate thread. Since the main thread is busy updating the screen, it's reasonable to poll the worker threads.

Wait Events

The second option is better suited for the scenario found in this chapter's code. Our threaded particle system spawns threads to update our particle objects, then draws the updated particles to the game screen. Since the main thread can't draw the particles until the updated particle data is ready, it doesn't want to continue until all the worker threads have terminated.

If we polled the worker threads in this scenario, we'd be wasting valuable CPU time in a loop that really doesn't do anything. With wait events, we can tell the operating system to suspend the main thread until the worker threads have finished their tasks. The main thread will basically sleep until it's awakened by the operating system. And while it's sleeping, it's not using any CPU time.

The New Update Method

In the original ParticleSystem example, the Update method performed three basic tasks, illustrated in the following pseudo code.

```
Begin Update Method
    For Each Particle in the Active Particle List
        /* TASK ONE -- Update Active Particles */
        Update the Particle
        /* TASK TWO -- Manage Particle Lists */
        If Particle is Inactive Then
            Remove Particle From Active Particle List
            Add Particle To Inactive Particle List
        End If
    End For
    /* TASK THREE -- Generate New Particles */
    Create ParticlesPerUpdate New Particles
End Update Method
```

Of the three tasks in our emitter's `Update` method, two tasks (TASK TWO and TASK THREE) make updates to shared resources—the active list of particles and the inactive list of particles. When we make changes to a shared resource, we need to be concerned with locks. When we're just reading data from a shared resource, we can avoid synchronization. So the TASK ONE looks like the easiest place to take advantage of threading. Each particle is a completely self-contained object. As long as no two threads are trying to update the same particle, we don't need to worry about resource locks.

Threading TASK THREE would require locks because it updates the two lists of particles (inactive and active). As long as the number of `ParticlesPerUpdate` is relatively low (i.e., you're not trying to create tens of thousands of new particles per frame), then TASK THREE shouldn't need to be threaded anyway. Similarly, TASK TWO updates the two lists of particles, so locks would be a concern if we wanted to implement threading for that task. And like TASK THREE, TASK TWO shouldn't need to be multithreaded as long as the number of newly inactive particles is relatively low. In practice, the number of particles that become inactive during a given update should be roughly the same as the number of new particles that are generated per update.

Notice that the first two tasks are processed within the same loop. As a particle becomes inactive, it is immediately moved from the active list to the inactive list. We can't split TASK ONE into a separate thread as long as it's being processed in a loop that's managed by our main thread. We need to redesign this logic to make it more thread-friendly. The following pseudo code is a good first attempt.

```
Begin Threaded Update Method
    Create ThreadCount New WorkerThreads

    For Each WorkerThread

        Assign (ParticleCount / ThreadCount) Particles to WorkerThread
        Start WorkerThread

    End For

    Wait for All WorkersThreads to Finish

    For Each Particle in the Active Particle List
        /* TASK TWO -- Manage Particle Lists */
        If Particle is Inactive Then
```

```
                        Remove Particle From Active Particle List
                        Add Particle To Inactive Particle List
                End If
        End For
        /* TASK THREE -- Generate New Particles */
        Create ParticlesPerUpdate New Particles
End Threaded Update Method

Begin WorkerThread Method
        For Each Particle in the Assigned Subset of the Active Particle List
                /* TASK ONE -- Update Active Particles */
                Update the Particle

        End For
End WorkerThread Method
```

Using this basic logic, we can process many more particles in parallel, and then perform clean up on our lists of particles in the main thread once the worker threads have finished updating the individual particles to which the lists refer. Until we determine that there's a legitimate performance need for parallel processing of the clean-up tasks, we won't bother adding the extra complexity to the code.

A Somewhat Serious Flaw in This Design

This example was created to illustrate some common threading concepts. It's a good start for creating a multithreaded particle system, but it's not gospel. One of the more obvious issues with our new design is that the pool of active particles to be processed is divided evenly among a fixed number of threads. When we're processing 40,000 particles across four threads, each has 10,000 particles to manage. That's a good thing. But as the number of active particles drops, the number of threads remains constant. At some point, we may be down to four active particles, with each thread processing just one particle. That's a very wasteful use of resources. A smarter design would use the number of threads requested by the caller as a hint (or maximum), creating a reasonable number of threads to balance the work load, avoiding threading altogether in some scenarios.

Update Method Implementation

This version of the Update method for the Emitter2D class mirrors the pseudo code that we developed earlier. TASK ONE is handled by one or more threads, which run the DoUpdate method. TASK THREE is handled by the DoPostUpdateWork method (called from the main thread). And TASK TWO remains within the Update method (also called from the main thread).

```
// run update as a single thread
public virtual void Update(float elapsed)
{
    Update(elapsed, 1);
}


bool[] m_ThreadDone;
public virtual void Update(float elapsed, int numThreads)
{
    if (Enabled)
    {
        // bad way to wait for threads
        m_ThreadDone = new bool[numThreads];

        // multi-threaded implementation
        if (numThreads > 1)
        {
            // good way to wait for threads
            ManualResetEvent[] MRE_Array =
                new ManualResetEvent[numThreads];

            // simple struct to pass to thread to let it know what
            // to work on
            Emitter2DUpdateInfo[] updateInfo =
                new Emitter2DUpdateInfo[numThreads];

            // the number of particles each thread will process
            int range = (int)Math.Round(
                (double)m_ActiveParticles.Count / (double)numThreads);

            // temp variables to save some typing
            int count = m_ActiveParticles.Count;
            int max = 0;

            // kick off each thread
            for (int i = 0; i < numThreads; i++)
            {
                // good way to wait for threads
                MRE_Array[i] = new ManualResetEvent(false);
```

```
            // data that the thread will need to process
            updateInfo[i].Elapsed = elapsed;
            updateInfo[i].Min = i * range;

            // account for rounding errors to make sure that
            // we are processing every last particle
            max = updateInfo[i].Min + range;
            if (i == numThreads - 1) max = count;
            if (max > count) max = count;
            updateInfo[i].Max = max;

            // bad way to wait for threads
            updateInfo[i].ThreadIndex = i;

            // good way to wait for threads
            updateInfo[i].MRE = MRE_Array[i];

            // actually kick off a thread, passing its relevant
            // subset of data
            ThreadPool.QueueUserWorkItem(
                new WaitCallback(DoUpdate), updateInfo[i]);
        }

//// while this code works, it's a bad way to wait for
//// threads to wrap up. there's no point in polling
//// when the Framework provides a method that won't
//// waste CPU cycles.
//bool done = false;
//while (!done)
//{
//    Thread.Sleep(0);
//    done = true;
//    for (int i = 0; i < m_ThreadDone.Length; i++)
//    {
//        done &= m_ThreadDone[i];
//    }
//}

// this is a better way to wait for the threads to finish
// unfortunately, it's not supported under the Compact
// Framework, and therefore not supported on Xbox 360
//WaitHandle.WaitAll(MRE_Array);
```

```
            // here's the next-best thing
            int mreComplete = 0;
            while (mreComplete != MRE_Array.Length)
            {
                mreComplete = 0;
                for (int i = 0; i < MRE_Array.Length; i++)
                {
                    if (MRE_Array[i].WaitOne(10, false))
                    {
                        mreComplete++;
                    }
                }
            }

            // don't forget to release your handles
            for (int i = 0; i < MRE_Array.Length; i++)
            {
                MRE_Array[i].Close();
            }
        }
```

If the numThreads parameter is equal to or less than one, the threading logic is ignored.

```
else
{
    // single-threaded
    Emitter2DUpdateInfo updateInfo = new Emitter2DUpdateInfo();
    updateInfo.Elapsed = elapsed;
    updateInfo.Min = 0;
    updateInfo.Max = m_ActiveParticles.Count;
    updateInfo.ThreadIndex = 0;
    DoUpdate(updateInfo);
}
        DoPostUpdateWork();
    }
}
```

The DoUpdate Method

The DoUpdate method is the code that each spawned thread runs for us. Each worker thread processes the data that is assigned to it via the stateInfo parameter. The stateInfo parameter is an instance of the Emitter2DUpdateInfo structure.

```
public struct Emitter2DUpdateInfo
{
    public ManualResetEvent MRE;
    public int ThreadIndex;
    public int Min;
    public int Max;
    public float Elapsed;
}


    // manage active particles
    protected void DoUpdate(object stateInfo)
    {
        if (stateInfo != null)
        {
            Emitter2DUpdateInfo updateInfo =
                (Emitter2DUpdateInfo) stateInfo;
            int min = updateInfo.Min;
            int max = updateInfo.Max;
            float elapsed = updateInfo.Elapsed;

            // temp variables to save typing
            bool outOfBounds;
            int parX, parY;
            for (int i = min; i < max; i++)
            {
                Particle2D particle = m_ActiveParticles[i];

                // when particle leaves emitter bounds, mark inactive
                parX = (int)Math.Round(particle.Position.X);
                parY = (int)Math.Round(particle.Position.Y);
                outOfBounds = parX < EmitterBoundsRect.Right;
                outOfBounds &=
                    parX + TextureRect.Width > EmitterBoundsRect.Left;
                outOfBounds &=
                    parY < EmitterBoundsRect.Bottom;
                outOfBounds &=
                    parY + TextureRect.Height > EmitterBoundsRect.Top;
                if (outOfBounds) particle.IsActive = false;

                // process active particles
                if (particle.IsActive)
                {
                    // allow active modifiers to update particle
```

```
            foreach (Modifier2D modifier in m_Modifiers)
            {
                if (modifier.Enabled)
                {
                    // tell the modifier to update this particle
                    modifier.Update(particle, elapsed);
                }
            }
            // tell particle to update itself
            particle.Update(elapsed);
        }
    }
    m_ThreadDone[updateInfo.ThreadIndex] = true;
    if (updateInfo.MRE != null) updateInfo.MRE.Set();
    }
}
```

The DoPostUpdateWork Method

The DoPostUpdate method performs the particle housekeeping tasks for us.

```
// clean up our active and inactive particle lists
protected void DoPostUpdateWork()
{
    // move inactive particles to inactive list for later reuse
    for (int i = 0; i < m_ActiveParticles.Count; i++)
    {
        Particle2D particle = m_ActiveParticles[i];
        if (!m_ActiveParticles[i].IsActive)
        {
            m_InactiveParticles.Add(particle);
            m_ActiveParticles.RemoveAt(i);
            i--;
        }
    }

    // only generate new particles if active
    if (IsActive)
    {
        // try to generate "ParticlesPerUpdate" new particles
        for (long i = 0; i < ParticlesPerUpdate; i++)
        {
            if (m_InactiveParticles.Count > 0)
```

```
        {
            // reset particle and add it to our pool of
            // active particles
            Particle2D particle = m_InactiveParticles[0];
            particle.Position = m_EmitterRV2.RandomValue();
            particle.Movement = m_RangeMovement.RandomValue();
            particle.Color = m_RangeColor.RandomValue();
            particle.IsActive = true;
            particle.LifeTime = m_ParticleLifetime;
            m_InactiveParticles.Remove(particle);
            m_ActiveParticles.Add(particle);
        }
        else
        {
            // no more particles in our inactive pool
            break;
        }
    }
  }
}
```

Summary

In this chapter, you learned how to appropriately apply threading to your game to handle multiple game tasks simultaneously. You also read about several design considerations that must be taken into account when implementing threads in your game code—considerations such as sharing data between threads and synchronizing threads.

Review Questions

Think about what you've read in this chapter (and the included source code) to answer the following questions.

1. What are the primary logistical concerns that must be addressed when retrofitting your existing game logic with threaded code?

2. List some benefits and consequences of using pooled threads.

3. Multithreaded code is faster than single-threaded code. True or False? Explain.

4. What does C#'s `lock` keyword do? When might you use it in your code?

5. What are two options for synchronizing your main thread and its worker threads? How do they differ? When might you use each?

Exercises

EXERCISE 1. Fix the flaw mentioned in the section labeled "A Somewhat Serious Flaw in This Design," found earlier in this chapter. Be smart about how many threads you spawn, using the requested number of threads as a maximum, and only spawning new threads when some minimum number of particles are queued for processing.

EXERCISE 2. Design a completely new multithreading strategy for this problem. See if you can find some way to process particles for the next game frame while the main thread is rendering the results of your work on the last game frame. This new design will likely involve maintaining at least two copies of the particle arrays so that you can avoid resource locks.

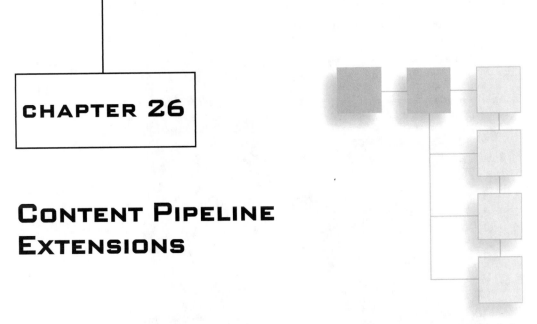

CHAPTER 26

CONTENT PIPELINE EXTENSIONS

By this time, you've used the Content Pipeline enough to know how useful it is in providing a unified interface for importing media and other data into your game from content creation tools. The Content Pipeline makes it easier for artists and designers to collaborate with programmers, each working in the environment with which he is most familiar.

Out of the box, the Content Pipeline provides importers for the most common 3D and 2D game content file types, as well as an importer for audio. Importers are just part of the pipeline, though. The pipeline also provides several standard processors for cleaning up that imported data, as well as classes to read and write that imported and processed data in a platform-agnostic format (.xbn files).

In this chapter, we will create custom Content Pipeline components to import the game fonts (that we created in Chapters 20 and 21) at compile-time, rather than loading and processing those source files within our game logic (see Figure 26.1).

Instead of loading a texture and creating a GameFont object from it, the Content Pipeline's ContentManager will be able to hand us a reference to a GameFont object that was serialized to our data stream when our game was compiled.

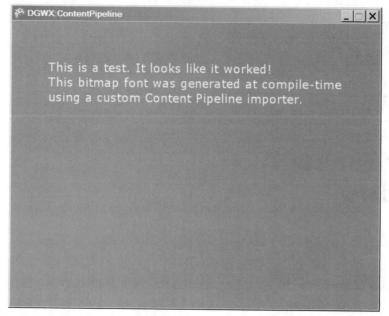

Figure 26.1
This chapter's example "game."

In this chapter, you will learn how to:

- Better understand how Game Studio Express manages your digital content

- Identify the four stages of the Content Pipeline

- Plug your own custom file types into the Content Pipeline

- Process existing file types to skim tagged data out into specialized game objects

Content Pipeline Stages

The four basic steps for importing external content via the Content Pipeline are described in detail in the following paragraphs.

Import

The importer is responsible for taking content in its raw form and converting it to a format that's compatible with the XNA content DOM (Document Object

Model). Once imported, all game content of a particular type looks the same to the XNA Framework, regardless of what file it came from. This is important because it means that every step in the pipeline after the import phase will work exactly the same way, no matter what tool was used to create the content.

Note

The XNA content DOM is just a logical grouping of game data that has been converted to one of the well-defined DOM types as it was imported. It provides an easy way for pipeline components to sift through related data. Since the data is stored in the content DOM in a generic way, stages that come after the import step don't have to know anything about the source data files of the content that they're processing—they just have to understand the content DOM and its members.

Importing data files into the content DOM can be described as a "lossy" process because the importer will ultimately only include data in the pipeline that is compatible with the content DOM. For example, you may have a custom image format that has descriptive data about the author of the image or some other metadata. That information isn't relevant to an instance of Texture2D, so it won't be included in the image data that gets imported into the content DOM.

In most cases, importers map to file types on a one-to-one basis. Individual importers can handle multiple file types, and several importers can process the same input file, though. Each importer is given its chance to process the file as if it were the only importer. Each importer will extract the bits that it is interested in. Content is mapped to importers and processors using the ContentImporter attribute of the importer class.

Game Studio Express provides several standard importers for the most common file types. Up until this point, we've been using those standard importers without really having to understand what's happening under the covers. The standard importers are shown in Table 26.1.

For a detailed description of what each of the standard importers do, see the article entitled "Standard Importers and Processors" in the XNA Framework documentation.

Table 26.1 Standard Importers

Content	Import As	File Type(s)
Texture	TextureContent	.dds, .bmp, .png, .jpg, .tga
Autodesk	NodeContent	.fbx
DX X File	NodeContent	.x
Effect	EffectContent	.fx
XNA XML	object	.xml

Process

The processor takes content that has been converted into a format that's compatible with the XNA content DOM and inspects it, manipulates it, or converts it to a new type. In many cases, content will have the same XNA content DOM type after processing that it did before processing. But, that's not always the case.

For example, the standard effect processor accepts shader content and produces a compiled effect. We will take advantage of this when we develop our custom processor by wrapping the standard texture type within our own class so that later stages of the pipeline don't confuse our bitmap font texture with general-purpose textures.

This stage of the pipeline can also be used to inspect content for special tokens and take different actions based on the tokens encountered. For example, you could implement a racing game as a single 3D content file where the starting point, checkpoints, and power-ups are named according to a certain standard. When your custom processor discovers these special objects within your mesh content, you can create specialized game objects that are tied to your main track object or set properties on the track object.

Another real-world scenario that could easily be handled using a custom Content Pipeline processor is generating a 3D height field mesh from a 2D texture. Of course, you could perform this conversion within your game logic by processing the texture at runtime, but placing that code in the pipeline allows you to perform those tasks at compile-time, leaving the conversion code out of your game logic. You eliminate in-game processing time and reduce the size of your game's assembly by removing the conversion logic.

Game Studio Express provides several standard processors for the most common content types. The standard processors are shown in Table 26.2.

Table 26.2 Standard Processors

Processor Type	Input	Output
Pass-Through	object	object
Effect	EffectContent	CompiledEffect
Material	MaterialContent	MaterialContent
Model	NodeContent	ModelContent
Model Texture	Texture Content	TextureContent
Sprite Texture	Texture Content	TextureContent
Texture (Generic)	Texture Content	TextureContent

A great example of a useful standard processor is the `SpriteTextureProcessor`. The `SpriteTextureProcessor` takes a texture and processes it so that the resulting texture is ideally suited for use as sprites, HUDs (heads-up displays), or other user interface elements—no mipmaps are generated and the texture is not compressed.

For a detailed description of what each of the standard processors do, see the article entitled "Standard Importers and Processors" in the XNA Framework documentation.

Write and Read

XNA-managed content is stored in a proprietary file format (*.xbn files). The `ContentTypeReader` and `ContentTypeWriter` classes handle streaming data to and from these proprietary files. Content that is stored in these files can easily be loaded into your Windows and Xbox 360 XNA games. If you only deal with standard content types, you will never need to write a custom data reader or writer. But these stages of the pipeline are available to your custom pipeline logic, if you need them.

The Content Pipeline Namespace

Much of the Content Pipeline functionality is contained within the `Microsoft` `.Xna.Framework.Content.Pipeline` namespace. By default, your XNA projects do not reference the DLL that contains these APIs. You will need to add a reference to the DLL for your project before you can use them.

Within the Solution Explorer, right-click the References folder for the project that contains your importer and add a reference to `Microsoft.Xna.Framework.` `Content.Pipeline.dll`. You will also need to add a `using` statement to your list of imports at the top of your source file.

Review of Pipeline Stages

The basic Content Pipeline workflow for adding content to your project is as follows:

1. Import data into the XNA content DOM.

2. Optionally process the data.

3. Write the imported and processed content out to the .xnb file.

The basic flow to reading that content back out of the .xnb file is as follows:

1. Read data from the .xnb into a game object.

The import, process, and write stages happen at build time, and they are completely dependent on Game Studio Express. That means you can use Windows-specific Framework APIs without worrying about cross-platform issues.

Reading your converted content is another story. Since your data needs to be used within your game, any custom code that you create to read your game objects from the .xnb stream must not use any Windows-specific APIs if you want your game to run on your Xbox 360.

GameFont in the Content Pipeline

To better illustrate writing custom pipeline extensions, we will write our own custom importer to load the bitmap game fonts that we developed in Chapters 20 and 21. There are several ways to approach this task.

My first thought was to take the image that is generated by the GameFontUtility and import it as is. Our importer would inspect the .png file to see if it was a valid game font source image (primarily by checking for the magic numbers). If it was a bitmap font image, we would hand it off to our custom processor and ultimately return a GameFont object.

That would have worked just fine, but it means that our importer would be competing with the standard texture importer (because our source image is one of the standard texture file types). There may have been some quirky side effects. Since two importers and two processors were handling the same texture data, the Content Pipeline would likely generate two resource files, one for use by our GameFont object and one for general use as a game texture, which would never be referenced in the game.

Another approach would be to write the options that the user selected in the GameFontUtility out to a text file without actually generating the source image. This text file would have a .bgf extension (bitmap game font) so that the importer could have exclusive access to its content.

Whenever our custom importer encountered one of these option files, it would generate the source image based on the options specified within the text file, and then add the newly created image as an XNA content DOM resource so that it can pass through the remaining pipeline stages. Ultimately, our game would receive a `GameFont` object, and only one texture would be generated in the .xnb stream.

In fact, this is the approach that we'll use in this chapter.

Changes to Existing Code

The following paragraphs detail the new code that we need to write and the changes to existing code that we need to make to support pipeline processing of our game font resources. When we're done, code that looked like this:

```
Texture2D texture = content.Load<Texture2D>(@"media\Verdana12Bold");
m_GameFont = GameFont.FromTexture2D(texture);
```

will look like this:

```
m_GameFont = content.Load<GameFont>(@"media\Verdana12Bold");
```

Rather than dropping a texture (a .png file) into your project, you can now drop in the new resource (a .bgf file). When the project is compiled, the importer automatically generates the texture for you, based on your settings. You can even tweak the settings in your .bgf file by hand, without having to run the `GameFontUtility` every time you want to make a small change to your font.

When the Content Pipeline reads in your persisted data at runtime, you get back a reference to an instance of the class that you were actually interested in (a `GameFont` object), rather than a texture that you'll never reference directly anyway.

GameFontUtility Changes

In addition to generating a texture that can be used to create a new `GameFont` object, the `GameFontUtility` now supports a special `-resource` output type. This flag generates a text file that describes the options that the user has selected, rather than actually using those selections to generate a texture. This new file type has the extension .bgf.

An example of our new .bgf file type follows.

```
Name:Verdana
Size:12
Bold:True
Italic:False
```

```
Strikeout:False
Underline:False
TextRenderHint:
StringFormat:
Chars: !"#$%&'()*+,-./0123456789:;<=>?@ABCDEFGHIJKLMNO...
```

That listing represents the output of our GameFontUtility when the following options are specified.

```
GameFontUtility.exe -fontname Verdana -fontsize 12 -bold -resource
```

Whenever the GameFontUtility encounters the new -resource command-line option, the other options that the user specified on the command line will be saved out to the text file, and no source image will be created.

Changes to the FontMaker Class

The FontMaker class has remained largely unchanged. The only addition was a new method (GetCharsToEncode) to retrieve a list of the characters that have been requested to be encoded. It was easier to pull this data from the FontMaker class (where it already lives) than to parse the user input from the command line again—especially in the case where a script was used to populate the list of characters (a common scenario in localization, where certain characters cannot be typed at a command line prompt).

Changes to the GameFontLibrary API

Remember when I said that it's okay to use Windows-specific code in the importer, processor, and writer, but not in the reader? We will need to have at least two DLLs to support the Content Pipeline—one that uses Windows-specific APIs to create our XNA-compatible content, and one that uses XNA Framework APIs to read that content back in for use in our game. The first will be used by Visual Studio; the other will be used by our game.

The GameFontLibrary is the obvious place to stick our new reader code, since it's where our cross-platform code belongs and the GameFont class (on which our custom reader relies) lives there.

Other than the addition of the new GameFontReader class, the GameFontLibrary also remains largely unchanged. The new reader class is pretty simple.

```
// GameFontReader.cs
using System;
using System.Collections.Generic;
using Microsoft.Xna.Framework;
using Microsoft.Xna.Framework.Audio;
using Microsoft.Xna.Framework.Graphics;
using Microsoft.Xna.Framework.Input;
using Microsoft.Xna.Framework.Storage;
using Microsoft.Xna.Framework.Content;

namespace Codetopia.Graphics
{
    public class GameFontReader : ContentTypeReader<GameFont>
    {
        protected override GameFont Read(ContentReader input,
            GameFont instance)
        {
            // read our font texture from the content stream
            Texture2D texture = input.ReadExternalReference<Texture2D>();

            // return a reference to a new GameFont object
            return GameFont.FromTexture2D(texture);
        }
    }
}
```

The real work is done in the importer. So, let's cover that new code now.

The Importer

The first stage in the Content Pipeline is to convert raw data into media that is compatible with the XNA content DOM. Clearly our proprietary .bgf text file isn't a file type that the XNA Framework is natively aware of. We need to write an importer to read in the options in the text file, and then use those settings to create a new game font source image.

To associate our importer with our new, custom file type, we need to use the ContentImporter attribute. This attribute also associates our custom processor to this importer. The class declaration for our new importer follows.

```
[ContentImporter(".bgf", DefaultProcessor = "GameFontProcessor")]
public class GameFontImporter :
```

```
ContentImporter<ExternalReference<TextureContent>>
{
    // TODO: implementation goes here ...
}
```

We need to override the Import method of the ContentImporter class to perform our GameFont tasks. We'll begin by setting some default values that can be used if the import fails (due to an IO error or a malformed option file). Then we will scan the option file, parsing out the valid settings, and overriding our default values.

When we're done parsing the file, we'll use the FontMaker class to generate the source game font image. Rather than list the entire method here, I've placed comments to show where the option file is parsed. Please see the CD-ROM that came with this book for a complete source listing.

```
public override ExternalReference<TextureContent>
    Import(string filename, ContentImporterContext context)
{
    // open our game font resource (text) file
    StreamReader reader = new StreamReader(filename);
    string line;
    // establish defaults, just in case the import fails
    string name = "System";
    float size = 10;
    char[] chars = (
        "abcdefghijklmnopqrstuvwxyz" +
        "ABCDEFGHIJKLMNOPQRSTUVWXYZ" +
        "01234567890").ToCharArray();
    bool bold = false;
    bool italic = false;
    bool strikeout = false;
    bool underline = false;
    // create an instance of our FontMaker helper class
    FontMaker maker = new FontMaker();
    // read each line from the resource file
    while ((line = reader.ReadLine()) != null)
    {
        // TODO: read each line, parse out valid options, override the
        // default values that we set before entering this loop.
    }
    // note which characters to encode
    maker.ClearCharsToEncode();
```

```
    foreach (char c in chars)
    {
        maker.AddCharToEncode(c);
    }
    // generate the source image for our font
    maker.Encode(
        new Font(
            name,
            size,
            MakeFontStyle(bold, italic, strikeout, underline)),
            filename + ".png");
    // return a reference to this new file
    return new ExternalReference<TextureContent>(filename + ".png");
}
```

N o t e

The design that I've outlined here has a small flaw that makes maintenance a little more difficult. I needed to use the functionality found in the FontMaker class in the importer logic, so I copied that class from the GameFontUtility project into the GameFontImporter project. The smart thing to do here would be to have the GameFontUtility link to the Game-FontImporter project, and move the FontMaker class to the importer project. That way, there would only be one copy of the source file to maintain.

The Processor

Once the source game font image has been generated, it's an XNA content DOM-compatible texture resource. The importer returns an ExternalReference to the new texture, and the processor applies the standard SpriteTextureProcessor to the texture so that it's better suited for our purposes—the texture will be uncompressed, and no mipmaps will be generated.

```
[ContentProcessor]
public class GameFontProcessor :
    ContentProcessor<
        ExternalReference<TextureContent>,
        GameFontTextureReference>
{
    public override GameFontTextureReference
        Process(
            ExternalReference<TextureContent> input,
            ContentProcessorContext context)
        {
```

```
        // take the PNG that we created in the import step and
        // build a new XNA-friendly resource from it
        GameFontTextureReference reference =
            new GameFontTextureReference();
        reference.Content =
            context.BuildAsset<TextureContent, TextureContent>
            (input, "SpriteTextureProcessor");
        // return a custom class, rather than a TextureContent
        // object this may seem a little silly, but returning
        // a normal texture object would cause a conflict with
        // the standard texture writer. by using a custom
        // class, our writer is sure to catch references to
        // our new media type.
        return reference;
    }
}
```

Since the result of our work is a standard texture, we need some way to note that this texture is reserved for use with our GameFont class. If our processor just returned a generic texture, the Content Pipeline manager wouldn't be able to distinguish our texture from any other game texture. We'll wrap our texture in a custom class so that the content manager sees our wrapper class and calls our custom writer and reader logic.

```
public class GameFontTextureReference
{
    public ExternalReference<TextureContent> Content = null;
}
```

The Writer

Our custom ContentWriter class performs three tasks—write our game font texture to the .xnb content stream, associate our texture with the GameFont class, and tell the content manager to use our custom ContentReader to load this texture from the .xnb content stream. The implementation is fairly straightforward, so I won't go into too much detail here. See the source comments for more information about what each method is doing.

```
[ContentTypeWriter]
public class GameFontWriter : ContentTypeWriter<GameFontTextureReference>
{
    protected override void Write(ContentWriter output,
```

```
                GameFontTextureReference value)
{
        // just write the new texture out to the content stream
        output.WriteExternalReference<TextureContent>(value.Content);
}
public override string GetRuntimeType(TargetPlatform targetPlatform)
{
        // associate our GameFont with this new content type
        return typeof(GameFont).AssemblyQualifiedName;
}
public override string GetRuntimeReader(TargetPlatform targetPlatform)
{
        // associate our reader with this new content type
        return typeof(GameFontReader).AssemblyQualifiedName;
}
}
```

Using the New Importer

Once you've created your importer and compiled it to a DLL, you can tell Visual Studio to use it by adding a reference to the DLL for your project. Right-click your project in the Solution Explorer, and open the project properties. Click the Content Pipeline tab, and then add your importer DLL to the list of XNA Content Pipeline Assemblies.

The next time you drag a .bgf file into your project, it will be associated to your custom importer and the game font source image will be generated. Since you added this reference to your DLL using the project properties, it's not actually loaded with your game at runtime; it's loaded by Visual Studio whenever you open the project.

The next step is to add a reference to your custom content reader. In your game project, right-click the References folder and click Add Reference. Select your reader DLL (in our case, the reader class is contained within our GameFontLibrary project) and click OK.

Debugging Importers

Since your import logic is contained within a DLL that is hosted by Visual Studio rather than being hosted by your game, the typical debugging scenarios won't work. If you have a debugger that will attach to a running process (like the professional version of Visual Studio), you can debug your importer by adding the following line of code to your importer wherever you would like the debugger to be invoked.

```
System.Diagnostics.Debugger.Launch();
```

When you build your game or add new content, that statement will open up a dialog that will give you instructions for attaching your debugger. From that point, you'll be able to debug your importer in a familiar environment.

If you're unable to get debugging to work, you can always fall back to the old-fashioned way of debugging—create a text file and log status messages to the file, or display a standard Windows message box with whatever diagnostic message you like. You'll need to add a reference to the System.Windows.Forms.dll before you can display a message box, though.

Summary

In this chapter, you learned what the four stages of the Content Pipeline are, how they process your game data, and how to hook your own custom code into each stage so that you can affect the way that your content is processed.

Review Questions

1. List the four stages of the Content Pipeline and briefly describe the responsibilities of each.

2. What is the XNA content DOM? Why does it exist?

3. Processed content is stored in a proprietary file. How does your code write data to and read data from this file?

4. How many importers may be associated with the same file type? Explain.

5. What application hosts the DLL that contains your custom importer? What application hosts the DLL that contains your custom reader?

Exercises

EXERCISE 1. Per the note at the end of the discussion on the importer, this example maintains two copies of the `FontMaker` class. That's a hassle for code maintenance, and it's an easy way to introduce bugs as you make changes to that class. Follow the steps mentioned in that note to eliminate the `FontMaker` implementation that lives in the `GameFontUtility` project.

EXERCISE 2. Write a custom processor that inverts the red, green, and blue components of every pixel in a texture.

EXERCISE 3. Choose a simple, well-documented graphics file format like .pcx or .rle and write a custom importer for it.

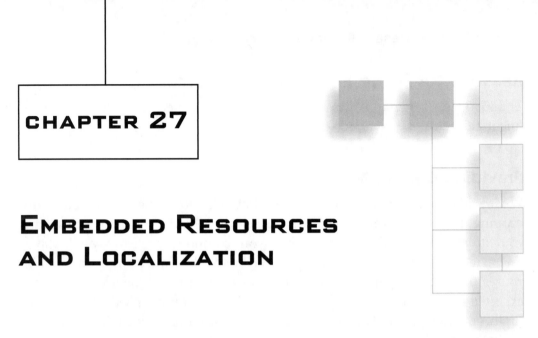

CHAPTER 27

EMBEDDED RESOURCES AND LOCALIZATION

Even if you're not working on a game that will be marketed across the globe, or writing next big best-selling, third-party game component, you will still benefit from the basic concepts found in this chapter. Writing stable, error-resistant code that's easily configurable and customizable will make your long-term maintenance and enhancement work easier to manage.

When designing your next game, invest the time to make it as data-driven and component-centric as possible. Building your game on generic, reusable, adaptable code blocks will make tasks like localization, falling back to default resources, and adding date-based themed content much easier.

In this chapter, you will learn how to:

- Load embedded resources from a game library (DLL)

- Gracefully handle missing resources or programmer error

- Extend the life of your game by implementing features to improve its replayability

- Adapt your game for distribution to any number of countries

- Identify potential localization issues early in your design

Reasons for Using Embedded Resources

The following paragraphs describe some scenarios where embedded resources might be useful.

Providing Default Media

When you develop a reusable component that relies on media, like the game font drawing library that we created in an earlier chapter, there may be cases when your attempts to load the assets on which your component relies may fail. Maybe the image data has become corrupted. Maybe the developer forgot to initialize your component properly. Whatever the reason, your component won't work as expected if it doesn't have media to work with. You could embed a failsafe asset for those scenarios and fall back to the embedded resource when things don't go as you expected.

Themes and Mods

Embedded resources are a great way to implement pluggable themes in your game. Color schemes, special effects, and stylized icons can be embedded in theme-specific DLLs. Then your game can change its look, on the fly, by referencing a different theme DLL. These changes in theme may be player initiated (via an options menu), based on the current level, or based on date-specific events (like a Christmas theme). Of course, you could achieve this same effect by storing your assets in parallel structures on the file system, but where's the fun in that?

These external resources could also include executable code or specialized game objects, like end-level bosses. You could even support game mods by allowing user content to extend your base game objects to do things you never dreamed of in your initial design. Game mods are a great way to enhance the replayability of your game and drive interest in your game for communities of hard-core gamers.

Localization

Gaming is a multi-billion-dollar industry. Those dollars don't just flow from American pockets, though. If you want to distribute your game to markets that span a variety of languages and cultures, you will need to create localized versions of your game assets for each region. Localization encompasses much more than simply translating game assets, though.

It takes planning and a good design, but varying your game's content based on the culture of the player is made a lot easier with Visual Studio, the .NET Framework, and the Common Language Runtime. We'll discuss writing localizable code in more detail a bit later.

Protecting IP Assets

You could embed your resources in a proprietary format in an attempt to foil players from easily copying the images, 3D models, and sounds that you worked so hard to create. But, this is perhaps the silliest use of embedded resources. While it is clearly harder to copy resources from a DLL than it is to drag-and-drop them from a file share, a motivated copyright-infringer will be able to rip any asset that your game can access. Even if you use encryption, any keys or algorithms that are embedded in your game code to load your media are available to a would-be hacker.

The Design

The example game (shown in Figure 27.1) that we'll develop in this chapter will showcase XNA's support for embedded resources and localization. There are three basic methods for loading content into your game: using the standard content manager (like all of the other examples in this book do), loading content that's embedded within another assembly (embedded resources), and loading culture-specific content from a satellite assembly (similar to embedded resources; most of the locale-specific tasks are handled by the XNA Framework and runtime). This example game will utilize all three methods.

In this game, an incredibility handsome cartoon avatar (a likeness of yours truly) is shown standing in a simple, cartoon park. Whenever the player presses the A button on his controller, the avatar will say "Hello", "How are you?", and "Goodbye" in a language that is appropriate for the region code of the Xbox 360 game console on which it is running.

I'm going to assume that you don't have an Xbox 360 from every supported region to test this game on. To test our new game, we'll add some code to trick our game into thinking it's running on consoles that are encoded for various regions. This game contains content that has been localized for English, German, Italian, Spanish, Russian, and Japanese. To cycle from language to language, the player will press the Y button on his controller.

Figure 27.1
Four screen shots from the example game, showing the idle animation and three localized versions of the same dialog.

In the real world, localization encompasses much more than the simple translation of dialog from language to language and making sure that currency, dates, and times are properly formatted for each locale. There are specific cultural norms that must be taken into account. Something that's humorous or completely benign in one culture may be horribly offensive, or even criminal, in another culture.

For a real game, you might load a different texture to replace red blood splatters with green splatters (or remove blood splatters altogether). You might need to replace in-game uniforms or insignias with culture-neutral equivalents. Testing may reveal that some dialog or situations in your game don't make any sense in your target culture. Localization won't always be a one-to-one mapping of your content.

To demonstrate this, I've added a "toot" action for the avatar. As long as the player is pressing the X button on his controller, the avatar will squint while he and the controller shake. This action can be disabled for a specific culture by editing the AllowCrude field within the content for that culture.

Implementation Details

This game is split into four basic projects.

The Example Game Project

The ExampleGame project is where the actual game logic lives. It has no content of its own. Its sole purpose is to manage the on-screen sprites and process player input. Each sprite on the screen is represented by a specialized class that is derived from a common SpriteBase class.

The SpriteBase Class

The SpriteBase class handles the common tasks of our sprite instances like maintaining common member variables and properties, drawing the sprite to the screen, and updating internal state. Some sprites, like the flag images, don't contain any additional logic and are able to use the base sprite class as is. Others, like the background sprite, contain few extensions to the base class. While others, like the dialog sprite, are highly specialized.

The SpriteBase class manages the reference to the sprite's texture, including the texture rectangle, which defines the location of the source image within the (possibly) larger texture. It also keeps track of the tinting that is used when the sprite is drawn to the screen, as well as the current state of the game pad for player one. Basic implementations of the Update and Draw methods are also provided by this class, which many of the derived classes can benefit from with no extra code.

In addition to these generic sprite-based properties and methods, the SpriteBase class also manages an internal variable that indicates the amount of time (in seconds) that the game has gone without interaction from the player. This information is used by the AvatarSprite and BackgroundSprite classes to trigger idle animations.

The code for this base class is fairly straightforward, so I won't list it here. You can view the code for this example on the accompanying CD.

The BackgroundSprite Class

The background image for this game is a simple park scene that I threw together after watching an episode of the *PowerPuff Girls* with my girls. The image is the same height as the game screen, and twice as wide. The player can actively scroll the scene using the left thumbstick on his controller. When the background hasn't been moved by the player for some number of seconds, it will begin to scroll automatically, at a much slower rate.

```csharp
public class BackgroundSprite : SpriteBase
{
    // handy constants for scrolling background
    protected const float IDLE_DELAY = 3.0f;
    protected const float RATE_IDLE = (1280.0f - 640.0f) / 120.0f;
    protected const float RATE_MOVE = RATE_IDLE * 8.0f;

    // rate and direction of scroll, in pixels per second
    protected Vector2 m_Movement = new Vector2(-RATE_IDLE, 0);

    // initialize our source texture rectangle
    public BackgroundSprite()
    {
        TextureRect = new Rectangle(0, 0, 1280, 480);
    }

    // process player input and update object states
    public sealed override void Update(float elapsed)
    {
        // determine the change in position of the background sprite
        float deltaX = -RATE_MOVE * GamePadState.ThumbSticks.Left.X;
        m_TimeIdle = (deltaX == 0.0f) ? m_TimeIdle + elapsed : 0;

        // update the location
        if (TimeIdle > IDLE_DELAY)
        {
            Location += m_Movement * elapsed;
        }
        else
        {
            m_Location.X += deltaX * elapsed;
        }

        // reverse direction whenever we hit an edge
        if (Location.X > 0 || Location.X < -640)
        {
            m_Movement.X = -m_Movement.X;
```

```
        m_Location.X = Math.Min(m_Location.X, 0.0f);
        m_Location.X = Math.Max(m_Location.X, -640.0f);
    }
}
}
```

The AvatarSprite Class

The avatar image for this game is a cartoon image of myself that I built using the Create-A-Character game on the southparkstudios.com website, tweaking the generated image in my photo editing software to personalize it. People who know me in real life probably think it's a photograph, but now you know the secret.

I created multiple versions of the avatar so that his facial expressions can change over time. Each image is the same size as the others, and there are a lot of unchanging pixels that are common to each image. In a real game, I would have taken the time to split the images up, building the on-screen images from their composite parts.

To keep things simple, I have a single sprite class to represent the avatar. Internally, this sprite actually contains references to multiple sprites—one for each expression. The main class manages the state of the avatar, and when it's asked to draw itself, it pulls the image from the sprite that represents the current state.

```
// idle states for the avatar
public enum AvatarStates
{
    Blink,
    LookLeft,
    LookRight,
    LookAhead,
    Smile,
    // -----
    Count,
};

// the state of the avatar, used to make the character
// more interesting when the player is idle
protected AvatarStates m_State = AvatarStates.LookAhead;
public AvatarStates State
{
    get { return m_State; }
    set
```

```
        {
            if (m_State != value)
            {
                CurrentSprite.TimeIdle = 0;
                m_State = value;
                CurrentSprite.TimeIdle = 0;
            }
        }
    }

    // an array of base sprites, one for each avatar state
    protected SpriteBase[] m_Avatars =
        new SpriteBase[(int)AvatarStates.Count];

    // in indexed property to get a reference to a sprite
    // based on the avatar's current state
    public SpriteBase this[AvatarStates state]
    {
        get
        {
            if (state == AvatarStates.Count)
            {
                state = AvatarStates.LookAhead;
            }
            return m_Avatars[(int)state];
        }
    }

    // get a reference to the sprite that's associated
    // with the avatar's current state
    public SpriteBase CurrentSprite
    {
        get { return this[State]; }
    }
```

When the game is presenting dialog to the player, the avatar's mouth is open. To detect this condition, the AvatarSprite class maintains a reference to the DialogSprite that's used by the game. When the VisibleLineCount is greater than zero, the dialog bubble is visible.

```
// reference to the dialog sprite
// certain actions are prevented while the dialog
// is transitioning from one size to another
```

```
protected DialogSprite m_Dialog = null;
public DialogSprite Dialog
{
    get { return m_Dialog; }
    set { m_Dialog = value; }
}

// true whenever the dialog sprite is visible
public bool IsSpeaking
{
    get { return Dialog != null && Dialog.VisibleLineCount > 0; }
}

// process player input
protected void ManageState(float elapsed)
{
    // ...
    if (IsSpeaking)
    {
        // dialog sprite is visible, ignore everything else
        State = AvatarStates.Smile;
    }
    else if (IsToot)
    {
    // ...
    }
    else
    {
    // ...
    }
}
```

When the player is idle, the avatar randomly looks around his environment, occasionally blinking.

```
// process player input
protected void ManageState(float elapsed)
{
    // ...
    if (IsSpeaking)
    {
    // ...
    }
```

```
        else if (IsToot)
        {
        // ...
        }
        else
        {
            // we're not speaking or tooting,
            // randomly select an idle state
            if ((State == AvatarStates.Smile) ||
                (CurrentSprite.TimeIdle > CurrentSprite.TimeDelay))
            {
                State = (AvatarStates)m_rand.Next(
                    (int)AvatarStates.Smile);
            }
        }
    }
```

If the current culture settings allow it, the avatar will enter the toot mode while the X button on the controller is being pressed, squinting his eyes and shaking with an intensity that grows over time.

```
// true when toot action is requested by the player, and
// allowed by their culture-specific settings
public bool IsToot
{
    get
    {
        return LocalizedContent.ResourceHelper.AllowCrude&&
            GamePadState.Buttons.X == ButtonState.Pressed;
    }
}

// time spent in toot mode, used to
// increase intensity of the effect
protected double m_TimeToot = 0.0f;

// shake offset, used in toot animation
protected Vector2 m_LocationDelta = Vector2.Zero;
public Vector2 LocationDelta { get { return m_LocationDelta; } }

// process player input
protected void ManageState(float elapsed)
{
```

```
    // we've just come out of toot mode
    if (!IsToot&& m_TimeToot > 0)
    {
        // reset counters, kill shaking
        m_TimeToot = 0;
        m_LocationDelta = Vector2.Zero;
        GamePad.SetVibration(PlayerIndex.One, 0.0f, 0.0f);
    }
    if (IsSpeaking)
    {
    // ...
    }
    else if (IsToot)
    {
        // we're in toot mode, set avatar state and increment timer
        State = AvatarStates.Blink;
        m_TimeToot += elapsed;

        // calculate the shake for the controller
        float motorLeft = (float)Math.Min(1.0f, m_TimeToot / 4.0f);
        float motorRight = (float)Math.Min(1.0f, m_TimeToot / 10.0f);
        GamePad.SetVibration(PlayerIndex.One, motorLeft, motorRight);

        // calculate the shake for the sprite
        float deltaMax = (float)Math.Min(4.0f, m_TimeToot / 3.0f);
        m_LocationDelta.X = m_rand.Next((int)(deltaMax + 1));
        m_LocationDelta.Y = m_rand.Next((int)(deltaMax + 1));
    }
    else
    {
    // ...
    }
}
```

The DialogSprite Class

This is, by far, the most complicated of the sprite subclasses. To make the logic for this class more manageable, I split the work into two classes. The Dialog-Sprite class is the main interface to the game logic, and it has an instance of the DialogRectangle to make sizing and animating the dialog easier.

The main texture for the DialogSprite class is the dialog bubble. The Texture, TextureRect, and Tint properties that we inherited from the SpriteBase class are used to draw the dialog image to the screen. But this sprite is also responsible for drawing localized text on the dialog bubble. The following properties support that task.

```
// color of the text within the dialog
protected Color m_TextTint = Color.Black;
public Color TextTint
{
    get { return m_TextTint; }
}


// a helper class to draw text to the screen
public GameFont GameFont = null;


// the (localized) three lines of text and
// their on-screen widths
protected string[] m_Text = new string[3];
protected int[] m_TextWidth = new int[3];
```

Since our dialog sprite is the only game object that concerns itself with localized resources, it makes sense to have it manage our flag sprite's texture. To do that, we'll need a reference to the FlagSprite instance that's used by the game.

```
// reference to the flag sprite
// the DialogSprite class is responsible for using
// localized content, and the flag is locale-specific
protected SpriteBase m_Flag = null;
public SpriteBase Flag
{
    get { return m_Flag; }
    set { m_Flag = value; }
}
```

When the DialogSprite is shown and hidden, it doesn't just pop into and out of visibility. It grows and shrinks to its target size as a simple animation. The current size of the dialog is stored in the Size property. The desired size of the dialog is stored in the TargetSize property. Whenever these two values don't match, we're in the middle of a transition from one size to the next. During this time, text is not drawn, and player inputs are ignored.

```
// time to transition between dialog sizes
protected const float TRANSITION = 0.25f;
```

```
// change in size of the dialog (in pixels per second)
protected Vector2 m_SizeChange = Vector2.Zero;

// the current size of the dialog
protected Vector2 m_Size = Vector2.Zero;
public Vector2 Size
{
    get { return m_Size; }
    set { m_Size = value; }
}

// the size we want our dialog to be
protected Vector2 m_TargetSize = Vector2.Zero;
public Vector2 TargetSize
{
    get { return m_TargetSize; }
    set
    {
        m_TargetSize = value;
        m_SizeChange.X = (TargetSize.X - Size.X) / TRANSITION;
        m_SizeChange.Y = (TargetSize.Y - Size.Y) / TRANSITION;
    }
}
```

The preceding code snippet just prepares the animation to run. The actual animation is handled by the Update method.

```
// process player input and update game objects
public sealed override void Update(float elapsed)
{
    base.Update(elapsed);
    if (Ready)
    {
        // we're not transitioning, check the A button
        if (GamePadState.Buttons.A == ButtonState.Pressed)
        {
            // cycle between no, 1, 2, and 3 lines of text
            int lines = VisibleLineCount + 1;
            if (lines > 3) { lines = 0; }
            Show(lines);
        }
    }
```

```
else
{
    // we're in the middle of a transition from one
    // dialog size to another
    // update horizontal size
    m_Size.X += elapsed * m_SizeChange.X;
    if ((m_SizeChange.X < 0&& m_Size.X < m_TargetSize.X) ||
        (m_SizeChange.X > 0&& m_Size.X > m_TargetSize.X))
    {
        m_Size.X = m_TargetSize.X;
        m_SizeChange.X = 0;
    }

    // update vertical size
    m_Size.Y += elapsed * m_SizeChange.Y;
    if ((m_SizeChange.Y < 0&& m_Size.Y < m_TargetSize.Y) ||
        (m_SizeChange.Y > 0&& m_Size.Y > m_TargetSize.Y))
    {
        m_Size.Y = m_TargetSize.Y;
        m_SizeChange.Y = 0;
    }
}
}
```

When we're ready to display the dialog bubble, we'll capture the current localized text and determine the size of the smallest dialog that will contain the text. The animation is kicked off whenever we set the TargetSize to a value other than the one stored in the (current) Size property.

```
// number of lines that are being displayed
protected int m_VisibleLineCount = 0;
public int VisibleLineCount { get { return m_VisibleLineCount; } }

// show or hide the dialog, cycle between no, 1, 2, or 3 lines
public void Show(int lines)
{
    // make sure line is between 0 and 3
    lines = Math.Min(lines, 3);
    lines = Math.Max(lines, 0);

    // set the desired line count
    m_VisibleLineCount = lines;
    if (lines > 0)
```

```
{
    // we're showing text now, capture the localized text
    m_Text[0] = LocalizedContent.ResourceHelper.Hello;
    m_Text[1] = LocalizedContent.ResourceHelper.HowAreYou;
    m_Text[2] = LocalizedContent.ResourceHelper.Goodbye;

    // measure the localized text
    m_TextWidth[0] = (int)Math.Round(
        GameFont.MeasureString(m_Text[0]).X);
    m_TextWidth[1] = (int)Math.Round(
        GameFont.MeasureString(m_Text[1]).X);
    m_TextWidth[2] = (int)Math.Round(
        GameFont.MeasureString(m_Text[2]).X);

    // determine the height of the client area
    float y = (lines + 1) * GameFont.FontHeight;

    // determine the width of the client area
    float x = 32.0f; // minimum width is 32
    for (int i = 0; i < lines; i++)
    {
        x = Math.Max(x, m_TextWidth[i]);
    }

    // set the desired size to initiate the transition
    TargetSize = new Vector2(x + 32, y);
}
else
{
    // we're hiding the dialog, shrink it before hiding
    // by setting desired size to kick off transition
    TargetSize = new Vector2(32, 32);
}
}
```

Drawing the localized text is pretty straightforward at this point. As long as we're not transitioning and our VisibleLineCount is greater than zero, we will draw the text. Otherwise, we'll draw the dialog bubble (if we're transitioning) or nothing (if VisibleLineCount is zero and we're not transitioning).

```
// true when the dialog is done transitioning
// from one size to the next
protected bool Ready { get { return TargetSize == Size; } }
```

```
// actually draw our dialog
public sealed override void Draw(SpriteBatch batch)
{
    if (VisibleLineCount > 0 || !Ready)
    {
        // we won't draw text if the dialog is hidden or the
        // dialog is transitioning between sizes
        m_DialogRect.Draw(batch, this);
    }
    if (VisibleLineCount > 0&& Ready)
    {
        // dialog is full-size and has visible lines
        // center the dialog within the drawable area
        Rectangle rect = m_DialogRect.DrawableArea;
        int centerX = rect.Left + rect.Width / 2;
        int centerY = rect.Top + rect.Height / 2;

        // determine the location of the first line of text
        int y = centerY - VisibleLineCount * GameFont.FontHeight / 2;

        // draw each line, centered, each below the previous
        for (int i = 0; i < VisibleLineCount; i++)
        {
            int x = centerX - m_TextWidth[i] / 2;
            GameFont.DrawString(
                batch,
                m_Text[i],
                x, y,
                TextTint);
            y += GameFont.FontHeight;
        }
    }
}
```

The DialogRectangle Class

The dialog bubble is drawn to the screen, centered with a drawable area that is
defined by the following property.

```
// on-screen area where dialog is to be centered
protected Rectangle m_DrawableArea = Rectangle.Empty;
public Rectangle DrawableArea
{
```

```
    get { return m_DrawableArea; }
    set { m_DrawableArea = value; }
}
```

The image for the dialog bubble is a simple rounded rectangle. This image is scaled to accommodate the text that is drawn to the screen. If we just scale the source image, the border will shrink and grow as the scale changes. To keep the border consistent, we'll split the rounded rectangle into nine parts, one part for each of the four corners, one part for each of the four sides, and one part for the center of the sprite.

```
// break the dialog texture rectangle into its nine components
public void InitTextureRects(Rectangle rect, int border)
{
    // handy local variables to save some typing
    int top = rect.Top;
    int left = rect.Left;
    int right = rect.Right;
    int bottom = rect.Bottom;
    int width = rect.Width;
    int height = rect.Height;

    // corners
    m_TextureRectNW =
        new Rectangle(left, top, border, border);
    m_TextureRectNE =
        new Rectangle(right - border, top, border, border);
    m_TextureRectSW =
        new Rectangle(left, bottom - border, border, border);
    m_TextureRectSE = new Rectangle(
        right - border,
        bottom - border,
        border,
        border);

    // top and bottom
    m_TextureRectNO = new Rectangle(
        left + border,
        top,
        width - 2 * border,
        border);
    m_TextureRectSO = new Rectangle(
        left + border,
```

```
        bottom - border,
        width - 2 * border,
        border);

    // sides
    m_TextureRectWE = new Rectangle(
        left,
        top + border,
        border,
        height - 2 * border);
    m_TextureRectEA = new Rectangle(
        right - border,
        top + border,
        border,
        height - 2 * border);

    // center
    m_TextureRectCenter = new Rectangle(
        TextureRectNO.Left,
        TextureRectWE.Top,
        TextureRectNO.Width,
        TextureRectWE.Height);
}
```

We'll never scale the corner images, and we'll only scale the side images in such a
way as not to affect the width of the border pixels (we'll scale the vertical sides
vertically and the horizontal sides horizontally). The central image will be scaled
(horizontally and vertically) to fill the inner area of the dialog bubble.

```
// draw the dialog bubble
public void Draw(SpriteBatch batch, DialogSprite sprite)
{
    // dimensions of target rectangle, centered in drawable area
    int width = (int)Math.Round(sprite.Size.X);
    int height = (int)Math.Round(sprite.Size.Y);
    int top = DrawableArea.Top + DrawableArea.Height / 2 - height / 2;
    int left = DrawableArea.Left + DrawableArea.Width / 2 - width / 2;
    int border = TextureRectNW.Width;

    // draw corners (they don't scale)
    Vector2 loc = new Vector2(left, top);
    batch.Draw(sprite.Texture, loc, TextureRectNW, sprite.Tint);
    loc.X = left + width - border;
```

```
batch.Draw(sprite.Texture, loc, TextureRectNE, sprite.Tint);
loc.Y = top + height - border;
batch.Draw(sprite.Texture, loc, TextureRectSE, sprite.Tint);
loc.X = left;
batch.Draw(sprite.Texture, loc, TextureRectSW, sprite.Tint);

// draw sides (they only scale vertically)
Rectangle rect = new Rectangle(
    left,
    top + border,
    border,
    height - 2 * border);
batch.Draw(sprite.Texture, rect, TextureRectWE, sprite.Tint);
rect.X = left + width - border;
batch.Draw(sprite.Texture, rect, TextureRectEA, sprite.Tint);

// draw top and bottom (they only scale horizontally)
rect = new Rectangle(
    left + border,
    top,
    width - 2 * border,
    border);
batch.Draw(sprite.Texture, rect, TextureRectNO, sprite.Tint);
rect.Y = top + height - border;
batch.Draw(sprite.Texture, rect, TextureRectSO, sprite.Tint);

// draw client area (scales both ways)
rect = new Rectangle(
    left + border,
    top + border,
    width - 2 * border,
    height - 2 * border);
batch.Draw(sprite.Texture, rect, TextureRectCenter, sprite.Tint);

// draw the arrow for the dialog bubble
loc.X = left + border;
loc.Y = top + height - 4.0f; // yuck: hard-coded.
batch.Draw(
    sprite.Texture,
    loc,
    sprite.TextureRectQuote,
    sprite.Tint);
}
```

The ContentStaging Project

The ContentStaging project is not directly referenced by any of our game projects. Its sole reason for existence is to make the job of converting our source images into XNA-friendly XNB files easier. When we add images to this project, they are automatically converted to XNB files when the project is built. We can then embed those XNB files into our EmbeddedContent resource file to access them as embedded content within our game.

To help us remember not to include a reference to this project in our game or content projects, I added a compiler warning to the only source code file in the ContentStaging project.

```
#warning Never reference the ResourceStaging library in your game.
```

Note

We could easily add a reference to this project from our game project, and the XNB files would be included in our game's resulting directory structure, but that's not the point of this example. We want to use embedded resources.

The EmbeddedContent Project

The EmbeddedContent project is an XNA game library project that contains a resource file. The XNB files that are generated by the ContentStaging project are added to this resource file using the Add Resource / Add Existing File menu options. When the project is built, the resulting DLL contains included content. There are no external XNB media files in our final game binaries.

To make accessing this content easier, I wrote a small helper class to make loading embedded content in our game as easy as loading content using the game's ContentManager class (which every other example in this book uses).

```
public class ResourceHelper
{
    // prep this class for use
    public static void Init(IServiceProvider provider)
    {
        m_ResourceManager = EmbeddedContent.Resources.ResourceManager;
        m_ContentManager =
            new ResourceContentManager(
                provider,
                ResourceManager);
    }
```

```
// used to extract embedded content
protected static ResourceContentManager m_ContentManager = null;
public static ResourceContentManager ContentManager
{
    get { return m_ContentManager; }
}

// used to extract (localized) embedded content
protected static ResourceManager m_ResourceManager = null;
public static ResourceManager ResourceManager
{
    get { return m_ResourceManager; }
}
}
```

To use this class, and access our embedded content, we just need to include a reference to this project from the main game project. Wherever we would have loaded content in the main game class (in the `LoadGraphicsContent`, for example), we'll use code similar to the following.

```
// our new code to load an embedded texture
EmbeddedContent.ResourceHelper.Init(Services);
ResourceContentManager embedded =
    EmbeddedContent.ResourceHelper.ContentManager;
m_background.Texture = embedded.Load<Texture2D>("background");
```

Compare that to the typical scenario you've used in our other examples, and you'll see that they're quite similar.

```
// typical code to load a texture
ContentManager content = new ContentManager(Services);
m_background.Texture = content.Load<Texture2D>("background");
```

The content that is contained within this project (and embedded within the resulting DLL) includes the dialog image, the avatar images, the background image, and the bitmap font image. Figure 27.2 shows the resource editor for the `EmbeddedContent` project.

The LocalizedContent Project

The `LocalizedContent` project is an XNA game library project that contains several resource files. Each resource file contains a string table where localized dialog and game settings are stored. Each resource file parallels the others, but the

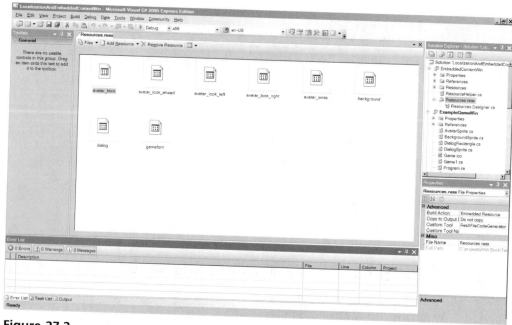

Figure 27.2
The resource file for our embedded XNB image data.

content of each is customized for the specific locale of the intended audience. Figure 27.3 shows the string table for our Spanish resource file.

Our main resource file is named "Localized.resx." Each of the localized resources is named similarly, but with a locale-specific code embedded in the file name. The two-letter codes represent a general culture. For example, the English content in our example game is encoded with "en," which is the culture code for English.

There are many English-speaking countries in the world, and each has its own unique take on the language. Each English-speaking culture has subtle differences in spelling ("color" versus "colour"), vocabulary ("truck" versus "lorry"), prepositions ("on a team" versus "in a team"), and number agreement ("Microsoft has released XNA" versus "Microsoft have released XNA"). Beyond the obvious translation issues, different cultures represent numbers, currency, dates, and times in regionally distinct ways too. I've only compared two English-speaking cultures here. As we move among Canadian, South African, Australian, Irish, and New Zealandean cultures, we find even more variety (and ambiguity).

To truly localize our content, we would provide each region with its own flavor of the language. To denote localized content as belonging to a specific subset of a general language, we can use another, more specific form of our culture code. For

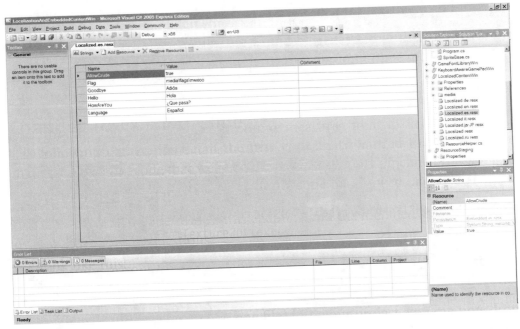

Figure 27.3
The string table for our localized Spanish content.

example, "en" is English in general; "en-US" is American English, "en-GB" is British English, "en-ZA" is South African English, and so on. With the exception of our Japanese content ("ja-JP"), we'll use the more generic culture codes in this example.

When the `LocalizedContent` project is built, each resource file is embedded within its own localized DLL. The filename of the DLL drops the culture code so that it matches our main resource filename, but each localized file is stored within a subdirectory, named for the culture code to which the resource belongs. Figure 27.4 shows the resource DLL for our Spanish content and the sibling directories for the other localized content.

We don't need to do anything special to access these DLLs; the runtime will load the appropriate DLL for us, based on the culture of the console or PC on which it is running. To test our localization efforts, I added some code to the main game class to trick the game into thinking that it is running on a computer with a different region encoding.

```
// list of our supported cultures
protected static readonly string[] m_cultures = {
```

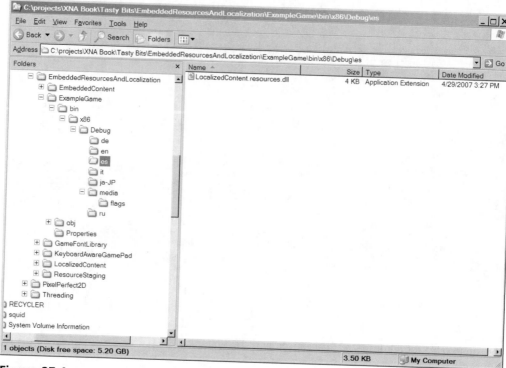

Figure 27.4
Directory structure for our localized content.

```
        "en",
        "es",
        "de",
        "it",
        "ja-JP",
        "ru",
};

// the current culture
protected static int m_cultureIndex = 0;

// select the next culture
public static void NextCulture()
{
    m_cultureIndex = (m_cultureIndex + 1) % m_cultures.Length;
}

// process the Y button press, don't repeat until they release
protected bool m_WasNextCulture = false;
```

```
public bool IsNextCulture
{
    get
    {
        bool pressed =
            SpriteBase.GamePadState.Buttons.Y == ButtonState.Pressed;
        bool result = pressed&& !m_WasNextCulture;
        m_WasNextCulture = pressed;
        return result;
    }
}


// have our current thread masquerade as another culture
public void UpdateCulture()
{
    Thread.CurrentThread.CurrentUICulture =
        CultureInfo.CreateSpecificCulture(m_cultures[m_cultureIndex]);
    LocalizedContent.ResourceHelper.Init(Services);
    m_flag.Texture =
        content.Load<Texture2D>(
            LocalizedContent.ResourceHelper.FlagPath);
}
```

This new code is used by the game within its `Update` and `LoadGraphicsContent` methods.

```
// is the player requesting another culture?
if (IsNextCulture)
{
    NextCulture();
    UpdateCulture();
    m_dialog.Show(m_dialog.VisibleLineCount);
}
```

To make accessing this content easier, I wrote a small helper class to make loading embedded content in our game as easy as loading content using the game's `ContentManager` class (which every other example in this book uses). This helper class parallels the `EmbeddedContent.ResourceHelper` class, so I won't list the source here. This class goes beyond the `EmbeddedContent` helper by adding a public, static property for each of the embedded strings. That way, the game can reference the properties directly rather than going through the resource manager every time.

To use this class, and access our localized content, we just need to include a reference to this project from the main game project.

When designing your game, avoid embedding text within images. Don't assume anything about the width of printed text—two characters in one language may translate to more than a dozen in another. Don't use automated translation tools like AltaVista's Babel Fish or Google's Translate. (For an interesting example of localization gone bad, search for "All your base are belong to us" in your favorite web search engine.) Be aware that certain gestures, signs, symbols, and images may be meaningless, offensive, or even criminal in certain cultures.

Summary

In this chapter, you learned how to embed XNA-friendly media into DLLs and use those embedded resources in your game, eliminating the need to ship XNB files with your game assemblies. We discussed some uses for embedded resources, such as providing default media when programmer-specified media fails to load, implementing date-activated themes for your games, and providing a mechanism for players to modify your game to enhance its replayability.

You also learned about some of the issues surrounding localized game resources and creating games that can dynamically adjust to the cultural idiosyncrasies of the region in which it is being played.

Review Questions

Think about what you've read in this chapter (and the included source code) to answer the following questions.

1. What are some good uses for embedded resources? What are some bad uses?

2. What is the ContentStaging project in this chapter's example used for? Is it needed?

3. List some issues that must be considered when localizing your game's content. What are some things you can do to make your code more conducive to localization efforts?

4. The avatar sprite and the flag sprite are separate images. How do they stay together when the avatar is shaking randomly?

5. How is the dialog bubble animated whenever its size changes? How is the target size of the dialog calculated? How is the size of the border that surrounds the dialog bubble kept constant?

Exercises

EXERCISE 1. Add some more culture-specific settings in your localize resources. Be creative. Here are a few examples to get you started: `AllowAvatarShake`, `AllowControllerShake`, `DialogColor`, and `DialogTextColor`.

EXERCISE 2. Use what you learned in the chapter on using audio in XNA to add sounds to this game. Add some background music, and add a looping sound for the toot action that increases in volume as long as the X button is being pressed. Be sure to account for the `AllowCrude` setting for the currently selected culture.

EXERCISE 3. The .NET Framework provides a mechanism for creating your own culture codes. I didn't include a description of this feature because those APIs require administrator rights to execute (a big no-no for a game). Add support for some creative, custom cultures—Pig Latin, L33t H4cK3r, and Klingon come to mind. You'll need to consult the XNA and .NET documentation on this one. Google may prove useful as well.

CHAPTER 28

PIXEL-PERFECT COLLISION DETECTION

Nothing irritates players more than thinking that they hit an opponent and the hit doesn't register, or thinking that they dodged a bullet only to find that they've lost a life. For most game programming tasks, "close enough" is perfectly fine. Collision detection isn't one of those tasks, though.

In this chapter, we will develop a reusable class to help us manage pixel-perfect 2D collision detection.

In this chapter, you will learn how to:

- Extract pixel data from a texture
- Quickly determine whether two on-screen sprites are touching

Opacity Data

Sprites are based on textures. Those textures are made up of pixels (see Figure 28.1).

To determine if two sprites are touching, you need to see if any common, opaque (non-transparent) pixels occupy the same on-screen pixel (see Figure 28.2). To do that, you'll need to access the pixel data for the texture(s) of the two sprites. Luckily there's a method in the Texture2D class that does just that.

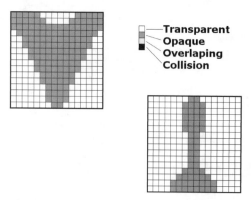

Figure 28.1
Two game sprites—a ship and a missile.

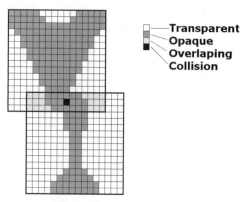

Figure 28.2
The missile is touching the ship.

To access the pixels for a texture, we'll use code similar to the following:

```
// an array to hold the pixel data from the texture
Color[] pixels = new Color[texture.Width * texture.Height];

// fill our array with the texture's pixel data
texture.GetData<Color>(pixels);
```

Now we can access any pixel in the single-dimensional array using code similar to the following:

```
Color pixel = pixels[x + (y * texture.Width)];
```

Remembering Opacity

The GetData method of the Texture2D class is fairly expensive in terms of performance and memory usage (and garbage collection churn). We'll want to get the data once, and then store it somewhere so that we can refer to that in-memory copy of the data rather than pulling it from the texture every time we need to inspect a sprite's pixels.

It's not important what color each pixel in our sprite is. We only need to know if the pixel is opaque or transparent. Rather than store the colors of each pixel, we'll store an array of Boolean values that tell us whether a given pixel is opaque.

```
// a handy interface to allow you to pass your game sprite into
// these helper methods, saving some typing in your parameter lists
public interface IPixelPerfectSprite
{
    Texture2D TextureData { get; set; }
    Rectangle TextureRect { get; set; }
    Vector2 Location { get; set; }
    bool[,] OpaqueData { get; set; }
}
```

Alpha Threshold

There may be some pixels that aren't fully opaque or fully transparent. For example, your sprite may have a drop shadow. In that case, you probably don't want a collision to be triggered when the missile hits the ship's shadow. To make our code configurable, we'll add a threshold value for the opacity. If the alpha is greater than or equal to this threshold, we'll consider that pixel to be opaque.

A Simple Collision Detection Optimization

Even though we saved some processing effort by storing our pixel data in an array of Booleans rather than repeatedly accessing the texture's pixel data directly, it's still rather CPU-intensive to scan an opacity data array for every pixel of every sprite that's on the screen with every call to our game's Update method. It's a complete waste of time to check for collisions, pixel by pixel, when the sprite textures don't overlap at all. To save ourselves some effort (and some valuable CPU cycles), we need to make sure that there's at least a chance for a collision, by checking to see if our sprite textures overlap.

The PixelPerfectHelper Class

The PixelPerfectHelper class contains a collection of static methods to help us detect 2D collisions.

GetOpaqueData

The first task in collision detection is to generate our opacity data array. Given a Texure2D object, the texture rectangle for the sprite, and an opacity threshold, the GetOpaqueData generates and returns an array of Booleans that represent the opacity of each pixel of the sprite.

```
// overload for GetOpaqueData(Texture2D, Rectangle, byte)
public static bool[,] GetOpaqueData(IPixelPerfectSprite sprite)
{
    return GetOpaqueData(sprite.TextureData, sprite.TextureRect, 255);
}


// overload for GetOpaqueData(Texture2D, Rectangle, byte)
public static bool[,] GetOpaqueData(
    IPixelPerfectSprite sprite, byte threshold)
{
    return GetOpaqueData(sprite.TextureData,
        sprite.TextureRect, threshold);
}


// overload for GetOpaqueData(Texture2D, Rectangle, byte)
public static bool[,] GetOpaqueData(Texture2D texture, Rectangle rect)
{
    return GetOpaqueData(texture, rect, 255);
}


// extract pixel data from the texture
public static bool[,] GetOpaqueData(
    Texture2D texture, Rectangle rect, byte threshold)
{
    // temp variables to save some typing
    int width = rect.Width;
    int height = rect.Height;

    // an array of booleans, one for each pixel
    // true = opaque (considered), false = transparent (ignored)
    bool[,] data = new bool[width, height];
```

```
// an array to hold the pixel data from the texture
Color[] pixels = new Color[texture.Width * texture.Height];

// I'd rather have used the overload for Texture2D.GetData
// that specifies the texture rect, but that function didn't
// work on the Xbox 360. This version pulls pixel data from
// the entire texture, but it should be OK since we're only
// using it briefly, and only on init of our game sprites.
texture.GetData<Color>(pixels);

// for each row of pixel data
for (int y = 0; y < height; y++)
{
    // for each column of pixel data
    for (int x = 0; x < width; x++)
    {
        // if the pixel's alpha exceeds our threshold,
        // note it in our boolean array
        if (pixels[
            rect.Left + x +
            (rect.Top + y) *
            texture.Width].A >= threshold)
        {
            data[x, y] = true;
        }
    }
}

// return our findings to the caller
return data;
}
```

DetectCollision

Once we have our opacity data, we can start checking for sprite collisions. The DetectCollision method encapsulates the two checks that need to be performed—do the sprite textures overlap, and, if so, do any of the overlapping, opaque pixels touch? These two checks are handled by the BoundsOverlap and PixelsTouch methods, respectively.

```
// overload for DetectCollision(Rect, Vec2, bool[], Rect, Vec2, bool[,])
public static bool DetectCollision(
```

```
        IPixelPerfectSprite one, IPixelPerfectSprite two)
{
    return DetectCollision(
        one.TextureRect, one.Location, one.OpaqueData,
        two.TextureRect, two.Location, two.OpaqueData);
}


// determine whether the bounding rectangles of the sprites overlap
// if they do, compare pixel by pixel within the intersection
public static bool DetectCollision(
    Rectangle rect1, Vector2 loc1, bool[,] data1,
    Rectangle rect2, Vector2 loc2, bool[,] data2)
{
    return BoundsOverlap(rect1, loc1, rect2, loc2)&&
            PixelsTouch(rect1, loc1, data1, rect2, loc2, data2);
}
```

BoundsOverlap

The BoundsOverlap method returns a Boolean value. If any part of the bounding rectangles of the two sprites overlap, this method will return true. The code in this method should look familiar. It's very similar to the bounds checking that we did in Chapter 13. If the first sprite is fully to the left, fully to the right, fully above, or fully below the second sprite, there is no overlap. Otherwise, the bounding rectangles of the two sprites do overlap, and we need to perform a pixel-by-pixel comparison.

```
// see if the texture rectangles overlap, if they don't, there's
// no need to do a pixel-by-pixel comparison
protected static bool BoundsOverlap(
    Rectangle rect1, Vector2 loc1,
    Rectangle rect2, Vector2 loc2)
{
    // determine the top, left, bottom, right for rect1
    int top1 = (int)loc1.Y;
    int left1 = (int)loc1.X;
    int bottom1 = top1 + rect1.Height;
    int right1 = left1 + rect1.Width;

    // determine the top, left, bottom, right for rect2
    int top2 = (int)loc2.Y;
    int left2 = (int)loc2.X;
```

```
int bottom2 = top2 + rect2.Height;
int right2 = left2 + rect2.Width;

return !(
    // rect1 fully to the right of rect2?
    left1 > right2 ||
    // rect1 fully to the left of rect2?
    right1 < left2 ||
    // rect1 fully below rect2?
    top1 > bottom2 ||
    // rect1 fully above rect2?
    bottom1 < top2
    );
}
```

PixelsTouch

This is the routine where pixel-by-pixel comparisons are performed. First, we calculate the bounds of the smallest rectangle that contains all of the overlapping pixels of both sprites. Then, we focus our search for a collision to that subset of the opaque data. If both sprites have an opaque pixel at the same location, a collision has occurred.

```
// perform a pixel-by-pixel comparison
protected static bool PixelsTouch(
    Rectangle rect1, Vector2 loc1, bool[,] data1,
    Rectangle rect2, Vector2 loc2, bool[,] data2)
{
    // update rects with locations of sprites
    rect1.X = (int)Math.Round(loc1.X);
    rect1.Y = (int)Math.Round(loc1.Y);
    rect2.X = (int)Math.Round(loc2.X);
    rect2.Y = (int)Math.Round(loc2.Y);

    // determine the intersection of the two rects
    Rectangle intersect = Rectangle.Empty;
    intersect.Y = Math.Max(rect1.Top, rect2.Top);
    intersect.X = Math.Max(rect1.Left, rect2.Left);
    int bottom = Math.Min(rect1.Bottom, rect2.Bottom);
    int right = Math.Min(rect1.Right, rect2.Right);
    intersect.Height = bottom - intersect.Y;
    intersect.Width = right - intersect.X;
```

```
    // scan the intersected rectangle, pixel by pixel
    int x1 = intersect.X - rect1.X;
    int x2 = intersect.X - rect2.X;
    int y1 = intersect.Y - rect1.Y;
    int y2 = intersect.Y - rect2.Y;
    for (int y = 0; y < intersect.Height; y++)
    {
        for (int x = 0; x < intersect.Width; x++)
        {
            // are both pixels opaque?
            if (data1[x1 + x, y1 + y]&&
                data2[x2 + x, y2 + y])
            {
                return true;
            }
        }
    }
    return false;
}
```

PixelPerfectHelper in Action

To keep our parameter lists small, we'll make sure that the game's custom sprite class implements the IPixelPerfectSprite interface. That interface exposes all of the sprite properties that we'll need to perform collision detection.

```
public class GameSprite : IPixelPerfectSprite
{
    // there's only one game texture, return it
    public Texture2D TextureData
    {
        get { return Game1.Texture; }
        set { }
    }

    // there's only one texture rect, return it
    protected static Rectangle m_TextureRect =
        new Rectangle(0, 0, 32, 32);
    public Rectangle TextureRect
    {
        get { return m_TextureRect; }
```

```
        set { m_TextureRect = value; }
    }

    // location of this sprite
    protected Vector2 m_Location = Vector2.Zero;
    public Vector2 Location
    {
        get { return m_Location; }
        set { m_Location = value; }
    }

    // opaque pixel data for this sprite
    protected bool[,] m_OpaqueData;
    public bool[,] OpaqueData
    {
        get { return m_OpaqueData; }
        set { m_OpaqueData = value; }
    }

    // draw this sprite, using current settings, and specified tint
    public void Draw(SpriteBatch batch, Color color)
    {
        batch.Draw(TextureData, Location, TextureRect, color);
    }
}
```

Now, our game just needs to create as many GameSprites as it wants, and then load the texture, populate the opacity data, and set the location for each,

```
// there's only one texture for this game, share it
public static Texture2D Texture
{
    get { return m_texture; }
}

// collidable, on-screen objects
public const int NUM_OBSTACLES = 20;
protected GameSprite[] m_sprites = new GameSprite[NUM_OBSTACLES];

// the player-controlled object
protected GameSprite m_playerSprite = new GameSprite();

/// Load your graphics content.
```

```
protected override void LoadGraphicsContent(bool loadAllContent)
{
    if (loadAllContent)
    {
        // recreate sprite batch and reload game texture
        m_batch = new SpriteBatch(graphics.GraphicsDevice);
        m_texture = content.Load<Texture2D>(@"media\game");

        // reset our obstacle course
        ResetSprites();
    }
}

// reset our obstacle course
protected void ResetSprites()
{
    Random rand = new Random();
    for (int i = 0; i < NUM_OBSTACLES; i++)
    {
        m_sprites[i] = new GameSprite();
        m_sprites[i].Location =
            new Vector2(rand.Next(SCREEN_WIDTH),
            rand.Next(SCREEN_HEIGHT));
        m_sprites[i].OpaqueData =
            PixelPerfectHelper.GetOpaqueData(m_sprites[i],128);
    }

    m_playerSprite = new GameSprite();
    m_playerSprite.Location = Vector2.One * 100.0f;
    m_playerSprite.OpaqueData =
            PixelPerfectHelper.GetOpaqueData(m_playerSprite,128);
}
```

Note

Since all of our sprites use the same image, they all have the same opacity data. The Reset-Sprites method could be made simpler by tweaking the GameSprite class to return a static reference to the same Boolean array for all instances. In most games, that won't be the case, however. Each unique sprite will need to manage its own opacity and texture rectangle data.

Now, we can process input in the Update method and render our sprites in the Draw method, just like we've done for all of our other games. We'll render any of the static sprites that our player-controlled sprite touches in a different color.

```
/// render game objects
protected override void Draw(GameTime gameTime)
{
    graphics.GraphicsDevice.Clear(Color.CornflowerBlue);

    m_batch.Begin();

    // draw each obstacle sprite
    foreach (GameSprite sprite in m_sprites)
    {
        if (PixelPerfectHelper.DetectCollision(sprite, m_playerSprite))
        {
            // collision detected between this sprite and the player
            sprite.Draw(m_batch, Color.Red);
        }
        else
        {
            // no collision detected
            sprite.Draw(m_batch, Color.Goldenrod);
        }
    }

    // draw the player
    m_playerSprite.Draw(m_batch, Color.LightGreen);

    m_batch.End();

    base.Draw(gameTime);
}
```

Summary

In this chapter, you learned how to inspect pixel data from a texture and use that data to perform pixel-perfect collision detection between 2D objects. You learned about some of the performance concerns with this method, and you picked up a couple of optimization tips for offsetting those penalties.

Review Questions

Think about what you've read in this chapter (and the included source code) to answer the following questions.

1. What are the two basic checks that are performed when detecting collisions using the methods described in this chapter?

2. Why are two checks performed?

3. Why is opacity data collected once, when the texture is first loaded?

4. How does this method of collision detection avoid false positives, for example, when one sprite touches another sprite's shadow?

Exercises

EXERCISE 1. Create a game, based on the code in this chapter, where any balls that the player touches become stuck to the player. Move the attached balls the same distance and in the same direction as the player as his location is updated.

EXERCISE 2. Similar to the first exercise, create a game, based on the code in this chapter, where any balls that the player touches begin to follow the player. Track the last NUM_OBSTACLES location of the player, and render each captured obstacle in one of those locations to achieve a growing snake effect.

EXERCISE 3. Create a game, based on the code and images in this chapter, that uses more than one obstacle image. Circles are a good test shape because they have transparent data on all sides, but it's a little boring. Add some stars, crescent moons, gears, or any other irregular shape that you like. To keep things simple, you can still use a single source texture, but you'll need to have distinct texture rectangles for each obstacle object.

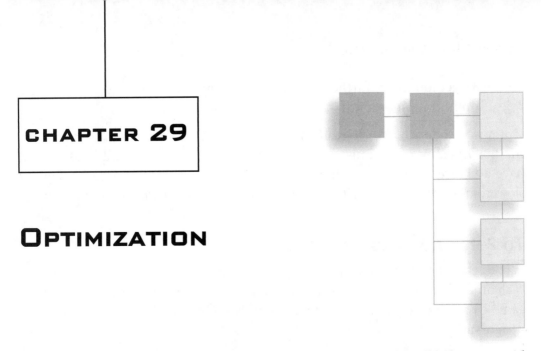

CHAPTER 29

OPTIMIZATION

This chapter covers several programming "best practices" that will help you avoid some of the most common pitfalls that make your games slower. The basic philosophy of this chapter is to write your games so that they rely on the performance enhancements that are built into the Common Language Runtime (CLR).

Spend more time focused on the things that make a great game—game play, user interface, replayability, and the like. When you're done with that, make sure that your code is logically grouped by related functionality, your code is readable, and your code is stable.

If (and only if) you have performance issues, fix them by eliminating unnecessary code, avoiding code that nullifies the built-in optimizations of the CLR, or by rethinking your implementation. Don't fix things that aren't broken.

In this chapter, you will learn how to:

- Budget CPU time for game tasks
- Know when to optimize your code
- Know when not to optimize your code
- Take advantage of optimizations that are built into the XNA Framework and the Common Language Runtime
- Avoid common performance pitfalls
- Use tools that provide measurable performance metrics to help you focus your optimization efforts

Before we get too much further into this topic, I need to remind you of the first rule of optimization—don't!

Optimized code is harder to read and it's harder to maintain. Attempts to extend the functionality of optimized code often introduce hard-to-find bugs. If you have a choice between a slightly faster, more-cryptic algorithm and a slightly slower, more-readable algorithm, always favor the code that is easier to maintain.

To Perf or Not to Perf

While reading this chapter, there may be certain topics that seem to contradict each other. That's the nature of code optimization. There are two components to game programming that seem to constantly fight each other—simplicity of design and processing speed.

Code reuse and readability are paramount, but your game code must perform well. You have to coordinate thousands of objects in a fraction of a second. And, as soon as you're done with those updates, it's time to do it all again.

Budget Time

As a part of your design process, identify your performance goals. If you want to maintain an average frame rate of 60 frames per second (FPS), then you'll have a budget of roughly 16.7 milliseconds to update and render all of your game objects for each frame. That time budget is divided over the tasks that you need to perform during every frame—graphics, audio, physics, AI, input, and any other tasks that your game performs.

By budgeting your time, you will have a measurable way to know when you're not meeting your performance goals. Your budget will likely need to evolve as your project moves from design to implementation. Maybe task A doesn't need all of its allotted time, and task B is a little over budget. It's okay to shuffle the numbers around, but ultimately, there can't be any deficits in this budget.

If you just can't squeeze it all into 60 FPS, you may be able to drop your frame rate to 30 FPS and double your budget. For most hobbyist games, a 60 FPS frame rate is a fairly arbitrary goal. The average player won't know that your game is running at 120 FPS or 30 FPS if you don't tell him. At some point, you can't drop the frame rate any more, though (the lower the frame rate, the "choppier" the movement). And that's where you'll need to optimize.

Set Measurable Goals

Near the end of this chapter, I'll introduce some tools that provide metrics that you can use to see how well your game is performing on Windows and on the Xbox 360 game console. Use them (or their commercial counterparts). If you can't measure your progress, you won't know if you're making any progress, and you won't know when to stop optimizing.

Benchmark your application regularly during the development lifecycle. Performance problems are often hard to track down. By testing often, you'll have a better idea of which recent code changes introduced new performance problems. Treat a failure to meet performance budgets like any other bug—fix the code or change the requirements so that the existing performance falls within your adjusted budget.

Having said all that, you need to make sure that you don't test your performance too early. Your code needs to be stable and fully functional before you start worrying about performance issues. Whenever you develop a game, you will throw away features that you've implemented. When you do so, you'll also be throwing out any optimizations that you've made. By only optimizing stable code, you'll reduce the risk of wasting your optimization efforts.

Be Willing to Rewrite Troublesome Code

When you find yourself having to fix a performance problem, always be willing to throw out your current implementation for a new algorithm. It's hard to let go of code that you've spent a lot of time developing, but many performance problems can be solved by doing the same task a different way.

For example, there are dozens of sorting algorithms out there. Every one of them has exactly the same goal, and every one of them has exactly the same end result, but each implementation approaches the same task in a drastically different way. Rather than patching and propping up a bad algorithm, consider a new, cleaner approach that's easier to maintain.

JIT Compiler (Freebies)

We will cover some performance coding best practices in this chapter, but I want to spend a little time explaining some of the performance benefits that you get "for free" when using managed code under the Common Language Runtime (CLR).

The CLR provides a technology for converting your managed code to native code that is specially optimized for the platform on which it's running. This feature of the runtime is known as the Just In Time (JIT) compiler.

Inlining

Whenever possible, the JIT compiler will inject small methods directly into the calling code. These methods have to meet some very restrictive size and code complexity requirements. Property getters and setters are ideal candidates for inlining. They're typically very small, and they generally don't have complex logic or conditional branching.

Inlined methods improve performance by eliminating the overhead of making a method call. Whenever a method is called, space on the stack frame is allocated to store its arguments and local variables, and parameters are copied into this local storage. By directly injecting the code into the calling method, it performs just as if you had cut and pasted the code into your method.

Virtual methods cannot be inlined since the JIT compiler cannot know which version of the overridden method will ultimately be called. There are ways to work around this limitation, though. We'll cover those options later in this chapter when we discuss the performance impact of virtual methods in more detail.

Of course, you could manually inline code using your old friend, cut and paste. But managing multiple copies of redundant code blocks is a maintenance nightmare. Whenever you find a bug in your manually injected code, you're less likely to remember to make the same fix everywhere else it was pasted.

Range-Check Elimination

Managed code is anal about restricting your code's access to memory that it doesn't own. For example, if you try to read from (or write to) the 11th element of a 10-element array, the CLR will generate a runtime exception (an Index-OutOfRangeException in this case). While that makes your code more crash resistant and less vulnerable to security exploits, those checks do take precious CPU time.

There are some simple cases where these range checks can be eliminated. The JIT is smart enough to see if there's no way that your code will ever access array indices that fall outside of the bounds of the array. Consider the following simple code snippet.

```
// JIT knows that you're not doing anything naughty here
for(int i = 0; i < objArray.Length; i++)
{
    objArray[i].SomeProperty = i * 2;
}
```

Loop Unrolling

For tight loops with relatively few iterations, the overhead of setting up loop variables and conditional branching logic can be greater than simply executing the same code several times in a row. Consider the following code snippet.

```
// the loop
for(int i = 0; i < 3; i++)
{
    obj.DoTask();
}

// the same set of tasks, unrolled
// avoids the overhead of setting up and managing the loop
// don't do this yourself; JIT will do it for you if it makes sense to
obj.DoTask();
obj.DoTask();
obj.DoTask();
```

Code Hoisting

Blocks of code within loops that perform the same task on every iteration (with the same result) are candidates for code hoisting. In this optimization, the JIT compiler is smart enough to recognize the blocks of code that will produce the same results whether they're executed once or a million times. There's no point in executing that code more than once, so the JIT will pull that code outside of the loop.

Constant Injections

Whenever the JIT compiler encounters a constant, or it can determine the results of a calculation at compile-time, it will inject the value directly into the code. That way, the native code that is generated doesn't have to access variable storage, and runtime calculations are reduced or eliminated altogether.

Enregistering

Another common JIT optimization is to try and store data in CPU registers rather than CPU cache or RAM, since it's the fastest storage available. Unfortunately, there are only a certain number of CPU registers available. Limiting the number of local variables and parameters in your methods will help the JIT compiler store values in CPU registers rather than on the stack frame.

To take advantage of this optimization, you will also want to avoid marking variables with the `volatile` keyword, since that tells the JIT compiler that your variable may be updated at any time. This prevents it from being stored in a CPU register because the generated native code will need to keep coming back to the value in RAM to make sure that it hasn't changed.

A Final Note on JIT

JIT does an incredible job of generating high-performance native code from our managed IL (Microsoft Intermediate Language, or MSIL), but it doesn't produce code that is as fast as that generated by an optimizing compiler.

There is a trade-off between the time spent analyzing the source IL and the speed of the resulting code. For the rest of this chapter, we will discuss some general performance best practices that you can apply to your code that will augment the gains that you get from your JIT-compiled code.

If you come from a C/C++ background, you may have picked up some performance tips during your time in the trenches. Be aware that managed code is a different beast, and that some of those code optimizations may, in fact, result in slower code.

In most cases, it's better to just let the JIT compiler and GC do their thing. The following text will discuss some ways that you can keep from fighting the optimizations that are built into GC and the JIT compiler.

HLSL

I'll spend the rest of this chapter discussing optimizations that you can make to your C# code. But, if your game is graphics-intensive, you will also want to focus effort on making sure that you're using the rendering pipeline as efficiently as possible. Make sure that you're not doing things on the CPU that would be better handled by the GPU.

Spend some time getting familiar with the High-Level Shader Language (HLSL). When using shaders, you have the same performance potential as the professional console developers. HLSL doesn't run within the confines of the CLR; it's executed directly on the GPU.

Note

A good example of a performance no-no can be found in Chapter 25, "Threading in XNA." The particle system in that chapter would thrive on the GPU. Threading may (or may not) increase the performance of that code on the CPU. Either way, it's a waste of resources. It would be better to free up the CPU to work on other game tasks.

The goal of Chapter 25 was to illustrate key .NET Framework threading API concepts, not to write the fastest particle system ever made.

Release Builds

While not technically a JIT optimization, building your project in release mode is another "freebie" that's worth mentioning here.

While you're developing your game, you will want to configure your project (actually, your solution) to generate what are known as debug builds of your executable. This build type generates extra data for your game that the Visual C# 2005 Express Edition IDE can use to help you troubleshoot any problems that you have with your code. The executables that are generated in debug mode are larger and slower than the same code that's generated during a release build.

Make sure that you compile your game in release mode when you're done, or whenever you want see how well a stable milestone of your code base is performing.

General Best Practices

The tips in this section apply to programming in general, regardless of language or platform. These best practices will help you write better XNA games (and any other type of program that you want to create).

Less Is More

This may seem obvious, but the fastest code is code that never executes. Keeping your implementations simple and small will generally result in faster code. Don't over-generalize or over-architect your code. Your game object may support a gazillion features, but if you're only using a small subset of those features, then you're wasting time, effort, and resources.

Reuse Everything

Try not to calculate the same value more than once. This is especially true for calculations that you perform within loops. In many cases, storing the result in a variable, and then using that cached value wherever it is needed, will result in less work for your game.

```
void ReuseCalcsExample()
{
    // Bad. Calculating repeatedly.
    for ( int i = 0; i < 10 ; i++ )
    {
        obj[i].Y = Math.Sin(m_angle * 13.0f) + i;
    }

    // Better. Reusing calculation.
    float y = Math.Sin(m_angle * 13.0f);
    for ( int i = 0; i < 10 ; i++ )
    {
        obj[i].Y = y + i;
    }
}
```

Don't needlessly create new objects when you can recycle an idle object of the same type. Use an object pool or object cache where unused objects are marked and reclaimed when needed.

For an example of object pooling, read about thread pools in Chapter 25, "Threading in XNA." For another example of object pooling, see how the bullets and enemy ships were managed in Chapter 16, "Top-Down Scroller."

Object pooling improves performance in certain scenarios by eliminating the time it takes to create and initialize new objects (pooled objects are created once), and pooled objects reduce the impact on GC, since objects aren't constantly being released. Object pooling may also help when using objects that are tied to system resources, where the cost of reserving and releasing the resource can be even more expensive.

Lazy Initialization

Your game may contain hundreds (or thousands) of objects. Depending on what the player does, some of those objects may live in dormant code paths where they will never be used. There's no point in creating and initializing an object that will never be used.

Wherever possible, wait to create your objects until just before they're needed.

```
// Bad. Member object is created every time the host object is instantiated
private GameObject m_obj = new GameObject();
public PerformTaskBad()
{
    m_obj.DoWork();
}

// Better. Member is created when (and if) it is needed.
// Subsequent calls reuse the existing member object.
private GameObject m_obj = null;
public PerformTaskBetter()
{
    if(m_obj == null)
    {
        m_obj = new GameObject();
    }
    m_obj.DoWork();
}
```

If the object that you're instantiating is large or takes a while to initialize, you may see a spike in CPU utilization when you first access it. Try to initialize those objects in stages, early enough so that they're ready by the time you actually need them.

Psychology of Performance

There may be some tasks that you simply cannot perform in a fraction of a second. Whether it's managing player save games or loading data for a large game level, some tasks just take a while to complete. In those cases, try to avoid blocking your game data and screen updates. Players tend to get irritated if your game simply hangs while performing a long-running task.

You should provide some visual cue that your game is still doing something. It can be as simple as a static screen (perhaps sporting a progress bar or simple animation), or as complex as a mini-game. Just don't make the player stare at the last frame that was rendered before the task began.

Better yet, try to avoid long-running tasks altogether. Load game levels in smaller groups, break long-running tasks into smaller, more-manageable stages, or perform those CPU-intensive tasks on a background thread. There may even be scenarios where you can anticipate what data will be needed ahead of time, and load it just before it's needed.

Preprocess Content

Don't perform tasks in your game that you can just as easily perform at design time or compile-time. For example, it probably makes more sense to generate drop shadows on your sprites in your graphics editor (design time) rather than generating them in-game (runtime). Similarly, you don't want to process game data as you load it into your game (runtime) if that same data can be stored in a preprocessed form (compile-time).

.NET Framework Best Practices

The tips in this section apply specifically to the .NET Framework and the Common Language Runtime (CLR). The information in this section also applies to your Windows and Xbox 360 games, since they run within the CLR and rely on the .NET Framework APIs, but the next section includes additional information that's specifically tailored to the .NET Compact Framework (CF) on which your Xbox 360 XNA games run.

Beware Boxing

Objects within the CLR are broadly grouped into one of two categories— reference types and value types. In the case of reference types, variables store a pointer to your data, which lies somewhere on the heap (an area of memory that is managed by the Garbage Collector [GC]). For value types, variables store the actual data of the type on the stack (scope-specific memory that's allocated to store local data and parameter data for method calls). Assigning a reference type to a variable copies the address of the type's data, whereas assigning a value type to a variable actually copies the type's data into the targeted variable.

Since all objects ultimately derive from a common base class (System.object), you can treat value types as objects. When you do this, though, the CLR allocates memory on the heap for the data in your value type. Then, the object behaves like a reference type (which it is). Just like any other reference type, this new object will need to be garbage collected at some point in the future. Consider the following snippet.

```
public string SimpleBoxingExample()
{
    return 1234.ToString();
}
```

The `int` type is a value type. But, because it ultimately derives from `System.object`, it supports the `ToString` method. The CLR will quietly create an object reference on the heap so that it can call `ToString` for that object. After the example method returns, the newly created object is no longer referenced, and it will eventually be released by the Garbage Collector.

```
public int SimpleUnboxingExample(object intData)
{
    return (int)intData;
}
```

In the preceding example, passing an `int` value into the method will result in a boxing of that value into an object (since the method requires an object), then the object is cast to a value type (unboxing) and eventually falls out of scope, to later be collected by GC.

So, what's the big deal about boxing? Value types are optimized to handle simple data, and they're designed to live outside of the heap. Avoiding garbage collection and reducing heap fragmentation are two of the best-selling features of value types. When you box a value type into a reference type, you've just forfeited those benefits.

Also, boxing and unboxing don't come for free. To box, the CLR has to allocate storage, initialize objects, copy data, and eventually release the memory (and possibly compact the heap).

If you expect that your value type will be boxed in its typical usage, it's probably a good idea to rewrite it as a small class instead.

Use Strongly Typed Collections

If you know the type of the data ahead of time, favor collections that are built on C# generics rather than collections that are based on `System.object`. In the case of value types, using loosely typed collections will result in implicit boxing and unboxing of your data. Consider the following code snippet.

```
// Bad. Results in unintended boxing of value types.
public void UnTypedCollectionExample()
{
    ArrayList list = new ArrayList();
    for(int i = 0; i < 10; i++)
    {
        list.add(i);
    }
}

// Better. The collection is aware of your specific type.
public void TypedCollectionExample()
{
    List<int> list = new List<int>();
    for(int i = 0; i < 10; i++)
    {
        list.add(i);
    }
}
```

A less-obvious implicit boxing example can be seen in the following code snippet.

```
public string HashtableExample()
{
    // create hash table
    Hashtable hash = new Hashtable();

    // populate hash table
    hash.Add(1, "one");
    hash.Add(2, "two");
    hash.Add(3, "three");

    // reference the hash table
    return (string)hash[2];
}
```

The Add method and the indexed getter for the Hashtable are general-purpose, so they accept an object as their key. Your value type (an integer) will be implicitly boxed whenever you assign data to the Hashtable or recall data from it.

That means that there will be another managed object on the heap that will need to be collected after it falls out of scope. The following snippet represents the method signature for the Hashtable class' indexed getter.

```
// method signature for Hashtable's indexed getter
public object this[object key] { get; set; }
```

One alternative in this case is the generics-based Dictionary class. Like a Hash-table, the Dictionary stores values, which are indexed by keys (rather than ordinal indices). Unlike the Hashtable, the generic Dictionary allows you to specify the type of both the value and the key.

```
public string DictionaryExample()
{
    // create dictionary
    Dictionary<int, string> dict = new Dictionary<int, string>();

    // populate dictionary
    dict.Add(1, "one");
    dict.Add(2, "two");
    dict.Add(3, "three");

    // reference the dictionary
    return dict[2];
}
```

Use Strongly Typed Parameter References

The same caveats apply to method parameters. If you know the type of the data that you're passing, use the specific type in your parameter declaration. To support multiple types, provide multiple methods, multiple overloaded versions of the same method, or declare your method using C# generics.

```
// multiple methods
public int   GetDataAsInt   (int index) {...}
public float GetDataAsFloat(int index) {...}

// multiple overloads
public void GetData(int index, out int   data) {...}
public void GetData(int index, out float data) {...}

// generics
public T GetData<T>(int index) where T : struct {...}
```

Strings

To help the compiler optimize the native instructions that it generates, strings are immutable. So any changes that you make to a string result in the creation of a new string object whose reference will eventually need to be collected after it falls out of scope.

The .NET Framework provides a helper class that allows you to build strings by appending new substrings—StringBuilder. The StringBuilder class doesn't use an immutable buffer, so the data can grow as needed.

I ran a simple (non-real-world) benchmark a while back that demonstrates the difference between concatenating strings using string objects versus using the StringBuilder class.

```
public void AppendingStringsExample()
{
    // this takes 12 seconds to run on my old laptop
    string x = "";
    for (int i=0; i < 100000; i++)
    {
        x += "!";
    }


    // this takes less than 9 milliseconds
    StringBuilder x = new StringBuilder( "" );
    for (int i=0; i < 100000; i++)
    {
        x.Append( "!" );
    }
}
```

You may not have much reason to do a lot of string appending in your games, but when you do, keep the earlier caveats in mind. String concatenation using the overloaded "+=" operator isn't entirely evil, though. There are times when the overhead of the StringBuilder class just isn't worth it.

StringBuilder is very efficient at concatenating many strings together, but it really doesn't save you anything on smaller sets of data, and it's generally less readable than using the concatenation overloaded operator. Consider the following code snippet.

```
public void StringBuilderExample()
{
    // Pretty clear.
    fullName = firstName + " " + lastName;

    // Harder to read. No more efficient in this trivial case.
    fullName = new StringBuilder()
```

```
        .Append( firstName )
        .Append( " " )
        .Append( lastName )
        .ToString( );
}
```

Exception Handling

The C# language provides a convenient mechanism for handling unexpected error conditions that your code may encounter—structured exception handling (SEH). By wrapping statements in special wrappers, known as try-catch blocks, the runtime can take special actions whenever an unexpected error occurs. Exception handling makes your code more crash-resistant. Rather than simply locking up or crashing, your code can try to recover from the error gracefully.

The keywords here are "unexpected" and "exception." Wrapping your code in try-catch blocks has almost no effect on performance. But actually catching exceptions is another story.

When an exception is thrown, the runtime has to perform a lot of behind-the-scenes work, which will kill your game's frame rate. So it's important that you don't rely on exception handling for trivial cases like testing for null objects, checking for the existence of a file, or preventing divide-by-zero errors. Consider the following code snippet.

```
// Bad. Uses SEH for trivial case, which should be anticipated by the code.
public void ExceptionHandlingExampleBad(GameObject obj)
{
    try
    {
        obj.PerformTask();
        obj.SomeProperty = 2;
    }
    catch(NullReferenceException ex)
    {
    }
}
// Better. In the case where obj is null, this code will perform much better
// than the earlier example. Don't use SEH for easily testable conditions.
public void ExceptionHandlingExampleBetter(GameObject obj)
```

```
    {
        if(obj != null)
        {
            obj.PerformTask();
            obj.SomeProperty = 2;
        }
    }
}
```

Exception handling isn't completely evil, even when it comes to game pro-gramming. Crash-resistant code is a good thing. But you'll need to use a little common sense in how you check for error conditions. Save exceptions for exceptional conditions.

Working Set

By referencing a single method of a single class, you may unwittingly be loading dozens of supporting classes. The CLR's class loader will resolve the dependencies of a referenced class until all of the subordinate classes are also loaded.

If you find yourself using a small fraction of the features of a certain Framework API, and that reference is bloating your working set (your game's memory foot-print), consider implementing that (simple) functionality within your own code.

In general, you don't want to reinvent the wheel, though. It's better to rely on proven, stable libraries like the .NET Framework that have a large community of users. But, in some cases it just doesn't make sense to load large groups of objects whose functionality will go mostly unused. Don't be afraid to bite the bullet, trim the fat, and roll your own helper method—but only when absolutely necessary.

Threads and Thread Pools

For simple, short-lived tasks use thread pools rather than creating your own thread. When the time to create, initialize, and reclaim the thread outweighs the time it takes to actually perform the task, pools make a lot of sense. If you expect your task to take a while to run or you expect it to perform some blocking action, it probably makes more sense to create your own thread.

When you do use thread pools, remember that the current task isn't the only one that may be performed on that thread. Once the thread has been reclaimed by the pool, it may be assigned to work on another task. Don't change the priority or affinity settings on a pooled thread unless you're absolutely sure that you understand how it will affect future tasks that may run on the same thread or you take great care to return the thread to its initial state before returning it to the pool.

Thread Synchronization

Threading is covered in more detail in Chapter 25. Review that content if you want some more background information on threading in general.

Limit the number of locks that you perform, and limit the amount of work that you do while data is locked. While that data is locked, no other threads can access it. The benefits of having multiple threads are negated when you're blocking all but one thread.

Remember, locks aren't free. There is some overhead associated with coordinating the efforts of your independent threads. Avoid synchronization within loops, where you multiply the chances for contention, which may make your threaded code slower than its well-designed, single-threaded counterparts.

Threaded code works best when threads are truly independent of each other. Try like heck to design your game so that you can avoid locks altogether.

Initial Size of Collections

If you know approximately how big a growable collection will be, and the collection supports specifying the intended size, go ahead and set it. Most collections default to a relatively small initial size, and grow by some amount whenever you try to add a new element when the collection is full. If you're adding a thousand objects to a collection whose initial size is four, you'll spend a good bit of time waiting for the collection to repeatedly allocate new space and copy the exiting contents into their new, larger home.

Value Type Overrides

There are some methods that are inherited from System.object that other classes use to gather information about your derived classes. Since System.object cannot know about every class that you will ever write, the generic implementation for those inherited methods may rely on reflection and object-based parameters to get their job done. In the case of value types, that may mean unnecessary boxing and unboxing.

If you're experiencing problems that you think may be related to object-inherited methods like `Equals` or `GetHashCode`, you may want to consider providing your own, overridden implementation of those methods within your custom value type.

Jagged Arrays

The JIT compiler has specialized optimizations for accessing single-dimensional arrays. Multi-dimensional arrays are managed using the same general code for all types, which will result in boxing for your value types. So, in many cases, your performance may be better if you replace your multi-dimensional arrays with single-dimensional arrays or with another data structure known as jagged arrays.

A jagged array is simply a single-dimensional array where each element is, itself, a single-dimensional array. The following snippet demonstrates each array type.

```
public const int ARRAY_WIDTH  = 10;
public const int ARRAY_HEIGHT = 10;

// a multi-dimensional array
private float[,] m_arrayMD = new float[ARRAY_WIDTH, ARRAY_HEIGHT];
public float MultiDimensionalArrayExample(int x, int y)
{
    return m_arrayMD[x,y];
}


// a single-dimensional array
private float[] m_arraySD = new float[ARRAY_WIDTH * ARRAY_HEIGHT];
public float SingleDimensionalArrayExample(int x, int y)
{
    return m_arraySD[x + y * ARRAY_WIDTH];
}


// a jagged array
private float[][] m_arrayJA = new float[ARRAY_WIDTH][];
public void InitJaggedArray()
{
    for(int i = 0; i < ARRAY_WIDTH; i++)
    {
        m_arrayJA[i] = new float[ARRAY_HEIGHT];
    }
}
```

```
public float JaggedArrayExample(int x, int y)
{
    return m_arraySD[x][y];
}
```

.NET Compact Framework Best Practices

The tips in this section apply to the .NET Compact Framework and the CLR for the Compact Framework (the version of .NET on which the Xbox 360 CLR is based).

GC Differences

Most of the topics that we've covered regarding performance best practices up to this point are generally applicable to the Compact Framework as well, and they should benefit your Xbox 360 games, but it's important to remember that the Compact Framework is its own creature, independent of the .NET Framework that runs on your desktop. One key difference is in how the Garbage Collector manages memory.

On the desktop, the Garbage Collector is generational. That means that an object on the heap is promoted to successively higher generations (or groups of data on the heap) the longer a reference is kept to the object.

Each generation on the heap is managed differently. The key difference is in how often the objects in a particular generation are checked to see if they're ready for collection. The logic here is that if the object has been kept around for a while, it's likely to be kept around a little longer. Most objects will be created and fall out of scope rather quickly. Those objects live in generation 0.

The Compact Framework was designed to work on devices with limited memory and limited processing power. Part of that design dictates that the Garbage Collector on the Compact Framework is non-generational. Every object lives in the same heap, and every garbage collection is a full collection.

While the specifications are subject to change with future releases of the Compact Framework, garbage collection is generally triggered with every 1MB allocated, or when there's an OutOfMemory exception.

Per the Compact Framework team blog, benchmarks seem to indicate that there is no major difference in the collection times of deeply nested references versus shallow references. Smaller objects are collected slightly faster than larger ones, but the largest factor in collection times is the number of objects that are being managed.

So, how do we minimize the impact of garbage collection on our games? Use fewer heap-managed objects. An easy way to reduce heap storage is to use fewer reference types, favoring structs in place of your smallest classes so that they never touch the heap.

Structs are value types, and they prefer to live on the stack rather than the heap. Keep the earlier warnings about boxing and unboxing in mind, though, or you may nullify the benefits that you think you're gaining.

Don't Pass Large Value Types as Parameters

It may seem obvious, but copying large value types takes longer than copying smaller value types. Those values are copied whenever you assign them, pass them as arguments to a function, or whenever boxing or unboxing occurs.

If you have a method that needs access to a large value type, pass the value type by ref or as an out parameter to avoid copying its content to a local parameter variable. Consider the following code snippet.

```
// Bad. Data for the value type is copied to local storage.
public void ProcessLargeValueType(MyBigValue val) { ... }
public MyBigValue GetLargeValueType(int index) { ... }

// Better. A simple reference is passed to the method. No data is copied.
public void ProcessLargeValueType(ref MyBigValue val) { ... }
public void GetLargeValueType(int index, out MyBigValue retval) { ... }
```

So, what is "large"? It depends. If your type is larger than 32 bits, you might want to start considering its impact under the conditions described above. For example, it's probably not a good idea to pass a bunch of Matrix objects from method to method, by value.

Floating Point

The CLR for the standard Compact Framework doesn't traditionally support floating-point hardware, since most of the mobile devices that the CF targets have limited hardware. The Compact Framework team recognized the need for floating-point math in high-performance games, and they've implemented hardware support for floats in the version of the CLR that runs on the Xbox 360 game console.

Their implementation isn't fully optimized in version 1.0, but they have plans to improve the performance of floats in future releases of the CF CLR. For now, you may find that your floating-point operations perform better on the Windows CLR than they do on the Xbox 360 CLR.

It's not as big a deal as it sounds, though. Chances are small that the impact of these platform differences will result in significant performance issues in your game. Focus your optimization efforts on the other best practices that we discuss in this chapter before turning your attention to floating-point math.

If testing reveals that floating-point calculations are causing you grief on the Xbox 360, then you can turn to an old programming trick known as *fixed-point* math.

Fixed-point math is a crude replacement for floating-point math where you store your numbers as an integer, multiplied by some preset value. Then, you can perform simple calculations as you normally would, dividing your fixed-point variables by that same preset value just before you actually need to use them. Consider the following snippet.

```
public const int   FIXED_POINT       = 256;
public const float FIXED_POINT_FLOAT = (float)FIXED_POINT;
public float SimpleFixedPointExample(float start, float delta)
{
    int x  = (int)(start * FIXED_POINT_FLOAT);
    int dx = (int)(delta * FIXED_POINT_FLOAT);
    for(int i = 0; i < 1000; i++)
    {
        x += dx;
    }
    return (float)x / FIXED_POINT_FLOAT;
}
```

I'm sure that you can find better examples on the web (the loop in this example can be replaced with a single multiplication), but this should give you a good idea of how fixed-point math works. There is some overhead when converting floats to and from fixed-point values, so you'll want to minimize casting by working with the fixed-point values as much as possible, only converting back to float when you call out to APIs that don't know about fixed-point numbers.

Virtual Methods

The Compact Framework Common Language Runtime does not use a vtable for virtual function calls. The CF CLR was designed for smaller devices. It's hard to justify building a complete vtable on a low-memory device when many of those virtual functions may never be referenced.

Instead, the CF CLR walks the object hierarchy when it needs to locate the specific overridden method to call. Once the method has been located, it's added to a cache so that it can be accessed quicker in future calls to the same method. In general, this results in around 40% slower performance on the first call.

The additional overhead of calling a virtual method on the CF CLR is relative to the overall time spent in the method over the life of the game. So the performance hit on smaller methods or methods that aren't called very frequently will be greater, as a percentage of the total time spent in the method.

There are several things that you can do to limit the performance impact of virtual function calls. The first is to avoid virtual methods altogether. If you find that your design needs virtual methods, perform as much work in each method as possible so that the overhead of locating the method is a smaller percentage of the time spent in the method.

Another trick is to mark your derived method or class as sealed. This allows the JIT compiler to know which method to call without using the vtable-esque look-ups. Consider the following snippet.

```
// a base class with a virtual method
public class BaseClass
{
    public virtual void OverrideMe() {}
}

// derived class that implements the method,
// and marks the new method as sealed
public class ChildClass : BaseClass
{
    public override sealed void OverrideMe() {}
}
```

Don't sacrifice your game's design just because there's a potential for a perfor-mance hit. If it makes sense to use virtual functions in your design, use them. If it doesn't make sense, don't use them. Remember, you don't need to spend time fixing performance problems that don't exist.

Tools

The following tools will help you focus your optimization efforts by providing you with meaningful, measurable performance metrics. To put it simply, you'll want to keep the good metrics high and the bad metrics low to make sure that your code is performing well.

When you do identify performance problems, keep testing your game's performance as you make changes to your code. Make sure that these metrics show that your changes are actually making a difference and that you're moving ever closer to your performance goals. If the new benchmarks don't show a measurable improvement in the performance of your game, trash your changes and keep the unoptimized code.

Remember the 80/20 rule—20 percent of the code does 80 percent of the work. That 20 percent is the area to focus your efforts on. You can spend time making a certain method perform a million times faster by optimizing its code, but there won't be any noticeable improvement in your game's performance if the game spends a small fraction of its overall time in that method. Use some common sense and pick your battles.

Windows Performance Monitor

The Windows Performance Monitor (Perfmon) is a general-purpose tool that lets you monitor key performance metrics on your PC and see how your Windows-based programs affect those metrics.

Perfmon is installed as a part of the operating system. It was not designed specifically for XNA games, and it will not provide any performance data for your Xbox 360 game console.

Perfmon has dozens of performance counters that track the state of system components. These counters are grouped by the system component that they monitor. Real-time data from these counters is displayed graphically so that you can easily identify changes in usage. You can combine a variety of counters into the same graph and see how performance events relate to changes in the graph. For example, you can graph the performance counters that monitor available RAM and CPU utilization, side by side.

When you installed the .NET Common Language Runtime, several .NET-aware performance counters were added to the Perfmon tool for you. There's a lot of useful information that can be gained by tracking these counters over time.

The .NET performance counters include: thread locks, value type boxing and unboxing, garbage collections, GC compactions, bytes allocated, bytes collected, and many more. You can even write your own performance counters and plug them into this tool.

For example, a frame rate performance counter for your game might help you more easily locate the changes in system performance that lead to a drop in frame rate. By graphing your game's frame rate alongside performance counters like the garbage collection and thread lock performance counters, you can more easily identify simple cause-and-effect relationships.

Remote Performance Monitor for Xbox 360

The Remote Performance Monitor for Xbox 360, like Windows Perfmon, provides a way for you to monitor your game's impact on certain key system metrics. Unlike Perfmon, this tool was designed with XNA in mind, and it will communicate with a connected Xbox 360 game console once you've properly configured your development PC and have deployed at least one Xbox 360 game project.

CLR Profiler

Monitoring performance counters is a great way to know when there's a problem with your game's performance, but rarely will a spike in a performance counter pinpoint the cause of your problem. That's where a specialized tool, known as a *profiler,* comes in.

Profilers let you know where your program is spending most of its time. By knowing how many times a particular method is called, or how much time your game is spending in repeated calls to that method, you can focus your optimization efforts where they are likely to do the most good.

The CLR Profiler is a free code profiling tool, from Microsoft, whose primary focus is on reporting how your application is affecting the Garbage Collector and the heap. This is a general-purpose profiler, and it was not developed specifically for XNA.

The CLR Profiler is intrusive. That means it will affect the performance of the application that it is profiling. In some cases, you can expect your application to run as much as 10 or 100 times slower while it's being profiled. That means that it's useless to see how long methods are taking to run, but it's still useful to know how many times they're called, and how those calls are affecting the heap.

Third-Party Profilers

When it comes to profilers, you can definitely do better than the CLR Profiler. Commercial profilers (like VTune and others) will give you a much better picture of where your game is spending its time. Call graphs can be broken down into the number of times each method is called or the percentage of time spent in each method. You can use that data to focus your optimization efforts on the methods that are doing the most work.

Many of the commercial profilers offer free trial downloads. Also, there are several vendors that provide free, "community edition" versions of their tools for hobbyists and students (for non-commercial use).

While these tools are typically only supported on the Windows platform, profiling your game under the standard CLR on Windows will often (although not always) provide insights into how your game is behaving on the Xbox 360.

In-Code Timers

If you're as cheap as I am, or you just want to perform some timing investigations using your own custom code, the .NET Framework provides a high-resolution timer API called System.Diagnostics.Stopwatch. There are a few simple tips that you should keep in mind when you write your own timing functions.

For short-lived tasks (most game tasks are short-lived), you'll want to run your code within a loop so that the time the function takes is multiplied by the number of iterations. For tasks with smaller execution times, it's hard to accurately measure changes in performance. By running your task a thousand times within a loop, you're amplifying any performance issues that may be plaguing your code.

Since JIT compilation happens when you first access a managed-code method, you'll want to run your loop for a little while before you actually start timing your function. That way, you eliminate any startup costs that the CLR may have added when first preparing your method.

Since performance measurements typically vary from run to run, it's also a good idea to run your test loop multiple times so that you can get an average of how long the task takes and determine the standard deviation for those runs (a measure of how "noisy" statistical data is).

Shader Analysis with PIX

Microsoft distributes a really useful tool in the DirectX SDK called PIX. PIX is an acronym that expands to Performance Investigator for Xbox, but it has been ported to Windows for use in your DirectX projects and given a new name (Performance Analyzer for DirectX).

Whether you're writing games in native DirectX, managed DirectX, or XNA, this handy tool will allow you to inspect the underlying Direct3D calls and resources that were used to generate a frame in your game. You can capture all of the frames in a running game into a stream, or you can capture a single frame. Either way, you have access to the detailed steps that DirectX used to create the frame, and you can play back that data to recreate the image that was seen at the time the frame was captured.

This isn't just a screenshot—it's a re-creation of the frame using the same calls and textures as they were captured during the run. You can incrementally step through the process of building the frame, moving forward to create or backward to deconstruct the frame. Using this data, you can make sure that your code is doing what you expect.

Gray Matter

Of course, the best free performance tool that you have is located between your ears. Take the time to thoughtfully analyze performance data and think about how your game is processing its data.

How does your code perform a specific task? What is the CLR doing when it executes that code? How is your code affecting garbage collection? Are there any sync points in your code or calls to Framework APIs that may be blocking for a time? Are you performing any tasks more often than you need to? Are there any objects or calculations that you're referencing that can be reused at a later stage? Are there any tasks that your game is performing that can be done before your game is ever launched? Are you processing objects that will never appear on the screen or will never affect the game play?

Summary

In this chapter you learned the importance of establishing a time budget for your game tasks, measuring your game's performance via system counters, code profilers, and custom timing code. You read about some common best practices that will help you avoid writing code that negates the performance optimizations that are built into the CLR, the .NET Framework, and the JIT optimizing compiler. You learned the importance of not optimizing code arbitrarily, not optimizing code too early in the development process, and (many times) not optimizing code at all.

Review Questions

Think about what you've read in this chapter (and the included source code) to answer the following questions.

1. When should you optimize your code? Explain.

2. What are boxing and unboxing? How do they affect your game's performance?

3. What is a profiler? How is it useful?

4. What is JIT compilation? How does it affect performance? What steps do you have to take to benefit from the JIT compiler?

5. How does garbage collection on the Compact Framework's CLR differ from the CLR that runs on a typical Windows desktop? How do those differences affect your game's performance? Explain.

Exercises

EXERCISE 1. Download and install the CLR Profiler. Use it to collect performance data for one of your game projects. Examine the data that was collected. Think about how that data (number of calls to a method, heap space used) might be useful when trying to track down performance problems.

EXERCISE 2. If you haven't already done so, download and install the DirectX SDK. Locate the PIX tool, and use it to capture a run of one of your XNA game projects. Get familiar with the tool now so that you'll be more comfortable with the interface before you actually need it.

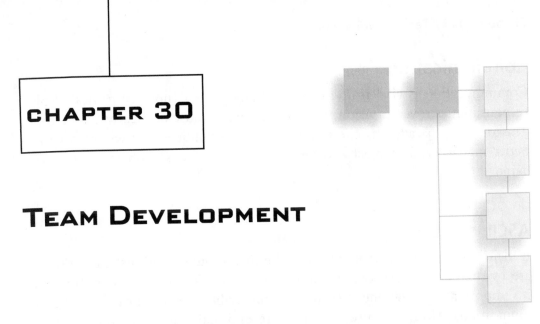

CHAPTER 30

TEAM DEVELOPMENT

You have a passion for game programming. And you just found some coworkers, classmates, or online buddies who share your passion, and you want to work together to write a complete, full-featured game.

But wait. Your game programming hobbies have always been solo efforts. How do you work with a team to develop a project? How will you divide up tasks? How will you coordinate code changes? How will you focus the team so that members don't waste time on wild tangents (like you frequently do with your own hobby projects)?

In this chapter, you will learn how to:

- Keep your team focused on a single goal (writing a finished game)

- Use tools that facilitate collaboration between virtual development team members

- Break your project into smaller, modular, more-manageable tasks

- Communicate roles, responsibilities, and specific tasks more effectively

- Use best practices, development processes, and tools to make integrating work from several sources easier

- Use tools for common project management tasks like issue tracking, disaster recovery, task management, and source control

Communication

Communication is vital to the success of any project (not just games). Roles, responsibilities, overall vision, and specific tasks must be clearly understood. The following paragraphs cite some tools and techniques that will help you to better manage your project and keep your efforts focused on making a great game.

ASCII Issues

E-mail, private forums, mailing lists (or e-mail groups), and instant messaging are a virtual team's best friends. Your team's dynamic will evolve over time, but it's important to remember that tone is impossible to read in casual text communications. Always use proper netiquette, and make sure that your criticisms are constructive and professional. When possible, favor phone calls or instant messaging over e-mails or forum postings where misperceived tone can be quickly corrected. Never reply to e-mails when you're angry or irritated.

Private forums provide a great way to log conversations to see how the team came to certain design or architectural decisions. Most folks won't regularly check a forum or blog, though. E-mail groups, automated e-mail forwards, and list servers provide a similar historical record and are more convenient for most readers, since they arrive in everyone's inbox at near real-time.

Instant messaging provides the type of instant collaboration that the other media cannot match. Most popular instant messaging clients also provide options that support group meetings, complete with whiteboards and shared desktops. If you schedule a meeting with more than a few team members, be sure to provide an agenda so that you can keep the virtual meeting focused, and avoid too many tangent discussions.

Working as a team takes discipline. That's not to say that the project can't be fun. But, everyone is giving up his reign as dictator over his own projects. You need to be able to build consensus and keep team members motivated and excited about the project. There are certain areas of developing a finished game that your teammates will consider cool and some areas they will consider a chore. Keep morale in mind throughout the lifecycle of your project. Morale is frequently the key factor in productivity, especially in a hobbyist project.

N o t e

I haven't listed any specific software in this section because everyone has his own favorite clients, and it really doesn't matter which ones you use. I personally use PHPBB for forums, WordPress for blogs, GMail for e-mail, Windows Live Messenger for IM, and the e-mail forwarding feature that's provided by my web hosting service (easy-cgi.com). I don't use actual list servers, but there are several local programming user groups in my area that rely heavily on them.

Organization

I love the collaborative process. I think that brainstorming sessions are great. Working with other developers and designers multiplies the creative process. Building on each other's ideas, you're often able to take your vision to a whole new level. It's like reaching a critical mass on your design where new concepts explode. Great ideas don't finish projects, though. Without some basic organizational processes in place, your project is doomed to the hobbyist idea graveyard long before the first line of code has ever been written.

Document your goals for the game. What features will the game have? Who is your target audience? How will you divide the project into smaller, more manageable pieces? How will game objects interact? Who is responsible for which tasks? There are several design document templates available on the web, but you can just as easily create your own. This is an organizational exercise. The design document isn't the goal. The goal is to make sure that everyone on the team understands the vision for the game, and that they clearly understand their role in the process and what is expected of them.

Once you've documented the details and assigned tasks, you need to make sure that the team is actually making forward progress towards your ultimate goal of a finished game. Set realistic milestones. Build in extra time for the unknown/unknowable. To help you stay organized, you can use one of the great commercial or free project management tools that are available, or just track everything in a spreadsheet or a text file.

N o t e

I'm quickly becoming a fan of a project management and bug tracking tool called Gemini. It's a simple, web-based project management tool with a (very generous) free licensing model for teams of 5 or fewer people.

If you don't want to be that formal or you don't feel that your game project is complex enough to merit the overhead, then don't use a project management tool. It doesn't matter how you keep things on track, it just matters that you do.

The makers of Gemini (CounterSoft) have given me permission to include the free version of their tool on the CD for this book. You can find it under the 3rd Party\Install\Bug Tracking directory. There, you will also find the installation and user guides as PDF documents. Be sure to read the instructions before installing to make sure that you have the appropriate prerequisites.

Source Control, Sharing, and Backups

There are several commercial and free source control tools out there. Several of the vendors also provide free single-user licenses, free trial downloads, or free "community editions" of their products for hobbyists and students. However you manage version control, make sure that this isn't one of the steps that you skip. It's just too easy to accidentally delete or overwrite a file and lose a week's worth of work. Version control tools allow you to see the state of your code at any point in time since the project started.

To use source control tools effectively, you'll need to make sure that your design is modular, and that assigned tasks are sufficiently silo'd. I know that most modern source control tools support concurrent check-outs, but I've had enough problems in the past with them that I prefer to hold exclusive locks on the files that I am editing. That means you'll need to design to the interfaces of clearly defined, modular classes. (That's a good thing.) There are some files that must be accessed by multiple folks, like project and solution files. For those cases, get in, make your change, and get out as fast as you can.

Make sure that your source control server is secure from prying eyes and malicious attackers. Many version control systems rely on TCP/IP or network file shares. In the former case, you'll need to configure your firewall for outside access to your server, and in the latter case, you'll likely need to pick one teammate's LAN as the host server where you can set up a VPN connection.

If you don't want to go to all that trouble, there are several websites out there that are devoted to the concept of virtual development teams. Most of those sites are also dedicated to the concept of open source software, though. If you want to keep your intellectual property to yourself, be sure to read the fine print before signing up for one of those (usually free) services.

Note

In keeping with my tradition of using outdated development tools, I still run Visual Source Safe (VSS) at home—a commercial source control tool from Microsoft. VSS has a lot of issues when it comes to large teams (more than 12 or so people), large projects (tens of thousands of files), or large files (greater than 2GB or so, total), but it has always suited my purposes well. Another issue that I have with VSS is arguably its biggest weakness. VSS relies on file shares to perform its magic. That means you and your teammates will need access to a shared UNC directory. Yuck!

The makers of another popular commercial version control system (called Perforce) have given me permission to include the free version of their tool on the CD for this book. This version supports up to two users and five workspaces. You can find it under the 3rd Party\Install\Source Control directory. There you will also find the documentation for the various components of this tool as PDF documents. Be sure to read the instructions before installing to make sure that you have the appropriate prerequisites.

Another popular (and free) source control tool is the Concurrent Versions System (CVS). The last few times I've revisited CVS, I've found that it's not as user-friendly as VSS, but it is a full-featured version control system, and you can't beat the price (free). Also, many of those open source project hosting sites that I mentioned earlier support CVS.

In this same category is another popular open source offering called Subversion, which many consider to be superior to CVS. Unfortunately, I have no experience with this tool, so I can't offer any opinions. I just want you to know that you have a lot of choices when it comes to version control tools.

While Visual Studio provides support for a number of version control systems within the IDE (a very handy feature), the Express Editions of Visual Studio (like the one that Game Studio Express is based on) seem to have disabled that feature. You will have to be diligent in making sure that your source is committed to the repository regularly via an external client application.

Back up your code regularly. If you're using source control, back up the repository database(s). You never know when your computer will decide to take the celestial dirt nap. You can do something as simple as copying the files to a CD, DVD, network share, or external hard drive, or you can use a commercial backup package. It's a hassle, but you'll be glad that you were disciplined enough to keep regular backups when you have your first drive failure.

Building and Testing

There was a great saying that I learned from the testing department when I was working in Redmond. "I don't care if it works on your PC. We're not shipping your PC." Be sure to test your game on as many different systems as possible. If your game targets the Xbox 360 game console, your testing work will have a smaller focus, since an Xbox 360 is an Xbox 360 is an Xbox 360. That's one of the greatest appeals of programming for game consoles—identical hardware and identical software.

Consider using a dedicated build PC. It can be yours, or another teammate's, but using the same PC for every build will help you avoid quirks that may arise from hard-to-find differences in the settings, preferences, and versions of installed tools and components.

You may even want to consider using an automated build tool or custom build scripts to perform your builds. By automating your build, you eliminate any chance for introducing errors by skipping steps or performing build tasks out of order. Most of the tools that you use to create game code and content provide command-line interfaces for just this scenario. Source control tools, compilers, FTP clients, batch image converters, and more can all be automated from simple scripts.

If your code base is especially large or relies extensively on components with well-defined interfaces, you may also want to consider automated testing. By combining automated builds with automated testing and e-mailed error reports, you can quickly identify issues like degraded performance, miscalculations, and crashing bugs as soon as they're checked into your source control repository.

Programming Standards

When working as a member of a team, consistency is an important factor in how easily you and your mates' code will integrate. Always code to well-defined interfaces, write modular (black box) components, and agree on some common coding standards before you get too far into the project so that reading each other's code will be easier.

The following standards are provided as a starting point for you to develop your team's own standards. These aren't gospel; they're just some simple Joe-isms that I've stumbled across during my career as a software developer.

Once you've settled on a set of standards for your team, it's important that you try to adhere to them. Be disciplined, but don't be legalistic. If there's contention among the team over a certain coding standard, and that standard isn't absolutely necessary (it would just be really, really nice to follow), favor team cohesion over legalistic adherence to an arbitrary style.

I recommend having regular code reviews. Code reviews between peers will ensure that everyone on the team understands what's going on outside of their assigned silo. Plus, it's always good to get feedback on your own work.

Optimize Last

Optimized code is harder to read and harder to understand. Optimization increases the entropy and complexity of your code, makes it easier to introduce new bugs, and makes future optimizations to the same code blocks harder. Also, optimizations that are introduced early in the project are likely to be thrown out as the design of your game evolves.

When you do find yourself having to optimize a section of code, be sure to document the optimization thoroughly. If you don't, the next programmer may have trouble following what you've done, or he may remove your cryptic code, unaware of the reasons behind writing it in the first place.

Note

In this scenario, it might be helpful to leave the original version of the code in the source file commented out. That way, folks who have to revisit the code later will have a better understanding of the original intent. In general, I recommend against leaving obsolete, commented-out code blocks in your project, though. It tends to add more confusion than clarity.

For more information on optimizing your XNA games, see Chapter 29.

Code to the Interface

Helper classes can be a collection of loosely related methods that don't require formal interfaces. Most of your other classes need to have well-defined interfaces, though. OOP depends on the ability of siblings and child classes to be interchangeable without affecting the functionality of the overall program. If your class doesn't have a well-defined interface, create one.

The Principle of Least Astonishment

Keep it simple. The code that you write shouldn't confuse other programmers. Write simple, elegant code, not cryptic code that relies on obscure programming tricks.

Eliminate Warnings

Ensure that the code you write compiles without errors (duh!) or warnings. Warnings are there for a reason. They generally indicate that the compiler has made certain assumptions about your code. Future versions of the compiler may make different assumptions, and may generate different executable code. Be explicit.

Avoid Deprecated APIs

As classes are phased out, compiler vendors (and third-party component vendors) will mark those APIs as deprecated. There is no guarantee that deprecated code will function as you expect (or function at all) with each new version.

Typically, the author of the deprecated API will cite alternatives in their documentation. Vendors take great pains not to break existing (or "legacy") code. You can rest assured that if a publicly released API was deprecated, it was for good reason. Don't use deprecated APIs.

Where appropriate, mark your own deprecated APIs with the [Obsolete] attribute so that the compiler will warn your developers of changes to existing classes. Be sure to suggest alternatives within your warning text.

```
public class SimpleUtilityClass
{
    [Obsolete("AlwaysTrue has been deprecated. " +
        "Use SometimesTrue instead.", false)]
    public static bool AlwaysTrue(int a)
    {
        return true;
    }
    public static bool SometimesTrue(int a)
    {
        return a > 12;
    }
}
```

Avoid the Bleeding Edge

It's tempting to use the latest, greatest version of your chosen tools and APIs. In game programming, this is especially true. The game programming industry seems to evolve faster than any other. If you're able to wait until new releases become stable, do so. Let everyone else work the kinks out of the new product. Feel free to play with betas and release candidates all you want, just don't build your real projects on them. Give them time to mature.

Don't Fight the IDE

Many modern integrated development environments (IDEs) perform some form of automatic code formatting for you as you type. In many cases, those formatting tools follow the coding standards that were established by the community of developers that use them, so they're specifically tailored to the language that you're using.

Don't waste time reformatting code that has been automatically formatted by your IDE. If the preset formatting options don't agree with your team's coding standards, change the formatting options within the IDE. If your IDE supports exporting and importing those settings, share the exported settings with your team to eliminate potential "fat-fingering" of your options.

Whitespace Is Your Friend

For compiled languages, whitespace has absolutely no effect on the size or performance of your game executable. Use blank lines and spaces to logically group related code blocks together and make your code more readable. Begin each logical block with a brief comment. Document the "why" rather than the "how" of your logic. The "how" should be obvious by looking at the code.

Eighty Columns or Less

Make sure that each line of code that you write fits within 80 columns or less. Break long lines into multiple, more-readable lines. Use concatenation to break up long string literals. This tip will help you scroll less when reading code on the screen, and it will make hard copies of your code listings look better.

Use Spaces Rather than Tabs

Use spaces (rather than tabs) to indent your code and to align elements within code blocks. That way, your code will look the same in any editor and your formatting is preserved when printing. Tabs are based on arbitrary columns, so your code formatting may be thrown off when viewed in an IDE with different editor settings.

Note

This standard is possibly the most arbitrary of all those cited in this chapter. There are fanatics in each of these two camps (the Spacists and the Tabians). And, as with most religious arguments, there are even subgroups within each philosophy (e.g., "Tabs are OK at the beginning of a line, but not within a line"). Each flavor of this standard has its own list of merits and shortcomings.

I've waffled between the two camps over the years, but I've recently settled on spaces, since that's what Visual Studio uses after a default install. It's not terribly important which camp you and your team fall into. What is important is that the team is consistent in whatever it chooses.

Indent Nested Code Blocks

Indent nested code using four spaces for each level of nesting. As branching or looping logic becomes more complex and your code blocks expand to fill multiple screens (or printed pages), indentation becomes more and more important.

Combined with the other code-formatting best practices, indented code makes your logic easier to follow. Your teammates will thank you, and you'll thank yourself if you ever have to revisit this code after the details of its implementation have faded from your memory.

```
public int NestingIndentionExample(GameObject obj)
{
    int count = 0;
    if(obj != null)
    {
        foreach(GameObject child in obj.Children)
        {
            if(child.IsActive)
            {
                count++;
            }
            else
            {
                child.Init();
            }
        }
    }
    return count;
}
```

Align Variable Names, Types, and Assignments

Where practical, try to line up related variable types, variable names, and their assignments within logical blocks. Don't forget about the restrictions on the number of characters per line, and don't fight the IDE if it keeps stripping out your extra whitespace.

```
int    myInt    = 123;
float  myFloat  = 5.12f;
string myString = "Hello, World!";
char   myChar   = 'X';
```

```
double valueOne    = - 23.00;
double valueTwo    = 1234.56;
double valueThree =     5.00;
```

Wrap Code Blocks in Curly Braces

Always, always, always wrap conditional code and loops in curly braces. If you don't follow this simple rule, you're increasing the chances of accidentally introducing a new runtime logic error as the code evolves over time (one of the most difficult type of bugs to locate and fix).

```
// Bad. Asking for trouble.
if(obj != null)
    obj.Method1();

// Good. Less prone to error.
if(obj != null)
{
    obj.Method1();
}
```

Both of the preceding statements are perfectly legal. Both compile just fine. Both produce the exact same executable. But, one is more likely to result in an error when you later decide to add another statement to the conditional logic.

```
// Oops! Hard-to-find runtime logic error.
if(obj != null)
    obj.Method1();
    obj.Method2();

// Good. Works as intended.
if(obj != null)
{
    obj.Method1();
    obj.Method2();
}
```

Naming Conventions

Always favor longer, descriptive variable names over shorter, cryptic names. Longer names take longer to type, consume more of your 80-characters-per-line limit, and they're more prone to typos (although IDE features like IntelliSense help to reduce typos). But, descriptive variable names make your code more readable and serve as a simple way to better document your logic without source code comments.

Use a simplified Hungarian notation for variable names, prefixing your names with a few characters to indicate their type and scope. Use a modified camel notation for variable names, where the first letter of each word (except the first letter of the variable name) in the name is capitalized. This even applies to acronyms that appear within your variable name (e.g. `XmlSoapParser` rather than the less-readable `XMLSOAPParser`). Use nouns for variables. Use the singular form of the noun for a single instance and the plural form of the noun for arrays and collections.

Use camel notation when naming classes and interfaces where the first letter of every word is capitalized (including the first character). Use nouns for classes that represent objects (e.g., `EnemyShip`). Prefix interface names with a capital "I," and try to use adjectives for interfaces that define attributes or features (e.g., `ISerializable`). If your class is based on a common design pattern, include the name of the pattern in your class name (e.g., `GameObjectFactory` or `PlayerProxy`).

Use camel notation when naming methods where the first letter of every word is capitalized (including the first character). Use action verbs in your method names that describe what they do (e.g., `ProcessInput` or `DrawCardFromDeck`).

Name constants using all capital letters, separating individual words with an underscore (e.g., `SCREEN_WIDTH`).

Exceptions to Naming Conventions

There are a few exceptions to these naming conventions. For trivial, short-lived variables with highly localized usage, there's no need to use descriptive variable names. Examples include loop indices, variables related to exception handling, method parameters whose purpose is absolutely clear, and system resource handles. In many of these cases, longer, more-descriptive variable names might actually make your code less readable.

```
// Exception 1: simple parameters whose purpose is obvious
public void ProcessData(int x, int y)
{
    try
    {
        // Exception 2: loop indices
        for(int i = 0; i < 20; i++)
```

```
    {
        // do work
    }
}
// Exception 3: structured exception handling variables
catch(NullReferenceException ex)
{
    // handle exception
}
}
```

Even when the scope and lifetime of a variable are highly localized, it may make sense to use a longer, more-descriptive name anyway. For example, you should never store the results of a complex calculation, or the results of a multi-step task, in a variable with a non-descriptive name.

```
// Bad. Confusing enough to warrant explanation.
long g = (x * y) % 13 + o / j;
```

Don't Use Inline Constant Values

Rather than hard-coding constant values in your logic, assign the constant to a variable and refer to the variable in your code. The resulting executable will be the same, but maintenance will be much easier because the constant only appears in one place.

You may also want to consider replacing source code constants with values that are stored outside of your game's executable (perhaps in the app.config file or in an XML file). That way, you can tweak those values without recompiling your game.

Comments

Document everything (classes, interfaces, structs, variables, properties, and methods), regardless of their access modifier. Don't just comment your public methods and properties. Today's private class members may be public properties or methods tomorrow.

When commenting methods, include a brief, yet descriptive, header just before the method declaration. Describe what is expected for each parameter, what the return value (if any) contains, any exceptions that the method may throw, whether the method relies on any member variable states to be set before the call, and whether the method updates any state data during the call. If merited, include a simple example in your comments of how your method should be used.

It's pretty much a given that source code and source comments never stay in sync. Misleading comments are actually worse than having no comments at all. Be diligent about keeping your source code comments updated, use descriptive names for your source code elements to help reduce the need for excessive commenting, and make sure that your code follows the principle of least astonishment, cited earlier in this chapter.

IntelliSense Prompts

Decorate your class members with IntelliSense-compatible comment headers. Minimally, add this header to all public properties and methods. It's better if you take the time to decorate all members. The following steps will ensure that the Visual Studio IDE is able to locate and display your comments whenever a developer uses your class in their code.

1. Add the comment header after you've settled on the method or property interface. The IDE will automatically add a stub comment that includes the names of the elements, and a simple comment template that you can fill in. After you've created this comment block, you'll need to update it manually whenever there's a change in your code.

2. Type three slashes above your class, interface, member variable, property, or method declaration to have the IDE automatically create a comment header stub.

3. Fill in the comment header stub with descriptive text.

If the class lives within your executable, you're done. Just rebuild your project, and the next time you use the class in your game, you should notice that the IntelliSense tool tip includes the descriptive text that you typed into the comments. If the newly commented code is contained within a separate assembly (i.e., within a Game Library project), you will also need to take the following steps.

4. Right-click on the project that contains the class with the new comments, and select properties.

5. Select the Build tab.

6. Make sure that the XML Documentation File checkbox is checked, and that the name of the file matches the name of your assembly. For example, if your project produces an assembly named MyGameLib.dll, make sure that your documentation file is named MyGameLib.xml.

Rebuild your library, and you should see the new XML file in the bin directory for your library project. Be sure to always copy the XML file along with the DLL. Visual Studio should locate, load, and use the documentation file without any further intervention.

The following snippet illustrates a common commenting scenario. Each of the triple-slash comments was first automatically stubbed out by the IDE, which I then populated with descriptive text. Whenever I reference this newly commented class in my game, my descriptive text is displayed in the IntelliSense tool tip for every member of the class that is visible to the scope where my new code is being typed. In most cases, I won't see the private member (m_IsActive) or its descriptive text because private member variables aren't visible to external classes.

```
/// <summary>
/// A simple game object to demonstrate intellisense-
/// compatible comment headers.
/// </summary>
public class GameObject
{
    /// <summary>
    /// Don't use this variable directly, use the public property instead.
    /// </summary>
    private bool m_IsActive = false;
    /// <summary>
    /// Indicates whether this game object is actively being used. When
    /// false, this object is available to be reclaimed from the object
    /// pool and it will not update or draw.
    /// </summary>
    public bool IsActive
    {
        get { return m_IsActive; }
        set { m_IsActive = value; }
    }
    /// <summary>
    /// Update the state of this object, based on the time elapsed.
```

```
///   </summary>
///   <param name="elapsed">Time since the last call to Update(),
///   expressed in seconds.</param>
public void Update(double elapsed)
{
    // do some work here
}
}
```

Another benefit of commenting your classes and their members in this way is that there are third-party tools (like NDoc and Sandcastle) that will parse the comments out of your source code to generate compiled help files (CHM files).

Compiled help provides an easy-to-read overview of the classes in your API, and it allows the reader to drill down into the hierarchy of classes to get detailed information about each class and its members. This may not be useful for your typical game projects, but it really adds a professional flair to any game libraries or reusable components that you create and distribute.

Special Comments

Most hobbyist and student game programmers are easily distracted by new and interesting technology or methodologies. If you ever want to make a finished game, though, you will need to keep your focus on making your code feature-complete. Rather than deviating from your current task and starting a new research effort, mark areas of concern with one of the following special comments and come back to it when you have more time to research and experiment.

```
// TODO: code works as designed, but should probably be revisited
// FIXME: code has some design or performance issue, fix before releasing
// EXCEPTION: code deviates from best practices, reasons cited in comment
```

Some (totally fabricated) real-world examples of these comment types follow.

```
// TODO: This method is taking too long. If we cache the result from call
// to call, and only recalculate when the parameter values change, then I
// think we'll see a 10-20% improvement in this method's performance.
// I need to run more tests to be sure, but I don't have the time now.
// -- joe, 02/02/2005


// FIXME: We should trash our custom implementation for these controls
// and use the APIs in the new version of our third-party controls. They
// have all the functionality of our code, and seem to use much less
```

```
// memory. There's no way to get this done before the next deadline, but
// we need to triage this issue when we develop our task list for the
// next milestone.
// -- tin, 04/28/2006

// EXCEPTION: We noticed a critical performance issue under certain
// circumstances (cited in bug #234) just before last night's release.
// It's too late in the process to redesign this section of the framework.
// By exposing three of the private member variables of this class, the
// helper class that manages these objects can bypass the problematic
// code.
// -- jon, 03/31/2007
```

Summary

In this chapter, you learned about some of the most common processes, best practices, and tools for working with a team to develop your game project. You learned how important it is to break your project into smaller, modular, more-manageable tasks, and how important effective communication between team members is to ensure that your project gets finished on schedule (or finished at all).

You read about the importance of communication and its effect on morale and productivity. You learned some simple techniques to keep team members focused on the final goal of writing a finished game by keeping discussions on track, clearly documenting the project's design and tasks, and recording note-worthy research efforts in the form of new project tasks or as source comments.

And you also read about the importance of source control, disaster recovery, and security in protecting the investment that you and your teammates are making in your project.

Review Questions

Think about what you've read in this chapter (and the included source code) to answer the following questions.

1. List some ways that communication can positively and negatively affect a project.

2. What is a design document? What is its purpose?

3. How can a large project be broken into tasks that individual developers work on? How do those independent tasks get integrated into a single project?

4. What are the roles of programming standards and best practices in working as a team to develop a project?

5. Why is source control (or version control) important? Why is disaster recovery (data backups) important?

Exercises

EXERCISE 1. Search the web for examples of each of the tool categories mentioned in this chapter (source control, project management, issue tracking, virtual team collaboration, documentation, disaster recovery, and so on). How do tools in the same category compare with each other? What features are important to your team, your project?

EXERCISE 2. Search the web for various design document templates, specifically those with a focus on game projects. Create your own template by using the best features of each and by adding sections that you think should be included. Review the template with your teammates to get feedback and to solicit support for the concept. Work with your team to take this generic template and create an actual design document for your current project. (If you don't have a project in mind, make one up. Be creative. For this exercise, you don't have to write the game, just the design document.)

EXERCISE 3. Develop a list of programming standards, based on the text in this chapter (or from any other source), that's tailored to your team. Review the list with your teammates, and then revise the document based on your discussions.

Once you're done, describe the entire process as a sort of postmortem. Discuss the interactions between the team members during the process. Discuss the quality of the final document. Was the team unanimous in their acceptance of every standard? List five things that went right during this process, and five things that went wrong. How could this process have gone better?

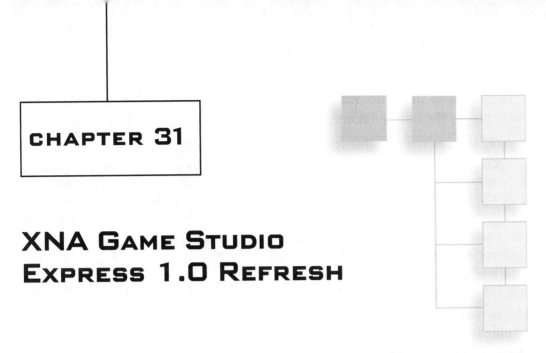

CHAPTER 31

XNA GAME STUDIO
EXPRESS 1.0 REFRESH

Even though it's referred to as an "incremental update," the XNA Game Studio Express 1.0 Refresh adds many much-anticipated new features. Expect to see regular updates from the XNA team. They recently announced version 2.0 of XNA, which is scheduled for release near the end of 2007. (Can you say, "networking"?)

Compatibility with Windows Vista

When XNA Game Studio Express was initially released, the only officially supported development platform was Windows XP with SP2. With the release of the XNA Game Studio Express 1.0 Refresh (the Refresh), all flavors of Windows Vista are also fully supported development platforms. Before the Refresh, many developers were able to successfully use Vista to write XNA games, but they were on their own if they ran into problems with that unsupported configuration. Users of the Windows 2003 Server operating system are still in that boat—XNA Game Studio Express 1.0 Refresh will install and run just fine on Windows 2003 Server, but it's an untested and unsupported platform.

Regardless of the platform, be sure to install the latest service packs, drivers, and updates for your operating system. You'll save yourself a lot of headaches by doing so. It's also worth noting that Service Pack 1 (SP1) for Visual C# 2005 Express Edition is now required. XNA Game Studio Express 1.0 Refresh (XNA GSE) will not install until you have updated your IDE with SP1. And don't forget to launch the IDE at least once before you install the XNA GSE refresh. You should also go ahead and register the IDE while you have it open. The documentation for XNA GSE cites registration as a prerequisite as well.

Note

If you're a security nut (like I aspire to be), you'll be happy to know that you don't have to be an administrator on your development PC to run XNA Game Studio Express. One of the most cited tenants of security is to grant processes the lowest privileges that they need to do their job. The number one cause for security issues is, arguably, running applications with elevated privileges.

Malicious software can't do anything that the user account that launched it can't do. Besides that, your users may not (read "should not") be running as administrators on their PCs, so it's smart to at least test your games under a normal user account to make sure they're not doing anything naughty. Believe it or not, you don't have to be an administrator to develop games. For a list of issues and caveats on this topic, search the web for "developing as a non-admin."

Building and Deploying

The following paragraphs list some of the improvements that have been made to the build and deployment process, which will help you as you develop your XNA games.

Clean Builds

Building your solution by clicking on the Build Solution menu item performs an incremental build, only generating new content when the compiler detects changes in the source files. Building your solution by clicking on the Rebuild Solution menu item forces the compiler to create your deployable files from scratch. There's a third build option that's pretty handy—Clean Solution—but it's not enabled in Visual C# 2005 Express Edition by default. The Clean Solution command will remove the results of previous builds from your file system, forcing the next build to regenerate all of your game's deployable files. This is especially useful when you run into issues with incremental deployment of your Xbox 360 games, or when you're developing custom Content Pipeline importers or processors.

To enable the Clean Solution menu item, you'll need to do the following:

1. Within the XNA Game Studio Express, right-click on the main menu at the top of the IDE.

2. Select the Customize option from the resulting popup menu.

3. Select the Commands tab.

4. Select the Build category.

5. Click on the Build menu item in the main menu of the IDE. The Build menu will remain open as long as the Customize dialog box is open.

6. Locate the Clean Solution command within the pane on the right side of the Customize dialog box and drag it to the Build menu, dropping it just below the Rebuild Solution menu item.

7. Click Close to save your change and dismiss the Customize dialog box.

Content Builds

Content builds have been optimized in this release, so your overall build times should be faster. In the process, the XNA team added support for cleanly canceling builds (whether the compiler is processing code or content), saving time, and reducing the frequency of deployment issues due to corrupt intermediate build data.

Sharing Games

The Refresh introduces one of the most anticipated new features—single-file deployment of XNA games for Windows and the Xbox 360. While your Xbox 360 audience is still limited to members of the XNA Creators Club, and they still have to have a working XNA development setup (as described in Chapter 3, "Using Visual C# 2005 Express"), you no longer have to ship your source code, project files, and raw game media. The Refresh includes a new tool (the XNA Game Studio Express Package Utility—xnapack.exe) for creating these files. Just send the package to your friends, and they can run your game by double-clicking on the file.

With the addition of the XNA Game Studio Express Package Utility, you now have three ways to share the games that you create.

- **XNA game package**—Share your Windows and Xbox 360 games with other XNA developers without sharing your source code, project files, or source media by creating an XNA deployment package. Recipients double-click on the package file to run your game.

- **Ship your source**—Share your Windows and Xbox 360 games with other XNA developers by sending them your source code, project files, and source media. Files are typically packaged as a single compressed (ZIP) file, which the recipient then builds and runs on his own system.

▪ **Windows-only distribution**—Share your Windows game with any Windows user by distributing the output of your Windows XNA game project. Gamers who have installed the (freely distributable) XNA runtime files can run your game by double-clicking on the executable.

The following steps describe the process by which you create XNA game package files.

1. Open your game project in the XNA Game Studio Express IDE.

2. Select the build type (Debug or Release).

3. Select Package as XNA Creators Club Game from the Build menu.

4. Locate your game package. If the build was successful, there will be a file in your output directory (under the bin subdirectory of your project) that has a CCGAME file extension. That's the only file that you need to distribute.

If you want to automate the packaging process, you can call the XNA Game Studio Express Package Utility from the command line. See the article entitled "Sharing Your Game Package" in the XNA Game Studio Express documentation for more information on this topic.

Xbox 360 Goodies

In addition to the improved support for incremental deployment to the Xbox 360, and the new single-file deployment mechanism, the following features have been added to this release to aid developers who are writing games for the Xbox 360 game console.

PC/Xbox 360 Connectivity

The user interface and overall experience of connecting your development PC to your Xbox 360 has been improved in the Refresh. You are now able to test your connection before committing it to your PC. For a list of common connectivity problems, and a more detailed description of the process by which you establish a connection, read the article entitled, "Deploying an Xbox 360 Game," in the XNA Game Studio Express documentation or read Chapter 12, "Coding for the Xbox 360 Game Console," of this book.

Game Thumbnails

You can now specify an image that will appear in the XNA Launcher when players are browsing the list of installed XNA games on their Xbox 360 game console. This may seem like a trivial addition to XNA, but this new feature will give your titles a more polished and professional feel.

There are some limitations that must be considered when designing your game's thumbnail image.

- Only PNG image files are supported.

- The largest dimension (width or height) of your thumbnail will be 64 pixels. If your source image does not meet this requirement, it will be scaled. The aspect ratio of the image will be preserved, but the scaling process may introduce undesirable visual artifacts, so it's best to create the thumbnail with this restriction in mind.

- The source image for your thumbnail must not exceed 2048 pixels in width or 2048 pixels in height, and the file size of the source image must not exceed 16 KB.

The following steps describe the process by which you change your XNA game's thumbnail image.

1. Open your game project in the XNA Game Studio Express IDE.

2. Right-click the game project in the Solution Explorer, and then select Properties.

3. Select the Application tab.

4. Select your thumbnail image from the list of project images in the Game Thumbnail dropdown list, or select another image by clicking the Browse button (labeled "...").

5. Click the Save All icon on the toolbar to save your change, then close the Project Properties page. The next time you build and deploy your game to your Xbox 360 game console, the thumbnail should appear in the XNA Launcher.

Note

The dropdown menu that you use to select your game thumbnail will list all PNG files in your project, regardless of image dimensions or file size. It's up to you to make sure that you heed the image restrictions cited earlier. If you don't have a suitable thumbnail image in your project, you can select any image from your hard drive by clicking on the Browse button (labeled "...") and selecting a PNG image file. The selected image will be added to the root of your project, and it will be configured as the thumbnail for the game.

XNA Launcher

The XNA Launcher has been updated to support the new features of the Refresh. The XNA Launcher is updated automatically. You are forced to update the XNA Launcher on your 360 any time there's a new release. Your XNA Game Studio Express 1.0 games will run just fine in the new launcher without rebuilding and redeploying them. That means you don't have to update your development environment right away when a new update is posted, but you won't be able to take advantage of all the new goodies until you do.

3D Audio

The sound APIs have been updated to include support for XACT's 3D audio positioning effects. This allows you to tie your audio cues to your 3D objects, greatly improving the immersive sensations of your games. The framework simulates the 3D positioning of sounds by adjusting the stereo balance of your audio cues on the fly, making them appear to move around within your game world. During this process, any stereo information in the cue is stripped to convert it to a mono cue. The new (dynamic) stereo mix information is managed by the audio engine.

To add this new effect to your games, you'll follow the same basic steps that were outlined in Chapter 10, "Using XNA Audio," to create a cue in XACT and load it into your game project. Two new classes have been introduced to describe the relationship between the player (represented by the AudioListener class) and the object that is generating the sound (represented by the AudioEmitter class). These two new classes have member variables to indicate the object's location and orientation in the 3D world (the Position, Forward, and Up vectors), as well as a member variable to indicate the object's speed and direction of movement (the Velocity vector).

Before you play the cue for the first time, you need to get a reference to it (using the SoundBank.GetCue method) and call a new method that has been added to the Cue class to alert the framework that this is a 3D sound (the Apply3D method).

See the article entitled "How to: Apply Basic 3D Positional Effects to a Cue" in the XNA Game Studio Express documentation for a simple demonstration of this new feature.

Math APIs and Common Structures

The math library has been expanded with more than five dozen new or updated methods. These changes were made based on user feedback. (See, the XNA team is listening!) And several familiar structures have received a facelift. Consider the following code from the example game in Chapter 6, "Using XNA Graphics for Basic 3D," which was written before the Refresh was released.

```
// helper method to convert Euler angles to a quaternion
protected void EulerAnglesToQuaternion(
    float pitch, float yaw, float roll,
    out Quaternion rotation)
{
    // deal with half angles, convert to radians
    pitch = MathHelper.ToRadians(pitch) / 2;
    yaw = MathHelper.ToRadians(yaw) / 2;
    roll = MathHelper.ToRadians(roll) / 2;
    // go ahead and calc our trig functions [cosine]
    float cosPitch = (float)Math.Cos(pitch);
    float cosYaw = (float)Math.Cos(yaw);
    float cosRoll = (float)Math.Cos(roll);
    // go ahead and calc our trig functions [sine]
    float sinPitch = (float)Math.Sin(pitch);
    float sinYaw = (float)Math.Sin(yaw);
    float sinRoll = (float)Math.Sin(roll);
    // quaternion voodoo, construct a quat from our angles
    Quaternion quat = new Quaternion(
        cosRoll * cosPitch * cosYaw + sinRoll * sinPitch * sinYaw,
        sinRoll * cosPitch * cosYaw - cosRoll * sinPitch * sinYaw,
        cosRoll * sinPitch * cosYaw + sinRoll * cosPitch * sinYaw,
        cosRoll * cosPitch * sinYaw - sinRoll * sinPitch * cosYaw);
    rotation = quat;
}
```

That horrible, bloated home-grown method can now be replaced with a call to the (newly) built-in method, Quaternion.CreateFromYawPitchRoll.

For another example of the new functionality that the Refresh brings, consider the following code that was introduced in Chapter 13, "Arcade," and refined in Chapter 28, "Pixel-Perfect Collision Detection," both written before the Refresh was released.

```
// see if the texture rectangles overlap, if they don't, there's
// no need to do a pixel by pixel comparison
protected static bool BoundsOverlap(
    Rectangle rect1, Vector2 loc1,
    Rectangle rect2, Vector2 loc2)
{
    // determine the top, left, bottom, right for rect1
    int top1 = (int)loc1.Y;
    int left1 = (int)loc1.X;
    int bottom1 = top1 + rect1.Height;
    int right1 = left1 + rect1.Width;
    // determine the top, left, bottom, right for rect2
    int top2 = (int)loc2.Y;
    int left2 = (int)loc2.X;
    int bottom2 = top2 + rect2.Height;
    int right2 = left2 + rect2.Width;
    return !(
        // rect1 fully to the right of rect2?
        left1 > right2 ||
        // rect1 fully to the left of rect2?
        right1 < left2 ||
        // rect1 fully below rect2?
        top1 > bottom2 ||
        // rect1 fully above rect2?
        bottom1 < top2
        );
}
```

Much of that code can now be replaced with a call to the (newly) built-in method, Rectangle.Intersects.

See the XNA Game Studio Express 1.0 Refresh documentation for a complete list of the supported Math functions and the changes to your favorite structures (including Quaternion.CreateFromYawPitchRoll and Rectangle.Intersects).

3D APIs

The `BasicEffect` class (used when you don't want to write your own custom effects) now supports per-pixel lighting. This new code is able to detect when your game is running on older 3D hardware that doesn't support per-pixel lighting, and it automatically reverts to per-vertex lighting.

The `SpriteBatch` class now provides an overloaded `Begin` method that accepts a `Matrix` as its parameter. This allows you to draw sprites using your 3D game's world coordinates.

The Content Pipeline

As mentioned earlier, the performance of content builds has been improved, content builds can now be cleanly canceled, and content files are now removed when you issue a Clean Solution command from within the IDE.

For those developers who are writing their own content importers and processors, there are improvements in the APIs that offer greater extensibility options. The Content Pipeline Graphics DOM now supports `Texture3D` content, useful for volume textures. Vertex and index buffers that were created by the Content Pipeline can now be read from. And, new methods have been added to allow pipeline extensions to determine the root directory from which the Content Pipeline is reading.

Font Support

Another much-anticipated new feature that was added in the Refresh was built-in support for bitmap fonts. These new font methods function much like the fonts that we developed in Chapter 20, "Game Font Maker Utility," Chapter 21, "Game Font Library," and Chapter 26, "Content Pipeline Extensions." As with our implementation, methods are provided to measure and draw text, and the generated bitmap fonts are based on Windows TrueType fonts.

But don't throw all that code out just yet. There are several features that you may want that the new built-in fonts don't support. Now you have the option of using the built-in game fonts (saving code), using the game fonts from this book as is, extending the functionality of this book's game font classes by tweaking the source, or using one of the many third-party game font classes that are freely available on the web.

The following steps describe the process by which you create and use the new, built-in game font classes.

1. Create a new Game project, or open an existing game project in the XNA Game Studio Express IDE.

2. Right-click your project in the Solution Explorer, and select Add then New Item from the resulting popup menu.

3. Select the Sprite Font icon, name your new font Arial.spritefont, and then click Add.

4. The new spritefont file is an XML description of your chosen font. You can make changes to the size, style, and other font attributes here, as well as specifying the range(s) of characters that you want to have encoded.

5. Declare a member variable of type SpriteFont to use the font within your game.

```
SpriteFont m_font = null;
```

6. In your game's LoadGraphicsContent method, add a line to load the game font from disk.

```
m_font = content.Load<SpriteFont>("Arial");
```

7. In your game's Draw method, add a call to the DrawString method of the SpriteBatch class.

```
m_batch.DrawString(m_font, "This is a test!",
    Vector2.One * 64, Color.GreenYellow);
```

Documentation Updates

The table of contents for the XNA Game Studio Express documentation has been redesigned to make finding important topics easier. Several great "How-To" articles have been added to the documentation with the latest update. Be sure to check out the "What's New in This Release" article in the XNA Game Studio Express documentation to get up to speed on the new features, and to explore topics where information was lacking in the previous releases.

Summary

In this chapter, you learned about many of the new features that are available in the XNA Game Studio Express 1.0 Refresh. We covered some updates from just about every area of the XNA Framework.

Review Questions

1. List four options that you now have to help you draw text in your games.

2. List three ways that you can distribute your XNA games.

3. How can you associate a thumbnail image with your game?

4. What is the difference between the following items on the build menu—Build Solution, Rebuild Solution, and Clean Solution?

5. What new operating system does XNA Game Studio Express 1.0 Refresh support? List another operating system where XNA Game Studio Express may work, but is not officially supported.

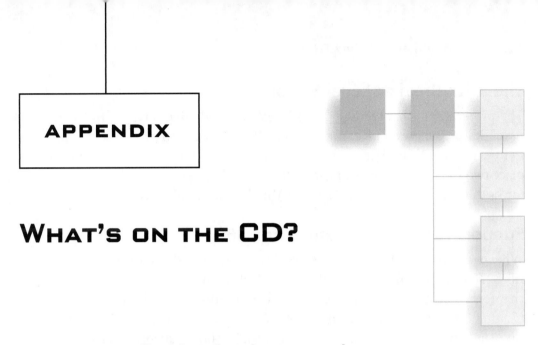

APPENDIX

WHAT'S ON THE CD?

Autorun Application (Welcome.exe)

I threw together a simple Windows application to let you browse the chapter descriptions and screen shots for each chapter. If the chapter about which you're reading has an associated demo game, you'll also be able to see a video of the demo and launch the Windows or Xbox 360 version of the demo right from the application. Please read the "Media Directory" section for important notes on this feature.

The application should automatically run when you insert your CD into your computer. If it doesn't, just open your CD drive in Windows Explorer and double-click the file named Welcome.exe. You don't have to run this program to use the CD, though. A description of the CD's contents follows.

Source Directory

The source code for the examples that we develop in this book can be found on the CD under the Source subdirectory. The sources are grouped according to the section of the book in which they appear (Introduction, Genre, Components, and Tasty Bits). I've also included the source code for the autorun application (Welcome.exe) that greets you when you insert the CD into your computer. That code can be found in the Source\Welcome subdirectory.

The Brick Breaker Level Editor

The projects for Chapter 14, "Brick Breaker," and Chapter 24, "Brick Breaker Level Editor," share some common code. It made sense to put those two projects in the same solution, sharing the common files between the two. I didn't want to place two (identical) copies of the code on the CD, so you'll find the source code for both chapters in the Source\Genre\BrickBreaker subdirectory.

Support for Windows and Xbox 360

Whenever possible, the examples in this book provide both a Windows and Xbox 360 version of the example code. The obvious exceptions to this are the chapters in which we develop Windows-based tools (like the game font utility in Chapter 20 or the level editor in Chapter 24) or when we use Windows-only APIs (like the mouse input example in Chapter 9). Without exception, cross-platform code is provided as a single set of source code files that are shared between Windows and Xbox 360 solutions and projects.

Note

> The XNA documentation suggests sharing code between separate solutions and projects, as I have done here, but it warns against placing those solutions and projects in the same directory. When you develop your own XNA games, be sure to use separate directories for your Windows and Xbox 360 projects, adding your source code directly to one project, and then sharing it with the other using the Add Existing option of the project's context menu (available by right-clicking the project within the Solution Explorer within the IDE).

Media Directory

The Media subdirectory contains videos of, and single-source executable packages (CCGAME files) for, the examples that were developed in the book. All of the videos can be found in the Media\Videos subdirectory. The precompiled example programs are segregated into subdirectories that mirror the structure of the Source subdirectory.

The next several paragraphs describe some things that you can try when you have problems launching the CCGAME files.

Problem: CCGAME Files Aren't Associated with Any Applications

Thanks to the new single-file packaging feature that was included in the XNA 1.0 Refresh, installing and running the examples is as easy as double-clicking the associated CCGAME file. The XNA Packaging Utility wasn't introduced until the XNA 1.0 Refresh, though. If you're still using the original XNA 1.0 runtime files, you won't be able to use the precompiled executables that are found in this directory.

I recommend that you upgrade to the XNA 1.0 Refresh, but I realize that some folks may have reasons not to do so. The source code for the examples will build and run under either version of the XNA runtime. If you're still using the old framework files, just copy the source files to your hard drive and build them for yourself to see what all the fuss is about.

Problem: The Xbox 360 CCGAME Demos Won't Run

The XNA Packaging Utility will automatically deploy Xbox 360 XNA games to your console, bypassing the development environment. It's not a magic wand, though. There are several things that you need to do before you can start deploying games to your console by double-clicking CCGAME files.

- You must have XNA 1.0 Refresh installed on the PC from which you want to deploy your games.

- You must have a properly installed and configured XNA Game Studio Express development environment.

- You should have successfully deployed at least one XNA game to your console. (Technically, this isn't a requirement, but it's a little easier to troubleshoot connection problems within the IDE than it is to interpret error messages from the packaging utility.)

- Your console must be connected to the LAN, it must be turned on (duh!), and the XNA Launcher must be running—sitting on the Connect to Computer screen, waiting for a connection from your development PC.

If everything is working as it should, double-clicking a CCGAME file that contains an XNA game for the Xbox 360 doesn't actually launch the game on your console. It simply deploys the game to your console, where you can run it from the "My XNA Games" screen. If you want to save some time, go ahead and deploy all of the examples in one sitting so that you don't have to keep switching between the Connect to Computer and My XNA Games screens within the XNA Launcher.

If you need more help with configuring your development PC or your Xbox 360 game console, please take the time to review Chapter 2, "Setting Up Your Development PC," and Chapter 12, "Coding for the Xbox 360 Game Console."

3rd Party Directory

The 3rd Party subdirectory contains free versions of some of the tools that were mentioned in the book. I'm grateful to Perforce and CounterSoft for giving me permission to distribute their software, and I appreciate the efforts of the people behind the groups that bring us free software like Audacity and Paint.NET.

These certainly aren't the only tools out there. Do some research and discover what tools work best in your environment, for your projects.

Audio

Audacity, a free (under the GNU GPL license) audio editor, can be found in the 3rd Party\Install\Audio\Audacity subdirectory. Within that directory, you'll find the installer, a link to the product's website, and product documentation.

Please read the license (found in _readme.txt) before using this software.

Bug Tracking

Gemini, a commercial bug tracking application, can be found in the 3rd Party\Install\Bug Tracking\CounterSoft subdirectory. Within that directory, you'll find the installer (only for new installations), a ZIP archive (for upgrades), a link to the company's website, and product documentation. Included with the documentation is an installation guide.

Gemini is free for use by small teams, with restrictions. Please read the license (found in ComplimentaryLicense.rtf) before using this software.

Graphics

Paint.NET, an open source graphics editor, can be found in the 3rd Party\Install\Graphics\Paint.NET subdirectory. Within that directory, you'll find the installer and a link to the product's website.

Paint.NET is free, open source (under the MIT License) software. Please read the license (found in _readme.txt) before using this software.

Source Control

Perforce, a commercial version control system, can be found in the 3rd Party\ Install\Source Control\Perforce subdirectory. Within that directory, you'll find installers for the various components, a link to the product download page, a link to the product documentation website, and local copies of the product documentation (as PDF documents).

Perforce is free for use by individuals or teams of two, with restrictions. Please read the disclaimer text (found in _readme.txt) and the license (found on the company website) before using this software.

INDEX

License Agreement/Notice of Limited Warranty

By opening the sealed disc container in this book, you agree to the following terms and conditions. If, upon reading the following license agreement and notice of limited warranty, you cannot agree to the terms and conditions set forth, return the unused book with unopened disc to the place where you purchased it for a refund.

License

The enclosed software is copyrighted by the copyright holder(s) indicated on the software disc. You are licensed to copy the software onto a single computer for use by a single user and to a backup disc. You may not reproduce, make copies, or distribute copies or rent or lease the software in whole or in part, except with written permission of the copyright holder(s). You may transfer the enclosed disc only together with this license, and only if you destroy all other copies of the software and the transferee agrees to the terms of the license. You may not decompile, reverse assemble, or reverse engineer the software.

Notice of Limited Warranty

The enclosed disc is warranted by Thomson Course Technology PTR to be free of physical defects in materials and workmanship for a period of sixty (60) days from end user's purchase of the book/disc combination. During the sixty-day term of the limited warranty, Thomson Course Technology PTR will provide a replacement disc upon the return of a defective disc.

Limited Liability

THE SOLE REMEDY FOR BREACH OF THIS LIMITED WARRANTY SHALL CONSIST ENTIRELY OF REPLACEMENT OF THE DEFECTIVE DISC. IN NO EVENT SHALL THOMSON COURSE TECHNOLOGY PTR OR THE AUTHOR BE LIABLE FOR ANY OTHER DAMAGES, INCLUDING LOSS OR CORRUPTION OF DATA, CHANGES IN THE FUNCTIONAL CHARACTERISTICS OF THE HARDWARE OR OPERATING SYSTEM, DELETERIOUS INTERACTION WITH OTHER SOFTWARE, OR ANY OTHER SPECIAL, INCIDENTAL, OR CONSEQUENTIAL DAMAGES THAT MAY ARISE, EVEN IF THOMSON COURSE TECHNOLOGY PTR AND/OR THE AUTHOR HAS PREVIOUSLY BEEN NOTIFIED THAT THE POSSIBILITY OF SUCH DAMAGES EXISTS.

Disclaimer of Warranties

THOMSON COURSE TECHNOLOGY PTR AND THE AUTHOR SPECIFICALLY DISCLAIM ANY AND ALL OTHER WARRANTIES, EITHER EXPRESS OR IMPLIED, INCLUDING WARRANTIES OF MERCHANTABILITY, SUITABILITY TO A PARTICULAR TASK OR PURPOSE, OR FREEDOM FROM ERRORS. SOME STATES DO NOT ALLOW FOR EXCLUSION OF IMPLIED WARRANTIES OR LIMITATION OF INCIDENTAL OR CONSEQUENTIAL DAMAGES, SO THESE LIMITATIONS MIGHT NOT APPLY TO YOU.

Other

This Agreement is governed by the laws of the State of Massachusetts without regard to choice of law principles. The United Convention of Contracts for the International Sale of Goods is specifically disclaimed. This Agreement constitutes the entire agreement between you and Thomson Course Technology PTR regarding use of the software.